A U S T R A L I A N
FISH
and how to catch them

AUSTRALIAN
FISH
and how to catch them

Richard Allan

LANSDOWNE

Published by Lansdowne Publishing Pty Ltd
Level 1, The Argyle Centre
18 Argyle Street, The Rocks, Sydney NSW 2000

First published by Weldon Publishing 1990

This limp edition first published 1999
© Copyright Lansdowne Publishing Pty Ltd 1990

National Library of Australia Cataloguing-in-Publication data

Allan, Richard, 1932-
Australian fish and how to catch them.

Includes index.
ISBN 1 86302 674 6.

1.Fishing - Australia. 2. Fishes - Australia - Identification. I. Title.

799.10994

CONTENTS

INTRODUCTION

Humans have fished as long as they have hunted, yet while hunting for food or recreation is rapidly diminishing, fishing continues to grow in popularity, a trend not easily explained in a developed country like Australia. It is certainly not from a need to supplement the diet. That can be achieved more conveniently at the local supermart or fishmonger — and probably more economically. Moreover nobody, it seems, from the passionately dedicated angler to the occasional line-dangler, can readily explain why they enjoy it so much.

Fishing can be a simple, inexpensive form of relaxation. No doubt about that. After all, the equipment need consist of only a length of line and a baited hook. And as for a venue, you can cast into a lonely backwater creek or listlessly hang the line from a crowded harbour jetty. You don't have to take it all too seriously, either. An angler at work may legitimately recline and contemplate; or perhaps make forgettable conversation with someone doing much the same. Such stalwarts may be vaguely aware that a fish could disturb their reverie by taking the bait, but not a hint of regret will be felt if one does not. Anglers such as these claim, with some authority, that "there's more to fishing than catching fish".

At the other end of the spectrum, fishing can be an expensive pursuit, requiring a crewed boat, rods, reels and accessories costing thousands of dollars. Such fishing is hardly relaxing. These anglers are driven by the challenge that the strike from a big fish offers. The really serious anglers of this persuasion, however, need not be any less eccentric than their comatose cousins on the shaded riverbank. They are just as likely, having eventually wrestled their great fish alongside, to let it go. If this seems perverse to some, I can only explain

from personal experience that seeing a fish swim free after having fought gallantly is as satisfying as the struggle that brought it in. Why slaughter what you cannot eat?

Of course fishing is not all beer and skittles. There may be bitter frustration when no fish are found and even anger if one is lost. Yet after the bleakest fishing trip the angler, it seems, can *always* salvage a pleasurable anecdote to recount. Fishing is like that, brimful with contradictions. Newcomers to fishing may be relieved to learn that most anglers fit between the two extremes. Certainly fishing need not cost a fortune. A generous range of tackle is available at prices to accommodate most pockets. And there are ample fishing methods and a diverse number of fish species to accommodate any predilection.

Some anglers prefer to fish alone, experiencing peace of mind through solitude. Others prefer to be more adventurous, deriving pleasure from discovering a wilderness waterway or a remote beach. Catching a fish is the bonus for their resourcefulness and effort. Then there are those with a competitive nature who, while fishing for records, trophies and championships, learn more about themselves than their quarry as they strive to win.

Still others find satisfaction through specialisation: the pursuit of a single fish species, or a few at most. These anglers enjoy long apprenticeships in mastering deft techniques in the crafty school of guile. There are many more of a less sophisticated bent who simply regard fishing as an outdoor activity, being happy to "wet a line" and share their optimism and expectations with family or friends, without regretting the time spent. They just enjoy the atmosphere and the occasion — and they can readily rationalise a good dozen reasons why the fish weren't biting the day they were there. And then there are those anglers who become so enthralled with every aspect of fishing that it becomes a way of life to them, almost a religion. They rejoice in fish and they have a deep respect for the waters that fish inhabit... people who care a great deal about both in a declining world environment. And the more caring anglers there are, the longer there will be fish to catch and a fragile ecology to appreciate. I commend their enthusiasm and zeal: it should be more infectious.

Finally, there may be diverse types of fishing and many more types of anglers but they all agree on one point. When it comes to taste, there is no comparison between the fish you catch and the fish you buy.

This book does not attempt to push beginners to a particular manner of fishing. Whether a fish is caught from a boat or from the shoreline — by any legal method — is a decision for the angler alone. There are libraries of books on particular fish, or specialised techniques and exotic rigs. This book takes the broader perspective of fishing, which I trust will be of help to the enthusiast, whether newcomer or the odd old hand. Certainly it will impart some knowledge of Australia's popular fish and how to recognise them. It may even help them to catch one occasionally. But never let yourself lose touch with the old maxim: the measure of the pleasure of fishing is never the size of the catch...

How we chose our fish

When we decided to use "popular" in the title of this book, it disinterred a memory long buried. I recalled approaching an old fellow — I was young then — who was dangling a line from a dilapidated jetty, somewhere in south-western Victoria.

"Which local fish are the most popular?" I asked.

"Mate," he said dryly, "any fish I *catch* is popular with me!"

I've heard worse evaluations. Popular fish for some anglers are: those that are easiest caught (if *any* are); those which make good eating; those fish that are present most of the time; or those that may be pursued without expensive equipment or extensive travel. Then there are those fish that some anglers find popular because they consider them demanding to locate or to deceive into taking a bait or lure; and there are others who prefer a fish that provides a challenging contest of skill or strength, or both.

In compiling the selection of fish in these pages, I hope, in one way or another, the fish I have chosen

are indeed "popular", but I will leave anglers to define the meaning of the word to suit themselves. Some fish have been arbitrarily omitted because of very confined distribution, or size, or numbers. Some native freshwater species fall into these categories. Some fish are included with nothing more than a description that should enable anglers fortunate enough to catch one to recognise it — and to hear my occasional plea to release it. Other fish, such as sharks and rays, for example, do not appear because of the limitation of space. I am fatalistic enough, from my years among anglers, to accept that there is bound be contention about the inclusion of certain fish and the absence of others. Somewhat controversially, with an aim towards uniformity of names (and it is an infinitesimal effort), I have used a main common name for all fish. For example, morwong will be found as the prime name, the various species being listed as morwong-blue, morwong-red, etc. Another example is swallowtail — a fish that is frequently listed separately in some references — which becomes nannygai-swallowtail (which is what it really is). I find myself in conflict here with the Australian Department of Primary Industries and some State fish marketing authorities, because I reject their recommended "marketing" names for some fish. In fact, not only have I ignored them but I was moved to comment in some fish entries about the deception of marketing fish under the name of an unrelated fish.

On the other hand, I have adopted or discontinued an international name for a couple of fish. Tanguigue is used for the narrow-barred spanish mackerel but tarpon is not used for the ox-eye herring.

Finding the correct scientific name was daunting. Only ichthyologists, fish biologists or studious anglers might judge if I have succeeded. A few fish will be found with two scientific names because I was unable to find a referee who was sure of the correct names. Should an expert expose any errors, I offer the same excuse as that well-known fish scientist who recently noted in his own book that "because of continuing research some of these (scientific names) may be incorrect by time of publication".

The often complex colouring of a fish is interpreted in the eye of the beholder. Two people examining the same fish may differ — at least in their perception — on a colour or a shade of it. The colours of a fish can also be very different when a fish is observed underwater alive, "lit-up" from the stress of being caught, or faded after having been dead for some time. Establishing recognisable colouring can be even more fickle because some fish undergo colour changes as they mature or change sex (or are separate colours from birth); and the same fish often have quite different hues when taken from clear water or turbid waters or from different habitats.

Nevertheless, every effort has been made to get it right. The descriptions are an amalgam of my own perceptions of colour, published references and the opinions of some experienced anglers who well know the fish they catch regularly.

Where I felt that the shape and colours of a fish were inadequate for the reliable recognition of a species, I have included simple taxonomic details, such as spine or ray counts or fins or the location of blotches or other marks, which might help anglers to make a positive identification.

The maximum sizes given have been thoroughly cross-checked. Some fish are given a length measurement only, while an approximate maximum weight is provided for others. As well as scientific references, I also used angling record charts (as at September, 1988) of such national organisations as the Australian Game Fishing Association, the National Sport Fishing Association of Australia and the Australian Angler's Association.

The breeding behaviour of many of the fish is described, particularly if I felt it was important for an angler to understand : Australia's native freshwater fish are such an example. Other have little or no information (an admission on my part of an arbitrary decision to save page space or an inability to obtain the information).

The distribution range of the fish has been gleaned from various reference books, individuall biol ogists or fish scientists, and fishing friends spread across this vast country. Only broad areas of distribution are mentioned. For anglers visiting a new territory, there are fishing tackle outlets, bait suppliers, fisheries offices, tourist information centres and fishing clubs from which more precise details about fish and fishing locations may be obtained. Local knowledge is invaluable.

A point worth mentioning is that too many people accept the view that members of the animal kingdom all behave in an absolutely rigid, genetically-programmed manner. Such behaviour is conveniently described as instinct. It is only humans, they claim, with their free will and superior learning ability that are uniquely unpredictable. Yet after years observing fish, I am convinced that despite the large component of instinctive drive in the behavioural patterns of fish, individuality is by no means uniquely human. An observant angler will find that fish are not always predictable. Nor do they recognise that they have entered waters that they are not supposed to inhabit. Expect the unexpected and at least your astonishment will be diminished.

I have tried to be both objective and informative, even educational, but certainly not parochial, which is always a risk with anglers. I trust this is reflected in my selection of fish and my descriptions of the various species of the same fish. Numerous fish within these pages, such as bream, flathead, garfish, morwong, rock-cods, trevally, trout, whiting and more, have several species detailed to show that a fish —a bream for example— that is popular with anglers of north Queensland is not the same bream caught in south-eastern Tasmania.

There are suggestions on tackle, rigs, bait and techniques, though there are as many opinions on such matters as there are fish in the waters. I have generally opted for simplicity in gear and rigs — those which I know from personal experience will work in most parts of Australia. They are unlikely to cause enthusiasts or newcomers any real problems. However, I would discourage any angler from accepting my suggestions as the *only* methods, baits or techniques. One of the great attractions of fishing is experimentation and innovation. Many ideas work well but the perfect fishing method has not yet been discovered.

Finally, it would be deceitful of me to claim I'd caught every fish in this book. As a truthful angler (and few anglers are not, despite the endless jokes), I *can* state that in my 40 years in the crazy pursuit of fish, I have landed more than 80 per cent of the individual fish in this book — though not all species — and I reckon that I've seen about another ten per cent caught, one way or another. Before my fishing days are reduced to recollections of wonderful, if sometimes exasperating, experiences, I hope to be able to say I've caught the lot...and a mermaid to boot!

RICHARD ALLAN
Wandandian, NSW

THE FISH

More than 30,000 fish species have been described so far in
the world and every year about another 100 fish are
discovered. It is estimated that more than 3000 species
exist in Australian waters.

The fishes comprise the largest group of the five recognised back-boned animals (others being amphibians, birds, reptiles and mammals). Not only are they the ancestors of all land vertebrates, but they outnumber them and are the most widespread. Fishes exist in waters of the polar and tropic regions; they prevail in raging mountain torrents and in the limpid pools of stagnant streams; some never rise from the bottom of the oceans, great abysses, others travel vast distances on the surface of the seas. Some can accommodate both salt and fresh waters during their life span; some leave the water to move to a new habitat; and others bury themselves in the mud to survive droughts. There are fish that will drown if put back into water during the time they must be in the air, and others must keep swimming or die.

Having evolved over hundreds of millions of years, fishes have shapes, colours and characteristics developed for their particular habitats. Such features may also help to identify their habits and behaviour. It is obvious, for instance, that flat fishes, such as flounder, are bottom-dwellers and that fish with pouting mouths grub for their food in the sand and silt. The fast hunting fish and pelagic species are torpedo-shaped for speed, while solid, thickset fish, such as the groper and tuskfish, need place no reliance on speed because their strong teeth and powerful jaws enable them to rip shellfish from rocks and to catch and crush crabs. Long-snouted fish mostly consume worms and crustaceans, which they can pull out of rock crevices or extract from weedy sand bottoms, and some species are equipped with sensitive barbels that enable them to detect food in muddy and silted areas. The swift pelagics have sharp teeth for grabbing or maiming their prey before swallowing. Fishes may be drab or as colourful as an artist's palette. Their colour is invariably linked to their preferred habitats. Most surface fish, for instance, have blue to green shades on their backs, but are silvery to white below. Bottom-dwellers very often change their colours like chameleons so as to blend with the rocks and weeds. Others are almost the colour of the bottom, such as whiting, scorpion fish or ox-eye herring. Colour may be used for camouflage, whether to hide from predators or to lie in ambush for passing prey. John dory is such an example. Because of its thin plate-like shape and an extraordinary ability to brighten or darken different sections of its body, it is almost impossible for its prey to identify. Others employ spotted, dappled or broken colouring to camouflage themselves against mottled backgrounds.

Some fishes as juveniles are not even a tone of the colour they eventually display on maturity; some change to another hue during spawning; while others assume new colour after changing sex.

Fishes may be herbivores, consuming only algae and certain vegetation; they may graze on corals and like organisms. Other species, use their gills and intestines to separate food from silt, sand and mud. Certain fish live on worms and small shellfish. Larger carnivores eat them and still bigger fish eat the smaller carnivores. And there are omnivorous fishes that eat vegetation and flesh.

Do fish see, hear, smell?
All fishes possess six senses, the sixth probably being the most important for their survival.
Their sight is mainly monocular, each eye transmitting separate "pictures" to their brain; and

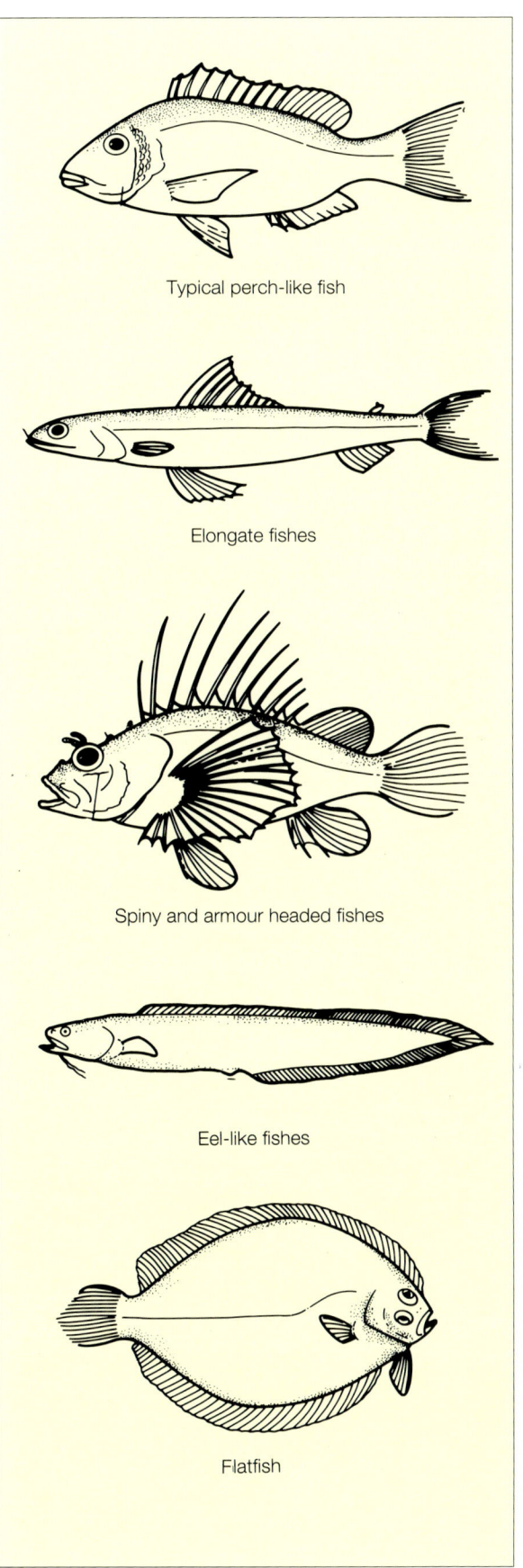

Typical perch-like fish

Elongate fishes

Spiny and armour headed fishes

Eel-like fishes

Flatfish

their range of view is probably limited to less than 30 metres, even in extremely clear water. Science believes that their underwater binocular vision is limited to focusing sharply on objects that are in a narrow area directly ahead of them. They rely on their sight to alert them to movement and their eyes correct refraction, a particularly vital function for fish — such as trout — which take insects above the water. Fishes see with little if any contraction of the iris. Most have no eyelids because the water continually washes their eyes.

Argument regarding the extent to which fishes can differentiate colours is unresolved. Evidence seems to suggest that they recognise some colours; it is not clear whether this is to separate sexes or species, or as a warning of danger. It seems there is, as yet, no scientific proof that fish recognise the colour of a lure or fly. Yet anglers who have caught fish after swapping an unsuccessful lure for another of a different colour or pattern, are convinced that fish do. Sceptics argue that the fish is more likely to have responded to some difference in the lure's action.

Similarly, the evidence that fishes hear underwater is doubtful. Certainly numerous species make noises but it is possible that only the vibrations thus caused are received and deciphered by their sixth sense. On the other hand, their sense of smell is highly developed. The noses or nares in a fish — a pair of small pits on the snout — have folds of membrane which are able to absorb and separate smells or scents. They use this sense, rather than sight, to alert them to predators and changes in water content — and to navigate.

Experiments by biologists in the USA have established that fishes react to numerous substances in the water, even in such minuscule proportions of one part to several million. Small fish of a particular species will panic, scatter or "ball" together (seeking the safety of greater numbers) if the odour of any of their known predators is added in the minutest quantity.

While nature has provided fishes with such delicate olfactory organs for feeding, navigation and an alarm system to signal the presence of likely predators, they have no taste organs in their mouth (except lung-fish). In any case, the vast majority of fish gulp in their food and its suitability has already been approved by the taste buds in their head, body, and whiskers or barbels around their mouths and, in some species, by modified fins.

A sixth sense...and pain

The fish's sixth sense is unique. It is contained in

their lateral line, being minute pores opening internally to a sensory channel and, to a lesser degree, in tiny openings on their head and face. These are called laterosensory pores. They signal to the fish any change in current or movements in the water. Experiments have proved that separating the base of the nerve that leads from these to the brain confuses the fish: it will not react to disturbances in the water or the re-direction of current flow, nor will it detect intruders as readily. It is believed that this remarkable sixth sense is a radar for finding shelter and, combined with the sense of smell, for finding drifting food in dirty water, and for measuring the size of an intruder or predator. It may also be a factor in enabling schools of fish to maintain formation and to find others of their own kind.

The other sense — that of feeling or pain — has become an issue with the anti-fishing lobby. The arguments are inconclusive but pain in humans is the result of information conveyed by nerves to the brain, where the cortex reacts. The more the cortex is stimulated, the more pain is felt. In some animals, and even between human individuals, the pain threshold can be higher than in others.

Fish have no cortex. Moreover, no other section of their brain seems to perform the function of a cortex.

The writer and countless other anglers have re-caught too many nuisance fish — almost before they had finished cursing their misfortune — to believe that fish react to pain as such. Even believing this is no excuse for treating a fish with disrespect or in a manner likely to be construed as cruel. It should be killed quickly by cutting through the neck, severing the backbone and main artery or by puncturing the brain with a sharp pointed knife. This is quicker than clubbing it on the head, and freshly bled fish keep better and taste better than those in which the blood is allowed to congeal in the blood vessels.

There is no excuse for anglers to toss live fish on to a beach or bottom of a boat to flap about in a slow death — bruising their flesh which, incidentally, starts a rapid deterioration of its eating quality. It provides those opposed to angling with evidence for emotional arguments about cruelty. The most insidious cruelty or stress inflicted on aquatic life of any kind is pollution. The fishes suffer a slow debilitating death from lack of oxy-

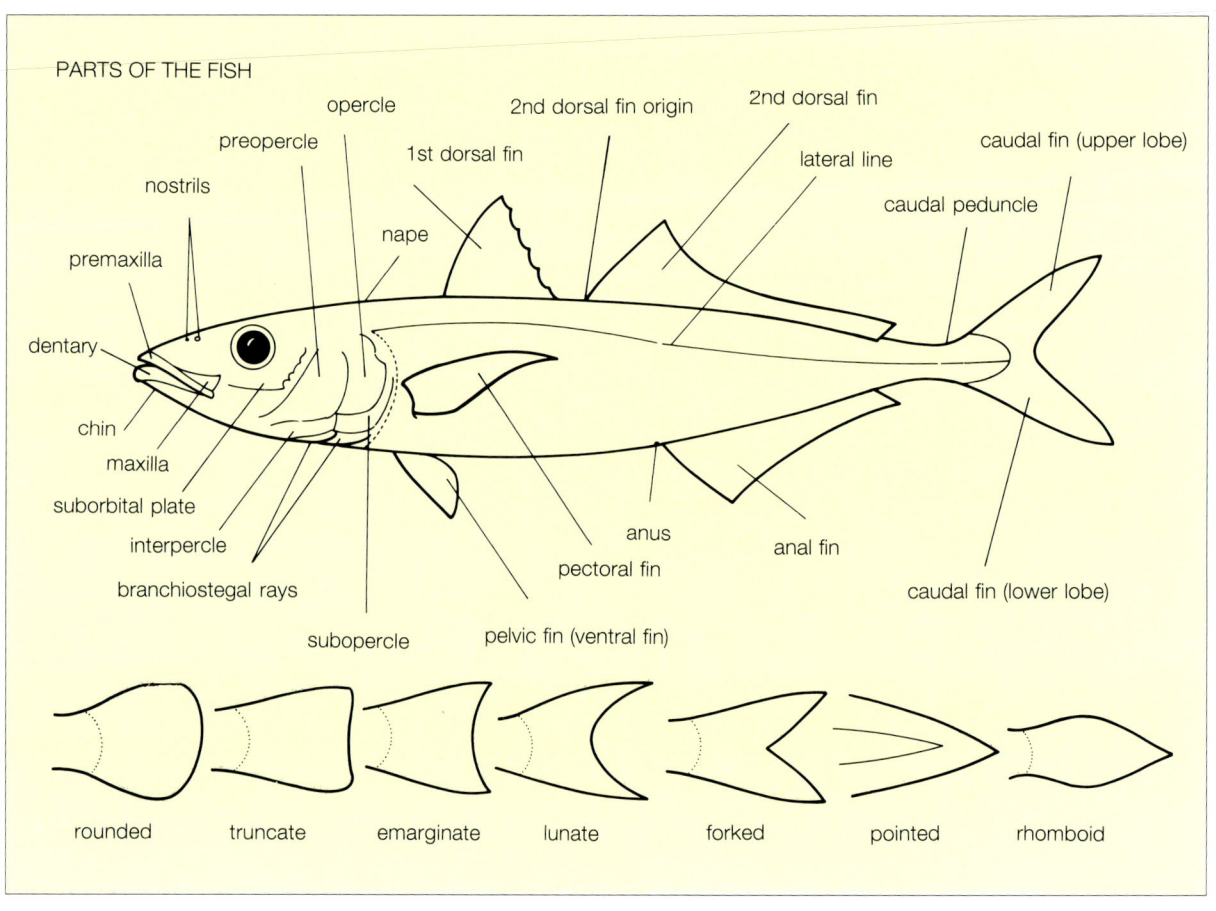

PARTS OF THE FISH

opercle · 2nd dorsal fin origin · 2nd dorsal fin · preopercle · 1st dorsal fin · lateral line · caudal fin (upper lobe) · nostrils · nape · caudal peduncle · premaxilla · dentary · chin · maxilla · suborbital plate · interpercle · branchiostegal rays · subopercle · pelvic fin (ventral fin) · pectoral fin · anus · anal fin · caudal fin (lower lobe)

rounded · truncate · emarginate · lunate · forked · pointed · rhomboid gen or loss of food as a result of water contamination. Some chemicals and pesticides can be mercifully quick but these usually enter water by seepage, poisoning and causing stress over a long period. The loss of habitat and unnaturally high water temperatures from siltation also affect them. It can lead to a slow death if they are unable to escape to cooler stretches.

It was anglers who first became aware of water pollution or waterway degradation and made it known. Yet the anti-fishing lobbyists overlook this and seem oddly less vocal about any "suffering" that might be caused by illegal netting (or approved netting for that matter).

The essential matter is that every person who enjoys the waterways and their aquatic creatures should respect both. Caring anglers do.

What makes a sporting fish?

A misleading belief exists — perpetuated by some writers and anglers with closed minds — that only certain fishes may be designated "sporting", with trout and barramundi most commonly heralded as such and the Australian bass and jungle perch accorded the accolade occasionally. The same expression is used to describe some saltwater species as sport or game fish.

This viewpoint is hard to understand but it has historical origins, involving early settlement and the conventions of the privileged English anglers of the early 1800s.

Most convict and early free settlers fished for Australian native fishes to supplement a sometimes meagre diet. They used set-lines and caught large fish more frequently than present or future anglers will ever encounter (more's the pity). By tall tale and myth it was accepted that such fish could only be caught on lines as thick as a little finger with a galah or other unusual bait on the hook. There is no doubt that strong cord was used for Murray cod and golden perch (other species in the same water went free because of the hook sizes and bait) as a matter of necessity and expediency to extract them from virgin waters full of snags. Those forebears who opened up the land knew nothing of the strange native fish nor had they the resources in time or money to study or to pursue them as a sport.

About this time, fishing in England began to be divided into a recreation or sport and a coarse pastime rather than simply a pleasurable means of catching dinner. Gentlemen fished for trout and salmon (sport) and the lower classes fished for other fish (a coarse pursuit). Such prejudices were reinforced in other ways too. The expansion of industries and the resulting pollution, combined with the urbanisation and the mounting inflow of effluents into waterways began to reduce stocks of the once plentiful trout and salmon; improving working conditions and transportation allowed the working classes to venture further afield on streams. As more of the landed gentry restricted angling in their estates to the privileged, the division between "sport" and "coarse" fishing widened. Such distinctions led the privileged to try to ban the forerunner of the threadline reel when it was manufactured in the 1800s, largely because it made casting a bait too easy and allowed *non-anglers* to use lures.

Some of these worthy gentlemen brought such views to the new world and when they found that the local fish did not behave like trout or salmon, they introduced them. Carp, tench and redfin followed.

There is no bias here, I hasten to add, against the good trout. The trout attracted the writer's first efforts and he is still content to catch trout or tuna, Murray cod or mulloway, golden perch or groper, river blackfish or rock blackfish. Trout are an admirable fish and a valuable addition to many waters. But I find it absurd that trout should be considered more sporting than most of our indigenous fish and a national tragedy that authorities spent so much research time and money introducing them to so many unsuitable Australian waterways while all but ignoring the propagation and protection of the native species. There is insufficient work done for the native species to this day and their habitats continue to be spoiled. Our native fish are a national resource that has yet to be properly appreciated.

Today, while the species of fish or how they are caught remains as sport or game or coarse fishing in some minds, the pastime is now available to all in Australia, without distinction.

Some anglers regard a sport fish as one which can be seen and tempted with an artificial representation, but this probably applies to all fish because many anglers are continually finding more fish which can be caught with a lure. Probably clearer in meaning as lure. Still other anglers consider sport fish are those which explode out of the water and complete sizzling runs and aerial acrobatics after being hooked, but one that struggles out of sight, albeit with great stamina, is apparently not. As far as I am concerned, all fish are sport fish when they are treated as such by matching the rig to the fish so as to make sport of the contest.

SALTWATER FISHING
A general introduction

There are between 31,000 and 37,000 kilometres to fish around the Australian coastline. In fact there is more if you extend the shoreline measurement of estuaries from their ocean entrance and add ocean lakes that open periodically to the sea, not to mention the shorelines of islands.

Such a shoreline, ranging from latitudes in the tropics to those of the southern temperate zone, encompasses the most disparate coastal terrain and environment, the like of which no other country may claim. And it is accessible to all. State restrictions are comparatively modest and generally very reasonable, involving the sizes or numbers of fish, or the methods of catching them. Only the tiniest areas have been designated marine parks or declared non-fishing zones.

There are remarkable contrasts for the angler to comprehend. Fishing the shallow waters of the Gulf of Carpentaria and the shallow waters of a South Australian bay are as different as fishing the Great Barrier Reef or a reef offshore from Albany. Anglers familiar with the tides of south-eastern Australia can expect an awesome experience if they ever witness the great racing tides of Western Australia's north-west.

In this broad introduction to fishing, the term "estuary" is used to describe rivers, bays and harbours and any other waterways that are saline or influenced by tides. Some are deep and extensive, with a whole diversity of shoreline and underwater habitats for fish; others are great expanses of sand and mud bottoms, with shorelines of mangroves; some are rivers which are broad and empty into the ocean from a coastal range, or drain saltpans and plains after the wet season in the north. Others are small creeks which may enter a lake or large bay or run directly into the ocean. Just as the terrain and the environment differ, so

A grand sky, a light swell, and a comfortable boat: all the best elements of salltwater fishing — if the fish are biting.

do the fish. Yet many fish of the same genus but different species are encountered. There are fish which migrate from fresh to brackish or salt water to spawn; fish which spend most of their lives in saltwater estuaries but migrate to sea to spawn; fish which spawn at sea though the young reach maturity in estuaries or bays or coastal lakes; others stay near the entrances. Pelagics, which are regarded as oceanic, may enter estuaries to hunt and come within casting distance of shoreline anglers. Many species regarded as tropical residents follow warm ocean currents down the coastline and occasionally provide game-fishing thrills for southern anglers: every so often a reef fish of the tropics is hooked well out of its usual habitat. And there are some fish, of course, which remain more or less in a confined area throughout their life.

Despite the diverse environmental and climatic conditions and the variety of fish which exists around the continent, there are some basic principles that apply when seeking fish from estuaries, beaches, ocean rock fronts or offshore reefs.

Estuaries

In *estuaries* — including bays and harbours — fish sought by anglers tend to congregate in areas of abundant food source. This can be rocky underwater reefs, beds of mussels or other shellfish, deep channels with weed growths alongside, rocky shorelines that are encrusted with shell and weed, sandflats and mangrove-fringed mudflat shorelines. Small fish, crabs, worms, shrimps, prawns, molluscs, which the anglers' fish prey upon, can also be found in these locations, and

often as not vegetation for some of the herbivores. Man-made structures in many estuaries may also provide shelter for small fish: wharf, jetty and bridge pylons, as well as breakwalls and groynes, become home to worms and crustaceans and weed growths. Navigation channel and reef markers, boat moorings and pontoons may also offer a protective home for the marine creatures that larger fish pursue.

In some estuaries a river or creek will flush in a whole variety of food and some breakwalls at river entrances act as a direction-changing obstruction, shepherding fish into estuaries or delivering a supply of food for fish.

During the day, small fish and crustaceans remain close to such structures or natural features, venturing away in dull light or on certain tides. Large fish are more likely to visit such locations when the residents are more active, or have a false sense of security created by dull light, or when schooling for a spawning migration. Some areas that can furnish excellent dining for fish are too shallow to reach except on a rising to full tide. The cautious fish will use a combination of tide and darkness to feed in such areas, which are usually shorelines of low rocks or mangroves around bays and creeks. Other fish are ambushers (flathead is an example, "chopper" tailor another). These fish will wait where a current or tide carries food items over the edge of a hole, or along a channel, or simply drag them from the crevices of rocks and similar sanctuaries. Still other fish will follow a tide over sand and mudflats to grub for worms, shellfish or crustaceans.

Whether you fish estuaries from the shore or a boat, you must establish where food is most likely to be available for larger fish, as well as how tides or current can be used to advantage. The principles that follow help, whether using bait or lure. Depending on the estuary location on Australia's coast, the fish you could expect are bream and barramundi, mullet, mulloway and mangrove jack, salmon, tailor and snapper, flathead, ox-eye herring, threadfin and trevally, garfish and whiting and numerous other species.

Beaches in bays that face the open seas are better "read" as ocean beaches.

Beaches

The writer likes the analogy that a beach is a take-away or eat-in restaurant, even a boarding house or motel. In the main, there are no permanent fish

Estuary fishing: deep channels with weed growth alongside.

populations on a beach. The various species visit for a quick meal, some stay for a short seasonal period, others use them for spawning. Still others are overnight transients.

When visiting a beach for the first time, it is essential to "read" or inspect it thoroughly. If time permits, do this at low tide. Make your survey from a headland or at least a high spot. Use binoculars, or at least polarised sunglasses.

The various forms of the beach are fairly obvious. These are *holes, channels, gutters, sandbars* and *sand spits.* A beach without these — one which is evenly sloped and appears similar from one end to the other — is called featureless or without formation. Lengthy shallow beaches or short deep beaches can acquire this condition as the sand is pushed onto the beach through long periods of flat seas and offshore winds. The few channels or holes in such cases will be shallow.

When examining a beach in good light, the shallow sandflats appear light green. Where there are channels and holes and gutters, the water will change to a light blue with deeper colour patches. The darker blue is the sign of deep water.

Channels are deepwater trenches that extend from behind the area of breaking waves, which may well be on the edge of a sandbar some distance from the water's edge. These are the "freeways" through which fish enter and leave the beach food zones. They may run more or less parallel to the beach before turning to sea again. Sometimes a channel divides, creating a foamy or deep flat area between two sections, often an excellent location for a bait. The same formation may be the result of a separate channel or a long gutter. Gutters are the sideroads by which fish move from the channels. These can run in the same direction or at different angles, but they have no direct access to the waters beyond the waves.

Holes, large or small, mark deeper sections of water within generally circular walls. They are surrounded by shallower water, usually (though not always) with a gutter from a channel on one side. Depending on the sand flat area there may be only one or several holes of different sizes.

Sandbars are similar to sandflats but they are mostly devoid of holes. It is a sandbar (or sandbank) which causes the swell to break with a drawback off it. Their shape, size and depth are determined by the wind conditions and wave power. The front of a large sandbar or flat is a prime fishing spot, because the water may have lost much of its force on the outer rim. Fish are not usually present, however, where wave action at the edge of sandbars continually clouds the water with a heavy content of sand.

Sand spits are fingers of sand which spread out from the beach. How high or large they are is subject to tidal and wind conditions and the run or sweep of the water along the beach. A gutter with a sudsy water cover alongside a sand spit can be a prime location for whiting and flathead.

If you spend a little time reading a beach, you can make further observations. Dark patches which tend to move with the waves are invariably weed, either attached or floating. If the dark patch seems to be moving at a different speed to the waves or if it appears to alter course, spread out and then reform, it will be a school of migrating fish such as bream, mullet, luderick, pilchards, tommy ruff or salmon. Many fish stay in fairly tight schools during migration. They visit beaches to feed or for shelter.

Rocky areas also can be discerned on any reasonable day. Make a mental note of rocks and weed areas and avoid casting over them during the fishing session.

While fish visit relatively featureless beaches from time to time, they prefer beaches with sufficient wave action and currents to shift sand, because it this action uncovers worms, and dislodges shellfish and crabs from their sanctuaries. The same forces then wash them along the edges of holes, channels or gutters, a smorgasbord that serves many species of fish. Where such conditions are reasonably accessible and there is a measure of wash or foam about to provide cover (for both predatory fish and the angler), the fishing is even better.

Many such "fishy" locations are quite close to the beach. Whiting and bream can be found in sudsy water quite near the shoreline and large flathead will bury themselves near a shallow gutter or on a shallow sandflat, lying in wait to ambush small fish. In general, fish avoid the pounding wave areas, where excessive amounts of sand are churned up. Food dislodged by this action will usually be washed towards the fish, and the same food is more easily obtained where the currents transport it over an edge of a hole or along the side of a sandbar.

Generally — there are always exceptions such as overcast days and gloomy-looking water — more fish feed at beaches when there is less light on the surface, which is normally from before dawn to shortly after sunrise and from late afternoon into

Mayhem off the beach at Fraser Island off the Queensland coast when the tailor spawn there in September.

the night. The pelagics, such as salmon, tailor, and even mulloway and tuna, are more often caught in numbers during these periods. On the other hand, fish such as whiting, garfish, tommy ruff and tarwhine are more a daytime fish. In northern areas such fish as queenfish, mackerel and others may be caught in daylight hours, especially near broken reefs at the ends of beaches.

Other locations that will harbour fish are the mouths of (or adjacent to) creeks, a lagoon or lake entrance on a beach, and at the end of a beach where a breakwater extends to sea, especially where rivers spill out (particularly after the top of the tide) or when they are emptying floodwaters.

The angler's bait should not be anchored; it should be weighted just sufficiently to be washed around sandflats or along the edges of channels where other food items are being presented to fish. If the seas are such that even with a heavy sinker the angler's bait is still pushed inshore or swept sideways, the conditions are perhaps too rough for that particular beach. Those who wish to cast and retrieve lures should fish in a gutter, channel or across a sandflat, and retrieve their lure in the direction of the current at a speed to keep it working near the bottom.

Beach fishing is a comparatively safe and dry way to catch fish, unless the angler wades into the surf to crib a few extra metres with his cast. Such practice can result in being dumped by a wave or overbalanced by a strong sweep or undertow. It can be particularly hazardous at night. There is always the possibility of a shark being in the vicinity, a not uncommon occurrence when numbers of fish are being caught or are present. It is a very sobering sight to see a pack of sharks herd a school of fish into the corner of a beach with such terrible ferocity that they drive their prey on to the sand.

Ocean rocks

If some caution is required fishing from a beach, special care must be taken around rocks. Anglers cannot be too conscious of their safety whenever they are working from ocean rocks, whether from a low platform or higher ledge. There are times when it is foolhardy to even contemplate fishing from such locations. The moment there is the slightest doubt about the situation, any sensible angler must retreat to a nearby beach or estuary if he must fish that day. The tragedies that have overtaken overconfident rock fishermen make a most miserable toll.

Experienced anglers never rush to a rockfishing spot anyway, even one with which they are familiar.

They spend at least a quarter of an hour watching the waves, noting how they are rolling in and breaking, their volume, size and velocity, and where they may be washing across to block an escape route. One of the most treacherous periods on the rocks can be at the turn of the tides.

Quite apart from inattention to the elements, too many anglers are washed in because of inappropriate footwear, and then they are handicapped by heavy clothing. It can be a dreadful price for rash enthusiasm. Calmly consider all the dangerous possibilities, including precisely how you will manage to land your fish.

But that is the negative side. And commonsense and caution can overcome it. On the positive side, rockfishing can be the most productive of all land-based angling. Almost all the fish available in an area to beach fishers can be caught from the rocks — and there is the prospect of hooking such esteemed fish as snapper, groper, mulloway, giant trevally, tuna, tuskfish, kingfish and even a juvenile marlin, as well as the more common luderick, rock blackfish, sweep, bream, wrasses, etc.

Rocks fronting the open sea are havens for small fish — yellowtail, sweep, garfish, mados, parrot fish, juvenile luderick and rock blackfish, as well as the common mackerel, mullet, pilchards and others during their migrations. The rocks are a source of a great variety of limpets and chitons, and often shellfish (including oysters in some areas) and several species of crabs, conjevoi and eels. There is also weed or algae growth for the herbivores. Along with the rock crevices, the weed beds provide some protection for all the small fish when predators are scouting. If a rock location is apparently devoid of much of the above, it is unlikely to be a consistent fishing spot.

Rock fishing often entails casting over rocks and rubble that extend out from a rock platform. It may also be over a relatively clear bottom between the cliff face and a reef, or in deep water below a headland. Any location with a deep inlet on one or both sides, or with a reef or obstruction such as a bombora, offers promising fishing.

In broad terms, the make-up of a good rock fishing spot varies around the coastline. The main locations are on the east and south-eastern coastline, along the Victorian and Tasmanian coasts and part of the eastern area of South Australia. The south-western corner of Western Australia and some of that State's mid-northern regions are also attractive. However, the opportunities for rockfishing in the tropics are very limited indeed.

Bait should be set close to the bottom on your rig,

amongst rocks and alongside weed or on sand patches between reefs. It may be floated just off the bottom, in midwater or close to the surface. A rig which allows the bait to sink slowly and move with the surges is usually more effective than one which a crab may have dragged under a rock or into weed. Even the activity of nuisance fish darting about and picking the bait can at least send a signal for a better fish to investigate. With few exceptions, luderick, rock blackfish and drummer are taken with a floating bait. By contrast, most kingfish, tuna, mulloway, mackerel, trevally, etc., are more often caught off the bottom or in midwater using an active live bait or a dead bait that is animated by a bobby cork or balloon. Snapper and morwong, usually regarded as bottom fish, will take a well-presented bait well off the bottom and groper have no hesitation in grabbing a red crab well off the bottom.

While flat seas without swell may make fishing more comfortable, the number of fish caught are usually few. In calm conditions, very few little fish move from the shelter of the rock crevices and shelves or weed growths, and crabs or weed are not likely to be dragged into deeper water by receding water. Moreover their predators are less inclined to come in search of food without the protection of disturbed waters, even on a rising tide, unless it is dark. Remember that they too are part of a food chain. Even luderick, drummer and rock blackfish prefer some water movement, with foam or soapy washes for cover, while they eat. The small fish are more active with a cover of disturbed water — and salmon, tailor, kingfish and members of the tuna family use white water to attack fodder fish.

The best times to fish rocks are in the morning before the light is too bright and in the afternoon and at night. A rising tide induces the deep water species to seek food close to the food sources and where migrating schools of fish may be sheltering. However, even at these more promising times of the day, a degree of choppiness on the water is desirable.

Bobby corks and bottom rigs, helped by off-shore winds or ebbing tides, are used to take baits into deep water beyond casting range. Depending on the fish targeted, the bait may be in midwater or near the bottom. The sudden disappearance of a float and the whir of line disappearing from a reel spool as an unknown fish streaks away with a bait is one of fishing's memorable moments — matched only by the perplexity felt if the fish is lost without having being seen.

Spinning from rocks is an energetic daytime form of fishing. It too is usually more successful in the morning and afternoon. Many fish can be caught on spoons, slicers or jigs retrieved at a reasonable speed; others such as tunas respond more to fast retrievals. Whichever lure is selected, lengthy and repetitious casting sessions are necessary to cover all the likely areas at different depths and speeds. But one good fish makes it worth all the effort.

Offshore

While fishing the centre of a large harbour or bay, well out from the shore, could be termed offshore, the common interpretation is fishing on reefs or drifting sandy or rubble bottoms or trolling in open ocean waters. In some instances, the offshore fishers are in reality much nearer land than anglers in harbours or bays when they fish inshore reefs, or cast lures to white water adjacent to a headland, or troll lures under a cliff .

The very first safety rule applies to both. The boat must be seaworthy for the conditions and at least all the legal requirements of safety gear must be fulfilled. Even this may be not be enough if the persons in the craft are too inexperienced to recognise the signs of changing weather (or they are mindless enough to ignore them).

For those contemplating offshore fishing, there is no better way to learn about it than by spending time with experienced boat anglers — or fishing regularly on charter boats. It is certainly wise to fish from other people's boats before investing in one yourself. Apart from the experience you will gain, you may well find that this particular form of fishing is not for you.

The sea floor is covered mainly with sand or mud; rubble areas with or without weed; kelp beds or seagrass meadows, and reefs. Some of the latter may be relatively small and in shallow water; others may be much larger and more extensive; and some will have peaks that rise steeply from deep water to close to the surface. Some reefs can have relatively shallow water on one side, others surprisingly deep chasms, and there may be several reefs close to each other. Their form, or their angle on the seabed, may create surges and currents around them; the dangerous ones are the bomboras that are often found close inshore. They can be a threat to boats, even in moderate seas.

Reef fishing can be within a few metres of the coastline or (from a suitable bluewater craft) as much as 200 kilometres offshore (such as the Swain Reefs of the southern Great Barrier Reef). Another form of offshore fishing involves finding warm water currents and trolling or drifting in

these in pursuit of tuna and marlin. Fishing from boats on the ocean is very much at the whim of the weather, but many anglers happily spend a lifetime chasing surface and bottom dwellers.

Most bottom fish are caught on baits but some, such as kingfish, respond to a form of lure fishing called "jigging". This is retrieving a lure from the bottom by cranking the reel with a short, stop-start action, combined with lifting and lowering the rod. It is much less tiring in sheltered waters with small lighter lures. It can be successful with snapper and other species. The more traditional form of lure fishing — apart from casting and retrieving saltwater flies or lures — is trolling with an array of lures for bait fish, or for pelagics such as tuna, tailor and salmon. This can be rewarding in water fairly close to the shoreline. Seagulls and other seabirds will often lead a boat to schools of such fish.

Some trolling is done with live or dead bait for tunas, marlin and sharks, etc.

Apart from using bait near the bottom while anchored over a reef or other underwater obstruction, or such fish attractions as a mussel bed or firm rubble bed (even a channel in a firm sand area), it can be done just as effectively if the boat is drifting on the current or with the wind. The bait bounces along on the chance it will encounter some fish. A heavier sinker — sometimes three times the weight — is required when fishing the bottom while drifting in deep water, compared to anchoring over a reef. This type of fishing, however, is not popular with experienced boat fishers. They have charts (and depth sounders) which not only indicate the nature of the seabed, and thus reduce the element of chance, but sometimes the echo sounder identifies a school of fish on its screen.

Whether fishing from an anchored position or while drifting, a floating bait is growing increasingly fashionable for catching a whole range of fish. This is most successful in a "berley trail" of minced fish or fish pieces, with some additives such as (poultry) laying or growing pellets. It is a much practised method for catching yellowfin tuna and in shallow water the berley will attract almost all pelagics, as well as raising snapper and many other reef-inhabiting fish towards the surface. The bait, in this case, is either completely unweighted or it is only weighted with sufficient lead to encourage it to sink and drift in the berley trail.

All fish have preferences on reefs. Some, such as

The ultimate challenge for the offshore angler — a strike for a fighting game fish, in this case a furious sailfish.

flathead and gurnards, will be found on the sandy bottoms near reefs; snapper can be caught on sand and rubble adjacent to reefs. Teraglin and mulloway often cruise the waters above a reef, john dory alongside a reef, and tuskfish and wrasses right in the heart of the reef. Morwong, sweep and nannygai can be found on or close to reefs. Kingfish and other hunters patrol on the current side of a steep slope or peak, even near the bottom. Some species of fish are more plentiful around reefs in certain seasons in different areas of Australia. With the exception of the northern parts of Australia, where massive extremes occur creating powerful currents, tides have less influence on offshore fishing than they have for estuary, beach and rock fishing.

While it is possible to fish offshore without them, particularly close to the coast where an idea of the bottom can be gauged from the land formations of cliffs, headlands and beaches, admiralty charts and depth sounders are an investment for those going to sea regularly in their own craft. The charts — in combination with some maps that help locate reefs within sight of landmarks, which are aligned to other reference points — only give the depth of water over the reefs and the extent of the reefs.

Depth sounders

Depth or echo sounders make locating of fish off-shore easier and quicker, but their use has resulted in many boat owners failing to develop the skills needed to navigate by landmarks and charts. And it must be said that this rapid location of fish, coupled with the speed at which modern craft can travel to and from the fishing grounds, encourages some to take gluttonous numbers of fish when they are running. This was less of a problem in the not too distant past because boat fishers had to rely on landmarks for the bearings of popular fishing spots and their boats were much slower. There simply was not as much time for the greedy to indulge themselves.

Modern depth sounders not only incorporate the latest sensitive electronics but they are much more compact, waterproof and robust — considerably less vulnerable to pounding from a choppy sea. While their basic function is the same, the breadth of information that the better of these devices can instantly supply is extraordinary.

Basically a depth sounder transmits a sound wave towards the ocean floor by means of a transducer fitted to the bottom of the boat. The signal bounces off the bottom and the "echo" is magnified and converted by the recorder to a graph for interpretation. Any interruption to the signal by an object such as fish or submerged timber between the

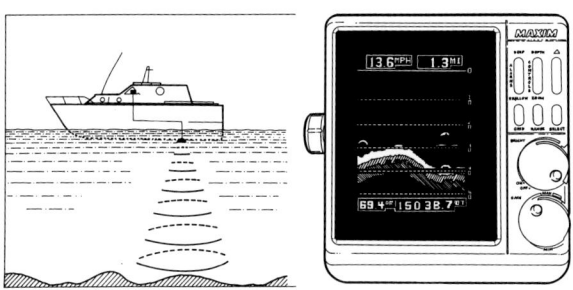

Depth sounder.

surface and the bottom is also indicated.

Originally the contours of the bottom were burnt into an electro-sensitive roll of paper by a stylus, or shown as flashing blips on a dial. The latest depth sounders, depending on the model, have a screen that interprets the signal in the form of graph-like solids and tones or as contoured bands altering almost instantly (or as fast as sound travels through the water which is approximately 1500 metres per second), as the sound echoes off the object or the bottom. The result, vividly displayed in most cases by liquid crystal read-out, is a detailed replica of the bottom, its formation of sand, mud, weed or flat rock and the peaks and hollows of reefs. The exact depth is indicated and anything separated from them by only a few centimetres — such as fish — are, on some of the electronic wonders, highlighted in a different colour. Almost all have adjustments to concentrate the signal to different depth ranges to obtain particular information about an underwater structure. The more the units cost, the more features are available at the press of a button or twist of a dial. Some include displays of water temperature at the surface and at various depths, the rate of the drift of the boat, or the speed of travel, including the distance from the boat the target is when searching at speed. Many offer "zoom" or "freeze-frame" adjusments for signal s on the screen, to help estimate the size of any fish that are located. Still others will retain a picture of an area and on future expeditions signal when the boat is in the same position as previously; on the drawing board are those which will give instant colour print-outs for reference and notations.

But I must confess that there is something about such sophisticated gadgetry that makes me uneasy as an angler. The fish really don't seem to have a chance if depth sounders are used to their full capability, especially if the angler has even the most rudimentary knowledge of the species and their habits in an area. The danger, of course, is that they can help overkill a finite resource when in indiscriminate hands.

A freshwater prize fit for a king: a beautiful Murray cod.

FRESHWATER FISHING
A general introduction

Despite Australia's reputation as the second driest continent
on earth, its freshwater rivers, lakes and impoundments
harbour a grand diversity of fish, many of which are unique.

At least one species of fish, and more often several, can be found in almost all of Australia's fresh waters. They exist in remote streams of the tropical ranges; in rivers which divide population centres; in creeks tumbling through gorges in the southern mountains of the mainland; and in the icy crystalline lakes of wilderness Tasmania. They can be found in wide stretches of turbid, slow-flowing rivers, lined with ancient gum trees, twisting across flat, almost featureless, landscapes, and among the debris of lush tropical lagoons. There are fish in the headwaters of most coastal rivers and creeks. Many man-made impoundments and lakes in all States have substantial fish populations; some of these waterways in the inland of eastern Australia have mixed fisheries that are the envy of anglers from other countries.

Fish of tropical freshwaters include jungle perch, sooty grunter, spangled grunter and sleepy cod, along with species which inhabit both freshwater and saltwater, such as barramundi and ox-eye herring. In the southern inland half of the continent there are Murray cod, one of the world's largest freshwater fish, golden perch, silver perch, Macquarie perch, river blackfish and others. There are species translocated from the northern hemisphere — trout, English perch or redfin and European carp — which are also present in freshwater of southern, central and south-western Australia, as well as Tasmania. In the fresh reaches of the coastal rivers of eastern Australia there are Australian bass, freshwater mullet, freshwater herring and marine species which extend from time to time beyond saltwater influence.

The threat of pollution

Freshwater fish have three inherent needs: pollu-tion-free water, shelter and food. Unfortunately man has sabotaged three out of three in many places.

Pollution is insidious and very difficult to isolate because so often it may not kill the fish directly. More often it will kill the fish's aquatic and terrestrial food list. It results from urban run-off, from the seepage of waste water and sewerage effluent, and from fertilisers and insecticides. Loss of shelter is generally caused by clearing trees and other vegetation from the banks of rivers and lakes to gain a few extra hectares for grazing or agriculture; it can also be the result of de-snagging river beds for flood mitigation. And not only does such action lead to the degradation of fish shelter habitats, it creates siltation from river bank collapses and soil erosion. The ultimate result is shallower warmer water. This in turn reduces the availability of food, constricts crucial fish migration, and destroys spawning zones.

Most of Australia's native fish are survivors (and artificial breeding of many of them will ensure they continue to survive in some waterways) but they are no longer in the numbers or of the size in waters where they once flourished. A biological requirement for breeding is water of a limited temperature zone. Cold water releases for irrigation purposes can kill their eggs and larvae. Upstream migration is often thwarted too by dam walls or weirs. Some have disappeared from upper sections of rivers to be replaced by introduced trout — yet these fish can be devastated by droughts and high temperature and low oxygen content of the water (for which the native species have a remarkable tolerance) and lack of suitable spawning areas.

Predators of freshwater fish are few. Anglers (and illegal netters) outnumber cormorants and other fish-eating birds, eels and crocodiles in some tropical waters. Larger fish prey upon fry and fingerlings, and small members of their own species, as well as others. Some small fish are taken by goannas and snakes. Australia is free of such predators as beavers, otters and bears.

The most successful anglers are those who understand something of fish habits; the importance of water conditions and temperature; and the significance of the underwater and above-water environment. Extremes of temperature and the clarity or turbidity of water will upset a fish's metabolism and they lose their appetite. When the water is very clear it can grow warm and a fish's natural instinct is to seek shelter from overhead predators, such as cormorants, and to seek a more comfortable temperature in deep holes or in the shadows. Dense muddiness, on the other hand, can irritate their gills and restrict the movement of underwater food, including other small fish, such as galaxiids, or shrimps.

Freshwater fish are reluctant to traverse clear shallow water, especially in bright sunlight. At night they will forage around the edges of sandy banks and explore weeds right to the water edge. During their spawning migrations, they have to cross shallow stretches but they try to pass them close to banks or under cover of darkness. Fish that are travelling are expending energy and the need to replenish it makes them hungry. Trout, golden perch and silver perch are noted migrators that eat constantly during their upriver movement and catadromous species, such as barramundi and

Canoes can provide access to overgrown or shallow waters. A sizable Australian bass is this angler's reward.

Australian bass, which must go downriver to find brackish or saltwater to spawn, become voracious eaters while they are fighting their way back to freshwater against the current .

In the main, freshwater fish (most marine as well) are opportunistic feeders, taking food which is presented to them by the current, or wind, or by downpours which wash terrestrial insects and worms into the water. In many instances they will occupy an area which affords protection, shelter and a regular food supply. Most larger fish, especially Murray cod, will control a territory that affords such luxuries. But this territorial dictatorship is also apparent in other fish; a large specimen taken from a safe location will be replaced by another dominant fish.

While the odd fish will display speed, and may surprise an observer with the distance it covers chasing a prey or lure, most do not expend energy in pursuit of food. The simple law of nature demands that a fish will not expend more energy chasing food than that food will ultimately deliver. Freshwater fish use speed to escape predators or presumed danger. Any angler who has disturbed a freshwater fish can vouch for it. ·

Trees, scrub, tussocks, briars and other bank vegetation with branches, and rocks and foliage overhanging the water, provide shelter and shadows in which a fish can hide. Other fish sanctuaries and food dispensaries are found in fallen trees or submerged logs, rock outcrops, reeds, water plants and undercut banks, deepwater channels or holes adjacent to them, and rock faces and clay cliffs. Insects and their larvae fall or are blown from trees and foliage, some breed in underwater rotting timbers and debris and amongst rocks, and shrimps, yabbies and small forage fish scavenge in such places.

Casting upstream and allowing the current to carry a bait into or past these spots is much more productive than having a bait anchored on a bare bottom. So is retrieving lures with the current, over and adjacent to underwater snags and obstructions. It is not possible to use the current in many areas of large lakes or dams, but a bait below a float that is moved by the wind (or the angler) can be very effective, creating just enough animation to attract a fish.

Other areas are where a spring or small watercourse or swamp enters the main river, especially when they are flushed by a quick downpour that may wash frogs, tadpoles, worms and beetles into the waterway. Streams receding after a minor flood, even if still discoloured, offer excellent

A stretch of the Namoi River in northern New South Wales. Moments of such beauty await the freshwater angler.

fishing, especially where the water below rapids slows down; and deep holes on the down-current side of a sandbar are often dining rooms for most fish, particularly silver perch, Macquarie perch and trout. Trout will often have a feeding station behind a rock or midstream, where the current is broken and food passes on either side. Even this fish does not waste energy when there are insect hatches; they cruise and rise but without real effort unless there is overpopulation in that waterway and food has been in short supply.

Almost all the foregoing conditions can be found in lakes and impoundments. They are sometimes fewer, and they may be beyond the casting limits of an angler on the shoreline, but there are ridges which disappear into the water, weed patches and springs or seepages, all of which offer some kind of aquatic or terrestrial food for fish. There are always the expanses where the current of an inflowing river or a creek are obvious. Look out for submerged trees in waterways for fishing with bait or lure or trolling amongst these can be very rewarding.

The most difficult waters in which to find fish are dams, where the shorelines have been denuded of trees and smaller vegetation, with few ridges or rocks or even submerged trees. Usually there will be weed beds for land based anglers to explore. Boat fishers should troll over and alongside these weed beds too.

It may not be pleasant fishing, but bays and inlets of impoundments towards which a wind is (or has been) blowing persistently, are really worthwhile fishing. Fish follow the insects that wind and waves sweep into these places, and the water slapping along the shoreline uncovers shrimps, worms or grubs. Casting baits or lures into the wind can be difficult and fishing from a boat uncomfortable in such conditions, but the fish in the creel after such a session can be satisfying compensation.

Where lakes are rising, fish during the night, using bait within metres of the water's edge. It can produce pleasing results.

Discoloured water should not deter freshwater anglers. Even what appears to be very muddy water can be fished with baits and even lures (which might also have a piece of bait attached). Fish possess reasonable vision for a limited distance but it is mainly to see movement and counter refraction when taking food from the surface and above, as do trout from time to time. They do have a sense of smell with which they separate the scent of familiar food from foreign odours. This alerts them to the possibility of a predator. (It is the sense of smell that guides salmon to the rivers and the same tributary in which they were spawned after years at sea. And the Australian native silver perch is so sensitive to pollutants and contaminants in water, they are more efficient at detecting them than much analytical machinery.)

The angler should remember this and ensure that their own hands, particularly when working with bait, are not tainted with foreign substances such as oil, kerosene, tobacco, insect repellents, deodorants, dog odour or citric fruits, for example. It is for this reason that many serious anglers exchange the soil in which they transport worms to a local soil from their fishing ground before using them, or they will immerse yabbies and shrimps for a time in the water they will be fishing.

All fish also have a unique sixth sense which is a form of radar for movement and current in the water. There are minuscule detectors in the skin along the lateral line and in branch canals over the head. These detectors help fish to avoid obstacles in turbid water and are believed to play a part in holding schools of fish in formation as they swim. When an object sinks into the water the current transmits the vibration which alerts the fish. It enables fish to detect the struggles of a sick or injured small fish and the flapping of insect wings. If, on the other hand, the object is larger than itself it will suspect a predator and flee for safety. And it is the sixth sense that makes it possible for fish to find lures in very turbid water. This is why, when fishing for trout for example, you are much more successful if you wade in and cast upstream, and why you are much more likely to draw a strike if you retrieve your lure with the current.

In general, fishing for freshwater species is most productive during the morning, in the late afternoon and during the night, much as for saltwater fishes. Fish seem to retreat to shelter and are less inclined to feed in the brighter periods (and often the warmest part) of the day, especially in summer. Water temperature and weather conditions, such as the air pressure associated with a change, or an influx of freshwater, or insect hatches or some other natural occurrence, can make mockery of such generalisations and induce sudden feeding sessions when the fish have been impossible to entice with a bait or lure for days!

Successful freshwater anglers are those who can relate to the significance of the environment and the behavioural instincts and habits of fish. The problem is that both the environment and freshwater fish of this great continent can be as different as soup and soufflé, though both may be enjoyed by the thoughtful and enterprising angler.

CHOOSING THE RIGHT GEAR

The most common error made by angling enthusiasts is to use a mismatched or unbalanced rod and reel. This can arise in any number of ways, the most common of which is an impulse purchase from a supermarket, where qualified advice is rarely available. Although some manufacturers offer packaged outfits through such outlets, specialist tackle shops generally offer a wider choice and thoughtful advice. Mismatched gear can also eventuate when the would-be angler receives only one part of the equation — rod or reel — as a gift. The delighted recipient, blissfully unaware of the pitfalls, then rushes out to purchase the missing component. The result can be a frustratingly clumsy combination. Tackle can also be unbalanced if the line used is of an incorrect breaking-strain for the weight of the terminal items, such as swivels, sinkers, bait or lures. This may not only snap lines, with consequent losses, but it can actually reduce the casting potential of the rod. The overall result is exasperation, particularly if a nearby angler appears to be casting and retrieving effortlessly.

The information here is necessarily brief but it should help the less experienced anglers equip themselves for fishing. There are no general purpose rods and reels but the suggestions that follow should help anglers to broaden their options without necessarily requiring a different rod for every purpose.

RODS

Rods may be made of fibreglass, graphite, a combination of these two materials, boron or kevlar. (Split cane is omitted because it is now used only for expensive fly-fishing rods). Newcomers and even casual anglers need not worry about boron or kevlar rods for their outfits. Both are costly and they are not dealt with here.

Tubular fibreglass rods are tough, longlasting and proven, requiring a minimum of maintenance. The newer glass cloths and improvements in manufacture produce lighter rods without loss of strength — and they have a quicker response or recovery in their action.

Graphite rods are a combination, in simple terms, of high -modular carbon fibre strands supported by a backing of fibreglass. The higher the percentage of graphite to fibreglass used, the more expensive the rod. But it will also be lighter and have a more rapid loading and recovery rate during casting.

In fibreglass-*and*-graphite rods, the mixture is usually distributed over the lower two thirds and the balance of the rod — or the tip section — is fibreglass only. These are very strong rods with a good casting action.

Rod action

The *action* of a rod — the way in which it bends from the tip under load while casting or when a fish is hooked — is termed *slow, medium, medium-fast* and *fast*:

• a slow rod curves more or less evenly from the tip to the butt

• a medium rod bends evenly from the tip to the middle

• a medium-fast rod has the bend in the top third of its length

• and a fast-action rod bends most in the top quarter.

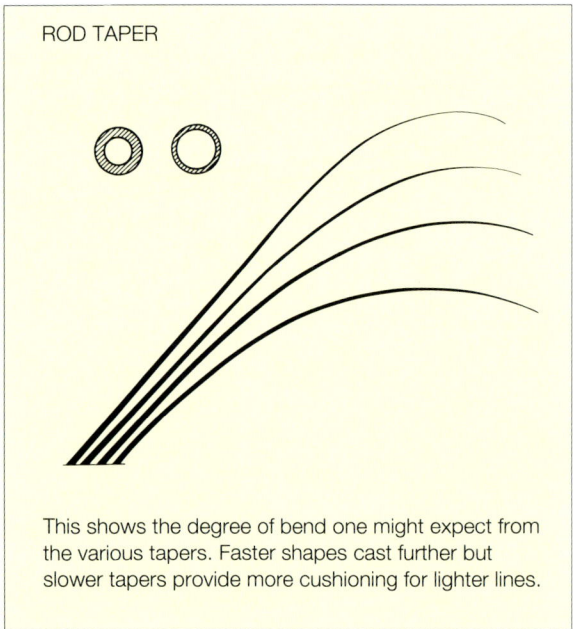

ROD TAPER

This shows the degree of bend one might expect from the various tapers. Faster shapes cast further but slower tapers provide more cushioning for lighter lines.

There are also rods with a multi-taper, which incorporate some aspects of the medium and medium-fast tapers.

Differences in the materials used in a rod and the rod's action or *taper* are really only noticed when an angler changes from one to another. Relatively small adjustments in technique and timing are needed to learn to control the maximum loading of which each rod is capable.

A safe choice for a newcomer is a medium-fast or multi-taper rod: one or two exceptions to this are mentioned later.

Rod weights

Ultra-light rods, mainly for single-handed use (some are made for two-handed casting), should not be considered during anyone's fishing apprenticeship. These are for specialist fishing by experienced anglers.

For this general summary, rods may be divided into *light*, *medium* and *heavyweight* (with some in the extra-heavy division). Weight is best described as the number of wraps of fibre which make up the thickness of the wall of the tube. The way the fabric is cut and wrapped can also give a rod a particular action: a rod with a fast taper and a heavy lower half, for instance, generates power while fighting a fish.

The choice of weight in a rod depends very much on the size of the fish sought — and by which method — as well as the weight of the line being used. For example, except for some estuary, lake and bay fishing, light threadline or baitcasting rods, with matching reels, are inadequate for ocean fishing. Such rods invariably lack the power to control a fish and the reels don't hold enough line for a contest with a big fish.

Medium-weight rods are suitable for most fishing, although a heavy model should be considered if you expect to hook a lot of large fish.

Threadline rods

These rods are built specifically for threadline reels. They can be identified by the line guides or runners, of which the one nearest the reel is larger and the remainder decrease in diameter towards the tip. When sighted from the butt, they form, if correctly spaced and mounted, a cone-shaped tunnel.

The reason for this is that the line spirals off a threadline reel. Those which are cast using one hand are *single-handed threadline* rods, usually about 1.6 metres to 2.2 metres long. They will have 4 or 5 guides between the large first guide and the tip guide. The reel seat, or mounting, will be approximately 15 centimetres from the butt. *Double-handed threadline* rods are obviously cast using both hands.

They should have about the same number of guides as the single-handed rod; but if the rod is 3 metres long, the reel seat will be about 35 centimetres from the butt; and if it is 3.75 metres long then it will be about 42 centimetres from the butt.

Note that the reel is fitted *underneath* the threadline rod for retrieving line or playing a fish.

Baitcasting rods

Baitcasting rods should be matched with baitcasting reels of a suitable size for single-handed casting. They are usually about 1.6 metres to 1.8 metres long, slightly shorter than threadline rods. In most cases they have a pistol grip so that the thumb is comfortably positioned near the reel during the cast. The reel seat is also closer to the butt. All the guides are much smaller than those of threadline rods because the line from a baitcasting rod runs out straight. There should be about five to seven guides, plus the tip.

The reel is *on the top* of this rod during casting, retrieving line or playing a fish.

Some rods are classified as *double-handed baitcasters*, being about 1.9 metres to 2.2 metres long. In such cases the reel seat is further from the butt and it does not have a pistol grip. This is often preferred for some forms of fishing, especially when pursuing large fish from a boat (*see* jig rods).

Overhead rods

These rods require overhead reels which, though they look similar to baitcasting reels, are usually larger and heavier. The reel mount is about 55 to 57 centimetres from the butt on a rod of 3.2 metres and 64 to 67 centimetres on a 3.6 metre rod. There should be about 6 to 8 guides, plus the tip.

Jig rods

These may be used with heavy-duty threadline reels, medium-sized baitcasting reels, or light overhead reels. The main difference is the distance from the reel-mounting to the butt and the line guides. They are versatile rods, which can be used for offshore trolling, bottom fishing, drift-fishing, fishing with live bait from boat or rocks, and casting-and-retrieving lures. If a lot of casting-and-retrieving is to be undertaken, then a threadline style rod without a roller tip guide is probably best, though some find this type of guide does not hamper their casting with a baitcasting or overhead reel either. Jig rods should be at least of medium weight, with a fast taper, and with power built into the bottom half.

A recent innovation is a short-stroke rod, somewhat like a jig-stick, measuring under 2 metres with a very powerful butt. It is mainly used from boats with live bait. This rod is not for beginners.

Sidecast rod

These are designed to mount a sidecast reel. They are identified by two features: their size — particularly of the first (or stripping) guide — and the position of the reel seat. The reel seat is closer to the butt, which is approximately 15 to 17 centimetres from the end on rods of 3 metres to 3.7 metres long — sizes suitable for beginners. The first guide is larger than that of a threadline rod and further from the reel. It is situated about halfway along the rod, because the line spirals off a sidecast reel in larger coils.

There are only another 5 or 6 guides, including the tip. On these rods there is often an open runner near the front hand-grip, which helps to stop "line-burn" on the fingers when a big fish strikes. This runner is usually of steel or chromed metal, as is the large first guide.

Boat rods

These are short rods — ranging from 1.3 metres — and fairly stiff. They usually have much less "flex", or cushioning factor, and in effect act like the arms of a hoist. The unsophisticated centre-pin style reel, usually spooled with a heavy breaking-strain line, is the winching mechanism. Cranking a fish to the surface is easier with a boat rod than hand-over-hand hauling — and with fewer tangles.

Fly rods

Almost all fly rods can be identified by the reel seat, which is on the end of the butt. Those of fibreglass are a slow or medium action. Newcomers who want to try fly-fishing should find a rod of about 2.6 metres for either a No. 6 or No. 7 fly line. This should be suitable for fly-fishing on most streams and impoundments, without overburdening the bank balance. They may have wire "S" shaped guides, although lightweight guides, positioned with extended feet, are becoming more commonplace: these will usually number between 8 and 10. (Saltwater fly rods are heavier, with stronger runners and a reel seat that is well away from the butt. But this method of fishing for saltwater species should only be tackled after the many other methods of fishing have been mastered.)

Float rods

The common name on the east coast for this type of rod is a luderick rod. It resembles a fly rod in many ways but the reel seat is about 15 to 20 centimetres from the butt. They are usually used with a centrepin reel, but similar diameter sidecast reels and light and medium threadline reels may be fitted. The runners are larger than those of fly rods and mounted higher. For estuary, lake or river fishing, a rod of 2.6 metres is adequate. But between 3 metres and 3.6 metres is needed for rock fishing in the ocean. They are usually of a medium to medium-fast action and have about 8 or 9 guides, including the tip. These rods are quite suitable for bait or float fishing and they may, with a threadline reel, be used for lure casting. Fly and float rods are used with the reel mounted *below* the rod.

Trolling rods/Game rods

These can be one and the same. They may be fitted with heavy-duty normal (but top quality) line guides, with a roller tip, or they may may be fitted entirely with roller guides. Many are built for line breaking-strain classifications under the rules of the Australian Game Fishing Association. They are used with the reels mounted *on top*. These rods are very much for the advanced specialist and are not examined in detail here.

REELS

There are threadline reels, baitcasting reels, overhead reels and trolling reels, sidecast reels, centrepin or Nottingham reels, and game reels. They are now lighter in weight, more precisely made, stronger, and less prone to corrosion than at any stage in the past. Their many improvements certainly make them much easier to use than reels made as recently as a decade ago. At least that is true of those made by established manufacturers who offer a wide range of models. These reputable manufacturers also provide good technical data so that reel buyers may be properly informed when comparing the various models and their features. Most also include an exploded diagram of the reel for maintenance and for identifying spare parts. (Doubtful brands can generally be avoided by seeking a brochure on the reel. In almost every case, detailed information will be unavailable.)

It is also wise to purchase a reel from a specialist tackle shop, which either carries spare parts or is willing to obtain them quickly. Such service more than offsets any seductive discounts elsewhere.

As with rods, the ultra-light or mini-model type of reels are not recommended for beginners.

Threadline reels

These reels are also called spinning reels or "egg-beaters". They have a fixed spool — one that remains stationary while the line is cast. The spool should not revolve when the line is being retrieved either, if the drag (brake) system is properly adjusted. With the correct adjustment, the spool will revolve only when a fish exerts that extra power that could break a line or tear out the hook. When combined with the cushioning effect of the rod (if it is suitable for the line being used) it helps the angler maintain a constant pressure on the fish. Various retrieval ratios are available through the gearing in these reels, as well as such features as front or rear drag (brake) system adjustments, automatic and manual line pick-up etc.

A guide to the classification of a threadline reel is

From left: Trolling or light game reel; light baitcasting reel; and overhead or double-handed baitcasting reel.

the diameter of the spool (measured across the front lip). In reels suitable for single-handed threadline rods, for example, a diameter of about 4 to 4.5 centimetres is light; 5 to 5.5 centimetres is medium; and 6 centimetres is heavy. The appropriate diameters of reels for double-handed threadline rods are about 6, 6.5 and 7 centimetres or more for light, medium and heavy rods respectively. Measurements may vary with different manufacturers, but these figures show that a heavy reel for a single-handed rod can be perfectly suitable on any light double-handed rod. Most of these reels will have a line recommendation (in breaking-strain or by diameter) displayed on them, along with the capacity of the spool. If you can afford a spare spool, fill one with the lightest line you might need and the other with a heavier line. In other words, use it to widen your options rather than simply doubling-up.

Threadline reels are mounted *under* the rod.

Closed-face or spin-cast reels

These reels are distinct because of their cone-shaped hood, from which the line emerges through

From left: Light, heavy and medium threadline reels.

a small hole in the point. They function somewhat like a threadline reel but they are used *on top* of the rod. These reels are restricted to light freshwater fishing, however, and threadline or baitcasting reels will prove more versatile tools.

Baitcasting reels

These are also called *multiplying* reels (larger versions may be called overhead, trolling, or game reels). During a cast, the spool revolves as the weight of the bait or lure pulls off the line. With the cast completed, a touch of the handle clicks the reel into gear. These are equipped with adjustable brake systems, magnetic centrifugal controls to reduce over-runs, level wind, etc. The rate at which the line is retrieved depends on the gearing. You can usually identify baitcasting reels that are too large for single-handed rods by single grips on the handle.

These reels are mounted on the top side of the rod.

Overhead reels

These are larger versions of a baitcasting reel. They are for use on double-handed rods. The lighter models are often used on double-handed baitcasting rods and they have a bigger line capacity than those used on single-handed models. Usually, though not always, they have a single grip with a counter balance on the handle. As the name suggests, these reels are used *on top* of the rod. The maximum weight for comfortable casting is about 500 grams, a limit that separates them from the larger reels.

Trolling/game reels

These are a still more rugged version of an overhead reel. Lighter models of both are preferred by some specialist anglers seeking large tuna or billfish from land-based fishing spots.

Both overhead and trolling/game reels are used on the *top side* of the rod.

Sidecast reels

This style of reel is comparable with the threadline when it comes to ease of casting, especially with light baits. It has a spool that is turned through 90 degrees by releasing a lever with a thumb-on action before a cast is made. It has to be returned to its original position before the line can be retrieved. In this very simple reel the spool revolves on a shaft. Various sizes in both diameter and spool width are available and in the main the drag or brake systems are simple. Their maintenance is minimal. They cast baits and float rigs exceptionally well but their use with lures is restricted to those which do not require a fast retrieval.

The sidecast reel is mounted *below* the rod.

Centrepin, Nottingham, fly reels

These reels, especially the Nottingham, can be traced back to the first reels fitted under a rod. They are (with the exception of a few fly reels) single-action, that is, one turn of the handle completes one turn of the spool. The difference between the centrepin and Nottingham is that the spindle of the centrepin has a tapered nose and the spool bushing bears on this taper. The Nottingham's shaft is straight.

Centrepins are made up to a diameter of 12 centimetres; Nottinghams to 22 centimetres; and a fly reel to suit a beginner should be about 10 centimetres in diameter.

These styles of reels are used *under* the rod.

LINES

Fishing lines are available in monofilament nylon, braided synthetics, lead core and wire. With the exception of freshwater fly-fishing, the standard

From left: Light-medium trolling or game reel; overhead or light trolling reel; light baitcasting reel; medium baitcasting reel.

From left: Sidecast reel; fly reel and centrepin or Nottingham reel.

nylon line can be used for any fishing. Braided synthetics and the other exotics have their roles for some gamefishing and specialised angling techniques, but they are disregarded here.

Monofilament nylon

This is available in breaking-strains from 1 kilogram upwards. Beginners should note that the thickness or diameter of a line is not the sole criterion of its breaking-strain. With lines of similar breaking-strain but different thicknesses, the thinner line will invariably be more expensive. Thicker line is usually wiry or springy, which can be a marked disadvantage on some reels. As a guide, anglers should buy the most limp or least springy line they can afford (unless it is for leaders or droppers on their terminal rigs, or for bottom fishing with heavy sinkers when using a handline or the winch type of reel).

Nylon is available in a wide choice of colours. Bright or fluorescent colours makes it visible while trolling, playing large marine fish, or when fishing in dull light for freshwater species, especially with lures. The writer prefers such shades as sandy, beige, grey, light green, fawn etc., which are less visible in the water, despite the fact that fish are supposed not to recognise much colour!

Nylon *does* deteriorate. Ultraviolet light is its worst enemy, so it should be kept away from sunlight when not in use. After use it should be washed in fresh water to remove salt and grime and inspected for bruises and nicks. Heat also weakens nylon, so knots should be lubricated (with spittle) when they are being tied. Nor should nylon be left in hot cars or stored close to hot areas. Petrol, acids, suntan lotions and insect repellents will also weaken it.

Fly lines

These synthetic lines are not classified by breaking-strain but by a number that indicates the weight of the first 9 metres of the working section of the line. A No. 1 fly line is very light (60 grams) while No. 12 is heavy (380 grams). A fly line may be the same diameter throughout its length (designated L), which is normally about 25 metres. Weight forward (WF) fly lines and double taper (DT) fly lines are usually 2 metres longer. A WF line has a thin diameter for about 12 metres, thickens for the next 5 metres, then further increases in diameter for another 6 metres, creating a better weight distribution for casting. Its final 3 metres taper off quite sharply with the last 50 centimetres being the thinnest portion of the whole line. On a line designated DT, the middle two thirds is the same

diameter and 3 metres at either end taper off sharply over the last two thirds of a metre. There are both floating and sinking fly lines.

Only level and double-taper lines are reversible. All require a "backing", usually of a heavy nylon line, to fill the reel correctly (and to allow a large fish to run more than 27 metres if necessary!). A fly line is matched to a fly rod in proportion to its stiffness (or more correctly, the resistance of its bend). The rods usually bear the number of the line to use. Flies are almost weightless, so weight is built into the first 10 to 12 metres of a fly line. A fly leader, which is a tapered length of monofilament nylon line between 2 and 5 metres, must be used.

HOOKS

There is a bewildering array of hooks manufactured. In every pattern of style there are different sizes, shank lengths, strengths and finishes, point and eye positions. The most confusing is the numbering system, which designates the size. Put simply, a hook size (distance between point and the shank, or the gap) starts from an arbitrary mid-point, a theoretical Size 0. From this point Sizes 1/0, 2/0, 3/0 etc. describe an increase in hook size. Sizes 1, 2, 3, 4 etc. describe hooks of descending sizes. Thus, the difference in gap measurement between Size 1 and Size 1/0 hooks is small, but between size 6 and 6/0 it is considerable.

The adage that any shape of hook will catch a fish if the point is sharp enough is sound advice — provided that the size is right for the bait. (The correct size hook can be better concealed, which helps the bait appear more natural.) A small abrasive stone or fine file is an essential item in the tackle box. Even new hooks may need a quick "touch-up".

Most hooks are available in a "bronzed" finish (several coatings of lacquer), tinned, cadmium or nickel-plated. Bronzed hooks are particularly prone to rust. They are also the cheapest and should be discarded after use. Other finishes delay the onset of rust but the points of these hooks are often duller. Unfortunately sharpening them breaches the rust-inhibiting finish. Hooks made from stainless steel are more expensive but certainly last longer, though they too require sharpening.

The following suggestion of hook patterns is given. An assortment of these — in sizes and strengths to suit the baits being used for the fish in the area — should equip an angler well.

• *Kendal Kirby*: a straight shank hook with a ball eye — for worms, slivers of fish bait, shrimps.
• *Beak* (or *Suicide*): a hook with a turne -up eye — for small live bait, pieces of fish bait.

HOOKS

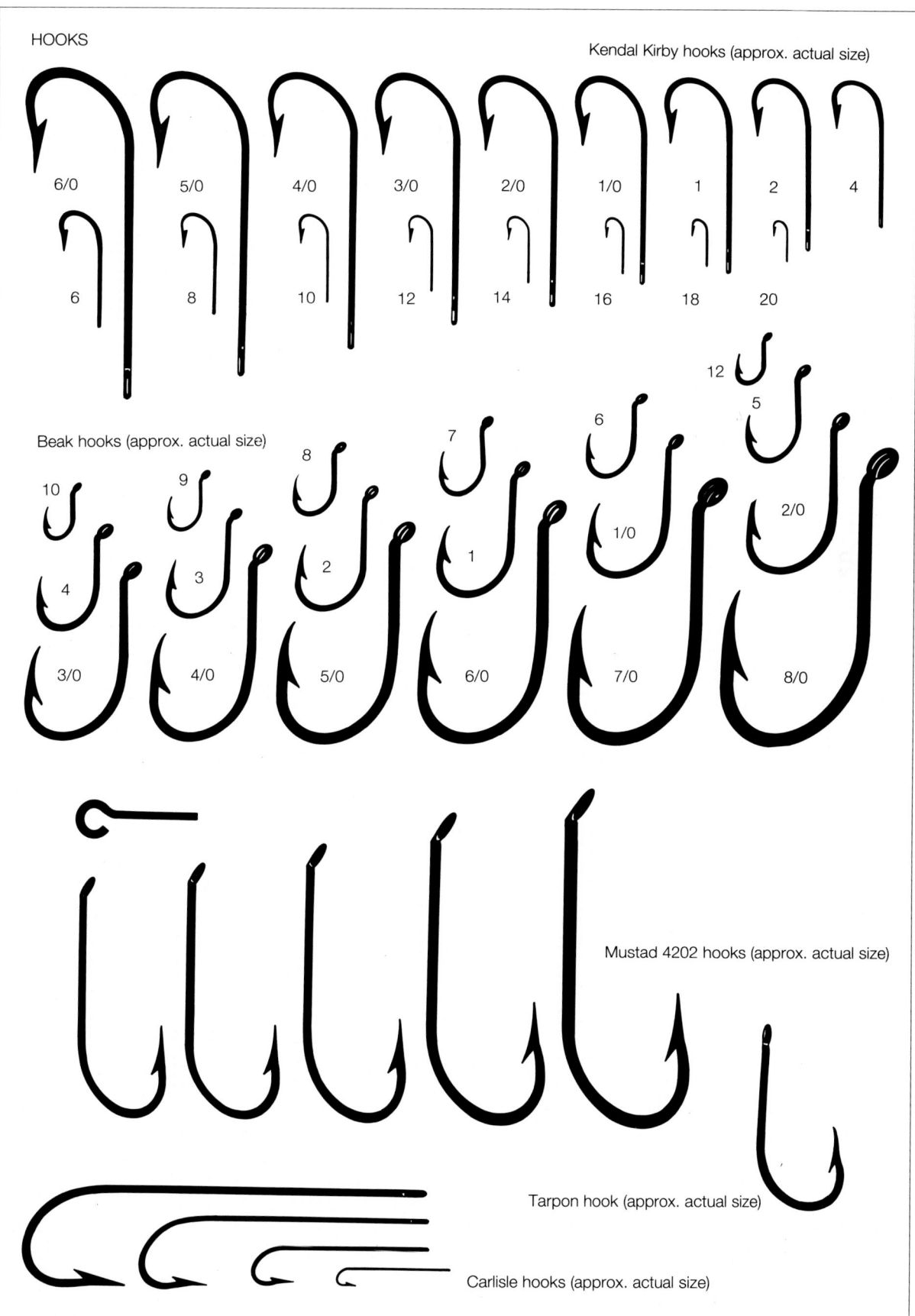

Kendal Kirby hooks (approx. actual size)

Beak hooks (approx. actual size)

Mustad 4202 hooks (approx. actual size)

Tarpon hook (approx. actual size)

Carlisle hooks (approx. actual size)

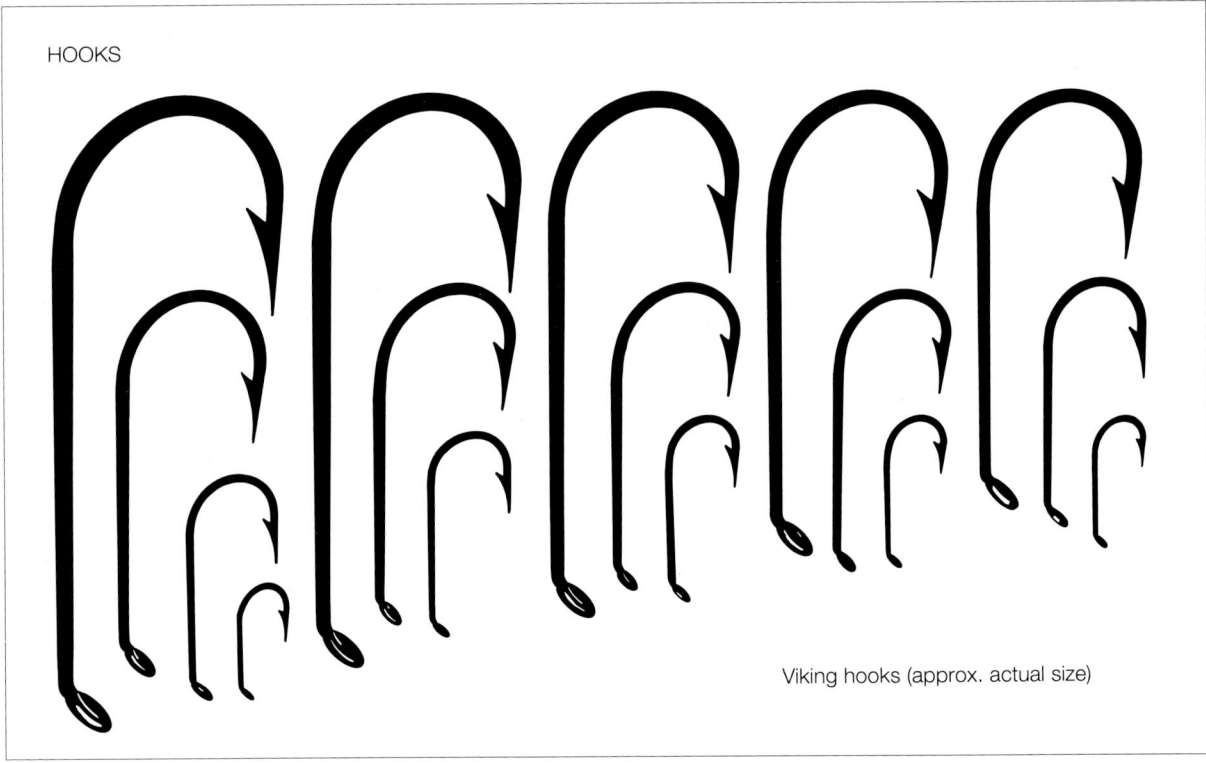

HOOKS

Viking hooks (approx. actual size)

• *Carlyle*: similar to the Kendal Kirby — suitable for whiting with worms, mulloway with beach worms, for flathead with large fillets of fish bait.

• *Viking* (or *French*): if only one hook is being selected, then a variety of sizes right through the range in this style will be adequate for any fishing (including ganging or linking).

• *Mustad 4200* or *4202*: popular for ganging for pilchards and garfish — No. 4200 requires the eye to be opened, No. 4202 has the eye opened ready to close after linking each hook.

• *Tarpon*: also popular for ganging and is another versatile hook.

SWIVELS

Swivels are not meant to be sinker stoppers. A swivel may have this effect in many rigs, but that is *not* its purpose. Swivels are employed to reduce line-twist caused by a bait or lure spinning during retrieval, especially when used on a threadline or a sidecast reel. They may also be used to connect a short leader or wire trace to a rig.

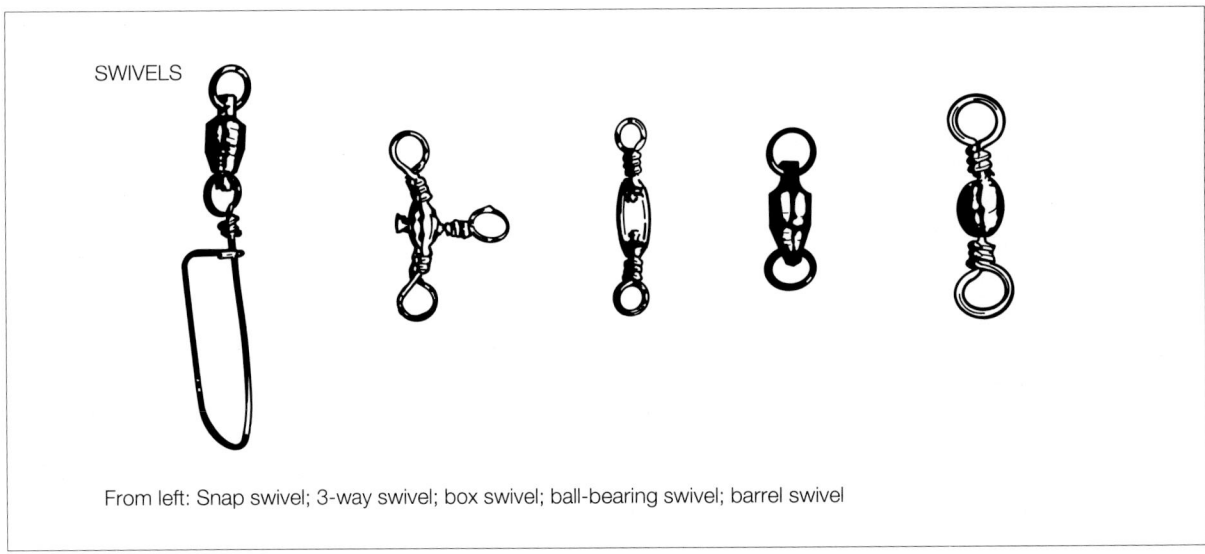

SWIVELS

From left: Snap swivel; 3-way swivel; box swivel; ball-bearing swivel; barrel swivel

In fact, a heavy sinker resting on a swivel reduces its effectiveness (as does a heavy bait or lure) by causing friction that retards or prevents it spinning freely. A guide to the right size swivel is the thickness of its wire : it should not exceed the diameter of the line being used.

Barrel swivels are the cheapest but the least efficient. *Box* or *rolling swivels* cost a little more. *Ball bearing swivels* cost even more but they are the most efficient. *Three-way* swivels are useful for bottom fishing on deep reefs. Some swivels have a snap attachment so that hooks and lures may be readily changed, though they can interfere with the action of some lures. Larger sizes are available in most of the styles that are used for trolling and gamefishing.

Some fish — tailor, leatherjackets, or large toads, for example — will grab bright swivels. Black swivels are available to reduce this unwanted attention, which frequently ends in a severed line.

RINGS

Rings are most useful as a sinker stopper for rigs in which line twist is unlikely to cause acute problems. But even when baitcasting with overhead reels, some lures have actions that can be bothersome. For this reason it is wise not to use ring connectors between the main line and the leader. They are excellent, however, when used in conjunction with swivels as a means of attaching sinkers (*see* rigs) Rings are satisfactory on handlines.

SINKERS

If you must use a sinker, it should be of the lightest practicable weight for the conditions. And it should be running or attached in such a way that it is not felt by a fish when it mouths the bait. Many freshwater fish, and saltwater species such as bream, will hesitate to take a bait that is unnaturally heavy. A sinker of suitable weight will allow the bait to move in any current or turbulence. If a sinker is used with a float, its weight should not spoil the float's balance and its ability to submerge easily.

For freshwater fishing, *ball, barrel* or *conical* sinkers will probably suffice. These same styles plus some *bean* or *channel* (or *picker's doom*) sinkers will be adequate for estuaries.

Ball sinkers are very good for beach fishing, but turbulent conditions can require *helmet* or *grip* sinkers. *Spoon* sinkers or small *snapper* sinkers are more practical when fishing from rocks, though small ball sinkers are suitable for many baits when bottom fishing and ball or barrel are best to balance a float. In some instances berley sinkers may be used (*see* rigs). Lastly, a caution regarding *split*

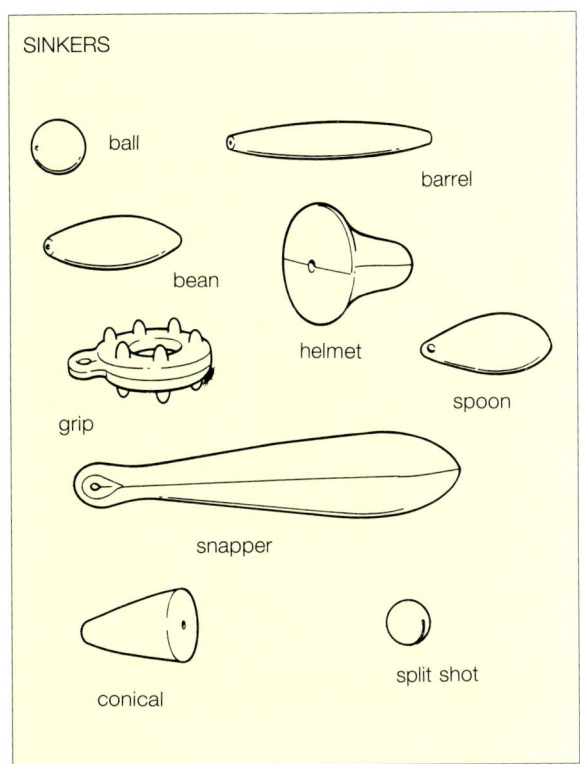

SINKERS

ball

barrel

bean

helmet

grip

spoon

snapper

conical

split shot

shot sinkers: they will weaken your lines if clamped on too tightly.

FLOATS

Floats are extremely effective when fishing for some species. This is certainly true for mullet, garfish, tommy ruff and luderick. They can be useful for many other fish too. In certain waters and conditions, a bait floated near the feeding area is more likely to be taken than one anchored to the bottom. They can also be effective with mid-water and surface roaming saltwater fish that are sought with live or dead bait, or fillets. A live fish under a float will transmit clearer signals of panic to a marauder; and a float can even create an impression of movement with dead bait as it bobs in the water or wind. Floats can also help carry a bait over a large area and prevent it from being snagged on rocks or lost in weeds or even dragged into crevices or holes by crabs. *Bobby corks* and *balloons*, assisted by currents or winds, can transport a bait well beyond casting range.

There are numerous styles of floats including *plastic bubbles*, which are popular for trout fishing. There are also large *round* floats and *quill* and *pencil* floats that resemble their namesakes. *Bodied stem* floats and *bobby corks* are mostly made from foam plastic these days. For the newcomer, the *quill* and *pencil* floats, a variety of sizes in the *stemmed* floats,

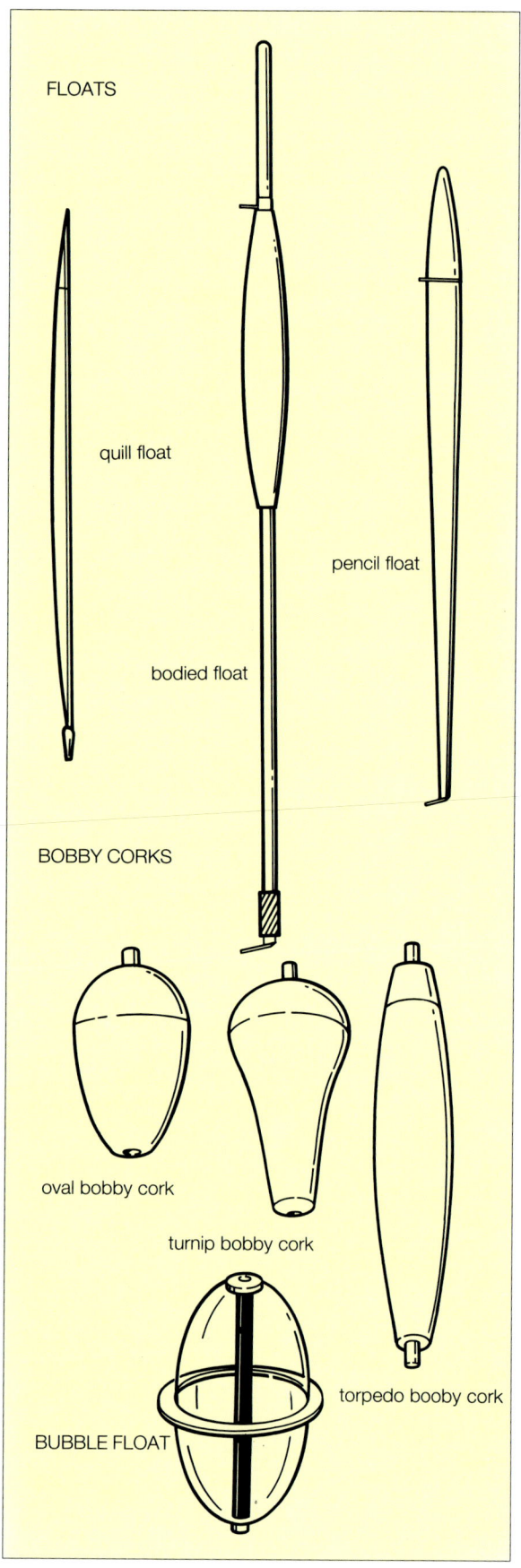

FLOATS

quill float

pencil float

bodied float

BOBBY CORKS

oval bobby cork

turnip bobby cork

torpedo booby cork

BUBBLE FLOAT

and some bobby corks, are all worth the investment. The secret of using floats is to weight them to hold the bait at the required depth. They should also be visible and slide easily beneath the surface when a fish bites.

LURES/FLIES

Whether the artificial lure is a *spinner*, a *spoon*, a *slicer*, a *plug*, a *jig*, a tiny wisp of a *dry fly* or a large lure that is too awkward to cast, each is a substitute for a bait. Some are exact replicas of a food item, some are imitations with which anglers try to deceive a fish. Others produce an action similar to an insect (or small fish, or injured fish) to mislead the opportunistic feeders that most fish are. Others will, by their action on or below the surface, do much the same as a known fish bait. And some do not remotely resemble anything a fish might naturally encounter.

• *Spinners* have a blade which revolves. The shape of the blade determines the speed it revolves.

• *Spoons* do not revolve. They dart and swerve as they are trolled, retrieved, or even jigged. Their action is dictated by the curves and/or weight distribution in their shape.

• *Slicers* may be as simple as a barrel sinker at the eye of a hook or a round, triangular or square length of metal. These are usually retrieved at a fast rate and if they are to have any sideways action, it has to be imparted by sweeping the rod. Spinners, spoons and slicers are mostly made of metal.

• *Jigs* or *lead-heads* place a weight at the eye of the hook. The body may be of plastic, fibres or other materials. They are usually fished with a lift and sink motion, though they may be trolled, or even cast-and-retrieved.

Many lures of the "twister" tail or soft plastic fish shape are basically jigs (the bodies of which can be purchased separately). They are frequently successful when threaded on a hook without any weight and retrieved in a stop-start motion near the bottom. The *trolling* and *game fish* lures are basically a metal or weighted head with a variety of coloured skirts attached (which may be fish-like, or squid replicas, or just strands of vinyl or other fabric). They are trolled at various speeds, skipping on the surface or at a depth.

• *Plugs* include lures of various shapes, some resembling fish or crustaceans. These may float, sink, or float-and-dive as they are retrieved, depending on their type. The float-only type are often referred to as *surface disturbers* or *poppers*. Their movement causes ripples or "glugs" as they are retrieved, which can be effective in bringing fish —

Above: Dry flies. Below: Spoons for casting.

Above: Spinners, mainly freshwater. Below: Metal slicers.

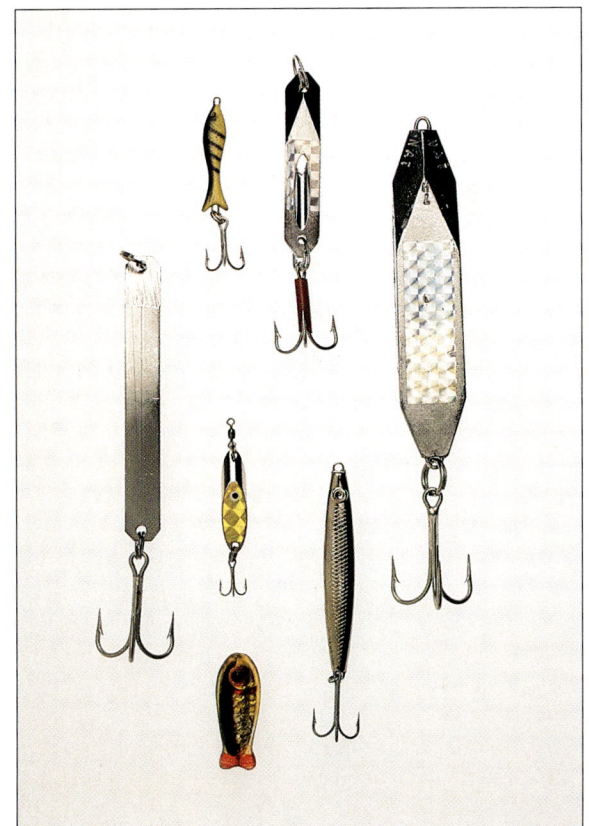

Surface and shallow diving plugs.

Deep-diving plugs.

bass, trout, barramundi, kingfish — to the surface. *Sinking* plugs require some action from the rod or they will trail straight at about the depth where the angler begins to retrieve them. Like spoons and slicers, they may be bounced along a clear bottom. *Float-dive* plugs normally have a shallow bib that pulls them below the surface. They may swim erratically. The *deep-diving floating* plugs have a much more elongated bib, which takes them down much deeper and often causes an exaggerated action.

The action of all lures can be varied by the speed of the retrieval, by stop-start cranking the reel, or by boat speed.

The display of lures in any well-stocked specialist fishing tackle outlet will demonstrate the wide variety and colours, or combination of colours, that are available. They are all made in sizes to suit the various lines and methods used by anglers for most freshwater and saltwater fish. A good salesperson, who understands their limitation, can steer a newcomer to those lures that have been proven by anglers over the years.

Lure fishing requires effort and perseverance. A quick cast here and there is often fruitless, but a complete exploration of each area — especially in inland waterways, estuaries, beach and rock locations — with one or several lures is the only satisfactory approach. Moreover, the angler should concentrate on locations where they would otherwise try bait.

• *Flies* can be minute, made of fur and feathers, hair and synthetics. Those which float on the surface represent terrestrial insects. Those which sink or are "worked" by the angler in the water are called wet. These may be imitations of the larvae of insects that rise to the surface to complete their life cycle, or small fodder fish — or "teasers" which trout, bass, Macquarie perch, silver perch (in fact most species) will all take opportunistically. There are many standard flies of all types and while some of these, in different sizes, should be carried in the fly box, a quick check with local anglers on what is being taken can save a lot of trial and error.

HANDLINES

All beginners or casual anglers should spend time fishing with a handline, even if they equip themselves with rod, reel, lures, floats, etc. They should not be regarded as either old-fashioned or simply primitive, though of course a rod is often more

Above: Surface disturbers or poppers. Below: Saltwater flies.

Above: Trolling lures for offshore. Below: Twister type of lures.

practical. There are many experienced anglers, however, who use only handlines for:
• inland and estuary fishing, whether from a bank or shoreline
• fishing from a boat
• when fishing for bait fish from jetties or rocks
• or when fishing for big fish on ocean reefs. There is no better way to learn about water drag on a line and bait, the different ways fish bite and run, and their strengths, because the movements are transmitted so directly along a handline. Several different breaking strains on plastic holders cost little. And reverting to fishing with a handline now and then is an enjoyable change, a change that can sometimes turn your luck!

OTHER ITEMS FOR THE TACKLE BOX

Anglers are reluctant to confess that their tackle invariably includes items (particularly bizarre lures and gimmicks) that they have never used and cannot remember why they bought them. Both newcomers and enthusiasts should resist the temptation to do the same.

There is no need, for instance, for a large and expensive tackle box when starting out. There are

From left: Folding net for freshwater fishing; large net with extendable handles; flying gaff; standard gaffs.

numerous small containers, with or without compartments, which will hold a range of lures, hooks, sinkers, swivels, etc., sufficient for most fishing excursions. Even when a tackle box is acquired, it should be used to store excess items, spare spools of line and sinkers, lures, boxes of hooks, etc. The smaller containers that can be carried in a suitable shoulder bag should be refilled from the larger tackle box. If you are on an extended trip, then take the tackle box by all means, but leave it in the boot of the car.

Apart from the items in the containers, the following are mandatory inclusions:
• *Two spools of line*, one about 50 per cent stronger than the line on the reel (for leaders) and a few light nylon-coated wire traces (in case toothy fish are about). The second spool of line should be lighter than the main line to be suitable for droppers for sinkers.
• *Small nail clippers* for snipping line and trimming knots are worth a corner in the bag. These can be replaced by a miniature pair and a larger pair of *side-cutters*. They not only do everything clippers can but they are also capable of opening hook eyes for ganging (a pair of pliers can be included for closing these and crimping). The large side-cutters are excellent for removing fish fins, cutting off stinging spines etc. before cleaning fish, or opening shellfish and conjevoi.

Two pairs of side-cutters don't cost much more than nail clippers. They require cleaning and a touch of oil to stop them rusting, but once an angler discovers the numerous tasks they do easily, they become indispensable.
• *Two knives*, one of which can be carried in a sheath, for cutting and trimming bait, removing heads, etc. It will retain its edge if a small piece of plywood or plastic is used while cutting bait. This knife can be fairly solid, with a serrated section on the back for scaling fish, or a small scaling tool can be added to the kit bag. The second knife should be more flexible, kept very sharp and used *solely* for filleting fish.

LANDING NET, GAFF

For many fishing situations a *landing net* is a valuable asset. While a lot of fishing from the shoreline of lakes and estuaries and river banks may not pose difficulties for the angler, anyone fishing from a boat should not be without one. The net should be as large as possible across the metal frame, whether circular or triangular, even if the fish expected to be caught are only pan-size. There is always the possibility of having to boat a larger species — and trying to get a big fish into a small net has its problems.

For those walking and fishing through difficult country, there are collapsible or folding nets available. There are also nets with extendable handles, which are convenient for use from jellies or wharfs or high banks. Nets, even with a long handle, are not easy to use when fishing from ocean rocks, where the wave action can reduce their efficiency by twisting the mesh — which in turn can catch on shellfish, conjevoi or jagged rock edges.

For rock fishing, a long-handled *gaff* is the best. These can have handles from 2 to 4 metres and some rock-hoppers buy the steel hook assembly and attach even longer handles. Both *fixed* and *flying* gaffs are available in many sizes — the size being the gape of the hook — to suit the requirements of those seeking various species of fish. In *fixed* gaffs, the handle is firmly attached; the handle of a *flying* gaff is removable but attached by a strong rope or cord. This enables the "gaffer" to have both hands free while he performs a task that can be a hectic few minutes if a large gamefish is brought alongside the boat.

CLOTHING

The angler should be comfortable. In summer a drill shirt and trousers or shorts are often adequate for inland and saltwater fishing. Where there is a breeze which chills, a good quality lightweight showerproof jacket may be all that is needed for warmth. These are much better if they are the longer safari style — waist-length jackets tends to ride up, exposing the kidney area. They should also be at least one size larger than the size normally worn. Even if the sleeves have to be turned up, the extra room should accommodate a light flotation vest or a pullover without unduly restricting your movement.

Boat fishers and beach fishers may also invest in full-length plastic waterproof trousers, though these are not recommended for anglers fishing from ocean rocks. Women's stretch pantyhose under shorts or trousers can provide surprising warmth without extra weight or constriction.

It is obviously better to prevent sunburn than treat it: applying blockout cream requires less time than baiting a hook. A hat is also important as well as good polarised sunglasses. Together these two will reduce reflections and allow anglers to see the underwater terrain (and fish) more clearly, especially when fishing inland waterways, estuaries and from ocean rocks.

Shoes should be worn in any form of fishing. They will prevent many otherwise inevitable and painful cuts from shells or broken glass, stabs from fish spines (even bites) and injury from falls caused by slipping on boat decks, wharves or jetties. Sandshoes with non-skid soles are suitable for boats and beach locations, including some types of rocks on the ocean fronts. Lightweight boots with good non-skid soles are also suitable for inland walking, shoreline fishing and for beach fishing, as are gum boots. They should always be reasonably easy to kick off but even then they should never be worn by rock fishers.

Depending on the rocks, the best footwear is sandshoes with herringbone pattern soles or shoes with rock plates. These may be attached to other shoes and there are sandals with built-in studs for rock fishers. Bare feet, thongs or smooth-soled shoes are particularly unsafe when fishing from rocks or slippery banks — and the consequences can be dire indeed.

Waders are worth considering if you are fishing inland streams or impoundments. They can be worn on sheltered shallow sandflats and beaches of estuaries, coastal lakes and bays. These are available in waist length and armpit lengths. Their cost usually indicates their quality.

Wading while wearing these big boots is not easy. It is prudent to practise in shallow, reasonably flat water with a rocky bottom. The waist-high style can fill if the wearer slips or steps into a deep hole (as can the armpit-high style). Find a stretch of water with some current, deliberately fall and learn how to regain an upright position in waders that have been partially or completely filled with water. It is not easy and there have been tragic accidents. Do it from several positions while wearing normal fishing clothing. Now, holding a rod, wade ashore to empty them. One such excursion is not enough and any angler practising this recovery should be accompanied by a friend in case of difficulty.

CHOOSING AND EQUIPPING
A SMALL BOAT

The expectations that a boat can generate almost unlimited fishing opportunities can lead even experienced anglers to a hasty purchase. As with boats for any purpose, buyers in their enthusiasm frequently put aside questions that can cause financial and other worries later. A common irony of this situation is that the reason many of the boats are put up for sale in the first place is that their previous owners have already made precisely the same mistakes.

Very light — very tight! — certainly portable and it will float in millimetres of water. Punctures can be disconcerting but rubber dinghies are surprisingly robust.

By answering the following questions honestly and dispassionately, many future frustrations or disappointments can be avoided.

• How often will I really use a boat?
• What sort of fishing do I really want the boat for?
• Can it be used for other purposes besides fishing?
• Are the rest of the family keen?
• Will I have a member of the family with me every time I go fishing or will I have to find a fishing friend to accompany me? If neither, then will I enjoy fishing alone on a boat?
• What size boat can I handle myself?
• How big should it be?
• Should it be open or have a cabin?
• Would a car topper do?
• Will I need a trailer? If so, how much more will that be?
• If not, then where will I keep the boat? And how much will that cost?
• Is my vehicle capable of towing the boat and trailer that I have in mind?
• Will I invest to my budget limit in one large motor or settle for something less powerful but with a

small auxiliary motor for an emergency?
• What are insurance and registration costs?
• How much will compulsory safety gear cost before putting in other equipment?
• How much can I afford to pay outright; or to repay regularly if the boat is bought with borrowed money?
• Can I really get the type of boat I want for that amount or will it lead to a fruitless compromise?

Most anglers have some idea of the fishing they want to do from a boat, but they can only profit from making excursions to the waters they want to fish with experienced boat-owners. Inspecting popular boat launching ramps should provide answers for some of the problems of general handling, launching and retrieving boats on trailers. A selection of craft and their uses follows.

Kayaks, Canadian canoes etc..
These are limited to very sheltered waters. Kayaks and other one-person craft lack room for gear and really are unsuitable for fishing. On the other hand, the two-person Canadian canoe can take another angler with room for gear and, once the technique of balance is mastered, they are surprisingly stable. These allow fishing in areas of creeks, rivers and estuaries that are unreachable from the banks. They can be used in calm open waters but at the first indication of a wind their nose should be pointed promptly to the shoreline and shelter.
Usually made of light plastics, such as fibreglass, or aluminium, these canoes are easily paddled and can take a fair degree of rough treatment. Timber canoes are rarely as light and require much more maintenance. Launching as well as lifting from the top of a vehicle is reasonably easy. Whenever afloat, canoeists should wear flotation vests (they need be neither bulky nor uncomfortable these days) and

Light timber punt powered by an electric motor provides mobility and silence for the serious angler.

the paddles should be attached to the canoe with a length of light cord. It can be disconcerting to watch the paddles float awa if you drop one with a swift current running, or capsize. In fact, well-prepared touring canoeists stow their belongings in a plastic drum (a home-brewing drum with its wide screw-top lid is ideal) for just such an eventuality. Properly designed canoes are extremely manoeuvrable in experienced hands and they are particularly handy if the water is very shallow and if portages become necessary.

Rowing dinghy

Most boats can be rowed, of course, but I refer here to yacht tenders, dinghies and flat-bottomed punts. Dinghies too can be manoeuvred stealthily to fish creeks, rivers and estuaries otherwise out of reach, though they are less so than canoes and rarely as light. Their significant advantage, however, is their relative stability. If loaded sensibly, there is room for equipment and ice-boxes and the like — and room to stretch and move around a little. Depending on the size, they can accommodate two anglers (large ones a third). A small outboard or electric motor can usually be accommodated. This will not only enable you to troll, but it minimises the rowing effort (and thus creates more room in the dinghy) and reduces the travelling time between fishing spots. The commonplace error here is to get an outboard that is too powerful. This can make the dinghy at best skittish to handle or it may be just plain dangerous. Every dinghy is a little different, so seek proper advice (responsible manufacturers and retailers of boats and outboards should help, if not ask your local authority). And remember, even if your dinghy happens to be stable enough to handle a more frisky little motor, the more powerful motor is always going to be heavier to lift .

Yacht tenders and dinghies are available in wood, aluminium or fibreglass. The flat-bottomed punt is generally made from aluminium or heavy marine ply . All three craft are easily loaded and unloaded by two persons; smaller ones by the angler alone. Aluminium dinghies or punts will withstand the wear and tear of being dragged over rocks and rough surfaces to be launched. All types should have built-in buoyancy, generally under the seats, so that they remain afloat if swamped. Occupants should wear flotation jackets and oars and a suitable anchor should always be aboard. If being used on waters where there is traffic at night, it is wise to have bow and stern lights.

The punt is not really a rowing dinghy, but it has the greatest initial stability of any small craft because of its flat bottom, the same feature that enables it to be rowed, paddled or poled into the shallowest of water. It is not, however, suitable in more exposed waters where there is any chop.

Anglers fishing from canoes and dinghies should keep the weight in the boat centralised (keep weight out of the bows) and the centre of gravity as low as is practicable (*don't* stand). Be wary of bow waves from larger craft.

Remember that rising or receding floods in inland waters, and extreme tidal flows in estuaries or bays may make rowing heavy work : if under power these conditions will slow you and use more fuel.

Car-toppers

For our purposes, a car-topper is a boat of about 3 metres but less than 4 metres. It will usually, but not always, be equipped with an outboard that will propel it below the speed which requires a licence. Of course there are smaller dinghies and larger ones that can be slung on a roof rack, but we are using a widely accepted definition. Despite the

An aluminium punt — or "tinny" — and a smallish outboard are rugged, light and extremely mobile in flat waters.

A swift runabout, with few comforts and a powerful outboard, can get you offshore. It can also get you into trouble.

promise of the advertisements, car-toppers are generally too heavy to be handled by one person but they can usually accommodate between one and three anglers.

They are capable of reaching most waters that dinghies can but their design is usually more seaworthy in waters more exposed to chop — though still in waters that the maritime services would regard as protected waters — inland impoundments, large rivers, estuaries, bays and harbours. Because of their size (higher freeboard, more beam than rowing dinghies), volume and a shape of more ultimate stability, they can usually be fitted with more powerful outboards and larger fuel tanks. Some have a small covered area in the bow for storage. They should have oars and rowlocks, of course, as an emergency measure. They should also have built-in flotation.

Car-toppers should carry two anchors on appropriately long warps (chain/rope), not just to moor for fishing but as a safety measure. If the boat is to be used at night it should carry the correct lights. Lifejackets should be carried for each person. Check with your local marine authority for other safety requirements. Though these slightly larger boats are better equipped to handle the wash from passing vessels and small wind waves — a small chop — or a mild swell, these little boats are not intended for use in the open sea.

They are made of marine plywood, aluminium or fibreglass. Aluminium is normally the lighter.

Trailer boats

These are the popular runabouts, centre console and half-cabin boats. If the runabouts are less than 4.5 metres, they should be restricted to the same waters as car-toppers. All of them, through size and weight, require a trailer to transport them and they are launched at launching ramps or over firm sand by means of rollers.

Runabouts can be used for more recreation than fishing, of course, and often are fitted with outboards powerful enough for water-skiing. Though motors range from about 20 hp to 70 hp, the high range is quite unnecessary for fishing. And if fishing is to be its prime purpose, then a middle range motor is more than adequate and a smaller auxiliary motor is a prudent addition. Runabouts usually have a little foredeck that terminates at a windscreen, and forward steering with remote controls and fixed or swivel seats.

Half-cabins are general purpose boats with small forward cabins that open to a control bridge covered by a canopy of some sort which provides protection from sun and spray. The cost of the boat will dictate how elaborately the cabin is fitted out. It may well have a step-through facility to reach the bows which can be more reassuring when anchoring in bumpy conditions than clambering around the superstructure on a narrow, slippery deck. Whether the cost of additional cabin comforts is worth the loss of valuable fishing space is something for the fisherman to ponder. Depending on their size, they may be fitted with a single or twin high-powered motors or a single middle range plus a smaller auxiliary motor.

Centre consoles are strictly functional boats that are designed to provide the largest stable working platform in a given volume. They make ideal work boats, diving boats or, more commonly, fishing boats. They are invariably open boats with the controls concentrated in and around a central pedestal console. Though they may have cathedral or even deep-vee underwater shapes they tend to have very shallow draught and pronounced beam for stability. This creates a large flat area inside the boat and with the driving station confined to a very small area in the centre of the boat, the maximum amount of boat space can be exploited for fishing, stowage, and fuel tanks, etc. The central console area is not only the part of the boat that experiences the least motion, it also provides excellent all-round visibility.

Some runabouts or half-cabin boats, are suitable for limited offshore use. Their design and size will govern how far they may be able to go as well as the prevailing conditions. Much the same applies to any boat, but centre consoles, because they tend to be shallow-draught open boats, are best confined to protected waters.

Needless to say — or it should be — before any such boats are taken to sea, the owners should familiarise themselves with the boat in calm waters and in changing conditions of wind and chop. They should be accompanied by an experienced boat driver in these initial runs and short outside excursions, which should include as many different weather and sea conditions as practicable. I also recommend a course in small craft navigation and maintenance. Such courses are conducted by technical colleges, boating groups and the volunteer coastal patrol organisation.

Sensible precautions

Regulations regarding the registration of recreational vessels, the restrictions that apply to their use, and the licensing requirements for helmsmen, all vary from State to State. But it is your responsibility to check these requirements with your local marine authority.

Equipping your boat well with quality safety equipment (especially if it is to be used offshore) is sound investment. After all, you can use the same gear in your next boat. Such equipment includes lifejackets (or in some circumstances buoyancy vests) for the maximum number of persons who might be carried, distress or smoke flares (which should be stored in a dry and accessible place), a fluorescent international-orange "V" distress sheet, Admiralty or Australian Hydrographic Charts for the areas you propose to work in, and a fire extinguisher(s).

Fuel and gas for cooking utensils should be stowed carefully and, on enclosed craft, detectors for leaks are worth installing. All batteries should be fully charged and suitable anchors with adequate warps should always be aboard. A strong bucket with a 2-metre lanyard should always be carried as well as a good first-aid kit.

Before leaving a launching ramp or mooring, all this safety equipment should be checked along with all the fishing gear.

It is compulsory in some States for any boat traveling beyond a prescribed distance offshore to have a radio transceiver fitted (and any boat, even in estuaries, should have a transistor radio aboard to listen for the latest broadcasts of weather conditions). A good liquid-damped compass with a rotating card clearly showing the cardinal points should also be installed.

Having chosen a sound craft and equipped it well with safety equipment, the angler can add accessories to increase the comfort and versatility of his fishing. Often inspections of fishing boats at ramps will provide many ideas. Among the early installations there should be rod holders, storage racks, secure places for tackle boxes and spare reels, ice boxes or fish storage containers, a live bait tank, berley bucket, and an extra fuel tank. The best fitted-out fishing boats have an efficient arrangement for cleaning fish so that these chores can be completed before they get back to the wharf or launching ramp.

An additional marine radio can be helpful and a depth sounder is a very useful tool too, though not absolutely essential.

An ongoing problem with boats is that we tend to add extras — little features or gadgets here and there. This can be a very satisfying side to boat-owning, particularly if you are good with your hands, but it is important that nothing be allowed to interfere with the safe operation of the boat or its fishing potential. Be a little weight conscious too. Every superfluous item in a boat is simply dead weight. It will require more fuel for the boat and the car (if the boat is trailered) and it will reduce the boat's efficient cruising speed.

There are fish to be caught in all the seas of Australia. It beckons both the old salt and the inexperienced alike. Unfortunately neglect, whether in learning to operate a boat properly or equipping it correctly, can endanger lives when least expected.

No fish has ever been worth that.

CHOOSING THE RIGHT RIG

Of the hundreds of rigs — that business end of the fishing line — used throughout Australia, only the following are suggested. They are simple and versatile enough to suit any fishing, from shallow, still water, to deep ocean bottom.

A rig should present a bait or lure in the most natural manner possible. These do just that, provided the correct one is selected for the prevailing conditions. With few exceptions, they are suitable for handlines and all styles of rods and reels. (On sidecast rod and reel outfits, it is advisable to add a second swivel further up the main line to minimise the risk of line twist.)

RIG 1

The angler is able to cast a fly because weight, which loads the rod, is built into the line. The "perfect" cast depend on whether the right weight of line is matched to the rod (fly rods are usually branded with the suggested fly-line number). However, whether it is a floating or sinking line in the weight forward, level or double taper type, it is too wide to tie to a fly or lure. Hence a tapered nylon leader, which is at least the length of the rod and up to twice as long, is attached. The taper is achieved by knotting lengths of various breaking-strain nylon together (they are also available ready-to-use). The last length is called the tippet. It is usually about 1 to 2 kilograms breaking-strain for the tiny dry flies that are tied to hooks between size 18 and 30.

On the other hand, a tippet for saltwater fly fishing may be 10 kilograms breaking-strain, which is suitable for a fly tied on a 1/0 or 2/0 hook. If a fly line is used to fish bait or lures — and they can be — it is unnecessary to taper the leader and it does not have to be as long as when fishing flies.

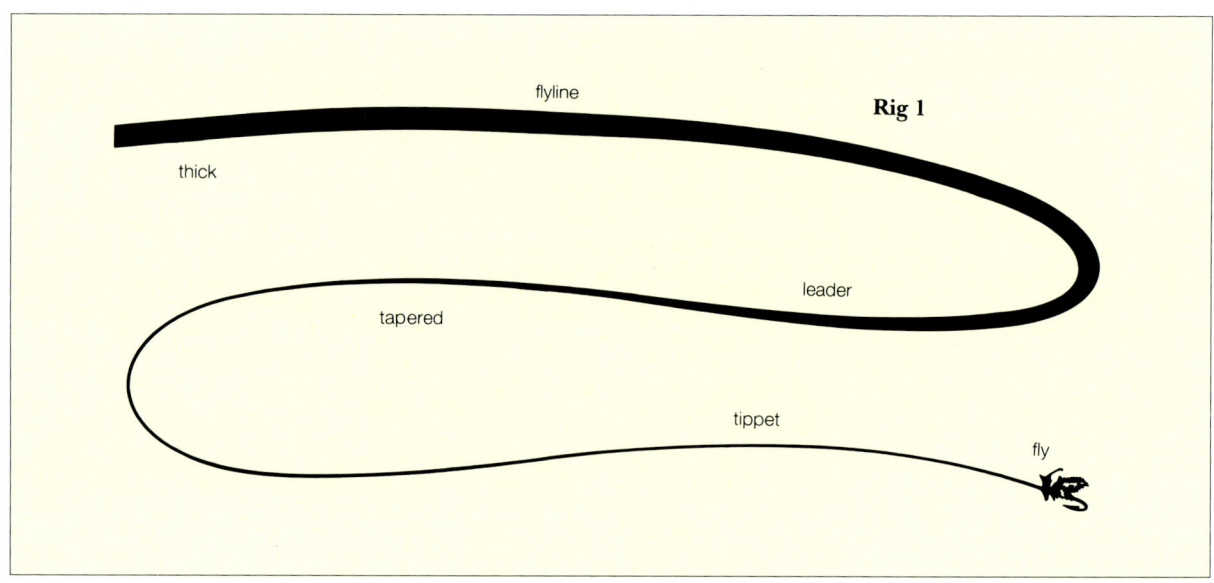

flyline

Rig 1

thick

leader

tapered

tippet

fly

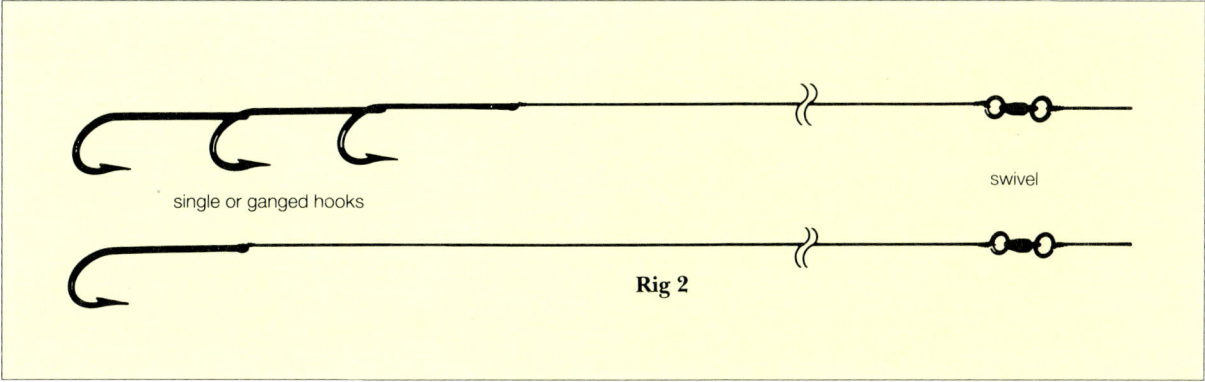

single or ganged hooks

swivel

Rig 2

RIG 2

This rig, without a sinker, is recommended wherever conditions of current or surge permit. It is suitable for the lightest baits, such as worms, grasshoppers, or maggots for freshwater, and all saltwater baits. Connect a leader of approximately 50 to 60 centimetres with a (preferably) ball bearing or box swivel that is of a size suitable for the weight of line. The leader can be about 50 per cent stronger than the main line. Where very toothy fish are likely to be encountered, a wire trace instead of a nylon leader may be substituted, though ganged or linked hooks often make this unnecessary.

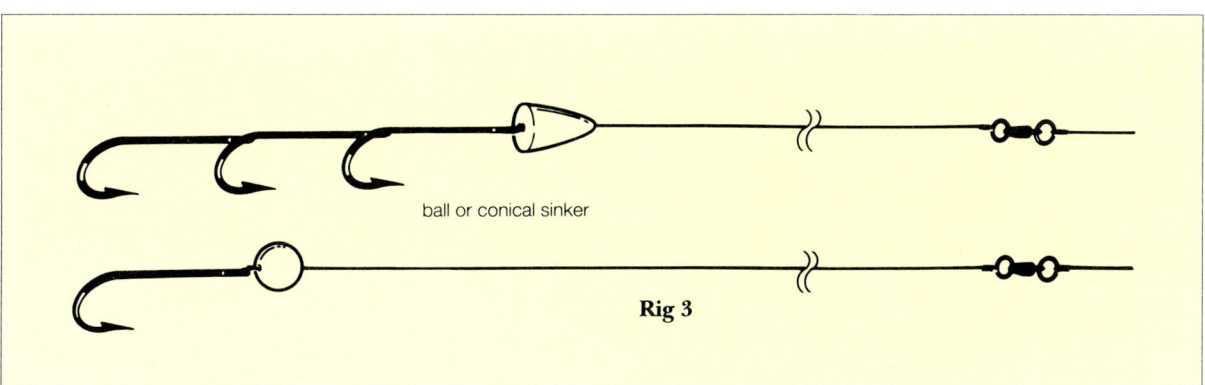

ball or conical sinker

Rig 3

RIG 3

This is about the same size as rig 2, except that only the smallest ball or conical sinker is added above the hook. It should be closer to the hook so that the bait is taken towards the bottom, where wind, surface chop or current prevents this, especially if the bait is to be retrieved, such as when using pilchards, garfish, whitebait etc. It is also a popular rig with the lightest weight for bream fishing and is excellent for fishing from the rocks for many fish when seas are settled.

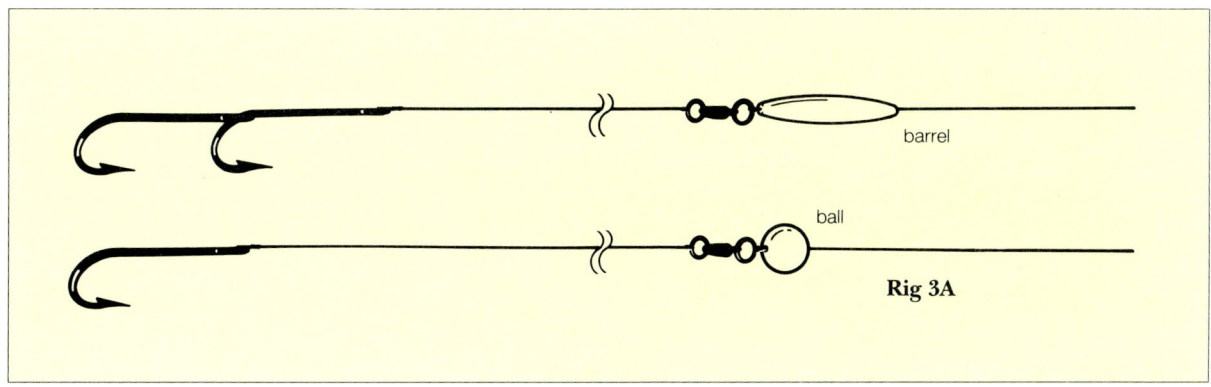

barrel

ball

Rig 3A

RIG 3A

A variation of rig 3. This rig is suitable for river, lake, estuary fishing. If conditions are calm, it is also suitable for beach fishing or fishing in the shallower offshore waters and when drift fishing or slowly retrieving the bait along the bottom — for flathead, whiting, etc. A barrel, ball, beam or channel sinker may be used. The barrel is recommended because it pulls more easily through weed and mud.

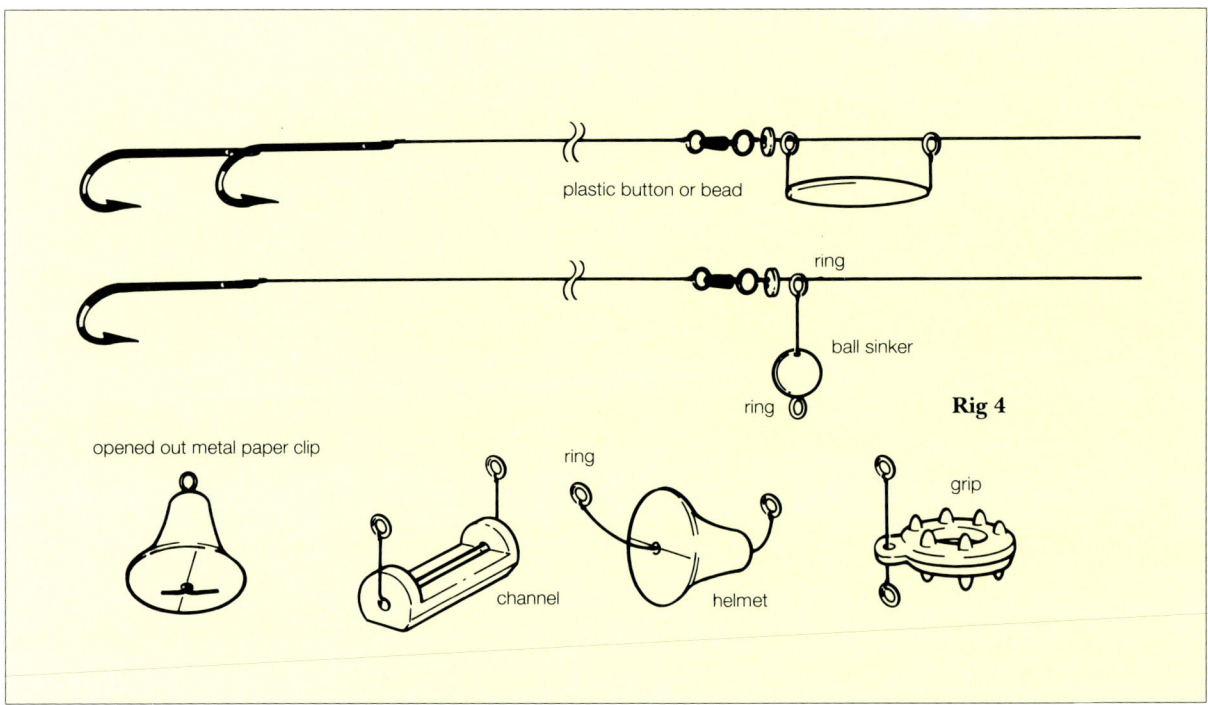

RIG 4

This is a much better rig than rig 3A. If you use a ring and a short length of line (about 2 or 3 centimetres) to attach the sinker, the line runs more freely when the bait is taken. If the ring slides over the swivel being used, a small ball (size 00) sinker, button or a plastic bead between the ring and the swivel will prevent it. This is an excellent beach rig. For barrel sinkers, two rings are used. This rig ensures sand or silt does not block the hole preventing line from pulling through. [Hint: use an opened cut metal paper clip, attached through the hole of one of the sinkers or another ring, rather than tying them to the line.]

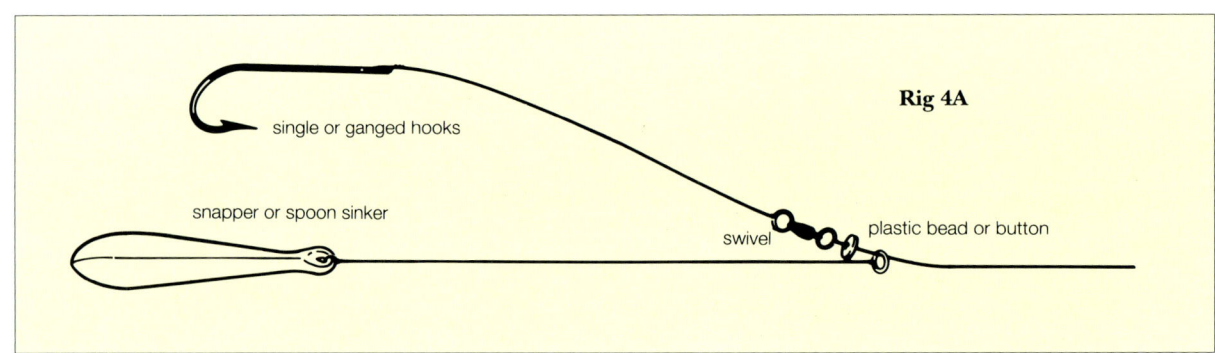

RIG 4A

This is rig 4 with a longer sinker dropper (about 60 to 80 centimetres) and a shorter leader (about 20 centimetres). It is an excellent beach and rock rig. A ball or helmet sinker is suitable when fishing from the beach, while a spoon sinker or small snapper lead is more practical from the rocks. [Hint: a piece of white styrene or plastic foam can be used at the eye of the hook to keep the bait off the bottom and moving in the surge.] The line used to attach the sinker should be of a lower breaking strain than the main line, so that if the sinker becomes snagged, the dropper breaks instead of the main line.

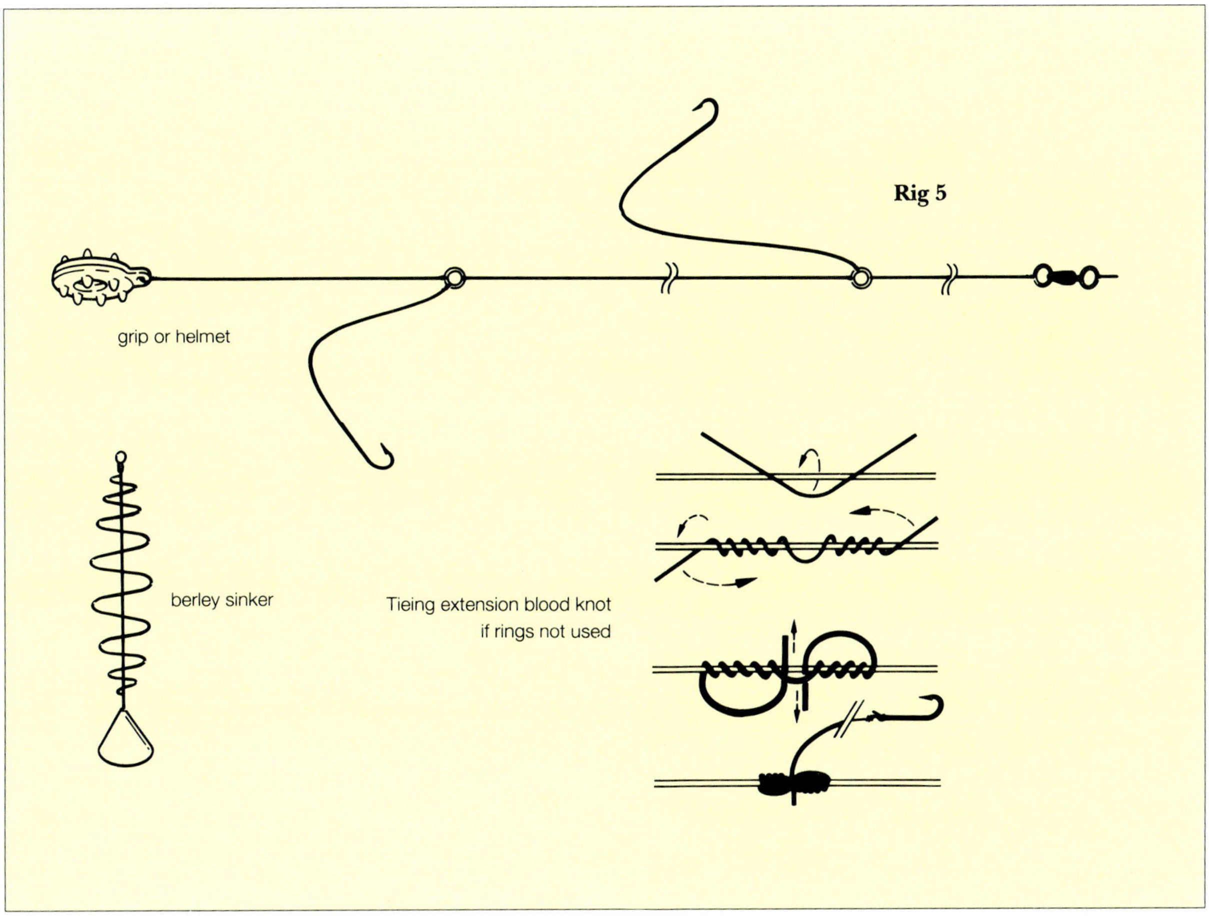

Rig 5

grip or helmet

berley sinker

Tieing extension blood knot
if rings not used

RIG 5

This is an estuary or beach rig favoured by some anglers when fishing for bream, whiting, tommy ruff, mullet, etc. The two leaders for the hooks are tied to the line, or to rings between the swivel. The sinker can be ball, bean, or gripstyle, but a burley sinker is also popular.

RIG 6

This rig is mainly used for bottom fishing. Several versions are popular. The hook droppers can be tied to the main line separately (using an extension blood knot); formed with a dropper loop or harness knot above the swivel; or 3-way swivels can be used. Sometimes 3 rings are used with a swivel further up the main line. Droppers should be spaced so that they do not overlap. The sinker is usually a small lead, snapper, or ball type, of sufficient weight to take bait to the bottom. Depending on the bottom and type of fish, the sinker is usually 80 to 100 centimetres below the first hook.

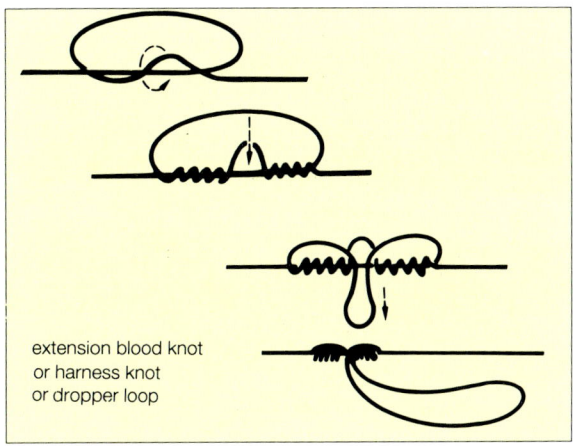

extension blood knot
or harness knot
or dropper loop

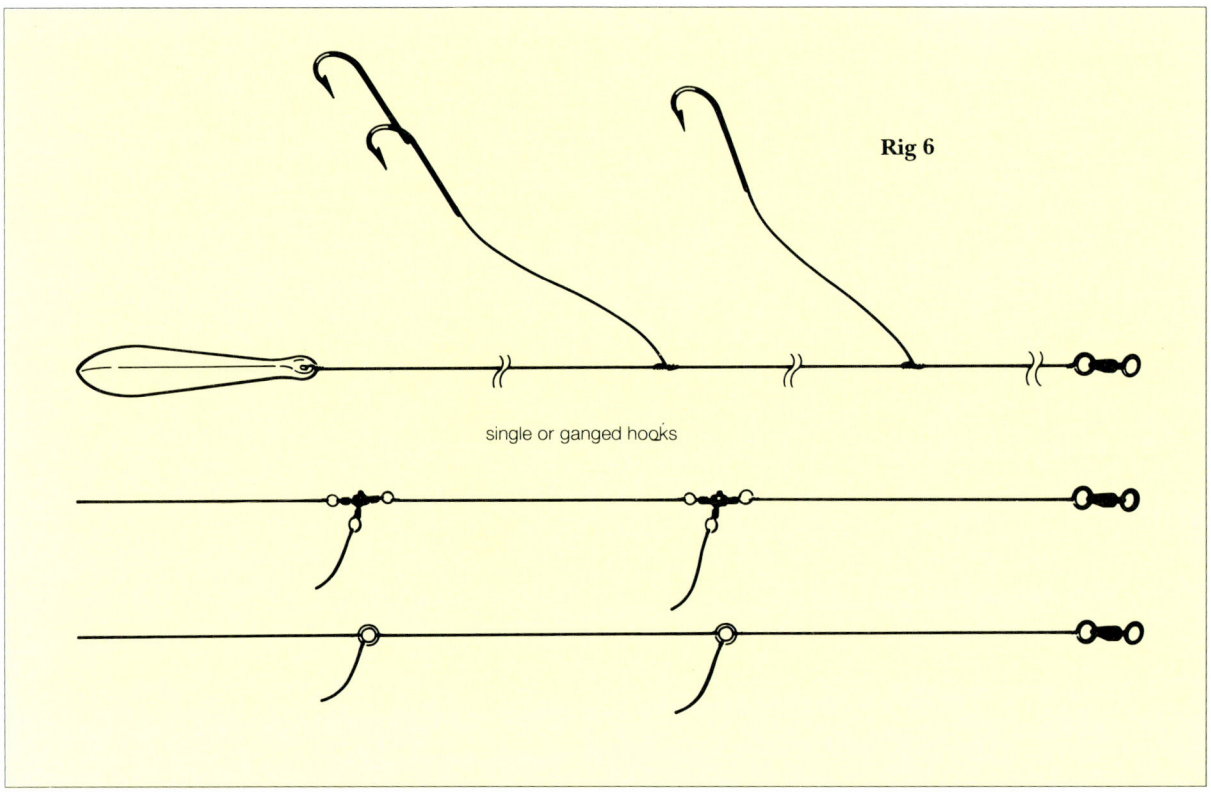

single or ganged hooks

Rig 6

RIG 7 (*see over*)

This popular luderick rig of the east coast is equally suitable for many other species, such as bream, mullet, tommy ruff, trout, native species, etc. The float type depends on the conditions, with quill or pencil suitable for calm conditions, and long stemmed bodied floats for choppy waters, or when fishing from the rocks. Either a fixed or running float may be used, but the running float allows quicker adjustment to the depth of the bait.

RIGS 7A/7B (*see below & over*)

This is a good "bobby cork" rig for ocean-front fishing for rock blackfish, luderick and many other species. The only difference is that a small sinker rides on the hook for light baits or when there is some surge (rig 7B). It is also an effective method of fishing for Murray cod and golden perch, as well as barramundi and other species in tropical bays, etc. It is suitable for live or dead bait. A running float allows easy changes to the depth of the bait.

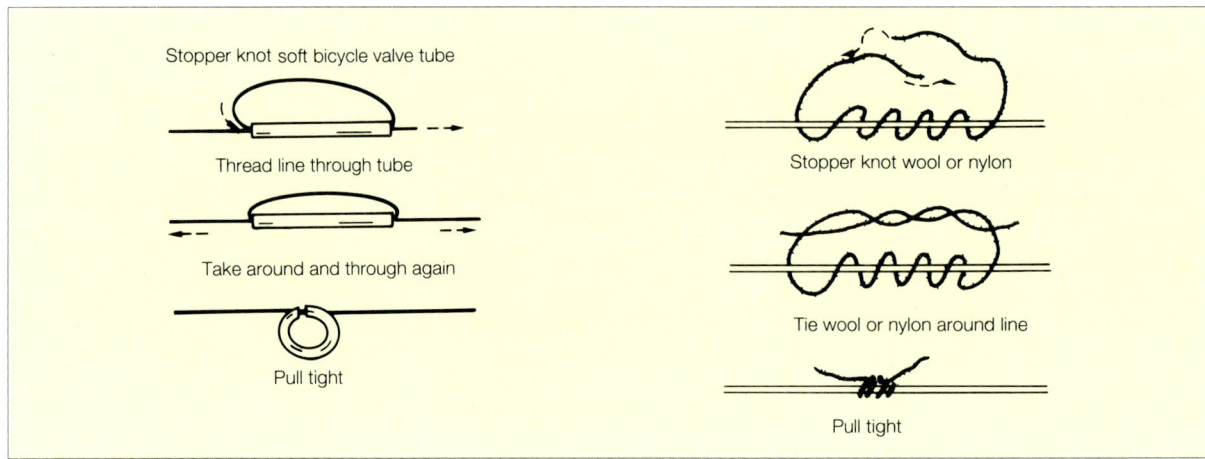

Stopper knot soft bicycle valve tube

Thread line through tube

Take around and through again

Pull tight

Stopper knot wool or nylon

Tie wool or nylon around line

Pull tight

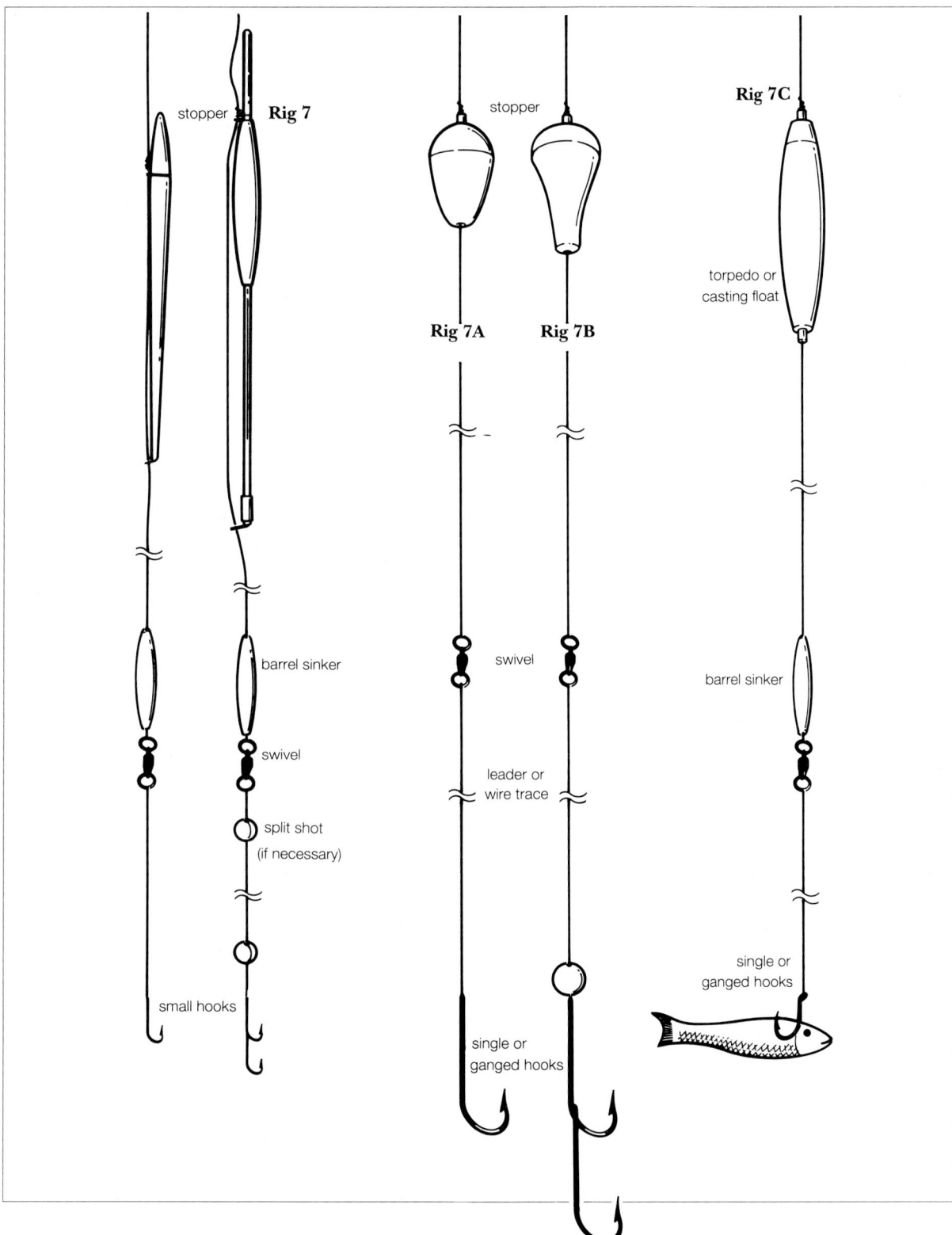

RIG 7C

This is the author's favourite for any bait, but particularly when fishing from the rocks. The torpedo or casting type of bobby cork is preferred with a barrel sinker (just heavy enough to take a lively yellowtail or similar bait to the depth re-quired) riding on a swivel with the hook about 30 centimetres below. The float runs on the line so quick depth adjustments can be made. The sinker above the swivel allows the live bait more freedom to swim around.

Rig 7D

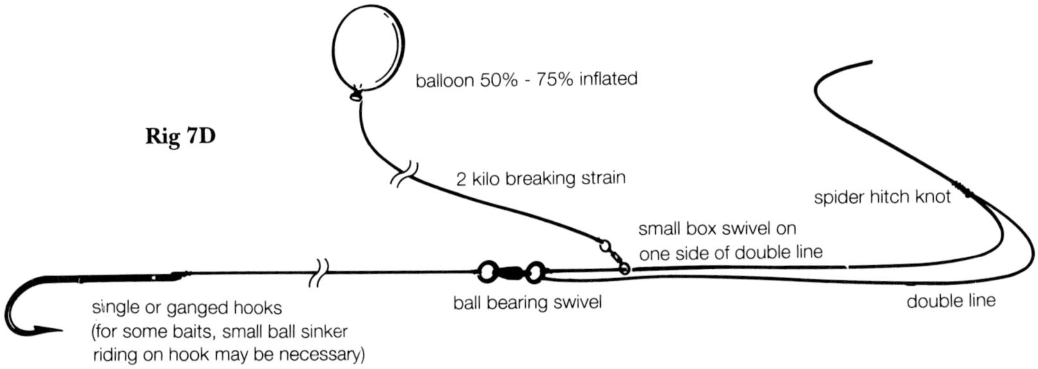

balloon 50% - 75% inflated

2 kilo breaking strain

spider hitch knot

small box swivel on
one side of double line

ball bearing swivel

double line

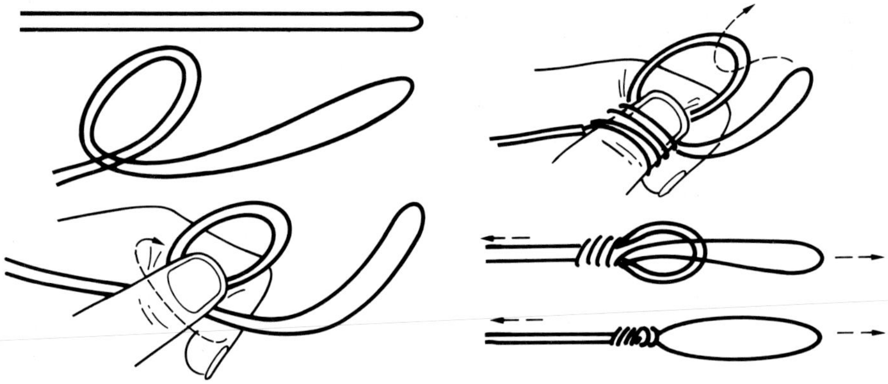

single or ganged hooks
(for some baits, small ball sinker
riding on hook may be necessary)

How to tie spider hitch hoop knot

RIG 7D

The balloon rig is popular for "live baiting" game fish and large pelagics such as tanguigue from a rock platform. It will cover a wide area of water with a suitable offshore wind. The balloon should be attached with a very light line or cotton which breaks when a fish takes the bait.

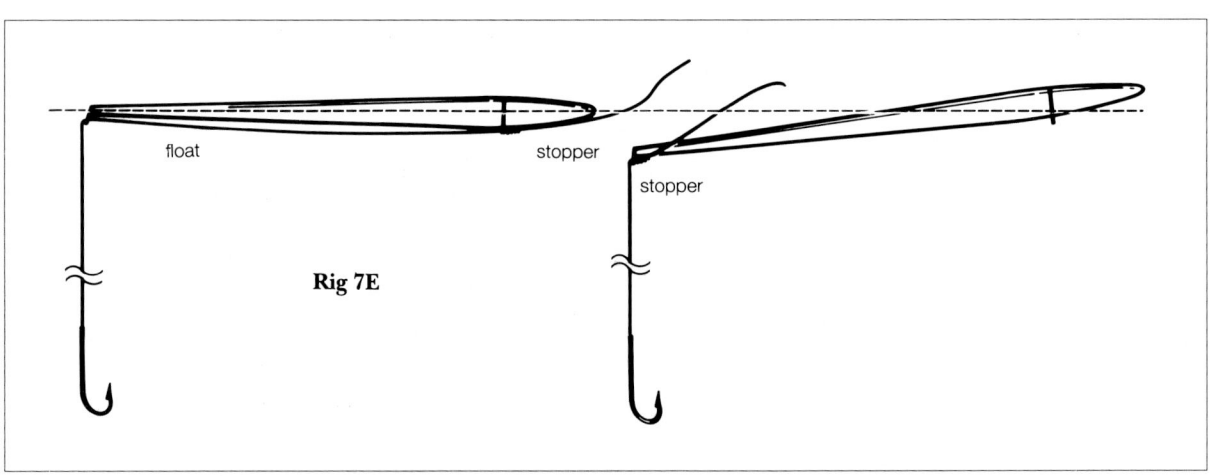

float

stopper

stopper

Rig 7E

RIG 7E

The very light quill or pencil float is used to fish for mullet, garfish and similar fish. It can be rigged to lay flat by threading the line through the two eyelets (or runners) but a very successful method is to use only the bottom eyelet or runner. The bait is usually sufficient weight to pull the float partly into the water so that it is at an angle. If the bait does not, add a pinch of lead. This makes the float very sensitive to movement, the slightest bite flipping it upright. If used at night for mullet, trout, bream, etc., it is much easier to see than a bubble float, which needs to be almost submerged to achieve the correct buoyancy for finicky biters.

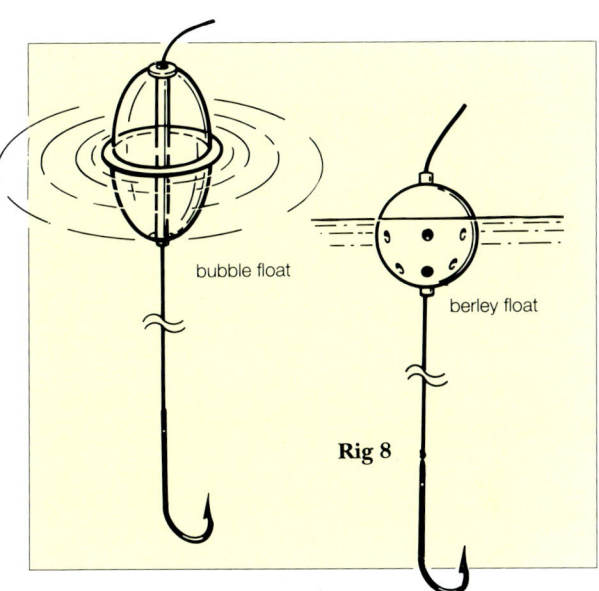

bubble float

berley float

Rig 8

RIG 8

This rig, which is popular in some areas of Australia for such fish as garfish and tommy ruff, features a "berley" float or "blob", a hollow, perforated float into which berley is packed. (A perforated practice golf ball can be used for the purpose.)

Fishing with floats has many advantages. Bait may be suspended at a governable depth — from just below the surface to just above the bottom. It can keep live bait away from rock snags and it allows the bait to move naturally with the current or waves, covering a wider territory than if anchored by a sinker to the bottom. With a running (or adjustable) float, it is easy to fish different depths.

The secret of float fishing is "fine tuning" the float so that it slides easily below the surface when a fish takes the bait. For this reason, slim or elongated bodied floats are recommended rather than round ball-type floats, which require excessive amounts of added weight to give them the correct flotation. Shown are two ways of fixing a "stopper" to allow quick depth adjustment of the float, using wool, nylon or thin rubber tubing. These will hold the float at the desired depth but can be moved up or down the line without difficulty. (The rubber tubing may have to be loosened, but is easily pulled tight.) If the "stopper" knot is too thick to pass through the runners, use a finer wool or nylon; if this tends to stick in the float ring or hole, a tiny plastic bead or button can be used.

RIG 8A

This rig is a variation of rig 8, with a bubble, cork or piece of styrene foam, used for fishing while drifting over relatively clean bottoms off-shore. It is generally a snapper lead attached to a shorter dropper between a ring and swivel. It is also a good rig for fishing in fast tidal flows, when the length from the ring to the hook may be several metres. On rigs used for saltwater bait fishing, single hooks or two or more linked eye to eye (ganged) may be used, especially when using fillets, small fish, squid or octopus tentacles as bait. Ganged hooks can make a wire trace unnecessary for many species.

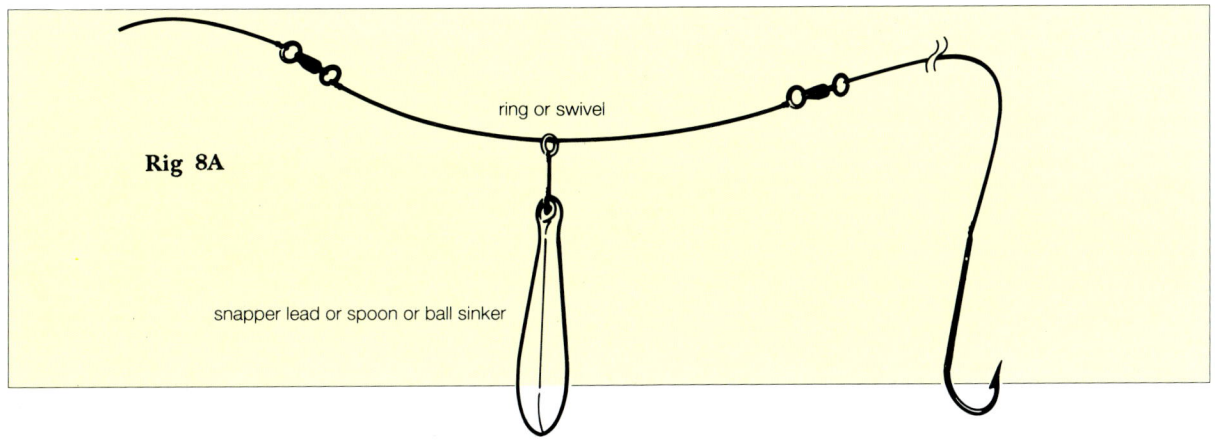

ring or swivel

Rig 8A

snapper lead or spoon or ball sinker

RIG 9/10

This rig can be used for casting and retrieving most types of lures in fresh or saltwater fishing. The length of leader, between the swivel and the lure, can be about 60 centimetres. As with bait, it should be approximately 50 per cent higher breaking-strain than the main line. The lightest wire trace can be substituted if the fish are toothy. Although convenient for rapid changes, a snap swivel can alter the action of weighted flies and many small lures. These are best tied to the leader with a clinched or locked half blood knot or with a Homer Rhode loop knot. A coastlock or McMahon snap can be used on large lures, for barramundi and saltwater species, with a heavy nylon leader or wire trace. If the weight does not alter their action, surface and shallow diving-lures may be used with a ball or barrel swivel to take them deeper.

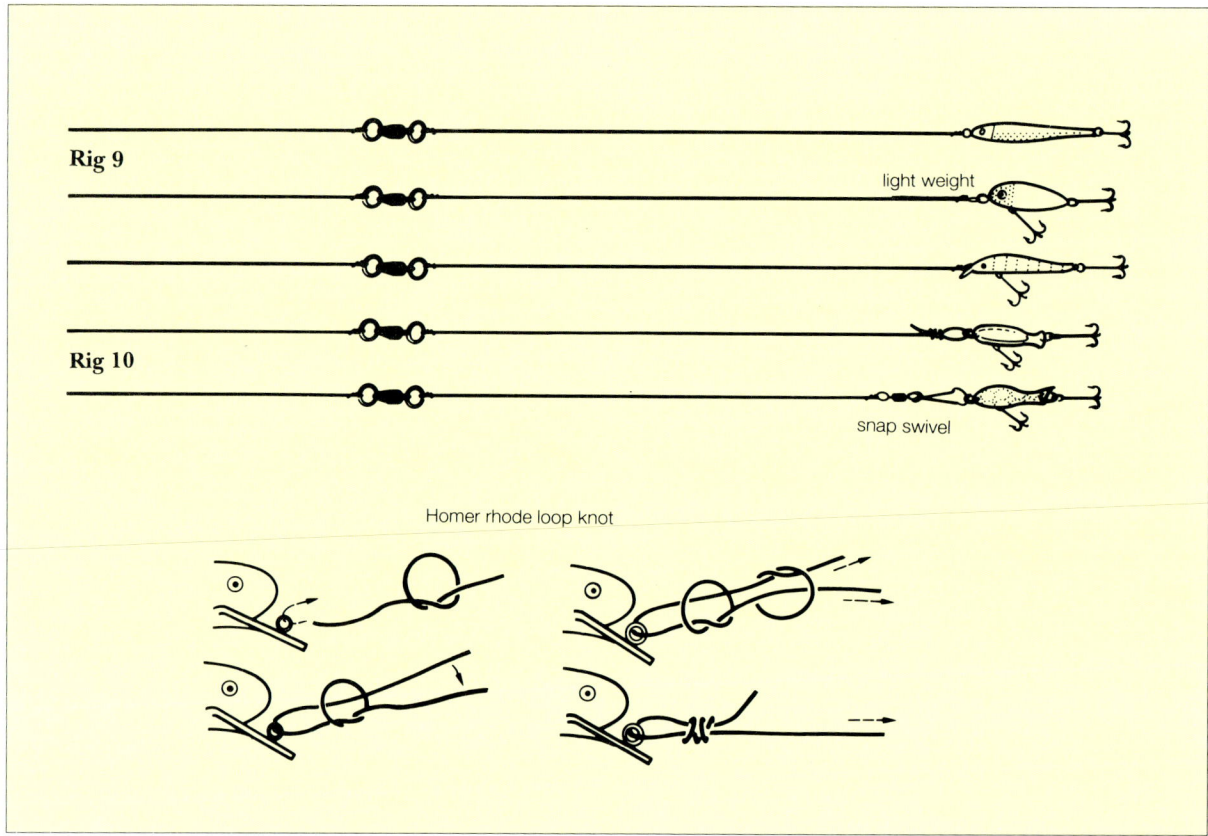

Rig 9

light weight

Rig 10

snap swivel

Homer rhode loop knot

RIG 11

These are common trolling rigs. Depending on the fish being sought, and the depth at which the lure is being trolled, a plastic or lead keel sinker (top) or paravane (bottom) may be used with or without flasher attachment. The plastic keel with flasher attachment is usually restricted to shallower freshwater trolling (and sometimes only the flasher with a barrel sinker is used). The lead keel and the paravane are for deeper water trolling.

A series of barrel sinkers and swivels can be an effective trolling rig (bottom) and are quickly made. Flies, lures and bait can be trolled.

These rigs may not comply with the rules under which records may be claimed. Anyone fishing for records should use the rigs which are set out in the rules of the club to which they belong or which are specified by the Australian National Sportfishing Association or the Game Fishing Association of Australia.

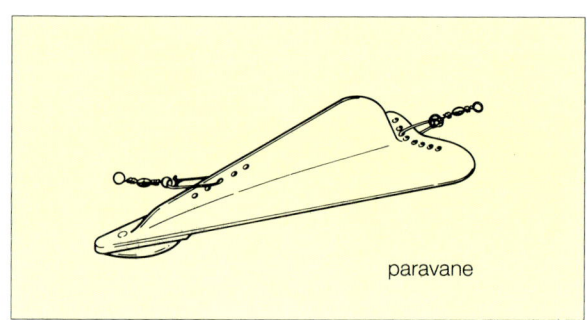

paravane

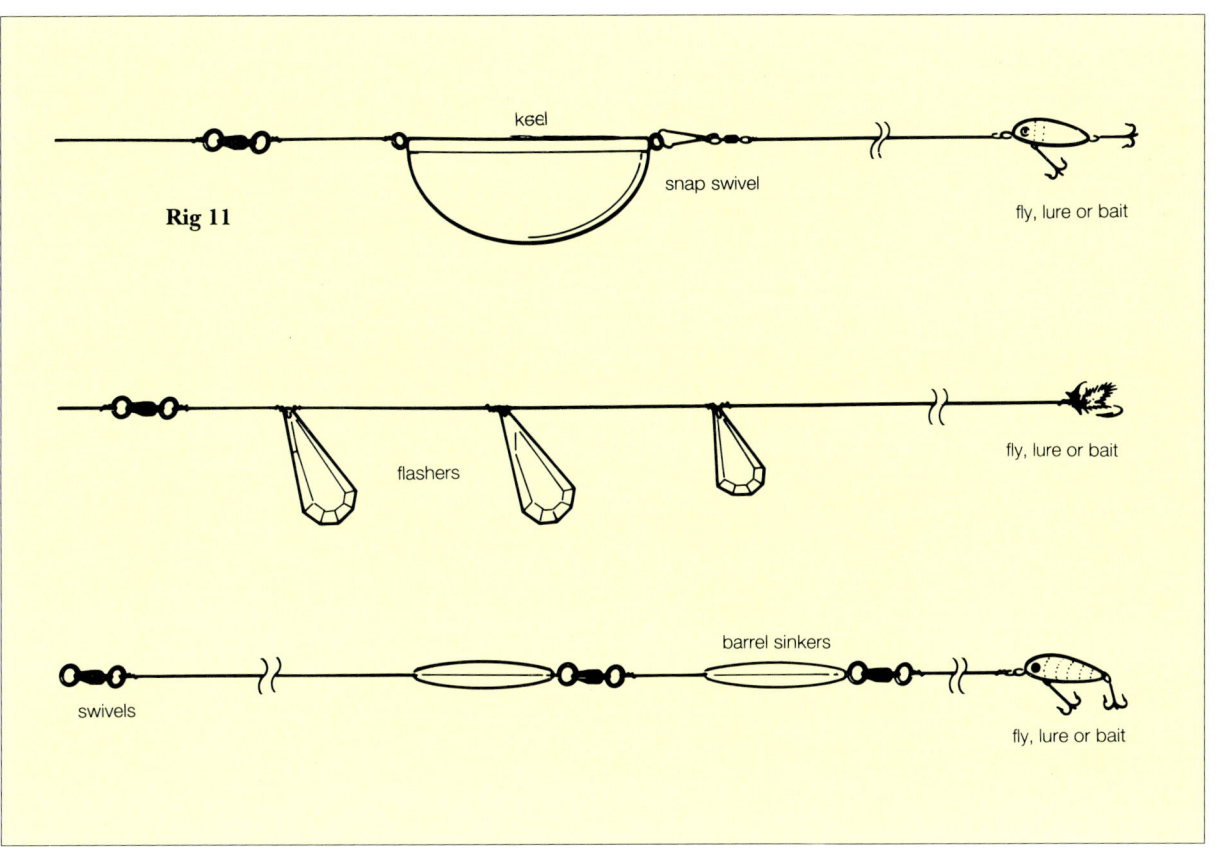

Rig 11

keel

snap swivel

fly, lure or bait

flashers

fly, lure or bait

swivels

barrel sinkers

fly, lure or bait

CHOOSING BAIT & BERLEY

Only those anglers who gather their own bait can be absolutely confident that the bait is fresh, the best proof of which is if it is alive. And live bait catches more fish. This chapter briefly details a variety of baits, most of which are available throughout Australia. If the effort of finding their own bait is too energetic for some anglers, don't be too concerned: much may be purchased — alive, fresh, preserved or frozen — from fishing tackle or other outlets.

Some States have regulations governing the netting or trapping of baits, together with limits on the quantity of certain bait fish or shellfish that an angler may possess. There are also areas, especially in estuaries, where crustaceans or worms may not be harvested. The guides to fishing regulations issued by the various State fisheries departments or divisions contain this information.

A WORD OF CAUTION

Collecting bait has a few hazards for the unwary. Apart from the obvious risk of stepping into a deep hole while wading, being caught in a fast current, or failing to keep an eye on the seas while seeking baits along ocean rock fronts — all of which continually get anglers into trouble — the following should be remembered:

• Be alert for land or *sea snakes*, though neither are likely to bite unless annoyed.

• Be conscious of *sharks* and *crocodiles*.

• In the tropics, check locally about the *stinging jellyfish* or *irukandji*, a smaller version of the deadly *box jellyfish* (or *sea wasp*). Both have translucent box-shaped bodies. The irukandji has four tentacles of varying length. Body and tentacles have tiny red spots which are the stinging mechanism. The sea wasp has as many as 16 tentacles extendable to more than 2 metres. These are covered by literally hundreds of thousands of stinging mechanisms. Effects are immediate pain, swelling and skin discolouring. Seek urgent medical attention. If available, use vinegar to soak the areas affected to kill the stingers. While the irukandji has not been associated with killing anyone,

the sea wasp has killed within minutes. Hospitals do have an antivenene for this deadly stinger.

• The common octopus of both the southern and northern waters of Australia are harmless. But the *blue-ringed octopus* also exists in these waters, and with a maximum size of about 20 to 22 centimetres, it makes a tempting sized bait for the unwary. It has a tiny parrot-like beak at the junction of its tentacles, which injects a potent venom. The bite is usually painless but the results are almost instantaneous: numbness, loss of senses, difficulty with speech, swallowing, paralysis in the limbs. No antivenene is available. Treatment is mouth-to-mouth resuscitation and heart massage, which must be continued till medical help arrives .

This little octopus is often found in rock pools or rocky holes, and even empty shells. It is a beige colour on which there are dark brown bands with blue rings or circles superimposed. If annoyed — touched, taken from the water — the brown darkens and the blue becomes vivid. If unsure of any small octopus, anglers should leave well alone. Their life may depend upon it.

A description of various berley mixtures and how best to use them follows the section on saltwater baits.

SALTWATER FISHING BAITS

Almost every marine creature will be eaten at some time by fish; even the herbivore will take prawns or conjevoi or worms from time to time.

Prawns: For the best results, anglers should make live, or at least fresh prawns, a priority (rather than frozen prawns). Live prawns can be kept alive in a bucket of saltwater with the use of an aerator. They can be kept alive for shorter times in damp weed or a wet bag. Prawns are easily scooped up in a net when making their migration to sea from the estuaries.

Nippers: These hard green relatives of prawns have an outsized claw. They are obtained from mud areas, usually under weed on estuary tidal flats. Most fish relish them. They will remain alive in wet ribbon weed or saltwater.

Yabbies (sand shrimps): These are shrimps, pinkish in colour, with a large pincer. They are usually found in mud-sand areas of coastal rivers between the tide levels. This is a bait that all fish find hard to refuse. Yabbies can be kept alive in the water from which they are taken.

Worms: About half a dozen worms are found in the saltwater environment. All are acceptable to fish. Beach or sand worms are collected from beaches by using a rank piece of fish or meat to entice them to raise their heads clear of the sand. They are then grasped by the fingers or special pliers and pulled free. This "art" is best learned by watching a skilled wormer. Roll the worms in dry sand to remove the slime from their bodies. Keep them in cool, dry sand in a can. They can also be kept alive in a thick potato bag, if it is properly soaking with saltwater.

Bloodworms: These worms are harder and brittle, often breaking into segments (which need not prevent them being used to fill up a hook). They can be dug or pumped from the mud beneath sandflats and the shorelines of bays and estuaries. They darken and thicken in captivity but will stay alive in damp ribbon weed.

Wriggler worms: These are slimmer and more

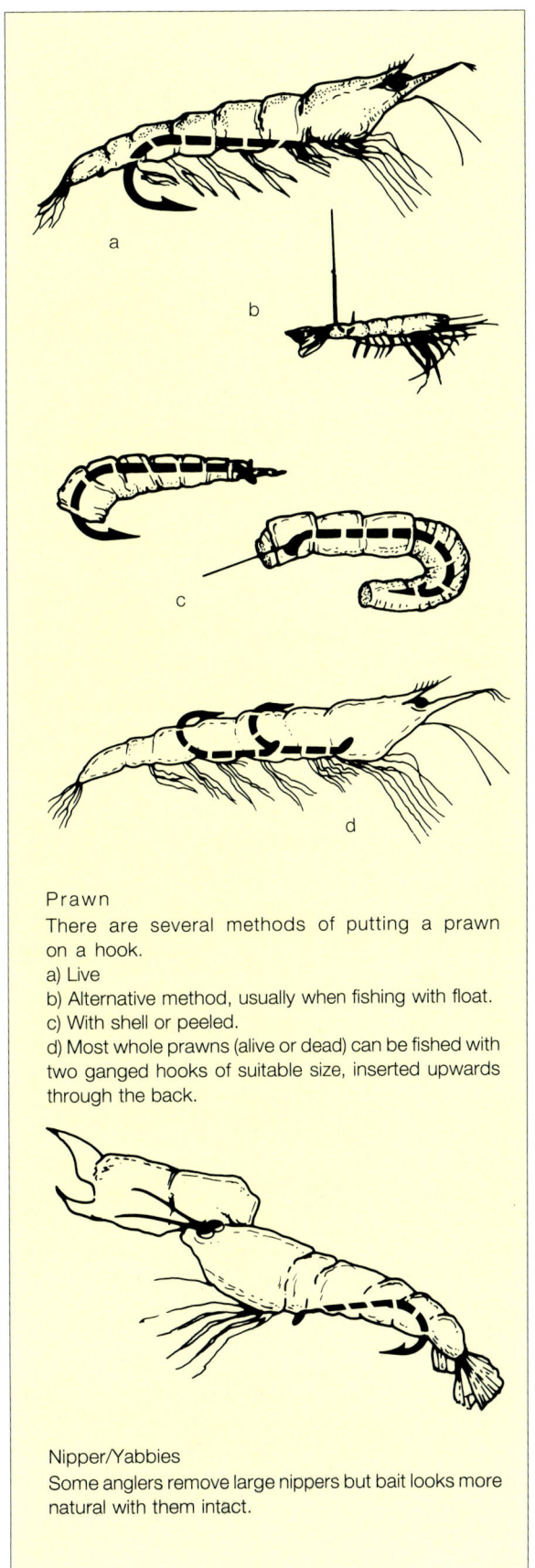

Prawn
There are several methods of putting a prawn on a hook.
a) Live
b) Alternative method, usually when fishing with float.
c) With shell or peeled.
d) Most whole prawns (alive or dead) can be fished with two ganged hooks of suitable size, inserted upwards through the back.

Nipper/Yabbies
Some anglers remove large nippers but bait looks more natural with them intact.

active worms that are found in mud and the sand beneath rocks or tree branches at low tides along estuary shores. They also nip fingers like their relatives the bloodworms.

Squirt worms: These softer worms live in sandflats between high and low water levels of lakes and calm bays. They can be pumped for or dug up, however squirt worms can be stubborn to separate from their self-made tubes. Both the wriggler and squirt worms shrink in length when collected but they become plumper if kept in wet ribbon weed.

Poddy worms: Small and pale by comparison with the other worms, these are dug from beneath damp sand under rubbish and rotting weed etc. near the high tide mark on beaches in big bays and estuaries. They should be kept in the material from which they were taken.

There are, of course, some very large worms amongst the coral of the Great Barrier Reef. Some anglers use them as bait — when they are able to extract them from their habitat.

Gentles or maggots: These are an effective bait for garfish, whiting, tommy ruff, yellowtail, some mullet, and even bream. Keep them in bran or pollard. Many keen anglers breed them and give them a rich cream or pink shade by feeding them a special diet. Some retail outlets sell them.

Conjevoi: Anglers often ignore this readily available ascidian or sea-squirt. It grows in a leather-like casing in clumps or alone, between high and low water, on rocks and piers. Its inside flesh, which is reddish coloured, tends to attract some rubbish fish but despite this shortcoming rock blackfish, drummer, snapper, bream, trevally, sweep and many other worthwhile fish won't refuse it either. Place it fresh in its own juices in an ice-cream container and freeze it for the future if you wish. It thaws well.

Pipis: Also known as the Goolwa cockle, this bivalve mollusc can be found by shuffling your feet in the sand under the water on beaches. They are a large soft bait but most fish that visit the surf can be caught with them. They can also tempt many rock fish species if suspended beneath a float or bobby cork.

Cockles, shellfish: Some cockles in the northern waters of Australia seem more like pipis, but the flesh of cockles, chitons, limpets, mussels etc., all

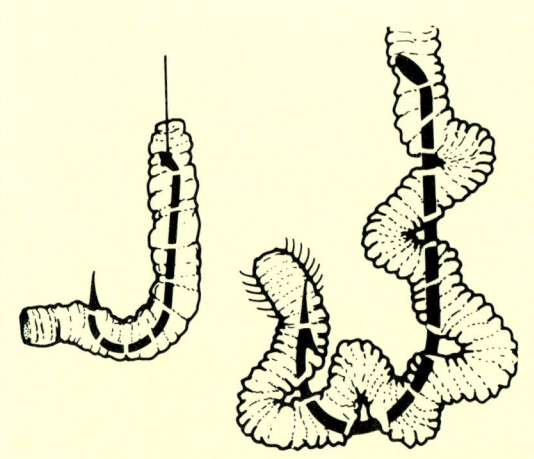

Worms
Large beach worms (for mulloway etc) should be chunky baits, with some length threaded above eye of hook.
Smaller worms such as blood worms (or pieces) are used in a neat manner for bream, whiting, etc. Can be threaded over eye of hook.

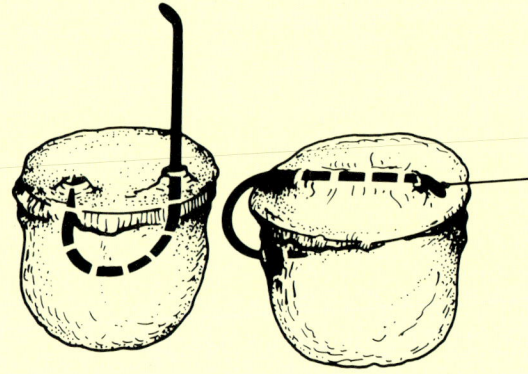

Conjevoi
Bait held firmly by inserting hook through one of the valves and bringing it out the other, then turning it over and pushing the hook point back into soft flesh. The conjevoi will be more compressed than in illustration. Conjevoi is excellent for rock blackfish and groper but most species will take it.

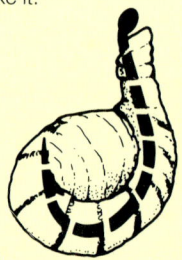

Pipis/Other Shellfish
Thread hook around the firmer edge of the flesh for whole baits. (Slim pieces of this flesh can be used to fill hook by threading on the shank). Bream, whiting and many other fish, particularly trevally, will take most shellfish.

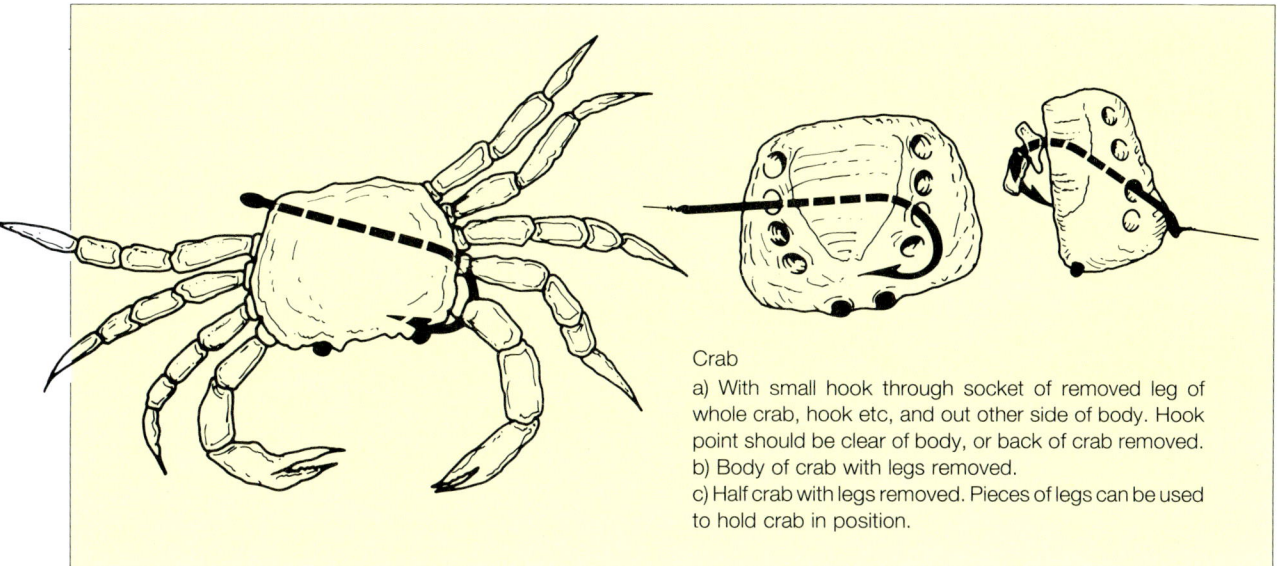

Crab
a) With small hook through socket of removed leg of whole crab, hook etc, and out other side of body. Hook point should be clear of body, or back of crab removed.
b) Body of crab with legs removed.
c) Half crab with legs removed. Pieces of legs can be used to hold crab in position.

make attractive food for most carnivorous fish. These can all be gathered and crushed for a useful berley if fishing bays and estuaries, or off rocks. They also add a dash of special flavour to berley made of other ingredients.

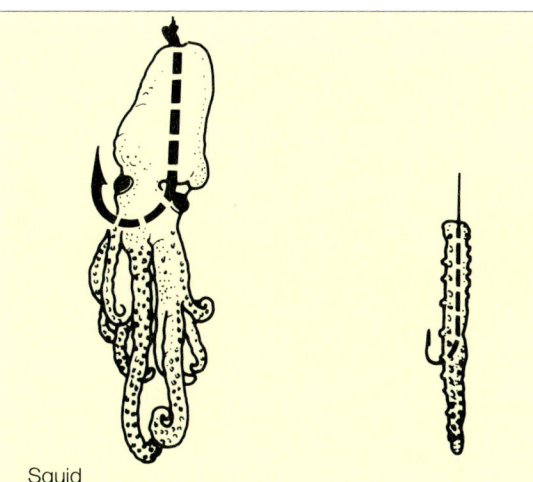

Squid
Small or medium size squid can be used on a single hook. Large squid or cuttle fish can be used on two linked hooks. Slivers of fillets of the flesh may be baited same fish flesh. A floated live squid is almost irresistible to kingfish, snapper, mulloway and many other fish.

Octopus
Octopus tentacle is tough bait, favoured by many anglers for snapper, mulloway, reef species. Tentacle is best skinned, slightly hammered but not mashed, and slit so that the shank of the hook fits in this cut. Half-hitch with the line round the end will hold hook in position. The hook point should be clear of the flesh. Some of the tentacle should extend beyond the end of the hook.

Crabs: Any crabs that are found on ocean rocks and in estuaries are eaten by fish. The little black crabs found by lifting rocks on estuary shorelines are excellent as a bream bait, but the black crabs in the crevices and rocks above the waterline on the ocean front seem to have less appeal to most fish. The red, green, ghost and soldier crabs used whole, if small, or cut and legless are excellent for most fish that feed around reefs or rocky terrain.

Mullet/chicken gut: Much of the odour and messiness of this bait can be overcome by mixing it into dry bran or pollard while still fresh. If frozen or salted, it can also be thawed out in the same ingredients. When coated with these cereals, mullet or chicken gut is easy to handle, and acts as a berley as the bran and pollard washes off. It is excellent for bream, though other fish do take it.

Squid and cuttlefish: A bottle (or baby) squid on a single hook is a welcome meal for all carnivorous fish. A larger live squid is almost irresistible to kingfish and mulloway and other big fish. Fillets of squid or cuttlefish, or the tentacles or hands, can also be used on single or ganged hooks to take many species. Neither squid nor cuttlefish keep well: the best results are obtained when they are live or at least fresh.

Octopus: The tentacles of octopuses are tough and can thwart small pickers, but they are readily taken by snapper, tailor, flathead and practically all reef fish. The skin should be removed and the flesh hammered, but not mashed, before use. Octopus freezes quite well. Anyone seeking octopus

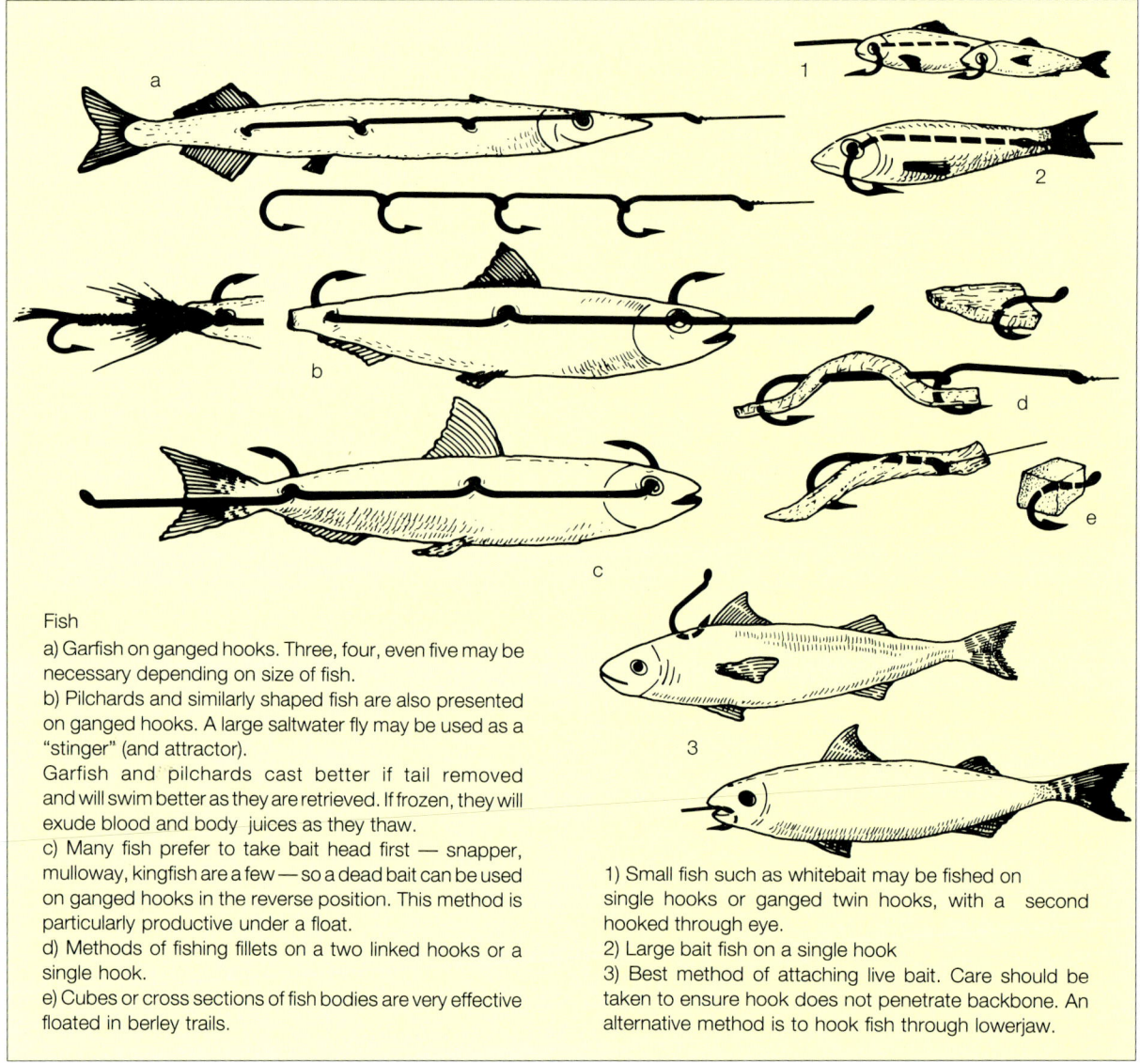

Fish

a) Garfish on ganged hooks. Three, four, even five may be necessary depending on size of fish.

b) Pilchards and similarly shaped fish are also presented on ganged hooks. A large saltwater fly may be used as a "stinger" (and attractor).

Garfish and pilchards cast better if tail removed and will swim better as they are retrieved. If frozen, they will exude blood and body juices as they thaw.

c) Many fish prefer to take bait head first — snapper, mulloway, kingfish are a few — so a dead bait can be used on ganged hooks in the reverse position. This method is particularly productive under a float.

d) Methods of fishing fillets on a two linked hooks or a single hook.

e) Cubes or cross sections of fish bodies are very effective floated in berley trails.

1) Small fish such as whitebait may be fished on single hooks or ganged twin hooks, with a second hooked through eye.

2) Large bait fish on a single hook

3) Best method of attaching live bait. Care should be taken to ensure hook does not penetrate backbone. An alternative method is to hook fish through lowerjaw.

in weed and rocks along the eastern seaboard of Australia should be cautious of the deadly blue-ring species.

Fish: Many small fish make prime live baits for bigger fish, ranging from bream to bonito, snapper to samsonfish, mulloway to marlin, and from tailor to tuna. In fact, game fishers often use large fish as bait, fish that are regarded as top-class table fare by other anglers. Some of the small baitfish include: yellowtail, slimy mackerel, garfish, pilchards, bluebait (blue sprats), mullet, sand sprats (whitebait), hardiheads, tommy ruff, etc. Fillets and cubes of these may be used as well as whole fish. Fillets of most fish — the smaller tunas, sweep, salmon, tailor, luderick, pikes, etc. — are also good baits. Some such as garfish freeze very

well, others, such as slimy mackerel for example, do not — though they can be salted.

Some anglers rationalise that using undersized fish for bait only does not circumvent the law. It not only breaks the law but threatens the very species that the minimum size requirements are designed to protect. And do not overlook the likelihood that a small bait fish might be protected in this way to preserve another species, often much larger, in a delicately balanced food chain.

Weed and cabbage: Herbivores such as luderick, zebra fish, and rock blackfish (perhaps milkfish, drummer, and some mullet) are primarily vegetarians, but they do eat flesh, such as worms, fleas, and small crustaceans etc. from time to time. The popular luderick, rock blackfish and drummer

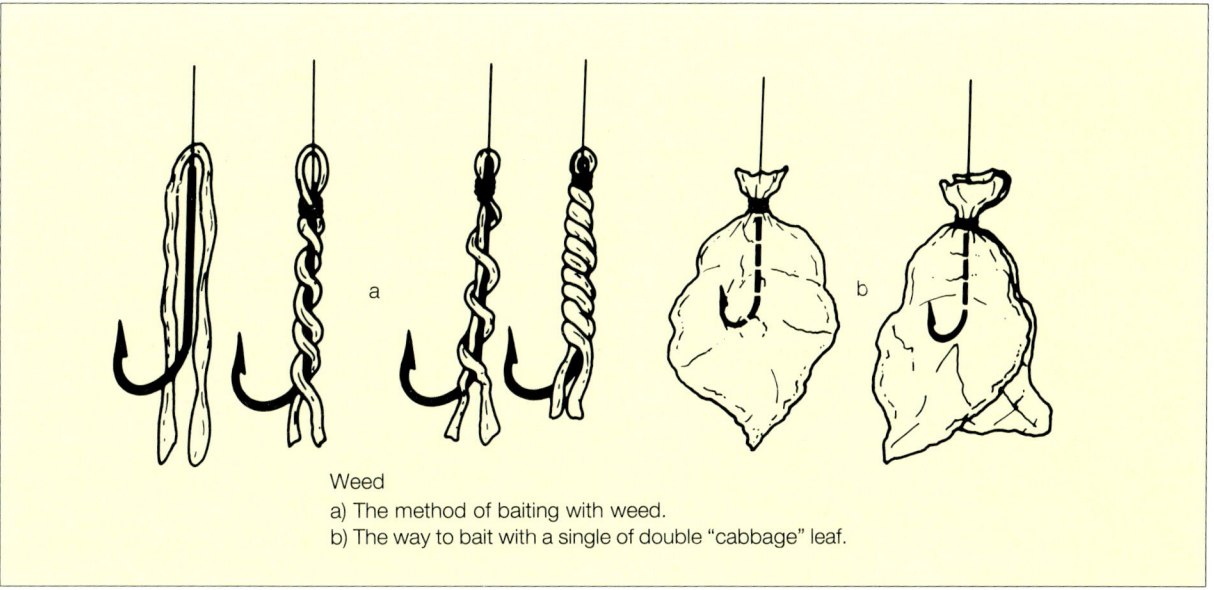

Weed
a) The method of baiting with weed.
b) The way to bait with a single of double "cabbage" leaf.

can be caught on the long-stranded grass-like weed or algae, which grows on rocks and pylons in estuaries, bays and harbours. The broad-leafed cabbage or lettuce on ocean rocks is a better bait for these fish when fishing these locations. Both weeds can usually be obtained where you fish but the long-stranded type is often available from bait suppliers. If fresh it freezes surprisingly well.

Dough, pudding, bread: These encompass a wide range of baits: from cubes or slices of bread, flour, water and sugar (with or without cottonwool to reinforce it) and other additives, to exotic mixtures of sausages of all kinds, cheeses, and fish oils etc. Both plain and the fanciful concoctions do catch bream, mullet, tommy ruff, garfish, rock blackfish, milkfish and, quite frequently, a surprising variety of other species. With the exception of bread, the dough and pudding baits are usually of a consistency to be squeezed into a pear or worm shape around a hook.

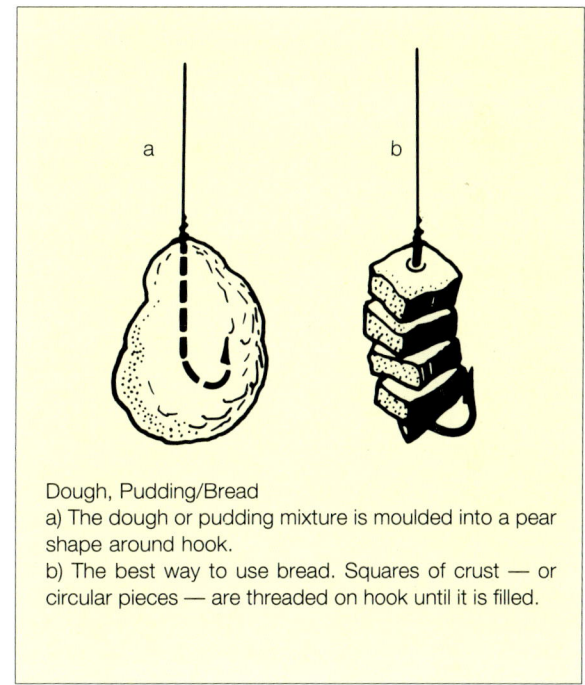

Dough, Pudding/Bread
a) The dough or pudding mixture is moulded into a pear shape around hook.
b) The best way to use bread. Squares of crust — or circular pieces — are threaded on hook until it is filled.

BERLEY FOR SALTWATER FISHING

Most estuary, beach, rock or offshore fishing catches can be improved by using berley. Fish such as luderick, zebra-fish, rock blackfish, drummer and mullet are obvious examples that are readily tempted, but a good berley will also attract, and sometimes hold, many others in a feeding mood. Particular berley mixtures are suggested with the relevant fish entries but anglers are encouraged to concoct their own.

For estuary fish, berley can be dropped to the bottom to be dispersed by the current, or it may be tossed out to spread over the surface and sink, drawing fish towards the anglers bait(ideal for luderick or mullet).

If you are seeking bottom-feeding fish, try lowering the berley in a porous bag attached to a cord, releasing clouds of the mixture regularly by lifting or shaking the cord.

Another effective method is to saturate a thick foam pad with pilchard and sardine oil, with a heavy sinker (attached to the top side) tied to a thick nylon line. When you lift or jiggle the line the weight of the sinker squeezes out the oil to attract fish. In some waters, berley sinkers and berley"blobs" or floats need to be used to carry the berley into the area of your choice.

Beach fishing requires some pre-planning. You will need to establish where there is a suitable back-wash or undertow that can be used to carry berley out from the water's edge. The most effective method to exploit this is a weighted, porous bag, which can be thrown out to a sand spit or gutter and anchored by a rope pegged in the sand, away from the waves — and where the rope will not interfere with other beach anglers (or even the user!) when retrieving their lines or landing fish. The rock anglers can use the hand dispensing method when fishing for luderick, rock blackfish and drummer. Depending on conditions, a porous bag can be hung over a rock front where the action of the waves and wash will release the berley. Oily fish, with the flesh exposed with a few slashes, or fish skeletons, can be used to the same purpose. Another method is to break up solid berley blocks (available commercially) and toss them into the area where you want to cast. A much better method — faster sinking and slower to disintegrate — is to make a mince of old fish scraps and baits and conjevoi and crabs etc. Freeze the mix in plastic or paper cups. Remove the cup when you get there and you have a conveniently-sized projectile to throw. But don't forget to take the used paper cup away with you when you leave. This same berley block frozen in a large container can be used when fishing inshore reefs, or even those in quite deep water. Remove the container and drop them to the bottom. Unless there is a powerful current flowing, they should not stray far. Where currents and wind permit, berley "trails" (of unfrozen pre-mixed concoctions) can be laid by hand so that they drift down to reefs to bring many fish — even snapper — to the surface. And when further out to sea, berley trails can be laid manually from a large container or from a berley bucket attached to the stern of the boat.

When a school of tailor or the like is attracted to the surface, the fish can be held with judicious use of a berley that floats. Some which work are chicken pellets, boiled rice (if dry) and minced dried-out fish, or a mixture of these.

Where a berley is used in a porous bag suspended under a boat in an estuary or shallow off-shore waters, it is wise to use a nylon line or rope that is easily broken. The writer does not suggest the oil-soaked foam for offshore use, and in fact discontinued its use after an episode in which a large shark swallowed the foam that was attached to a very strong rope. It tried mightily to pull the boat under, while an equally startled angler tried to saw through the rope with a blunt knife!

FRESHWATER FISHING BAITS

As with the marine species, freshwater fish have quite catholic tastes. Hot weather, low water and lengthy droughts can reduce the supply of some insects and crustaceans but plagues of grass-hoppers, on the other hand, can induce a preference for these while they are in abundance. Some species' appetite can also be affected by warm or excessively cool water.

Worms: All freshwater fish will eat worms. Some more regularly than others, and with a preference for certain worms, but they will all eat them. A worm of universal popularity is the large milky scrubworm. The ordinary garden or earthworm (the darker the colour, the better) is also popular. Fish will eat the striped tiger worm or bright red worm, but reluctantly, even when they are desperately hungry. The reason for this appears to be the fact that the tiger and red worms are manure worms and experiments suggest that their aroma causes them to be rejected if other food is available. Some anglers cultivate their own worm supply. And don't go for overkill when baiting your hook with worms. Fish will take a single worm that is well presented on a hook in preference to a bunched number on a hook.

Yabbies: The real yabbies are freshwater crayfish which inhabit the dams, creeks, backwaters and rivers of the inland. They may be caught in commercially available traps or fished for with bait or meat or fish flesh on a line or in a nylon stocking. Where possible use yabbies alive under a float, so that they do not burrow or hide on the bottom; a dead one is given some form of animation by drifting it unweighted in a current or under a float. A piece of yabbie tail makes an excellent addition to one of your hooks if casting or trolling lures in turbid water. Yabbies live well in damp grass and leaves.

Shrimps: These are a favourite food of most fresh-water fish. They are distinguished by their long single pincer. Usually found among weed, they can be trapped using fish flesh (or plain unscented soap) or scooped by dragging a small hand net through weed patches. They are difficult to keep alive.

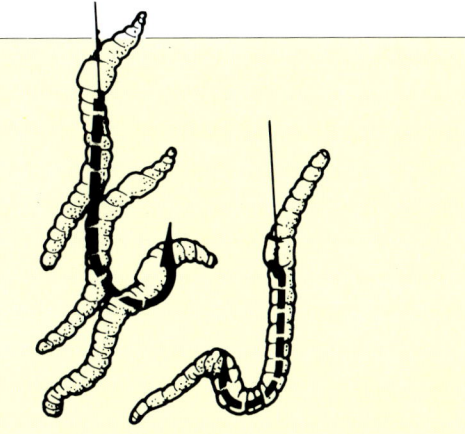

Worms

Several small worms can be threaded on a hook or a large single worm used. The hook should not penetrate the clitellum — the small girdle like section — towards the mouth of the worm which holds the heart and other organs. The worm remains alive and active when not damaged in this area.

Shrimp

Hook size depends on the size of shrimp. Insert in tail or thorax. It should only penetrate the body segments.

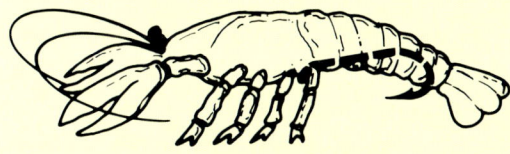

Yabby

The hook is inserted into the soft tail section, where it joins thorax. This ensures yabby remains alive. Fished below a float, off the bottom, a yabby is prevented from hiding in weed or other shelter. Yabby tail is also good bait. A piece can be used to add "smell" to hooks of lures in muddy water.

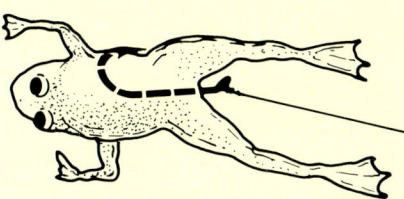

Frog/Tadpole

Hook size depends on the amphibian's size. Insert under the skin of the stomach area. Frogs, sometimes requiring a small sinker on eye of hook. Can be productive below a float.

Frogs and tadpoles: It may well be that European carp is the only fish in Australia's inland freshwater that will not eat frogs. But even they will eat tadpoles. There is argument about whether the brown or green frog makes the better bait: they take both. The amphibians should be hooked through the skin of their bellies.

Grasshoppers: There are many grasshoppers and trout will consume all of them. The most popular bait is the large green/yellow grasshopper (more correctly a locust) and trout, Macquarie perch, silver perch, bass and redfin take them readily. Other freshwater species will also eat them.

Grubs: The two most popular grubs are the larvae of the long-horn beetle which are called wood grubs or wattle grubs. They can be obtained by opening logs and stumps and the dying branches of casuarinas, wattles and kurrajongs.

Their presence is often indicated by sawdust-like waste exuded from a hole. The witchetty grub, which is the larva of the jewel beetle is found in soil near large river gums mostly. A thin wire with one end made into a corkscrew is used to extract them from the holes.

A big juicy witchetty grub is a favourite food of Murray cod, but all other freshwater fish take them as well as the wood grub. Both are popular with trout or Macquarie perch.

Gentles or maggots: These grubs seem to be regarded as a delicacy by trout and European carp but if other freshwater species are not quite so tempted by them, they will take them nevertheless.

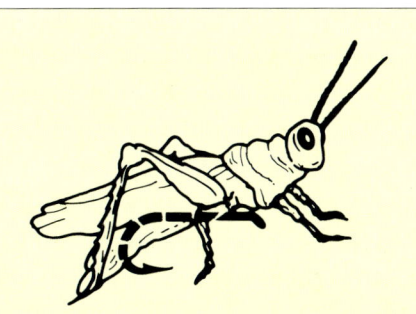

Grasshopper/Crickets

This insect may hooked as illustrated, or reversed with hook emerging from the point of insertion in the illustration. It's important that the hook only penetrates the abdomenal segments of insects. Moths can used as baited in the same manner. Hook size depends on size of insect.

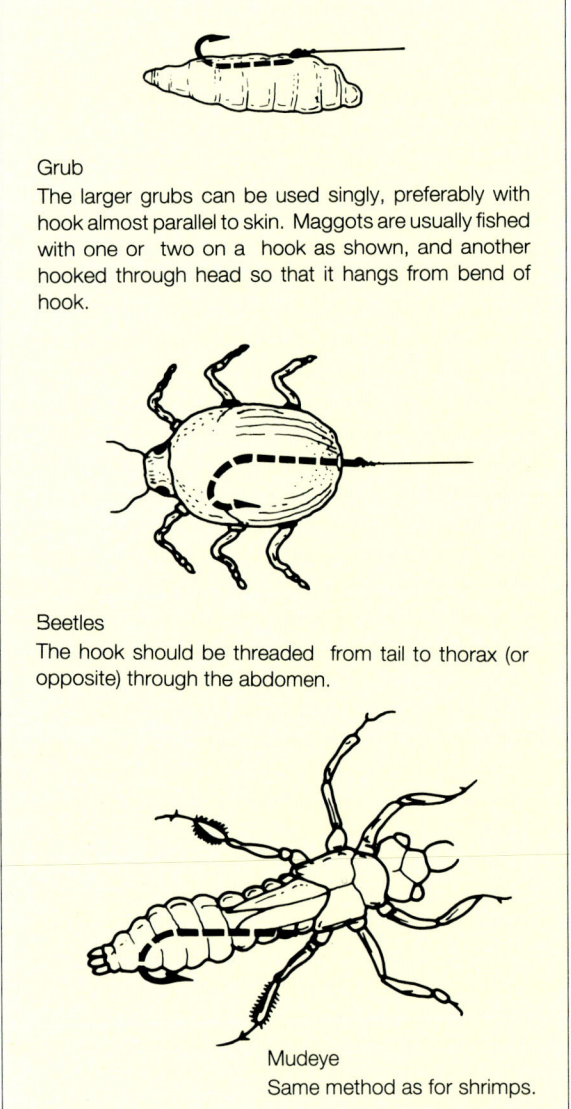

Grub
The larger grubs can be used singly, preferably with hook almost parallel to skin. Maggots are usually fished with one or two on a hook as shown, and another hooked through head so that it hangs from bend of hook.

Beetles
The hook should be threaded from tail to thorax (or opposite) through the abdomen.

Mudeye
Same method as for shrimps.

Beetles/crickets: Almost any beetle is acceptable food for the majority of freshwater fish. Christmas beetles and similarly large ones are extremely effective when fishing at night for trout and bass.

These same fish will not reject a cricket either. Nor, for that matter, will most of the main freshwater angling species.

Mudeyes: Trout eat dragonflies but definitely prefer their larvae (or mudeyes). Anglers can find these in damp rotting logs on the edges or submerged in the shallows of impoundments and rivers. They are best fished under a light float or bubble.

Corn/potatoes/dough: European carp have a broad taste in food that includes worms, crustaceans and insects. But it does not stop there by a long haul. They will take small boiled potatoes (or pieces of them), kernels of corn (boiled or from the can) and flour and sugar dough. Moreover they will frequently take such baits greedily if they are attracted with a berley that has a small amount of the bait being used minced in with it.

In general, the variety of food that freshwater fish will take is likely to astonish anglers as long as they fish. So will some of the baits that are suggested from time to time. However, there are authentic instances of snakes and water dragons and small birds (even a duck) being found in Murray cod stomachs. Lizards and mice have been eaten by trout and bass and nothing on or in the water would be safe if a barramundi needs to assuage its hunger.

Using any kind of small live fish as bait is not recommended for freshwater species. Not only has it caused environmental problems, but it is also illegal in the majority of States.

Some galaxiids or gudgeons are scarce or endangered and use by unthinking anglers of European carp, tench, roach and mosquito fish for bait can lead to their introduction to waters that have been mercifully free of foreign fish. It was this action which introduced many of the exotics to other waterways — and translocation of fish from one area to another may also spread diseases.

PREPARING THE CATCH

All fish taste better if some rules are followed during preparation. This applies just as much to those species that are not well-regarded as table fare, perhaps more so.

Fish retained for eating should be killed and bled immediately. This can be done by various means. On smaller fish, the backbone (and main artery) can be snapped by placing the index and second fingers behind the gill covers and forcing the head sharply back towards the dorsal fin. Be careful to avoid the sharp edges to the gill covers of some fish, or sharp spines. You may prefer to use a knife to cut the fleshy flap (the opercular membrane) between the gills on the throat, slicing through to the artery and backbone. The head may be retained on the fish by not cutting the flesh and skin on the top of the backbone. This method can be reversed, cutting from the back of the head through the backbone and down past the gills.

Another method that kills and bleeds a fish is to puncture the brain with a sharp-pointed knife, though the head will have to be removed before the fish is dressed.

All these methods are more satisfactory than hitting the fish on the head with a blunt instrument, usually a solid piece of timber, called a "priest". This does not properly bleed the fish and bruising the flesh detracts from the taste of many species. Though holding fish in a pool, a keeper net, or tethered can be convenient when fishing, the confinement can affect their flesh, because the stress causes some fish to produce enzymes that result in soft flesh spots when the fish is eventually killed. And many fish, tailor for example, can bruise their flesh if they are left to flap around on rocks or sand or on the bottom of a boat.

It's a matter of choice whether to scale a fish prior to cleaning (gutting and gilling) or after this has been done. However, it is much easier to remove scales from a fish before rigor mortis sets in. This is best done with a stiff knife with a serrated back edge, or with a scaling tool — there are several around and they all work. How well depends on the type and size of the fish's scales. A few fish, leatherjackets are one, can be skinned and gutted in one operation while other fish, trout and garfish, are often not scaled.

After cleaning, during which all intestines, gills, and blood along the backbone are removed, particular attention should be paid to removing any black lining of the stomach cavity that is prevalent among some fish, such as luderick, some mullet and rock blackfish .

A fish may be cooked whole or filleted, and the fillets may or may not be skinned. Large fish may be cut vertically through the body to produce cutlets.

It is better not to skin cutlets, because the skin helps to hold the flesh together around the bone in most methods of cooking, including barbecuing.

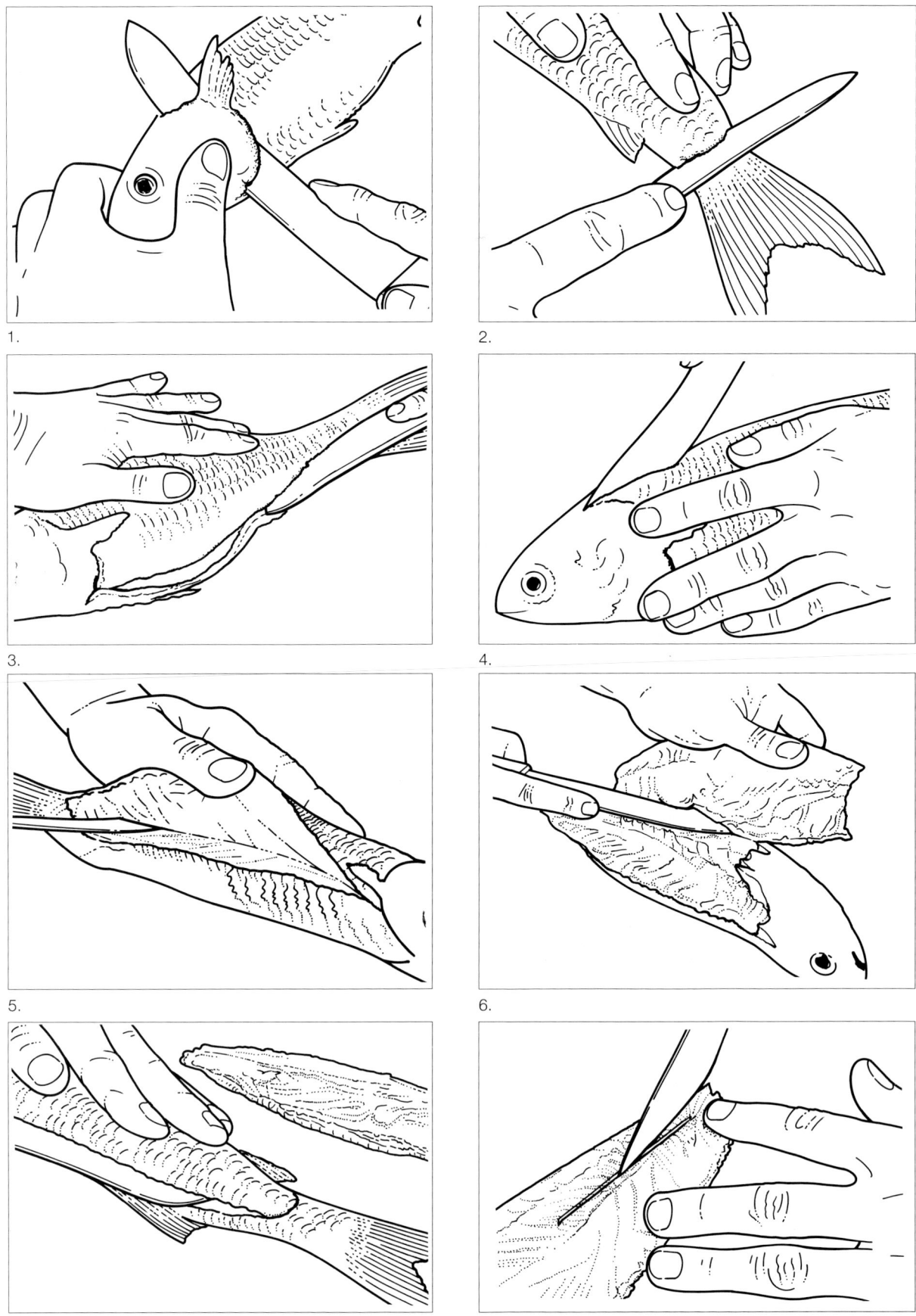

1.

2.

3.

4.

5.

6.

7.

8.

Fish intended for barbecued cutlets need not be scaled or skinned.

Anglers fishing from a boat well out to sea should kill, bleed, clean, gut and remove the gill rakers and backbone blood from any fish they plan to eat as soon as it is unhooked. The intestines, rakers and blood are the first to deteriorate, giving flesh an "off" taint. A few minutes' lost fishing time will ensure a better fish, for eating or freezing for later use. Scaling can be done later, although it will be somewhat more difficult.

Fish should be placed on ice without delay — throughout the year in the tropics, and in the summer months or during unseasonably hot days in most other regions of Australia. The availability and variety of ice boxes (some operated by batteries) and suitably large plastic containers makes this easy. And bags of ice should be as important as having bait. If the fish and ice are being kept in an open container, cover the lot with a damp canvas or cloth of some kind. If you are not using ice, at least keep the fish in the shade.

Land-based anglers should follow the same rules. However, the ice boxes and large containers are a burden when fishing from a beach, or rocks, or along inland waterways, where you are obliged to stray some distance from your vehicle. If you are at a beach, put the fish in a damp bag and bury it in the cooler wet sand, just above the waterline. Mark the spot for later retrieval. If you are fishing from rocks with no suitable sand within reach, at least place the bag in the shade.

Inland anglers of rivers and impoundments will probably be obliged to carry their catch. A porous hessian bag with a shoulder strap attached is best. Plastic-lined bags may be waterproof but they heat up, causing the fish to "sweat". If bank-wandering anglers plan to return along the same route, they can wrap their dressed fish in damp gum leaves, bracken or grass and bury them in a damp shady location for collection on the way home. But again, mark the spot well.

FILLETING (opposite)

1. Cut at an angle from behind the gill cage to the backbone, on both sides of the fish.

2. Make another cut near the tail, again on both sides.

3. Slice open the belly, crossing cuts (1) and (2) as close to the backbone as practicable.

4, 5, 6. Similar cut made along the back, again cutting very close to backbone, till previous cut (3) is met, freeing fillet.

7. Repeat 4, 5 & 6 on opposite side.

8. After having removed the rib cage, angle a slice down both sides of the blood line, and then lift it free.

Freezing fish

If a fish is left uncleaned for too long, or if it has not at least been kept cool on ice, whether whole or as fillets, its suitability for freezing is jeopardised. And some soft flesh fish, such as tailor or beardies, do not freeze well anyway and are better cooked fresh.

Before freezing fish, consider that a thawed whole fish does not produce satisfactory fillets or cutlets (or steaks as they are sometimes called). Moreover fillets from a properly cleaned and treated fish have a much longer refrigerator life than fish frozen whole.

Fillets or cutlets should be washed in water and thoroughly dried. If you wrap each one separately in plastic wrap, you need only thaw the number required for a meal, rather than waste any. You must *never* re-freeze seafood. Label and date each package. As soon as the fillets or cutlets are frozen, dip the package in cold water. This forms an ice glaze over the wrap, which that further seals the package to help prevent the fish from drying out. The packaged fish will freeze best if they are not stacked on top of each other. If this is impractical because space is at a premium, at least keep the layers to a minimum. Never stack other frozen packages on fish. Fillets or cutlets that have been properly frozen have a maximum freezer life of 4 to 5 months, but oily or fatty fish should be eaten within 3 months.

Keeping in mind that it is practically impossible to fillet a fish after it has been frozen — or even cut steaks — a whole fish can be frozen. It merely takes a little more effort. Thoroughly wash and dry the fish and wrap in a waxed paper. When the fish is frozen, a pan of near frozen water is required and the fish is unwrapped and dipped into this. Allow the water film to freeze and repeat several times so that a skin of layered ice completely covers the flesh. Then wrap it in aluminium foil and envelope in a freezer bag.

Frozen fish can be defrosted for about 24 hours prior to cooking. But defrost it in the bottom of the refrigerator, not at room temperature and certainly not with hot water. Alternatively it can be cooked at once in its frozen state.

When cooking, avoid being heavy handed. Whether baked, broiled, grilled, poached, deep-fried, barbecued or pan fried, defrosted fish should never be overcooked. It will only toughen the flesh and diminish the flavour. If you have got it right, fish should still be cooking on the way to the table...and so should fresh fish for that matter. Bon appétit!

POISONOUS & VENOMOUS FISH

Over the years there have been far too many tragedies caused by ignorance — particularly amongst newcomers — of the dangers of eating Australia's poisonous fish. And with a good deal less severity but not without pain, countless anglers have also been hurt handling fish carelessly, particularly those whose defence mechanisms include a venomous sting.

[This excludes, of course, the most common form of poisoning from fish, that is food poisoning, which can be caused by any fish having been kept too long, or improperly frozen. It cannot be stressed enough that fish must be properly cleaned and iced as soon as practicable, particularly in the tropics. — *see* Preparing the Catch]

POISONOUS FISH

The following fish may not be eaten in any circumstances.

Toadfish (blowfish)/pufferfish

There are about 20 species of these fishes in Australian waters, ranging in size from about 15 centimetres to 50 centimetres, with the silver toadfish of temperate and tropical waters measuring about a metre. A small piece of this fish very nearly killed Captain Cook and some of his crew. All toadfish and puffer fish, some quite colourful, are smooth skinned. They inflate their body with either air or water when they are alarmed.

Porcupine fish

Much easier recognised, the bodies of porcupine fish are covered with spines. These become erect when the fish feels threatened. They too inflate themselves with air or water.

Boxfish, cowfish

These fish can be recognised by the bony plates which enclose and protect the body. They can be colourful and the various species may reach a length of 50 centimetres.

Stinkfishes

To some degree the stinkfishes resemble gurnards. They are found in both shallow and deepwater reefs and weed areas. They are best distinguished by the wide triangular head when viewed from above, with a rounded corner at the mouth and behind the eyes. These fish have an offensive smell and their flesh is extremely bitter even when cooked.

The spines on these fish are not poisonous. The flesh and organs contain a poison known as tetrodotoxin which they manufacture themselves (unlike poisons ingested by eating other fish — such as ciguetera).

Symptoms, treatment

Within 5 to 30 minutes of consuming flesh containing the (tetrodotoxin) poison , muscular paralysis develops to such an extent that it can cause respiratory failure. The victim experiences dizziness and weakness. The lips may swell and become numb. Vomiting usually occurs and this should be induced as soon as the symptoms become apparent, provided the victim is not unconscious. Seek urgent medical attention and if the victim lapses into unconsciousness give mouth to mouth resuscitation. A period in hospital is normally necessary.

STINGING FISH

Almost all fish that have strong spines in their dorsal or anal spines can inflict painful wounds. Fortunately most injuries caused this way — usually the result of hasty or careless handling by anglers — merely hurt a little . The best treatment is to induce little bleeding before cleaning the wound prior to apply an antiseptic and covering with sticking plaster is all that is necessary. A deep puncture or a spine broken off in the wound will require medical attention.

Some fish have extremely sharp teeth (which are usually obvious). Bites from them are painful and can cause profuse bleeding. Tailor are notorious in this regard but most of the well-fanged fish will sink their teeth in if given a chance. Large yellow leatherjackets or chinaman leatherjackets are capable of removing a finger and peg-toothed fish such as snapper and tusk-fish can lacerate and bruise a finger carelessly placed in their mouth while removing a hook.

Unless the bite has removed a sizeable piece of flesh, the cleansing and dousing with antiseptic and a pad to staunch the flow of blood will generally allows the angler to continue fishing.

The best protection is prevention, of course, so do not rush when handling and unhooking fish. If in doubt about the spines of a fish, fold some old cloth or canvas in several layers to handle them. Most dorsal spines can be pushed flat (except on triggerfish) without too much effort and the rag helps to hold the fish firmly.

The gill covers of some fish are finely honed and can cut deeply, but simple first aid is usually sufficient treatment.

VENOMOUS FISH

Venomous fish are those whose spines contain a venom. In almost all cases the venom glands are protected on the spines by a sheath or skin, membrane or tissue. When the spine punctures the skin of the victim, the insertion into the flesh pushes the skin back, which ruptures the protective membrane or tissue around the spine and the venom is released. The deeper the puncture the more venom is released.

CIGUATERA POISONING

Fish that are not properly cleaned and kept cool (preferably on ice), can cause severe food poisoning, particularly in the tropics, but elsewhere too during hot weather. An obvious difference in the symptoms between the more commonplace food-poisoning and ciguatera is that only the latter causes tingling in the lips, mouth, hands and feet of its victim.

Ciguatera is caused by eating various carnivorous tropical reef fishes. The toxin originates in a single-cell algae known as *dinoflagellates,* which grow on coral reef surfaces. These are ingested by algal grazing species such as parrot-fish and surgeon-fish, which in turn fall prey to the carnivores. The best-known of these carnivores are the red bass or kelp sea-perch, paddle-tail sea-perch and the chinaman-fish (*see* sea-perch). The toxicity in any of these fish can vary, depending on the locality. They may well be safe to eat in some areas. However, common sense suggests that the only prudent course is to regard them all as hazardous and release them.

When fish ingest the toxin, it is retained in their flesh. Thus the larger and older the fish, the more toxin it is likely to have accumulated.

The symptoms of ciguatera usually — though not always — surface within two hours of eating contaminated fish. Sometimes there will be no signs for up to 12 hours.

One of the first reactions is a feeling of weakness and dull, aching limbs. A tingling sensation in the mouth, lips, hands and feet usually accompanies the weakness and aches. The palms and the soles of the feet may become itchy. Vomiting and diarrhoea occur. This is often accompanied by a reversal of the victim's perceptions of hot and cold: hot drinks will feel cold, cold drinks seem hot. Convulsions can follow, and vision (particularly focussing) may be difficult. Paralysis may occur.

Should these symptoms surface soon after a meal, vomiting should be induced and medical assistance sought. Experienced anglers of the tropics are aware that many other reef fish they like to eat are just as carnivorous as the worst carriers of the toxin — including emperors, javelin-fish, job-fish, mackerels, tanguigues etc. They minimise any risk of ingesting dangerous levels of the toxin by restricting themselves to only small quantities of bigger reef fish, and with less frequency than meals of smaller fish of the same species (which might reasonably be supposed to have accumulated less toxin in their shorter life). While ciguatera poisoning has only been reported from Queensland and Papua-New Guinean waters, this policy may be a wise one for all anglers fishing Australian tropical waters.

Common fish which sting, and may even cause pain severe enough to require medical attention (depending on the reaction by the victim) are:

Catfish

These fish have three venomous spines, one in the front of the dorsal fin and one in the front of each pectoral fin. The membrane over these cover numerous small venom glands. The spines are serrated, which causes a deeper spread of the venom as they tear the flesh when extracted. This sting can be extremely painful.

Boarfish

With a long dorsal spine, the boarfish also carries venom. Reaction to its sting can be much the same as with a flathead wound.

Flathead and gurnards

The dorsal spines of these fish contain a venom so mild that it causes no reaction at all in some anglers but quite a severe reaction in others. If you experience a reaction that is worrying, follow the treatment below.

Scorpion-cods, stingfish, others of the scorpaenidae family

The spines of the dorsal fin of these fish (and in some members, spines on the sides of the head) have several grooves running along them containing venom glands. Each spine is covered with a sheath of skin and a membrane which is ruptured when the spine punctures the victims skin. Most scorpion-cod and gurnard perch produce a severe sting but the firefish seem to cause the most severe pain and reaction, with swelling and flesh discolouration.

Other fish

Among other fishes that release a venom are **stingrays** (and **stingarees**). They have 1 to 3 long serrated spines on their tail and the way they thrust it can cause deep lacerated wounds as the spines tear the flesh on withdrawal. They are not illustrated in these pages nor are fish called **spinefoots, velvet fish** and **stargazers**, all of which sting in the same manner as scorpion-cods.

Port Jackson sharks and dogfish: Even these fish have a spine on the leading edge of each dorsal spine and can inflict a venom if it punctures the skin.

Symptoms and treatment

The recommended treatment is suitable for stings from all venomous fish though it is aimed at the more severe stings.

The pain is usually immediate when a spine punctures the flesh. This pain steadily increases as the venom moves up the affected limb. In the case of the scorpion-cod and related species, the pain can be severe for several hours. There is almost always quite noticeable swelling in the area of the wound. It may even become discoloured. In very severe cases some difficulty with breathing may result and mouth to mouth resuscitation may be necessary.

The wound should be immediately washed with water to remove any dirt or other foreign material from the puncture. The wound should be allowed to bleed, assisted by some slight pressure. If possible, the wound and limb above the area should be immersed in water as hot as can be borne by the victim because heat breaks down the venom: this should be continued until the pain eases, which may be several hours. If the area of the wound cannot be immersed in hot water continuously apply towels soaked in hot water. Do not apply hot water to an unconscious victim, only water hot enough (about 50° C) so as not to scold. And please seek urgent medical attention.

STONEFISH

Two species of these **deadly** fish are reasonably common in Queensland waters and a third exists in Northern Territory and north-west waters of Western Australia.

Reef Stonefish (Synanceichthys verrucosus) inhabit the lagoons and reef-flats of the Great Barrier Reef.

Estuarine Stonefish (Synaneja trachynis) are found in muddy bays and estuaries of the Queensland coast as far south as Moreton Bay.

Spotted Stonefish (Inimicus sinensis) are found in tropical waters of the Gulf, Northern Territory and north-western Western Australia.

The fish are ugly, the smooth skins are covered with warts and protrusions and it is often camouflaged with marine growth such as algae and polyps. Stonefish use their paddle-shaped fins to bury themselves with their eyes and mouth barely exposed, waiting for prey. When disturbed they are a very clumsy and slow swimmer.

Their 13 dorsal spines, with a fleshy sheath, contain twin venom glands which have a duct near the tip.

Not a pretty sight: the scorpionfish out of water.

These spines are raised, the tips protruding through the sheath. When a weight, such as a foot forces the sheath down, this constricts the two venom glands, squeezing out the venom, which is injected deep into the puncture. Thick-soled shoes are necessary if wading in stonefish territory because the spines can penetrate soft rubber soles and sandals. Handling this fish is not recommended.

Symptoms and treatment

The venom is potent, causing immediate searing pain and swelling, irregular respiration, a lowering of the blood pressure and often partial paralysis. An anti-venene exists but the victim should be treated with hot water (as for other venomous fish) and hot vinegar forced into the puncture (an eye-dropper is helpful) until medical treatment is received (as fast as possible). Mouth-to-mouth resucitation may be necessary before medical assistance arrives.

The grotesque stone fish, almost indistinguishable among the coral of the Barrier Reef.

FISHING REGULATIONS

Australian fisheries are a valuable resource under tremendous pressure from exploitation. Each State or Territory maintains legal controls to protect this resource. The controls also try to ensure that fish are available on a equitable basis to the growing numbers of recreational anglers.

The author has made every effort to include legal size limits or any "bag limits" (number of fish per angler per day) where applicable, along with occasional cautions regarding fish that are partially or totally protected.

Brief mention is also made of those waters that are closed seasonally — periods when fishing is forbidden. Such regulations may be changed by State authorities, however, and the author and publishers accept no responsibility for the information, published in good faith, that is thus superseded.

Obligations required of recreational anglers differ from State to State. These include various license requirements; restrictions of fishing methods; the types of equipment permitted; the sizes and design of nets or traps for catching bait fish; size and quantity limits on bait fish and shellfish that anglers may use or have in their possession; even regulations regarding where baits may be sought. Each State has its own rules, its own calendar for closed seasons; and its own gazetted non-fishing areas, such as aquatic reserves and marine parks, etc.

It is the recreational angler's responsibility to be informed of these local regulations . Copies of fishing regulations and guide-lines are usually available from tackle shops as well as the relevant government fisheries departments.

ALBACORE
Thunnus alalunga

OTHER NAMES: **LONGFIN TUNA**

This fine "white flesh" member of the tuna family is probably the most sought-after by commercial fishers and recreational anglers. Unfortunately, the albacore does not come within reach of the shore-based anglers and the exhilarating sport they provide is restricted to those with a boat suitable for fishing waters over the continental shelf.

Identification
It is easy to distinguish the albacore from other tunas because of its relatively heavy body and — more particularly — by the extreme length of its pectoral fins, which reach back past the dorsal and anal fins. Its second dorsal fin lacks the distinct sickle shape of the yellowfin, and its tail has a white edge. The body is mainly a deep blue, though almost black on top. The blue fades to an off-white or creamy belly. There is a hint of yellow in the dark fins.

Size
The world all-tackle record is 40 kilograms, which would appear to be close to its maximum size. The Australian all-tackle record (at September, 1988) was 23.20 kilograms. A catch is usually between 7 and 10 kilograms in size, though often smaller in the far south of its range.

Breeding
Spawning is believed to occur in subtropical waters around late spring. This may be subject to water temperature.

Habits
Albacore roam widely throughout the Pacific, remaining offshore all their lives. They seem to prefer a water temperature of about 15° C to 21° C. Schools shoal in what appear to be age groups, with fish up to about 15 kilograms more likely to be found close to the surface. Larger fish gather in smaller schools, which move at greater depths. Like all tuna, they can display frantic feeding when attacking a school of small fish.

Distribution
Because of its preference for a narrow water temperature range, the albacore is more likely to be

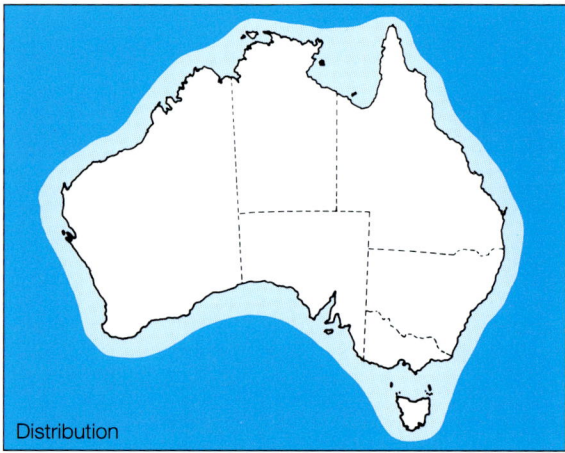

Distribution

found along mainland Australia's eastern coast, as far south as Tasmania and into Bass Strait between October and April. There are reports of this fish having been present in southern waters of the mainland, and off Western Australia, but these sightings would seem to be mistaken identification. The appearance of albacore may also be linked with the migration or shoaling of its main food fish.

When to fish
The ideal time is during the migrating movement which covers late spring to early autumn. Most anglers prefer to fish for albacore in the early morning or late afternoon. The fish will bite on bait well into the dark.

Where to fish
Albacore are unlikely to be found inside the continental shelf.

Tackle
Medium to heavy baitcasting (even top-of-the range

threadline) rods and reels, spooled with about 10 to 12 kilograms breaking-strain line, provide for fine sport with the hard-running albacore. Light game outfits become more suitable when fish at the top end of the size range are running.

Baits
Albacore will respond to live bait such as yellowtail, anchovies, squid and slimy mackerel. However, dead mullet, pilchards, squid, mackerel, etc., may be taken.

These fish can also be attracted with a wide range of the smaller skirted lures, especially those which imitate or simulate the food they may be chasing. The lures should be trolled at between 7 and 10 knots. It is also often possible to cast to a school, using the metal minnow type of lures.

Rigs
Use an unweighted rig (No. 2) for casting baits to a school or rig 11 when trolling lures or bait.

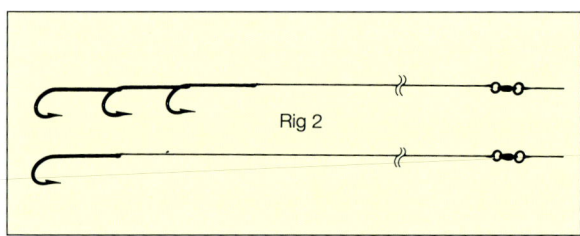

Rig 2

Hint
A school may be held with a berley of live bait and fish pieces.

Edibility
This white-fleshed tuna should be bled quickly, dressed and kept on ice. It is excellent eating, whether fried, grilled, steamed or baked.

AMBERJACK
Seriola dumerili

OTHER NAMES: **GREATER AMBERJACK, ALLIED KINGFISH**

Of the nine species of the genus Seriola in the world, four are
called amberjack. This explains much of the confusion among
Australian anglers trying to distinguish between amberjack and
samsonfish (*Seriola hippes*). Some, in fact, have been driven
to settle on the name "samberjack" for both!
The amberjack is a fine sports fish, as are all fish of the genus
Seriola, and it will test the skill and equipment of
the most skilled angler.

Identification

There is some variation in the amberjack's colouring, which is probably related to age or sexual
maturity, and it alters quickly after death. Nevertheless, the dorsal area and the caudal fin of the
fish are generally purplish-brown and the belly a
creamy white. These colours are usually separated, though not always, by a broad gold to
amber band that runs from the eye to the tail. The
other fins are olive green, the anal fin showing a
white edge. Young specimens have a relatively
deep body that becomes more elongated as the
fish grows. The head is steeper than that of a
yellowtail kingfish but not as blunt as that of the
samsonfish. The preoperculum (or cheek bone)

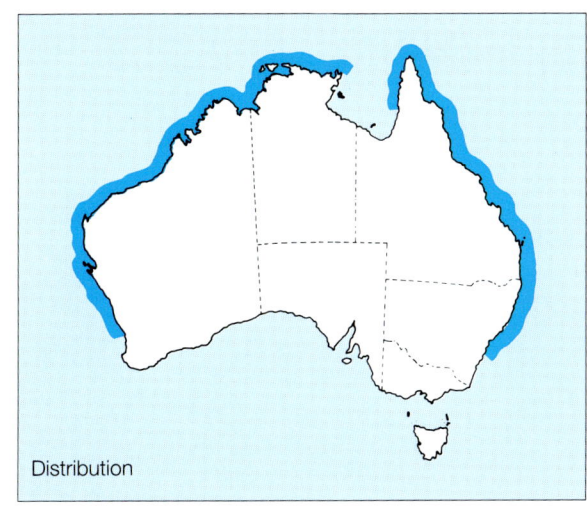

Distribution

reaches a point above the middle of the eye. The rays in its anal fin total 19 or more (compared with a maximum of 17 in samson fish).

Size

The maximum recorded weight for the fish is 70.59 kilograms; the Australian all-tackle record (September, 1988) is 36.7 kilograms, taken at Flinders Reef, Queensland.

Breeding

Little is known of the breeding cycle of the amberjack in Australian waters.

Habits

Amberjacks are often encountered in schools over shallow and mid-depth off-shore reefs and off headlands that terminate in broken reefs or rock outcrops. They feed on many small bait fish such as yellowtail, pilchards, sardines, hardiheads, garfish, mullet, etc., and they may also take bait that is being used on reefs for other bottom-dwelling species, such as squid or fish fillets. The amberjack also displays the same behaviour of its cousin, the yellowtail kingfish, by aggregating around a tethered member of its own kind.

Distribution

Amberjack are found throughout the world. They inhabit tropical, subtropical and temperate Australian waters along the eastern and western coastlines, preferring a water temperature about 20° C to 25° C. Only occasionally are amberjack found as far south as Sydney in the east, or Perth in the west.

When to fish

The best time to fish for amberjack is when the water current falls to its preferred range of temperatures throughout the area of its distribution. This is usually from late spring to autumn.

Where to fish

This is an offshore fish that is usually found over reefs or off headlands — and even in open water when chasing food.

Tackle

Medium to heavy threadline and baitcasting out-

fits are adequate for small amberjack but light game gear is required for the larger fish. Lines of between 6 and 10 kilograms breaking-strain are suitable. The fish responds to a wide range of lures, either cast or trolled.

Bait

This fish likes smaller fish, such as yellowtail, garfish, mullet — live or trolled — or cubed pieces of fish floated in a berley trail. A good burley of fish pieces can draw them to the surface.

Rig

Use a lightly weighted bait rigs and trolling rigs (No. 3, 11).

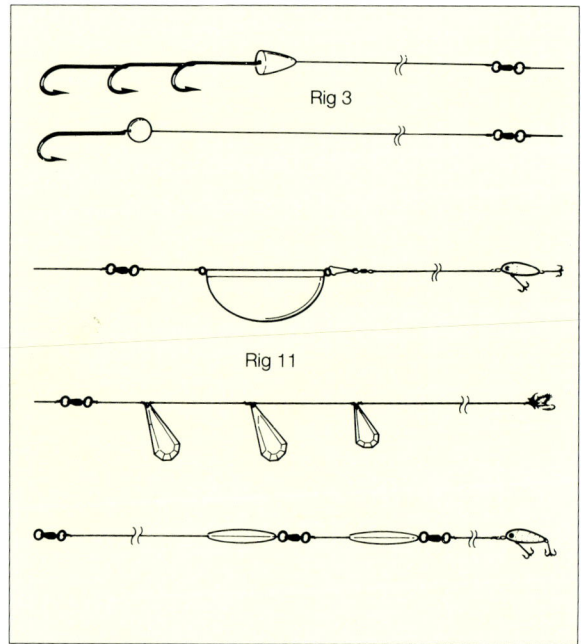

How to hook

When the amberjack attacks a bait or lure, it tends to gulp it and hooks itself. With bait, tightening of the line is usually enough to embed the hook.

Edibility

The smaller amberjack make reasonable table fare, provided that they are killed, bled, gilled and gutted, and kept on ice immediately after having been caught. If a bigger fish is not required for a record claim, it should be released.

BARRACOUTA
Thyrsites atun

OTHER NAMES: **COUTA, PICK-HANDLE**

Anglers' opinion of the barracouta is sharply divided. In some
areas it is highly regarded as a food fish, in others it is cursed
as a nuisance. It is least popular when it turns up on the east
coast around the Illawarra region, because its arrival usually
indicates a cold current, which deters more desirable fish from
biting. (It has been known to travel occasionally as far north
as the subtropical waters past Coffs Harbour.) Even the
barracouta's ability to provide good sport, with often hectic
action on light gear, fails to assuage its detractors.

Identification

This fish should not be confused with the barracuda, which is a tropical water species, though it
does bear a resemblance. The barracouta is a
streamlined fish with a dark, sail-like dorsal fin
connected to its second dorsal fin, directly above
the anal fin. Between the dorsal and anal fins there
are six separate finlets on the back and bottom of
the caudal peduncle. Its scales are small and readily rub off, sticking to the angler's hand. The top
of the body is dark blue to black fading to silver on
the underside of the belly. This is a ferocious-
looking fish with a mouth full of extremely sharp
teeth, particularly those in its protruding lower
jaw.

Size

A barracouta measuring about 1.5 metres may
weigh up to 6 kilograms, but immediately after
spawning in the summer period, the same fish

might be half that weight. A more common size is
about 70 to 80 centimetres.

Breeding

These fish spawn in the summer.

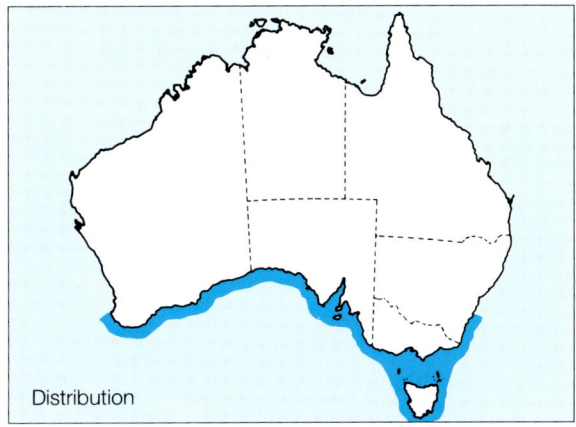

Distribution

Habits

If you hook a barracouta it invariably means that a school is present, whether offshore (they rarely travel more than a few kilometres to sea) or around wharves, piers, breakwalls and ocean rock fronts. They will enter bays, harbours and ocean inlets, where small local or migrating fish seek shelter. Once induced to feed, they attack with a frenzy that scatters their prey in panic. Barracouta generally swim 2 or 3 metres beneath the surface, though they are encountered on the bottom in deeper water.

Distribution

Barracouta prefer cooler waters, being largely distributed from the far south coast of New South Wales, around Tasmania and the south-eastern coastline of Victoria, west past Port Phillip Bay, into South Australian waters, and off the south-west coast of Western Australia.

When to fish

In the colder areas of their range, the summer and autumn periods produce large schools of big fish. The best time in more northerly regions is from autumn-spring. Water temperature has a decisive influence. Overcast or rainy days often offer more productive fishing than bright sunny days.

Where to fish

Fish for barracouta by trolling in open waters, or by casting-and-retrieving bait or lures from wharves, piers, breakwalls and ocean fronts, especially in small sheltered bays with good weed beds.

Tackle

For small boat or pier or wharf fishing, use light to medium threadline or baitcasting reels. Rods are ideal for trolling lures, casting-and-retrieving lures, or for baitfishing for barracouta. When fishing from rocks, use a light or medium rod of about 3.5 metres, with a matching sidecast, threadline or overhead reel. They are more suitable for lures and baits. Lines need not exceed 5 kilograms breaking-strain.

Baits

Try fish flesh, small sprats, yellowtail, sardines, etc., squid fillets, octopus tentacles and so on. All are readily devoured by this voracious fish.

Rigs

The long-shanked single hook (with a light nylon-covered wire trace) or two or three ganged hooks (either rig 9/10 or 2) but with a black swivel. The barracouta will grab at bright brassy or silver swivels. For this reason, it is best to use cadmium-plated or stainless hooks: if the bait is removed from the hook by a barracouta without being hooked, it or another is likely to "hit" the bare hooks.

The same rigs can be used with lures, especially spoons and slicers, that are shiny or bright. It is prudent to use lures made of metal or some other material that cannot be ripped or punctured by the barracouta's teeth.

How to hook

Once the bait or lure is below the surface, a slow retrieval should be maintained, even if there is a "hit and miss" strike by this fish. The barracouta can turn in its own length for a second attack.

Hint

If a school is found when trolling it is much better to stop and fish by casting and retrieving. As soon as the fish start biting again, change from bait to lures—the catch is rarely diminished.

Barracouta often follow krill schools. An effective lure is a long-shanked hook, with silver paper or mylar wound on the shank. Slip a clear plastic tube (with a couple of slices in the end a few centimetres longer than the shank) up to the eye of the hook and fasten it at the eye with a couple of twists of nylon or wire. But still use a light wire trace.

Edibility

Some times, more often in the northern area of its range, the barracouta can be infested by a cestode worm or have soft milky sections in its flesh. Despite its many fine bones, the barracouta is much sought after as a food fish, especially in Tasmania.

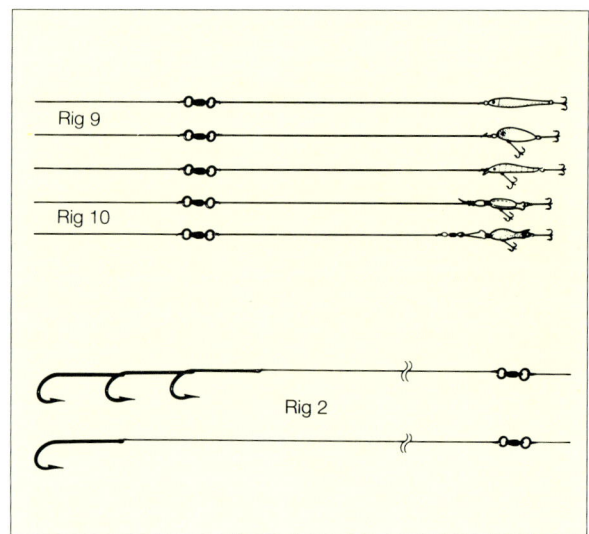

Rig 9

Rig 10

Rig 2

BARRAMUNDI

Lates Calcarifer

OTHER NAMES: **BARRA, GIANT PERCH**

Folklore to the contrary, the barramundi is not found only in Australia. It can be found in the rivers and estuaries of Papua-New Guinea, throughout the Indonesian archipelago, most of South-east Asia, including Malaysia, and up into the Persian Gulf. Moreover, there is evidence to suggest that its "Aboriginal" name — by which it is known throughout Australia — was not bestowed on this fish by the country's original people. That aside, the barramundi is without doubt one of the   world's grand sport fish and a very fine food fish. Sadly, the universal recognition of these attributes — and its reputation as a tourist attraction — is also cause for concern. Numbers are declining, distribution is shrinking. It remains to be seen whether the introduction of fewer commercial licences, closed seasons, catch limits, size restrictions and other steps, will reverse the trend.

Identification

There is a marked difference in the colours of a barramundi that has spent time isolated in a freshwater billabong and one which has remained in the saltwater or brackish sections of an estuary. The estuarine fish is greyish-green with a bronze tint on the dorsal and silvery on the sides; the freshwater fish is much darker and duller in colour. The fins are basically grey with a gold-bronze hue at the bases. The body is solid and elongate-oval, the mouth large and the tail paddle-shaped. Its profile rises distinctly — from about the eye— to the back. The barramundi's eyes are large, pink-red, and will reflect bright torchlight and even sunshine.

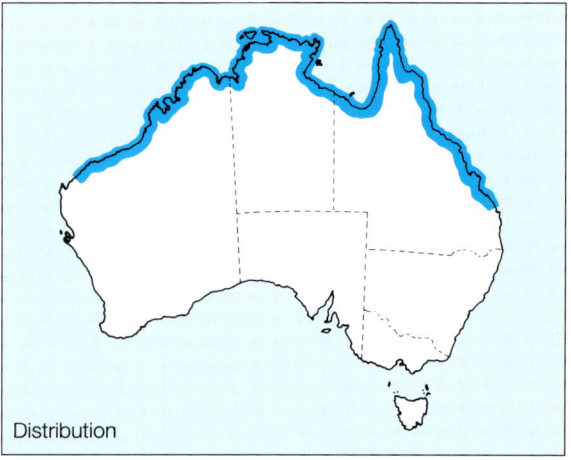

Distribution

Size

The fish is known to exceed 50 kilograms, but one of 30 kilograms is exceptional today. The great majority of fish caught by anglers are now below about 6 kilograms. A fish of maximum weight would measure about 1.7 metres.

There are scientific arguments supporting a maximum size above which a barramundi should be released, as its survival in numbers depends on its life cycle.

The minimum size for a legal catch in the Northern Territory and Queensland is 50 centimetres.

Breeding

Sexually mature barramundi run down-river to spawn in the sea. This may begin in September. The first breeding fish are those which have remained near the ocean (in bays or estuaries) or those which are not impeded in their run from rivers or creeks. Those barramundi that have been isolated in billabongs wait for the floods of the wet to escape to the sea, sometimes as late as February, because they will not spawn in water with a salinity of less than 20 parts per thousand. After spawning, adult barramundi may remain in salty water or return upriver. Juveniles stay in mangrove areas, move into tidal creeks and migrate into freshwater, if their progress is not stopped by weirs, waterfalls, dams, etc. Some even reach freshwater areas that close off to become billabongs when the floodwaters recede. Barramundi reach approximately 30 centimetres long in their first year.

If the barramundi's breeding is fairly straightforward, its sex life is not. A barramundi is unlikely to be sexually mature before 3 years — and the female barramundi may be regarded as non-existent. The male spawns regularly, producing sperm for 3 to 4 years after maturity. It then changes sex, and becomes not only female but one of the most abundant breeders in the fish world. A CSIRO study concluded that, in the main, small barramundi are male (which rarely if ever reach 10 to 12 kilograms). Large barramundi (about a metre or more) are females. Thus, if the bigger fish are retained and small specimens released, the sex ratio in populations can become unbalanced. The case for a maximum rather than a minimum size limit may be a more practical proposal for the conservation and preservation of this magnificent fish. And a photograph of a large barramundi, together with the memory of the thrill it provided, remains considerably more vivid and lasting than its taste as a meal.

Habits

A predator of the first order, the barramundi is a hunter that likes to ambush its prey. It will follow and feed on a shoal of small fish as they move with incoming or outgoing tides; it will wait around the edges of deep holes behind a sandbar until the fish enter; it will station itself at the mouth of a draining creek and prey on food the current brings; and it will take up shelter (often displaying a territorial behaviour) near mangroves, under fallen trees, and submerged snags at a creek entrance — but invariably where a current will help bring food. While it eats near the bottom it will attack, with explosive force, surface fish, small animals, etc. It appears to be ready to attack or devour interlopers to its territory at any time.

Distribution

Living in rivers and estuaries in subtropical and tropical regions, the barramundi ranges from about the Mary River in Queensland (though its numbers are thin south of Cairns), around the Cape York Peninsular, through the Gulf of Carpentaria, across the Northern Territory, and down the north-west coastline of Western Australia to about the Asburton River.

The distance barramundi penetrate a river depends on a clear passage upstream. Weirs, rock bars, even rapids not far above tidal influence, may be the extent of its travels.

When to fish

Outside the closed periods in the Northern Territory and Queensland (*see* Other regulations), the conditions of many inland waters can delay access till after the wet or extended floods. Some estuary areas can usually be reached. Water levels or tidal heights are a factor, many anglers preferring not

A good sized barramundi.

forms its head-shaking aerial antics. Strong hooks are as necessary for bait as for lures, and the lure bodies should be strong too.

Baits

Probably the best bait is a live mullet, though the barramundi will accept other small fish and large live prawns. It may take dead baits but they make a poor substitute. Attracted by a wide range of

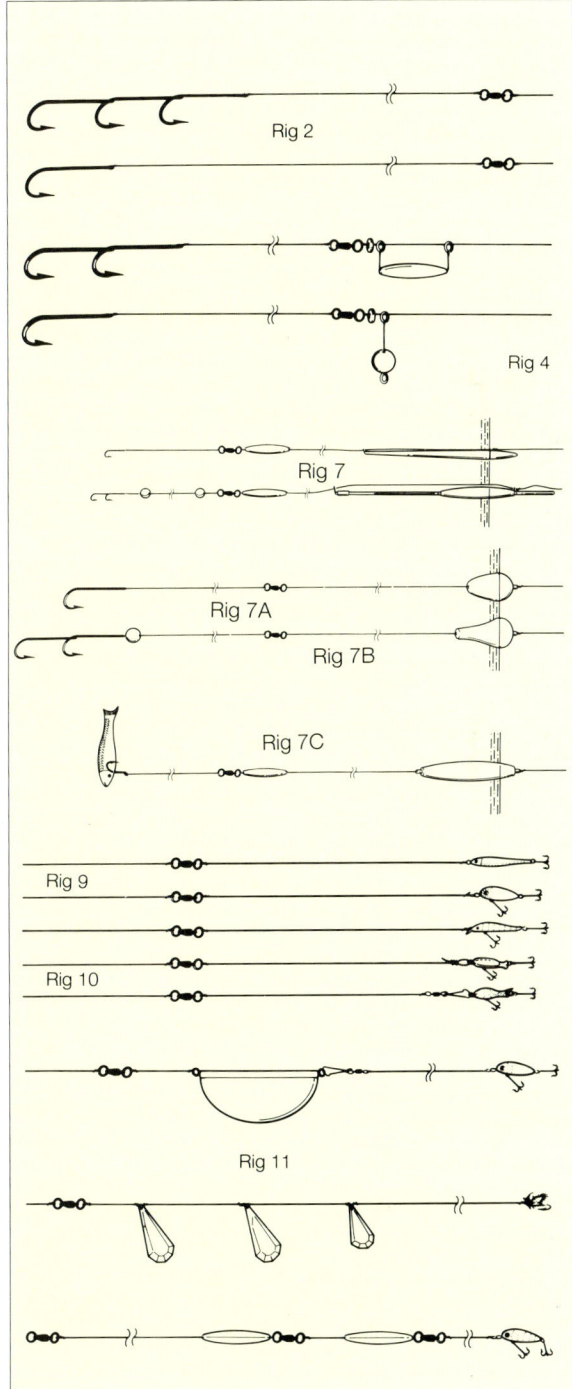

to fish in faster running waters. Night fishing with bait or surface lures is usually successful where the underwater snags are not too bad.

Where to fish

If there are obvious signs of agitation amongst schools of small fish, this may be a good place to start fishing. If, however, you get no signals — it may have been another fish worth trying for — then seek out deep holes, particularly deep waters that are overgrown with branches or fallen trees in the water, rocky outcrops, small creek inflows and patches of lily pads or similar in billabongs.

Tackle

Handlines can be used when fishing with live or dead bait. By far the most efficient outfits are light to medium (even heavy) threadline or baitcasting rods and reels, for bait fishing, trolling or lure casting. Some experienced anglers use saltwater fly equipment. A line on a handcaster of about 20 kilograms breaking-strain is adequate. If using reels, a line of about 6 to 8 kilograms breaking-strain is recommended.

Light nylon-coated wire, or a heavier strength leader, can prevent the razor sharp saw-toothed gill covers cutting line when the barramundi per-lures, the most popular would be the minnow-type (in shallow or deeper swimming models) and surface disturbing plugs, poppers etc. All attract barramundi, as do plastic fish imitations and even feathered jigs.

Rigs

With bait on handlines or rods, rigs No. 2 or No. 4 are satisfactory. If currents permit, try rig No. 7B or No. 7C. If casting lures, rig No. 9 is suitable and it also can be used for trolling. Rig No. 11 will work only if depth of water and absence of snags is suitable for handlines and/or rods for trolling. Strong hooks, strong swivels and tough lures are needed. A nylon-coated wire leader or strong nylon trace is necessary.

How to hook

It is usually worth giving a barramundi four seconds to swallow the bait. With lures, the fish usually hooks itself. The barramundi can quite unpredictably display a hesitation in hitting a lure, transmitting a feeling that the lure has been bumped. It can be a snag, of course, or it may be another fish. Usually the diffident biter can be tempted by repeated casts to the same location. If that fails, change to a slightly different size in lures or one with a different action.

Hints

The experienced barramundi angler alters his speed of trolling or lure-retrieval often: the slower speeds probably catch more fish. Many first-time anglers are so astonished by the ferocity of a barramundi hit that they lose their concentration and let the fish throw the lure. Be ready at all times.

Edibility

A small barramundi, caught and prepared soon after the catch, is excellent eating. Fillets that have been iced, frozen and transported are edible but there are many other fish that taste better. The saltwater barramundi are more tasty than river fish. Occasionally other fish are substituted for barramundi in restaurants, the result of the market demand and inflated prices. Its huge demand, however, may have more to do with the fashionable than a discriminating public taste. It is a most enjoyable fish but somewhat overrated.

Other regulations

In Western Australia and Queensland the legal limit for barramundi is 5 per angler per day. The same limit applies in the Northern Territory, with a maximum of 10 in 2 or more days. The exception is the Mary River where the maximum catch is 2 for a day's fishing and 4 for 2 or more days.

There is a closed period for barramundi fishing in Queensland between November 1 and January 31 inclusive. In the Northern Territory no fishing is permitted for barramundi in an area of the Mary River and the Daly River between October 1 and January 31 inclusive.

BASS, AUSTRALIAN
Macquaria novemaculeata

OTHER NAMES: **PERCH, FRESHWATER PERCH,
EASTERN FRESHWATER PERCH**

It is only in the last 20 years that research has been directed
towards conserving this excellent fish, an indigenous species
that stands proud alongside the likes of trout and salmon as a
sport fish — and the dedicated bass angler regards the bass
with much more respect than either of them! The Australian
bass, which is no relative of the big-mouth and small-mouth
bass so revered by American anglers, has been exploited by
both commercial fishermen and anglers. Agricultural and
chemical pollution has seriously depleted stocks; its habitats
have been destroyed; its waters have been silted; and its life
cycle disrupted by the construction of weirs and dams.
Despite these pressures it has managed, thankfully, to survive,
if in much smaller populations. But it rarely gets the chance
to reach its maximum weight, a sad loss to the anglers
who so appreciate this tough fighting fish.
The plight of the bass reflects the general lack of appreciation
for our native fish, by the community in general and government bureaucracies in particular. Though some steps are at
last being taken to conserve these native fish, they are provided with far less stringent rules to protect them than the
introduced trout. Surely most native fish have unlimited
potential as tourist attractions? After all, they are unique.

The bass is an elongate to oval, somewhat compressed fish, and more torpedo-shaped than its close relative, the estuary perch (*see* entry). It has an almost even profile from the snout to the back of the head, whereas the estuary perch has an obvious concave profile, especially above the eye. There is some variation but the colours are usually dark olive-green to grey on the dorsal surface and sides, which lightens to yellowish off-white on the belly. There are white tips on its anal and pelvic fins and the front ray of the pelvic fin is white.

Size

Though there have been claims that bass may grow to 8 kilograms, it is generally accepted that 4 kilograms is about the maximum weight. Today a specimen of more than 2 kilograms is newsworthy and even one over 1 kilogram is satisfying to catch. The bigger fish are always females.

The minimum legal catch in Queensland is 30 centimetres long. In Victoria the legal minimum is 25 centimetres.

Breeding

Bass must spawn in saltwater: freshwater kills both sperm and eggs. Eggs may hatch in water with low salinity (8 to 10 parts per thousand), but better results but apparent when the salinity is higher than 14 parts per thousand. The fish spawn in winter, moving down from the upper reaches of rivers in June, but cold and dry weather may delay this. Depending on the location, adults usually start returning to the freshwater about August but it can occur as late as November. Young bass of 1 to 1.5 centimetres in length have been found in freshwater at the end of October.

Bass males congregate in large schools in the estuaries prior to spawning, making them vulnerable to illegal netting.

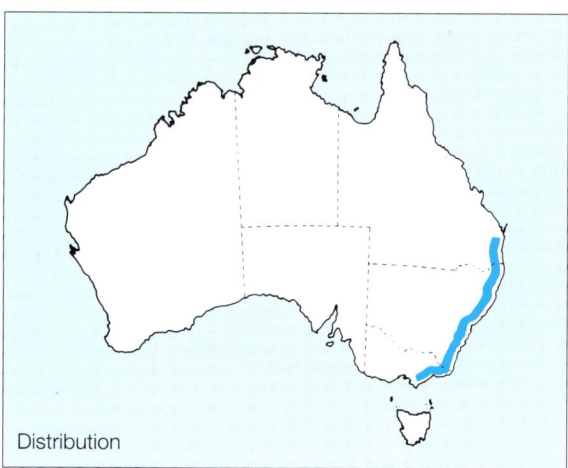

Distribution

A fine bass hooked and almost in the bag.

Bass prefer overgrown shady water. They can be found in deep holes near banks or rock faces; beneath water lilies and around reed beds or other obstructions; and about submerged trees. They do not like open or shallow water, though they will move to the edges of shallows when the water is cooler, but under the cover of darkness. The clearing of land, particularly riverbank trees and other vegetation for agriculture, has hit the bass habitat hard. And the removal of snags from river beds, in the name of flood mitigation and the deforestation by timber industries, has caused siltation in many creeks and rivers, creating further loss.

The biggest bass seem to have retreated to remote and tiny creeks that are impossible to fish from the bank and difficult from a small one-man canoe because of trees and overgrowing bankside vegetation.

The bass is a territorial fish. It will emerge from its hideaway to attack any food-like object which passes or falls on to the surface. It is not unusual to see a bass explode from the water and smash a leaf or twig which drops off a tree. Any small wriggling, floating or swimming insect or creature, such as a cricket, lizard or mouse is similarly disposed of. It also eats frogs, tadpoles, grasshoppers, cicadas, beetles and insects of any size, crustaceans, shrimps, prawns, small fish etc.

Distribution

The bass exists in river and creeks, from Tin Can Bay in Queensland, south to Wilson's Promontory in Victoria. There are suggestions it once inhabited rivers in Tasmania. The estuary perch is often mistaken for bass.

Bass may be found upriver from its spawning areas of brackish water until a natural barrier such as a waterfall prevents it passing, though it can overcome many obstacles a metre or so in height when there are floods. On many of the rivers in which the bass traditionally thrived, weirs have been built, making it impossible for the fish to pass, even in floods. High dam walls also restrict them, effectively corralling them into a vulnerable target for excessive fishing. Bottom (cold water) releases from dams also affect the fish.

When to fish

There are no restrictions — other than a closed period in Victoria from August 1 to November 30 inclusive — on where or when to fish, but any responsible angler would regard the spawning period in New South Wales and Queensland as a closed season as a conservation measure. Early morning, late afternoon, and during the night are more productive than during bright sunlit hours.

Where to fish

Start looking for bass near rock-faces, beneath overgrown banks, near snags or fallen trees, lily patches and similar, with deepish water and shade cover. At night, the bass will venture along the edge of shallow sandbars and banks, seeking food.

Tackle

If fly-fishing gear can be used in the dense overgrown areas likely to hold the best bass, it is exciting fishing. Light single-handed threadline or baitcasting rods and reels will enable the angler to use large weighted flies as well as a profuse array of surface, floating, sinking, shallow swimming and deep-diving lures.

Baits

Bass will swallow a bait so far that it is usually difficult to free the fish in good enough condition to survive. It eats worms, yabbies, shrimps, frogs, beetles, etc., and prefers them live and active.

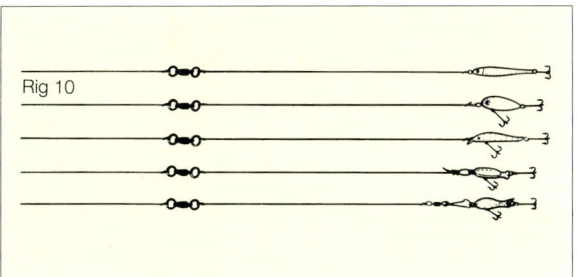

Rig 10

Rigs

A fly line for bass is better with a shorter heavier tippet, allowing the larger-bodied, heavier flies to be used. Casting and retrieving with a threadline or baitcasting outfit (rig10) may need a stronger leader, as the gill covers on bass are sharp enough to cut light line. The heavier leader helps when the fish dives into snag territory.

How to hook

Usually flies are taken quickly and it's a matter of timing technique to set the hook. The bass chasing sub-surface lures usually hooks itself. Often the bass smashes into but misses a surface lure. Whether such attacks are meant to stun its prey or are simply misjudgment is a matter of argument. The angler's instinctive reaction is to jerk the lure away, but it is better to leave the lure sitting for a period, then use the rod to twitch it as if it is about to move away like a wounded or stunned insect or animal. Bass rarely miss on the second attack.

Hint

"Bass-bugs", a type of streamer fly with cork or plastic bodies that is extensively used by anglers in the U.S. for their bass fishing, is also effective on Australian bass, especially when plopped on the water after dark. (By the way, they work on trout as well.)

Edibility

The bass has a firm flesh, of good texture and is first class fare.

Other regulations

Anglers in New South Wales may legally catch only 5 bass a day. The legal limit in Queensalnd is 2. Though there is a closed season in Victoria (August 1 to November 30 inclusive), the Australian bass deserves the protection of more regulations than now exist. There should be a closed season in New South Wales and Queensland, fishing methods should be limited, and size restrictions should be imposed in New South Wales. Netting should be banned in the limited waters that are now inhabited by bass. This fish is a grand survivor, but for how long? Thoughtful anglers should make this fish a catch-and-release species, being satisfied they have enjoyed the thrill of encountering a fast disappearing native.

BLACKFISH, ROCK
Girella elevata

OTHER NAMES: **BLACK DRUMMER, PIG, AND MANY
UNCOMPLIMENTARY NAMES**

The rock blackfish is frequently confused with the silver
drummer but there is no relationship — and the blackfish is a
much better eating fish. Both fish are capable of breaking lines
much stronger than their own weight, and some anglers regard them as the most challenging of any rock fish. Rock
blackfish prefer the disturbed white water along ocean fronts,
and the pursuit of them has often seduced anglers into taking
unnecessary risks when big swells or heavy seas are running.

Identification

The rock blackfish gives every appearance of brute
strength. It has a solid, stocky body, with a powerful broad tail. The pectoral, pelvic and anal fins are
broad and rounded. The dorsal fin stretches back
to the caudal peduncle. Its colouring is mainly a
very dark slate-grey to black with a lightening of
the colour on the belly area. This fish's head and
mouth appear oddly small for the size of the body.
[**Note**: A very similar fish, western rock blackfish,
Girella tephraeops, which is bluish-black to brownish
black, exists in West Australian waters between the
Recherche Archipelago and Carnarvon. It is distinguished mainly by the blue eye in adults, and
it grows to more than 60 centimetres.]

Size

The rock blackfish has been caught weighing in excess of 8 kilograms, but fish half this weight are not uncommon and they will test the best of equipment.

A minimum legal size of 25 centimetres applies in New South Wales.

Breeding

The fish probably spawns in early summer, as fish full of roe may be taken during October to December.

Habits

The rock blackfish is an inshore fish, being most abundant among ocean rocks where there is a prolific growth of green weed — the lettuce and cabbage type — and conjevoi outcrops. Juveniles and smaller fish, perhaps to a kilogram in weight, are often in large schools. The bigger fish gather in smaller aggregations, but one or two can appear suddenly to the dismay of an angler fishing with lighter gear. The fish moves to deeper water or retreats to rock crevices or caves in smooth or very clear seas. They feed on a rising tide in the early morning, or late afternoon and evening, when the light is not bright. The water should provide sufficient turbulence and wash — or a milky surface — for the fish to feel secure as it ventures into shallower water for its natural food.

Distribution

The fish is largely confined to the New South Wales coastline. Only an occasional fish is caught near or north of the Queensland border or south into Victorian waters. It seems not to move into water over 8 to 12 metres.

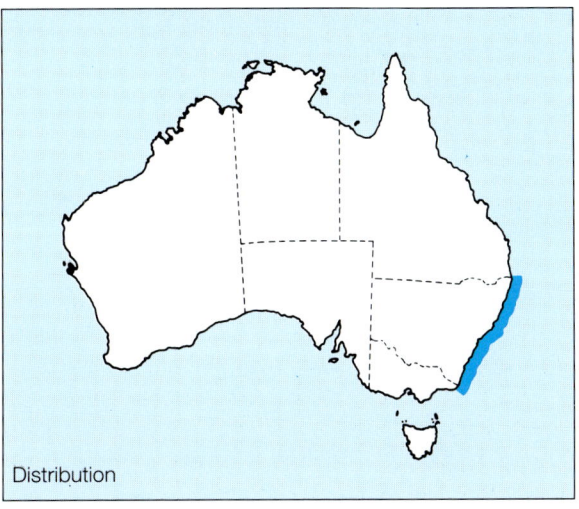

Distribution

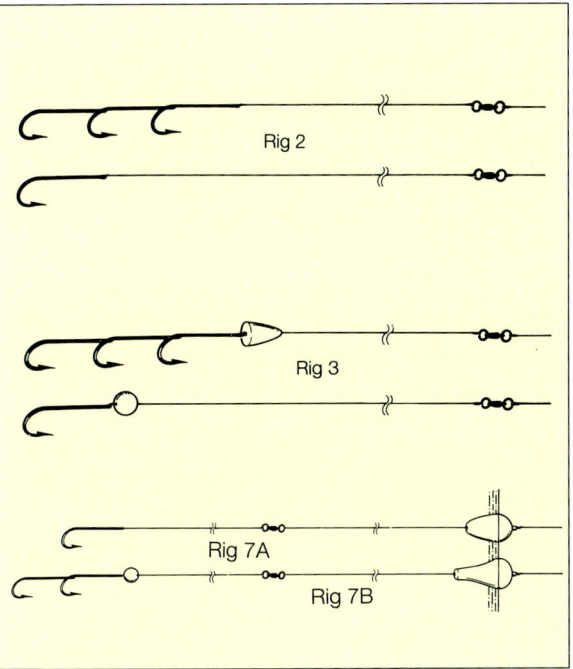

Rig 2

Rig 3

Rig 7A

Rig 7B

When to fish

Undoubtedly the best fishing for rock blackfish, which are around throughout the year, is during the autumn and winter months, into spring. This may have something to do with the lower daylight temperatures not drying out and killing off the green weed exposed by low tides.

The fish is more likely to be taken on the last of the rising tide — to the turn — early in the morning or late afternoon. It can bite all day after really heavy seas, when overcast weather gives the water a darker look. It will bite during the night in very shallow gutters or potholes.

Where to fish

Rock blackfish can be found where there are headlands, rock platforms and inlets, with growths of weed and conjevoi, preferably when there is a wash — or at least in sloppy conditions if the seas are windless.

Tackle

A medium-weight rod of about 3.5 metres long, with a fast-taper tip, is ideal. It can be one which takes about a 15 centimetres-diameter sidecast reel or a heavy threadline or medium overhead reel. Line should be between 5 and 7 kilograms breaking-strain. (For night fishing, a shorter rod, and even lighter line, can be used for pot-holing.) Strong hooks (1/0 is a good size) and swivels are necessary.

Baits

The fish is basically a herbivore that feeds on green lettuce or cabbage weed, but it is partial to conjevoi. It also eats red crabs and limpets. Prior to and during the spawning period, rock blackfish will take peeled prawns and pieces of squid. And they relish abalone gut.

Rigs

A widely used rig is the lightly weighted bait rig No. 3 with a small ball or barrel sinker. In some conditions, the unweighted rig No. 2 may be used. On fishing grounds where the bottom is so rugged that it frequently claims gear, use a bobby cork which has a fixed or adjustable depth (rig No. 7A) to keep it clear of the snags.

Rig No. 2 is usually sufficient for night-time gutter or pot-hole fishing.

In the main, lengthy distance casts are not required. The bait should reach the tail end of the wash or white water and sink. A bobby cork can float back or forth in this area.

Berley

A steady stream of berley is essential if you are to attract and hold rock blackfish in an area. The luderick mix of sand and chopped up weed works, but by far the most effective for rock blackfish is plenty of soaked, sloppy bread. This may require making contact with a bakery to obtain stale buns and bread.

The area should be heavily berleyed on arrival and an input continued during the fishing period. Some weed scraped from the rocks may be added.

How to hook

Bait for the rock blackfish should be kept under tension and slowly retrieved. The bite, even from a big specimen, is very like that of the picking of small fish. It may also be that the fish trims the bait to the right mouthful, because usually the first inkling the bait is in the fish's mouth is a fast downward dive. The faster the angler reacts by lifting the rod to halt the downward movement, the more likely the fish is to be held away from rocky crevices. It is almost impossible to move a rock blackfish once it reaches such a sanctuary.

Hint

The crust of unsliced bread is an excellent bait. The crust can be about 6 or 7 mm thick and trimmed to a roughly circular shape of 12 to 15 millimetres in diameter. (A piece of metal conduit can have the edge sharpened to punch out perfect "buttons".) The pieces are put on the hook through the centre until the whole hook is filled, with even a piece above the eye.

Edibility

All rock blackfish should be killed, bled and gutted immediately and the black stomach lining completely rubbed away. This ensures the fish will not have an iodine or weedy taste. The flesh is firm, flaky and tasty, and can be fried, grilled or baked. Fish over a kilogram should be skinned, though this size and larger tend to be tough when. Holding rock blackfish in a keeper net causes the fish stress, which precipitates the release of enzymes and lactic acids in the body, which affect the flesh.

BOARFISH, GIANT
Paristopterus labiosus

OTHER NAME: **DUCKFISH, SOWFISH, YELLOW-SPOTTED BOARFISH**

Five boarfish inhabit the southern waters of Australia. They are, in the main, fish of the deepwater reefs and are only occasionally caught by anglers. All can be recognised by slightly upturned long snouts and the steep concave head profile.
In some areas they are called duckfish, while the Australian Government Department of Primary Industries recommends penfish as the commercial marketing name.

Identification

Deep-bodied and with the characteristic pig-like snout, this boarfish is variable in colour, ranging from a dull silver with brown oblique stripes, to brown-red with yellow spots. The mouth is large. Juvenile and immature fish have very long dorsal fin spines but these become proportionally shorter as the fish grows.

Size

The giant boarfish grows to about 90 centimetres.

Distribution

The most widespread of the boarfish, the giant extends from the north coast of New South Wales

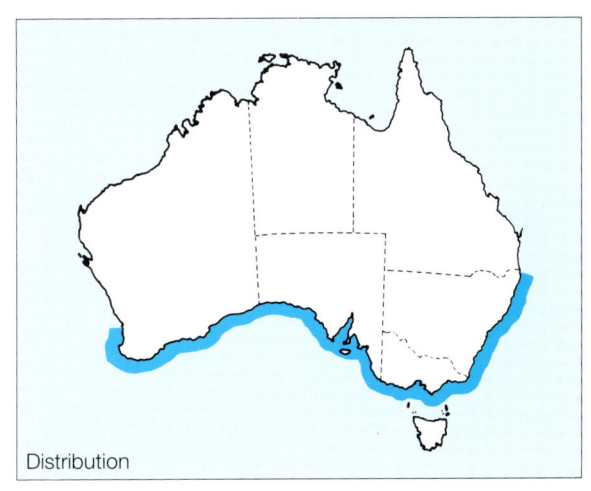

Distribution

91

along Victoria (and off Tasmania), South Australia and Western Australia to north of Perth.

Habits

The fish inhabit deepwater rocky reefs and mud bottoms. Those taken by anglers are usually juvenile or immature specimens that have come inshore to shallow coastal reefs adjoining deep water. Boarfish are hooked while fishing for other species such as snapper, morwong, etc. The fish is carnivorous and its snout shape indicates that it seeks marine worms, crustaceans and sea-urchins off the bottom.

When to fish

This fish is usually hooked by anglers fishing for snapper, morwong and other offshore bottom fish.

Edibility

The boarfish, despite the looks and name, have a firm white flesh and are excellent table fish. They can be prepared by all methods.

The giant boarfish in its element.

BONEFISH
Albula neoguinaico

OTHER NAMES: **GREY GHOST, LADY FISH, BANANA-FISH**

This is no eating fish but it is an exciting challenge: first to find the fish, then to cast a bait or lure to it, and then to experience the extraordinary power, velocity and distance of its several runs after you have hooked it.

Identification
It is a streamlined fish with a single prominent dorsal fin, midway along the back, and a steep-forked tail. Its eyes, set high in its head, will swivel to watch anglers unhooking it. Its mouth is smallish and rubbery, with an underslung lower jaw. There are no spines in any of its fins nor sharp edges to its gills. The body is deceptive in profile because it is as wide as it is deep. It has a shiny silvery colour overall but there is a faint green tone along the dorsal. The fins and tail are a grey colour.

Size
The maximum size is probably 12 to 15 kilograms.

Breeding
Little is known.

Habits
The bonefish moves in with the tide over inshore sandy flats from deep water. Large schools of these fish tend to be in the smaller-size range, the bigger fish congregate in smaller numbers. Large bonefish are sighted singly or in pairs. The fish are often found in very shallow water sifting shrimps, prawns, worms, small crabs, etc., from the sand, its mouth-down attitude causing its tail to break the surface. While cruising, its tall dorsal fin or tail can cause a ripple on the water surface. It is easily scared off by shadows, splashes on the water and other fish.

Distribution
Bonefish are found throughout the world's tropical regions, on sandflats, beaches and estuary mouths, though it has been hooked on baits in deeper waters.

In Australia, bonefish are found from mid-Queensland, around the top end, and down to the north-west of Western Australia. There have been isolated reports of bonefish having been caught as far south as Sussex Inlet on the east coast, mainly in estuaries and sandy bays.

When to fish
The best time is during days when the water is relatively calm. Ruffled water makes spotting the pale shimmery fish difficult. A rising to full tide over any sandy flat or beach is generally best.

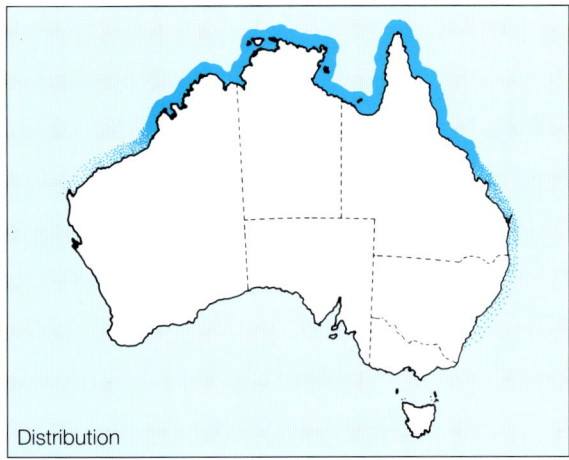

Distribution

Where to fish

The angler stalking a bonefish is likely to find one in very shallow water or nosing around a sandbar with an escape channel to deeper water on one or more sides. The fish may also be found by drifting over shallow water in a boat and casting towards the fish. It is important to place the bait or lure without excessive splashing because the bonefish is so flighty when alarmed, though it will return fairly quickly if you have the patience.

Tackle

The challenge is to use light lines to enable long casts to be made with small lures, jigs, flies and baits. Rods should be light to medium with a whippy or quick taper tip, about 3 metres long. Either threadline or baitcasting outfits are used. Line between 3 and 6 kilograms breaking-strain is adequate, provided the reel can hold at least 250 metres. If drifting, single-handed outfits may be used. The ultimate tackle for this fish is a fly rod and reel with a weight forward line, provided there is ample backing on the reel behind the flyline. There are many saltwater fly patterns suitable to tempt a bonefish.

Baits

Bonefish take sandworms, small crabs, shrimps, prawns and small shellfish. They have a distinct preference for live bait.

Rigs

Try a fly line and saltwater fly (rig No. 1) or un-weighted baits (rig No. 2) and lures or jigs (rig No. 9 or 10). If you use baits, then hooks should be between sizes 4 and 1.

How to hook

When it decides to take a lure or bait, the bonefish is lightning quick and the unforgettable speed it exhibits is usually enough to set the hook. The fish is a clean fighter, usually running straight and hard. One run is not the end; when the angler works the fish back it is likely to make two or three equally breathtaking long bursts. Sometimes the fish will return directly past the angler at the end of one of these.

Hint

It should not be too difficult to spot these fish feeding with a pair of good quality sunglasses. An angler can often get a strike by using some of the tiny lead-headed jigs (with feathers or fibre-tail) tossed into deep water ahead of the feeding fish and retrieved in jerks past them, to stir up the sand.

Edibility

It did not get its name for nothing! The bonefish is a catch-and-release fish unless a record claim is being considered.

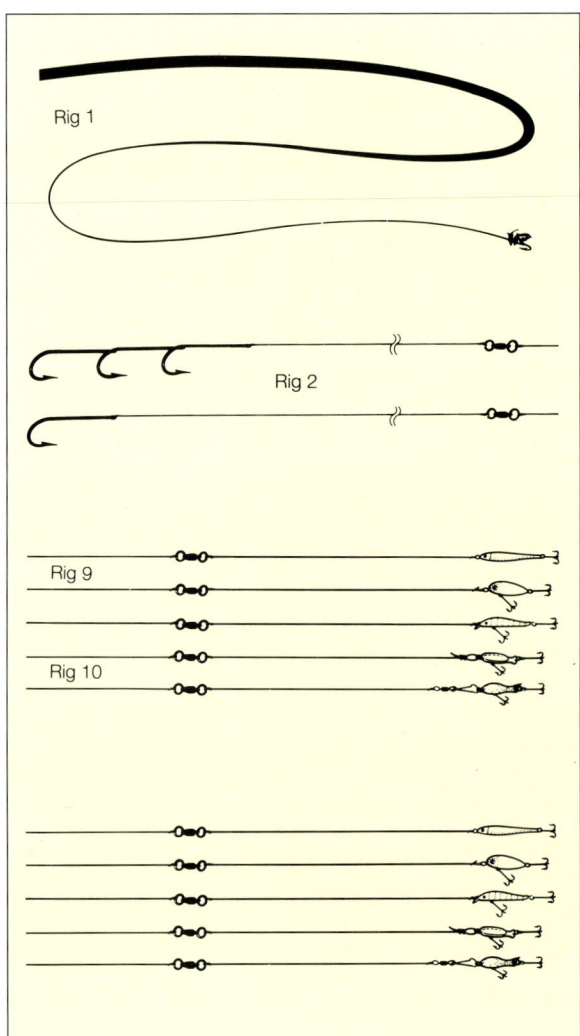

Rig 1

Rig 2

Rig 9

Rig 10

BONITO, AUSTRALIAN
Sarda australis

OTHER NAMES : **STRIPED BONITO, BUNNIES, HORSIES, HORSE MACKEREL, SKIPJACK, SKIPPIES, COMMON BONITO**

This fish is used by many anglers, particularly game fishers, as a bait fish for marlin, sharks, snapper and others. While it is still sought predominantly for bait, it should be regarded as a sports fish, by boat and shore-based anglers, if fished for with the right tackle. Though not normally regarded as a food fish, when prepared correctly the bonito is first class fare.

Identification

Bonito has the streamlined solid shape of the tuna family, and the Australian bonito can be readily distinguished by the 10 to 12 straight, clear stripes which run horizontally along the back and sides. The odd specimen has blackish-grey stripes that are broken along the belly region. It is an usually bright blue along its back with a tinge of green, and grey to silverish towards the belly. Bonito have strong, curved and quite sharp teeth.

Size

The Australian bonito is known to grow to more than 10 kilograms, but they are usually caught below the 5 kilogram mark.

Breeding

Bonito are believed to spawn in summer.

Habits

This fish is migratory and appears to range in water with temperatures between 16 and 22° C. The schools, which vary in numbers, can be found close into ocean rocks and well off-shore. These fish live in the open ocean, but the hunt for food can bring them in to rock platforms, headlands and beaches — they may even invade inlets — at any time of the day. Bonito generally pursue small fish near the surface but larger bonito have been taken from deep water reefs.

Distribution

Their range extends from southern Queensland waters south to Victoria, although rare in that region. In the north they are in abundance in the winter months. Further south they are more plentiful in summer and autumn. But small schools

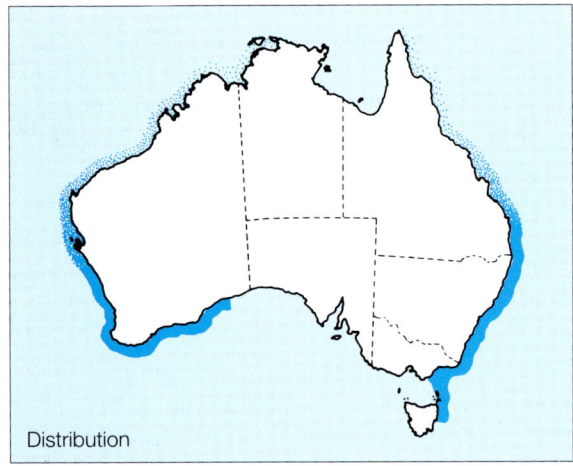

Distribution

seem to be present throughout the year.

When to fish

While bonito can be found throughout the year, the autumn-winter months in the north and summer to autumn in the south are generally the best periods.

Where to fish

As this fish can appear at any time, off-shore boat fishers usually find a school while trolling. Rock anglers will often be alerted to the presence of bonito when they see the swift arrival of one or two along the rocks. Occasionally birds will signal a school of bonito feeding on small fish, though this can indicate any number of other fish.

Tackle

When trolling for other surface bait fish, boat and game fishers catch bonito on a wide variety of line weights. For lure and bait fishing — and for trollers with a sporting instinct — there is no need for lines to exceed 5 kilograms breaking-strain. Use lures or baits, with light to medium weight threadline or overhead rods and reels that are usually used from the rocks. Smaller rods as well as light game outfits are adequate for small boat trolling, or lure tossing. Handlines may be used for trolling as well.

Baits

Bonito have a marked preference for small fish such as yellowtail, pilchards, mullet, garfish, sardines, hardiheads, etc. They will take them live or dead (when cast and retrieved or suspended beneath a float). They can also be caught with squid.

Rigs

Use saltwater fly rods and reels and try a variety of

The Australian bonito, a gracefully streamlined predator.

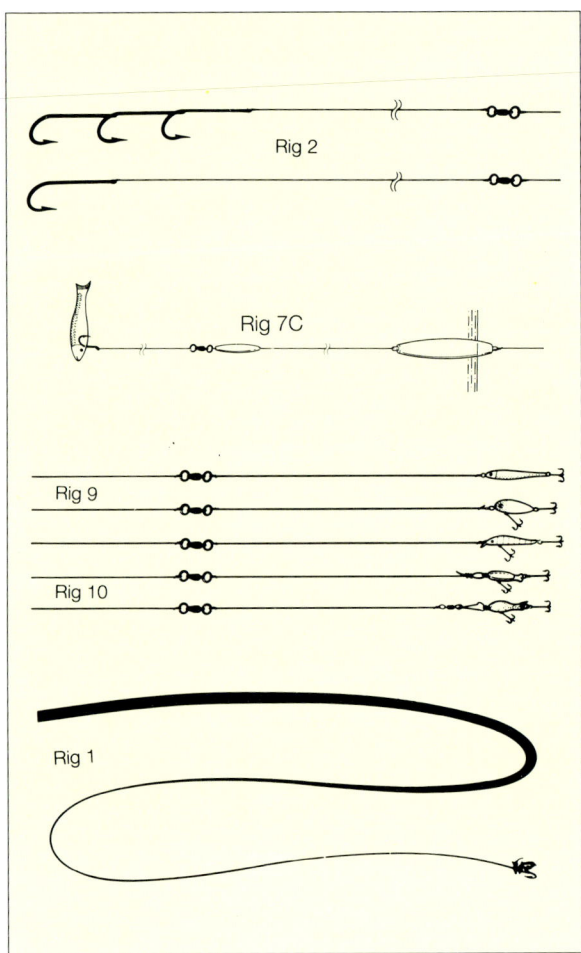

96

saltwater flies. When casting and retrieving from rock platforms, use rigs No. 9 or No. 10 if you are trying lures and rig No. 2 if you are using bait. Bait rig No. 7C is also successful with live or dead bait. Bonito will respond to a variety of spoons, slicers and fish-like lures and jigs in many colours, as well as smaller skirted game lures.

How to hook

When lures are employed, the fish usually hooks itself during its attack. If you are using baits, however, let the fish run for some distance before lifting the rod.

Hint

If you can see bonito but cannot attract their interest with your lure, try a smaller size in a different colour.

Edibility

The bonito should be killed, bled, gilled and gutted immediately it is landed. Thin fillets removed and skinned at the same time and kept on ice (and lightly fried in breadcrumbs or batter) are excellent eating.

[**Note:** The Australian bonito is a small game fish that is available to many anglers who may not have the opportunity to tangle with the glamorous big species. On the right gear it can provide some idea of the reason large game fish are sought, and the experience is equally satisfying.]

Watson's or **Leaping Bonito,** *Cybiosarda elegans,* is a smaller fish and is more common in winter months in the tropical and northerly temperate areas of the east and west coasts. It visits inshore reefs, coastal shorelines, estuaries and bays, and probably grows to a maximum of 3 kilograms. This bonito can be distinguished by the broken and blotched appearance of the lines above the lateral line of the body and it usually has 3 unbroken grey lines below.

On the West Australian coast, the **Oriental Bonito,** *Sarda orientalis ,* which has no stripes on the lower half of the body, is encountered in the oceans from the Great Australian Bight to Shark Bay. This bonito offers the same sport as its east coast relative and grows to about the same size.

BREAM

"Bream" is incorrectly used to describe a wide variety of fish in Australia, including some freshwater species and many reef fish of the tropical regions. To compound such confusion, the Australian Department of Primary Industry suggests the species *Nemadactylus valenciennes, cheilodactylus* and *macropterus,* which includes such fish variously known as queen snapper, blue morwong, rubberlip, grey morwong, jackass morwong, deep-sea-perch, sea bream, be marketed under the names of Blue Sea Bream and Sea Bream. With so many freshwater and saltwater species already commonly called bream, when not even belonging to the family, it is very hard to understand.

[**Note:** Fish frequently called bream — either freshwater or saltwater species — will be found under a more correct name elsewhere in these pages. The "bream" name will appear among their other common names.]

The classical bream, in this case a yellowfin.

BREAM, BLACK
Acanthopagrus butcheri

OTHER NAMES: **SOUTHERN BREAM, SILVER BREAM, BLUE NOSE BREAM**

Identification

This is a deep-bodied fish with a large head and rounded nose, with a moderately large mouth, the upper jaw being larger than the lower. The mouth is full of well-developed teeth with several incisors in the upper jaw. The eyes are large. The dorsal fin is long-based with strong spines at the front and soft rays at rear, separated by a small notch. The colour is variable but usually brown to black with a bronze to greenish tone on the back and sides. The head is darker but the stomach area is off-white. Pectoral, pelvic and anal fins are a dirty yellow to brownish. Mature fish often have a blue tinge on the nose area.

Size

Catches have been recorded at up to 4 kilograms but most caught by anglers rarely reach a kilogram.

This fish *must be released alive* by recreational anglers if it is under 23 centimetres in Tasmania; under 24 centimetres in Victoria; under 25 centimetres in Western Australia; under 28 centimetres in South Australia; under 25 centimetres in New South Wales.

Breeding

Black bream spawn in August through to January, occurring first in eastern Victoria and later the further west you go. The fish aggregate in large schools prior to spawning in deep water areas in the lakes and estuaries, requiring a salinity level of between 11 and 18 parts per thousand. The fish scatter after spawning.

Habits

The black bream is principally an estuarine species, preferring lakes and rivers. It is not commonly found in open ocean waters, and if it is, it has probably been flushed there by floods. There is some indication that migration may take place between estuaries. Black bream do enter freshwater.

The black bream has a partiality for shellfish of all kinds (its teeth and strong jaws equip it well for crushing these) and crabs. It also eats prawns,

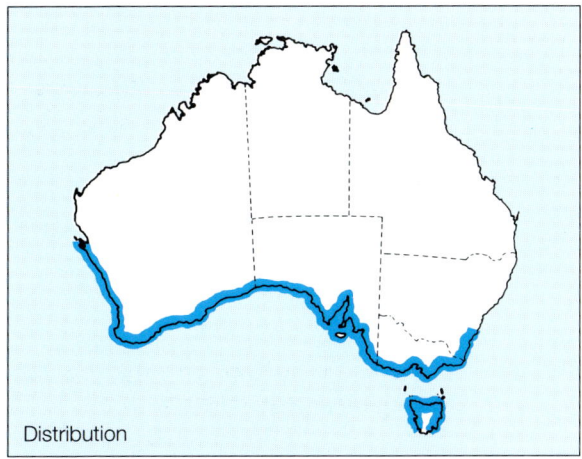

Distribution

worms, yabbies, small fish and even algae.

Distribution

This fish is common in the far south of New South Wales, throughout Victoria, Tasmania, South Australia and in Western Australia as far north as Shark Bay, mainly in estuaries, rivers and saltwater lakes.

When to fish

There are times when black bream will be found during the day but the afternoon, the early morning and during the night are usually more productive. Depending on location, a rising to high tide often allows the fish to seek food in places it cannot otherwise reach. In most areas bream are around all year but their locations and numbers vary.

Where to fish

Black bream can be widespread throughout its habitat but areas with a good supply of its favourite food items are more productive. These are around shellfish encrusted rocks, mussel beds, weed patches where crustaceans are likely to be, sandy areas where worms are located, etc.

In South Australia, some Aquatic Reserves may contain black bream. Check locally to establish whether fishing is allowed.

Tackle

A handline of 3 or 4 kilogram breaking-strain is quite suitable for catching bream from many banks and jetties or boats. Light single-handed threadline or baitcasting rods and reels with the same line is also used. Longer medium to soft-action reels for threadline or baitcasting and sidecast reels may suit some locations or anglers.

Baits

Shellfish, mussels, pipis, crabs, yabbies, squirt, sand

and bloodworms, prawns, small fish such as white-bait and fish pieces — are all accepted by the bream, and dough is favoured on occasions.

Berley
The fish can be attracted and held with judicious use of berley. Try breadcrumbs, rice, bran or pollard, particularly if it is flavoured with some of its favourite food items.

Rigs
The water flow or tide current governs the rig. Where possible an unweighted bait with rig No. 2 is recommended. Rigs 3, 3A, 4 or 4A, with the lightest weight for the conditions, should a sinker be absolutely necessary. Hooks need not exceed size 1.

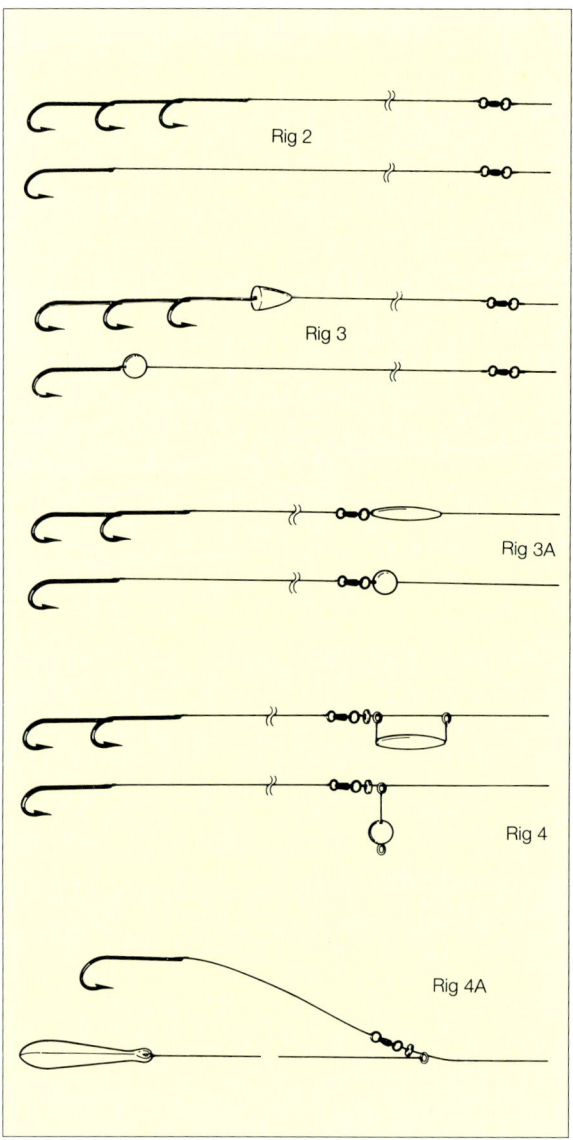

How to hook
The black bream is usually a shy biter, giving the impression that it is tasting the bait. It is best to allow the fish time to mouth the bait and move away before tightening the line and setting the hook. Many fish are missed by wild swipes, jerking the bait away and frightening the wary fish.

Hint
Try an oyster, pipi or squirt worm for bait, suspended beneath a float.

Edibility
The black bream has firm white flesh which can be prepared for the table in many ways.

Other regulations
In Western Australia, a maximum of 30 black bream per angler per day applies. A bag limit of 10 fish per day applies in the Sydenham Inlet and Bemm River in Victoria.

In South Australia the Onkaparinga River is closed to bream fishing between November and January inclusive.

BREAM, PIKEY
Acanthopagrus berda

OTHER NAMES: **BLACK BREAM**

Identification
The same shape as the black or yellowfin bream, this member of the family has a slightly more pointed mouth area. Its main name is derived from the long and strong second spine of the anal fin. When caught in some mangrove areas of creeks, it is so dark that black appropriately describes its colour. In other waters it is similar in colour to the black bream, darkish grey to olive-brown with definite reflections of brassy or deep gold tones.

Size
In Papua-New Guinea this fish has been weighed at more than 7 kilograms. Most taken by Australian anglers, however, would be less than 2 kilograms. That is not to say that some specimens, particularly those caught in the Gulf of Carpentaria and the remote north-east corner, have not been real heavy-weights.

The minimum legal length for a catch in Queensland is 23 centimetres.

The pikey bream: The breams are not easy to separate.

Breeding

Little is known about its breeding. Its habits and location suggest that the Pikey bream is basically an estuarine species.

Habits

Pikey bream seems to remain in the estuaries of creeks and rivers in the tropic waters and feeds along banks of creeks, adjacent to obstructions in the water, and the piles of jetties etc. It feeds on crabs and other crustaceans and small fish.

Distribution

A fish of tropical waters, the Pikey bream is found from about Townsville around Cape York, across Gulf of Carpentaria and across the Northern Territory to south-west of Darwin.

When to fish

The wet season affects many rivers and estuaries which this fish inhabits. Autumn and spring are more comfortable — with better fishing conditions — when the weather is more settled. This bream is not as shy as its relatives but night fishing is productive.

Where to fish

Keep close to banks, obstructions, mangroves and jetties and you are likely to uncover a prime spot.

Tackle

Handlines are popular and single-handed threadline and baitcasting outfits are suitable in a medium size, with heavier breaking strain lines of at least 6 kilograms. This fish co-exists with barramundi, mangrove jacks, sea-perches, threadfin salmon and even trevally and queenfish. While a light wire trace is needed to be sure of handling some of these other fish, it does reduce the chance of catching the pikey bream.

Baits

Crabs, crustaceans, small fish, fish pieces or fillets will tempt this bream.

Rigs

The water or tidal current will restrict the use of unweighted or lightly weighted baits. The choice should be made from rig No. 2, 3, 4 or 4A (see previous page). Hooks about size 1/0 extra strong will help if some of the other predatory species are caught; even 2 hooks ganged in a fillet of fish will not be rejected by a pikey bream.

How to hook

The pikey bream is much less wary than its cousins because of the fierce competition from more aggressive fish. It is less hesitant, quickly mouthing and then running with the bait. Set the hook by simply stopping the line with a firm pull (if a handline) or lifting the rod.

Edibility

This bream is as good to eat as the other members of the Acanthopagrus family.

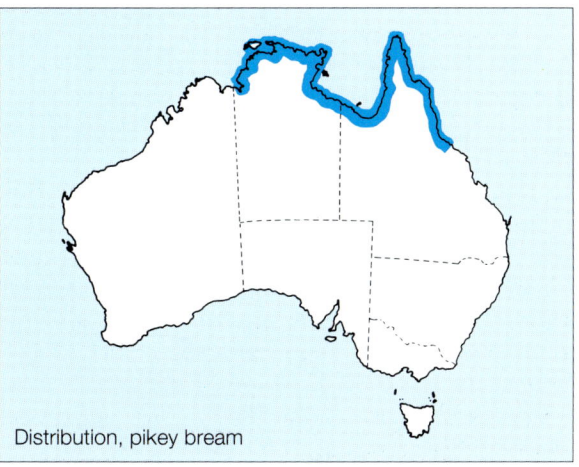

Distribution, pikey bream

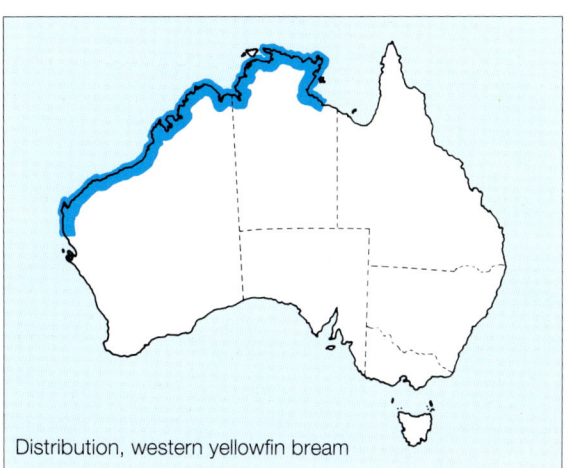

Distribution, western yellowfin bream

BREAM , WESTERN YELLOWFIN
Acanthopagrus latus

OTHER NAMES: **WESTRALIAN YELLOW-FINNED BREAM, BLACK BREAM, SILVER BREAM, JAPANESE BREAM**

The wide choice of common names explains a lot. Little wonder there is some controversy over the identity of this bream. It has been said to be a black bream, yet it tolerates water with a higher temperature, like that of the pikey bream on the eastern and northern coastline. It also overlaps the pikey bream in tropical waters and could be a lighter version of this fish — except that it does not have the required thick spine on the anal fin. In fact it is like the black bream and the yellowfin bream in much of its behaviour and habitat preference.

Identification
This fish looks much like both the black and yellowfin bream, though its colouring is more often similar to the black bream with fins more yellow than dusky or dull. It can be a very dark grey-brown, probably due to habitat. A bream called silver exists in the warmer waters of the African coast, the Red Sea and around India, which looks identical to this fish. Colour varies from silver to mid-grey.

Size
Western Yellowfin have been caught weighing up to 2 kilograms. The minimum legal length for a catch in Western Australia is 25 centimetres.

Breeding
Little is known.

Habits
Little is known but it is believed to inhabit estuaries, although they are also caught along ocean fronts and reefs.

Distribution
North from Shark Bay to the western side of the Gulf of Carpentaria.

When to fish
The western yellowfin bream is generally fished for in the same periods and with similar rigs and baits

as the pikey bream. It is often taken by anglers fishing for the more popular larger species in the waters it inhabits.

Edibility
This bream is also a good table fish.

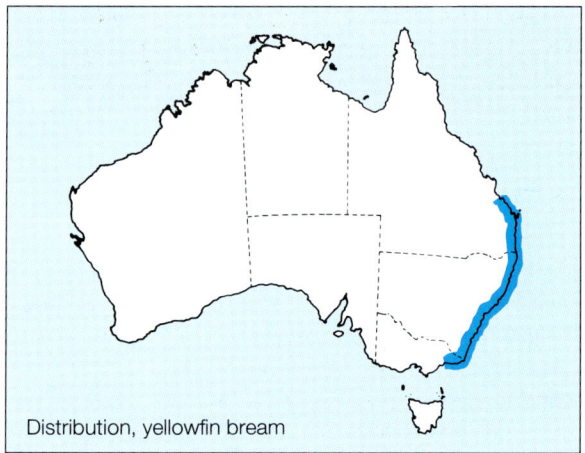
Distribution, yellowfin bream

BREAM, YELLOWFIN
Acanthopagrus australis

OTHER NAMES: **BLACK OR SILVER BREAM, SURF BREAM, SEA BREAM, YELLOW-FINNED BREAM**

Identification
The yellowfin bream is identical in shape to the black bream (*see* photograph introducing bream). It is usually quite dark grey in colour with obvious bronze tonings when taken from some estuaries, and even ocean fronts. In the ocean, especially from beaches, it tends to quite a silvery grey, with only the merest hints of the bronze colour. There is a black blotch at the base of the pectoral fins and there is a much brighter yellow colour to these and its anal fin. And if you really want to get down to details, this fish has less than 50 scales in series, from the base of the pectoral fin to the tail, compared with the black bream, which has more than 50.

Size
The yellowfin bream has been caught exceeding 4 kilograms, but even a fish of 2 kilograms is rare. Most would be up to 1 kilogram.
Yellowfin bream must be released alive by anglers

when they are less than 25 centimetres long in New South Wales, less than 24 centimetres in Victoria, and less than 23 centimetres in Queensland.

Breeding

This bream begins spawning about February on the south coast of New South Wales and eastern Victoria, in April-May on the central coast area, May-June on the north coast and in July-August in Queensland waters. At this time they can be abundant near estuary entrances and bars near ocean beaches. After spawning, bream stay in ocean waters for some time before returning to the estuaries.

Habit

The yellowfin bream's migratory habits mean that mature and large bream occupy different habitats at different times of the year. While some can be taken from most of their habitats all year round, the quantity is variable. This may be subject to water conditions and temperature. However, the best times to find yellowfin bream in estuary and river locations is spring to summer in the south and autumn and winter in the north.

Yellowfin feeding times are governed mostly by tides, because they need the depth of water from the incoming tide to get at their favourite meals of crabs, oysters and worms. While at sea, they will use the tide to approach rock areas and beaches in search of food. They seem more inclined to move to the shoreline when the tides are high during dusk to daylight hours. Nor are they averse to fast water in rivers or bumpy seas on beaches — probably because these conditions expose shellfish, crabs and worms.

Distribution

Yellowfin bream are found as far south as Lakes Entrance in Victoria, up along the east coast and tapering off along the central coast of Queensland. They can be found on inshore reefs, around ocean rocks, beaches, bays, estuaries, harbours and in rivers (sometimes into the edge of freshwater).

When to fish

As bream change their location because of breeding habits, the abundance of fish very much depends on the time of the year. The best fishing, however, is from late afternoon through the night and just before the dawn. This is not to suggest that they do not bite at other times. In fact bream can come on the bite during darkly overcast days.

Where to fish

The old saw that it's easier to find fish where the food is, applies to this bream. Likely spots are close to oyster or shellfish encrusted rocks, pylons and piers or breakwalls, alongside weed beds where crustaceans or small fish hide, on the edges of sand- bars and sandflats or other locations where worms live, in washes off ocean rocks.

Tackle

If fishing from a boat, a handline with a 3 or 4 kilograms breaking-strain line is easy to use and the same can be used from wharves, jetties and some banks. Light single-handed threadline or baitcasting outfits can also be used for these locations. For the beach or rocks, use a light rod with a medium fast action, of between 3 and 3.5 metres, to suit medium-size threadline, baitcasting or side-cast reels. Line may be increased to 5 to 7 kilogram breaking strain. Even the traditional luderick slow to medium-action rods can be very effective for bream fishing.

Baits

If any fish has a catholic taste it is a yellowfin bream. Apart from natural foods such as oysters, shellfish, mussels, prawns, nippers, yabbies, worms, small fish, etc., it will from time to time prefer mullet strips, mullet gut, chicken gut, other fish flesh, pilchards (tails in particular), skirt steak, chicken liver, bullock heart and "pudding" — concoctions of dough, cheese, preserved meats, herbs and a lot of other exotic non-fish food. The recipes are numerous and each is acclaimed as the best by those that use it. And they all seem to work!

Rig

Where conditions permit, an unweighted No. 2 rig should be used . Where a weight is necessary, only the lightest running sinker to suit the conditions should be used (rig No. 3, 3A or 4). The more commonplace 40 centimetre leader can be increased to 60 centimetres. The running rig, rig No. 4A, is suitable for beach and rocks fishing and

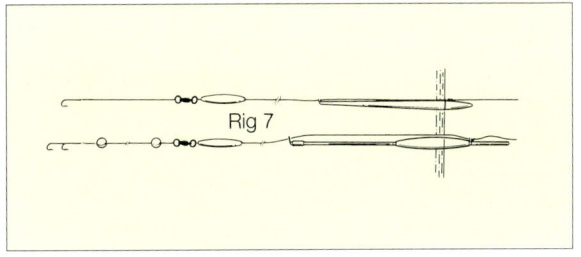

Rig 7 only. For other rigs see previous pages.

it is an excellent rig in rivers, bays or harbours where a very muddy or silted bottom can hide the bait. In calm waters, a float rig No. 7 is often successful where the bream are angler or line shy. About size 1 or 1/0 in hooks, subject to bait size, are satisfactory.

Berley

This fish is attracted to a berley and can be held in a feeding mood. There are opinions that too much can overfeed the fish, putting them off the bite — but once the fish are about a steady trickle keeps them biting.

One of the best concoctions is a mixture of boiled rice with soaked breadcrumbs, into which is stirred an over-boiled mullet or a can of pilchards — flavoured cat food. This works for many more fish than yellowfin bream.

How to hook

Much like its southern relative black bream, the yellowfin bream is a tentative biter, frequently seeming to taste before taking food into its mouth. For this reason, an unweighted or running rig allows the fish to taste the bait without detecting any restraining weight that might prevent it from moving off with it. Line should be allowed to run freely for the fish to get the bait well into its mouth. A tightening of the line and lift of the rod is then usually enough to hook the fish. In ocean beach or rock waters, bream grab and swallow the bait much more positively.

Hint

Berley with the rice mixture above. If over boiled mullet or minced pilchards is the added ingredient, use mullet strips or gut or pilchard pieces (the tail half or head half) as bait. Many people dislike using mullet gut because it is messy. This can be overcome by mixing it in breadcrumbs, bran or pollard. It is then coated and easy to put on the hook. The coating comes off in the water, adding to the berley trail.

In recent years more anglers are using small jigs and lures to tempt all species of bream, and even saltwater flies. The techniques and types of lures are still evolving but enough are being caught by anglers trying this method to suggest it is worth a change of pace or a challenge for those prepared to try it.

Edibility

The yellowfin bream has firm white flesh that can be prepared for the table in a wide variety of ways.

Other regulations

A bag limit of 10 per day applies in the Sydenham Inlet and Bemm River in Victoria.

CARP, EUROPEAN
Cyprinus carpio

OTHER NAMES: **COMMON CARP, ASIAN CARP, CHINESE CARP, GERMAN CARP, EDIBLE CARP, GREAT CARP, MIRROR CARP**

Species of the Cyprinidae family number about 1,500 and this carp, which was introduced to Europe in the 12th century, is probably the world's most widespread freshwater fish. In many countries it is cultivated as a food fish as well as being admired as a recreational fishing fish in Britain and other European countries.

For over 100 years, two strains of carp existed in the ponds, dams, reservoirs and some irrigation systems in New South Wales and Victoria without causing concern to fisheries authorities or anglers. It was a third strain, which was imported to Victoria from Germany in 1960 to be grown commercially as a food fish, that adapted so well to Australian waters that it infested waterways throughout south-eastern Australia.

Despite Australian and State governments declaring the fish a noxious import, and an extensive eradication programme in thousands of Victorian dams, the fish was sold for stocking in farm dams.

Others were released by unthinking people into the Latrobe River system or in waterways draining into the Murray River. It is believed the German strain actually entered the Murray in only 1968.

The rest is history — it is now throughout the Murray-Darling system and other inland waters and coastal streams.

The explosion of its population and its incredible distribution followed droughts of the early 1970s (which had confined them to certain areas). The massive floods that followed in 1974 and 1975 spread them to many parts that were previously remote.

The fish that spread were, in the main, smaller fish. With a plentiful food supply in the invaded waters, the infestation coincided with a period when natural predators — Murray cod, golden perch and cormorants and pelicans — were present in fewer numbers because of the prolonged drought.

While the extent of the territory may have been prevented by dam walls, even some weirs, irresponsibility by some anglers in using live carp as bait for native fish and trout (and releasing any excess quantities) in water upriver from these barriers, aided the carp's distribution.

The carp has been blamed for many happenings. It has little (if any) effect in increasing the turbidity of rivers. Water level variations and flows have been shown to affect aquatic vegetation more than carp, and the major cause of undermined banks and siltation has been the destruction of river-bank vegetation and trees, usually as a result of the cultivation of adjacent land.

There is, nevertheless, increasing evidence that carp, which may not be guilty of consuming native fish eggs in quantities, do compete for plankton, plant materials, algae and small aquatic animals, especially insects, that are an integral part of the food chain for native fish. Larger fish readily eat worms and many are caught with shrimps, small yabbies, mudeyes and grasshoppers, all of which are consumed by aquarium and indigenous angling fish.

Carp numbers appear to have stabilised in many waters in recent years. Some incomplete research seems to support evidence that the numbers of small carp are much fewer, having themselves become a large portion of the diet of the golden perch, and even trout.

Unfortunately redfin, which are a predator of small natives and trout, are also relishing small carp. Now *they* appear to be increasing. Other signs of a decline are the failure by commercial carp fishers on inland waters in Victoria and New South Wales to become a viable operation.

Perhaps the carp will eventually be controlled as a result of its increasing popularity as bait for lobster and fish traps with coastal commercial fishermen — and similarly with saltwater anglers who find the flesh of carp excellent bait for snapper and the like.

Identification

The European carp is a stocky fish, elongated and slightly compressed, curving gradually from a blunt snout to the caudal peduncle. The head looks triangular and it has small eyes. Its mouth is small and protrusible, without teeth or jaws. It has four barbels, a long one at each corner of the mouth, and a short one on each end of the upper lip. Scales are large and thick.

The carp's colour is variable, from olive-green, yellowish to green to golden or orange tone on its dorsal surface, with a brassy or orange-yellow tone on the sides, fading to a greyish-yellow on the stomach. Fin colours vary but they usually have a reddish-orange colour at their extremities.

Genetic variations cause a difference in scale cover. In almost all populations there is a percentage, perhaps as high as 5 per cent, that do not have a completely scaled body: they have a varying number of large scales, often along the middle of the body, though they can be elsewhere. These fish are called "mirror carp" as the scales are silvery or mirror-like.

Koi carp are the result of selective breeding. There are many strains of this carp but it is the same species and subject to legal control. There are hybrids between the carp and goldfish (*see below*) which breed.

Size

In other countries carp have been recorded at more than 60 kilograms. In Australia there have been reports of the fish weighing over 10 kilograms. One has been authentically measured at more than 1.3 metres. Some Australian carp have been caught measuring 80 centimetres.

Breeding

Carp can mature as young as 3 months. Spawning is during spring and summer in waters between 14° C and 25° C but spawning has been detected throughout the year. The eggs are deposited by the female in batches over 3 or 4 weeks. These may amount to several million, which stick to the bottom or on underwater vegetation. Spawning takes place in shallow water, never deeper than a metre or so. The young feed on microscopic algae, minute insects and tiny crustaceans.

Prior to spawning it is not unusual to see a school of carp swimming in a tight ball near the surface.

When this breaks up, several fish, apparently a single female and two or three males, perform various antics very close to the water's edge.

Habits

Carp can be found in still water, or at least where there is only a slight current, with a muddy or silted bottom. It can withstand poorly oxygenated turbid water, a high pollution content, and even water with a salinity of up to 18 parts per thousand. Older, larger fish are often seen alone, but carp usually form schools that wander slowly about. This fish does not like extremely cold water. Researchers have found them on the bottom in large numbers after a severe drop in temperature.

When feeding on the bottom, carp use their protrusible mouth to suck in mud and then expel it after extracting any food. However, the carp will also feed on the surface and in midwater. Apart from plant matter and small animals they sift from the bottom or off aquatic plants, they feed on worms, larger insects, crustaceans, molluscs, maggots and grubs.

Carp are more active at night, moving faster and further than they seem to during the day.

Despite its preferred habitat of warm slow water, the carp has not only been observed in fast flowing water, but jumping to clear rock falls and low weirs during water level rises in what appears to be a bid to migrate upstream.

Distribution

The European carp is abundant in many waters in Victoria, particularly in the south-east of the State and in the Murray and its tributaries; and it is widespread in the Murray Darling system, up to southern Queensland in some tributaries and impoundments. It has certainly reached the Nepean River on the eastern side of the Great Dividing Range in New South Wales and it is now fairly common in South Australian waters. The Tasmanians believe they have eradicated it from their farm dams.

Hybrids of the carp will breed with one goldfish (*Carassius auratus*), which is also called golden carp. The goldfish have no barbels and the resultant hybrid usually looks a mixture of the two species but with smaller barbels, one pair reasonably discernible, the second pair often just knobs. The goldfish is found in many of the same waters as the carp and it has spread to the waters of Tasmania and the south-west of Western Australia. It is another exotic, best-known as an aquarium fish, but it is food for Murray cod, golden perch, trout and redfin in the wild.

When to fish

Depending on weather conditions, particularly during winter, the fish can be caught all year, though it does not bite as freely in cold water as it does during the spring, summer and autumn. It feeds during daytime and at night.

Where to fish

It doesn't often take much time to spot a few carp or a school of them. However, in the waters it inhabits, any reeds, obvious weed beds, under overgrowing trees and vegetation, or grassy banks that dip into the water, are all likely to have a resident carp population or at least be visited by the fish.

Tackle

The carp can be caught on handlines or rod and reels from the bank, or from boats in larger expanses of water. Heavy line or heavy rods reduce any sport the fish might give. Where multiple hook rigs are allowed, these can produce multiple catches.

Surprisingly, more and more carp are being taken by anglers using lures for Murray cod and golden perch and other natives and trout. These fish are usually of above average size and seem to prefer subsurface, slow-moving plug-type lures.

The carp is a fun fish and fair sport on typical trout outfits using tiny ant imitations.

Baits

These range from doughy bread, dough strengthened by cottonwool, worms, small potatoes or cubes of boiled potatoes, corn from the cob, creamed corn out of cans, maggots, worms, mudeyes, shrimps, small yabbies etc.

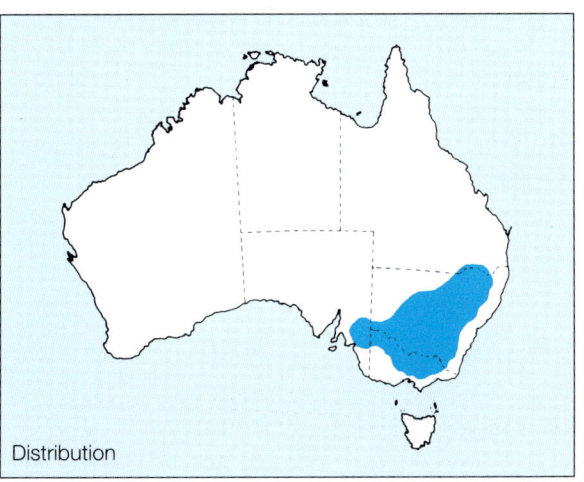
Distribution

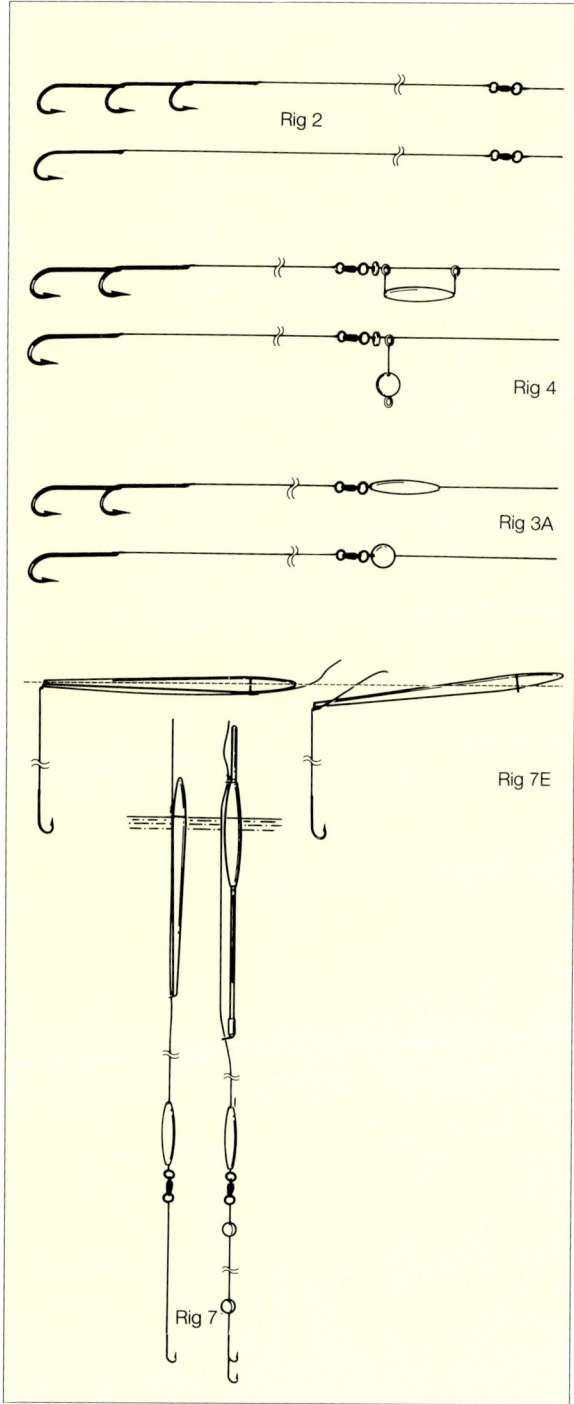

Rig 2

Rig 4

Rig 3A

Rig 7E

Rig 7

Berley

Carp can be attracted and held with berley. Soaked bran, pollard, breadcrumbs, minced corn, dehydrated potato mix and boiled rice are some which work quite well.

When berleying, it is a good idea to have a mix of ingredients, some of which tends to stay on the surface, some of which sinks slowly and some of which sinks quickly to the bottom. A smattering of the bait being used should be included in the berley. A rig with a suspended bait and a weighted one will often mean catching fish at the top and from the bottom. A fine surface berley is best if fly fishing.

Rigs

Unweighted or weighted rigs No. 2 and 3A, with the smallest sinker to suit conditions, can be used. In very weedy or heavy mud or silted bottoms, rig No. 4 will often keep the bait in the clear. The float rig for luderick rig No. 7 or the quill float rig 7E are very successful.

How to hook

The carp sucks in the bait, which is ground up by teeth in its throat area. When the line moves away, the hook should be well inside the fish's mouth. Stopping it, together with the weight of the fish, should ensure that a hook takes.

Hint

Berleying the same area for several days can produce large catches when fishing for carp.

Edibility

Most Australians would not regard the carp as a food fish. Perhaps because it has that "goldfish" association. (These are actually available from the Department of Rural Affairs and Fisheries in NSW.) On the other hand, attitudes may gradually change, because many European and Asian settlers in this actually prefer carp. And why not, particularly when it was a favourite table fish during the years they spent in their home countries.

CATFISH, EEL-TAILED
Tandanus tandanus, Tandanus bostocki

OTHER NAMES: **TANDANUS, EELTAIL CATFISH, FRESHWATER JEWFISH, DEWFISH, KENARU, COBBLER**

[In some coastal systems the catfish is probably confused with the saltwater species, especially *Cnidoglanis macrocephalus,* which in some localities is also known as the eel-tailed catfish and some of the other common names listed above. This saltwater catfish frequents coastal bays and estuaries and has been found in freshwater.]
The distinctly unprepossessing appearance of this fish inhibits many people from eating them. Many are killed or thrown away by anglers because they have taken baits meant for more desirable species such as Murray cod, golden perch or silver perch, especially in the Eastern States. Such conduct is considered absurdly wasteful by many dedicated inland anglers who contend that the catfish is more edible than the more conventional looking fish.
No such attitudes prevail in the south-west of Western Australia, where the fish — popularly known as the freshwater cobbler — is sought in the rivers and dams between the Moore River, north of Perth, and the Franklin River to the south.
All catfish have barbels or cat's whiskers around the mouth. And they all have sharp serrated spines on the front of the dorsal and pectoral fins. These are venomous and can inflict painful wounds and damage surrounding tissues: reaction to the sting can be severe. There is no sting in the barbels.

Handle this fish carefully. It is common for anglers who regularly fish for them to carry a small club or "priest" with which they kill the fish before attempting to unhook it. Others prefer to pin the fish with a knife through the head. The spines can still cause injury when the fish is dead, a warning that anglers should remember when carrying these fish or disposing of the heads. Do not leave them where barefoot children — or other anglers for that matter — might be hurt.

Identification

This fish is unlikely to be mistaken for any other fish or even an eel. Its whiskered snout, down-turned mouth and thick lips are evidence enough. The body is solid, with a continuous second dorsal tapering to connect with the caudal fin; the anal fin also joins the caudal fin to give an arrowhead shape. Colour varies considerably, depending on the location and the maturity of the fish. It usually has a mottled camouflage on its top and sides, ranging from light tan or beige through brown to olive-green. These shades fade to a dirty white on the belly. The skin is scaleless and slippery.

Size

The freshwater catfish (*Tandanus tandanus*) has been recorded at almost a metre in length and over 6 kilograms, but half this length and a weight

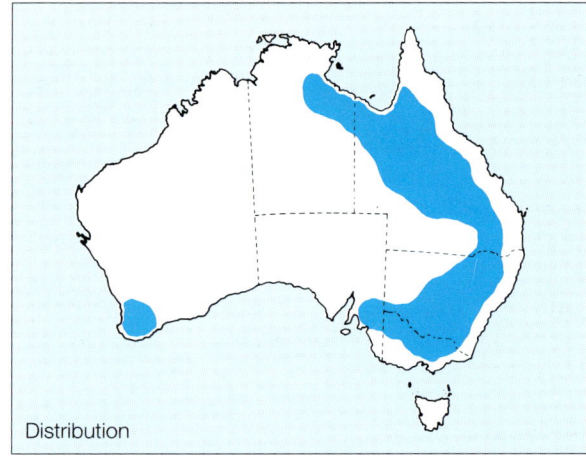

Distribution

of 2 to 3 kilograms are common. *Tandanus bostocki* is a smaller fish, one of 40 centimetres and 1 to 1.5 kilograms is a good specimen. The cobbler, as these fish are more commonly known in Western Australia, must be 23 centimetres to constitute a legal catch in that State.

In South Australia, the legal minimum size for a catfish (*Tandanus tandanus*) is 33 centimetres.

[**Note:** In Western Australia the length is measured from the beginning of the fish's continuous dorsal fin to the tip of the tail. In South Australia the fish is measured from the lip of the mouth to the tip of the tail.]

Breeding

The freshwater catfish builds a circular nest of coarse gravel or rocks in which to deposit its eggs. One parent remains on guard throughout the hatching period. Catfish may spawn from spring to early autumn in water above 24° C.

Habits

Freshwater catfish forage on the bottom, often close to shorelines of dams, lakes and the banks of rivers. They eats worms, shrimps, molluscs, terrestrial and aquatic insects etc., most of which are detected by smell. It tends to be more active at night but will take bait during the day. It much prefers still or slow moving water.

Distribution

The freshwater catfish inhabits most of the slow waters of the Murray-Darling system but it is confined to the lower sections of the Murray, Murrumbidgee and Lachlan rivers. This is said to be the result of cold water releases from Lakes Hume, Burrinjuck and Wyangla. They are also present in the Wimmera River and dams in Victoria; dams and other waters in South Australia; and dams and

One for the pot — a good catfish.

billabongs in New South Wales and Queensland; and it exists in upper reaches of several coastal rivers. The West Australian freshwater catfish, *Tandanus bostocki*, is confined to the south-western waters of that State.

When to fish

The catfish becomes less active in cooler water so the best fishing is to be had in late spring to early autumn. While it may be caught during the day, better catches are made in the late afternoon and at night.

Where to fish

A bait should be placed close to or on the bottom in still water, not far from the bank, close to weed areas and along rocks — where food it forages for is likely to be found.

Tackle

Handlines or light threadline or baitcasting rods and reels, or light rods with sidecast or centre pin reels, can be used. Line about 3 to 5 kilogram breaking strain will handle most fish caught with a hook in sizes from 2 to 1/0.

Baits

Try earthworms, woodgrubs, grasshoppers, mussels, shrimps, small gudgeons.

Rigs

Unweighted or weighted rigs 2 or 3A are popular. If fishing close to or over weed, a quill float (rig 7E) can be helpful.

How to hook

The usual indication of a catfish bite is a slow-motion movement of the line, a slow dip of the rod tip, or the float steadily submerging as the fish mouths the bait while slowly foraging about the bottom. Give the fish about ten seconds before setting the hook.

Once hooked, the catfish is a strong fighter and will invariably head towards weed, reeds or snags.

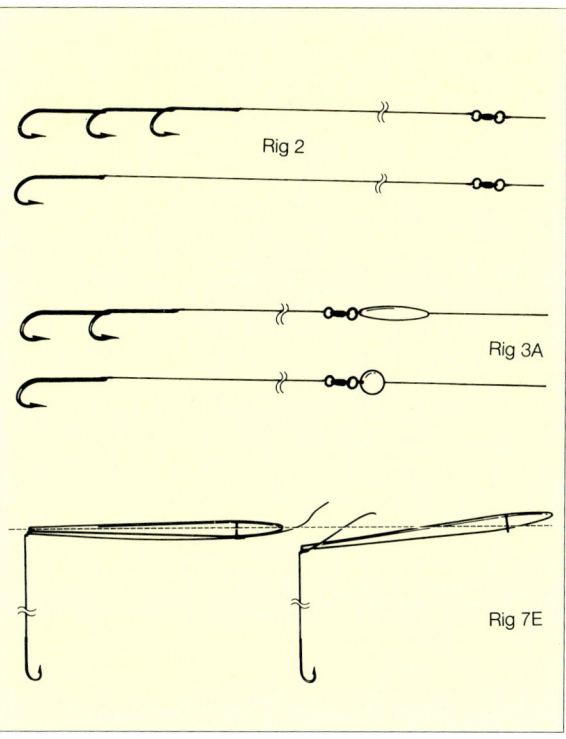

Hint

The catfish detects much of its food by smell, so use a bait with some aroma, such as yabby tail, half earthworms (the blood oozes into the water), squashed grasshopper or mussels.

After the fish has been killed, a pair of side-cutters make a marvellous tool with which to remove the spines.

Edibility

All catfish should be skinned and filleted. Both freshwater and estuarine species have white moist flesh, though the freshwater catfish is generally — though not universally — acknowledged as having more flavour. Simple cooking methods allow this flavour to be appreciated.

[**Note:** There are several other freshwater catfishes in Australian waters as well as the saltwater eel-tailed and fork-tailed species. All are edible.]

COBIA
Rachycentron canadus

OTHER NAMES: **BLACK KINGFISH, CRAB EATER, SERGEANTFISH, LING**

Anglers rarely set out after this game fish. They usually catch it while fishing for other species. The dark shape of its back is often mistaken for a shark, which it sometimes follows, or rays, which it may pursue into quite shallow water.

Identification

The cobia's shape is solid and tapered, with a broad, flattened head and a wide mouth that does not extend back to its eyes. Its front dorsal fin is a series of separate short and unconnected spines, which flatten in a groove. The rear dorsal is curved high at the front and dips to run to its narrow caudal peduncle. The anal fin is a smaller replica of its dorsal fin. In larger specimens, the top lobe of its tail, which is unevenly forked, is curved and longer at the lower point. It has small teeth, arranged in rows. Its colour is dark brown on the top with creamy or off-white bands alternating with brown-tan bands running along its sides, from the eyes to the tail. This banding is more evident on small or juvenile fish, the tail of which is straighter.

Size

The world all-tackle record is 61.5 kilograms, while the Australian all-tackle record is shared (at September, 1988) by two anglers with a fish of 49.44 and 49.66 kilograms. The reason for the tie is that under Australian game fishing rules, a fish weighing between 10 and 50 kilograms must exceed an existing record by at least half a kilogram.

Breeding

Little is known.

Habits

This is a surface fish, generally considered to prefer water temperatures in the range of 20° C and 32° C. It is most frequently found around offshore rocks, reefs or bomboras, but like yellowtail, kingfish and mahi mahi (dolphin fish), it may be present near large pieces of flotsam, often well away from its usual haunts.

The cobia does come inshore to maraud near wrecks and reefs, and often follows sharks and rays into water less clear than that offshore. It is said to follow sharks and rays because it feeds on crabs dislodged from the sand by them.

Distribution

The cobia is a fish of the world's tropic and temperate waters. In Australia it is more common from Port Stevens north, across the top of Australia, and from there south to about Geraldton, in Western Australia. Some are caught further south on the east and west coasts but this depends on the warmth of the summer currents.

When to fish

In the more southerly areas of its distribution, summer is more likely to have water temperatures to the fish's liking. Most catches seem to be made in the morning or afternoon and, when it comes inshore, at the top of the tide.

Where to fish

Your first choice should be to fish near its preferred habitats of offshore reefs, rocks and bomboras and near similar rock formations inshore. When a cobia is seen in shallow inshore waters, it can be cast for with bait or lure.

Tackle

Medium-weight single or double-handed threadline and baitcasting gear is adequate from boats, with bait or lures whether casting or trolling. These will suffice from jetties but a longer double-

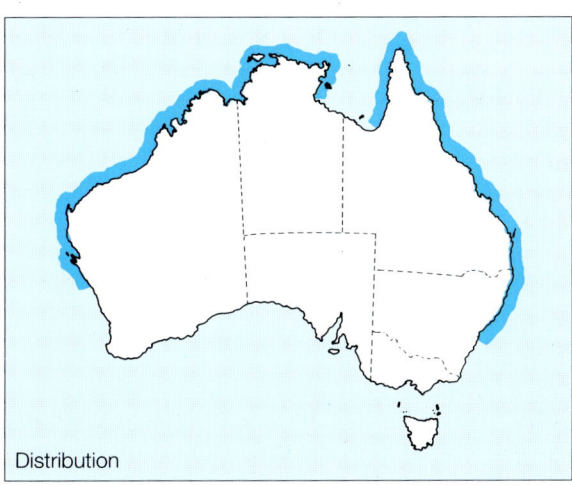

Distribution

Though rarely caught by design, the cobia can be relied upon to give a good account of itself before an angler can bring it alongside.

handed threadline or overhead rod and reel set-up is better for casting and retrieving lures from most shore locations. A 3 to 4 metre rod and sidecast reel is suitable for bait or lures. Light game outfits are also used from boats. Many reef fishers have captured cobia, not easily if it was a large size, while fishing reefs for snapper and other species. Heavy lines 30 kilograms breaking-strain upwards are used by most handline anglers. On rods the lines can be lighter.

Baits

Cobia relish crabs, which is what brings them into bays and even estuaries, as well as foraging around reefs. But they also eat fish, garfish being a particular favourite: try trolling or cast-and-retrieving with them, whether dead or alive. Whiting is another favourite, and perhaps a second reason for its visits to shallow water. Whole fish or fillets of this fish will be taken.

Berley

A berley of crushed crabs and fish pieces can be used to lure cobia away from some of its rocky (line-jagging!) terrain and it may well get them to bite more readily.

Rigs

Depending on the conditions and depth of water, as well as clear or snaggy bottoms, bait rigs Nos 2, 3, 3A, 4 or 5 are suitable.

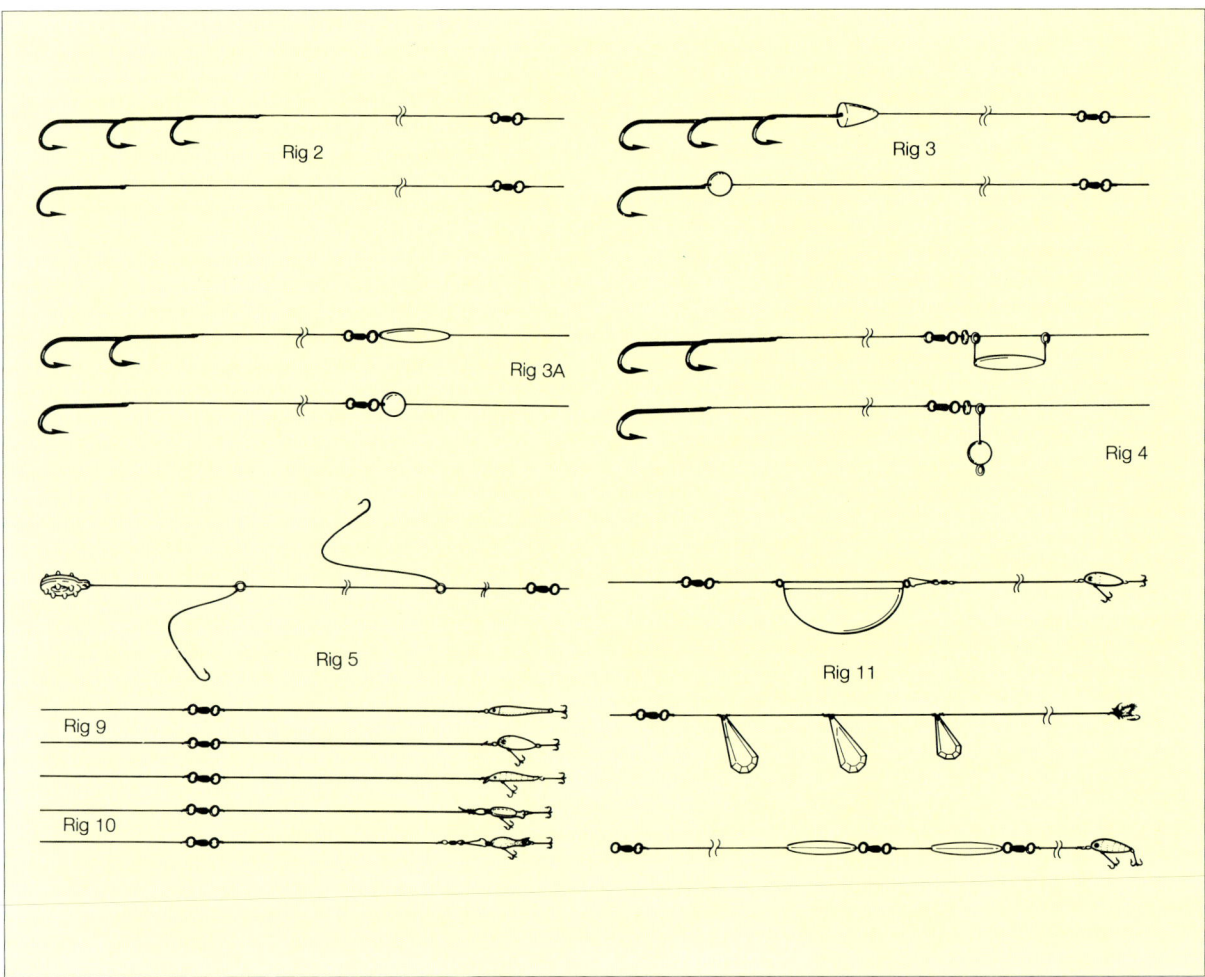

For casting and retrieving lures, use rig No. 9 and for trolling, rig Nos 11. Leaders need not be wire or nylon-coated wire, but should at least be of heavy nylon.

When hooked, cobia display both strength and an unerring ability to find line-cutting rocks. As other toothier fish are invariably present in waters when and where this fish is caught, a wire trace is at least a small insurance in case others should take bait or lure.

How to hook

Cobia usually take a bait or lure quickly. The angler's real challenge is controlling the fish — without breaking the line and before it reaches any underwater obstructions. This fish is strong, runs powerfully and has extraordinary stamina. It is never beaten until it is landed in the boat or ashore.

Hint

Cobia will at times follow a lure or trolled bait but display a reluctance to attack it. Sometimes — though not always, it must be said — a sudden change of pace, stopping or speeding-up the lure or bait, will tempt the fish to make a hit.

Edibility

The cobia is popular with anglers who catch it. It has a full flavour and eats well, however prepared.

COD, MURRAY

Maccullochella peeli

OTHER NAMES: MANY ABORIGINAL NAMES EXIST – PONDE (OR PONDI)
AND GOODOO ARE MOST WIDESPREAD

The Murray cod is not only extolled in legends of the Australian
Aborigines, it is the fish that has inspired Australia's inland anglers
with some of the tallest of tall fishing tales. In fact, these grand
myths became so pervasive that many began to believe that this
titan could only be caught on set lines that were as thick as a little
finger. Grand legends notwithstanding, the Murray cod is
certainly Australia's best known native fish, and it deserves its
pre-eminence. It is in fact one of the really great freshwater fishes
of the world, a fish that has had to wait till relatively recent years
to be recognised and more properly appreciated
by anglers and non-anglers alike.

The once abundant numbers of this fish are much
reduced now and the fish caught today are small
indeed. The Murray cod suffered grievously for
generations from commercial exploitations — now
controlled and being phased out — when thousands of tonnes were sold in Melbourne, Sydney,
Adelaide and Brisbane. And even the amateur
angler over-fished it in many waters. The uncontrolled destruction of its habitats, particularly by
riverbank clearing and the removal of snags and
logs from rivers, all caused siltation. The over-
grazing and cultivation of adjacent lands also affected fish stocks, as did the construction of weirs,
irrigation channels, and dams, all of which contributed to the release of cold waters that expose and/
or kill its eggs.

Even though it is successfully propagated for stocking waters by the New South Wales and Victorian
governments, and some private hatcheries, the
Murray cod is unlikely to ever be prolific again —
or grow to the monumental sizes they used to reach
up to the early years of European settlement.

Identification

The Murray cod is an elongate, deep-bodied fish with a broad head which is slightly concave above the eye. The top of its profile is gently convex from the top of head to the caudal peduncle. It has a large mouth. In large fish the lower jaw may be slightly longer. The front of the dorsal is spined and separated by a notch from the soft rear dorsal fin. The tail is large and rounded. Colour varies from olive-green to a yellowish-green, darker on dorsal area, with black, bluish-black, grey-green to pale green mottling on the back and sides that gradually fades away to off-white to white on belly area. There are varying amounts of white on the margins of its soft dorsal, caudal and anal fins.

Size

The largest recorded Murray cod ever to have been caught on a line weighed 113.4 kilograms and measured almost 2 metres. It was caught in the Barwon River in 1902, but it is probable others of equal size were caught prior to this. As late as early 1988, a Murray cod exceeding 100 kilograms is reliably reported to have been caught in the River-ina. Today fish over 50 kilograms are rare, fish of 30 kilograms exceptions, and fish of over 20 kilograms a trophy catch.

The Murray cod does not reach maturity until about 4 years old, and cod under 3 kilograms are regarded as future brood fish. Conservation minded anglers release them.

Any Murray cod that is caught measuring less than 46 centimetres in length in South Australia must be released. A minimum size of 50 centimetres applies in Queensland and it is 40 centimetres in Victoria, with the exception of Lake Hume and Lake Mulwala.

Breeding

Murray cod prefer a habitat where hollow sunken logs and stumps, or creviced rock areas, are present. The cod is known to deposit eggs on sloping banks and it requires water temperatures of about 16° C to 21° C, associated with a rising level. The eggs, which are adhesive and demersal, are laid in hollow logs or crevices. Spawning in some dams can be affected by water release exposing the eggs prior to hatching. Cold water releases from up-stream impoundments will also kill eggs or newly-hatched larvae.

Habits

The Murray cod cannot be described as an active fish. It will favour a hole where it will find plenty of food adjacent, or where food is swept to it by a current. Such locations are also suitable for it to remain during long periods of dry weather. Larger fish display territorial rights and they may not move when the water rises if the environment is suitable for spawning. The cod will rest in depressions and in hollow logs. It is probable that a migration of smaller maturing Murray cod occurs when they seek spawning sites.

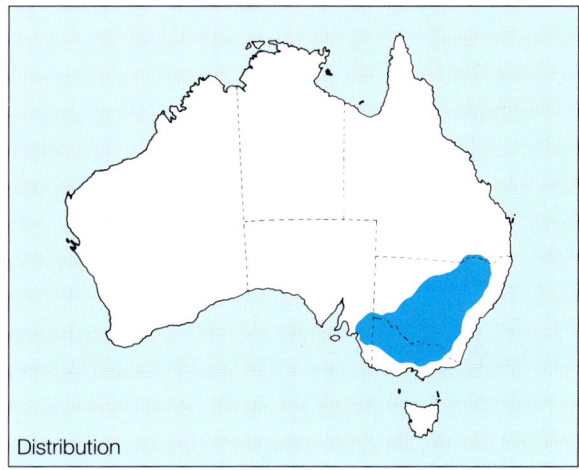

Distribution

Distribution

The fish is widespread throughout the Murray – Darling system, well into Queensland, but its numbers are sharply reduced in some of the upper reaches of many of the tributaries of this river system — and it is disappearing from some. For example, it existed in the Murrumbidgee river beyond Adaminaby. Today it rarely extends further than Canberra. It has been introduced to the Yarra River in Victoria and in several waters in the Wimmera district of that State.

An introduction to Lake Powell near Albany in Western Australia appeared successful and Murray cod in excess of 40 kilograms remained apparently until the 1950s, when pollution is believed to have killed them. Lake George near Canberra supported a commercial fishery in the early 1900s but when the fish could not be sold the catches were dumped or used as fertiliser.

When to fish

The cod is unquestionably more comfortable during warmer weather, though it can be caught during the winter when it is likely to respond to baits rather than take lures. There is much wisdom in two creeds of inland anglers. One is "when the bar's at a thousand and twenty, there's cod aplenty". The other is "start fishing when the wattle blooms" (or in other areas "when the willows bud"). Most of the inland freshwater fish react to atmospheric and water temperature changes.

In late winter and early spring the cod starts to eat greedily. It become ravenous because so many of its natural food items grow scarce in the cooler weather. It is also compelled by instinct to condition itself in readiness for spawning, and to fatten-up for possibly long dry spells in summer. Towards the end of summer they eat after spawning and to build-up tissue for the cooler water of winter.

Where to fish

The simple answer is: where food is most plentiful. And if there is shade cover nearby, all the better. The most likely locations that a cod might occupy or visit are deep holes around rock faces; rocky ridges which dip into the water; rocky outcrops; against deep or undercut banks; near submerged and fallen logs, amongst tree roots in the water, around weed beds. All these are places where the cod's natural food occurs.

Tackle

Handlines can be used for bank or boat fishing — with bait or for trolling lures. More convenient, however, are single or double-handed threadline or baitcasting outfits, which can be used for lure casting. Rods designed for sidecast reels are also useful. Handlines need not exceed 10 kilograms breaking-strain, lines on rods about 5 or 6 kilograms breaking-strain. Depending on the bait size, a hook size between 1/0 to 4/0 will do.

Baits

The Murray cod is not a fussy eater. This fish has been caught with water dragons, small snakes and ducklings in its stomach. Recommendations for such exotic baits as rabbit carcasses, parrots etc. abound in the outback. Without wishing to dispute the more bizarre baits, the Murray cod's normal diet consists of yabbies, shrimps, crayfish, molluscs, frogs and fish — such as bony bream, goldfish, carp, redfin, even silver perch and golden perch — as well as woodgrubs, grasshoppers, scrubworms.

Rigs

When using bait, the rig may be unweighted (rig No. 2), lightly weighted (rig No. 3A, or rig No. 4A where the bait is required to be kept clear of snags). The weight of the sinker will depend on the current, but remember that a moving bait is more likely to catch a cod than an immobile one. For casting andretrieving lures, use rigs No. 9 or

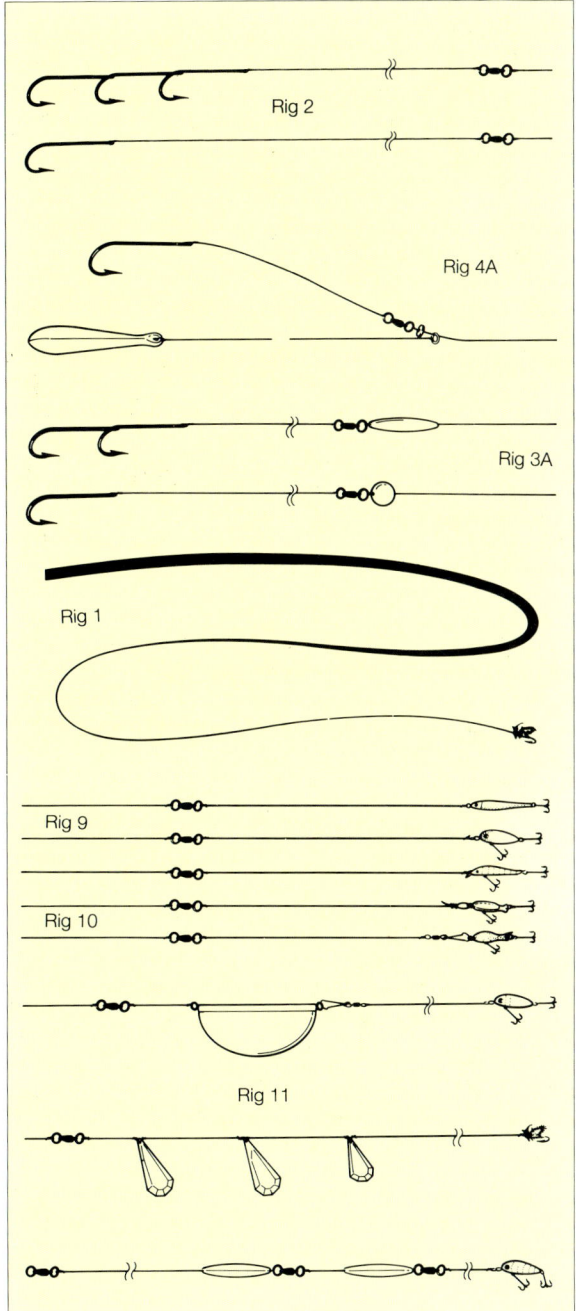

10; for trolling try rig No. 11. A stronger breaking-strain leader is recommended but a wire trace is unnecessary.

For those willing to try artificials on fly gear, salt-water flies or large wet freshwater patterns are worth a go, especially if fished deeply and slowly but erratically.

Only lures with plenty of action are satisfactory — wobbling, wriggling, darting or diving — and they should be retrieved slowly. If you are fishing in the river proper, then it is generally more productive

Murray cod

to retrieve lures with the current and as close to obstructions and banks that you can manage.

How to hook

Though Murray cod sometime grabs a bait, they are usually slow-takers. It is better to give the fish some line before tightening to set the hook. It will swipe or nudge a lure — as if harassing an intruder — which makes the line go slack. When this happens, persist with casting to the same spot. When the Murray cod hits a cast or trolled lure, it generally hooks itself.

Hint

The Murray cod is used to quite muddy waters that are often too turbid for lures. But some "colour" in the water is regarded by many as necessary for good catches. If a lure's action is not upset by it, attaching a piece of natural bait with a smell — such as yabby tail or woodgrub — to the hooks can induce cod to hit.

In clear water, particularly on moonlit nights, a large floating lure with lots of surface-disturbing action, can attract a big cod. It often indicates its presence with bow waves as it cruises in near the surface to investigate.

Edibility

Large Murray cod tend to be fatty and oily but smaller mature specimens have white and well-flavoured flesh. They are good eating, however

cooked, but they are delightful when stuffed and baked.

Other regulations

In South Australia there is a closed season for Murray cod between September 1 and November 30 (inclusive). No cod can be taken from a stretch of the Murray River near Yarrawonga in New South Wales. Check locally.

COD, SLEEPY
Oxyeleotris lineolatus

OTHER NAME: **SLEEPER COD**

If any fish has an appropriate description, this one is apt indeed. It's very nature of appearing to doze in shallow waters of some rivers and dams it inhabits has made it a relatively helpless target for hand spearing and even being captured in hand-held nets. On the other hand, when caught on a light line with baits or lures, you have a very scrappy tussler.

Identification

In some ways this fish resembles a large member of the gudgeon family — the mud gudgeon of some Queensland northern freshwaters. The sleepy cod is a dull brownish colour, lightening to a creamy to dirty white on the belly. It has a flattish head that is much broader than it is deep with a large mouth, the lower jaw of which is longer. There is a slight rise to its profile from behind the eyes and its back curves gently down to the edge of its rounded tail. The eyes are high in the head. The second dorsal fin is larger than the front and the anal fin is almost identical in shape and size.

Size

It is believed the maximum size is 50 centimetres and 3 kilograms.

Breeding

Little is known about its breeding.

Habits

The fish is most likely to be seen and caught during late spring to early autumn. It is invariably found in slow-moving or still water where there are submerged logs, trees and weedy vegetation. It feeds on crustaceans, aquatic insects and small fish.

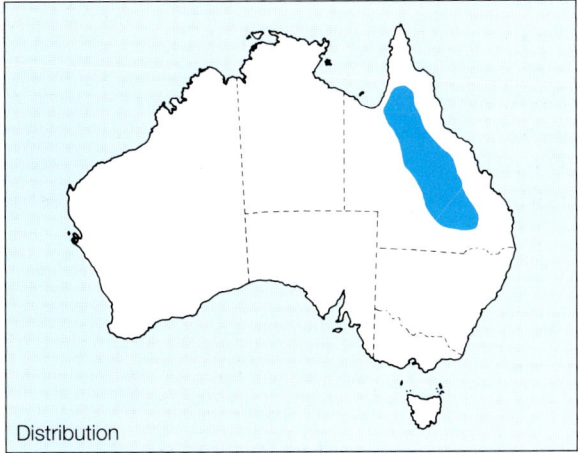

Distribution

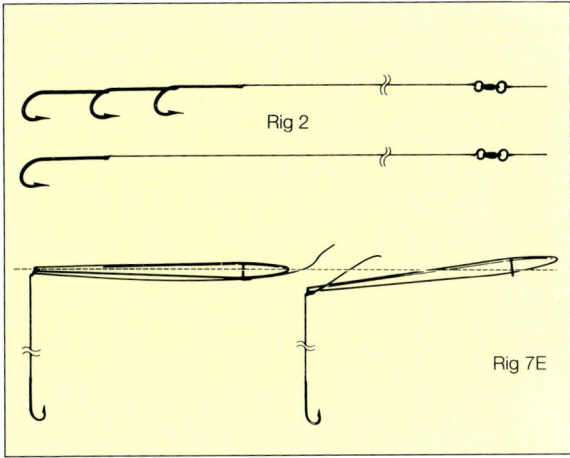

Rig 2

Rig 7E

Distribution
The sleepy cod inhabits freshwater rivers and lagoons on both the coast and inland of central and northern Queensland. It is now in some of the newer freshwater impoundments.

When to fish
Some of the waters inhabited by this fish are difficult to fish during the "wet" season. It is obviously preferable to fish prior to this, the most pleasant period being autumn, while the weather is still warm, and in the spring and early summer.

Where to Fish
The best locations are around snaggy areas, along weed banks and amongst submerged trees.

Tackle
Ultra-light threadline or baitcasting outfits are more sporting, but because some harder fighting fish inhabit the same waters, it is safer to use slightly heavier rods and reels.

Baits
Try crayfish, freshwater prawns, small bony bream and fillets of gudgeons.

Rigs
A sinker is not necessary in the still water where the fish prefers to rest. Rig No. 2 and a light float (rig 7E) method if over and alongside weed and snags are suitable. The hook should suit the bait but because of the capacity of the fish's mouth, can be larger than normally used.

How to hook
On many occasions the sleepy cod simply swallows a bait and can be so hard to detect that many an angler has only discovered he has a fish on his line when he begins to reel the bait in for an inspection. Despite its apparent laziness, it is surprisingly fast to hit a lure (deep-diving or sinking types) which passes close to it.

Edibility
Many regard the firm, flaky and white flesh as the best eating of all freshwater fish. And though this fish is often caught in muddy water, the flesh is never tainted.

COD, TROUT
Maccullochella macquariensis

OTHER NAME: **BLUENOSE COD**

The trout cod was the first inland fish to be described (in 1829), but it was not until the mid 1970s that the existence of the second species was confirmed. Until then, the Murray cod bore the scientific name *Maccullochella macquariensis*. This name then reverted back to the trout cod and the Murray cod became *Maccullochella peeli*.

Once quite widespread and as prolific as the Murray cod, the trout cod was more common in the cooler upper reaches and faster waters of many of the tributaries of the Murray – Darling system, though it was recorded as far downstream as Mannum in South Australia. It existed in numbers in Lake Sambell in Victoria until the population was wiped out in 1970 by an unexplained "kill".

This fish is now classified as endangered, with the only reasonable population living in a stretch of the Murray River and in a creek in Victoria. It is

Trout cod.

Identification

An elongate deep-bodied fish, the trout cod can be distinguished from the Murray cod by several characteristics. The colour of the dorsal area and upper sides is generally blue-grey with small dark grey to black spots that extend to the lower sides. (Murray cod is blotched, the marks appearing wiggly.) The spots are also on the base of its fins. Its belly is light grey to white and a dark, usually blue-black stripe extends from through the eye to the edge of the operculum. The upper jaw over-hangs the lower jaw and there is a bluish tone on the snout area.

Size

The trout cod is believed to have reached a maximum of 20 kilograms.

[**Note:** This description is to help any angler who unwittingly hooks this endangered fish to identify it so that he or she may release it promptly and carefully. Remember that it is much safer for the well-being of the fish to cut the line close to the lips rather than trying to remove a hook inside the mouth or throat.

It has been proved now that the **eastern freshwater cod** (*Maccullochella ikei*) that has been found surviving in the tributaries of only one river on the New South Wales north coast, was not a translocated Murray cod. Fishing for this species is totally banned. New South Wales fisheries biologists are trying to breed it in a hatchery by hormone induced spawning in an effort to save this fish from extinction.

The taxonomic state of another cod, called the **Mary river cod**, in Queensland, is uncertain. This fish is endangered and may be on the verge of extinction.]

possible a few fish are located in only one or two sections in another New South Wales and Victorian river. In a declared area of the Murray River, near Yarrawinga, the fishing for any cod is prohibited for the present in a determined effort to preserve this fish.

The Victorian Fisheries are trying to breed these fish in a hatchery in co-operation with Native Fish Australia. A breeding programme is also being undertaken by the New South Wales Fisheries.

The trout cod is a much more aggressive fish than the Murray cod and will leap from the water for large insects. It strikes lures hard and this very aggressiveness may have been one reason for its sad decline, being an easy fish for greedy anglers to catch.

Like so many other good freshwater fish, trout cod were also netted in commercial quantities.

Environment changes have been regarded as partly responsible for the trout cod's dwindling numbers. Biologists suggest that it may also have suffered as a result of competition from imported trout, which thrive in a similar habitat and on much the same diet.

COD

It is difficult to understand why this name has been given to such a wide variety of Australian fish. The majority bear scant resemblance to the codfishes of the northern hemisphere fishing grounds, such as cod, haddock, hake, whiting, codfish, rocklings and poutings. One would have expected Australia's early settlers, who first named the local fish, to have been quite familiar with the European cod family. (In fact only one true freshwater codfish has ever been identified, and that is the burbot of northern European waters.)

All true cods generally have soft fin rays which, with few exceptions, contain no hard spines, and their pelvic fins are located forward on the belly. Many of these fish have a single barbel — if not more — on the chin and sometimes elsewhere, and a distinct tail fin structure. All cod prefer cool to colder water temperatures; the few which inhabit tropical regions are found only in water deep enough to be cold.

Australian members of the cod family consist of deep-sea fish, but the beardie cod and bearded rock-cod [for red cod, *see* Scorpionfish] are the only ones a recreational angler is likely to catch. Some of the more popular marine fish that are wrongly referred to as cod — but that at least are accessible to recreational anglers — are included under the heading Rock-cod.

COD, BEARDIE
Lotella rhacinus

OTHER NAME: **LING**

COD, BEARDED ROCK-
Pseudophycis barbata

OTHER NAME: **TASMANIAN COD**

COD, RED
Pseudophycis

OTHER NAME: **LING**

The beardie and bearded rock-cod are closely related, especially the red and bearded rock species. They belong to the family Moridae — the morids — and are relatives of the cod family. They certainly have a very cod-like shape.

Identification
These two have a rounded, oval body, the profile tapering fairly evenly on the back and belly to the tail. The front dorsal fin is small and soft, with a narrow notch between it and the long soft rear dorsal fin which almost reaches the tail. The anal fin is a replica of the rear dorsal fin. They have large eyes, a snout which projects over the mouth and a whisker-like barbel under the chin.

The colour of the beardie is variable — from pale brown to reddish-brown to dark brown. Its dorsal and anal fins have a distinct white edge.

The bearded rock-cod can be tan brown, reddish-brown to dark brown. It does not have a lighter stomach colour and the black edge on its dorsal and anal fins is much wider than the red cod's.

Size
These cods grow to between 60 to 70 centimetres long. They have been caught exceeding 5 kilograms.

Breeding
Little is known, though some evidence suggests the fish aggregate at about spawning time.

Habits
These cod frequent rocky areas and reefs. The beardie is more likely to be found in reefs deeper than 7 or 8 metres; the bearded rock member of the family can be found near reefs with sandy, or even muddy areas, close inshore and well offshore;and the red in coastal inlets and bays where reef and rocks are protected from heavy seas. . The beardie is the most retiring of the three, holing up in caves or crevices during the day and emerging as the water darkens in the evening. Both are carnivorous, eating small fish, crabs and shellfish, such as limpets and cockles.

Distribution
The beardie is probably the more abundant, ranging from the central-north coast of New South

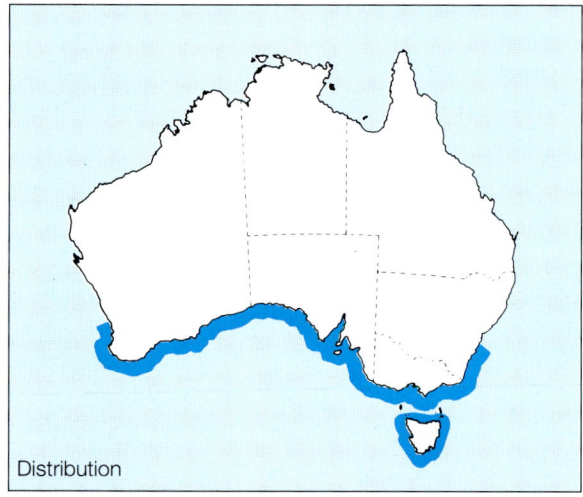

Distribution

Wales south around Tasmania, through Bass Strait, along the Victorian and South Australian and Western Australian coasts up to to Lancelin, a little north of Perth.

The bearded rock-cod is found from about Sydney, all round Tasmania, along the Victorian and South Australian coasts and along the south coast of Western Australia about as far as Esperance.

The red cod is found from the far south coast of New South Wales and into Victorian, Tasmanian and South Australian waters.

When to fish
You can occasionally catch these fish at any time of the year but more regular catches are made in the autumn-winter period. Either morning, afternoon or evening seems to be the best times.

Where to fish
These fish are found off the rocks among broken reefs and rocky areas and on or alongside reefs in sandy or muddy bottoms.

Tackle

Boat fishers may use a handline or small rod and reel. When fishing from the rocks, try a light to medium rod about 3 to 3.5 metres long with threadline, overhead or sidecast reel. Because some big wrasses or other fish may be hooked in the same habitat, lines of 8 to 12 kilogram breaking-strain are a suitable precaution for handlines, and 4 to 6 kilograms should be adequate for rods. Hooks should be about size 2, 1 or 1/0, depending on the bait being used.

Baits

Small fish, crabs, molluscs and shellfish, particularly limpets and cockles are accepted.

Berley

A mixture of minced fish, shellfish and rice (or bread), with canned cat food should entice these fish from their hidden sanctuaries.

Rigs

Use running bottom rigs such as No. 4 or 4A, with the hook closer to the bottom, depending on water conditions and the terrain being fished.

How to hook

These fish bite readily and are usually hooked once the weight of the fish is felt as you tighten the line or lift the rod tip.

Hint

These three cods can be tempted by jigging with small spoons or lead-head jigs, especially when a small school is attracted by berley.

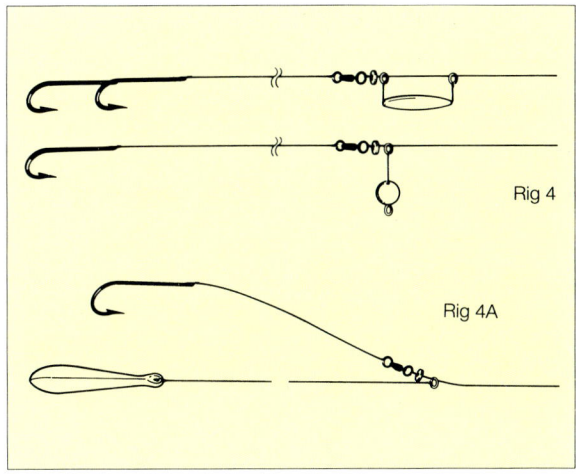

Rig 4

Rig 4A

Edibility

These cods are reasonable food fish but their white flesh is a little soft. Do not overcook.

[**Note:**Occasionally, anglers fishing for these cod — especially in Victorian and Tasmanian waters — may catch a fish that seems similar in all respects except for its longer length. This is the rock ling (*Genypterus tigerinus*). Its body shape is very much the same as a marine catfish, with a continuous soft fin from about its pectoral fins around to its anal opening. The fish is greyish to pink or greyish-fawn to brownish-green. Occasionally is can be a whitish-silver, mottled with a darker colour that lightens off in the stomach area. It has two barbels on the lower jaw — but no whiskers like a catfish. It grows to more than a metre and in excess of 6 kilograms. It is an excellent table fish. In Victoria the minimum legal catch for a rock ling is 33 centimetres.]

DART

Two of the three darts, all of which belong to the trevally family (called "pompano" elsewhere in the world), are very similar, though they are not encountered in the same waters. The swallowtail dart's distribution can overlap the others but it is easily identified. All three dart occupy similar habitats and can be caught by the same methods. They are furious biters and a tough fighting fish.

DART, BLACK SPOTTED

Trachinotus bailloni

OTHER NAMES: **DART, BLACK-SPOTTED SWALLOWTAIL**

Identification

This fish has an oval profile, though rounder on the bottom, and thin like trevally. It has a shiny silvery body with a bluish-green dorsal, lightening towards the lateral line, along which are several small round black spots, usually four. (The swal- lowtail dart with which it is sometimes confused, has larger spots of a smudged appearance.) The front dorsal fin is very short but the rear dorsal and anal fins are long and sweeping at the front. The tail is deeply forked.

Size

The black-spotted dart is probably the smallest of the family, with a maximum length of about 50 centimetres and perhaps 2 kilograms in weight.

Breeding

Little is known.

Habits

It is abundant along clear coastal waters near reefs, off beaches and in estuaries. They are a schooling fish and it is not uncommon to see large schools in the currents or close inshore.

Distribution

This is restricted to warm waters. The black-spotted dart is found mainly north of Gladstone and around to the Exmouth area of Western Australia, occasionally reaching as far south as Jurien Bay.

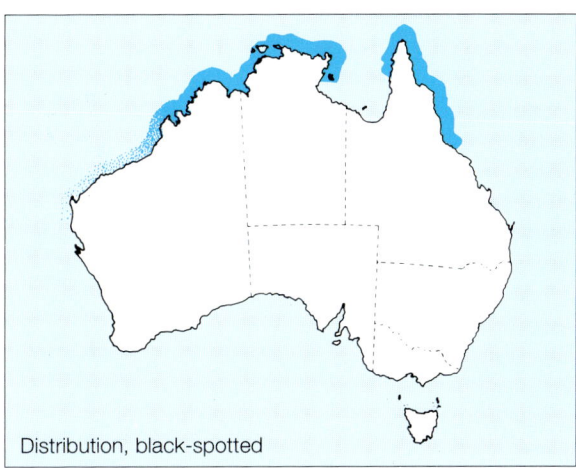

Distribution, black-spotted

DART, SNUB-NOSED
Trachinotus blochii

OTHER NAMES: **BUCK-NOSED TREVALLY, SNUB-NOSED SWALLOWTAIL, OYSTER-EATER**

Identification

This dart is much rounder and deeper in the body than the black-spotted dart. It has a similar curve on the top and bottom of its profile but it is straighter from in front of the rear dorsal and anal fins to a narrow caudal peduncle. Overall it is of a light silver colour with a blue-green dorsal area. It has no black spots. There is a yellow colour on the fins, face, throat and towards the belly. There is a dark to blackish edge to its long dorsal and anal fins and tail.

[**Note**: Some biologists believe this fish may be the same as another dart, *Trachinotus anak*, which is commonly called the oyster-eater.]

This is the largest of the darts, measuring up to 90 centimetres in length. It can reach a weight of more than 10 kilograms.

Breeding

Little is known.

Habits

This dart inhabits warmer waters, especially where bivalves, shellfish and oysters are in good supply. These are its favourite foods, which it crushes between a set of bony plates in its throat, a practice that led to one of its common names, oyster-eater. It is, in fact, sometimes accused of raiding oyster farms in the southernmost area of its range.

Distribution

This dart is found in the coastal and inshore waters of northern and central Queensland but it occasionally appears as far south as the Gold Coast. It also occurs through the tropics and on the West Australian coast. It is seen less commonly than the other two darts.

Satisfaction on the rocks: a good bag of dart and mackerel

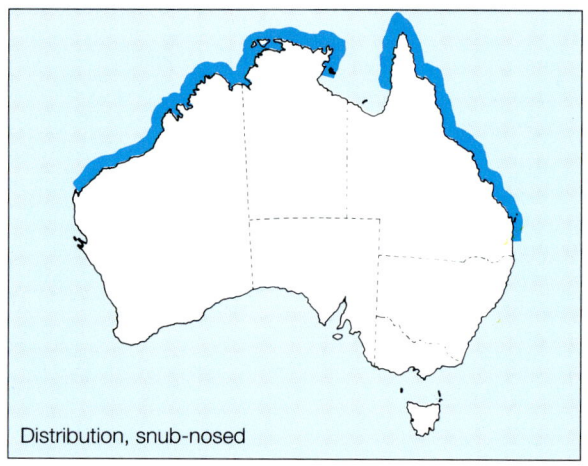

Distribution, snub-nosed

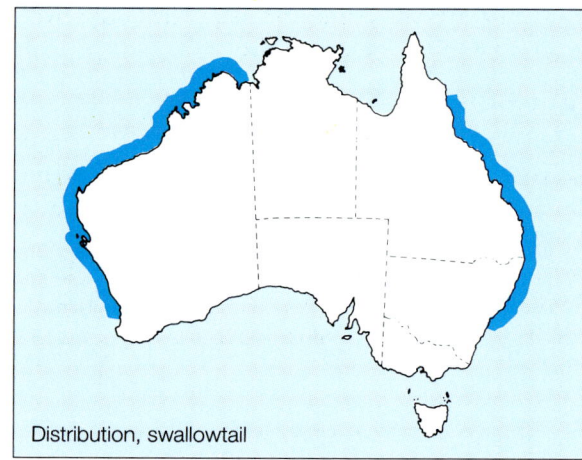

Distribution, swallowtail

DART, SWALLOWTAIL or COMMON

Trachinotus botla
(Eastern coast)
Trachinotus coppingeri
(Western coast)

OTHER NAMES: **SURF BREAM, SURF TREVALLY, COMMON DART**

Identification

T. botla is very similar to the *T. coppingeri*. Both are grey-green to blue along the dorsal area of a bright silver body. The distinguishing characteristics are the 5 to 7 smudged thumb-size blotches along the top edge of the lateral line. Those of the west coast have larger darker spots, with one located above the pectoral fin. The east coast species have smaller spots or blotches, with two above the pectoral fin.

Size

A swallowtail dart of 60 centimetres is a large fish. Its maximum weight is about 4 kilograms but most catches are about a kilogram.

Breeding

Little is known.

Habits

Swallowtail darts often school, and shoals — sometimes in the hundreds — may form. They visit surf beaches and enter clear estuaries, surpris-ing anglers by appearing in extremely shallow water, swimming very fast and on their sides. They are probably foraging for worms, shellfish and small crabs in such situations.

Distribution

T. botla of the west coast is probably most abundant where there are sandy beaches and estuaries, but it is found along the entire coast, from about Bun-bury to Northern Territory waters. Though con-sidered a tropical species, *T. coppingeri* of the east coast ranges as far south as Sydney on occasions. The black-spotted dart and swallowtail dart are the most popular and the more common angling and eating species. The following applies equally to both.

When to fish

In the more northerly regions, the dart is present throughout the year. Prime fishing time is from November through April. The fish is averse to dirty water, which can affect some of its preferred habitat, and it is very definitely a daytime target. Fishing for dart in late afternoon or for a short time from sunrise — especially if a high tide coincides with these periods — will generally produce the best catches.

Where to fish

Dart aggregate in holes and channels on the beaches and move into gutters that deepen at high tide. Channels, or deep water behind sand-bars in wide estuaries, are also locations worth trying. Feeding dart often betray themselves by flashing their reflection through the smaller waves break-ing against the sand.

The fish appear to seek food beneath the wide

foamy and relatively smooth areas in front of waves crashing on the outer surf break.

Tackle

You will require a lightweight rod, about 3 to 4 metres long, with a sensitive tip. It will have to suit threadline or sidecast reels, spooled with lines of a breaking-strain between 3 and 5 kilograms. These will cast the relatively light baits and small sinkers. While both reels will cast small lures, the thread-line is better for varying the speed of retrieval.

Baits

The ideal bait is whole or slices of pipi (also known as eugari and goolwa cockle) but the fish readily takes nippers, yabbies, peeled prawns and other molluscs, as well as small fish and fillets of fish.

Rig

As dart are not usually found in shallow and calm waters, a sinker as light as the conditions of surf and current will allow should be used — and it should be a running sinker. The rigs with running sinkers (No. 3, 3A or 4) are practical. Hooks should be around sizes No. 2 to 1/0.

How to hook

The line between the angler and the bait should be kept under tension. If the water is not moving it, the angler should reel in slowly. The fish shows no hesitation before grabbing the bait and it hooks itself. Fast and furious fighters, the dart can test the skill of the most experienced fisher with its speed, power and twisting directional changes in surf conditions.

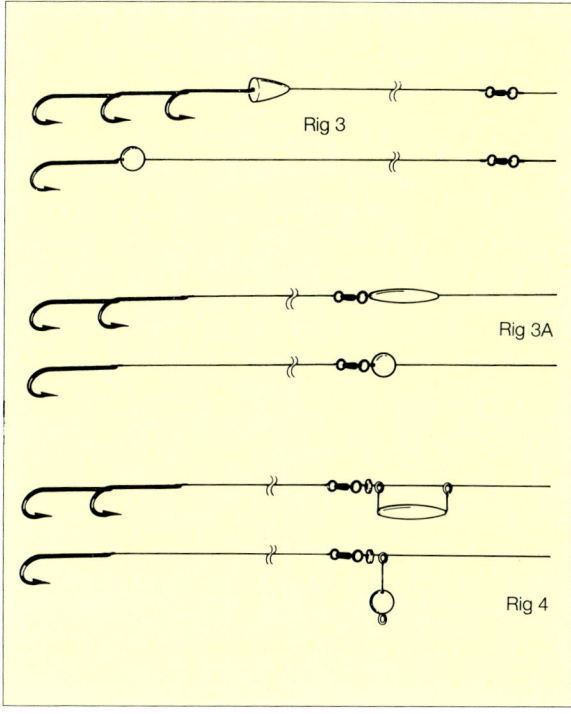

Hint

Exciting fishing is in prospect when a good school of dart is present if you use weighted saltwater flies, small lures and small jigs.

Edibility

The dart, which should be bled as soon as caught, has a flesh which quickly deteriorates if not kept cool. It will also dry out rapidly. Nevertheless, fresh fillets, lightly fried in breadcrumbs or batter are excellent eating.

DORY, JOHN
Zeus faber

OTHER NAMES: **ST PETER'S FISH (FROM THE GERMAN *PETERFISCH*)**

This is one of several fish that bear spots on the sides which —
as myth has it — were caused by the fingers of St Peter when
he picked one up to extract a coin from its mouth. The name
is also said to be a corruption of the Italian *Janitore* fish,
meaning door-keeper. But the name is more probably
derived from an English mispronunciation of the French
jaune dorée, reflecting this fish's yellow-gold appearance in
some environments. There are several other "dory fish",
mainly deepwater reef species. Nevertheless, the
john dory does venture inshore and well within
reach of the astute angler.

Identification

The fish at all times looks surly or mournful. It is
a deep oval shape, almost flat, with a large head
and big eyes. The head gives the impression of skin
stretched over bones with no flesh. The mouth is
drooping and the jaw structure is such that the
mouth can be extended or protruded to engulf its
prey. The first dorsal and pelvic fins are long and
there are lengthy filaments between the spines of
the dorsal fin, which in large john dory may reach
back past its tail. It has stubby spines along the base

of the fins but it has a small, neat tail. A large black spot on the sides has a yellow edge. The fish's overall colour is a mixture of greenish olive-bronze and yellow shades, but when caught it becomes a patchy greyish-olive.

Size

John dory grows to 60 centimetres and may weigh more than 8 kilograms, though most catches are less than half this size.

Breeding

John dory spawns in the shallower (40 metres to 100 metres) reefs off the continental shelf in the late summer to the early autumn. The eggs are buoyant.

Habits

The fish glides rather than swims but once it lines up a small fish, its speed to get within a range from which it can suck in and grasp its victim is quite extraordinary.

It hovers and rises and sinks with almost indiscernible movement of its second dorsal fin and the twitch of its tail. It also can rotate slowly while seeking food. The plate-like thinness of the fish makes it difficult to spot from head on. From above it looks like a pencil.

When it stalks its prey it tends to change colour, brightening in uneven patches with its dorsal fin erect and quivering. This is a marvellous camouflage, making it almost invisible to its prey and blending it into any weeds and rocks. It prefers broken — often isolated or separated — reefs with sand patches. It is usually found on the deep water side of these reefs.

The john dory feeds mainly on such small fish as yellowtail, pilchards, and reef species. It will also eat crabs and small squid, sucking these and worms

from the pylons of wharves or the crevices of deepwater rock faces on the shoreline.

After spawning, from late April to about September, it moves into shallow inshore reef areas, hunts in deepwater close to cliffs and favours deepwater channels or holes in rocky inlets (especially if there is weed and a sandy bottom). It enters harbours, bays and estuaries and will glide stealthily around pylons, buoys or moored boats.

Distribution

This is mainly a temperate to cool water fish, its range extending from about Bundaberg in Queensland, south to around Tasmania, in the Bass Strait; along the Victorian and South Australian coast; and then north to about Bunbury in the south-west of Western Australia.

When to fish

Depending on the capability of the boat, john dory are within the reach of off-shore fishers most of the year. The land-based angler will often find the fish around very comfortable fishing locations — from wharves or piers in harbours, from small boats in harbours or deepwater estuary spots — the end of autumn to the end of winter.

It is a daytime fish and usually between 8.00 a.m. and dusk is the best time, especially if a tide is low at about the starting time and then rises through the main fishing period.

Where to fish

The fish inhabits broken and isolated reefs offshore, usually on the deeper side of them. This may be associated with the presence of food or currents. Inshore it seems to head for locations where there are small fish. Any area where there are small fish present — particularly yellowtail — in reasonably deep water, is almost certain to be visited by john dory. It is also worth trying around wharves and amongst moored boats in season.

Tackle

For reef fishing, a handline or boat rod with a large centrepin style reel, about 10 to 20 kilograms breaking-strain is adequate. A handline may be used from boats or wharves or piers, as can threadline or baitcasting outfits, with lines of about 3 to 5 kilograms breaking-strain. In some locations, such as rocks or high wharves, a 3-metre light to medium rod with threadline, overhead or sidecast reel, but with a slightly heavier line, is more practical. Viking or French or Suicide style hooks about 3/0 – 4/0, depending on bait size, are all successful.

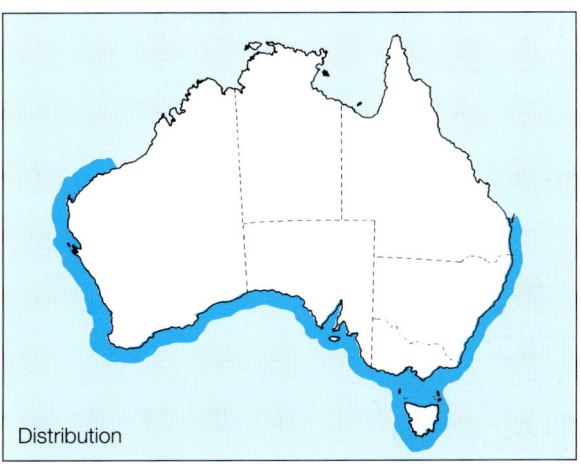

Distribution

Baits

The most readily available and particularly attractive bait to the john dory is a live yellowtail, between 7 to 15 centimetres in length. Similar sized slimy mackerel and tailor or reef species are also taken. The livelier yellowtail, mackerel and tailor baits can be slowed down in their activity when pinned to a hook by cutting off a half of their tail if fishing offshore waters. (It is illegal to use undersized bream, whiting etc.) Live squid and crabs are not as successful as fish.

Rigs

For offshore the running size rig 3A or 4A, with a sinker to suit the depth or current, can be used. On shallower reefs, off rocks or in harbours, bays or estuaries, the live bait rig 7C is recommended. Offshore, once the sinker has reached the bottom, it should be raised 1 to 1.5 metres.
If a float rig is used, the water should be sounded (plumb the depth by dropping a sinker on the end of the line if you have no depth sounder aboard). Adjust the float so that the live bait is swimming about 1 to 1.5 metres from the seabed or above weeds if they are present.

How to hook

The first hint of a john dory is often indicated by the panic of the bait.
Most predators take the bait and run, but the john dory sucks in the fish and glides off slowly as it readjusts its mouth and swallows the fish without chewing it.
It is a matter of feeding out line and giving the fish time to get its meal well down before applying pressure. On the suspended bait rig, the float usually bobs (the live bait panicking) and disappears slowly. Allow the fish to move for 2 to 3 metres before tightening up fairly hard. The fish, once hooked, is not an exciting fighter.

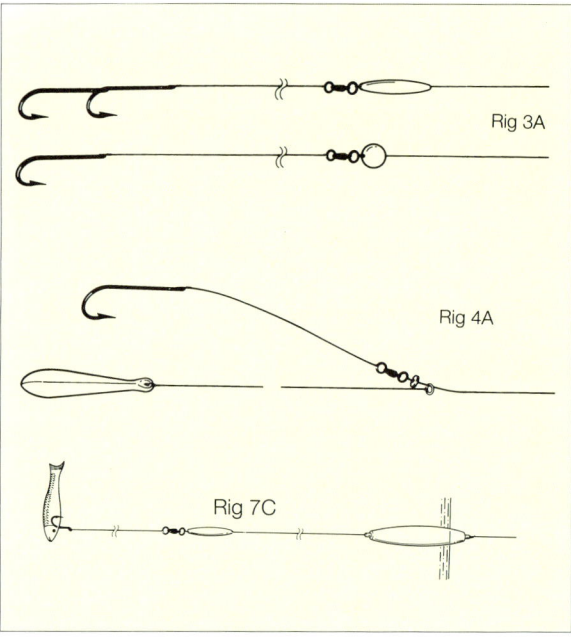

Hint

The live bait should be hooked forward of the front dorsal fin, just through the flesh and skin without injuring the back bone. This ensures the hook will be well down towards the stomach and will pull free easily to penetrate the dory's throat or mouth as the angler tightens up. (Some hook it through the lips but this is not as successful.)
While it has to be considered as a daytime fish, it can be caught at night with the floating rig in harbours near wharves with bright lights shining on the water surface. Fish in the lit area.

Edibility

The demand for john dory is always high — as are the prices — in fish shops and restaurants. Its white flesh makes excellent eating. Overcooking or too much "dressing" in the way of sauces etc. can spoil its flavour. Treat simply for the best results.

DRUMMER, SILVER
Kyphosus sydneyanus

OTHER NAMES: **DRUMMER, BUFFALO BREAM**

There are several members of the Kyphosidae family around the Australian coast. All are herbivorous, though from time to time they will take other bait such as conjevoi, peeled prawns, worms and abalone gut. These various drummers (with the exception of the luderick and rock blackfish which appear under their own entry) are described below with any particularly relevant comments: the general information about the silver drummer — methods of capture, rigs, etc. — applies to all drummers. The silver drummer is the largest of these fish and an extremely tough adversary for even experienced anglers.

Identification

This is a solid deep-bodied fish. It has a short head and a small mouth with fine teeth in both jaws. The dorsal fin is short and it dips between the front and rear, which reaches to the caudal peduncle. The pectoral fins are short and rounded. Colour ranges from a darkish silver-grey to dark grey and almost black on the dorsal area, head, fins and tail. Some fish display an easily seen olive-green shade to-wards the stomach. Light longitudinal stripes may also be discernible on some fish.

Size

The silver drummer grows to more than 90 centi-metres and can weigh in excess of 12 kilograms but they are considerably more common between the 4 and 6 kilogram mark. These fish can, however, be larger in South Australian and West Australian waters.

Breeding
Little is known.

Habits
The silver drummer lives close to inshore reefs and along ocean rock fronts. It is found where there are good growths of the broad-leafed brown and green weed and conjevoi. It may gather in schools and it is not unusual to see numbers holding on to weed as a wave recedes from a sloping rock where they have come to feed. It may also eat immature or soft conjevoi.

Distribution
The fish inhabits inshore waters, to about 40 metres deep, from the north coast of New South Wales to about the Victorian border. It is more scarce on the Victorian and north-east Tasmanian coastline but it reappears in South Australian waters and is found right along the coast of the Great Australian Bight, and north beyond Perth in Western Australia.

When to fish
The fish is around all year, though the best catches seem to be made from the late summer through the winter. A high tide before the sun is too high from the horizon or in the mid to late afternoon, enables the fish to move in to feed close to the rocks. A disturbed white water or plenty of suds provides a preferred cover for them.

Where to fish
The best locations will be found along ocean rocks where there is evidence of water-washed green

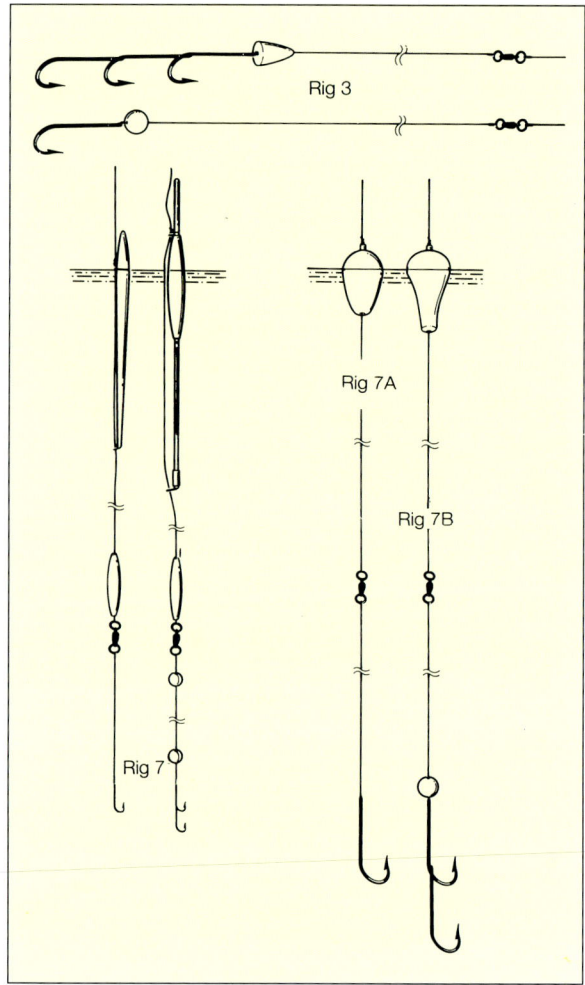

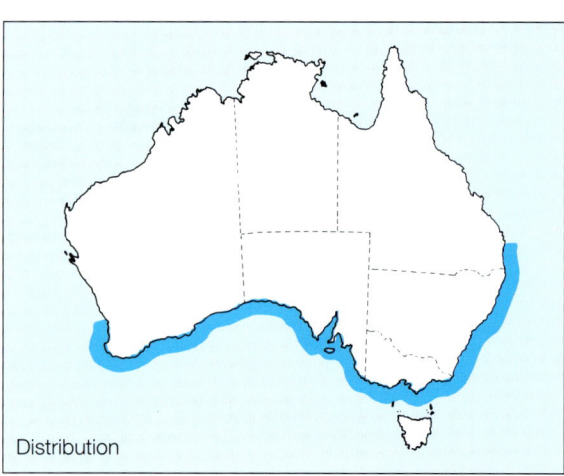

Distribution

weed and conjevoi beds. Unfortunately, the very best of such sites may also be subject to hazardous swells, so caution is needed.

Tackle
A medium rod of about 3.5 metres with a medium fast taper, which will suit a sidecast reel, is an excellent outfit. A similar rod may be used for threadline or overhead reels. Line of not less than 8 kilograms breaking-strain is needed to handle this fish. Extra strong hooks about size 1/0 are needed (French or Viking types being a safe choice).

Baits
First choice of weed is the broad-leafed green "cabbage" or "lettuce" but a silver drummer, as well as rock blackfish, will often take the finer long-stranded weed used by luderick anglers. From time to time it may also prefer dead or brown cabbage or lettuce. Conjevoi is usually accepted and occasionally peeled prawns, limpet flesh and abalone gut are also taken.

Berley

The silver drummer can be attracted and kept in an eating mood with berley. This can be sloppy bread used liberally (with the occasional dry crust that will float to indicate the direction of any current), supplemented by weed scraped from nearby rocks.

Rigs

The lightly weighted bait rig No. 3 with a strong leader is very effective. The weight of the sinker should be able to carry the bait slowly towards the bottom. The floating bait method can be used with rig No. 7 or 7A.

How to hook

The bait should be cast to wash around as it slowly sinks where no float is used. With a float, the bait may have to be adjusted to find the depth at which the fish are feeding. The line between the angler and the bait should be direct. The silver drummer is less likely to nip at the bait like a rock blackfish and the strength of its fast dive will invariably hook the fish. It is then the angler's problem to overcome the power of this stocky fish, which is almost immovable side-on in any swell, begins. It is less likely to dive for rock crevices or cover but the areas in which it is caught will have many line-parting rocks.

Edibility

The large fish are coarse and tough. Smaller fish should be killed and gutted and wellcleaned as soon as caught.

The fillets, which should be skinned, are quite palatable.

EMPEROR

There are numerous fish called emperors in the sub-tropical and tropical waters of Australia. Three have been selected arbitrarily but many other emperors, which are usually smaller, are caught in the same environments while fishing. As the emperors inhabit similar waters and possess similar habits,the fishing information is applicable to all and appears after the individual descriptions. The very popular **red emperor** belongs to a different family, the genus *Lutjanus*, and it is treated separately. Nevertheless, for practical purposes its entry follows the others, which are: long-nosed (*shown below*), spangled, sweetlip, and red-finned emporers.

EMPEROR, LONG-NOSED
Lethrinella miniata

Identification

This emperor identifies itself. If the long-pointed and slanting snout does not provide the evidence, then the very distinct red mark around the lips will. It is also an attractively coloured fish, its body being a greenish shade, with brown markings towards the dorsal area. The green tone fades to white on the belly. Its bright red spots tend to be arranged in rows on the dorsal fins and the same colour is quite clear in the tail, ventral fin and anal fin.

There is more of a blue look to the pectoral fins. The long-nosed emperor has curved canine-like teeth in the front of its mouth.

Size

This emperor can reach as much as 8 kilograms in weight.

EMPEROR, SPANGLED
Lethrinus nebulosus

OTHER NAMES: **GREEN SNAPPER, MORWONG, SAND BREAM, SAND SNAPPER, YELLOW SWEETLIP, NORTH-WEST SNAPPER, PIG-FACED BREAM**

Identification

This fish is regarded by some as the most handsome of the emperors. The body is a yellow-gold colour with lines of blue spots on its scales — which run lengthwise — tending to produce an olive-yellow hue on the dorsal area and sides. The spots are less conspicuous on the lighter yellowish belly but there are obvious blue dashes on its head and cheeks. Its top lip is yellow and there is a lot of yellow-orange in the fins as well as blue spots and patches. The spangled emperor's front teeth are small and canine. Though its snout is shorter than that of other emperors, it is nevertheless quite prominent.

Size

This fish has been recorded at 8 kilograms in weight. Fish from Western Australia's north-west

coast can be larger. In Western Australia the minimum legal size for a catch is 28 centimetres. Any fish caught below that figure must be released.

EMPEROR, SWEETLIP
Lethrinus chrysostomus

OTHER NAMES: **SWEETLIP, LIPPER, NANNYGAI, RED-THROAT, TRICKY SNAPPER, RED-THROATED SWEETLIP**

Identification

The sweetlip is a very common emperor in the subtropical and tropical waters of Queensland, across the Northern Territory and about half-way down the coastline of Western Australia. Its body is olive-green along the top fading to a silvery belly and it is straddled by distinct dark bands which grow faint as they narrow towards the belly. These bands disappear shortly after death, so it may well be that they are caused by stress rather than being a permanent marking. The fish is said to be a dull silver colour when caught at night, but the same bands are present and similarly disappear on death. The head and dorsal fin are a reddish-brown; the other fins range from pink to red. The inside of its mouth is red, particularly the area near the corner of its lips. It has several canine teeth at the front of each jaw.

Size

It is relatively common to catch this emperor at around 2 to 3 kilograms, though it is known to grow to 8 kilograms. Fish from the north-west Australian coastline are perhaps heavier.

EMPEROR, RED-FINNED
Lethrinus fraenatus

OTHER NAMES: **BLUE-LINED EMPEROR, BROWN KELP-FISH, BROWN MORWONG, CORAL BREAM, GREY SWEETLIP, PIGGY, RED-THROAT SNAPPER BREAM, SQUIRE, SWEETLIP**

Identification

This emperor has the most extensive southerly

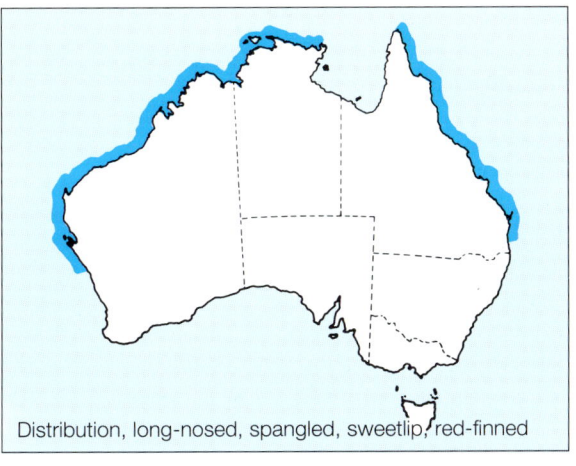
Distribution, long-nosed, spangled, sweetlip, red-finned

range of the emperors, having been caught in waters below the Queensland — New South Wales border, though it is more abundant in the north. It has the prominent pointed nose of other emperors, but with a slight dip in the vicinity of the eye instead of a straight line. It is fawn to olive with a blush of pink on the top of its body, which grows paler towards the belly. This fish also exhibits a change of colour after death — the brownish splotches on the body becoming almost indistinct after death. The head is a brownish shade and there are red-pink shades on the dorsal fins and a bluish edge to its pectoral and pelvic fins. It has the canine front teeth on both jaws.

Size

The maximum size reached by the red-finned emperor is about 60 centimetres, though it is usually caught at half this size.
The minimum length for a legal catch in Queensland is 30 centimetres.

Breeding

Little is known about the red-finned emperor's breeding habits but juveniles spend time in coastal estuaries and mangrove creeks.

Habits

All the emperors are predators that devour a wide range of fish, prawns, crustaceans and molluscs. They inhabit coastal and reef waters, feeding over sandflats, above dead coral areas, and amongst the coral niggerheads.
These fish will bite during the day or night. In fact, all emperors are voracious biters and strong fighting fish. When hooked, they surprisingly show less of the survival instinct that urges them to run for their rocky or coral environment than most other reef fish when hooked.

Distribution

The more southerly range varies but in general the emperors are confined to the warmer waters, the exception being the red-finned emperor. These and other emperors are common on most reefs throughout the tropics and down the west coast as far as Geraldton.
The spangled emperor is often encountered in water shallower than the others will enter. There are few such locations where land-based anglers can fish for them on Australia's east coast but the fish is regularly taken by anglers employing baits or lures in many parts of the north-west of Western Australia.

When to fish

The habitats of emperors are located in the regions of the long wet season. While the fish will bite all year the more comfortable months to fish are autumn to early summer. All emperors bite during the day or night. In the north-west, with its extreme tides, the top of the high tide in some areas is best for shore-based anglers or at the bottom of the tide if they are fishing reasonably deep water.

Where to fish

Emperors are usually found on the edges of reefs in deep water and on sandy openings between reefs. Unweighted baits floated over seabed rubble or dead coral is a good place to try, particularly for spangled emperor, and deep holes in rocky areas close inshore.

Tackle

Heavy handlines of 30 kilograms breaking-strain are used when bait fishing from boats or with boat rods and the winch type of reels. A medium fast taper rod of about 2.5 metres, with power in its mid-section and butt, matched with either a medium to heavy baitcasting reel or a heavier style of threadline reel, are an effective combination, bottom fishing with bait or casting and retrieving lures and jigging. In this case, use about 12 to15 kilograms breaking-strain line. If fishing from the shore, use a rod of about 3.5 to 4 metres long that is suitable for overhead, threadline or a sidecast reel.

Baits

The emperors are not fussy. They eat fillets of most fish, small fish such as pilchards, mullet, whitebait etc., and octopus tentacles, squid, crustaceans etc.

Rigs

For bottom fishing, rig No. 3A, 4 or 4A with a sinker to suit the current or depth are satisfactory. If you are floating your bait, the unweighted rig No. 2 is a sound choice or rig No. 3A if a little weight is needed. If casting and retrieving select rig No. 7. Hooks can be in sizes 4/0 or 6/0 — extra strong. A ganged hook set-up is prone to snagging but it can be used with a heavy leader instead of nylon-coated wire trace. A wire trace is a safeguard against large well-fanged species as well as reducing break-off on coral.

How to hook

These fish are competing for their food against many equally voracious fish, yet they do not have a

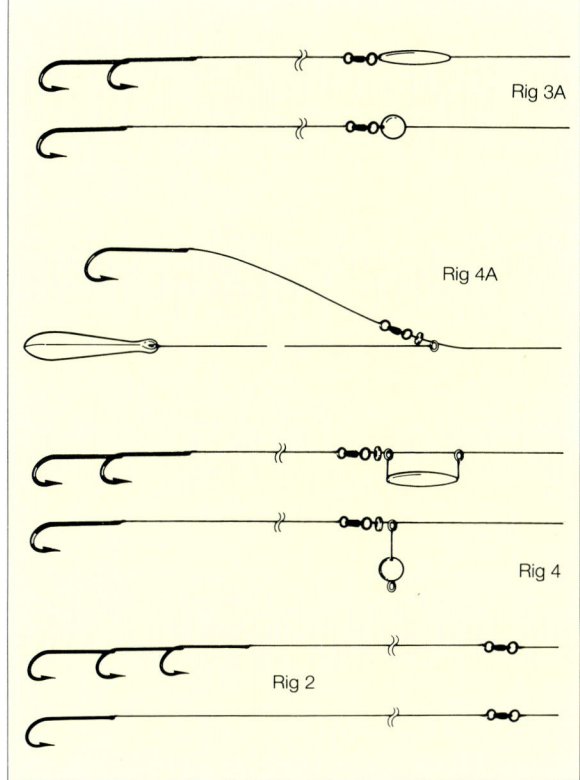

particularly hungry bite. To hook these fish the angler should simply tighten the line as he feels the weight of the fish.

Hint

The emperors — sweetlip in particular — can be attracted to the surface with a berley of oily fish pieces or cubes. Float a bait in the berley trail.

Edibility

The emperors are all fine food fishes and can be cooked by any of the usual methods. One cannot emphasise how imperative it is that all fish caught in tropical waters must be quickly killed, cleaned and kept on ice.

EMPEROR, RED
Lutjanus sebae

OTHER NAMES: **KING SNAPPER, GOVERNMENT BREAM, QUEENFISH, RED KELP**

This fish should really be called a sea-perch or snapper, belonging as it does to the Lutjanidae family. But though it looks least like the other emperors, it is known as one far and wide. This is a popular fish with all anglers because it is a tough hard fighter that is relatively common. Anglers visiting the tropics for the first time who have not had the good fortune — or good management — to catch a barramundi, a coral trout or some other game fish of the area, are quite satisfied if they can land a good-sized emperor, especially if they can find someone to provide the photographic proof.

Identification

This is a vividly-coloured fish with a rich salmon-red body. Three dark bands form a broad arrow on its scales — one from the mouth along the head to the beginning of the back; the second running vertically in the vicinity of the pectoral fins; and the third sweeping from the bottom tip of the tail through the peduncle to the rear dorsal fin. These markings led to one of its common names, government bream, though they disappear or are indistinct in large red emperors.

They are very prominent on immature specimens, which have pale bodies. This fish has a less pointed snout than other emperors and an almost square tail.

Size

Red emperors grow to more than a metre long and about 25 kilograms in weight. In Western Australia the minimum legal size is 28 centimetres; it is 35 centimetres in Queensland.

Breeding

Little is known.

Habits

This emperor is a reef dweller that is usually taken in deep water of about 30 metres. A reef edge with a series of scattered coral niggerheads and a sandy bottom is one area the fish is found. It is a fish which is less active and less eager to eat during the day.

In the main, the best red emperors are caught at night. They frequently school, so when one is caught the chance of landing several is high. They feed on fish, crustaceans, and molluscs.

Distribution

This is a tropical water fish and while the occasional red emperor is caught as far south as Moreton Bay, it is usually found in numbers from about Rockhampton north. On the north-west coast of Australia, the red emperor is caught as far south as the Abrolhos Islands.

A magnificent red emperor.

When to fish

The night is by far the best time to catch a red emperor, though fish can appear in catches made during the day.

Where to fish

Though the red emperor strays into relatively shallow waters from time to time, you are far more likely to find them in waters at least 30 metres

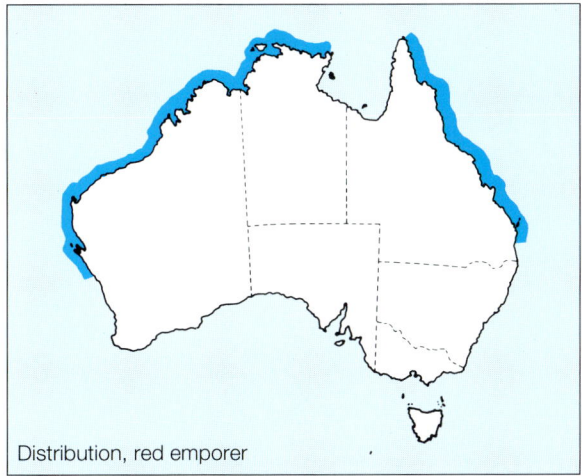

Distribution, red emporer

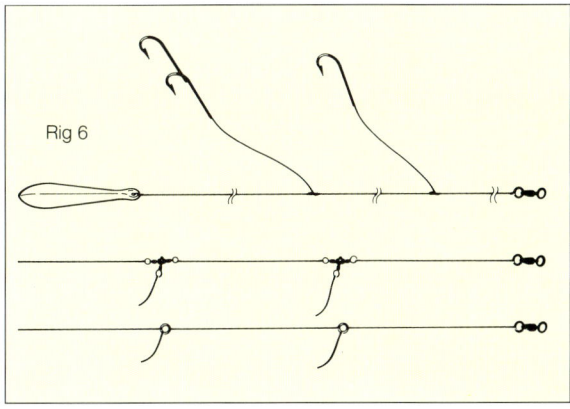

Rig 6

deep. If you can find the edge of a reef that plunges to this depth or deeper, from which niggerheads are scattered and the bottom is sandy, you have a promising location.

Tackle

By far the most practical outfits are a handline (on a caster) or a line on a deck winch or a short boat rod with a simple winch type of reel. Line should of 30 kilograms breaking-strain or more. A heavy-weight rod of about 2 metres, with a strongly geared threadline or baitcasting reel, is also suitable.

The lines on these should be about 15 kilogram breaking-strain. Hooks in sizes about 6/0 or 8/0 and extra strong are best.

Baits

Fillets of almost any fish are good bait but strips of the belly of mackerel or fillets of tuna are excel-lent. The red emperor will also take half garfish or blue pilchards.

Rigs

The bottom rig with the sinker about 50 centi-metres to a metre below the bait and one or two droppers (rig No. 6) is suitable.

How to hook

The bite of a red emperor is not tentative. As soon as the weight is felt a firm tightening of the line should hook the fish. This will precipitate a battle of strength between the angler and the fish, a battle long recalled if the angler boats a large red emperor. It is a powerful fish that resists power-fully!

Edibility

The red emperor is an esteemed table fish. It is one of the few examples of a fish whose flesh is equally tasty, whether from a large and old fish or a younger and smaller one. The flesh is white with good flavour. A whole fish bakes magnificently.

FLATHEAD

OTHER NAME: **LIZARDS**

Though the flathead has always been appreciated as a fine food fish it was until recently regarded as without merit as a sporting fish. In the past decade, however, increasing numbers of anglers are learning that if they use lures with light spinning or baitcasting (even saltwater fly) outfits to tempt some of these fish, they can find themselves engaged with a surprisingly fast predator and a very worthy sporting fish.

There are more than three dozen species of flathead in Australian waters. The following members of this fish family (over which genus and species the ichthyologists, biologists, and sundry experts are left to their continuing arguments) are those readily available to anglers from shore or boat. For convenience in identification, all of these flathead are first described together. Fishing methods follow the individual descriptions — and thankfully they apply equally to them all. Initial descriptions include their distribution, distinguishing features and habitats together with size and any particular habits or behaviour that each might have. There is one behavioural aspect that all flathead share: they conceal

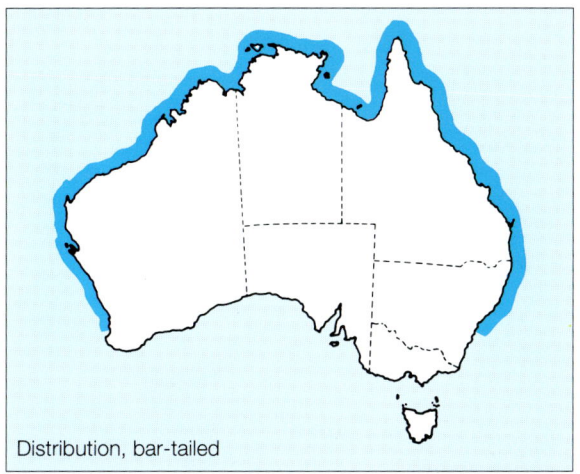

Distribution, bar-tailed

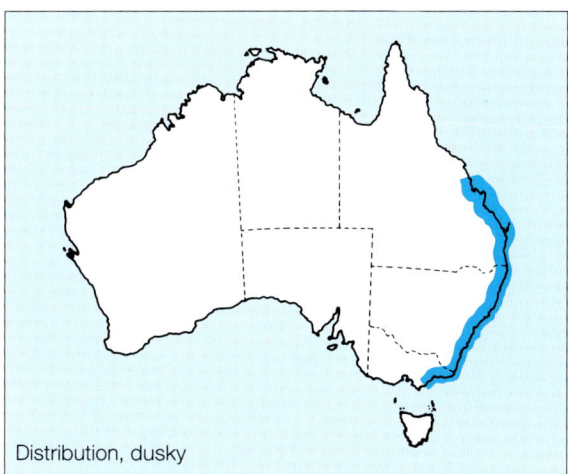

Distribution, dusky

themselves on the sea floor with excellent camouflage and wait for food to come to them, whether it is swimming, crawling or being swept helplessly by the currents.

FLATHEAD, BAR-TAILED
Platycephalus endrachtensis

Identification
This flathead is brown to dark brown with numerous darker spots. It also has an uneven yellow marking on the top of the caudal fin, above black bars.

Size
The bar-tailed flathead grows to a metre in length. A minimum legal size for a catch in Western Australia and Queensland is 30 centimetres long.

Habits
This fish has a preference for silted bottoms in estuaries and rivers.

Distribution
Bar-tailed flathead are found in northern New South Wales, along the Queensland coast, the Northern Territory coast, and it is one of the most common flathead on the West Australian coastline as far south as Fremantle.

FLATHEAD, DUSKY
Platycephalus fuscus

OTHER NAMES: **BLACK FLATHEAD, MUD FLATHEAD, RIVER FLATHEAD**

Identification
Easily the largest flathead in Australia, its colour varies from a light sandy shade with small brown spots and darkish blotches, to almost black with white spots (that disappear after death). The dusky flathead can be distinguished from the others by a blotch or spot on the top area of its tail. This flathead is relatively common on sand and silt bottoms in coastal rivers, bays, harbours, along beaches, and near inshore rocks in waters up to 30 metres deep.

Size
This flathead grows to at least 1.5 metres and is said to reach 15 kilograms in weight. All dusky flathead over 60 centimetres are female.
The minimum legal size for a dusky flathead catch in New South Wales is 33 centimetres; in Queensland the minimum size is 30 centimetres; in Victoria the minimum size is 25 centimetres..

Habits
Large dusky flathead are frequently caught well up rivers or creeks in winter, though they are supposed to move to the lower reaches and even to sea for spawning during the summer — autumn period, returning to upriver in spring. This fish has been caught beyond the tidal influence in rivers. Their numbers increase in the lower reaches of estuaries and along the beaches before spawning.

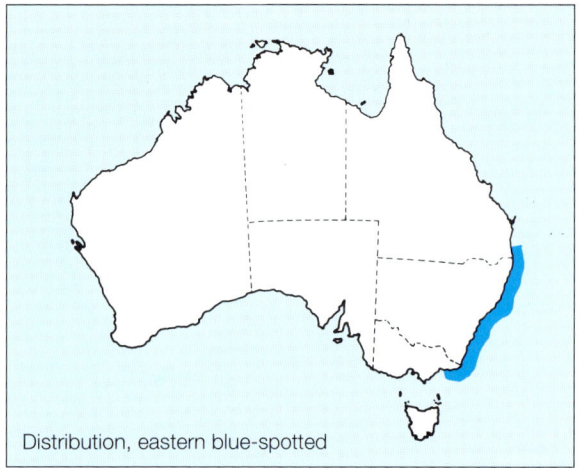

Distribution, eastern blue-spotted

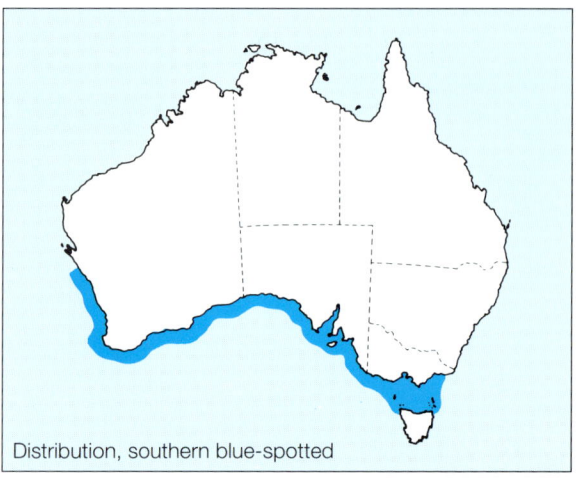

Distribution, southern blue-spotted

Distribution

Dusky flathead inhabit waters from mid-Queensland down the east coast to Wilson's Promontory, mainly in estuaries and bays and coastal lakes.

FLATHEAD, EASTERN BLUE-SPOTTED
Platycephalus caeruleopunctatus

Identification

Closely related to the southern blue-spotted flathead, this fish is either sandy coloured with white spots or a reddish to dark brown with blue spots. It has unevenlyshaped blotches on the tail.

Size

The eastern blue-spotted flathead grows to about 70 centimetres. The minimum legal size for a catch in Victoria is 25 centimetres.

Habits

This flathead prefers sandy bottoms and is usually found in coastal waters.

Distribution

Eastern blue-spotted flathead are found along the New South Wales coastline and in eastern Victorian waters.

FLATHEAD, SOUTHERN BLUE-SPOTTED
Platycephalus speculator

OTHER NAMES: **YANK FLATHEAD**

Identification

This fish is easily mistaken for the eastern blue-spotted flathead. It has a sandy to darkish brown colour with white or blue spots on its back and a row of 3 to 5 round black marks on the end of its tail fin.

Size

The southern blue-spotted flathead grows to 90 centimetres.
The minimum legal size for a catch in Victoria is 25 centimetres; it is 30 centimetres in Western Australia and Tasmania.

Habits

It prefers sand and weed sections of shallow bays where there is protection from rough waters.

Distribution

The southern blue-spotted flathead is found in Victoria, northern Tasmania, South Australia and around the West Australian coast as far north as the Murchison River.

FLATHEAD, LONG-HEADED
Leviprora inops

Identification

There are two forms of the long-headed flathead in West Australian waters: one is wideheaded and the other narrowheaded (marine scientists speculate that the latter may in fact be a separate species). These fish are recognised by their long head and a band on the rear half of the front dorsal fin —

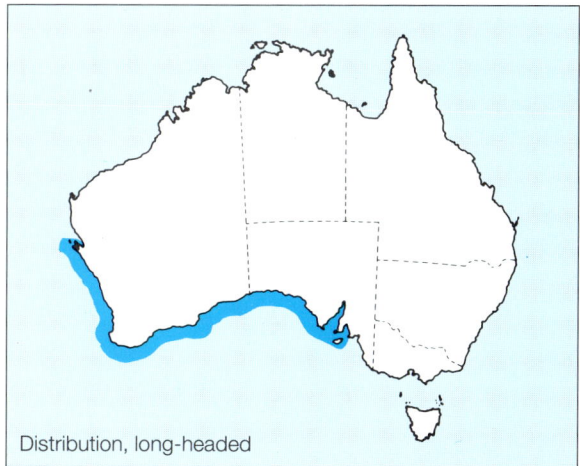

Distribution, long-headed

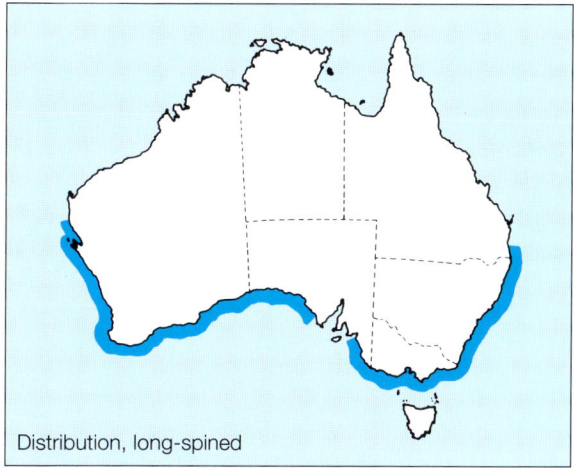

Distribution, long-spined

from the rear base towards the front top. The colours of these fish vary but they are usually sandy coloured or mottled with brownish blotches, which turn a dark brown after capture.

Size

These flathead grow to approximately 61 centimetres.

Habit

Long-headed flathead are quite common in coastal sand and weed zones.

Distribution

These fish are found from Kangaroo Island in South Australia across to Western Australia and as far north as Shark Bay.

FLATHEAD, LONG-SPINED
Platycephalus longispinis

OTHER NAMES: **SPIKY, WESTERN SAND**

Identification

The long-spined flathead is sandy to light brown in colour. It can be identified by the long spine on the side of its head and the yellow colouring on the upper half of the tail.

Size

This flathead is known to grow to 34 centimetres. Minimum size for a legal catch in Western Australia is 30 centimetres; it is 25 centimetres in Victoria.

Habits

This is a common flathead, which inhabits sand and weed areas, preferring deeper offshore waters of up to 100 metres.

Distribution

The long-spined flathead is found from Moreton Bay in Queensland down to about Lakes Entrance in Victoria and in South Australian and West Australian waters as far north as Carnarvon. It is probably more abundant on the east and west coasts of Australia.

FLATHEAD, MARBLED
Platycephalus marmoratus

Identification

The colours of this flathead range between a reddish to yellowish-brown that is mottled — "marbled" — with pale and dark spots and blotches. It has a distinct white border to its caudal, anal and pelvic fins.

Size

The marbled flathead grows to 60 centimetres approximately.

Habits

These fish dwell in deeper off-shore waters, ranging from 40 to 100 metres.

Distribution

The marbled flathead is found in Queensland and New South Wales waters south to the Eden area and on the opposite side of the continent, between Geographe Bay and Ocean Reef, north of Perth.

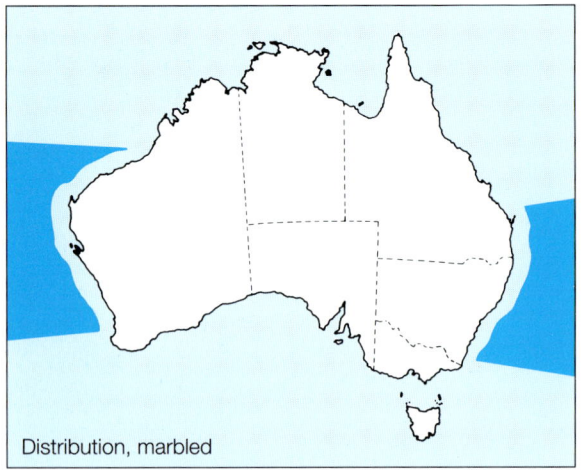

Distribution, marbled

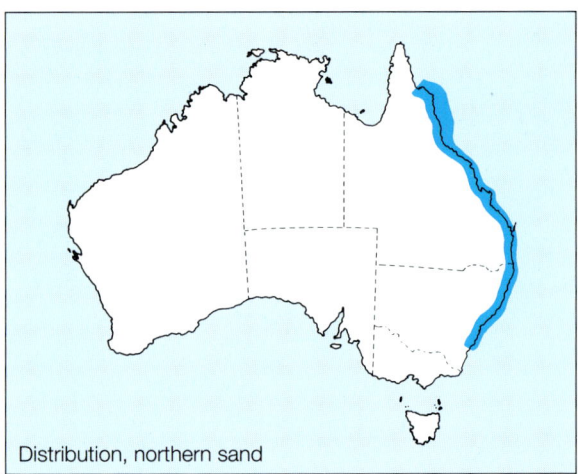

Distribution, northern sand

FLATHEAD, NORTHERN SAND
Platycephalus arenarius

Identification
The northern sand flathead is very similar to the bar-tailed flathead, the most pronounced distinction being that it lacks the latter's yellow colouring on the top of the caudal fin.

Size
Northern sand flathead grow to about 45 centimetres. A minimum legal catch in Queensland is 30 centimetres. The limit in New South Wales is 33 centimetres.

Habits
This flathead prefers the sandy bottoms of estuaries, bays and coastal waters.

Distribution
Northern sand flathead inhabit waters north from northern New South Wales to north Queensland, though fish have occasionally been sighted as far south as Jervis Bay.

FLATHEAD, SOUTHERN SAND
Platycephalus bassensis

OTHER NAMES: **SLIMY FLATHEAD**

Identification
This light brown flathead has dark brown to red-dish-brown spots. It also has a dark marking of almost triangular shape at the base of its caudal fin. The area between the edge of the marking and the end of the fin is off-white.

Size
Southern sand flathead grow to 46 centimetres. The minimum legal size for a catch in New South Wales is 33 centimetres; in Victoria it is 25 centimetres; in Tasmania and Western Australia it is 30 centimetres.

Habits
This fish is usually encountered when fishing on sandy bottoms in reasonably shallow coastal waters — to about 40 metres — and in inlets, bays and coastal saltwater lakes.

Distribution
Southern sand flathead are present south from around the middle of the New South Wales coast. Numbers are greater in Victorian and Tasmanian waters. This fish is comparatively scarce in South Australia and rarely seen in Western Australian waters.

FLATHEAD, ROCK
Leviprora laevigatus

OTHER NAMES: **GRASSY FLATHEAD**

Identification
This flathead has a very short snout and obvious brown to greenish-brown spots along its sides. The top spine on the side of its head is longer than the lower spine.

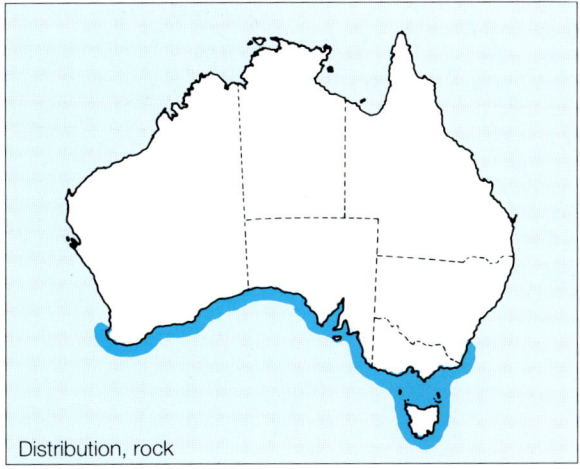

Distribution, rock

Distribution, tassel-snouted

Size

This fish can reach a maximum size of 81 centimetres.

The minimum legal size for a catch is 25 centimetres in Victoria and 30 centimetres in Tasmania.

Habits

The rock flathead prefers seagrass beds and reefs in the same area in off-shore waters from 3 to 40 metres.

FLATHEAD, TASSEL-SNOUTED
Thysanophrys cirronasus

Identification

The colour of this fish can be white, brown, orange, red and purple. It has prominent spines on the head and a dark bar on the rear edge of its front dorsal fin.

Size

The tassel-snouted flathead grows to about 38 centimetres.

The minimum size for a catch in Victoria is 25 centimetres. The limit is 30 centimetres in Western Australia.

Habits

This flathead inhabits sandy areas around the rocks and weed beds of inshore waters up to about 30 metres deep.

Distribution

Tassel-snouted flathead may be found from Newcastle in New South Wales, down the east coast, and

around the southern coast to west of Australian waters. It is not, however, found in Tasmanian waters.

The tassel-snouted flathead relies on its effective camouflage.

FLATHEAD, TIGER
Neoplatycephalus richardsoni

Identification

This fish is readily recognised by the bright red-orange spots on its head and body — the older the fish, the more spots it displays. It also has large teeth on the roof of its mouth.

Size

This flathead grows to 65 centimetres. The minimum legal size for a catch is 33 centimetres in New

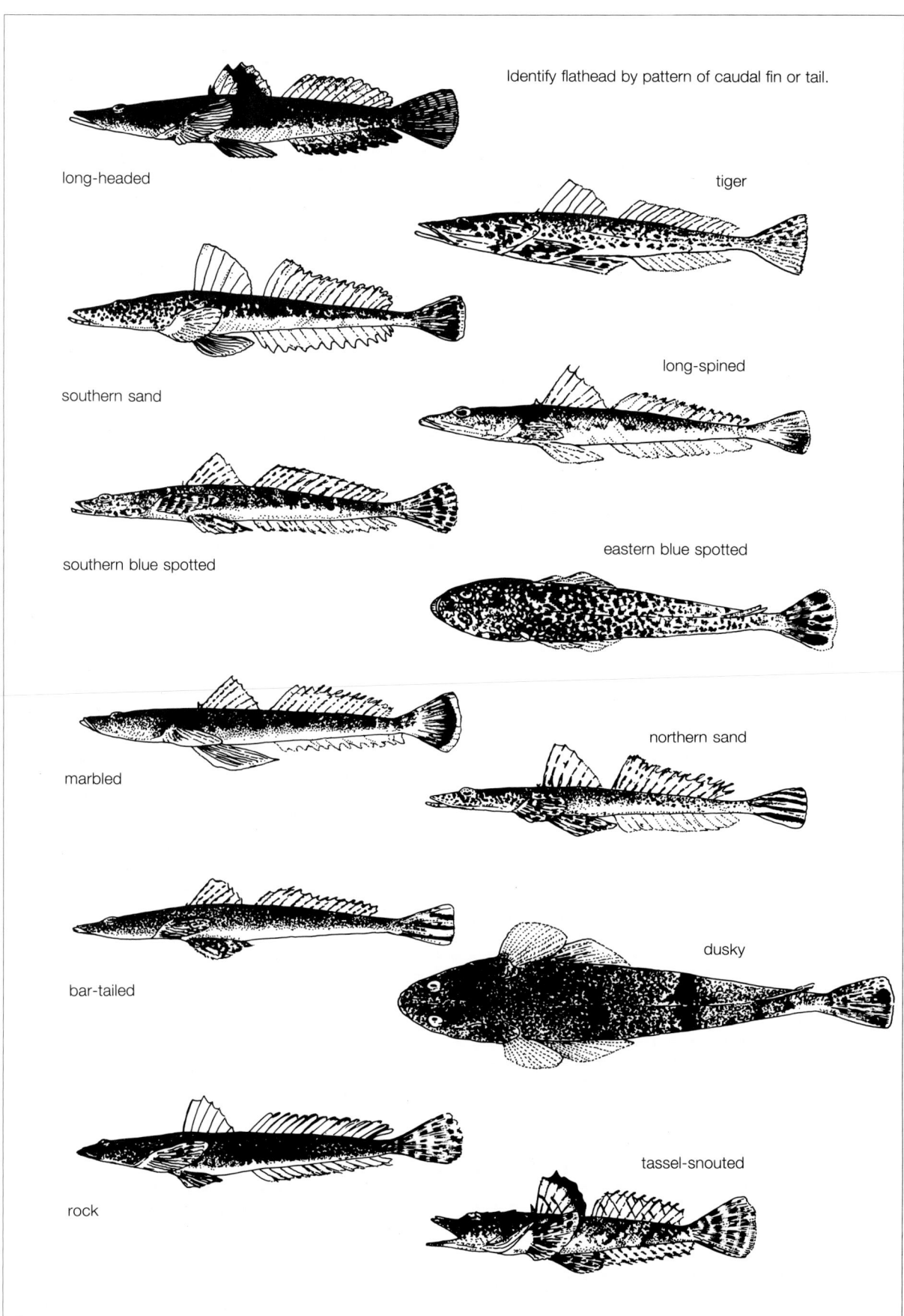

Identify flathead by pattern of caudal fin or tail.

long-headed

tiger

southern sand

long-spined

southern blue spotted

eastern blue spotted

marbled

northern sand

bar-tailed

dusky

rock

tassel-snouted

South Wales, 25 centimetres in Victoria, and 30 centimetres in Tasmania.

Habits

The tiger flathead is found in coastal waters at depths of 50 to 300 metres. Larger fish move in from the deep to the shallow range to spawn in summer to autumn. This fish will venture into the deeper inshore bays of Tasmania.

Distribution

The tiger flathead is limited to an area from the northern coast of New South Wales to near the southern extremity of eastern Tasmania. It may also be present in the eastern end of Bass Strait. It is claimed that commercial fishing has severely reduced its numbers in New South Wales waters.

In those States where these minimum lengths are proclaimed, no self-respecting angler would consider retaining a flathead of less than legal size. While the foregoing information will help to identify the different species, I should warn you that variations in their colour, which are not uncommon, can make accurate identification very testing. It is always far better to err on the side of caution and release all flathead below the legal minimum of that State regardless of whether it applies only to some species.

Forunately for the bewildered angler, at least all flathead *behave* in much the same way. The following fishing information applies to them all.

When to fish

Flathead can be caught throughout the year. Those inhabiting the rivers, estuaries and beaches, however, are caught in greatest numbers in the late spring, summer and early autumn months. These are the times when the fish congregate to spawn in the lower parts of the estuaries or inshore areas. [For unknown reasons, some very large flathead remain in the uppermost reaches of coastal creeks and rivers. Such specimens may be caught in the autumn and winter months.] The deeper water species also move to shallower inshore areas in the same periods. Most anglers seek flathead during the day, although bright sunlight on relatively shallow water is usually an unproductive time. Early morning and late afternoons are the best times.

Where to fish

For inshore members of the flathead clan, the ideal locations are those where this ambushing predator can bury itself in the sand or mud or in weed and

Tiger flathead.

pounce on any prey that swims into range or is carried within striking distance by the current. Such spots are at the ends or edges of sandbars, the borders of weed beds, the sides of channels, and alongside sea walls, breakwaters or groynes, particularly where the rocks in such constructions meet the sand, mud or silt. In places where there are mangroves or where other tree trunks and branches have fallen into the water, it is not unusual for a flathead to take up a position on a limb — still and perfectly camouflaged — from which it attacks any small fish, crabs, prawns, etc. that pass. Flathead of the deep, or those that feed around rocks in somewhat shallower waters, will similarly blend into their preferred habitat in a position from which they can pounce on any passing food.

Tackle

If you are drifting in a boat in estuaries, ocean bays or offshore, the humble handline can be more effective than rod and reel. It gives the angler a more sensitive "feel" or "touch" as the bait drifts across the bottom or is "yo-yoed" (jigged up and down). The breaking-strain of the line need not exceed 5 kilograms for estuary or inshore fishing. Some of the offshore flathead, however, are located where snapper or other large fish are also likely to bite as well, so lines can be heavier there. Single-handed threadline or baitcasting outfits can also be used from boats in estuaries for drifting, casting and retrieving baits or lures. Lines about 3 to 5 kilograms breaking-strain are adequate.

If casting baits or lures from the beach or rocks, use a longer rod of about 3 to 4 metres with medium threadline, overhead or sidecast reels, spooled with line between 5 to 8 kilograms breaking-strain line. Hooks — single or ganged, depending on the bait — should be of a wide gape style.

Baits

The flathead lives on small fish, prawns, crabs,

crustaceans, worms, etc. If there is a flathead in the area, a live "poddy" mullet or yellowtail is almost irresistible to them and live prawns are taken greedily. Dead bait is also acceptable if it is yellowtail, pilchards, whole bait, sardines and similar, as well as fillets of many other fish. Sand or beach worms, nippers, squid, octopus tentacles etc. are also taken. Even a fillet of another flathead's belly can be a very successful bait.

Lures that catch flathead are the wobbler type, plastic fish imitations, "twister" types and deep diving plugs. So do lead-head jigs jerked along the bottom. These fish may also respond to large saltwater flies fished close to the bottom.

Berley

A berley of minced stale bait, prawn heads, rice with canned dog food or similar can bring flathead to the area and set them on the bite. It can be used from a moored boat or off a breakwall etc. and from shore positions where the angler's bait can be drifted in the berley stream.

Rigs

If you are using live bait, the running sinker rig (No. 3A or 4, both with a leader about 1 metre) is suitable if you are fishing from a moored or drifting boat, as well as when casting from banks in estuaries. The best sinker is a barrel or ledger type. Both will stir up the bottom to alert the flathead and slide through mud and weed patches. In still estuary water, it is worth trying a float rig (No. 7E for example) with live or dead bait suspended just above the bottom. When fishing offshore, use Rig Nos 4A and 5, depending on the bottom and depth. The movement of the boat should animate the bait sufficiently to attract a flathead. If casting and retrieving baits or lures, rig Nos 2 or 9 work well.

A wire trace is not necessary for flathead. This fish rarely, if ever, bites through the line until it has been brought to the surface, when it will shake its head vigorously from side to side, sawing the line with its fine teeth. The fish should be netted below the water surface. Where a net is not practical, the same rigs with ganged hooks can be used, provided you are not using live bait. Lures usually hook a flathead in the jaw area.

How to hook

Despite its reputation as a skulking ambusher, the flathead indicates interest in most baits by a tentative shake or "picking" bite. There is some evidence that the flathead may grab a prey from the

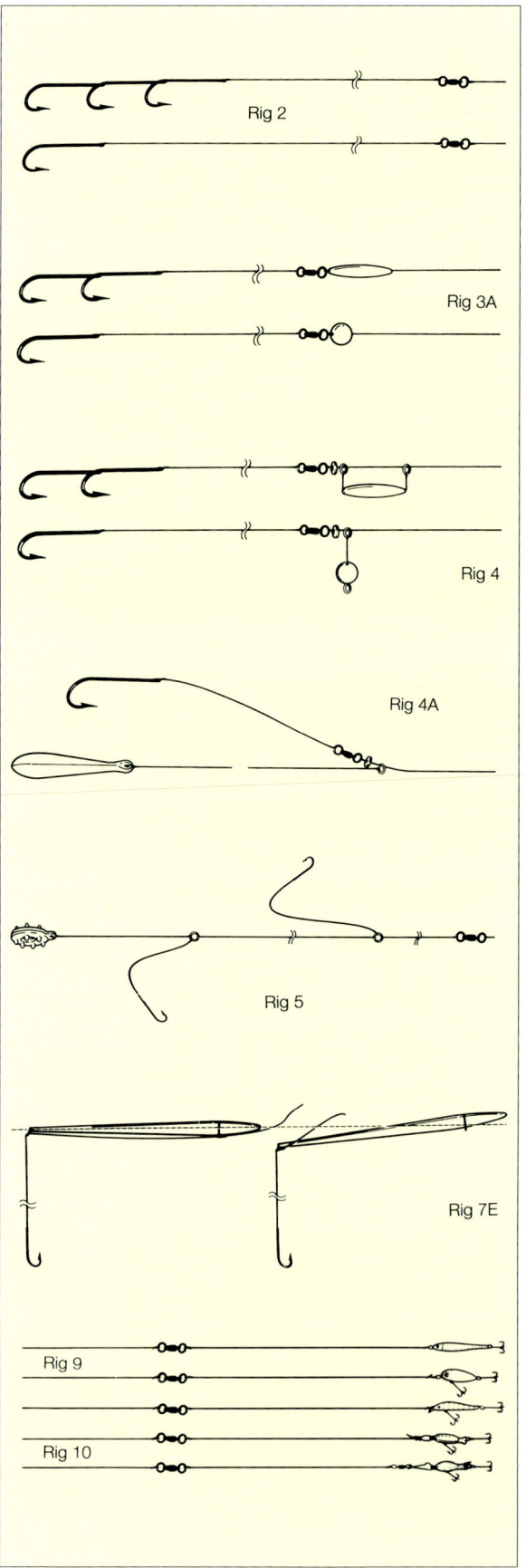

side and the action felt by the angler is the fish manipulating the bait to a swallowing position. When this shaking is felt the angler should let the flathead have a metre to 1.5 metres of line, before tightening the line and maintaining pressure once the weight of the fish is felt. Flathead are adept at dislodging a hook or lure if the pressure is eased for a moment.

Hint

In estuaries where there are regular prawn runs in the summer, large flathead can often be caught at night. Either fish with a live prawn by casting and retrieving over or alongside weed beds, or float a live prawn in the same area under a light float. The prawn should be hooked on two or three ganged hooks (Tarpon style are ideal). When casting and retrieving the prawn should be retrieved with the current.

Handle all flathead with care. They have dorsal spines capable of inflicting painful wounds and the sharp edges of their gill covers can cut.

Edibility

Any one of the three dozen or so flathead in Australia are excellent eating. The flesh is white, firm and flaky. Its fillets are a tasty meal, grilled or fried.

Other regulations

Flathead can be found in aquatic reserves, marine parks and closed areas of estuaries in some States. Check whether fishing is permitted there with the local fisheries officials or angling organisations.

[The author acknowledges with gratitude the assistance of Mr Barry Hutchins, a Curator in the Fish Department of the West Australian Museum, and co-author of *Sea Fishes of Southern Australia* (Swainston Publishing, Perth, 1986) for the scientific names of the flathead described, along with some particular descriptions and locations.]

FLOUNDER

A large number of flounder inhabit Australian waters. These flat fish undergo a remarkable change between the time they hatch and grow to a few centimetres in length. Though the fish starts life swimming in a "normal" upright position, it gradually tilts, during which time one of its eyes move around or through its head to locate itself near the other. The sightless side then becomes its underside, the fish's body begins to flatten, and its swimming action changes. The flounder eventually becomes a perfectly adapted bottom dweller, with an ability to alter its colour like a chameleon to blend into the surrounding sand or silt. Some flounder have their eyes on the left or right side of their body, when viewed from above. These are identified as "left-handed" or "true" flounder or "right-handed" flounder.

All flounder have similar habitats. Their location and appropriate angling methods follow the identification, size and distribution details. Flounder can be distinguished from sole by the prominent lower jaw and distinct cheekbone.

Queensland flounder or halibut.

FLOUNDER, GREENBACK
Rhombosolea tapirina

Identification

This flat fish has a wide range of colours and may or may not have different sized blotches scattered over its body. It may be green, a greenish-grey, grey, or tan to brownish. It has a quite pointed head and a square tail.

Size

The greenback flounder grows to about 35 to 40 centimetres.
The minimum legal catch for all flounder in Western Australia, Victoria and Tasmania is 23 centimetres.

Distribution

This fish is found in southern New South Wales, Victoria, Tasmania, South Australia and southern Western Australia, mostly on the sand or silt floors of estuaries and coastal bays.

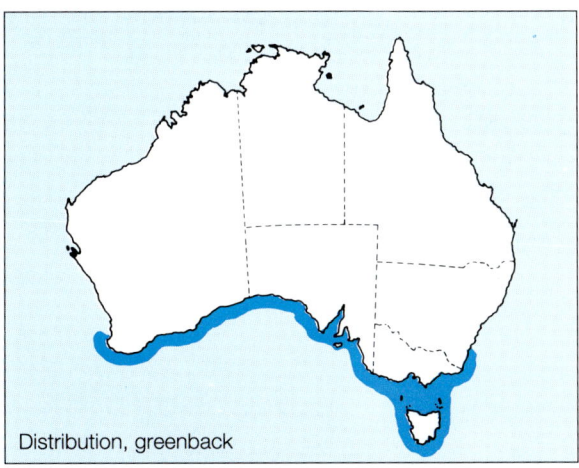

Distribution, greenback

FLOUNDER, HALIBUT
Psettodes erumei

OTHER NAMES: **QUEENSLAND HALIBUT, TROPICAL HALIBUT**

Identification

This flounder-like fish is distinguished by its large mouth and obvious sharp teeth. Its eyes can be located on its left or right-hand side. Broad dark bands on younger fish disappear with age. The adult is dusky brown. Unlike the other flounder,

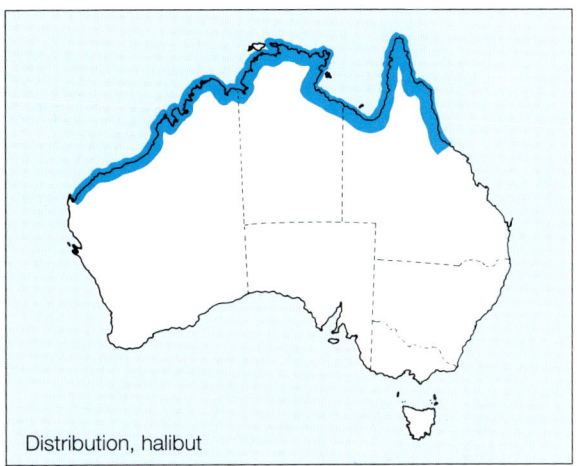

Distribution, halibut

this fish swims upright, but it usually "rests" on its side on the bottom.

Size

This flounder may grow to more than 60 centimetres in length.

Distribution

This is a fish of the deeper waters and estuaries in northern Queensland, the Northern Territory and Western Australia.

FLOUNDER, LARGE-TOOTHED
Pseudorhombus arsius

Identification

This flounder's colour varies from fawn brown to dark, depending on habitat. It has two clearly visible dark spots on the body. There are several prominent teeth at the front of the mouth. Its tail tends to be pointed.

Size

The large-toothed flounder grows to 50 or more centimetres.
The minimum legal catch for all flounder in Western Australia, Victoria and Tasmania is 23 centimetres.

Distribution

This fish is present in waters right around mainland Australia, though not in Tasmania. It is common in estuaries and bays and in sandy-bottomed offshore waters to 50 metres.

FLOUNDER, LONG-SNOUTED
Ammotretis rostratus

The large-toothed (above) and long-snouted (below) flounder.

Identification
This is usually a pale fawn to greenish-tan flounder but it can occasionally be quite dark with pale spots.

Size
The long-snouted flounder is much smaller than the others and it is rarely caught at its maximum size of 30 to 35 centimetres.

Distribution
Flat fish are found from southern New South Wales to Tasmania, Victoria, South Australia and Western Australia.

The following applies to all flounder:

Breeding
Flounder are believed to spawn in inshore and ocean waters, in the late summer to early autumn.

Habits
Flounder are usually found in bays, inlets and estuaries but these fish also inhabit inshore coastal waters as deep as 60 metres or so. They prefer sandy or silt bottoms, where they can feed on small crustaceans, all marine worms and shellfish. A startled flounder displays surprising speed with its undulating swimming action, described by Australian ichthyologist, Gilbert Whitley, as a motion "like the flying carpet of Arabian Nights".

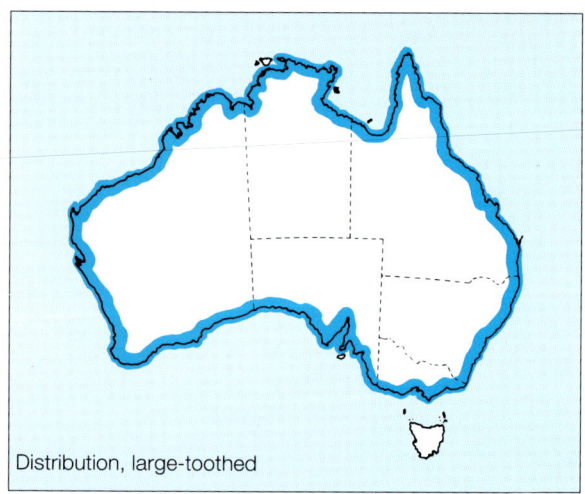

Distribution, large-toothed

When to fish
A flounder is often an incidental catch while fishing for other fish, especially flathead or bream. The spring to autumn period appears to be the best time for flounder in the estuaries.

Where to fish
Flounder can be caught on sandy or silt bottoms where there are indications of small shellfish or crustaceans; or sand-mud areas occupied by worms. It inhabits areas with scattered weed growth and seagrass meadows, which offer an already well-camouflaged fish further protection and a source of food items.

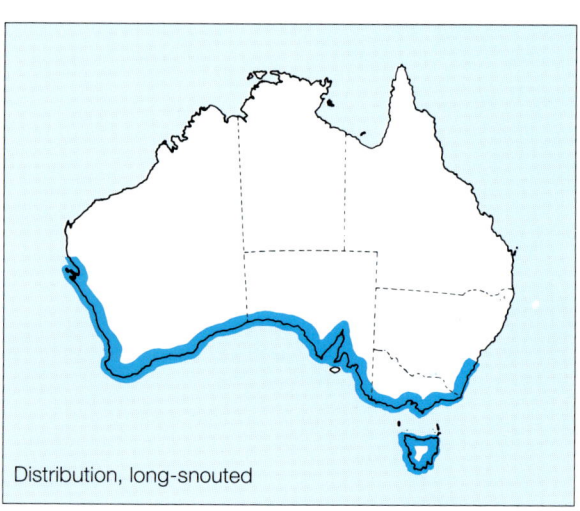

Distribution, long-snouted

Tackle

Despite the fact that the lines, sinkers and rigs used for flathead are much too heavy and the baits too large for flounder, many are caught on such rigs. Gear similar to that used by whiting fishers (who regard the fish as a pleasant bonus) is much more suitable.

Light handlines can be used from a moored or drifting boat, but the ideal is a light rod with a sensitive tip and balanced threadline reel, spooled with 2 or 3 kilograms breaking-strain line. The sinker need only be heavy enough to hold the bait on the bottom. Avoid over doing it. Hooks can be in almost any pattern in sizes about 1 to 4.

Baits

Successful baits are small baits of bloodworms, sand or beach worms, small prawns, live nippers, the flesh from almost any shellfish or bivalve, and slivers of fresh mullet flesh.

Rigs

An unweighted rig No. 2 or a lightly-weighted rig for bait No. 3A are most satisfactory for flounder. Where a current or other conditions require a heavier sinker, the running rig variation No. 4 is suitable. There are some anglers who use tiny trout-size jigs or spoons for flounder — and quite successfully.

How to hook

The bait should be trailed slowly along the bottom with the angler maintaining a direct feel for the bait. The flounder ambushes its food, grabbing a passing meal. Simply continuing to reel in the line will ensure the hook sets.

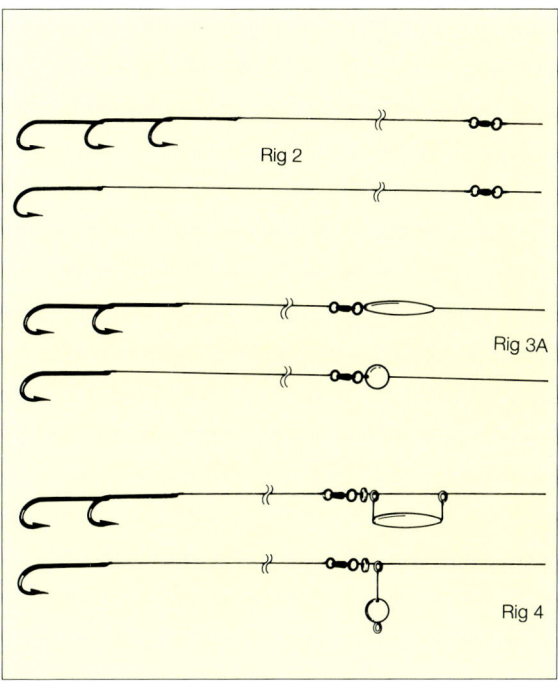

Hint

After having selected a sandflat, or silt bank, or the edge of a weed area to fish, cast and retrieve the bait in a grid pattern until the whole area is covered. A flounder will often follow a bait briefly but then unaccountably settle again and wait— facing in a different direction.

Edibility

Flounder are fine eating but the taste is so delicate it can easily be lost by over cooking or with the use of strong sauces or dressings in the preparation.

GARFISH

One of the oddest facts about the half-dozen garfish most regularly sought by anglers is that although they are all algae and weed-eaters, they are often caught on baits that play no part whatsoever in their normal diet. These baits include dough, gentles (maggots), prawn pieces, shellfish, red meat, even fish cubes — especially if they are of their own kind! All garfish are hectic fighters, quite willing to leap and skitter across the surface. They are fished as much for bait as the table. Fishing information that applies to all garfish follows the individual descriptions.

GARFISH, RIVER
Hyporhamphus ardelio
(Eastern)
Hyporhamphus regularis
(Western)

OTHER NAMES: **BEAKIE, NEEDLE GAR, SPLINTER GAR**

Identification

This garfish, which is very similar to the sea garfish, has a light greenish back with a greyish tinge to the front of its tail fin. It has brownish streaks running along its back. As with all species of garfish, the jaw is full of fine teeth.

Size

The river garfish grows to a maximum length of about 40 centimetres. They are measured from the front on their top jaw to the tip, or top lobe, of the tail.

The minimum legal size for a catch in Victoria is 20 centimetres; the limit is 23 centimetres in Western Australia.

Breeding

River garfish move down from the upper reaches

of estuaries to spawn near the sea entrances, depositing eggs on weeds and sea grasses.

Habit
This fish can be found occasionally in both the brackish and freshwater sections of rivers. It swims close to the surface, especially over weed beds and eel grasses.

Distribution
Hyporhamphus ardelio is regarded as the eastern species and *Hyporhamphus regularis* as the western species, though in reality they are considered indistinguishable. Populations of this fish thrive in the rivers, estuaries and coastal lakes from southern central Queensland to Lakes Entrance on Victoria's eastern coast; and in Western Australia from the Murchison River in the north to Bunbury in the south-west.

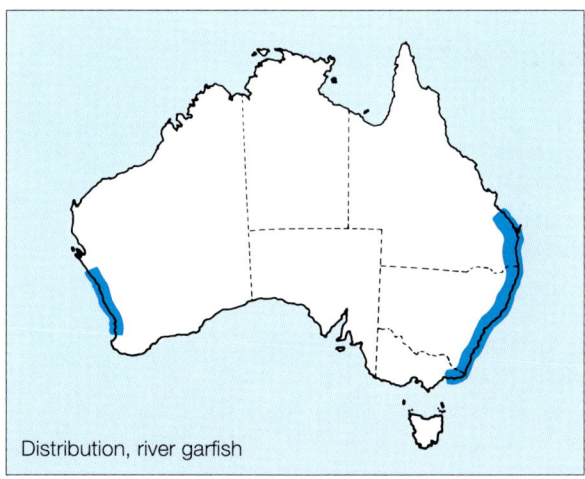
Distribution, river garfish

GARFISH, SEA
Hyporhamphus australis
(Eastern)
Hyporhamphus melanochir
(Western)

OTHER NAME: **BEAKIE**

Identification
Most authorities find it difficult to separate these two related species, preferring to let their location identify them. The sea garfish is a slender fish, very silvery overall with a bright bluish-greenish back.

Sea garfish.

There are three brown lines along its body from the pectoral fins to the tail — a silver band underlines these. The bill or beak has a red colour. Its top jaw is longer than it is broad.

Size
The sea garfish grows to more than 50 centimetres. The minimum legal size for a catch in Western Australia is 23 centimetres; it is 21 centimetres in South Australia, 20 centimetres in Victoria and 23 centimetres in Tasmania.

Breeding
This garfish enters the inlets, bays and estuaries in spring and early summer to spawn.

Habits
For most of the year sea garfish remain in open water but they will congregate in large schools over sea grasses and algae areas prior to and during spawning. They seem to be much more wary of attack from predators than other species of garfish, being easily "spooked" and scattering quickly.

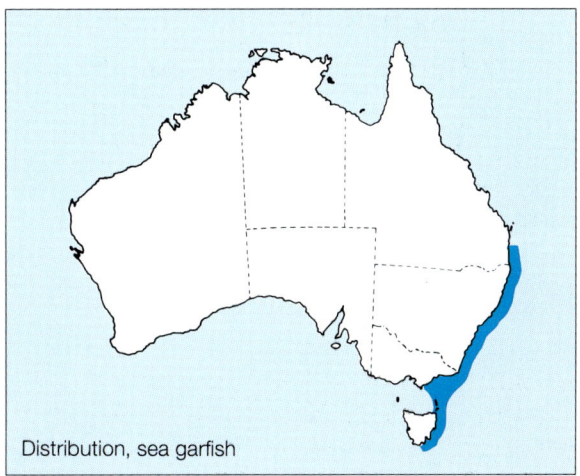
Distribution, sea garfish

Distribution

Sea garfish are found from the Moreton Bay area of Queensland down to the eastern side of Tasmania and south-eastern Victoria. The eastern species most likely overlaps with its western relative in the Bass Strait. The western species extends across the southern coast and then north beyond Perth.

GARFISH, SHORT-NOSED
Hyporhamphus quoyi

OTHER NAMES: **HALF-BEAK, SEA GARFISH**

Identification

The bill on this garfish is nearly as long as its head. The top of its body is greenish coloured and the rest silver. A distinct silvery flash along its sides — from head to tail — has a thin black line edging the top of it.

Size

The short-nosed grows to about 35 centimetres.

Breeding

This fish is believed to spawn inside estuaries or in shallow ocean waters.

Habits

Though this garfish inhabits both ocean beaches and saline estuaries, it does not venture far upstream.

Distribution

The short-nosed garfish is found all along the Queensland coastline into the tropics.

GARFISH, SNUB-NOSED
Arrhamphus sclerolepis

OTHER NAMES: **SHORT BILL, NO BILL, SNUBBIE**

Identification

This fish is easily identified because it is the only garfish with practically no beak or bill. Its bottom jaw is only slightly longer than its upper jaw. Colouring is a sea-green overall which fades to a silvery belly. There are three thin but distinct stripes along the middle of its body. This is a heavier-bodied garfish.

Size

The snub-nosed garfish grows to about 38-40 centimetres.

Breeding

It is believed to breed in the lower reaches of estuaries.

Habits

This garfish prefers water with extensive weed beds or sea grass meadows in estuaries and rivers. Like the river garfish, it will visit brackish and freshwater sections.

Distribution

The snub-nosed garfish is widespread from central New South Wales throughout the tropical north and southward down the West Australian coast to about Carnarvon. Primarily estuarine, the numbers of the fish increase in the more northerly regions.

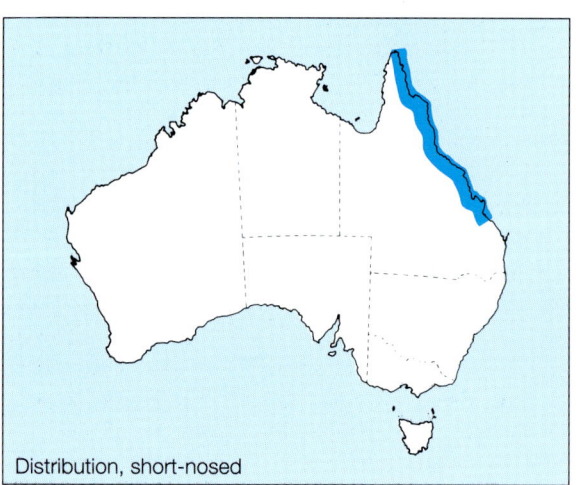

Distribution, short-nosed

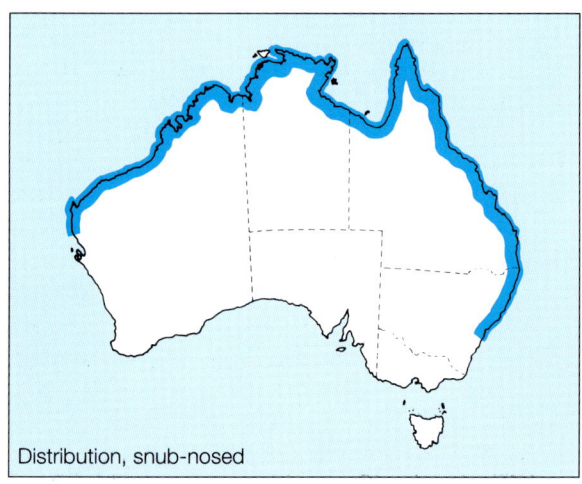

Distribution, snub-nosed

GARFISH, ROBUST
Hemirhamphus robustus

OTHER NAMES: **THREE-BY-TWO, FLAT-SIDED GARFISH**

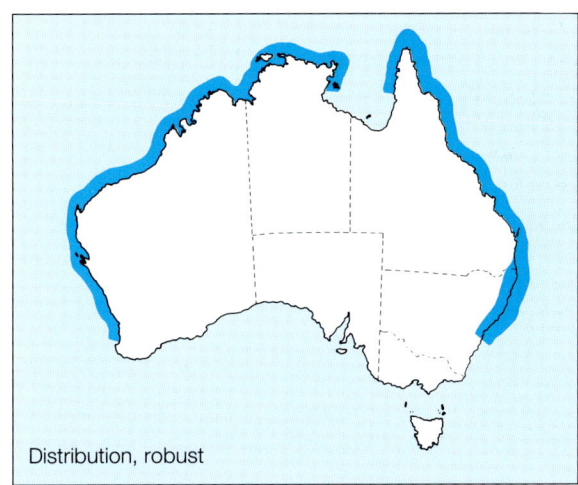
Distribution, robust

Identification
This solid-bodied garfish receives one of its common names, Three-by-Two, from its angular flat-sided shape. If further proof is needed there is usually a dark mark on the back below the dorsal fin. It also has a longer bottom lobe of the tail.

Size
The robust garfish grows to approximately 50 centimetres in length.

Habits
This fish inhabits the inshore coastal waters and tolerates turbidity.

Distribution
This garfish is found from about the New South Wales central coast and northward along the Queensland coast, across the Northern Territory and south to Geographe Bay in Western Australia. In the clear waters, sandy bays and coral reefs of the Great Barrier Reef, however, this garfish appears to have been displaced by the distinctively marked **black-barred garfish** (*Hemiramphus far*) in the Great Barrier Reef. This fish has anywhere between 1 and 9 vertical oval black splotches along its lateral line.

When to fish
Garfish are present all year round in many parts of Australia but spring to late summer provides excellent fishing. Even the sea garfish, however, can be encountered during winter — though relatively close to shore on mild winter days. The best time seems to be morning and late afternoon and an almost mandatory requirement for the best catches is a flat unruffled sea. Cold winds and rain will drive these fish from the surface.

Where to fish
The ideal locations are over sea grass meadows and weed beds in inlets, bays, harbours, estuaries and rivers.

Tackle
The preferred tackle will depend on the location, but the ideal choice would be an ultra light or light single-handed threadline rod of about 2 metres with matching reel, or a 3-metre light beach rod with threadline reel or medium-size sidecast reel. These will very effectively cast the light baits and floats normally used to catch garfish. Lines of a breaking-strain of around 2 to 5 kilograms will handle the garfish and standard or long shank hooks between sizes 6 and 10 will suit the small baits used for this fish.

Baits
Garfish will take gentles (maggots), dough, prawn pieces, shellfish flesh, red meat and cubes or thin strips of fish, especially garfish.

Rigs
Most garfish anglers use floats, usually a plastic bubble, quill, light-bodied stem types or even special floats that can be filled with berley. Use rigs No. 7, or 7A and 7C, often with an extra hook on a dropper at a shallower depth than the hook on the leader. If the fish are reluctant to rise to berley, a light sinker and droppers with hooks above it can be tried: when sunk in the vicinity of garfish it will often tempt the fish's appetite. A totally unweighted bait (rig No. 2) cast beyond the berley and retrieved through the school is also successful.

Berley
This is almost essential for a successful catch of garfish. The choices are many, such as bread, bread crumbs, bran and pollard, boiled rice, minced fish scraps, sardines in oil mixed with any of these. The berley should be damp enough to sink slowly and break up. More dry berley should be used on the surface. Excessive use of berley is claimed to put garfish off. It also tends to attract

other fish (especially tommy ruff or Australian herring) in southern and western States. Remember that garfish will not compete with other fish and will usually disappear the moment other fish arrive.

How to hook

Garfish bite rapidly and strongly. It's a matter of timing to lift the rod to set the hook. Vigorous swiping can tear the hook out of the fish's jaw.

Hint

If berley attracts tommy ruff, yellowtail, sweep or other fish — and the garfish disappear — anglers should try increasing the berley nearer themselves to draw the intruders closer. The garfish will often hang back and pick up the "left-overs", so cast beyond the other fish.

Garfish are a flighty fish. Sudden disappearances or scattering can mean a predator under them. Birds overhead frighten them as do anglers' shadows on the water or large sinkers cast near them.

Edibility

Garfish are caught for bait by some anglers and others regard this as wasteful. Here is one quick and tasty preparation: Clean and scale the fish and remove head, fins and tail. Split the fish along the backbone (not through the flesh or skin) and spread open. Sprinkle with pepper, add several small dollops of butter and squeeze with lemon juice. About 3 minutes under a hot grill produces a quick and delicious meal.

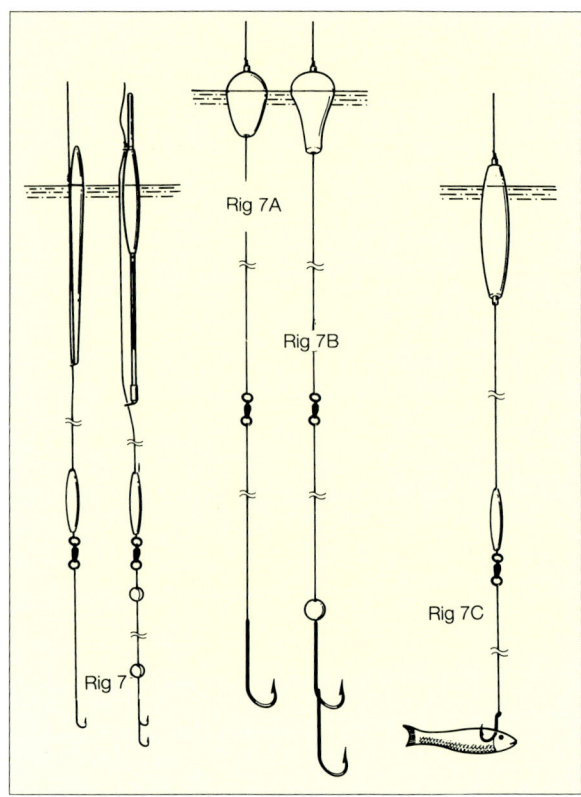

Rig 7A

Rig 7B

Rig 7C

Rig 7

GOATFISH

One of the world's most widespread fish, goatfish are
abundant in Australian waters. No angler sets out to catch
a goatfish; they are hooked while fishing for other reef fish.
These are often on the smallish side and are thrown back if
larger or more desirable species are plentiful. Only the
few goatfish that reach pan size or larger are listed
here. Each is excellent eating. All goatfish possess a
most distinguishing feature, a pair of barbels
(like a goat's beard) on the lower jaw.

GOATFISH, BLACK-SPOT

Parupeneus signatus

Identification

With the characteristic barbels and elongate body
of all goatfish, the black-spot (*see above*) has a light
base colour with brownish to red colouring, often
in bands.

There is a purplish shade in the tail and body of the
larger fish. This goatfish is easily identified by a
black spot on the top of the caudal peduncle.

Size

The black-spot goatfish grows to about 45 to 50
centimetres.

Distribution

Though it is generally considered a tropical species,
schools of black-spot goatfish are often found in
the southern areas of western and eastern Australia
— as far south as Geographe Bay in Western
Australia and Mallacoota Inlet in Victoria.

Blue-striped goatfish

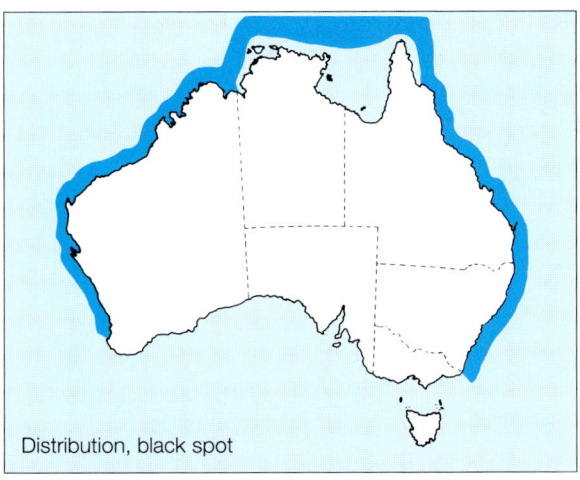

Distribution, black spot

GOATFISH, BLUE-SPOTTED

Upeneichthys vlamingii

OTHER NAMES: **BLACK-STRIPED GOATFISH, RED MULLET**

GOATFISH, BLUE-STRIPED

Upeneichthys lineatus

OTHER NAME: **BLUE-STRIPED RED MULLET**

Identification

The base colour of these goatfish is usually off-white but variable, with greenish and orange tones often evident. Their colour turns a pinkish shade after death. The red-brown-black stripe on the body is usually more distinct in the blue-spotted goatfish but it too fades on capture. The blue spots on body and fins of this species are sometimes so faint that they are almost impossible to distinguish. The blue-striped obtains its name from the purple-blue stripes and spots on its head and body. The blue-spotted species has a slightly longer head.

Size

Both fish grow to about 35 to 40 centimetres in length.

Distribution

The blue-spotted goatfish is common in waters on the central and southern regions of the east coast, around Tasmania, in Victoria, South Australia and in West Australian waters north of Perth.
The blue-striped goatfish occurs from central New South Wales waters to at least the Gold Coast of Queensland. The two species may overlap in New South Wales waters.

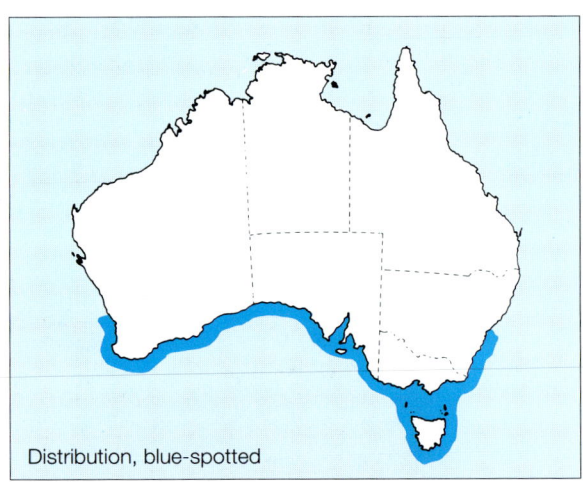

Distribution, blue-spotted

GOATFISH, GOLD-SADDLED

Parupeneus cyclostomus

OTHER NAMES: **BRIGHT GOATFISH, RED MULLET, SURMULLET**

Identification

These fish have an elongate body and an almost flat belly. Their profile curves from the mouth to first dorsal fin and sweeps back to a forked tail. They have a long first dorsal; the second dorsal and anal fins are almost identical in size and shape. The overall colour of this goatfish is a rich rose pink with a browner pink along the dorsal area which grows lighter towards the belly. A saddle of gold is located between the rear dorsal fin and tail. There are blue lines between the mouth and the eyes. The barbels reach back towards the pelvic fins, but can be hidden in grooves when not being used.

Size

This fish grows to approximately 45 to 50 centimetres in length.

Distribution

The gold-saddled goatfish inhabits all the tropical reef areas of Australia's north.

GOATFISH, YELLOW-STRIPED (Western)

Parupeneus chrysopleuron

GOATFISH, GOLD-STRIPED or BANDED (Eastern)

Mulloidichthys vanicolensis

Identification

These two goatfish are very similar in appearance. They are basically white, with the western or yellow-striped fish having a bright yellow band from eye to tail; the eastern or gold-striped has bright yellow fins in addition to the other markings. The latter is also more slender bodied.

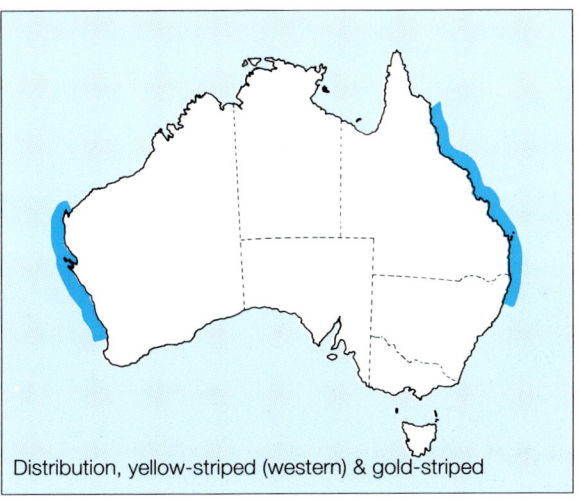

Distribution, yellow-striped (western) & gold-striped

Yellow-striped (western) goatfish

Size

Both the goatfish grow to 35 to 40 centimetres in length.

Distribution

Though the western species is much more likely to be encountered on the north-west coast of Western Australia, it is caught from time to time well south of Perth. The eastern species is frequently encountered on the northern coast of New South Wales.

The following applies to all goatfish.

Breeding

Little is known.

Habits

Goatfish are basically bottom dwellers. Their flattish belly and the shape of their mouth are an indication that they feed by grubbing on the bottom. The barbels, which they fold into grooves when not seeking food, are used to detect edible items in sand, weeds and rubble. The fish appear to be able to brighten or subdue their colour to suit their habitat and will often display brighter shades when disturbed, hunting or hooked. The fish appear to sleep or rest in the daytime and become more active in the late afternoon and during the night. They form small or large schools when feeding.

Goatfish prefer sheltered reef areas with sand, rubble bottoms and scattered weed beds in close proximity. Long broken reefs jutting out from a headland are favoured habitats.

When to fish

The goatfish is usually caught when fishing from a boat over inshore reefs early in the morning or in the late afternoon or night. Rock fishers seeking other fish often hook them in these periods.

Where to fish

These fish are almost always encountered in reef

areas, with sand or rubble patches, from a few metres to perhaps 70 or 80 metres deep.

Tackle

A handline on a caster or winch type of reel with line of 10 to 15 kilogram breaking-strain is adequate when fishing from a boat — or a short boat rod. If fishing from the shoreline you will need a rod of about 3.5 metres — in threadline, overhead or sidecast styles — with suitable reels spooled with 8 to 10 kilogram breaking-strain line. Hooks in sizes 1/0 to 4/0 are suitable, depending on the bait.

Baits

The goatfish is likely to take bloodworms, beachworms, prawns, crabs, even fish fillets, shellfish flesh, conjevoi.

Rigs

Goatfish are caught while fishing for bottom fish from boats or rocks. Depending on the depth of water and the bottom, rigs 2, 3A, 4 or 4A can be used.

How to hook

This fish is more of a slurper than a biter. The baited hook is often well into the fish's mouth by the time the angler detects the weight and tightens up to impale the hook. The larger fish can swallow surprisingly large baits.

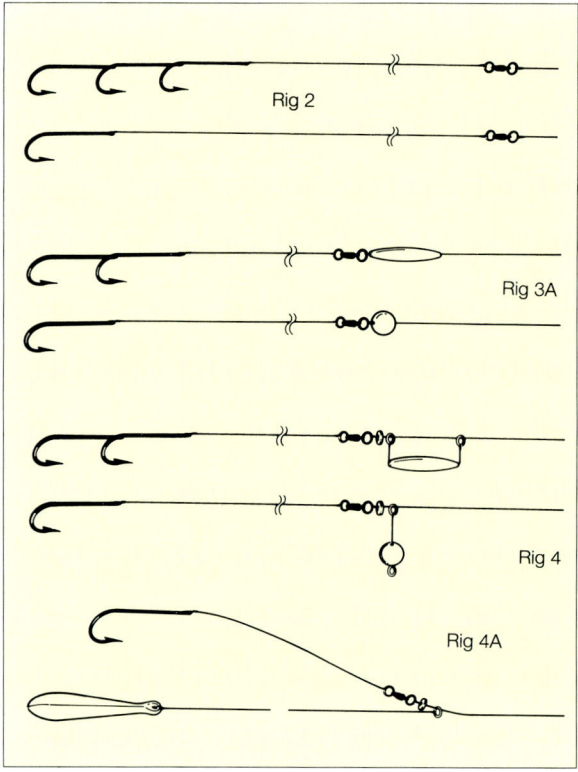

Edibility

The angler who discards or releases a goatfish of pan size or bigger is wasting an excellent eating fish. The flesh is white and firm and can be prepared in many ways.

GROPER

The true groper belongs to the Serranidae family of fish. (It is spelt "grouper" outside of Australia and is believed to be derived from a Portuguese word *garupa,* which in turn was a corruption of a South American Indian word for the fish.) Australian fish in this family include wirrahs, sea-perches and rock-cods. The only true groper in this array of fish is the Queensland groper: three others follow here because of popular usage of this name, but they should more correctly be listed as wrasses or tuskfishes elsewhere.

GROPER, QUEENSLAND
Promicrops lanceolatus

OTHER NAMES: **GIANT GROPER**

Excluding sharks and the billfishes, the groper is Australia's largest fish. It is also much maligned, being denounced as the scourge of other fish by recreational and professional anglers when many other species may have been responsible. It has also been accused of being a danger to divers, though there is precious little evidence to support this contention. (A diver feeding other groper had his hand bitten, but it seems likely that the fish mistook the white hand for part of the offerings.) The groper is an inquisitive and passive fish, much exploited by anglers and spearfishing enthusiasts; so much so that numbers are so reduced in the more populated areas that spearing them has been mercifully prohibited.

Despite its name, this groper is not confined to Queensland waters.

Identification

This is a powerful solid-bodied fish that can grow to an enormous weight. The body colour of a mature groper may vary from brown with a green tinge to a very dark grey-green to almost black. Fins and tail can sometimes appear to be dirty yellow with some blackish spots. The young fish are black to brown with yellow blotched bands, though these are a rare sight. A groper's mouth is filled with very sharp teeth.

Size

This groper is known to grow to more than 3 metres in length. One has been recorded at more than 300 kilograms. In Queensland anglers may not retain any groper *over* 120 centimetres long.

Breeding

Little is known. There seems to be no pre-spawning migration.

Habits

Groper are slow-moving fish that take up residence where food is plentiful. This can lead them to reef caverns or overhangs, and even sunken ships. They will also visit and loiter around wharves or boat anchorages where fish are cleaned and the skeletons and scraps thrown into the water. They seem totally unafraid and will swim across shallow reefs and sand bars. They will closely inspect intruders in their territory, whatever their size, such as scuba divers. Groper are voracious feeders with very catholic tastes.

Distribution

Groper are most common in the tropic waters of the Great Barrier Reef, the Gulf of Carpentaria, across the Northern Territory and in north-west waters of Western Australia. They are much reduced in the southern parts of the Barrier Reef and southern Queensland waters. They have been found as far south as the central coast of N.S.W. and on the west coast as southward as Rottnest Island.

When to fish

The groper is present all year round.

Where to fish

An angler's chances of catching a groper are improved the further north they travel. Those chances will improve even more along edges of reefs where there are overhangs, caves with adjacent sandy areas, around wrecks, and inshore reef

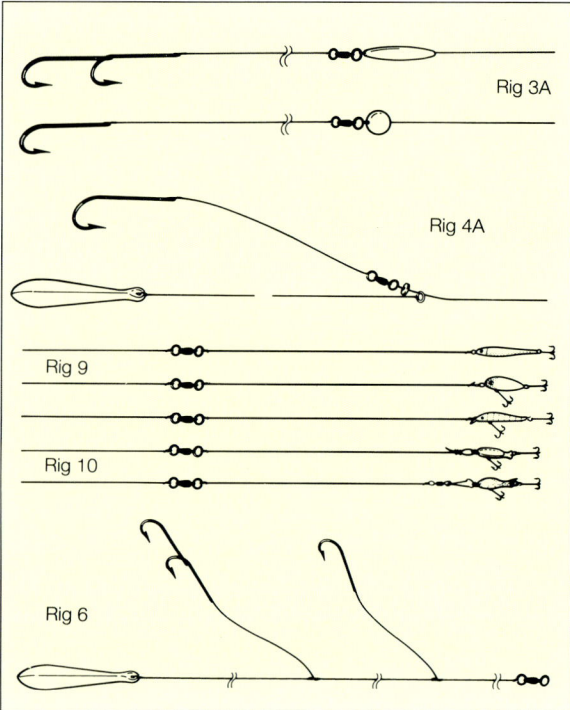

outcrops as well as wharves and fishing boat anchorages.

Tackle

Some anglers still persist in fishing for large groper with a handline that might better be described as a tow rope! The reason for this somewhat barbarous approach is all the more difficult to fathom when you appreciate that any groper over 12 to 15 kilograms is going to be coarse and tough. Even if any trace of sporting instinct is abjured, there is no logical incentive to land larger fish. For this very reason lines should be no more than 20 kilograms breaking-strain and even lighter when

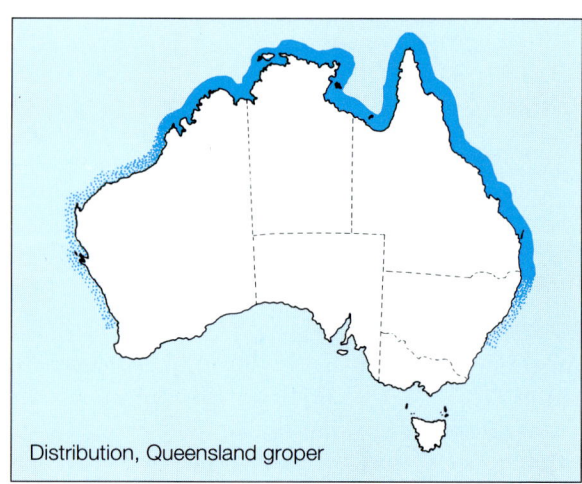

Distribution, Queensland groper

used on boat reels, or heavy duty overhead or sidecast reels used with short powerful rods. Hooks should be large and extra strong. The sinker should only be as heavy as is absolutely necessary. With this gear any angler should be able to handle a groper of a size suitable to eat.

Baits

Groper are scavengers but their main diet consists of crabs, large prawns, rock lobsters and seemingly any fish, including skates and small sharks. It is documented that a large groper has taken a whole fish in excess of 50 kilograms, which is less surprising when you realise groper of about 100 kilograms will try to swallow fish more than half their weight.

Rigs

Try to use an unweighted rig if possible, or at least a lightly-weighted rig No. 9 or 3A. The bottom rig (No. 4A or 6) is also satisfactory. It helps if the groper is hooked off the bottom. The groper will take lures but these must be of game fish strength to withstand the power of its crunching jaws.

How to hook

The angler's problem with groper is not in hooking it but matching his strength — and that of his gear — against the groper's massive power when its a large one.

Edibility

Groper in excess of 12 kilograms become coarse and tough. Smaller fish have white flesh with good texture and flavour. It grills, bakes and fries well.

Other regulations

This groper is protected in New South Wales.

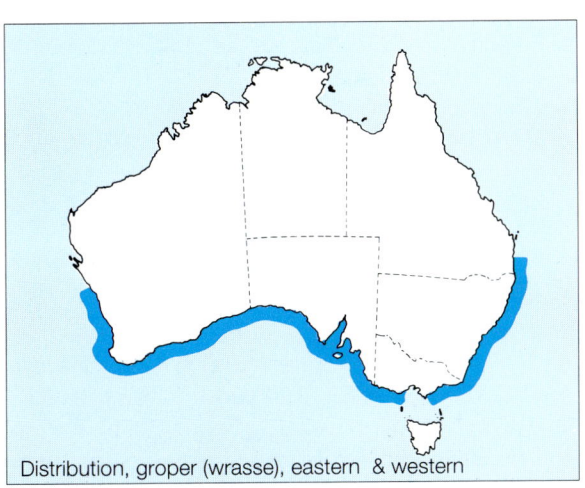

Distribution, groper (wrasse), eastern & western

Gropers (wrasse): Eastern blue (above), western blue (below)

GROPER (WRASSE), EASTERN BLUE
Achoerodus viridis

OTHER NAMES: **BROWN OR RED GROPER**

GROPER (WRASSE), WESTERN BLUE
Achoerodus gouldii

OTHER NAMES: **BLUE GROPER**

As these two fish belong to the family Labridae, they would be more correctly listed as wrasse. It seems an almost impossible task, however, to change the name used by anglers since the fish were first caught. Even State Fisheries publications on regulations list these fishes as groper. Perhaps my emphasis on wrasse in this reference will prompt a few more anglers to use the proper name.

Identification

The location of the fish is a clear indication of the species. Nevertheless there are distinguishing features. The colour of the eastern and western blue wrasse males are exactly that — a dull bluish hue with the western fish perhaps slightly darker. In females, the eastern is a red-brown colour (not a different fish as many believe) and the western species is green.

Small juveniles of the eastern wrasse are brownish or orange-brown and the western wrasses are a greyish-tan. The eyes of the eastern wrasse are surrounded with yellowish-orange lines, those of the western wrasse have spots.

Both fish are solid with a short spine-front dorsal fin and a deeper second dorsal. The western species' dorsal and anal fins are longer. Both have thick fleshy lips and strong peg-like teeth.

Size

The eastern blue wrasse grows to a metre and weighs about 50 kilograms; the western fish grows to a larger size of about 1.6 metres.

New South Wales places no size restrictions on the eastern blue wrasse (groper). In Western Australia, the minimum size is 40 centimetres and; South Australia's minimum size for the western blue wrasse is 60 centimetres.

Breeding

Little information is available but wrasses seem to make no definite spawning aggregation or migration.

Habits

Both wrasses inhabit close inshore reefs and rocky headlands or platforms where there are holes, crevices or caves in which to take up residence. In some areas uncontrolled spearfishing has depleted local populations because of the fish's retiring nature. This is now banned. Apart from a place to retreat, the fish seek a territory where crabs, sea urchins and conjevoi are plentiful or nearby. Juveniles are much more active than the adults. On coastal rock fronts it is not uncommon to see a blue wrasse lazily rise near to the surface in search of crabs and conjevoi.

Distribution

The eastern blue wrasse inhabits rock fronts and reefs in waters from about 5 to 40 metres deep. Their range extends from about Moreton Bay in Queensland to Wilsons Promontory in Victoria. The western blue wrasse will be found in the same type of habitat from Port Phillip Bay along the southern coastline and north to about the Abrolhos islands off Western Australia. Despite the protective measures of fisheries authorities, the numbers of both fish have declined in readily accessible locations because of fishing pressure.

When to fish

Both wrasses are around throughout the year but are more plentiful close-in to the rocks in spring through to early autumn. The rising tide from half to full and from half to low are favoured when fishing holes or rock faces from the shore. Tides seem less important when fishing from a boat in deeper water.

However, early morning and late afternoon usually produce more fish which could be due to the light on the water. Whether fishing for these two wrasses from a boat or from a rock location, the water conditions have to be watched. These fish reside in areas where rough seas can be hazardous.

Where to fish

Rock anglers should try deep water alongside rock faces and in holes in reefs within casting range as their first priority, particularly where there are conjevoi beds and weed beds containing crabs (especially the red variety). Boat anglers should seek out holes in reefs or fish alongside reefs.

Tackle

If using a handline it should be at least 15 kilogram breaking-strain. When fishing from the rocks, use a rod with plenty of power throughout its length and about 3.5 metres long. It should be suitable for heavy duty threadline or overhead reels — which are adequate — but a sidecast reel of about 12 to 15 centimetres diameter provides much more winching power to stop the fish.

A similar reel on a short rod is recommended in preference to a handline for boat fishing. Lines on rods can be about 8 to 12 kilogram breaking-strain. Anglers using a handline should wear rubber finger stalls or gloves. The pull of these wrasses can zip line through fingers and burn deep cuts that are painful and slow-healing. Hooks about 4/0 to 8/0 and extra strong are needed.

Baits

The red crab, whole or cut, is the first choice for bait. No other crabs are as readily taken. Conjevoi is also very good, as is abalone flesh. Flesh of shellfish from the area being fished can also tempt the wrasse. Bear in mind when you make your choice, however, that most baits except whole crab attract "rubbish" fish.

Berley

Legs of crabs, crushed crabs and sea-urchins, and crushed shellfish all make a successful berley.

Rigs

The conditions of the water and the terrain being fished are factors in the choice of rig. Where possible a lightly weighted bait rig No. 3 is excellent. The running rig No. 4A with the sinker on a dropper (short length off line of the main line with a hook or a sinker attached) of a lower breaking strain than the main line is frequently used from

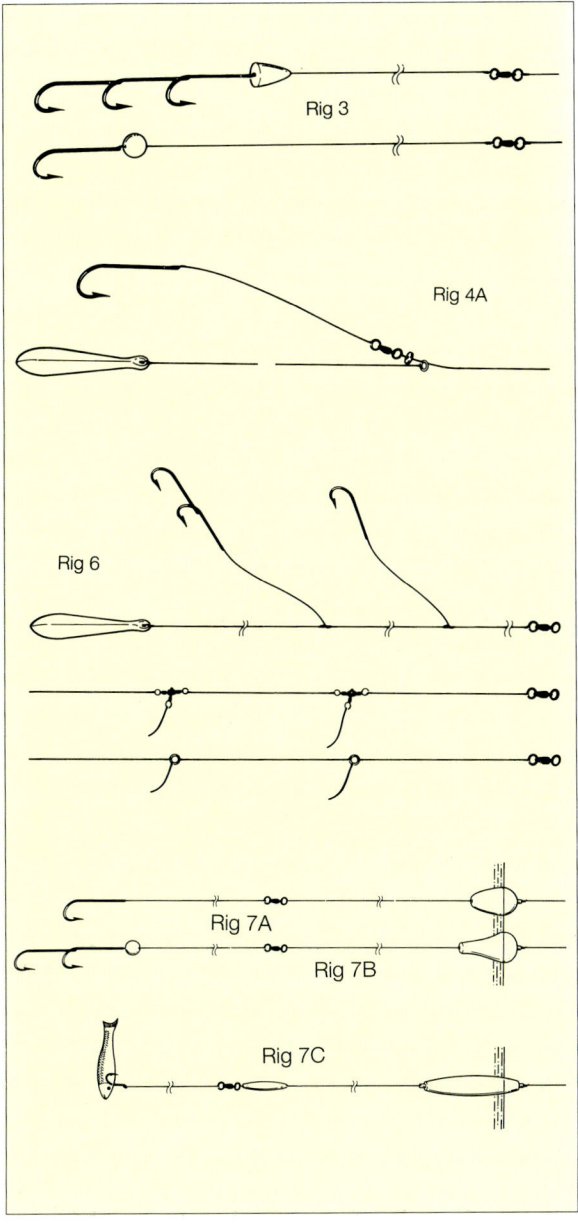

rocks or boats. (The running rig is also helpful in case a snapper or some other desirable species take the bait.) Bottom rig No. 6 is also useful. With the running rig or fixed bottom rigs, the leader is often shorter. The dropper for the sinker should be about a metre long. Many anglers prefer the floating bobby cork rig No. 7A or 7C with the bait suspended about a metre off the bottom.

How to hook

The first indication of a blue wrasse bite is a slow steady pull, similar to the way an octopus or squid might drag on a bait. Do not give too much line before stopping it firmly to set the hook. The next few seconds are usually spent in a contest of strength between the angler and the fish. And wrasse are not beaten until they are gaffed or until they have been swum clear on to the rocks. A sudden stop — with exactly the same feeling you get when a line is snagged — invariably means that the fish has reached a crevice. In the great majority of hook-ups the wrasse will then be immovable.

Edibility

The best eating blue wrasse is between 2 and 6 kilograms. Should an angler catch one outside of these weights, the fish should be admired and then returned to the water — either to grow up or to continue to breed.

The flesh is white with good texture and flavour. It is easier to skin the fish than scale it, particularly in the larger sizes. It grills, fries and bakes well.

Other regulations

New South Wales anglers are permitted to take only 2 of these fish per day; in Western Australia the limit is 1 fish per day; and no limit applies in South Australia.

GROPER (TUSKFISH), BALDCHIN
Choerodon rubescens

OTHER NAMES: **BALDCHIN TUSKFISH, BALDCHIN WRASSE**

This is another fish that is wrongly known as a groper. It belongs to the genus Cheorodon and is therefore a tuskfish. Perhaps some day we will see

Groper (tuskfish) baldchin

it listed in publications under its other name "baldchin tuskfish". This fish is confined to a section of West Australian waters.

Identification
The well-developed and light coloured chin of this fish makes it unmistakable, these features even being discernible in juveniles. It has a solid, high-forehead, which varies in colour from a tan-brown to pink-brown, and even a greenish-grey. The lips are less fleshy than the western blue wrasse and it has the prominent teeth that characterise the tuskfishes.

Size
The baldchin reaches approximately a metre in length and more than 30 kilograms. A baldchin of less than 40 centimetres cannot be retained.

Breeding
Little is known of their breeding but juveniles are often seen in the protected shallows of sand and weed areas.

Distribution
This fish is occasionally hooked in deep off shore waters as far south as Cape Naturaliste, but is much more abundant towards the northern end of its range, around Exmouth in the north-west of Western Australia.

When to fish
Weather and sea conditions probably dictate the best times to fish, as they do for many reef fish. Strong winds and rough seas in the areas these fish are caught can be very dangerous for small boats. This fish is available most of the year.

Where to fish
The baldchin tuskfish inhabits reef areas and nearby sandy patches or rubble. It is carnivorous, eating fish, molluscs, small squid and crabs. Though normally located in the deeper areas of its range, it is quite common in shallow areas around the Abrolhos. Baldchin tuskfish cruise around more than wrasses.

Tackle
Handlines of 20 kilogram breaking-strain or 12 to 15 kilogram breaking-strain lines on short powerful rods are satisfactory. Reels may be heavy duty baitcasters or overhead models or 15 centimetre diameter sidecast style. Hooks about 4/0 to 6/0 size and extra strong are suitable.

Baits
The baldchin tuskfish will take crabs, shellfish, crustaceans, squid, fish pieces or fillets.

Berley
If conditions and depths allow, the baldchin groper can be attracted and lured towards the surface — as can other reef fish — with a berley of fish pieces, crushed crabs, etc.

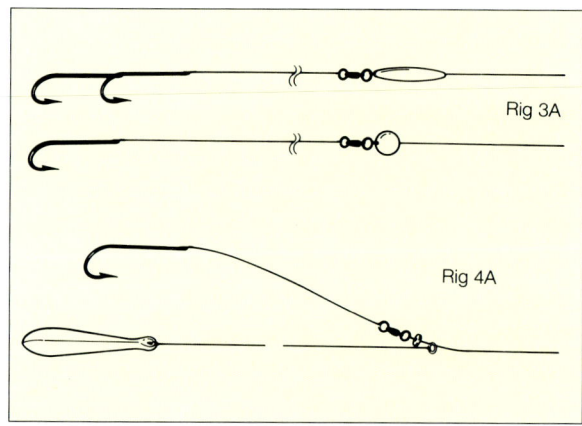

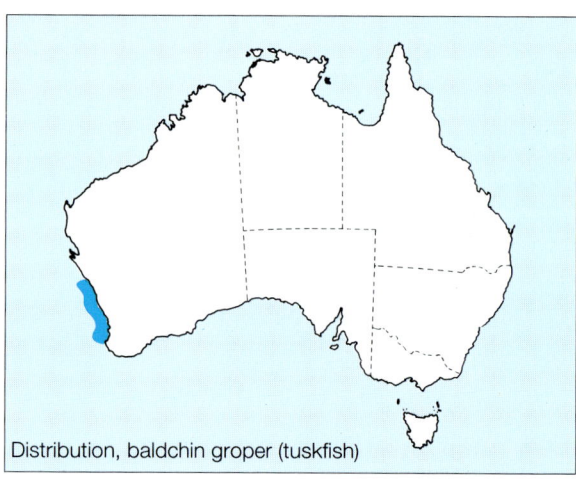
Distribution, baldchin groper (tuskfish)

Rigs

Try a lightly weighted rig No. 3A with a sinker of a weight to reach the bottom or a running bottom rig No. 4A.

How to hook

The baldchin tuskfish readily takes a bait but be ready for a struggle.

This fish is a powerful fighter and a test for even the experienced angler.

Edibility

Fish of between 2 and 8 kilograms are good eating. The flesh is white, flaky and tender. A whole fish bakes particularly well.

Other regulations

There is a regulation governing "grouped species" in Western Australia that puts a bag limit on the angler of 10 fish in any day. The baldchin tuskfish is one of these fish.

GRUNTER

Many freshwater and saltwater fish are called grunters — some
say too many — including several members of the perch
family: these are listed by their appropriate names elsewhere.
Those marine fish that are called grunters include many small
fish such as the trumpeters and yellowtail perch as well as
javelin fish and the long-nosed trevally. What follows under
this heading are only those fish that anglers (rather than
scientists) will probably call grunters — along with other
names — as long as they are available to be caught!

GRUNTER, SOOTY

Hephaestus fuliginosus

OTHER NAMES: **BLACK BREAM, PURPLE
GRUNTER, BLUBBERLIPS, KHAKI BREAM**

The variety in the other names given to this fish
demonstrates the wide variations in colouring, but
such differences are probably dictated by the level
of turbidity in its water as well as the current flow.
The sooty grunter has been over-exploited. Its
numbers are reduced in many populated areas,
and four-wheel drive vehicles and other advances
such as lightweight canoes and fold-up boats, have
breached its hitherto inaccessible sanctuaries.
Except for some stocked impoundments, it should
be considered a catch-photograph-and-release fish.
It requires care when being handled.

170

Identification

The sooty grunter is more oval than elongate with a deep body, especially between the front of the dorsal fin and the pelvic fin. The dorsal fin, supported with strong spines, is lower in the front and the rear dorsal fin is connected with only a small depression indicating a change from spines to soft rays. The anal fin also has strong spines at the front. Its tail is broad. Colour ranges from a yellow-gold-tan to a grey to blackish-brown. There are also hints of a yellow-gold sheen on some of the darker fish. Occasional fish are marked with large contrasting colour-change blotches. The mouth is small with obvious lips. It may omit a grunting sound on capture.

Size

This fish has been known to reach about 8 kilograms but rarely does an angler catch a sooty grunter of more than 1.5 kilograms today.

Breeding

Some current research is incomplete but there are indications the sooty grunter spawns after the major "wet" floods towards autumn and that the eggs are deposited where there is a gravelly or rocky bottom and a slow water movement.

Habits

The sooty grunter inhabits waters that may be fresh with tidal influences or small fast-flowing headwaters of rivers. They adapt to a range of water temperatures, surviving in cooler tropical tableland waterways. It is often found in schools in any substantial fishing hole, particularly where there is an overhang from a tree. And it will have even greater promise if any overhang produces berries, or if thickets of vegetation on the bank droop into the water. These fish have been found with berries and fruits in their stomachs, though it is probably not the berry it eats so much as the eggs or larvae of minute insects that may have lodged in them. Sooty grunters also sup in mud, again probably feeding on tiny aquatic insects or fleas. The main diet is shrimps and other crustaceans, tadpoles, frogs, insects of all kinds and even small fish.

This fish is not easily startled and exposes itself to over-fishing by not fleeing from an area when one or two from a school have been caught.

Distribution

The sooty grunter is mainly of the tropical rivers of Queensland and the Gulf country, including those of the Atherton Tableland. It can be caught anywhere from the uppermost reaches down to the freshwater stretches that are influenced by tides. It is also distributed in Northern Territory waters and in the north-west of Western Australia. It has been introduced to freshwater impoundments in Queensland, but may only breed if there are good inflows from rivers or creeks with suitable spawning beds.

When to fish

The tropical wet season, with floods creating access problems to many streams the fish inhabit, can curtail fishing at this time of the year.

Where to fish

Seeking out overgrowths on the banks, along undercut banks, near deep rock shelter or underwater snags, the angler should place his bait or lure in the vicinity of these. The fish will also hang about where a current from another creek enters a river or creek. The faster flowing areas are more successful.

Try fishing while drifting in a canoe or punt or walking along the bank. A small boat can open up otherwise unreachable areas.

Tackle

Handlines can be used, of course, yet fishing with a light to medium threadline or baitcasting outfit with bait or lure is not only easier but it provides for a better appreciation of this fish's strength and fighting ability. Lines of about 3 to 5 kilogram breaking-strain are suitable. If you choose to bait your hook, size 1 or 2 is satisfactory. A sinker is not usually necessary as the sooty will rise to a current-floated bait. Fly gear is also successful.

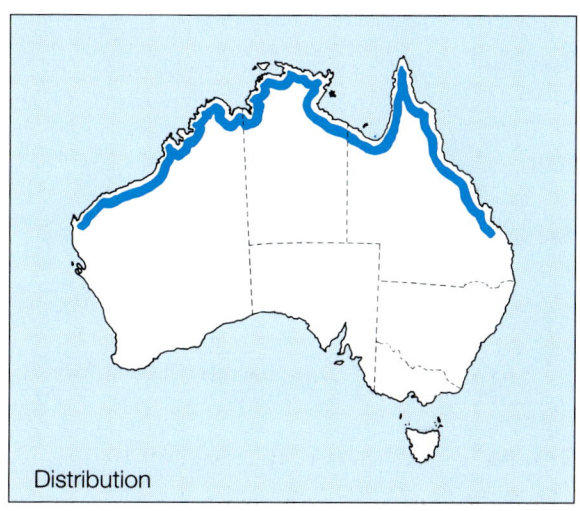

Distribution

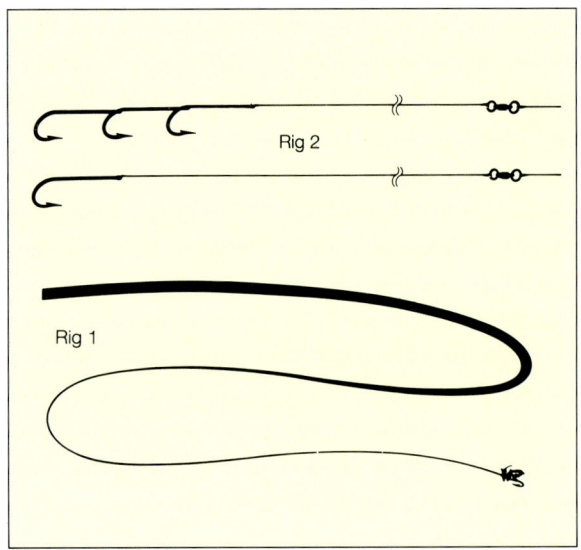

Baits

Try shrimps, worms, yabbies, large insects of any kind, thin wriggly fillets of fish, etc.

The sooty grunter is taken on surface, mid-water and bottom-swimming lures of all kinds. Those with plenty of action at a slow retrieval rate often prove the most effective.

Rigs

The unweighted bait rig No. 2 or lure rig No. 9 may be employed to good effect. Light fly-fishing outfits and a wide variety of wet flies — mostly dark coloured — are used also.

How to hook

This fish is not a fast attacker, but displays resolute intent and rarely misses taking any bait or lure it decides it wants. In many of the clear waters it is possible, as it is with other fresh and saltwater fish, to see when to lift the rod for a hook-up.

Edibility

The eating quality is excellent provided the fish or its fillets are placed on ice soon after capture. It can be cooked by most methods but is well worth trying smoked.

GRUNTER, SPANGLED
Leioptotherapon unicolor

OTHER NAMES: **JEWEL PERCH, JEWEL PERCH, BOBBY PERCH OR COD, TROUT COD (QLD)**

This is one of Australia's most widely distributed indigenous freshwater fish. It is also an outstanding angling fish and excellent table fare.

Identification

The spangled grunter lacks the more oval body and beak-like small mouth of the other "perches" or grunters. It has a longer head (somewhat like the Murray cod) and a large mouth. It has a spined front dorsal fin connected by a clear rise to a tall, narrow second dorsal. The tail is almost square or faintly curved, rather than forked. Its colour variations, which are most likely associated with its environment, range from almost black to brown: the majority are a blue-black with a dark grey back. The sides are golden to silvery and the belly off-white. The fish is spotted with ochre, rust-coloured, or dull red spots, in a random or mottled pattern, or in rows that create an impression of bands. The spots are said to increase in colour intensity when the fish is captured or disturbed.

Size

The spangled grunter has been recorded at 25 centimetres and half a kilogram.

Breeding

The spangled grunter is one of the few freshwater perches of the Teraponids family that will breed in still-water dams or impoundments. It spawns from November through the summer, randomly depositing its eggs over the bottom. Though it is not yet proven, this fish probably aestivates (survives in wet or bottom mud) which may account for its appearance in large numbers after rain in previously dry areas before any inflow of water occurs from elsewhere. It is a prolific breeder and can over populate an impoundment or billabong, resulting in a mass of small fish.

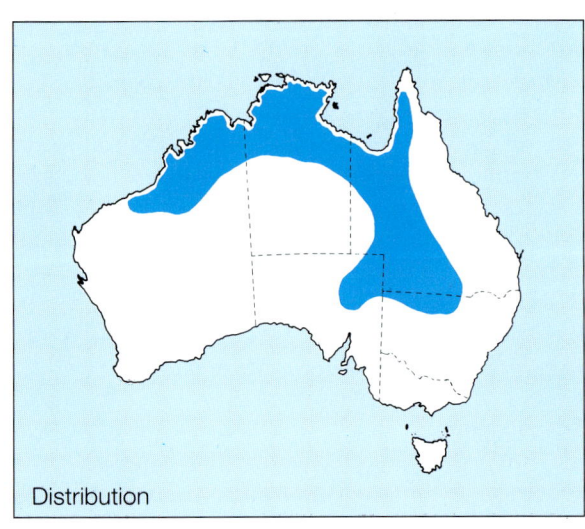

Distribution

Habits

The spangled grunter, especially the small or immature fish, tend to school in large numbers. It eats a variety of aquatic inhabitants such as worms, insects, crustaceans, molluscs, plus some vegetation and terrestrial insects and beetles. It has a wide water temperature tolerance and not only is it found in most of the warmer freshwaters of Australia, it can also be found in billabongs and bore drains. This fish has a preference for warm, still, or slow-flowing turbid waters.

Distribution

This fish is found in the northern reaches of the Darling River, including its tributaries. It also occurs in the Lake Eyre and Bulloo drainage systems, the freshwater rivers draining into the Gulf of Carpentaria and those emptying into the Timor Sea and Indian Ocean.

When to fish

The spangled grunter is inactive in times of long droughts, though in its more northern regions it can be fished for through the autumn, winter and until the wet season. It bites more readily in the morning and late afternoon as well as during the night.

Where to fish

These fish can be found throughout the water depths but shallower water with bushes, rocks, weed beds or overhanging greenery that may attract insects, one of its foods, offer better angling opportunities.

Tackle

This is a light tackle fish. Handlines need not exceed 3 to 5 kilogram breaking-strain. If you use a light single-handed threadline outfit — which will enable you to cast the tiny baits and lures better than a baitcasting rod and reel — then a 2 to 3 kilogram line is all you will need. Sinkers are largely unnecessary: just let the bait sink slowly in the slow water. Hooks about sizes 6 to 2, depending on the size of bait, will do.

Light fly gear and a wide range of wet and dry flies can be successful if the water is clear.

Baits

Shrimps, grasshoppers, small yabbies or pieces of yabby tail, worms etc. are all taken at different times.

Rigs

The unweighted bait rig No. 2 is ideal.

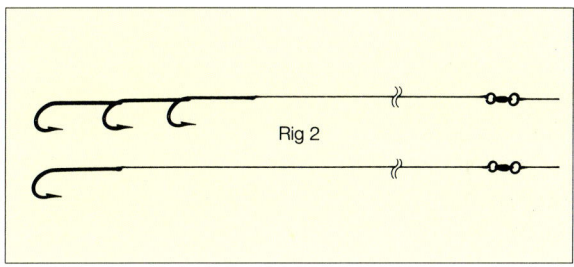

Rig 2

How to hook

The spangled grunter is a surprisingly voracious feeder. When it decides to eat, it shows no reluctance and swallows its meal quickly. It just about hooks itself. It is a scrappy fish for its size, a quality that is best appreciated when the angler uses appropriately light gear.

Edibility

Some regard the small pan-sized fish as superior to its close relative, the silver perch, to eat, despite the number of small bones. It smokes well.

GURNARD

There are many gurnards in the oceans of Australia but they are not a fish the angler actively pursues. All of those likely to be encountered — and most anglers encounter them sooner or later — are accidentally hooked while fishing the bottom for other species, especially on sand or gravel areas alongside reefs. The description of the following provides a guide to the species anglers are likely to catch. With only a couple of exceptions, gurnards have three feelers in the front of the pectoral fin that enable the fish to "walk" along the bottom.

GURNARD, RED

Chelidenichthys kumu

OTHER NAMES: **GURNARD, LATCHET**

Identification

Most gurnards can be readily identified by the severe lines of their head, which is encased in a bony shield, coupled with the extremely large, usually rounded and wing-like pectoral fins. The body of the red gurnard is coloured a pinkish-red to red, to red-brown, and it can appear more of a sandy colour if seen on the bottom before it has been caught or before death. Its large fins are a vivid deep green with blue spots and margins. They also have a large black patch with scattered blue and white spots.

Size

The red gurnard grows to 60 centimetres.

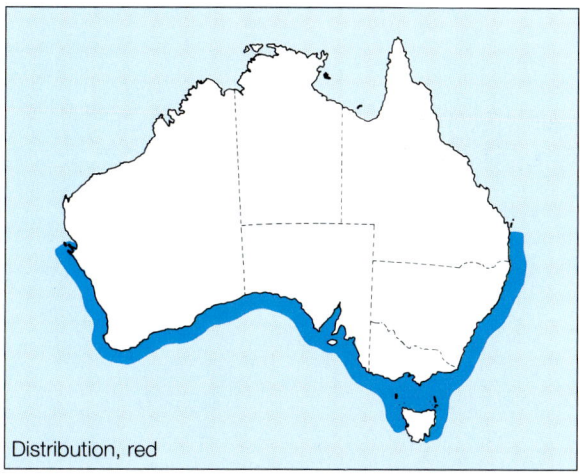

Distribution, red

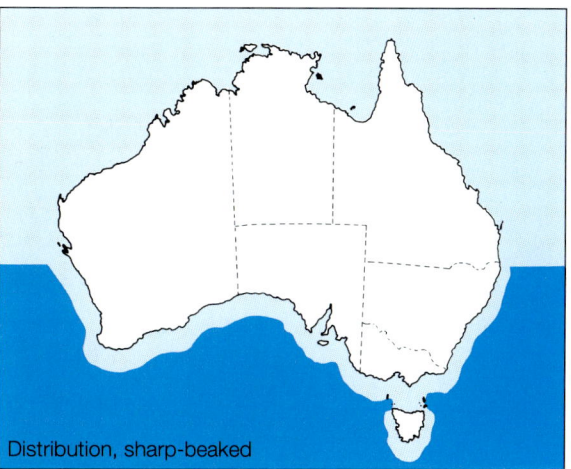

Distribution, sharp-beaked

Distribution

This fish is reasonably common in southern Queensland, New South Wales, Victoria, Tasmania, South Australia and Western Australia (up to Shark Bay). It is usually caught on sandy, gravelly, or rocky bottoms, or around reefs in coastal and estuarine waters.

GURNARD, SHARP-BEAKED
Pterygotrigla polyommata

OTHER NAME: **BUTTERFLY GURNARD, LATCHET**

Identification

The profile from nose to forehead on this species is quite convex (a part of the profile that is almost straight on the red gurnard) and there are two distinct spines on its snout. Its body colour changes from sandy to red on capture. The fins or wings, of which the upper surfaces are vividly blue with bright yellow spots, are obviously more circular than the red gurnard.

Size

The sharp-beaked gurnard grows to about 54 centimetres.

Distribution

This fish also inhabits the sandy areas adjacent to rocks and reefs in deeper off shore waters of New South Wales, Victoria, Tasmania, South Australia and Western Australia.

The gurnards are taken by anglers fishing with bottom rigs from boats in deep water estuaries, close in along ocean rocks and from the rocks by land-based fishers. They will "quietly" take a wide range of baits and are singularly unspectacular in their resistance on the end of the line.

Edibility

All gurnards—if skinned—are reasonable eating, although surely only a desperately hungry angler would not release them.

[**Note**: Neither of these gurnards are the true butterfly gurnard, which has a greenish-red colour to the wings. The majority of gurnards change colour out of water. The colours, which can range through a yellow to reddish-brown, become more vivid with the stress of being caught.

It has been claimed that some gurnards have venomous spines in their dorsal fin, but this appear to be unsubstantiated. It is more likely that the culprit with the poisonous spines is a fish called the stingfish that is also called a "gurnard perch" (*see* stingfish, scorpionfish; *see also* venomous fish.)]

HAIRTAIL, AUSTRALIAN
Trichiurus savala

OTHER NAMES: **COX'S HAIRTAIL, RIBBONFISH**

HAIRTAIL, LARGE-HEADED
Trichiurus lepturus

OTHER NAMES: **AUSTRALIAN HAIRTAIL, COX'S HAIRTAIL,
LARGE-HEADED HAIRTAIL**

There is as much mystery about this fish as there is with its scientific name (*see* identification). This is of little importance to the angler who encounters one because it is extremely difficult to mistake it for any other fish (the frostfish which looks similar in other respects has a forked tail). It can appear unexpectedly, linger for a time, and then disappear as mysteriously as it came.

Identification
The hairtail has a flat, ribbon-like body with no scales. Nor does it have a caudal fin, the body terminating in a thin whippy point. There are no pectoral fins either and the anal fin consists of spines or spinules buried in the flesh. This fish has a singularly fearful-looking head and a mouthful of the meanest teeth. Its colour is silver. (*T. savala* is not usually encountered in tropical waters; *T. lepturus* is said to inhabit waters of the northern and north-western continental shelf of Australia. It is also described as brilliant blue-silver.)

Size
Both species grow to a length of nearly 2.5 metres, and a weight of about 6 kilograms.

Breeding
Nothing is known of their breeding but an invasion of Botany Bay, which began in the January of 1976 and lasted several months, had a high proportion of ripe females.

Habits
Hairtail are usually found in deep water near the

A pleasant surprise when it happens: a good catch of hairtail.

Where to fish
The deepest water of an inlet, harbour, bay, or estuary that shows no diminishment of salinity, seems to be the most hopeful location to "fluke" a hairtail. It can be caught from the bottom to near the surface, so set lines at different depths until you get a bite.

Tackle
Because of the shape of the fish, a handline gives better control. If using a small rod, the wire trace (it's essential) should be grabbed to lift or slide the fish on board. Lines should be heavy: of at least 12 to15 kilogram breaking-strain if it is a handline, 5 to 8 kilograms breaking-strain on a rod. A nylon-coated wire trace of about 50 centimetres is needed. (Old time hairtail anglers often use a curtain ring but a suitable swivel prevents line twist and is just as effective.) Hooks can be large, size 6/0 to 8/0 for live bait or ganged (Mustard 4202 or Tarpon style) to fit the fish fillet or dead bait (such as sardines, pilchards, yellowtail). All hooks must be needle sharp.

Baits
Try live or dead yellowtail, poddy mullet, pilchards, garfish, etc. Fillets of any of these small bait fish will also work.

Berley
Berley is an important factor on hairtail expeditions. It can be a concoction of mashed stale prawns, fish scraps, left-over soft pilchards, bread, bran, pollard —with sardines or cat food included. This mixture should attract any hairtail and keep them around.

Rigs
The unweighted rig No.2 or lightly weighted rig No. 3A with nylon-coated wire trace is suitable.

entrances to saline estuaries; in deepwater channels or holes; in harbours or bays; or near rocky foreshores. It relies on the power of its body to swim in the absence of pectoral and caudal fins. Hairtail eat crabs from the bottom and relish small fish, especially yellowtail. They also eat their own kind. Not proven is a theory that it may swim upright in the water. Except for a few out-of-season appearances, it is usually regarded as a winter fish.

Distribution
It was thought that the fish visited Cowan Waters of the Hawkesbury River in New South Wales in the autumn-winter period. It is now believed that this is a resident population. From time to time, apart from the lengthy stay in Botany Bay in 1976, the odd occurrence has been noted in southern waters of Queensland, in Pittwater, Sydney Harbour, Botany Bay, Port Kembla Harbour, Jervis Bay, Newcastle Harbour and Bateman's Bay (New South Wales) and Bunbury (Western Australia). These visits occured at various times of the year.

The population in Cowan Waters is present all year but the most prolific fishing is in the autumn and winter months. The best catches are made during the night.

When to fish
In the Hawkesbury River it is best to fish at night in the autumn-winter period, particularly in the Cowan Waters arm. It is regarded as a rare catch if one is taken during the day or in other months. When the fish have appeared elsewhere, the season or the time of the day do not appear to have been significant.

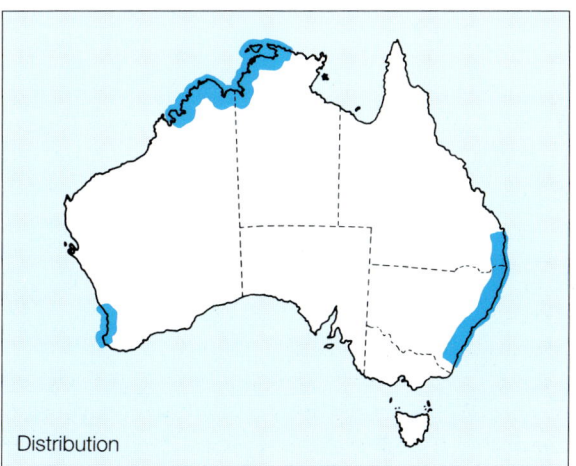

Distribution

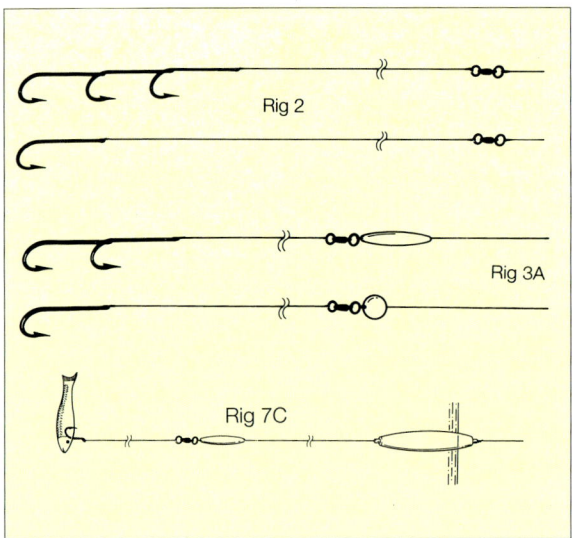

Some anglers use an adjustable float rig No. 7C because it accommodates quick adjustments to fishing depths in the search for the hairtail.

How to hook

The bite of a hairtail is indicated as the fish takes hold of the bait and moves down or away, not unlike the motion of a squid taking a bait. Let the fish have more line —about 2 metres — and then tighten the line firmly. If there is no hook-up, let the bait stay in the water. A hairtail will often attack again, especially if the bait is jigged. It is important to allow time for the hairtail to swallow the bait. They have a disconcerting habit of holding the bait between their teeth and letting it go at the surface.

Hint

The hairtail has a nasty disposition. It will snap at anything when brought aboard, including fingers, toes and ankles. If it is grabbed and held firmly behind the head, below the gill covers, it becomes immobile. It is worthwhile having a quantity of pre-rigged nylon-covered wire traces ready. It is quicker — and safer — to change a snap swivel than to unhook a hairtail by torchlight. The rigs can always be recovered when the catch is cleaned.

Edibility

There is no need to remove the bright silvery coat (it has no scales) from this fish. With the head removed, it can be prepared by most methods but for the best results cook hairtail whole, or at least in sizeable slabs.

HERRING, GIANT
Elops machnata

OTHER NAMES: **BANANA FISH, LADY FISH, PINCUSHION FISH, TEN-POUNDER**

[There is some confusion regarding the Australian" herring" *(Arripis georgianus),* as so many West Australian anglers prefer to call it. It is not a herring but a relative of the Australian salmon. With apologies to those who like it that way, the author submits that for a national list it is better to accept the name used by the Eastern State anglers — the tommy ruff (*see* entry) — to avoid or reduce the confusion already surrounding the names of so many fish.]

The giant herring is quite another fish. This fish is a stimulating sport fish, providing an angler with an exciting attack on the bait or lure and then following up with some breathtaking runs and a hard fight. Any angler who bests one of these fine fish should then release it: the giant herring is a worthy adversary but it provides precious little enjoyment as a meal.

Identification
The giant herring is a streamlined fish with bluish-olive colour around the dorsal area and bright silver on the sides and belly. Its fins are a dusky yellow with a tinge of black. The caudal fin is deeply forked. It has a large mouth.

Size
This fish grows to 1.2 metres long and can weigh as much as 7 kilograms.

Breeding
Little is known but larval specimens are like a transparent ribbon.

Habits
Though it is normally an inhabitant of coastal sand-flats and adjacent clear water, the giant herring will enter rivers and estuaries. It often aggregates and attacks schools of small bait fish. Its high leaps through such schools make a spectacular sight.

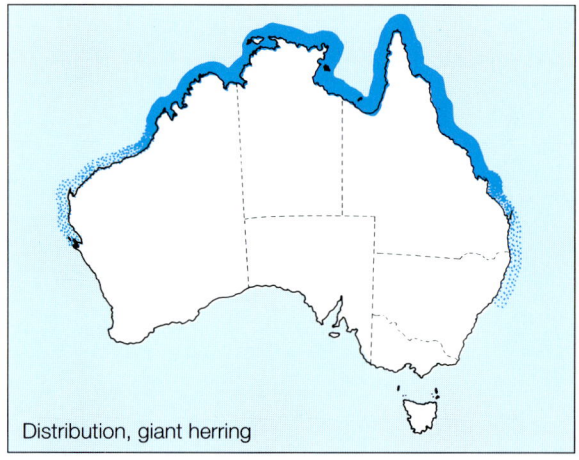

Distribution, giant herring

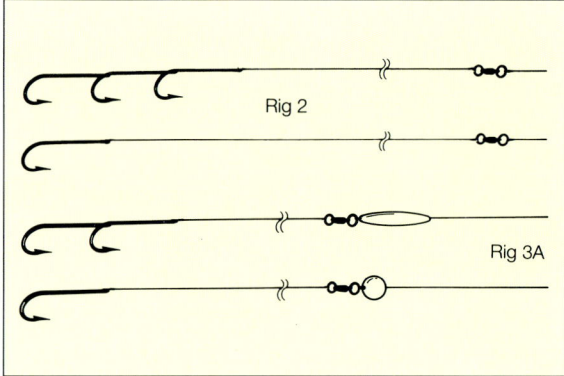

Distribution

A tropical fish species, the giant herring grows to its largest size in the far north of Queensland, in the Gulf of Carpentaria, in the Mornington Island area of the Northern Territory, and the north-west of Western Australia. Smaller sizes are more likely to be caught in the southern area of Queensland and in New South Wales and off the West Australian coast as far south as Shark Bay.

When to fish

The fish is present all year round but it often enters estuaries and rivers in the summer months, particularly in the central and northern areas of its range.

Where to fish

Many giant herring are caught near the edge of sandflats, particularly where they drop into deeper water, or alternatively in deepwater estuary channels.

Tackle

Rods will need medium-weight threadline or baitcasting reels with a capacity for 300 metres of line of about 8 kilogram breaking-strain. These should enable the angler to cast lures, cast-and-retrieve, or troll baits, but with a reserve of line for

when the hooked herring makes a long, sustained run, often leaping from the water.

Baits

Giant herring are generally only interested in other small fish. These can be used alive or cast and retrieved dead. Fish-shaped fillets are also acceptable. This fish is also a relatively easy target for a whole range of lures, either trolled or cast and retrieved.

Rigs

The unweighted or lightly weighted rigs (No. 2 or 3A) are successfully used for bait or lures. Single or ganged hooks can be used depending on the bait. A nylon-coated wire trace is unnecessary for a giant herring. The trouble is that the territory occupied by the giant herring is also home to a number of other fish, some with ferocious bites. The trace can be a small price to pay for some insurance.

How to hook

The angler very rarely has the chance to worry about hooking this fish as it charges in for the strike. It hooks itself and the angler can save his wits for the battle joined.

Edibility

The fish is so full of fine bones that it is inedible. Photograph the fish and release it.

HERRING, OX-EYE
Megalops cyprinoides

OTHER NAMES: **TARPON, BONY MULLET**

There is an increasingly worrying tendency about to call this fish a tarpon. Granted it is closely related, but to suggest that it is the same fish as the mighty tarpon *(Megalops atlanticus)* does both an injustice. The ox-eye herring grows to less than half the size of its tropical Atlantic relative, which has been recorded at an astonishing 2.8 metres (but a questionable weight of nearly 80 kilograms). The Australian National Sportfishing Association's record for an ox-eye herring is 3.4 kilograms (to December 1988), which would be very close to its maximum size.

Comparisons are ever odious, and the ox-eye herring derives its recognition as a sport fish in its own right, not by a comparison with the tarpon.

Identification

This fish is not as streamlined as the giant herring, its body being considerably thicker in the midsection. It also has a smaller and noticeably more upturned mouth. The ox-eye herring's most distinguishable feature is a long trailing filament at the back of its dorsal fin. Its overall colour is silver with a dullish green back. The ox-eye's tail is more deeply forked than that of the giant herring.

Size

Ox-eye herring grow to about a metre in length and perhaps as much as 5 kilograms.

Breeding

Breeding takes place at the beginning of the wet season and juveniles spend about the first year in upstream lagoons and headwaters of rivers.

Habits

The adult fish are known to spend time in freshwater, especially in deep water near mangroves, but the majority are seen in schools near the entrances to mangrove creeks or rivers. The fish will be near the bottom in deepwater.

Distribution

This fish is more common in the tropic regions. They normally range from northern New South Wales around the coastline of Queensland, Northern Territory and south of Shark Bay in Western Australia, though they have been caught as far south as Albany in the west and Port Hacking on the east coast.

When to fish

Fish are present all year but because many of the estuaries they inhabit are affected by monsoonal weather, the best time to catch ox-eye herring is autumn and through the winter in the northern region. Further south and anglers have to wait for the summer months to tangle with one.

Where to fish

These fish are found in estuary entrances, mangrove-lined rivers and creeks. They may also be seen "working" or "patrolling" over shallow sand flats. But any deepwater shelf around the mangroves may hold schools of these fish, especially near corners where the current sweeps past.

Tackle

Light threadline or baitcasting outfits — rods can be from 2 to 3 metres — will help cast the lighter lures or thin fish fillet baits to the fish. Lines of about 3 to 5 kilogram breaking-strain are adequate. Single or double-ganged Tarpon style hooks of about size 2 to 1/0 size will do their job. Saltwater fly outfits and flies are also used to catch ox-eye herring.

Baits

Ox-eye herring will accept small sprat-like fish, fillets of mullet and other fish. However, these fish

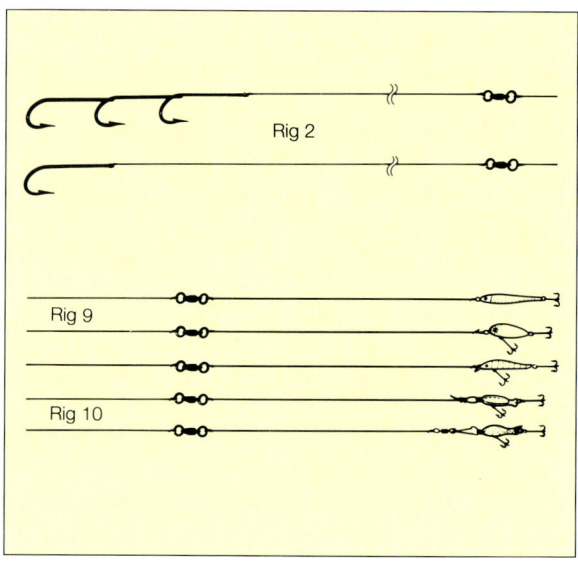

are exciting sport on small plastic lures, feathered or bucktail jigs, poppers, etc. and weighted flies.

Rigs

The unweighted bait rig or lure rig (Nos 2 or 9), with a stronger nylon leader, are suitable.

How to hook

The ox-eye herring may be a fast striker but it can be every bit as fast rejecting or throwing a hook. The angler must react just as fast when tensioning the line and maintaining sufficient tension to keep the hook embedded in the fish's mouth.

Hint

The stop-start, sink-and-lift type of retrieval with jigs, flies or sub-surface plugs, often results in a strike from ox-eyes that are resting or feeding on the bottom.

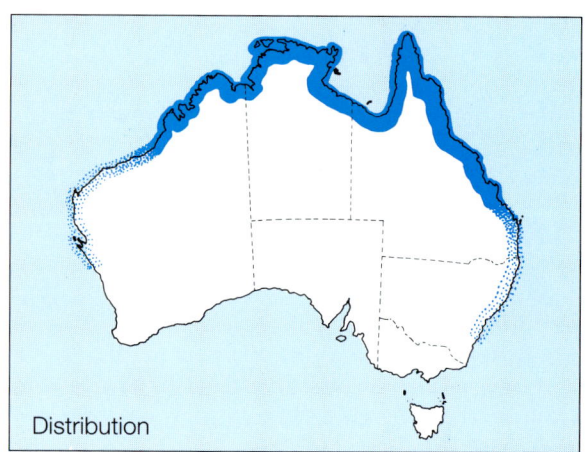

Distribution

Edibility

If a "million" fine bones do not worry you, then the absence of any flavour should.

The **Wolf Herring** *Chiocentrus dorab* (other names : knife-fish, ribbon- may be encountered in the tropics while fishing for the giant oxe-eye herring. It has an ugly mouth full of protruding fang-like teeth.

It grows to about 1.5 metres and is a shimmering silver-coloured fish with a shiny blue-green back. This fish is often caught while trolling inshore waters but it is known to enter estuaries during winter in the southern and central areas of Queensland.

This herring is certainly not regarded as a food fish butmany anglers its flesh an appealing bait for many other fish.

JAVELIN FISH

There are several javelins inhabiting the inshore and estuary waters of tropical Australia. They are frequently referred to as "grunters". And though these fish *do* make a grunting sound when caught, it is made by grinding together the sharp teeth (called pharyngeal) they have in their throat. Their swim bladder, which is located close by, tends to amplify the sound, so that a large specimen manages quite a loud "grunt". This fish's name is said to be derived from the strong, pointed spine in its anal fin. Javelins are near relatives of some sweetlips.

JAVELIN FISH, SPOTTED or YELLOW-FINNED

Pomadasys kaakan

OTHER NAMES: **GRUNTER, GRUNTER BREAM, QUEENSLAND TRUMPETER, TRUMPETER, LARGE-HEADED HAIRTAIL**

Identification

This is the largest member of the javelin family. It has a superficial resemblance to bream though it is not as deep-bodied. The body colour is a silvery-grey with a blue tinge. Bands of blotchy dark spots run from the dorsal to the stomach area. The tail is almost square. It has a relatively small mouth.

Size

This fish grows to approximately 60 centimetres and reaches about 6 kilograms. The minimum

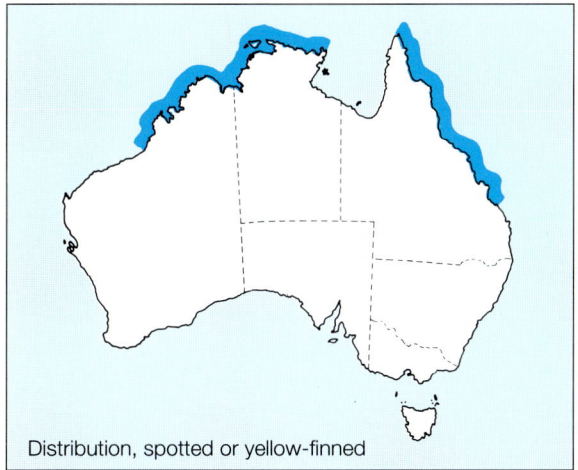

Distribution, spotted or yellow-finned

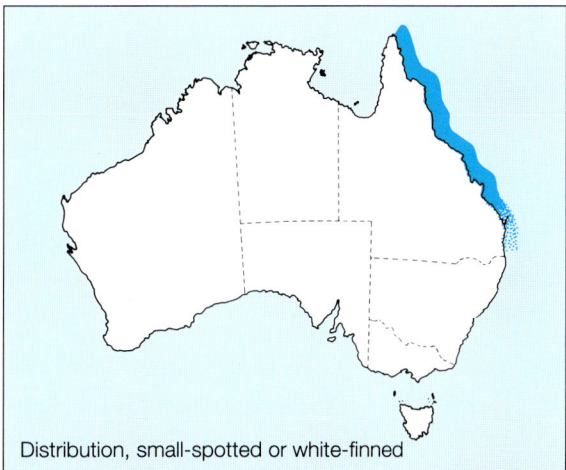

Distribution, small-spotted or white-finned

legal length for a catch in Queensland is 30 centimetres.

Breeding
Little is known.

Habits
The spotted javelin fish of northern Queensland and other tropical regions inhabits the mangrove estuaries and bays. It can also be found along rocky foreshores near the entrances. It prefers to dwell on firm or rocky bottoms, mainly in deep water, with a strong current flow. However, it will roam, feeding on sandflats on extremely high tides. Its diet is largely small fish, crustaceans and molluscs.

Distribution
It is commonly found from the central Queensland coast northward across the top end and down to the north-west of Western Australia.

JAVELIN FISH, SMALL-SPOTTED or WHITE-FINNED

Pomadasys argenteus

OTHER NAMES: **GRUNTER, GRUNTER BREAM, TRUMPETER**

Identification
This is a smaller, somewhat darker fish, being silver with visible olive/fawn undertones. It is easily distinguishable from the spotted relative by its overall spots, though they diminish towards the stomach. The spots are also prominent in its dorsal fins. Pelvic and anal fins are yellow.

Size
This fish grows in length to about 50 centimetres. The minimum legal length for a catch in Queensland is 30 centimetres.

Breeding
Little is known.

Habits
This fish is rarely caught outside sheltered mangrove creeks and estuaries. It, too, prefers deep water with a hard or rocky bottom with some tidal movement. It eats small fish, crustaceans, molluscs, etc.

Distribution
The small-spotted javelin fish can be found around the Gold Coast but bigger populations will be found the further you move north. They are present across Australia's north coast and down as far as the north-west of Western Australia.

When to fish
The javelin fish is around all year but the wet season, with its flooded estuaries and muddy conditions, has to be considered, but at least this is a fish that bites during the day *and* night. There is usually some area at the southern end of their distribution that can be found and fished during this period.

Where to fish
Try deep holes where a current runs past on either

tide, particularly if it has a clean hard sand or rocky bottom. Deepwater eddies close to mangroves or rock areas in estuaries are also likely to produce javelin fish. They can be found at the confluences of creeks and main bodies of water.

Tackle

Light single-handed rods with threadline, baitcasting or sidecast reels, with spools of 3 to 5 kilogram breaking-strain line, are suitable from some shoreline positions or from small boats — even light handlines are not inappropriate. For estuary shoreline fishing, use light 3 to 4 metre rods with matched threadline, overhead or sidecast reels, and with the same line weight. Hooks need not be larger than 1/0.

This fish is caught where larger species can be found, but the anglers may have to risk their lighter lines to improve their chance of catching javelin fish. All species are shy biters. If they are not as fussy as the true bream there is very little in it.

Baits

This fish will take very small hardiheads, mullets or sprats, fillets of garfish, pilchards, mullet, shellfish flesh, prawns, marine worms.

Berley

The javelin fish responds to a berley of minced fish, crabs, etc., made in a compound thick enough to reach the bottom before disintegrating or to be lowered in a mesh bag. Unfortunately, this also attracts many line-biting inhabitants which disperse the javelin fish and can cause quick "bust-ups".

Rigs

Try the lightly-weighted running rig No. 3 or 3A, or the running rig No. 4 with a sinker weight just heavy enough to hold the bottom. Some drift of the bait is helpful.

How to hook

The javelin fish nibbles, tasting the bait, often giving the impression of a small fish. The angler

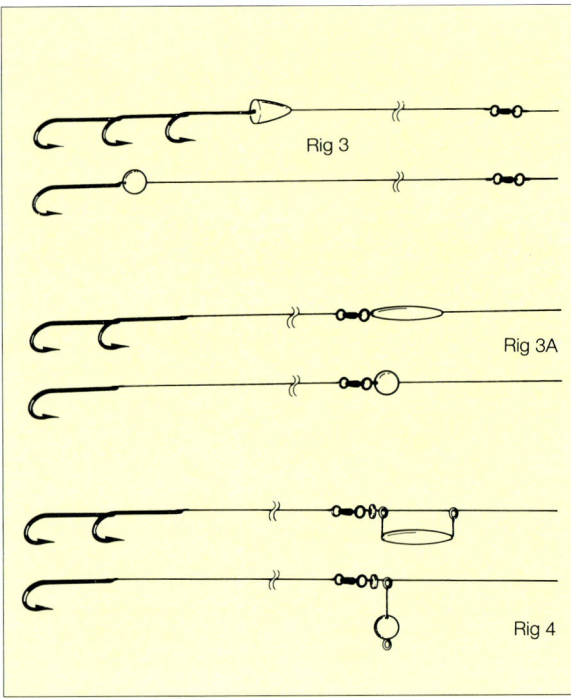

has to allow the fish time to take the bait well down where it begins the grinding process in its pharyngeal teeth before swallowing. When hooked it is a strong fighter.

Hint

If you slowly retrieve soft plastic-bodied jigs, in a shape resembling a little fish, about 2 to 3 centimetres long, through a berley trail, you stand a good chance of hooking a javelin fish.

Edibility

The javelin fish has white tasty flesh that makes excellent eating, however prepared, but the simpler methods allow the flavour to be savoured.

[Note: Other javelin fish encountered in tropical Queensland are the blotched javelin fish (*P. maculatum*), and the chunky member of the group, the lined javelin fish (*Hapalogenys kishinouyei*), which are also found in the Northern Territory and the north-west of Western Australia.]

JEWFISH, WESTRALIAN
Glaucosoma hebraicum

OTHER NAME: **DHUFISH**

Old names die hard and "dhufish" is still widely used for this magnificent West Australian fish. Unfortunately the reputation of the jewfish as one of the best eating fish, amongst anglers and in the restaurant trade, led to its exploitation by amateur and commercial fishers. The jewfish [*see also* close relative, the pearl perch] is endemic to a stretch of the West Australian coast and thankfully the local State fisheries authorities realised — perhaps not quite as soon as they might have — that this fish was threatened. The recreational angler's catch is now limited to no more than 5 per day and all must be at least 50 centimetres long. But it is a greedy angler, not to mention a lucky one, who catches that many. This fish should not be confused with the mulloway (*see* entry) which are commonly called jewfish.

Identification

This is a thick-shouldered fish, with a curved profile from its mouth to the back beyond its gill covers, from which point it curves to its thick caudal peduncle. The dorsal fin lays backwards and — in males only — a filament on the front of the dorsal reaches back to the base of its tail. There is a slight curve from the chin to the bottom of the gill cover, then the belly, and then fairly flat to the anal fin, from which point it rises to meet the caudal peduncle. The tail is broad and square. Its mouth is huge and its eyes are large. Jewfish are silvery-grey with purple and bronze reflections on their back. They often display a black line that curves from the bottom of the gill covers, through the eye, to the forehead. Juveniles possess longitudinal body stripes which disappear as they grow.

Size

These fish grow to about 1.2 metres and specimens of more than 30 kilograms have been recorded. An 8 to 10 kilogram fish is now a trophy catch. The minimum legal length for a catch in Western Australia is 50 centimetres.

Breeding

Jewfish are known to migrate in the late autumn-winter months from deep offshore reefs to shallow inshore waters which have less rugged terrain. This movement may be associated with water temperature or spawning.

Habits

The jewfish is a bottom-dweller that inhabits reefs with caverns or wide overhanging ledges. Occasionally a few fish may aggregate but it is more common to find individuals in such locations. Jewfish eat other fish and crabs. They are also partial to squid and, more particularly, octopus. When hungry they will slurp in their food from a distance (though not with bait hiding a hook!).

Distribution

The jewfish is found in reef areas from inshore to 30 or 50 kilometres off-shore. Its West Australian range is from Shark Bay in the north to the Recherche Archipelago near Esperance on the south coast.

When to fish

These fish can be caught throughout the year, seas permitting, as they inhabit some of the roughest waters on a hazardous coast, especially in the south of its range. Autumn and winter months offer the best chance of catching this fish in some of the inshore reefs.

Where to fish

Boats equipped with modern echo sounders are more likely to find a promising reef structure, but others drift in known haunts. The Shark Bay and the Houtman Abrolhos areas are popular target areas, but local knowledge is invaluable.

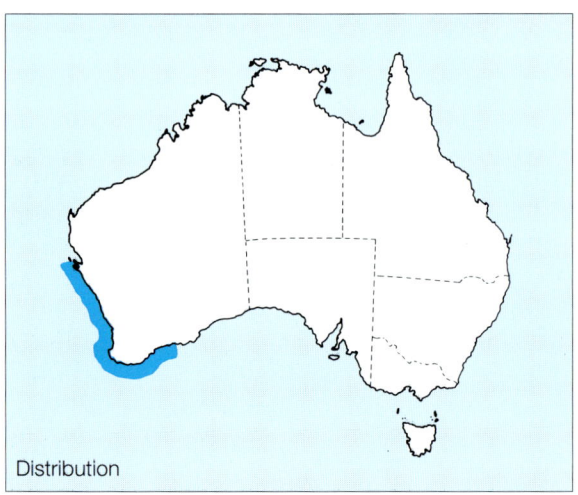

Distribution

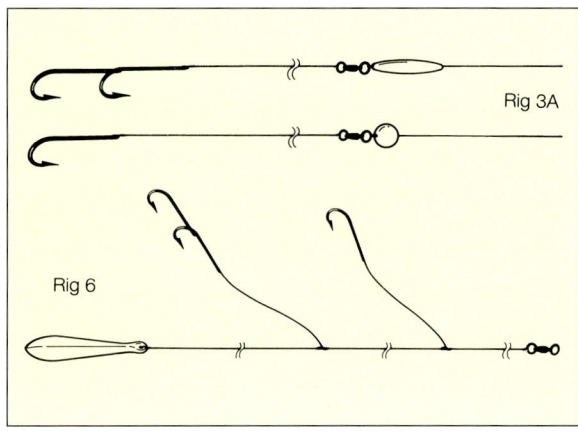

Rig 3A

Rig 6

Tackle

A handline with a breaking-strain as heavy as 30 kilograms or more, with up to a couple of kilograms of sinker, is suitable if drifting in deep waters. Gunwale-mounted winches are also used. There is no need to reduce the breaking-strain for handline fishing in shallower waters but lighter sinkers can be used if drifting or fishing from a moored boat. Strong, short, boat rods are not favoured as they do not facilitate the sensitive touch required to feel a jewfish's bite. Leaders and hooks must be strong. Hooks from 6/0 to 12/0 are most commonly used.

Baits

The number one bait among experienced jewfish anglers is a fresh skinned octopus with whole fresh squid a suitable substitute. Live fish up to 20 centimetres long are excellent, especially when fishing from a moored boat or in shallower areas where snagging is not a problem. Parrot-fish, wrasses, whiting, herrings and sardines are all used.

Berley

An effective berley in some areas and conditions—perhaps to a depth of 20 to 30 metres — and conditions is minced fish such as pilchards, mullet, shellfish, etc. It can be in a weighted onion bag dropped to the bottom or scattered from the surface. It may also attract other desirable species such as snapper.

Rigs

One approach is to use a bottom rig with a snapper lead of sufficient weight to reach and hold the bottom, whether drifting or moored. Rig 6 is suggested, with one or two three-way swivels and a metre-long tracer about 1 to 1.5 metres above the

The Westralian jewfish, a massive fish for the table.

metres and it loses its fight.   It's a different situation when a jewfish is caught in shallow water: the fish and angler find themselves in a sometimes formidable test of strength.

Edibility

One word expresses it perfectly — excellent! Do not over cook the fish in any circumstances, or spoil its delicious flavour by over-dressing. It is best savoured by pan-frying fillets, coated with bread crumbs, or grilled and sprinkled with lemon juice. West Australian anglers have every reason to boast about their grand jewfish.

The dorsal and anal rays, and the top of the caudal fin, end in long trailing filaments.

PERCH, PEARL
Glaucosoma scapulare

Identification

This close relative of the westralian jewfish can be a silvery dusky-grey though it lacks the black band of the jewfish that runs from the forehead through the eye to bottom of the gill cover. It does, however, have a distinct dark blotch on the top of the gill opening.

Size

The pearl perch grows to about 70 centimetres. It is found in small schools in deepwater reefs from about Yeppoon in Queensland to Seal Rocks in New South Wales, though it is more common in the waters off northern New South Wales. It is generally caught by anglers who are bottom fishing for snapper. Nevertheless, the pearl perch is as highly-regarded as its West Australian relative as a table fish.

sinker..   In shallower water, a running sinker rig with a large swivel, with bean or barrel sinkers of the weight required riding on this, is effective (No. 3A).   Use a metre or so of strong leader with a strong 6/0 to 8/0 hook— some use a three-way swivel with a second leader attached in this rig.

How to hook

The jewfish, for all its size, and some eating habits, is a frustrating biter. It sucks in many baits, the feel of which is acquired only by experience. Many anglers, especially while drift-fishing, will let off several metres of line just in case what may feel like a snag is in fact a jewfish holding on to the bait. The extra line gives it time to swallow.

Once hooked, the jewfish is all power. However, its swim bladder bursts once it is lifted through a few

Pearl perch.

JOBFISH

There are three jobfish (members of the Lutjanidae family of snapper and sea-perches) which are available to anglers fishing the Great Barrier Reef. They can also be found in the Northern Territory and the north-west of Western Australia. The general fishing information applies to them all.

JOBFISH, GREEN
Aprion virescens

OTHER NAMES: **KING SNAPPER**

Identification

This is the largest of the jobfish. It is an olive green-brownish colour on the dorsal fading to off-white towards the stomach. There is a deep blue edge to its yellowish spiny dorsal fin. The deeply-forked tail is dull yellow. The mouth is large with obvious canine teeth.

[**Note**: This fish is very similar to the **gold-banded snapper** (*Pristipomoides multidens*) of the reef areas of the Northern Territory and North-west coast of Australia.]

Size

This fish grows to about a metre in length and 12 kilograms.

Breeding

Little is known.

Distribution

The green jobfish is more plentiful in the reef areas from about Brisbane and north to beyond the Cape.

JOBFISH, ROSY
Aprion microlepis

OTHER NAMES: **KING EMPEROR, KING SNAPPER**

Identification

This solid elongate fish has a pale pink body with a silvery-white belly. The scales on the dorsal and upper sides have a blue tone and golden edge. The top of the head is a deep pink to red. There is a backward sweep to the bottom of its rear dorsal and anal fins.

[**Note**: This fish closely resembles the threadfin snapper (*Pristipomoides typus*) of the reef areas of the Northern Territory and north-west coast of Australia, also a member of the Lutjanidae or sea-perch family.]

Size

This fish grows to about 80 centimetres.

Breeding

Very little is known.

Distribution

The rosy jobfish inhabits reef waters stretching north from the southern area of Queensland.

JOBFISH, SMALL TOOTHED
Aphareus rutilans

Identification

This jobfish has a brownish hue along the dorsal with gold-copper undertones. Its most distinguishing features are the long filaments from the end rays of the rear dorsal and anal fins. It also

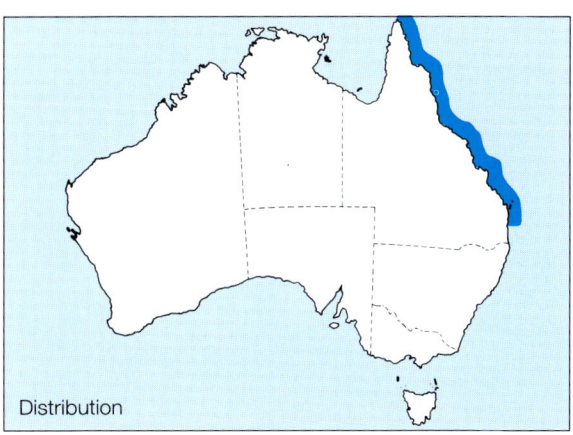

Distribution

has long tips to both lobes of its deeply forked tail. Though this jobfish has a large mouth, its teeth are less prominent than those of its relatives.

Size

The small-toothed jobfish grows to 80 to 90 centimetres in length and 8-plus kilograms.

Breeding

Little is known.

Distribution

It is mostly encountered towards the northern end of the Barrier Reef and beyond.

Habits

Jobfish appear to be gregarious; when one is caught, it is almost certain that a number of others will be found within a small area, hunting and eating together. This can deliver a good catch or a problem, depending upon what fish you were after in the first place. They are often caught on the edges of reefs in waters between 10 and 40 metres deep — and very often by anglers fishing the bottom for snapper, or coral trout etc. Jobfish are aggressive predators that display no hesitation before boldly attacking lures being trolled for such surface fish as mackerel. They eat a wide range of fish, crustaceans, molluscs, etc.

When to fish

Jobfish are present all year. Weather conditions for safe boating is the main consideration.

Where to fish

Reef ledges and chasms between reefs are likely to hold communities of jobfish. In clear water it is sometimes possible to see an aggregation of the fish swimming about, sometimes well off the bottom.

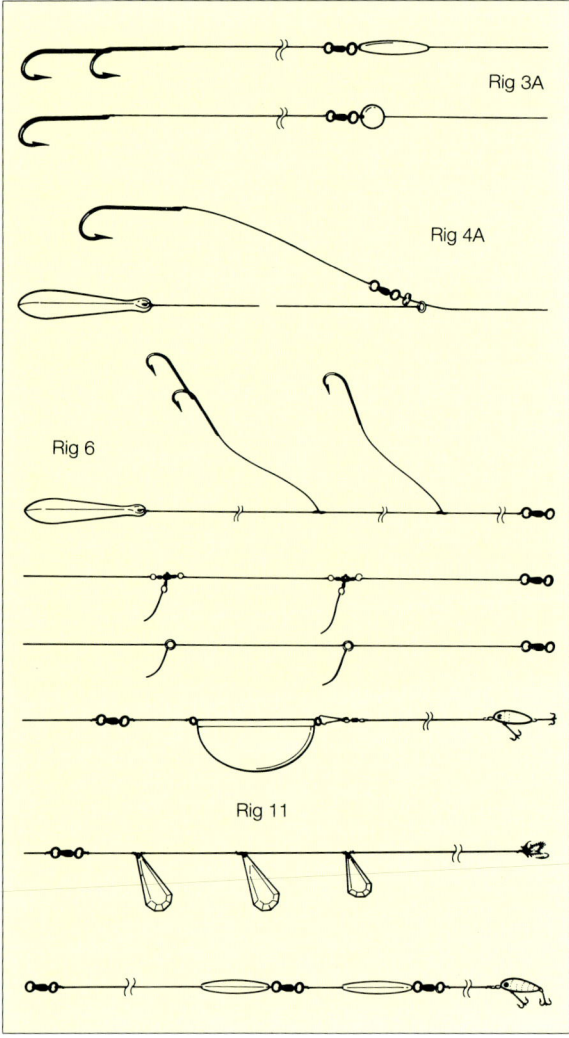

Rig 3A

Rig 4A

Rig 6

Rig 11

boat rods and the winch type of reels are also used. If you are using fish baits, lines of about 8 to 12 kilograms breaking-strain may be employed on medium to heavy single-handed threadline or baitcasting rods that are fitted with heavy duty reels to match: bait or lures can be cast and retrieved or jigged with them. They are also suitable for trolling. Nylon-coated wire traces are an insurance and hooks at least as strong as 6/0 are required.

Baits

Fillets of practically any fish will do, but try whole or half garfish, pilchards, mullet, hardiheads, octopus tentacles, etc. And provided they are tough and fitted with strong hooks, almost any lure seems suitable for trolling or jigging — they are taken without hesitation by these fish when they are in the mood.

Rigs

The conditions and the depth of the water govern the choice. Running rigs, such as No. 3A or 4A, as well as bottom rigs (No. 6) are satisfactory. Rig No. 9 is fine for casting and retrieving lures and for trolling (with a weight added as in trolling rig No. 11).

How to hook

The jobfish is not a selective eater. It will grab at almost any offering. The angler has to concentrate on besting a strong hard fighting fish. Unlike so many reef fish it is less inclined to rush for the protection — with line cutting consequences — of coral shelves or niggerheads.

Tackle

Because these fish share the environment with many larger fish, the prudent angler uses a heavy handline — a minimum 15 kilogram breaking-strain — for bottom fishing and trolling. Heavy

Edibility

Provided practical safeguards of cleaning, filleting and icing are taken, the flesh of the jobfish is excellent eating. Smaller ones can be baked whole.

KINGFISH, YELLOWTAIL
Seriola lalandi

OTHER NAMES: **KINGFISH, KINGIE, YELLOWTAIL, SILVER KING, KING AMBERJACK**

The yellowtail kingfish is a game fish that is accessible to many recreational anglers. Catching a large kingfish — especially from rocks — is regarded as an achievement by the most experienced anglers. For those inexperienced or casual anglers who get lucky enough to land one, it remains a most mem-orable highlight of their fishing experiences.

By the way, the yellowtail or scad or "bung", which are caught for bait (or for fun by youngsters) from wharves, piers or rocks, are *not* juvenile yellowtail kingfish.

Identification

This is a streamlined, torpedo-shaped fish with a solid body. When alive, it is a deep blue along the back. There is a hint of green where the blue merges with a rich yellow-gold band that separates the blue back from the silvery belly. The dorsal and pectoral fins are grey-blue, the pelvic and anal fins yellowish, and the tail a bright yellow. It has a mouth full of small teeth.

Size

The kingfish grows to about 2 metres in length and can weigh more than 50 kilograms. The Australian all-tackle record (as at September, 1988) is 39.91 kilograms; the world all-tackle record stands at 52 kilograms.

The minimum legal size for a catch in South Australia is 40 centimetres in length.

Breeding

The only conclusions reached by current research is: "offshore", and even that is with a question mark.

Habits

The kingfish is pelagic, the majority following their food source of small migrating fish such as pilchards, sardines, garfish and squid. However, it is not uncommon for larger fish to become permanent residents in an area, particularly deepwater locations with a constant or stable source of small fish, crabs, octopus and squid.

Juveniles are often found in large schools, the numbers of which shrink as the fish grow. By the time they become large kingfish they are usually found in twos, threes or fours, if not "loners".

Adult fish prefer rocky or reef areas, often aggregating in or near formations that rise sharply from the ocean floor. They will enter harbours via shipping channels and visit deep waters near wharves or jetties, usually hunting small fish. Kingfish feed at all levels and often attack schools of surface fish. They can be berleyed to the surface and can provide some of the most exciting fishing action when using lures or poppers.

The kingfish will also aggregate around floating objects. In recent times this trait has resulted in the development by professional fishers of a floating trap. Fisheries authorities are watching the method — and recreational anglers are concerned — because the traps are taking small or "rat" (juvenile) kingfish. And when these traps lose their marker buoys or break free in rough seas, they can pose a threat to small craft.

Distribution

The yellowtail kingfish is wide-ranging. It can be found from about Rockhampton in Queensland

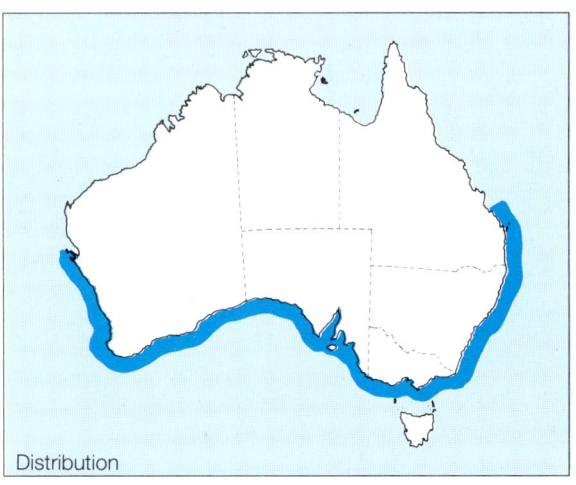

Distribution

south to northern Tasmania, along the Victorian, South Australian and Western Australian coasts as far north as Shark Bay.

It was thought that the populations of the east coast of Australia were separate from those of Lord Howe Island and New Zealand. Yet in recent years, fish tagged in Australia have been discovered in New Zealand waters. This could be explained away as a rare event, with those fish following the tongue of an unusual current, but it has researchers intrigued.

When to fish

These fish are not frequently caught at night. The morning and afternoon yield more fish when working from rocks, or off-shore in a boat, though they can be seen during the day. Some will be caught at any time of the year but the best chance of catching a good sized kingfish is during summer and early spring, often in deeper waters. Catches tend to be smaller at other times of the year .

Where to fish

There are in most States well known off-shore locations which produce fish consistently. But boat fishers with an echo sounder fitted to their boat should look for reefs with high points and deep water at least on one side. Sometimes the fish will be present on the tops of shallower reefs. Land-based anglers can find kingfish in the front of ocean platforms where there is deep water with broken reefs extending to sea and under cliff faces with a deep hole. Do not overlook wharves or jetties with dredged channels leading to them.

Tackle

The fish can be caught on handlines with a minimum breaking-strain of 20 kilograms, with live or dead baits. Stopping them is a hand-over-hand test of strength and the angler should wear protective finger-stalls. The winch type of reel fitted to the gunwale is less strenuous.

Medium to heavy threadline or baitcasting outfits with 8 to10 kilogram breaking-strain line can be used from boats for trolling, bait fishing and tossing lures and poppers to the fish. Special jig rods, often fitted with a roller tip, work well. Light game outfits are used also for trolling or bait fishing from boats. From the rocks a 3 metre to 3.5 metre rod, suitable for a heavy-duty threadline or overhead reel, will cast lures satisfactorily and can also be used to fish with floated live bait. Any rod will require a medium-fast or fast taper, with plenty of pulling power in the butt area. Line on these

A splendid yellowtail kingfish caught off Montague Island.

rods needs to be 8 to 12 kilograms breaking-strain.

Baits

Use live squid, yellowtail, pike, sweep, garfish, small salmon, tommy ruff etc., or fresh kills of these fish. If you are using dead fish bait, pieces sliced off the side seem to give the better results. Large fillets of most tunas are accepted — but live bait will always be more effective than dead bait and the slim type of fish are best for trolling. Hooks of a size to suit the bait should be strong and sharp. The kingfish can be taken on almost any lure used for trolling or casting and retrieving, and the speed does not seem to be a factor (which it is with many other pelagics). These include spoons, slicers, skirted game lures, poppers and plugs.

Berley

Yellowtail kingfish can be induced to the surface with good oily berley, especially in shallower in-shore waters. Once they are feeding they will take bait, lures or poppers.

Rigs

For bottom fishing, the running rigs No. 4 or 4A work well, the bottom and depth deciding the type and weight of the sinker. In shallow water with live bait, unweighted or lightly-weighted rigs No. 2 or 3 are suitable.

When fishing from rocks, the floated bait rig No. 7C or with a balloon instead of a float, is very effective as are standard game rigs when fishing offshore.

How to hook

With lures trolled, jigged or cast and retrieved the kingfish virtually hooks itself. The same can be said for trolled baits. With live bait — perhaps with the exception of squid — the kingfish is less positive and takes time to swallow. Allow the fish some metres of line before applying the pressure to set the hook. Once hooked, this fish is determined to reach the bottom by the most rugged path, or find a cave or niggerhead — even a wharf pylon — on which to cut the line.

It is a powerful fish and stopping and turning one requires good equipment and steadfast effort, especially if the angler is fishing from the shore.

Hint

When fishing from the shore using dead fish bait such as yellowtail, pilchard, mullet, garfish (with beak removed) or similar under a float or balloon, hook it on 2 or 3 ganged hooks in the reverse manner. That is, the point of the bottom hook is put through the fish's eye, not the tail area as is normal. The kingfish which swallows bait head first is less likely to ignore such a fish bobbing

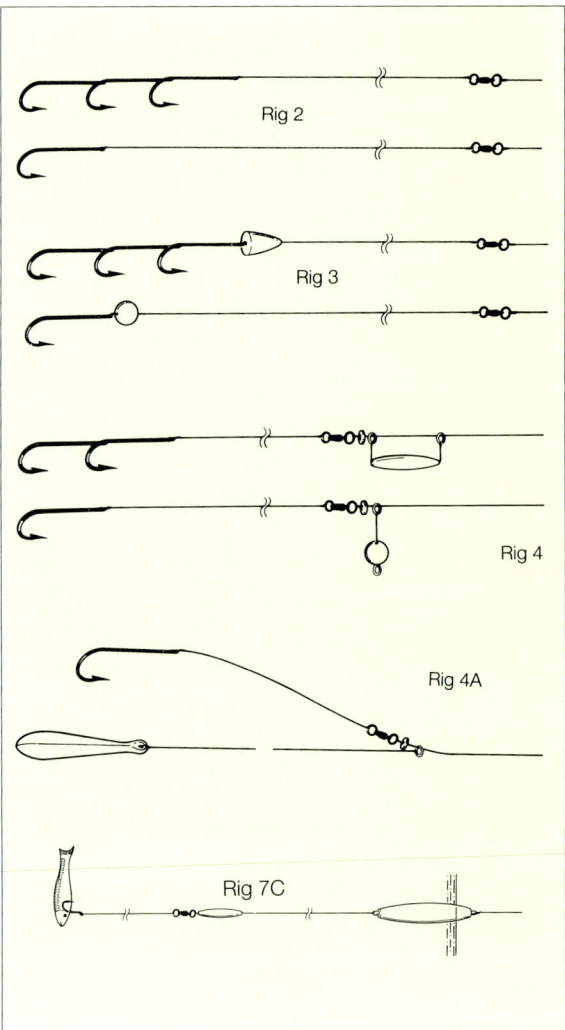

around. A dead squid on a large single hook can also be threaded so that the hook point is exposed at its "blunt" or mantle end. The arms can be half-hitched above the hook eye.

Tethering a kingfish to a boat will attract other kingfish. It will also, unfortunately, attract sharks.

Edibility

The kingfish caught in the south of their distribution area are regarded as better than those taken in the north.

This fish is not a top-rate table fish, though the smaller fish of up to 6 kilograms are palatable, provided that they have been killed, bled, cleaned and kept out of the sun. Steaks from large specimens are considered satisfactory when barbecued.

LEATHERJACKET

There are more than five dozen different leatherjackets in Australian waters and the confusion of names among them — both common and scientific — might have arisen from the numerous colour variations between the sexes and the diverse habitats that these fish occupy. A lack of co-ordinated research might also have contributed: this commercial and recreational species attracts little expensive research.

It is easy to distinguish the differences between leatherjackets and triggerfishes. Leatherjackets have a single dorsal spine and soft rear dorsal and anal fins. The dorsal spine is much more forward on the head than the three spines of the triggerfish's dorsal fin. Elsewhere in the world, the leatherjackets (a name bestowed on them by Captain James Cook) are called file fish — their skins are covered in fine, tooth-edged scales.

The triggerfishes, which in general are thicker through the body than leatherjackets, have a covering of quite large, horny plate-like scales, especially near the gill openings. Their dorsal spine consists of three strong sharp spines, the second of which locks the first spine in position. The first spine cannot fold back until the second spine is depressed. Triggerfishes are mainly tropical and are generally of spectacularly gaudy colours.

What follows is an arbitrary selection of leatherjackets, chosen mainly because they grow to a reasonable size and are relatively common. It is quite probable that other leatherjacket species will be caught. If they are of a reasonable size (caution is needed; *see* unicorn and scribbly leatherjacket) and more desirable fish are unco-operative, they can be a tasty meal.

[**Warning**: By contrast, some triggerfish are *known* to be poisonous, if only at certain times of the year. Don't risk eating them at any time.]

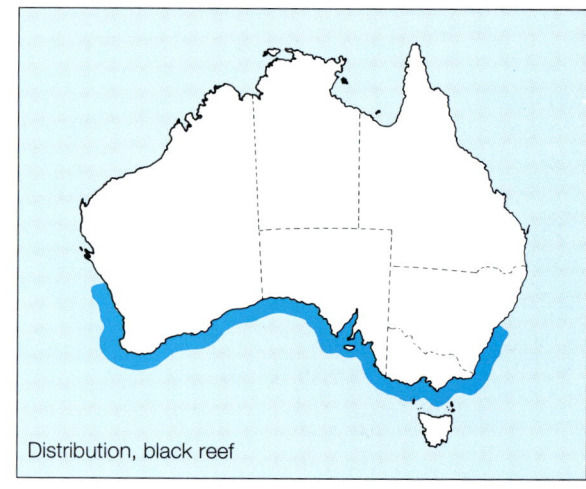

Distribution, black reef

LEATHERJACKET, BLACK REEF
Eubalichthys bucephalus

Identification
The body colour of this leatherjacket varies from a pale brown to a blackish-brown. The area around the head of the fish is usually much darker than the body. There may be faint stripes along the body and it has a white ring around the eye.

Size
This leatherjacket grows to approximately 40 centimetres in length.

Distribution
The black reef leatherjacket inhabits the coastal reefs of central and southern New South Wales, Victoria, South Australia and Western Australia, north to about Geraldton.

LEATHERJACKET, CHINAMAN OR YELLOW
Nelusetta ayraudi

Identification
This leatherjacket has a much longer head and elongated body, although the male's is deeper than the female. Its colour can be sandy to fawn to tan to a red-brown. This is one of the largest of the leatherjackets with extremely strong teeth. It is said to be capable of biting through hooks that are used for large reef fish.

Size
The chinaman grows to more than 80 centimetres in length and weighs up to 3 kilograms.

Distribution
It is found around the deeper offshore reefs from southern Queensland, around the eastern and southern coastline (including Tasmania) to the north-west region of Western Australia. Juveniles of up to about 0.5 kilograms are frequently encountered in harbours and bays.

LEATHERJACKET, FAN-BELLIED
Monocanthus chinensis

OTHER NAME: **FAN-TAILED LEATHERJACKET**

Identification
This leatherjacket is distinguished by the larger fan-like extension on its body in the belly area and a long filament on the top lobe of its tail. It also has spines on each side of its caudal peduncle. The fish's colour varies from green to a sandy-fawn in juveniles and a yellowish-brown to dark brown in adults. There are blotches or variations of these colours on its sides.

Fan-bellied leather jacket.

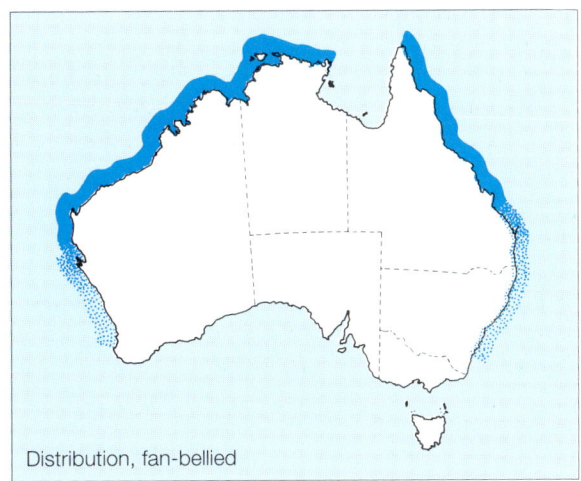

Distribution, fan-bellied

Size

This fish grows to 25 or 40 centimetres long — depending on your source.

Distribution

Mainly confined to the tropics, this leatherjacket prefers areas of seagrass adjacent to reefs and in bays and inlets, though it has been found on off-shore reefs. It is often found as far south as Batemans Bay on the New South Wales coast, throughout Queensland and Northern Territory waters and as far south as Busselton in Western Australia.

LEATHERJACKET, HORSE SHOE

Meuschenia hippocrepis

Identification

Yellow-green to olive in colour, the male of this species has a dark area across its forehead that curves around the eye to below its mouth. Both sexes have an elongated horse shoe shape on the sides. This fish also has 4 spines on each side of the caudal peduncle.

Size

The horse shoe leatherjacket is said to grow to 61 centimetres in length.

Distribution

These fish inhabit coastal reefs and rocky inshore

areas from Wilson's Promontory in Victoria to the Houtman Abrolhos in Western Australia and along the northern coastline of Tasmania.

LEATHERJACKET, MOSAIC
Eubalichthys mosaicus

OTHER NAMES: **DINNERPLATE LEATHERJACKET, DEEP-BODIED LEATHERJACKET**

Identification

The body colour of this leatherjacket depends upon its size. It ranges from light grey in very small

Distribution, horse shoe

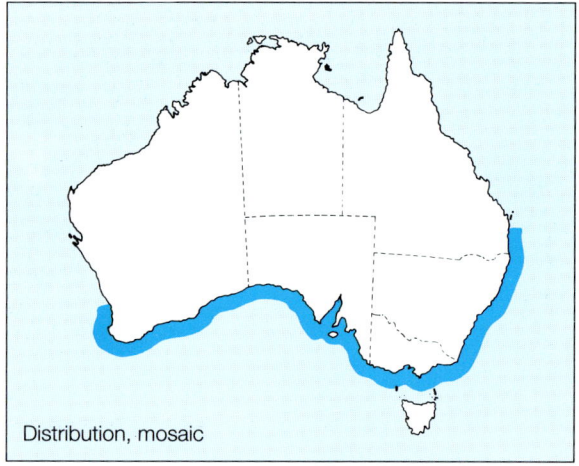

Distribution, mosaic

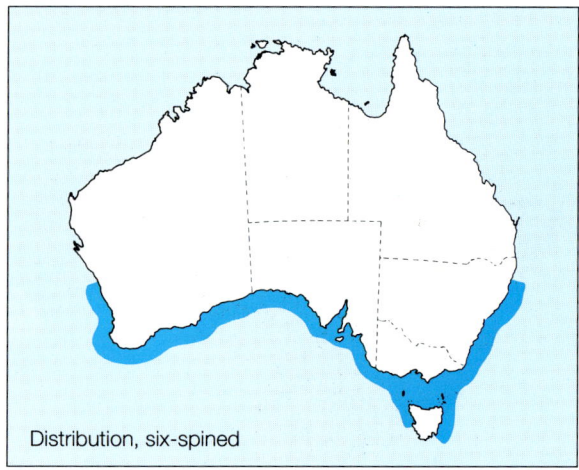

Distribution, six-spined

fish, through a yellowish-orange in juveniles, to a bluish-grey with yellow patches in adults.

Size
The mosaic leatherjacket is reputed to grow to 60 centimetres in length.

Distribution
Though this fish inhabits the deep offshore reefs of southern Australia, off Victoria, northern Tasmania, South Australia and Western Australian waters north of Perth. It has also been located on some inshore reefs in New South Wales and on occasion as far north as southern Queensland.

Size
This leatherjacket grows to about 60 centimetres in length and 2 to 3 kilograms in weight.

Distribution
These fish inhabit coastal reefs from central New South Wales, all along the southern coastline and north to Jurien Bay in Western Australia. It is also found in Tasmanian waters. Juveniles school in estuaries, harbours, bays and coastal lakes but they move out to the reefs as they mature. The smaller fish are commonly found where artificial reefs have been formed in some of New South Wales' lakes and estuaries.

LEATHERJACKET, SIX-SPINED

Meuschenia freycineti

OTHER NAMES: **VARIABLE LEATHERJACKET, REEF LEATHERJACKET**

Identification
This leatherjacket, which is more elongate than most of the others, except for the chinaman, is most easily distinguished by the Maori-like pattern of blue or olive tones on the head area, which extend along the body. Its dorsal and anal fins are yellow and most males have yellow and black marking or blotches on the sides. The east coast variety usually sports brighter colours and displays a very dark vertical stripe in its caudal fin.

LEATHERJACKET, SCRIBBLED

Alutera scripta

LEATHERJACKET, UNICORN

Alutera monoceros

Identification
These two tropical water leatherjackets are elongate but without the belly flap. The unicorn is a drab olive-brown to black colour. It has a short and thin dorsal spine easily broken.
The scribbled species is olive-yellow and its body is covered with bright blue wiggly lines and many

brown spots. It also has a tiny dorsal — so fine that it is easily snapped — and a large caudal fin.

Size
Both these fish grow to between 60 and 70 centimetres in length.

Distribution
Both are primarily tropical water fishes but occasional smaller species have been found as far south as the central coast of New South Wales and as far south as Fremantle in West Australian waters

[**Warning**: Both these fish have been suspected of causing an illness similar to ciguatera if eaten. This is usually only caused by larger specimens of the fish (*see* Ciguatera, page   ) but anglers in doubt should check with the locals about these two leatherjackets.]

The following applies to all leatherjackets.

Habit
Leatherjackets are omnivorous fish. Their mouth shape and strong front teeth are perfect for cracking the hard covers of shellfish, bivalves and mussels to extract the flesh, as well as nipping algaes and tiny growths from rocks. The erect dorsal spine is locked in position as a precaution against predators and there is no doubt it would injure the mouth of any fish trying to clamp its jaws around most leatherjackets. It is also believed that the leatherjacket uses the spine to fasten itself in crevices and holes in rocks. These fish use their rear dorsal and anal fins as part of their forward and backward propulsion, fins that help it to hover or remain motionless. The scribbled and unicorn

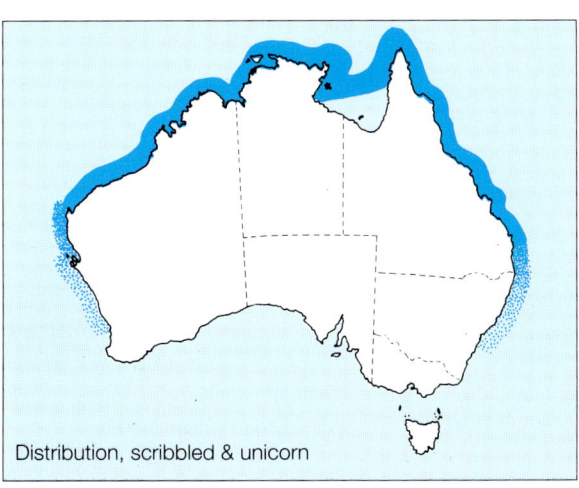

Distribution, scribbled & unicorn

Unicorn leatherjacket.

leatherjackets can swim in a perfectly vertical position.
Leatherjackets are a schooling fish.

When to fish
In harbours and estuaries leatherjackets are considered a spring and summer fish, but on reefs they can be encountered throughout the year. Regular leatherjacket anglers tend to take a more jaundiced view, when they say of this fish: "They're always absent when wanted and present when they're not!"

Where to fish
These fish provide endless fun for youngsters (and adults) when the small ones are biting around the wharves and jetties of harbours and estuaries, and near breakwaters and groynes. Otherwise leatherjackets are invariably encountered while fishing from rocks or from boats over or near estuary reefs or offshore reefs.

Tackle
The basic handline with a breaking strain of 3 to 6 kilograms is adequate for estuary fishing. So is a light single-handed threadline rod and reel. If you are fishing from rocks, or from boats offshore, the handlines and rods used for reef fishing will catch leatherjackets—provided the hook is small enough and a short wire trace is employed.

Baits
Any bait will do. Small pieces of prawn, small cubes of fish flesh (with a piece of skin to help keep it on the hook), pieces of octopus tentacles and squid, small pieces of bacon rind, etc.

Rigs
For estuary fishing, use a lightly weighted running rig No. 3A or a running bottom rig No. 4 or 4A, depending on the bottom terrain and the strength

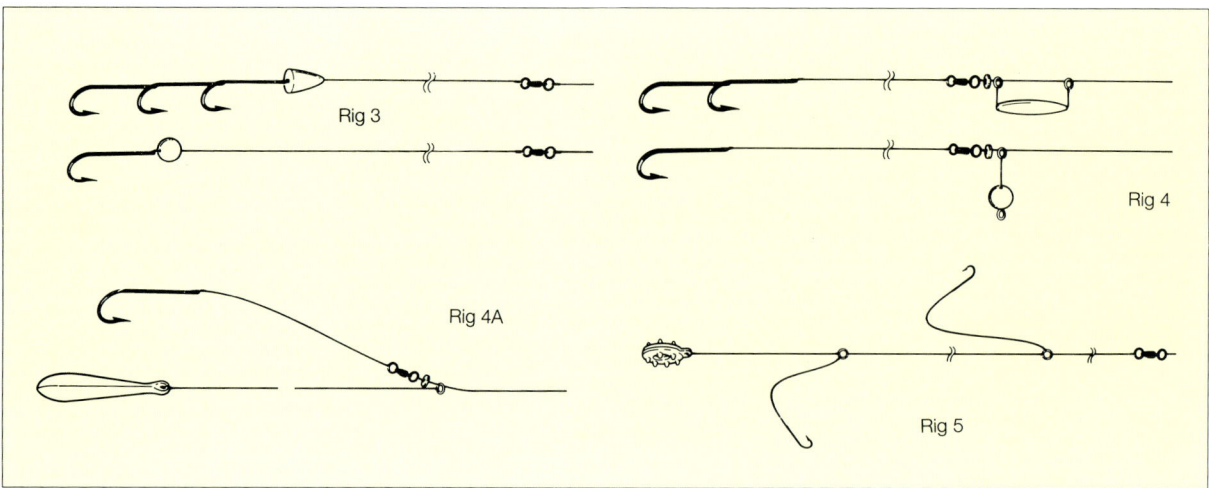

Rig 3

Rig 4

Rig 4A

Rig 5

of the current. Running sinkers or fixed sinker rigs (Nos. 4 or 5 respectively) can be used in reef areas. The use of a wire trace is almost mandatory where larger fish are likely to be hooked. Long shank hooks are necessary for much the same reason if you are fishing in estuaries (and a short length of light nylon-coated wire trace is an extra safeguard).

How to hook

It is crucial for the angler to maintain touch or tension on the line to feel the picking bite of a leatherjacket. This tension will help to hook the fish when the leatherjacket takes the point of it into its mouth.

Edibility

The flesh of a leatherjacket is firm and white. Fish to be eaten should be cleaned and iced (or at least kept cool).

The flavour of a leatherjacket is much better when fresh.

LUDERICK
Girella tricuspidata

OTHER NAMES: **BLACKFISH, DARKIE, NIGGER, ROCKPERCH, SWEEP**

This is a case in which the traditional Aboriginal name for a
fish is slowly but surely replacing its European common
names. Luderick is increasingly appreciated as both
appropriate and distinct. In New Zealand this fish is
known by its Maori name of parore.
The luderick deserves to be ranked near the head of any
sportsman's list of fighting fish, and the anglers who specialise
in them deserve their dedicated reputation as sport fishers.
This fish is tougher and imbued with more staying power — if
not as spectacular — than the revered trouts. The dedicated
do battle with them on what is almost inadequate gear and in
some habitats and conditions where the fish hold
almost all the advantages.

Identification

This is a solid, oval fish with a short front dorsal fin connected to a higher soft second dorsal. The tail is broad and slightly forked. Fish taken from river estuaries are usually darker, being a brownish to black in colour that becomes lighter at the belly. The 6 to 8 dark bands around its body are not as distinct as those on fish that have spent some time in the ocean. The latter become a more bronzed-brown-to-black on the dorsal area and light tan to grey on the abdomen, and the bands appear much more pronounced. There is a hint of bronze in the pectoral fins. Its mouth is small.

Size

The luderick has been recorded at 71 centimetres long, and weighing more than 5 kilograms, but it rarely exceeds 0.75 kilos in estuaries. And even out in the ocean a 2.5 kilogram fish is some catch. In New South Wales the minimum legal size catch that may be kept must be 25 centimetres long. The regulations in Victoria stipulate a minimum of 22 centimetres.

Breeding

Adults make an offshore spawning run during winter months in the north and during or after spring in the south. Extensive schools move northwards along the southern coast of New South Wales at these times.

Habits

The luderick is a schooling fish, but the schools vary considerably from a few to a great many. There are generally mixed sizes in a school. Luderick move frequently, both within estuaries and along the ocean fronts between estuaries. They are basically herbivores, eating algae and particularly the thin stranded ribbon weeds of rivers and estuaries and the broad-leafed lettuce or cabbage of the ocean rocks. Nevertheless, they can often be tempted to eat conjevoi, prawns and abalone gut in the early spring. In Victorian and South Australian waters, luderick are usually caught using baits of squirt worms or other marine worms. Luderick bite freely during their spawning migrations.

Distribution

This fish can be found in estuaries, bays and coastal lakes, as well as along ocean rock fronts. It is abundant along the New South Wales coast, thinning out towards its northern limits in the most southern of Queensland's waters. It similarly thins out to the south and then westward along the Victorian coast. Having said this, luderick *are* occasionally caught as far west as Adelaide.

When to fish

These fish are present throughout their range in varying numbers all year round. There are some areas in rivers and estuaries where these fish will feed on a rising tide and there are others — often not far away — that offer better fishing as the tide ebbs. When fishing off the rocks, the last quarter before the top of the tides and the first third of the run-out is frequently productive. Where there is a sandy gutter or rock split leading into deep water, look for the fish on the bottom at the deep end, apparently waiting for the ebbing tide to carry weed to them. Luderick bite during the day.

Overcast and choppy water is more productive than very clear water, calm conditions and bright sunshine. A high tide in mid-morning or mid to late afternoon is usually preferred by anglers.

Where to fish

In rivers and estuaries luderick enthusiasts concentrate their efforts over or alongside weed beds, near weed-encrusted rock walls or groynes, and around bridge pylons and wharf piers. Many such spots are best fished from a moored boat.

Along the oceanfront, try fishing around those platforms or rock formations where there are growths of green cabbage or lettuce, especially if there are foamy suds in the water or washes to provide cover for the fish. The sides of inlets where rough seas may push out torn-away weed is also a good spot to start looking for luderick. Some rock areas can only be fished, for the angler's safety, in flat seas or low swell conditions. In such positions use good footwear, with rock plates.

Tackle

A specialised outfit has evolved for luderick fishing. The rod is a slow taper style, of 3 to 4 metres in length — the shorter and usually lighter model being used only when fishing from boats, rocks, walls, or wharves in the calmer waters of estuaries or harbours. Those in the longer size, usually of a medium weight, are much better for rock locations where the fish has to be controlled and kept clear of rocks in much rougher conditions, and often swum ashore on a wave. However, if you only have a faster medium-tapered rod in similar lengths it should be no handicap. The reel is usually a free-spinning centrepin type. This allows line to be spun off to keep the float in an upright position as the

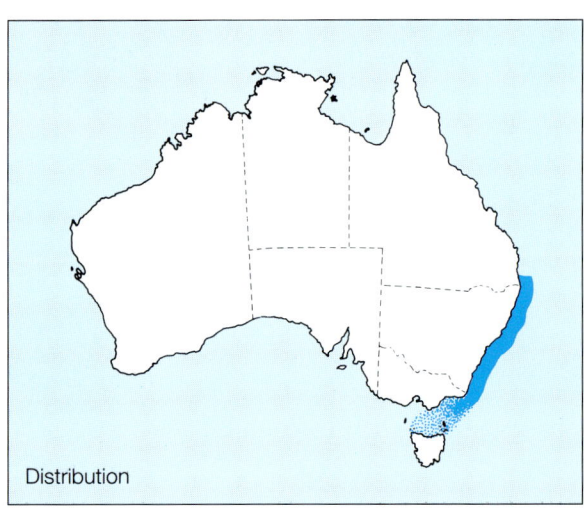

Distribution

current or wash takes the float away from the angler. These reels are positioned almost as low on the butt as a reel on a fly rod.

Some luderick anglers use the same rods as above, but made to suit a threadline reel. The reel should be one which allows manual operation of the bail arm. It can then be left open for easy stripping but instantly switched to its line-retrieval mode when needed.

When fishing in estuaries, use about a 3 kilogram breaking-strain line and try a lighter leader. When fishing the rocks, make the main line about 5 to 8 kilograms breaking-strain, with about a 3 to 4 kilograms breaking-strain line for the leader. Your float should usually be a quill or pencil type for estuaries; a light, medium or heavy long-stemmed model is best when fishing from the rocks. However, wind, current and the sea conditions may dictate your choice. Hooks should be about size 6 to 10, viking or sproat being suitable.

Baits

Basically vegetarian, the luderick is generally caught in the fine-stranded algae weed in estuaries and harbours and sea-cabbage or lettuce on the ocean front. In some areas, however, and especially prior to their spawning run, luderick will greedily devour squirt and other marine worms as well as peeled prawn flesh. After rough seas, conjevoi will often be taken. Luderick will also eat the white of hard-boiled eggs, but cutting this into cubes and threading it on the hook is a tedious task.

Berley

The most most popular berley for luderick in the protected waters of estuaries, bays and harbours, is a quantity of the weed being used for bait, chopped

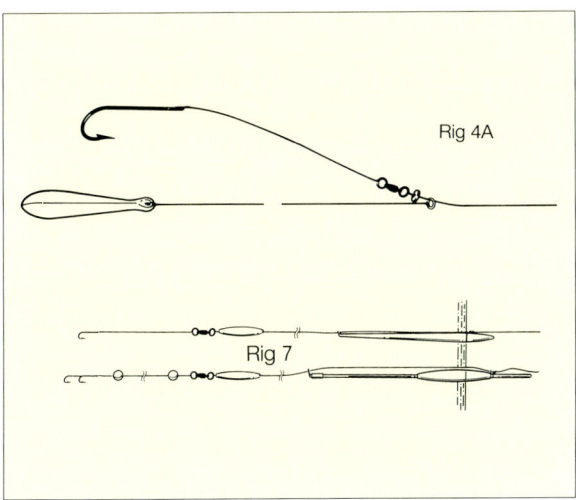

Rig 4A

Rig 7

finely and mixed with sand. It is a good berley from the rocks but any cabbage weed in the vicinity should be chopped and added. Chopped cabbage weed with sand and some sloppy bread make an excellent rock berley.

Rigs

An adjustable float rig with which the depth of bait can be quickly and easily regulated is the normal rig No. 7 or a running bottom rig No. 4A for fishing the bottom, sandy gutters or rock splits.

How to hook

As with most angling, time spent with an experienced angler in such specialised fishing can be invaluable for the newcomer. However, in the absence of such a paragon, here are a few tips. The small sinkers must be heavy enough to get the bait down to the correct depth and keep the float upright. It will then submerge easily at the most timid bite for, in the main, luderick are quiet sippers, even though there are those times when they will suck in greedily. Keep the line straight between the rod tip and the float. Any wind or water "belly" will delay the setting of the hook. If the float is correctly weighted, one old expert advises to "say ninety-nine, and not too quickly" as the tip of the stem goes under, then lift the rod firmly to set the hook. The luderick will make a powerful fight of it, so pressure on the line must be maintained, even with such light breaking-strains. When fishing from the rocks, there is a great deal of "give and take" in the waves as the fish tries to dive. Anglers must also maintain pressure to steer the fish away from sharp rock edges or shell-encrusted surfaces. They should expect more powerful surges from the fish when it is brought near the surface.

Hint

Run the line above the float through a light coating of petroleum jelly (or a commercial fly-line coating) between your fingers. It will keep that section of the line floating — and it will lift off the water's surface much easier than if it was beneath the surface when you come to set the hook.

Edibility

Luderick is an excellent eating fish, but it should be killed, bled and thoroughly cleaned, paying particular attention to the removal of all the black stomach lining. Some people skin the fish. I prefer this fish as crumbed or lightly-battered fried fillets, eaten with a squeeze of lemon juice, though it can be most satisfactorily cooked by other methods. [**Note:** Anglers may accidentally hook a zebrafish or bluefish when fishing for luderick.]

ZEBRAFISH
Girella zebra

More often netted than caught on a line, this fish is relatively small, though shaped like its near relative, the luderick. It also has a distribution from northern New South Wales to the south-west coast of Western Australia as well as around Tasmania. It is easy to understand why it is called "zebrafish", having about 9 broad vertical stripes between the head and the tail of its body. They are wide at the top cut come to a point on the belly. They stand out on the silvery-tan body colour which fades after death to almost the same shade as the bands. It schools over algae and weed-covered reefs that have plenty of water movement around them, at depths of 2 to 20 metres. These fish are particularly common in the Bass Strait.

The zebrafish has hybridised with the rock blackfish (*Girella elevata*) and the hybrid is often referred to as a banded rock blackfish.

BLUEFISH
Girella cyanea

This fish is mainly encountered around New Zealand but it does visit the coast of New South Wales from time to time and it is common around Lord Howe Island and Norfolk Island. It is often caught by anglers fishing for rock blackfish, luderick and silver drummer. It grows to 40 to 45 centimetres and is easily identified, being of an overall violet-blue colour speckled with gold spots.

MACKEREL

There are about half a dozen mackerel in Australian waters and they can all be classified as game fish if caught on the appropriate gear — even the mackerel that is so popular as a bait fish. These fishes, which generally roam the tropical waters, are a dashing sporting fish that is accessible to the recreational angler. Moreover, some are worth catching for their fine eating qualities.

The narrow-barred spanish mackerel is listed as **Tanguigue**, the name used by the Game Fishing Association of Australia *and* the International Game Fishing Association. We have listed it as such in the interests of establishing some sort of uniformity for anglers. Another fish that is popularly called a frigate mackerel can be found under **Tuna**, which it properly is.

MACKEREL, BROAD-BARRED
Scomberomorus semifasciatum

OTHER NAMES: **BROAD-BARRED SPANISH OR SPANIARD MACKEREL, BROWNIE, GREY MACKEREL, SCHOOL MACKEREL, STRIPED MACKEREL, TIGER MACKEREL**

Identification

This fish can be quite a vivid blue or dark bluish-grey on the dorsal area, with an off-white to grey belly. Its blue-black bars are broader and fewer than those on the much larger tanguigue (narrow-barred spanish mackerel). These bars tend to become dull and blotchy after death and often appear to be broken — more like big uneven spots

—in larger specimens. The broad-barred mackerel has a deeper body than other mackerel of similar size. The mouth has a single row of fine teeth in both jaws.

Size

The broad-barred mackerel grows to about a metre in length and can weigh about 8 kilograms. The size taken by anglers, however, is usually around 2 to 3 kilograms.

The minimum legal length for a catch in Western Australia is 76 centimetres. The minimum in Queensland is 45 centimetres.

Breeding

These fishes are believed to breed during winter in tropical waters.

Distribution

This mackerel inhabits close-in coastal waters, sometimes in estuaries, along the Queensland coast for most of the year, although August to November are regarded as better months. Depending on the warm-water currents, it can be found as far south as the New South Wales central coast, any time between January and May.

Habits

The broad-barred mackerel is a schooling pelagic. It feeds ravenously on almost any small fish such as hardiheads, garfish, sardines, etc. It will follow the schools of these fish into quite shallow water and herd them into cays.

Other regulations

A bag limit of 5 fish per angler per day applies in Western Australia.

MACKEREL, QUEENSLAND SCHOOL
Scomberomorus queenslandicus

OTHER NAME: **BLOTCHED MACKEREL, DOGGIE, DOGGIE MACKEREL, SCHOOL MACKEREL, SHINY MACKEREL, SNOOK**

Identification

This mackerel is an iridescent bluish-green along the dorsal area, but silvery white below. It has 3

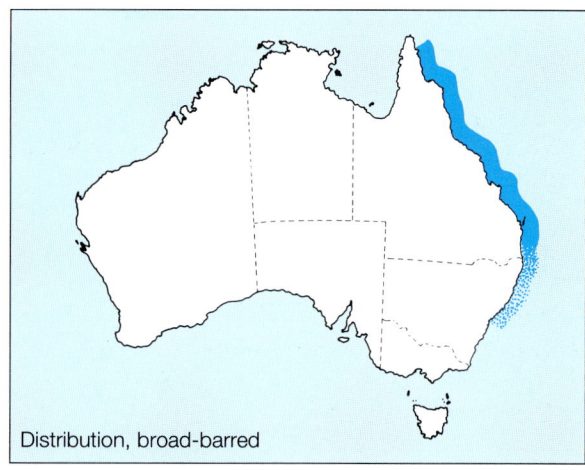

Distribution, broad-barred

rows of bronze-to-grey black spots scattered thinly along the flanks that appear blotchy in large specimens. The spots are larger than the eye. The dorsal fin is whitish on the leading edge and black towards its trailing edge.

Size

Though the Queensland school mackerel is known to grow to about a metre, catches by anglers are invariably much smaller, with a weight ranging between 1 and 3 kilograms. The minimum legal length for a catch in Queensland is 45 centimetres.

Breeding

Very little is known, though it is believed to breed in the tropics.

Distribution

This fish, which is so prolific in Queensland waters during mid-winter, can also be found in waters around the northern coastline and north-west coast of Western Australia. It also extends into northern New South Wales waters around about April.

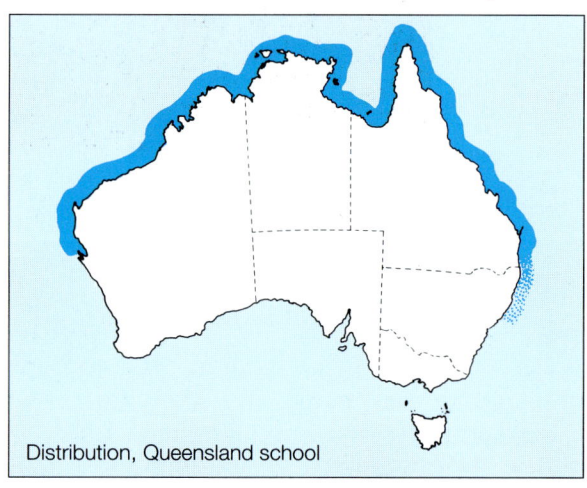

Distribution, Queensland school

Queensland school mackerel

Habits

The Queensland mackerel schools in quite large numbers. It will enter shallow coastal zones and can be found in bays and estuaries and around reefs. At night they will congregate in large schools over weedy sandflats. It mixes particularly freely in offshore reef areas with schools of that giant among mackerels, the tanguigue. It eats mainly small fish and will travel well into estuaries in pursuit of them when the water is clear.

MACKEREL, SHARK
Grammatoreynus bicarinatus

OTHER NAMES: **LARGE SCALE TUNA, SALMON MACKEREL, SCALEY MACKEREL**

Identification

The scales on this fish are much larger than on other mackerels, resulting in one of its other names. Its common name comes from the ammonia smell its flesh exudes when being cleaned — much like a shark. (This odour will disappear if the fish is frozen, or during cooking.) The body colour of the shark mackerel is silvery, with a greenish shade with a yellow tinge. The back is often darker with some spots evident. Its most distinguishing feature is a double lateral line along the body.

Size

This fish grows to about 1.3 metres in length, reaching a weight of about 12 kilograms. Anglers are more likely to land this fish in the 3 to 6 kilograms range.

Breeding
Little is known.

Distribution
The shark mackerel inhabits warm waters from northern New South Wales, all along the Queensland, Northern Territory and Western Australian waters as far south as about Geographe Bay. They are found further off shore in the south than in the north.

Habits
This fish aggregates adjacent to single or broken reefs and cays, but also moves into shallow water over reef flats on a rising tide, feeding on small fish such as pilchards, hardiheads, sprats, etc. The shark mackerel mostly feeds beneath the surface.

Other regulations
A bag limit of 5 fish per angler per day applies in Western Australia.

MACKEREL, SPOTTED
Scomberomorus munroi

OTHER NAMES: **MUNRO'S SPANISH MACKEREL, AUSTRALIAN SPANISH MACKEREL, JAPANESE SPANISH MACKEREL**

Identification
Though one of its smaller members, this tropical fish has the characteristically sleek body of the mackerel family. It has a deep blue (tending to purplish) back with 4 uneven rows of blackish spots. Some claim that these spots are never larger than the pupil of its eye. (The Queensland school mackerel is also spotted but is a larger fish.) The front dorsal fin is a deep blue to purple, verging on black. Other fins are greyish-white.

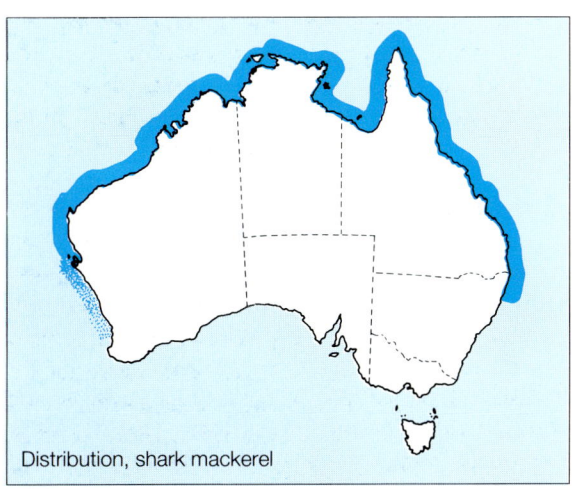
Distribution, shark mackerel

Size

The maximum size for this fish is about a metre, and though it is said to grow to about 8 kilograms, it is usually caught at around 3 to 4 kilograms. The minimum legal length for a catch in Western Australia is 50 centimetres; the minimum is 45 centimetres in Queensland.

Breeding

Little is known.

Distribution

The spotted mackerel is common in the tropical waters of Queensland, the Northern Territory and Western Australia. Some are encountered, if infrequently, as far south as Sydney on the eastern coast and as far south as off Rottnest Island in Western Australia.

Habits

This fish schools in shallow waters around reef areas. It eats small fish, though it is less likely to be seen in a feeding frenzy than other fish — nor is it as likely to chase lures. The spotted mackerel prefers a floated bait.

Other regulations

A bag limit of 5 fish per angler per day applies in Western Australia.

MACKEREL, NARROW-BARRED SPANISH*
Scomberomorus commerson

OTHER NAMES: **SPANIARD, SPANISH MACKEREL, KINGFISH, SNOOK**

*See TANGUIGUE entry for complete details

When to fish

There are prime periods to fish for all the foregoing mackerels, even though they may be found in varying numbers throughout the year (unseasonal appearances probably caused by water currents). The broad-barred mackerel and spotted mackerel are often in larger numbers in the southern part of Queensland in the summer and winter, and a little later further south. The Queensland school mackerel is prolific during the

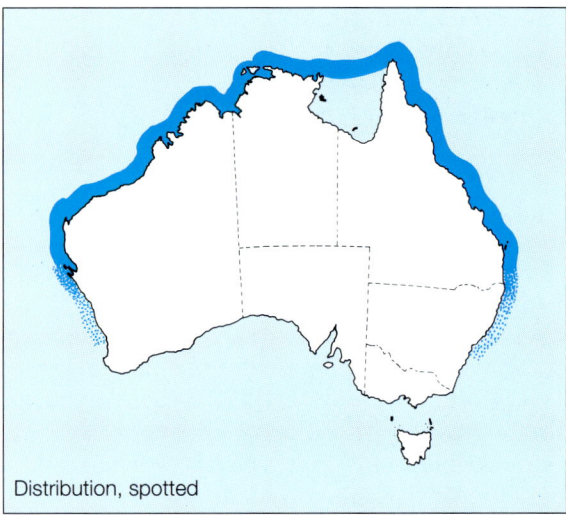
Distribution, spotted

months of winter and spring. Most anglers consider the shark mackerel to be available most of the year. The mackerel on the western coast follows a similar pattern. For the best information, ask local anglers or contact the angling clubs in the area.

In general, the best times of day are usually the early morning or late afternoon periods for the smaller mackerels, as they follow schools of bait fish into the shallower areas. Mornings are, in the main, cooler and less windy, with more comfortable sea conditions for the mackerel angler.

Where to fish

The flurry of small fish as they attempt to escape may reveal feeding mackerel (obviously it may also be many other pelagic fish). If there is no visible evidence of the mackerel, trolling baits or lures along the edges of reefs, on both shallow and deeper sides, and through openings in reefs, can attract these fish. In clear waters, schools of the smaller fish may be sighted as the mackerel roam in search of food.

Tackle

Much larger fish can be caught while trolling for mackerel, so if handlines are used they should be of not less than 30 kilograms breaking-strain line. If rods are used, choose from medium or heavy, single-handed or double-handed, threadline or baitcasting models, of between 2 metres and 2.5 metres. You will need suitably strong reels to match, spooled with 6 to 10 kilogram breaking-strain line. Such rods also allow casting and retrieving from small boats, whether drifting or moored. From shore-based fishing spots, a similar rod but of about 3 to 4 metres, is more convenient. All the rods will facilitate live or dead bait being fished, suspended beneath a float or balloon. Dispense with a wire trace if using ganged hooks with a heavier nylon leader, but wire is recommended with live baits or lures.

Baits

Pilchards, garfish, hardiheads, mullet, herrings, yellowtail and similar fish are effective for all the mackerel when trolled, or as floated baits, or when used for casting and retrieving. Yellowtail and mullet are particularly good live baits. Squid is sometimes used. The mackerel will take a wide range of lures — metal wobblers, spoons, minnows and skirted types. Surface swimmers and poppers are taken readily when cast to the side of a feeding school of the smaller mackerel.

Berley

Almost all mackerel respond to a berley of stale fish, fish skeletons, crabs, etc., crushed or minced. This is effective where the fish can be seen but seem uninterested in trolled or cast-and-retrieved lures. Once the fish mill around, they will usually take lures. Berley also attracts other fish but it must be used so that the fish are kept within casting range from a moored boat.

Rigs

The unweighted bait rig No. 2 with a heavy nylon leader or nylon-coated wire trace is satisfactory when fishing with baits, and with a light sinker rig No. 3A for reef areas with a reasonable bottom. For trolling, rigs 3A or 11 are suitable.

How to hook

Mackerel are predators that will strike a moving bait or lure hard and fast, rarely missing. If you are using a floating bait or live bait, it is best to give your quarry a few seconds to swallow before firmly setting the hook. Let the mackerel run but keep them under pressure. This fish tires surprisingly quickly and is then much easier to handle.

Hint

Mackerel will follow both trolled and cast-and-retrieved baits and lures, sometimes frustratingly so. Reducing speed or a sudden increase in speed can induce the fish to strike.

Edibility

The least popular of the mackerel is possibly the shark, because of its shark-like smell of ammonia, despite the fact that it disappears during cooking or freezing. All mackerel have firm-textured flesh

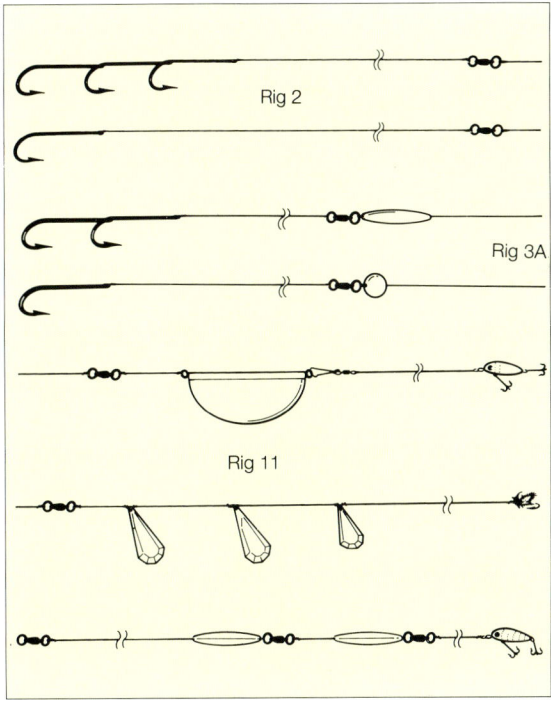

and excellent flavour. These fish are better filleted than cut into steaks. They can be fried, baked, grilled or used as sashimi.

Like all fish caught in warm water and warm climates, the mackerel should be bled and gutted. Any slime (especially on the tanguigue) should be washed off and the fish placed on ice or in a freezer box.

MACKEREL, SLIMY
Scomber australasicus

OTHER NAMES: COMMON **MACKEREL, SLIMIES, PACIFIC MACKEREL**

This is regarded as a bait fish. These little mackerel are excellent live bait for mulloway, kingfish, john dory, salmon and others. The fresh flesh of one is irresistible to most fish-eating species, including snapper, tailor, salmon, mackerels and all reef fish. They can, however, be eaten, if they are gilled, bled and cleaned when caught. They smoke well.

Identification

This mackerel has the same streamlined shape as its much larger relatives. Those fish taken from deeper ocean waters are more blue (fading to a green) after death. The smaller ones that invade inshore waters, harbours, bays and estuaries, are more green. The back and sides are covered with narrow bars and the abdomen area is spotted. The skin is soft and slippery.

Size

This fish grows to about 65 centimetres in length but is most commonly caught a little more than half this size. The minimum legal length for a catch in Western Australia is 15 centimetres.

How to hook

A light line — 2 to 3 kilograms breaking-strain is adequate — either on a handcaster, or a light threadline rod and reel. A hook about size 4 is usually suitable. It should be unweighted if conditions allow, to sink slowly or with a minimum of lead.

This fish will take a bait that is retrieved slowly after it has sunk to the bottom. A berley of bread, rice, pollard, bran, soaked dog biscuits etc., will attract and hold slimies.

[**Note:** This fish is difficult to keep alive unless in special bait tanks or a large keeper's net.]

MAHI-MAHI
Coryphaena hippurus & Coryphaena equisetis

OTHER NAMES: **DOLPHIN FISH, DORADO (OVERSEAS)**

The name mahi-mahi, which is used by both the Game
Fishing Association of Australia and the International Game
Fishing Association, is much more appropriate than the more
common "dolphin fish". Certainly the real dolphin — which
is of course a mammal — was named long before this fish was
recognised. Just how the fish came by the name is unclear
but it was probably given to the mahi-mahi by sailors who
confused its body shape and graceful leaps with the real thing
... then lamely added "fish" as a distinction.
Even though it is common in off shore waters, it is a fish
spoken of with a special appreciation by those who have seen it
or caught it. Though it is not as big as most of the other game
fish, its extraordinarily beautiful colours, astonishing
acrobatics when chasing food or hooked, and its bursts of
great speed, combine to mark it as a splendid sporting fish.
Moreover, unlike so many sporting fish, the
mahi-mahi is particularly edible.

Identification

The two species are identical except *C. equisetis* has
fewer rays on the dorsal fin than *C. hippurus* and is
much smaller in size; its maximum length being
around 75 centimetres.

The mahi-mahi is an elongate shape, with a deep,
blunt head, which in males forms an almost straight
line from the mouth to the front of the dorsal area.
This slope of the head is less severe on juveniles
and females. The body tapers to a thin caudal
peduncle. This fish has one long dorsal fin, which

starts above the eye and decreases in height, almost to the tail. It has long pectoral and anal fins and a deeply forked tail.

The colour of the fish in the water is a rich blue that fades into green and yellow-gold down the sides and on to a silvery stomach. Yet when in a hunting mood, while hooked and immediately after having been caught, it undergoes spectacular colour changes. The dorsal fin becomes a brilliant blue, with flashes of lighter blue on it and along the back. These and its other green and yellow colours can fade, then rekindle more vividly — and very rapidly. The usually bright blue or green spots on its back and sides switch from dull to bright quite frequently. With death, all the brilliance of these colours fade to an overall darkness.

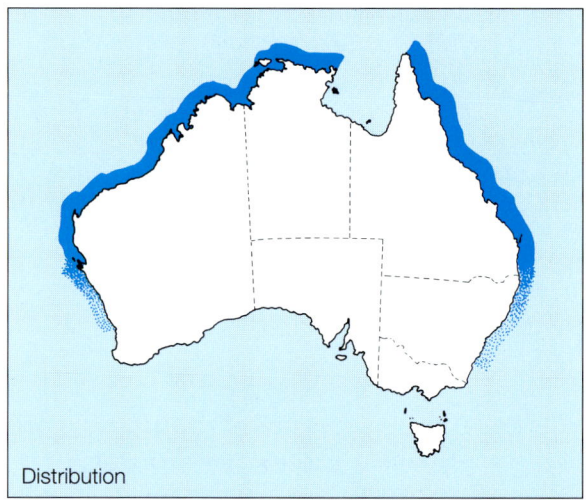

Distribution

Size

The *C. hippurus* grows to about 2 metres and about 40-plus kilograms. (*C. equisetis* has a maximum length of half its relative but is usually much smaller.) The Australian all-tackle record (September, 1988) is 31 kilograms caught at Port Stephens (New South Wales) and the world all-tackle record is 39.46 kilograms.

Breeding

Little is known about the mahi-mahi's early life, though there have been suggestions that it grows extremely fast, causing it to eat frequently. Researchers in the United States claim that the life span of a mahi-mahi may be only 3 or 4 years.

Habits

This fish is a pelagic of the blue water where the temperature ranges from 19°C to 30°C. It can be found alone or in schools. One of its favourite foods is flying fish, which speed out of the water when attacked, with the predator following. It also swims below the flying fish with such speed that it can anticipate where a panicky one will land and sweep into position. However, the mahi-mahi's diet is not restricted to flying fish — more than 30 species of fish have been found in a mahi-mahi's stomach — and they also eat squid.

Mahi-mahi will investigate floating objects, be it rubbish dumped from boats, or buoys etc. Whether they are naturally inquisitive, or are attracted by the probability of smaller fish gathering near the flotsam, is not known.

Distribution

The mahi-mahi is a tropical fish but it will follow

currents of the right temperature as far south as Bermagui on the east coast and Rottnest Island in the west. It is an off shore fish.

When to fish

In tropical waters it can be caught all year. The southern angler has to wait for the right current to move southwards.

Where to fish

The mahi-mahi is found off shore, in the deep blue water, where the temperature is in the preferred range. Circling frigate birds may provide a clue to its presence. Check around any flotsam too.

Tackle

This fish is caught on game outfits, often when baited and being trolled for large species, or trolling with a variety of lures. It can be trolled for, or cast to, with heavy threadline or baitcasting rods and

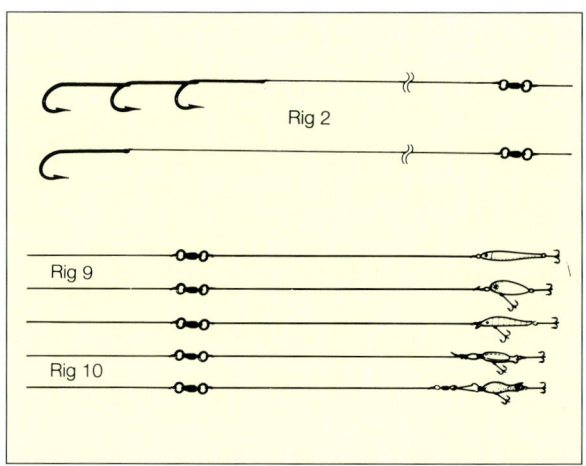

Rig 2

Rig 9

Rig 10

reels. Light game gear gives the fish a chance to realise its fighting potential for the sporting angler.

Bait

Mahi-mahi will take a wide range of fish, including yellowtail, saury, sea garfish, slimy mackerel, squid and well-presented fish fillets. It may well tear to pieces any bait that it finds too large to swallow, and it will attack a wide range of trolling lures, from spoons to slicers, even the metal-headed skirted types. Some jigs worked as lures can be effective.

Rigs

The usual rig is that used for game fishing, trolling baits or lures but rigs No.2 or No. 10 are satisfactory.

How to hook

The speed and power of a mahi-mahi attack means it hooks itself. The angler's efforts begin with trying to control the fish's runs — estimated at up to 60 kilometres per hour—and trying to anticipate and control its aerial leaps and twists and underwater dives.

Edibility

The table quality of this fish is held by many to be the very best of marine species. It can be prepared in many ways.

Other regulations

A legal limit of 3 dolphin fish (mahi-mahi) per angler per day is imposed in Western Australia.

MANGROVE JACK
Lutjanus argentimaculatus

OTHER NAMES: **CREEK RED BREAM, RED BREAM, DOG BREAM, PURPLE SEA-PERCH, RED BASS, RED PERCH.**

Some northern anglers believe this fine-looking fish challenges the barramundi for its rugged resistance when hooked and its determination to fight its way back to the snags where it lies in wait for prey. While it is classified as a brackish-saltwater species, there is always the chance of finding one in freshwater. And though it is caught on reefs well off shore, it is usually fished for along mangrove-lined inlets, rivers and creeks.

Identification
The fish has a perch-like shape. The colour varies from a pale pink to a dirty red-brown. It has an aggressive head, the mouth of which is equipped at the front with sharp and strong canine teeth capable of inflicting deep wounds to the unwary angler's fingers. Its fins are strong and the tail broad and straight. After death, the belly tends to turn a brighter red.

[**Note:** The mangrove jack can be distinguished from the red bass or sea kelp (*Lutjanus bohar*) — a fish regarded as a possible source of ciguatera poisoning — by the absence of a conspicuous pit in front of the eye. Another way to distinguish between the two fish is that the mangrove jack's scales come away easily; the red bass's scales are difficult to remove.]

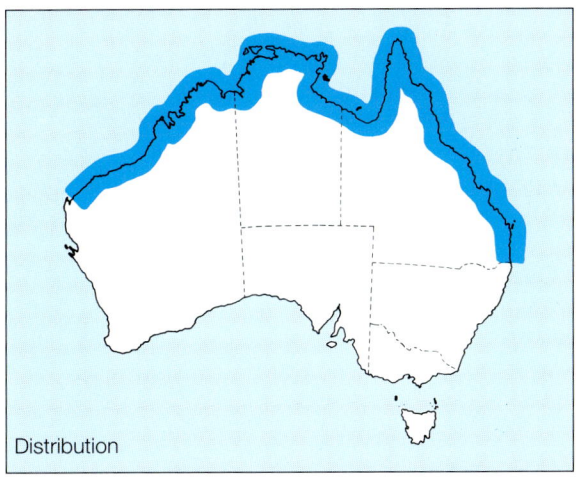

Distribution

Size

The mangrove jack is recorded as having reached about 90 centimetres and in excess of 10 kilograms, but those most commonly caught by anglers are between 2 and 4 kilograms.

Breeding

It is believed the fish grows to sexual maturity in the tidal mangrove areas and moves to off shore reefs when around 3 to 4 kilograms in weight.

Habits

This fish is an ambusher of the first order. The more tangled or knitted the mangrove roots or other plant growth is, the more likely is it to conceal a mangrove jack. From this underwater hide, any food — prawns, fish, crabs, squid, etc. — which swims nearby or is carried past by the currents or tide, is snatched in a swift attack. The mangrove jack returns to its haunt as quickly as it strikes.

Distribution

The mangrove jack inhabits the whole of the Queensland coast, across the Northern Territory, and the north-western coast of Western Australia. There have been catches recorded in waters as far south as Wollongong in New South Wales and also in south-west Western Australia, but these are rare exceptions, probably the result of unusual warm current movement.

When to fish

Many of the estuary and creek waters inhabited by the mangrove jack are flooded or inaccessible during the wet season. Nevertheless, that still leaves about three quarters of the year in which to seek this fish. Tides appear to be of little significance.

Where to fish

Banks and flats that are overgrown with mangroves, where there are plenty of underwater roots, are obvious locations. Mangroves near the confluence of two creeks can be a very promising spot, though in the majority of northern estuaries and creeks such areas can only be reached by boat or canoe.

Tackle

Because the angler is most likely to be confined to a boat or canoe, the ideal outfit is either a single-handed medium or heavy threadline or baitcasting rod with a suitably strong matching reel. Bait fishing is possible with a handline, but bait or lures can be better accommodated with a rod. If you use a rod, the line should be about 5 to 6 kilograms breaking-strain. A heavy nylon leader or coated wire trace is essential. Hooks in size 3/0 or 4/0 are suitable.

Bait

Any live or dead fish or fillets are accepted without hesitation by the mangrove jack. But mullet and sardines are natural baits in this fish's territory as are prawns, squid and crabs. Live baits tend to be more effective with larger specimens.

Almost any lure will tempt this fish. Deep-diving and sinking types (though they can be a problem in such snag-riddled waters), and the shallow-swimming models in shapes resembling fish, will all be hit — and hit hard. Reasonably sized lead-head jigs can attract the same result.

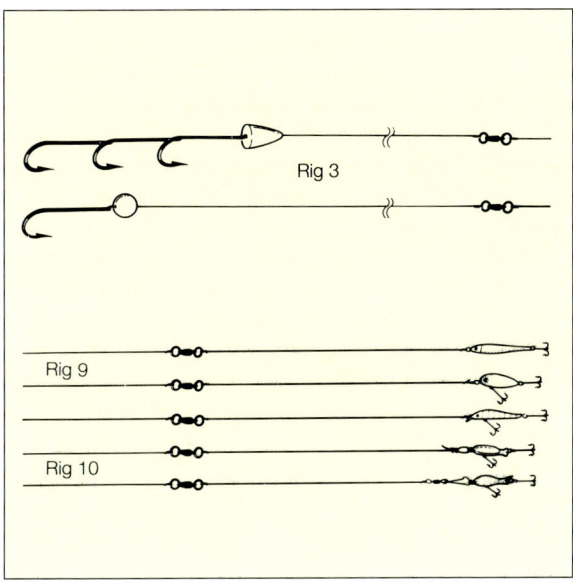

Rigs

Two rigs work extremely well. Whether using dead baits or live fish, rig No. 3 is satisfactory with a sinker sufficiently heavy to get the bait down to the fish. The leader on this rig can be nylon of 25 kilograms breaking-strain. For casting and retrieving lures, rig No. 9 with a short coated-wire trace will be adequate.

How to hook

The important factor in catching mangrove jack is neither the bait nor lure but the placement of these as close as possible to the fish's hide. Its strike is so hard that it invariably hooks itself. The real problem starts when it decides to sharply retreat among the roots and snags of its hide. Keeping it away until it tires is the long-term challenge.

Hint

Use a disgorger to unhook a mangrove jack. It has a habit of snapping at fingers and it can sink its teeth very deeply.

Edibility

The usual advice of cleaning tropical fish quickly and keeping them cool applies to the mangrove jack. The flesh is tasty and excellent eating, prepared in any manner.

MARLIN

Marlin are included here because they may occasionally be
sighted by recreational anglers, and even hooked now and
then by experienced rock-hoppers or boating anglers who are
pursuing juvenile marlin or altogether different fish —
though the latter have to be blessed by all the
deities to get that lucky!
The beautiful marlin is really the ultimate challenge for
experienced anglers who have the time, money and
equipment to fish for them. If, as an inexperienced angler,
you happen to hook a marlin, enjoy the breathtaking
encounter for what it is worth — and good luck to you.
The three marlin of Australian waters are described.

Black marlin.

MARLIN, BLACK

Makaira indica

Identification

This is the giant of the marlin family. Its body is
stout, the head is humped and its spear is thicker
than that of other marlins. The dorsal fin is low
and rounded (about half the body depth) and the
anal fin is almost a replica of the front part of the
dorsal, low and round. Another distinguishing
feature is the curved pectoral fins, which are aerofoil
in section and do not sit flat along the body (in
juveniles of up to 60 kilograms, these may be
movable). The black marlin's colour is a deep
steel-blue to black, that reflects a purplish hue,
and whitish around the belly.

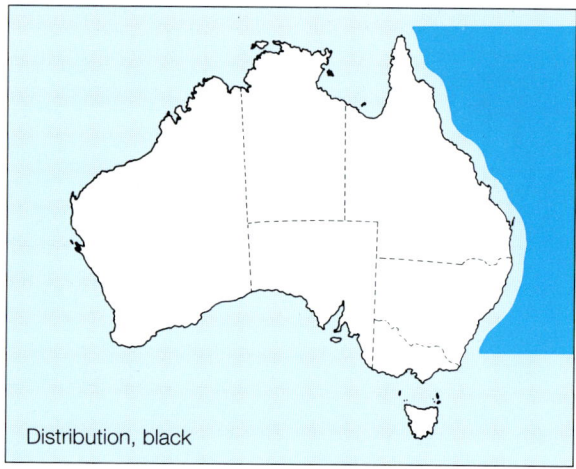

Distribution, black

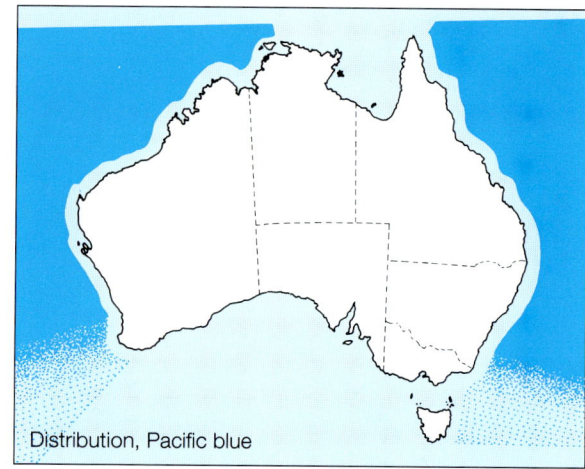

Distribution, Pacific blue

Size

Black marlin have been estimated at more than 5 metres in length and heavier than the present world record, which stands at 707.61 kilograms (caught according to International Game Fishing Association rules). The Australian all-tackle record was 654.08 kilograms (at September, 1988).

Distribution

The large fish all come from the Cairns, Lizard Island and Barrier Reef area in north Queensland. More than 30 black marlin exceeding 454 kilograms are caught, tagged and released from these localities each year. Many of the line class records created here have also been world records. Though fish under the 100 kilogram weight are found in this area, they are more often taken south from about Townsville to Bermagui in southern New South Wales. These figures are taken from records of the Australian Game Fishing Association, but it is likely that much larger black marlin, which are not records in the particular line classes, are caught, tagged and released.

MARLIN, PACIFIC BLUE
Makaira nigricans

Identification

Despite attempts to distinguish the Pacific blue marlin from the Atlantic blue marlin with the scientific name *M. mazura*, the taxanomic details are so minor that most icthyologists and game fishing asscociations use *M. nigricanus* for both. The body of the Pacific blue is not quite as stout as the black marlin, but the head is scooped to a moderately heavy spear. It has a dorsal fin that measures about two thirds its body depth and the pectoral fins are relatively straight-edged and fold flat along the body. The anal fin is of similar proportions to the dorsal fin. The Pacific blue marlin is a cobalt blue on top and silvery white below — sometimes with a yellow band apparent at the junction of the two colours. A pattern of wiggly lines follows its lateral line, which may not be visible in smaller blues. Vertical stripes of light blue and lavender fade rapidly after death.

Size

The Pacific blue marlin is known to reach about 5 metres and the world all-tackle record is not far below its black marlin relative at 624.14 kilograms. The equivalent Australian record is 319 kilograms (at September, 1988).
Commercial longline fishers in the Tahiti region have reported blue marlin in excess of 907 kilograms.

Distribution

All the Australian records (at September, 1988), with the exception of only two line classes, were set by fish caught in the temperate waters of New South Wales and Western Australia. The two exceptional records were set off Exmouth in Western Australia and Cape Moreton (Queensland).
Though the Pacific blue marlin is a tropical fish, it follows the warm currents south in the summer-autumn period, the most prolific numbers found around Bermagui on the east coast and Rottnest Island on the west coast. They are known to occasionallly reach south-eastern Tasmania.

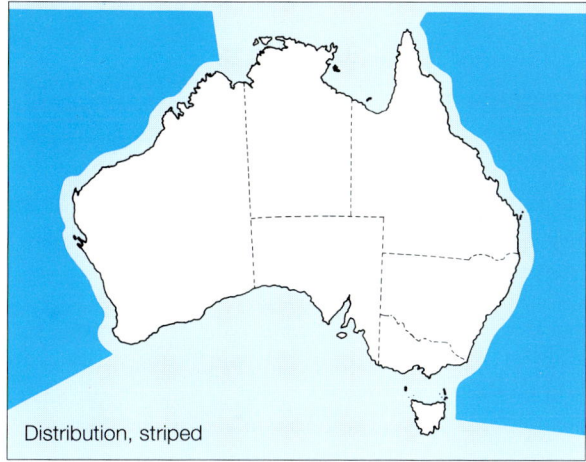

Distribution, striped

MARLIN, STRIPED

Tetrapturus audax

Identification

A sloped head and a slender spear make this the most streamlined marlin. The dorsal fin is high (about equal the body depth); the pectoral fins are relatively straight-edged and flatten along the side of the body. The striped marlin is a purplish-blue over a silvery white lower half, but it has distinct lavender-coloured vertical stripes along the body, that remain visible after death.

Size

In the main, only the smaller striped marlin are caught in tropical waters, with all-Australian record fish having been caught south of Port Stephens in New South Wales. The Australian all-tackle record is 169.5 kilograms and the all-tackle world record is 224.1 kilograms (both as at September, 1988).

Distribution

The most likely time to encounter a marlin is the period from January to April off the east or west coasts, though big fish have been caught in September/October. They range in numbers south of about Cape Moreton in Queensland, along the east coast of Tasmania, as well as south to Cape Naturaliste in Western Australia.

Habits

All marlin are pelagics that will rush into schools of fish, including tuna, slashing and swiping with their spears. Though scientists have been unable to confirm that marlin try to spear their prey,

whole fish have been found in their stomachs with a mark that could only have been caused by a spear. They mostly kill or maim their quarry with the spear. Some marlin have speared boats but it is not known if such attacks are deliberate or the accidental result of the speed with which it chases its prey or attempts to escape. In some instances the penetration through solid timbers and metal have been frightening. The impact invariably kills the fish.

Marlin hunt and feed at the surface and mid-water depths though they will take fish off the bottom and reefs. The predominantly off shore black marlins — certainly in juvenile sizes — are the marlins that have been taken by east coast rock-based anglers.

These splendid fish have enormous power and dazzling acceleration over short distances. In the

Mighty striped marlin reduced to a trophy picture.

221

fury of the fight, they will make plunging deep dives as well as dozens of great leaps. Blue marlin and (particularly) striped marlin, glow with colour during the contest, a remarkable phenomenon.

Bait

Their food ranges from tuna and trevally to pilchards, mackerel, queenfish, sardines, flying fish, and salmon, not to mention squid and octopus. All marlin will take dead fish trolled, but the striped and blue marlins are more often caught on live bait (though that is not to say that the striped marlin is not happy to take baits of fish fillets or chunks).

All marlin respond readily to a range of trolled lures.

Tackle

The only adequate equipment for the larger marlin are game rods and reels of the finest quality — which is beyond our "popular" brief — and a seakindly boat for fishing beyond the horizon.

Edibility

Striped marlin have a pinkish flesh, while black marlin and blue marlin have a white flesh. They are excellent eating. They are high priority targets for Japanese commercial fishing fleets because their flesh makes such prime sashimi (a raw fish delicacy). A recent agreement between the Australian and Japanese governments may reduce the commercial exploitation of these fish and, perhaps, help restore some of their numbers for Australian anglers.

Any angler fortunate enough to bring a marlin to the boat should consider its release, with or without a tag.

The contest it would have provided and its glowing colours are likely to be much more memorable than cutting up a once majestic fish (which would then be rather drab) for a meal.

MILKFISH
Chanos chanos

OTHER NAMES: **GIANT HERRING, MORETON BAY SALMON, SALMON HERRING**

This is a food fish in countries north of Australia. In the Philippines this fish is collected and reared in enclosed, brackish ponds. They grow to a marketable size quickly when protected from their predators and competitors for their main food items. Those who have caught the milkfish in Australian waters regard it as a major fishing achievement but rarely retain it to eat.

Identification

This fish has a brilliant silver colour. The dorsal area has a greenish hue, though it can become much bluer in turbid waters. It has a single dorsal fin and a large sweeping tail. The mouth is small and toothless. The body is streamlined and its eyes are large and located close to its mouth, features that — along with the absence of an overhanging jaw — distinguish the milkfish from the bonefish and the giant herring.

Size

Milkfish are known to grow to almost 2 metres, and specimens in excess of 1.3 metres and about 13 kilograms have been recorded in Australia.

Breeding

This fish enters shallow estuary waters to spawn in summer, when the wet has reduced the salinity. It is estimated that a female can disperse over 9 million eggs.

Habits

Apart from its spawning period, these fishes congregate in large schools in open waters close to those coastal bays where there are mangroves. Though they can also be found well offshore, it is usually close to islands or sand cays.

Distribution

Very large schools are found from the Gold Coast

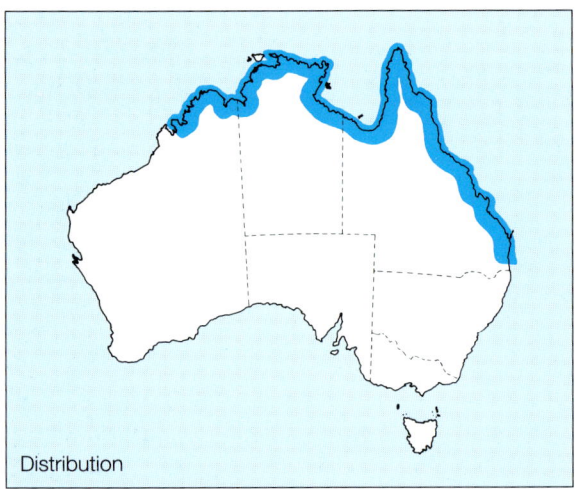
Distribution

region of Queensland north to Cape York, in the Gulf of Carpentaria and along the coast of the Northern Territory. Milkfish schools have been sighted in Jervis Bay and offshore in the same area of New South Wales. These were probably following a warm current with an algae or plankton food source.

This fish's diet is basically of algae or vegetable matter, which provides the challenge for line anglers. It feeds at the surface and below and it is an extremely powerful and fast swimming fish. The larger milkfish are capable of breaking taut nets in their efforts to escape. The milkfish can survive in remarkably warm water.

When to fish

The fish is present throughout the year in the northern areas. They are more readily available around estuaries and in rivers early in the wet season, before the floods make fishing difficult.

Where to fish

When a school is seen it can be attracted close to the angler with berley, especially if there is a current to take the berley to the fish. Areas to look for milkfish are bays, mangrove shorelines and over sandy areas close to reefs and shallow lagoons.

Tackle

The line has to be light to float the type of baits necessary to catch the milkfish, yet the rod has to be powerful enough (in the butt section at least) to exert pressure to control the torpedo-like thrust of the milkfish during its runs. The reel has to be strongly geared to prevent it stripping. My suggestion for this dilemma is a 3 to 3.5 metre rod with a multi-taper construction. It probably can be made for either a threadline or overhead reel (the former more suitable for casting the light bait or float, the latter better geared for fighting the fish). Either reel must be capable of spooling a minimum of 250 metres of line, which should be the best quality in the finest diameter for the chosen breaking-strain. Consider about 5 kilograms breaking-strain though the fish — if you catch it — may weigh as much as 12 kilograms or more. Stainless steel hooks, tarpon-style about size 1 are large enough, smaller if the angler is brave. Light saltwater fly rods may be more suitable with a floating line but the reel must have the capacity to hold sufficient backing.

Bait

Unlike mullet, luderick and some other basically vegetarian species, no particular weed or other bait has been satisfactorily established for milkfish. Reports of the fish taking lures might be considered an accident or a display of anger by the fish at an intruder amongst its food.

Dry flies on a floating line and tippet have had some success, though the type and size of flies are open to experimentation.

The writer admits that the only milkfish he has seen caught were taken on cottonwool-reinforced dough, which had been mixed in some slime-covered water and was woven around the hook shank. It was suspended a few centimetres beneath a small float. It is acknowledged that bread crust proffered in a similar manner will also take a milkfish. Perhaps button-shaped pieces of bread threaded on to a hook (so successful with black rockfish) are an answer.

Berley

Breadcrumbs and bread pieces (and probably pollard and bran) floated on the surface is a proven manner of attracting milkfish. A sloppy mixture with extremely finely chopped weed may also work.

Rig

If you can float an unweighted bait on the surface in the berley trail, it is much more likely to be taken by a milkfish. For that reason, the line should be greased with vaseline or a commercially available compound for fly lines. The rig No. 2, without a swivel, should be tried; but a tiny bubble float, with approximately 10 centimetres of line between it and the hook, is also worth considering. So is substituting a piece of white polystyrene foam on the shank of the hook next to the eye when bread crusts are used.

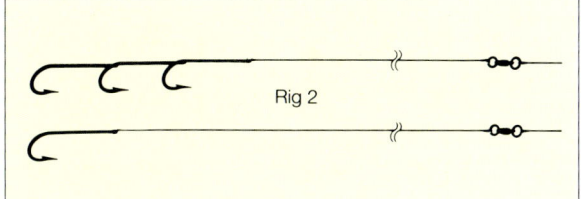

Rig 2

How to hook

If and when a milkfish takes a bait the hooking is done by the fish. It sips it in quite quickly. After that it depends on the angler's equipment and his ability to use it to its maximum efficiency.

Edibility

Though the milkfish is regarded as a delicacy in Asia it is regarded without enthusiasm at an Australian table. One suggestion from E.M. Grant, a marine biologist, is to soak it overnight in vinegar and pressure-cook it. It will be edible, he said, though without flavour.

[**Note:** The milkfish offers thinking anglers with an open mind the opportunity to experiment. What is a suitable method? Which is the best bait? Is dry fly fishing the answer to hook a sport fish of the first order? There is certainly much to challenge the angler when he sights a milkfish.

As at December, 1988, there was no milkfish of any size or in any category claimed in the Australian National Sportfishing Association's National Record Chart.]

The milkfish: excellent sport, but a very ordinary meal.

MORWONG

Commercial interests — with some government support —
are doing their best to have this distinctive Aboriginal name
replaced. In a move that is misleading both consumers and
anglers, professional fishermen and fish-marketing authorities
have decided that consumers didn't find the fish sufficiently
appealing under its traditional name so they renamed it "sea-
bream". Not only that, but the Australian Government
Department of Primary Industries recommended that the
southern blue morwong (or queen snapper) be sold as "blue
sea-bream" and all the other species "sea-bream". This is not
only misleading — the consumer is not sure what he is now
getting — but it may even contravene some trade practices
legislation. Morwongs belong to the *Cheifodactylidae* family:
they are not remotely related to the bream or *Sparidae* family!
Their nearest (but distant) relatives are the sea carps of
the *Cirrhitidae* or *Aplodactylidae* family.
In New Zealand, two popular species of morwong are
marketed without difficulty as tarikihi and porae,
their Maori names.

The blue morwong.

MORWONG, BANDED
Cheilodactylus spectabilis

OTHER NAMES: **BROWN-BANDED MORWONG**

Identification
The banded morwong is often mistaken for the red morwong, but it lacks the latter's horns in front of the eyes. Its colour is tan to red overall and there are wide dark brown bands running diagonally across its body.

Size
The banded morwong grows to about 65 centimetres.

Breeding
Little is known.

Habits
Its habits are much the same as the red morwong, preferring exposed and broken inshore reefs.

Distribution
This morwong overlaps with the red morwong in southern New South Wales; it is more prolific in Victoria, Tasmania and South Australia.

MORWONG, BLUE
Nemadactylus douglasii

OTHER NAMES: **MOWIE, RUBBERLIP, LUBRA-LIP, GREY MORWONG, GREAT PERCH, PERCH, SEA-BREAM**

Identification
This is a fish which has a perch-like shape, is silver-blue in colour with a tinge of tan to the upper half of its body. Immature fish have a grey-black blotch on the middle of their body. It has long pectoral fins of a bluish shade. The mouth seems small in relation to its size and the lips are thickish and rubbery.

Size
The blue morwong grows to 70 centimetres in length and can weigh about 8 kilograms.
The minimum legal length for a catch in Tasmania

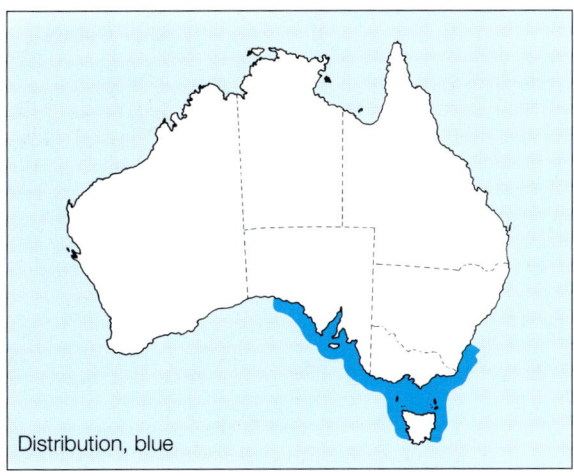

Distribution, blue

is 23 centimetres. The minimum in New South Wales is 28 centimetres.

Breeding
Research in New Zealand indicates that these fish spawn inshore — near the surface — in the autumn and early winter months. The fish move to deeper depths as they grow, in search of worms, etc.

Habits
Like all morwongs, the blue morwong is a bottom dwelling fish that feeds there. It can be found in water from about 12 to 100 plus metres, where it feeds on prawns and other crustaceans, molluscs and marine worms. It is also a schooling fish: catch one and you can reasonably expect that there will be others in the area. The fish is often present, though rarely fished for, in sand and gravel areas between reefs or off headlands along the beaches, especially in the autumn months.

Distribution
This morwong prefers the cooler waters of the east

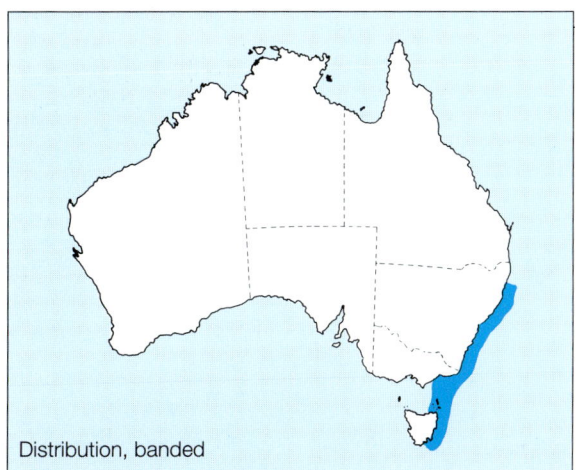

Distribution, banded

Southern blue morwong.

Jackass morwong.

coast, ranging from the north coast of New South Wales, the south-eastern coast of Victoria and the east to north-eastern coast of Tasmania. The most abundant populations are in the central and southern parts of New South Wales.

MORWONG, SOUTHERN BLUE
Nemadactylus valenciennesi

OTHER NAMES: **QUEEN SNAPPER, QUEEN MORWONG, QUEENFISH**

Identification
This fish is a much brighter blue than the blue morwong, with some appearing lighter because of a silvery undertone. Its caudal fin has a yellow colour. The vivid blue fades and becomes dull after death. Its distinctive features are its lines or dashes around the eyes and a dull or dark blotch on the mid-section of its body.

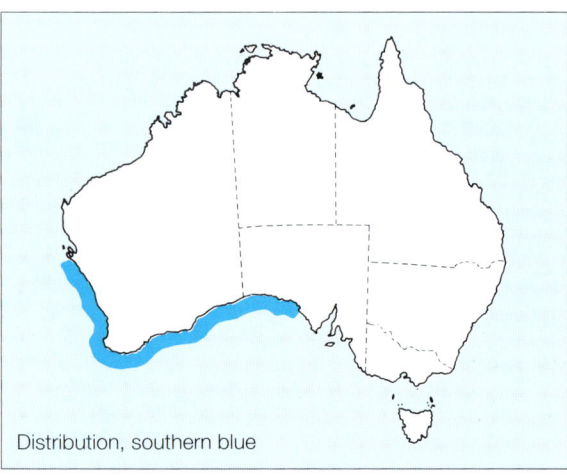
Distribution, southern blue

Size
The southern blue morwong is one of the largest of the morwongs, growing to about a metre in length and some 7 kilograms in weight.
The minimum legal length for a catch in Western Australia is 30 centimetres.

Breeding
It is also believed to breed inshore.

Habits
The southern blue morwong fish moves in schools that are common around inshore and off shore reefs.

Distribution
This fish is occasionally encountered in the waters of south-western Victoria, but it is comparatively abundant along the South Australian coast and in West Australian waters up to Lancelin, north of Perth.

MORWONG, JACKASS
Nemadactylus macropterus

OTHER NAMES: **JACKASS FISH, MORWONG, SEA-BREAM, SEINE BOAT MORWONG, DEEP SEA PERCH, MOWI, SILVER PERCH**

Identification
This fish is light blue-grey with dusky undertones, though it is best identified by the purple-black saddle marking between the head and first dorsal fins.

Size
This fish grows to about 70 centimetres in length

but most are caught at around 35 to 45 centimetres. The minimum legal length for a catch in new South Wales is 28 centimetres. In Tasmania the minimum is 23 centimetres.

Breeding
The jackass morwong breeds in late summer-autumn.

Habits
Its habits are similar to those of the blue and southern blue morwong, but occasional specimens enter deep coastal inlets and harbours. They prefer a broken or hard gravel bottom near reefs.

Distribution
The jackass inhabits mainly the deeper off shore reefs, from about Sydney south to Victoria, Tasmanian waters, across the southern coast and up the west coast to about the latitude of Rottnest Island, off Fremantle, in Western Australia.

MORWONG, RED
Cheilodactylus fuscus

OTHER NAME: **RED MULLET, SEA CARP, GOAT FISH**

Identification
Though the red morwong shares the typical morwong body shape, it can be distinguished from the others by its colour — pale to reddish-brown on the upper half with greyish to white belly. A few may be found that appear banded (similar to the banded morwong). Another identifying feature is a pair of small blunt horns in front of the eyes.

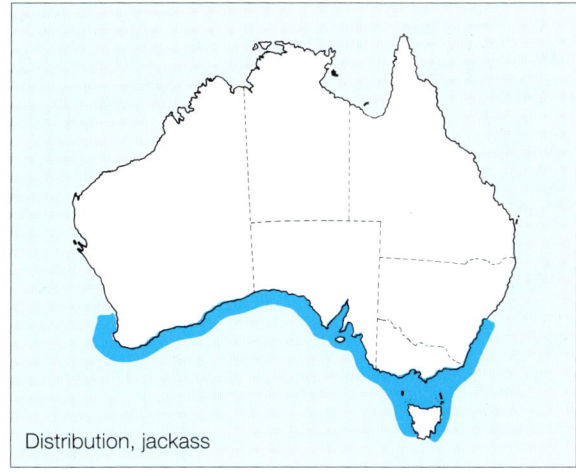
Distribution, jackass

Size
Red morwongs have been caught measuring up to 65 centimetres long and about 3 kilograms. The minimum legal length for a catch in New South Wales is 25 centimetres.

Breeding
Little is known.

Habits
This fish inhabits inshore reefs that may be exposed at low tide. It does not appear to school as much as other morwongs but it does like to locate itself on a rocky or rubble bottom where there is an abundance of shellfish and crabs. It does enter very deep locations in harbours, and is often found in deep holes near breakwaters.

Distribution
This morwong is limited to the coastal areas from the northern coast of New South Wales to the northern waters of Victoria.

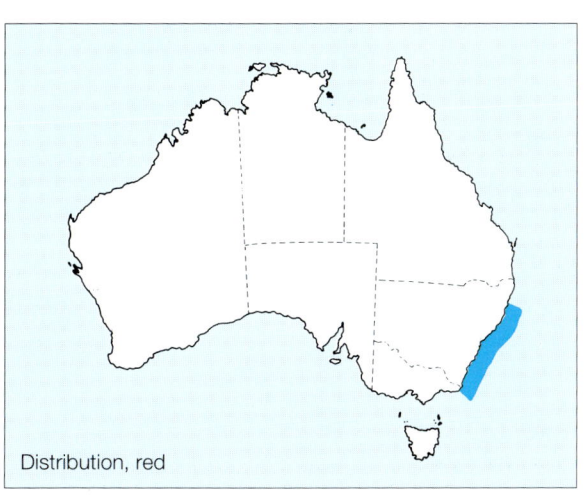
Distribution, red

Red morwong.

Other regulations
Anglers are limited to a catch of 5 red morwong per day in New South Wales.

MORWONG, RED-LIPPED
Cheilodactylus rubrolabiatus

OTHER NAME: **RED-BANDED MORWONG**

Identification
The red-lipped morwong cannot be mistaken for the banded morwong because of its vivid red lips and the intense brown spotting between the dark brown-black bands on its body and on its fins.

Size
This morwong grows to about 75 centimetres in length.

Breeding
Little is known.

Habit
The red-lipped morwong inhabits broken and exposed reefs and reefs in protected waters.

Distribution
This morwong is common in West Australian waters south from Coral Bay. It is in thinner numbers along the southern coast about as far as Ceduna in South Australia.

The following applies to all morwongs.

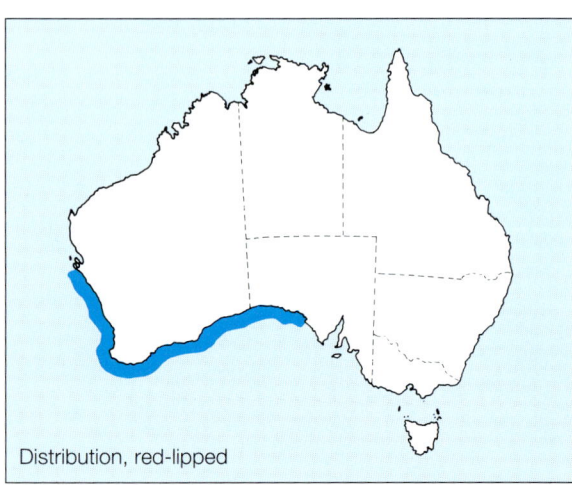

Distribution, red-lipped

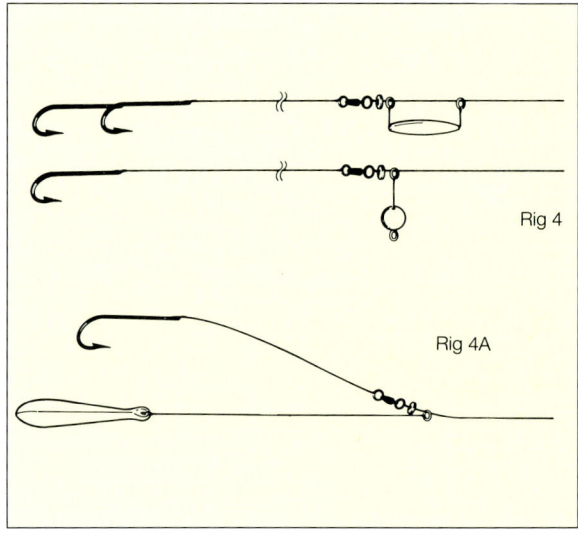

Rig 4

Rig 4A

When to fish
Those species of morwongs that prefer the deeper off-shore reefs are around all year. When these do move inshore they are often within reach of land-based anglers in late summer autumn. The species that prefer the shallower waters are also around throughout the year and the early morning seems the most promising time to find morwongs in a feeding mood.

Where to fish
Try sand, gravel, and weedy areas alongside reefs.

Tackle
For the deeper off-shore morwongs, the bottom rigs Nos 4A or 6A are suitable with a handline, deck winch or a small boat rod. If fishing from the rocks, use a rod of about 3.5 to 4 metres in length with a sensitive tip, fitted with a matching threadline, overhead or sidecast reel. Lines about 5 to 8 kilograms breaking-strain are adequate for the inshore species but they will need to be double that strength for off shore reef fishing.

Bait
The prawn is undoubtedly the number one for the deep water morwong. However, these fish will also take fresh fish fillets, and small fish such as sprats. Shoreline and off shore anglers will do much better with red crabs, mussels, limpets, etc. for morwong, but these are favoured by "pickers" and, of course, other popular species.

Rigs
On close inshore waters with a comparatively clean

bottom, the running rig No. 4 can be used. For rock fishing, rig No. 4A is fine. If specifically seeking morwong, the sinker dropper should be shortened as this fish is found close to the bottom. The hooks should be relatively small — never over 2/0 — and even smaller when inshore fishing.

How to hook

The morwong is a soft biter, a slow taker. It is a matter of experience to detect the bite and know when to apply pressure to set the hook. It is better to be a little slow than too hasty in this action. The fish fights strongly but rarely does it try to dive into reef holes or run around obstructions.

Edibility

The flesh of morwong is white, firm and good tasting. It can be cooked by all methods. Other morwong may be landed occasionally. They are equally edible.

[**Note:** The **dusky morwong** *dactylophora nigricans* is very rarely taken on a hook and it is not a good eating fish. It is confined to Victorian, Tasmanian, South Australian and Western Australian waters. It is sometimes called strongfish, butterfish and tillywurti. It grows to more than a metre. The fish minimum legal length for a catch of this fish in Victoria is 23 centimetres.]

MULLET

The confusion of common names — and to lesser extent some doubts about the scientific names — makes it very difficult to separate the 20-odd mullet of Australian waters. The writer has chosen the easy way out of the tangle here. Those mullet that are widespread in several States or those which are abundant in a particular area may be regarded as representative. Each mullet that the writer has chosen as representative is identified, by size, habits and distribution. Information on angling methods that apply to all follows thereafter.

The sea mullet.

MULLET, BLUE-TAILED
Valamugil seheli

OTHER NAMES: **BLACK-SPOT, BLUE-SPOT, LONG-ARMED, LONG-FINNED, EVEN SAND**

Identification
This is a bright, silvery mullet with a greenish-brown back and a white abdomen. It has light blue fins with a dark blue tip to the top of its tail.

MULLET, DIAMOND-SCALED
Liza vaigrensis

OTHER NAMES: **LARGE-SCALED MULLET**

Identification
This mullet is thicker or heavier in the body around the pectoral fins than the others. It is identifiable, if not by its olive-green colour, then by the yellowish

Diamond-scaled mullet.

tropical waters north of this area, across the top end, and down to the north-west of Western Australia.

MULLET, FLAT-TAIL or FANTAIL
Liza argentea

OTHER NAMES: **JUMPIN OR JUMPING, BROWN-BACK, GOLD-GILL, ROCK-MULLET, TIGER MULLET, TYGUM**

shade to its abdomen area and distinctive scale pattern — plus the five or six broken lines of a brownish colour along its body.

Size
Both the blue-tailed and diamond-scaled mullet grow to a large size. The blue-tailed reaches about 80 centimetres in length and can weigh as much as 10 kilograms. The diamond-scaled mullet has been recorded at 5 kilograms

Breeding
Little is known but they are believed to breed close to or in estuaries.

Habits
Both the mullet inhabit the estuaries and rivers of the tropics. Their feeding habits and behaviour are very similar to the sea mullet.

Distribution
The occasional specimen is found about Rockhampton but both fish appear to prefer

Identification
This is easily distinguished from other mullet by the gold or yellow markings on the gill covers. (The sand mullet or tallegalane also has a gold blotch in this area but it has only 9 rays to the anal fin compared with 10 on the flat-tailed mullet. The flat-tailed mullet is also thicker in the region of the anal fin and it has a larger caudal fin.)

Size
This mullet grows to 45 centimetres, but is more commonly found at around the 30 centimetres mark. The minimum legal length for a catch in Victoria is 22 centimetres; in South Australia it is 21 centimetres.

Breeding
This mullet is believed to spawn in estuaries in the late summer to early autumn.

Habits
The flat-tail mullet confines its movements to rivers,

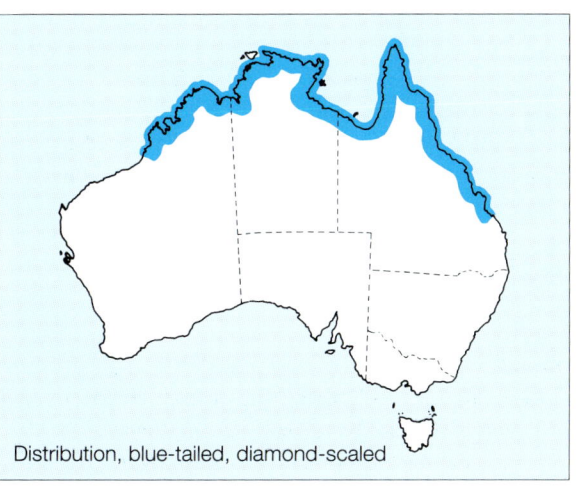

Distribution, blue-tailed, diamond-scaled

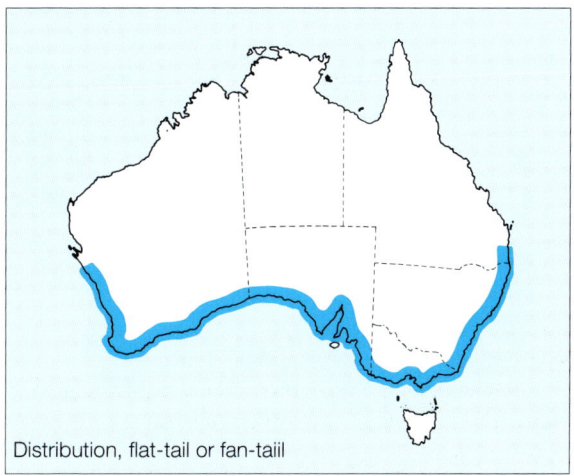

Distribution, flat-tail or fan-taiil

233

estuaries and adjacent ocean beaches. Some evidence exists that it may move to nearby estuaries. Adult fish have similar feeding habits as sea mullet. It is known that juveniles also consume insects and their larvae.

Distribution

To be conservative, this mullet can be found from about central Queensland, south around the mainland and up to the Murchison River in Western Australia.

MULLET, SAND
Myxus elongatus

OTHER NAMES: **TALLEGALANE, LANO, WIDE BAY MULLET, PODDY**

Identification

This mullet has a gold blotch on the gill cover but its body is not as thick in the region of the anal fin as the flat-tail mullet. It also has a more pointed snout than the other mullet and a row of identifiable teeth in the upper jaw. There is a blackish spot at the top of the pectoral fin base. It is a brownish-olive or brownish-blue on the back, depending on its habitat.

Size

This mullet reaches about 45 centimetres in length. The minimum legal length for a catch is 21 centimetres in South Australia; 22 centimetres in Victoria; and 20 centimetres in Tasmania.

Breeding

This is believed to occur in estuaries or close to them.

Habits

This mullet has a somewhat wider food intake than the other mullet, with the exception of the yellow-eye. It inhabits the sandy areas of estuaries and along nearby coastal beaches, preferring calm waters. The sand mullet forages in sand areas for marine worms as well as decomposed material. It does not appear to migrate any distance.

Distribution

Sand mullet can be found from the central region of Queensland, throughout New South Wales, Victoria, South Australia and Tasmania and on to Western Australian waters.

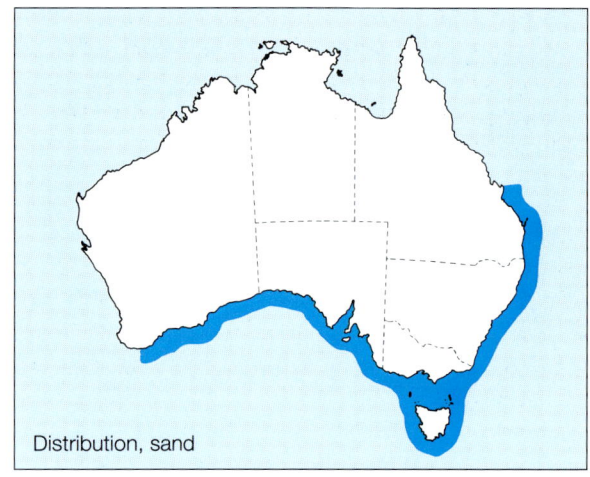

Distribution, sand

MULLET, SEA
Mugil cephalus

OTHER NAMES: **BULLY, HARDGUT, RIVER, MANGROVE, PODDY OR GREY MULLET**

Identification

As with most mullet, this fish has an elongate — even elegant — shape in profile. It is slightly compressed and the head is broad. Those growing up in rivers are a dull grey with a blue to brown back, often with brown lines along the bottom of the sides. Mature sea mullet are much more silvery with an olive-green back. There is usually a bluish spot on the base of the pectoral fins. It has a small mouth and bristle-type teeth on the lips. Their large, fatty or gelatinous eyelids become milky with death.

Size

This mullet grows to 80 centimetres in length and a weight of about 8 kilograms, but sizes between 30 and 50 centimetres are more common.
In Victoria the minimum legal length for a catch of sea mullet is 25 centimetres. In New South Wales the minimum size is 30 centimetres; in Tasmania 20 centimetres; in Western Australia 24 centimetres; in South Australia 21 centimetres; and in Queensland 30 centimetres.

Breeding

The sea mullet grows to maturity in rivers and estuaries. At 3 years and a size of 30 to 35 centimetres, they school and run to sea and northwards (except in South Australia where the fish appear to only move to sea), spawning over deep water. The eggs and larvae are carried back to estuaries and rivers by tides and wind. After spawning, the adults enter rivers to the north of their immature location. Spawning migrations occur in autumn-early winter.

Habits

Sea mullet congregate only during spawning. Otherwise the fish are spread out, though they will form into tight schools in panic. They feed on detritus (decayed organisms and debris) and microscopic organisms. They graze on blue-green algae and filamentous algae. A small amount of sand is always mixed with the food to help the grinding process in the fish's gizzard-like stomach. These fish will enter freshwater. On their spawning migration they may travel only a few kilometres or many hundreds. Two-year-old juveniles move between estuaries in mid-summer prior to the major spawning migration of the adults.

Distribution

The sea mullet are abundant on the east coast from at least the central Queensland coast to the north and eastern coasts of Tasmania. They are less common in western Victoria but abundant again in South Australian waters and through the waters of Western Australia well to the north. There is some doubt if it reaches the top third of Australia's coastline (marine biologists' opinions differ).

MULLET, YELLOW-EYE
Aldrichetta forsteri

OTHER NAMES: **PILCH, FRESHWATER MULLET, COORONG MULLET**

Identification

This mullet is distinguished by its yellow eyes and a much larger mouth than others of its family. It is a grey to silver colour overall with a blue tone to its back. It has minute teeth.

The yellow-eye mullet.

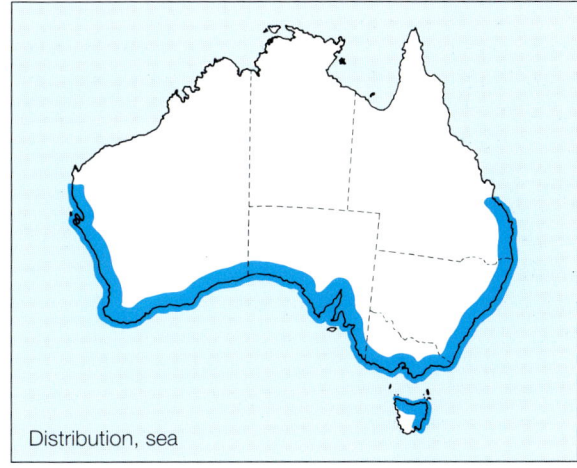

Distribution, sea

Size

Though this mullet grows to a maximum length of 50 centimetres, it is usually caught at about the 30 centimetres to 40 centimetres mark. The minimum legal length for a catch in Western Australia is 23 centimetres; 21 centimetres in South Australia; and 20 centimetres in Tasmania.

Breeding

There is some evidence that the yellow-eye of the western region breeds in the autumn to winter period, while those of the east breed in the summer to spring period, when these fish move to sea.

Habits

The main difference between the yellow-eye and other mullet is that it readily takes bait, eating a wide range which includes prawns, shrimp, pieces of lobster, beach or sand worms, bacon rind and slices of boiled mutton. It also moves from estuaries out to sea and on to other estuaries.

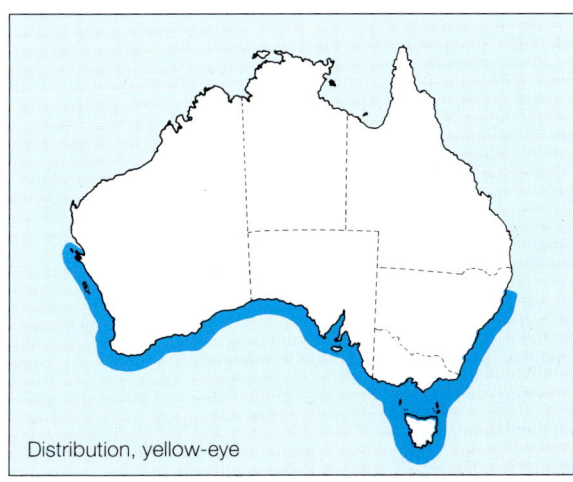

Distribution, yellow-eye

Distribution

Yellow-eye mullet inhabit estuaries and coastal bays that have clean sandy bottoms or low sea-grass meadows, preferring the more sheltered waters around pilings and sand-banks or embankments. They are found from the north coast of New South Wales, around Tasmania, Victoria, South Australia and on to Shark Bay in Western Australia. In some southern areas they are more abundant than the sea mullet.

The following applies to all mullet.

When to fish

All of the above mullet tend to follow the rising tide so that they have the protection of a tidal cover while feeding on the mudflats or sand areas. The best time to catch them is during the rising tide period in the morning or afternoon and at dusk. Anglers should proceed with silent caution: mullet are easily panicked by the shadows of an angler casting or by splashes on the water.

Where to fish

Try near the edges of the mud or sandbars and where the water surface is relatively smooth. In some areas, it is possible to moor a boat and "seed" a location which is known to be visited by feeding mullet.

Tackle

The operative word is light for handlines, although these are neither as convenient nor as successful as rod outfits. The same recommendation, however, applies to rods — light and sensitive — fitted with a matching threadline or sidecast reel, spooled with a maximum of 4 kilogram breaking-strain line. Hooks must be small, between size 8 and 12 for most species and perhaps 2 or 4, depending on the species and its size. When fishing from boats, some piers or banks, the rod can be a single-handed style about 2 metres long, but one about 3.5 metres (the slow action light luderick rod is suitable) is ideal from many locations. Fly outfits with small flies are growing increasingly popular.

Bait

For some mullet, dough will work and occasionally pieces of blood worm or sand worm, as well as bacon rind or the fat from the rind. The yellow-eye eats these baits much more readily as well as others (*see* Habits, yellow-eye).

Berley

All mullet can be "taught" to eat a wide range of readily available baits. However, the angler must reside close to an estuary where mullet gather or know someone who has access to a river or estuary. Once you discover an area where the mullet congregate on an incoming tide to feed, "seed" the spot on the last of the ebb and during the beginning of the flow. This must be done daily for five or six days, preferably on both high tides.

The mixture can be breadcrumbs, pollard or bran which contains some sand and a percentage of

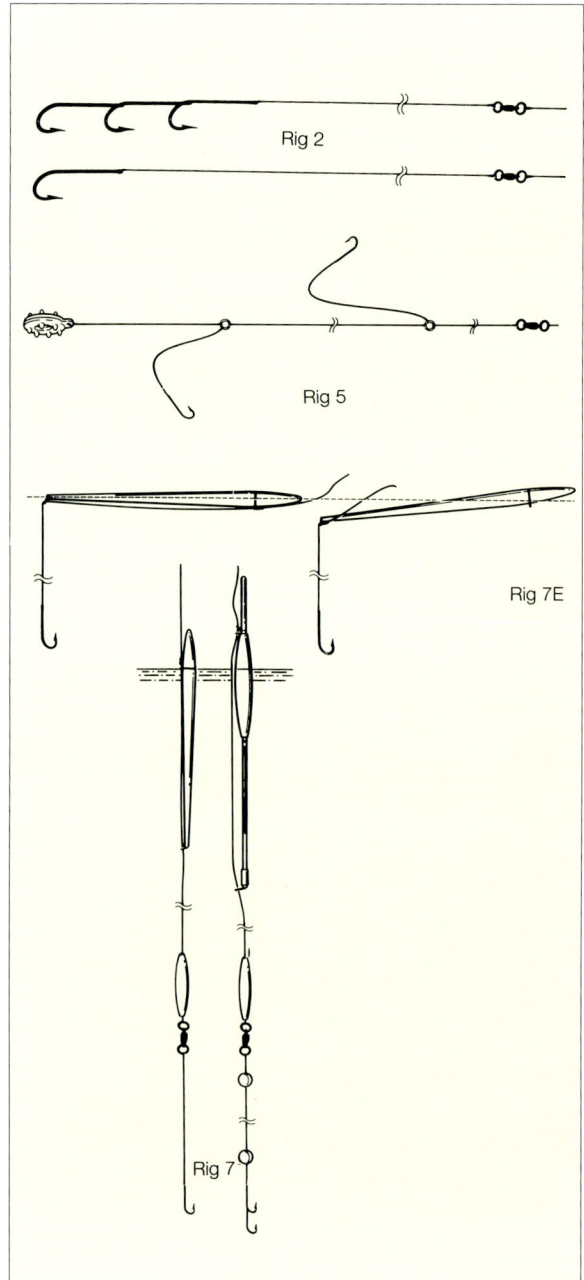

finely-minced weed from the local water. The additive to this is over-toasted or over-roasted (until it is crumbly) flesh which is to be used as bait. This is also finely minced and mixed with the crumbs, etc. Very successful additions are pilchards, beachworms, liver and bacon. The longer the seeding of an area is carried out, the more successful the result. When fishing, you then use tiny fresh pieces of the flesh used in the berley, floated amongst the mullet as they feed. They can become quite addicted to this berley or food mix.

Rigs

The lightest quill, pencil or bubble float is an important part of the rig for most mullet. In the case of the yellow-eye, when fishing from beaches or bays influenced by waves or currents, a sinker as light as the conditions will allow should be used, but if it can be dispensed with altogether, more mullet will result. Depending on conditions, the rig Nos.2 or 5 are satisfactory but float rigs Nos 7 or 7E are recommended. The depth to the bait should be between 10 and 20 centimetres.

How to hook

Where the bait can be seen, it is a matter of timing, setting the hook after the mullet has sipped in the proffered bait. Fishing on the bottom, as is the case with yellow-eye in many places, the hook should be set firmly the moment the bite is felt.

It is important for this reason to maintain a straight line with some tension between rod and bait.

Edibility

Mullet are often regarded as second-rate. Much of the problem arises from not killing, bleeding and thoroughly cleaning them immediately they are caught. All mullet are best filleted and skinned and can be prepared by most methods, but a sea mullet straight from the ocean and stuffed and baked is a gourmet's delight.

[**Note:** The distribution of the sea mullet and the yellow-eye mullet can extend well into some rivers, beyond the brackish limits, though they usually return with the tide. These should not be mistaken for the **freshwater mullet** (*Trachystoma petardi*), also known as pink-eye, Richmond and river mullet. The real freshwater mullet, which has a very pointed snout, is silvery with a dark green back and dirty, grey-brown fins and bright orange-yellow eyes. It has a mouth full of fine teeth and larger ones in the roof of the mouth. This mullet, which grows to 60-plus centimetres, spends its life in freshwater. It can be caught with floating rigs on light lines and small hooks baited with earthworms, small shrimp, pieces of yabby and sometimes grasshopper abdomens. If taken from clear water, it is excellent eating. It is limited to freshwater streams and lagoons from Moreton Bay, in Queensland, and south to around Nowra in New South Wales.]

MULLOWAY

Mulloway are high on the list of fish that recreational anglers dream of catching. Some of the most dedicated anglers are happy only when they are fishing for them, and with good reason: they are not easy to catch despite being one of the most widely-distributed species in Australia. Many an angler has proudly displayed the otoliths or ear-bones (which look like large pearls) from a large mulloway as evidence of his prowess.

The seriousness of the mulloway mystique to its aficionados is reflected in the special names that describe its status. It is a "soapy" while less than about 1.5 kilograms, a "school" or "schoolie" until it passes 5 kilograms, after which it becomes a "mulloway". It also has several common names.

There are, in fact, *two* mulloways much sought by anglers. Though very much the same, they are nevertheless different species that occur in different parts of the country. The difference will hardly affect most anglers. The major distinction is that one is confined to the tropics and the other is found around the southern half of the mainland coast. There are no mulloway in Tasmania.

[Note:
There are also two other fish, called jewfish, which look much like small mulloway. One, often thought to be a young mulloway *(A. hololepidotus)*, is the **little jewfish** or **river perch** *(Johnius belangerii)* which is found in estuaries from southern Queensland to about Rockhampton. The other is the **silver jewfish** *(Pseudosciaena soldado)*, also called silver perch, banana jew and grassy jew. It occurs in estuaries and rivers from mid Queensland and across the northern areas of Australia. Neither of these jewfish exceeds 35 centimetres.

These jewfish and the mulloway below belong to the Scianidae family, which are called "croakers" because they can make a similar noise — caused by a vibrating swim bladder — when caught.]

MULLOWAY
Argyrosomus hololepidotus

OTHER NAMES: **JEWY, JEWFISH, SILVER JEW, RIVER KINGFISH, KINGFISH, SOAPIE, SCHOOL JEW**

MULLOWAY
Johnius diacanthus

OTHER NAMES: **JEWY, JEWFISH, BLACK JEW, SPOTTED JEWFISH**

Identification

A. hololepidotus is a powerful elongate fish, whose colour tends to vary according to its habitat. Its colour is generally a shade of bronze with a definite green tinge on the upper half and a silver-grey belly. The lateral line is highlighted by a series of pearly blotches that fade rapidly after death. The inside of the mouth is orange and the powerful tail is convex or slightly rhomboid (curved tending to a point), two features which distinguish it from the teraglin.

J. diacanthus is similar in appearance but is a darker colour — blackish on the dorsal area, often in blotches — which gives it one of its common names. This fish has a prominent second spine in its anal fin, whereas its relative has short and weak spines in its anal fin.

Size

Both these fish exceed 50 kilograms when fully grown. The largest authenticated mulloway measured almost 2 metres long and weighed 60 kilograms; the largest mulloway caught on a line weighed 43.7 kilograms.

The minimum length for a catch in Western Australia is 33 centimetres. The minimum is 75 centimetres in South Australia (except those caught at Coorong, where 45 centimetres is the minimum); and 30 centimetres in Queensland.

Breeding

The mulloway spawns at sea on shallow coastal reefs, though not too far from the entrances of large estuaries. Spawning is believed to occur in the spring and summer months. This is the only time the larger mulloway aggregate.

Habits

Mulloway are an active fish both day and night. However, the larger ones seem to rest in sheltered reef areas and deep holes for long periods during the day. The "soapies" and immature mulloway tend to travel in schools, but large ones appear to roam alone or at most in twos or threes. Large numbers will gather and follow schools of migrating bait fish. They will also gather at the entrances to estuaries when floodwaters are pushing other fish into the ocean. The mulloway have a catholic taste, eating prawns, octopus, squid, large crabs, and fish — especially yellowtail, slimy or common mackerel, pilchards, tailor, mullet, garfish and luderick. The "thwack" of a mulloway, referred to as a "chop", when it is attacking a school of mullet or garfish in an estuary, is a memorable sound. It feeds on the surface and down to the bottom. It will also tolerate muddy water or sand stirred up by waves on ocean beaches. The larger fish are usually caught in the first few hours after dusk.

Distribution

A. hololepidotus can be found from about the Burnett River in Queensland, along the coast of New South Wales, Victoria, South Australia, and as far north on the West Australian coast as Exmouth. They are not present in Tasmanian waters. From those points, its tropical relative replaces it across the top of the continent, providing excellent fishing, for example, at Port Hedland, Dampier, Darwin, in the Gulf of Carpentaria and north of Townsville. At various times of the year mulloway will be found in the upstream waters of estuaries but normally they are caught in the lower reaches of estuaries and in deep harbours or bays, as well as off ocean beaches and rocks and inshore reefs.

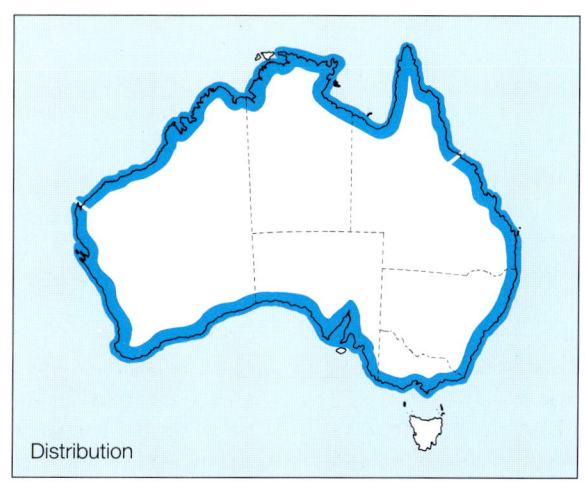

Distribution

When to fish

The best fishing times vary. A promising time along the east coast is when the smaller sea mullet change estuaries during the summer and during the spawning run of sea mullet. The mulloway also follow tailor on their northward migration in autumn. Thus the far south coast season is probably shorter than the northern area of New South Wales and southern Queensland. The movement of whiting and salmon also influences their whereabouts. As migrating fish thin out, the marauding mulloway will seek out other fish, particularly mullet in the estuaries. On the west coast of the continent, the fish are about inshore waters and reefs in the winter and spring in the south, and in the late spring to autumn further north. In many rivers and estuaries of their southern distribution, the mulloway are more numerous during late spring and early summer. This is also a good time in the more eastern coastal estuaries. However, the presence of preferred food, or the availability of any food, remains a major factor.

The fish can be caught during the day, but most of the larger ones from 6 kilograms upwards are taken at about dusk on a rising to high tide and beyond until it is halfway out again. Questionable arguments exist as to the best phase of the moon — full, the last quarter or the new moon.

Where to fish

Mulloway seem to be everywhere till you try to catch one. Try estuaries first, at locations that are known to be ideal territories for mullet, garfish or other small fish. Deep water near eddies or channels are likely spots too, and alongside underwater obstructions or reefs or near bridge pylons. The breakwaters on many rivers towards the ocean end are also consistent mulloway areas. The deep channels entering and running parallel to a beach may also yield mulloway as it seeks tailor, salmon, whiting, beach worms and sand crabs. Mulloway will often venture into the white water off a beach. Holes at the end of a beach near a reef or headland are also visiting spots. The same applies to rocks alonside a channel entering an inlet or a sand or gravel bottom between reefs or niggerheads. Mulloway can also be found over reefs off shore.

Tackle

When fishing from a boat in an estuary or the open sea, use a handline about 15 to 20 kilograms breaking-strain or a short boat rod. Heavy duty threadline or baitcasting rods of about 2 metres are suitable with a line of 8 to 10 kilograms breaking-strain. If fishing from the beach or rocks, use a medium-weight rod between 3.5 and 4 metres long, matched with a heavy-duty threadline, overhead or sidecast reel, spooled with the same (8 to 10 kilograms) breaking-strain line. Hooks should be between 5/0 and 8/0, depending on the type and size of bait. A higher breaking-strain leader is suggested rather than a wire trace.

Bait

Bait should, if possible, be alive. It can be (not in order of preference) slimy mackerel, small mullet, yellowtail, small tailor, squid and other fish (of a size which complies with legal length requirements), beach worms and large sand crabs. The same baits can be used dead as long as they are fresh — or large fillets of them.

Rigs

The running rig No. 4 with a sinker suitable for estuary conditions will do. If the current is running strongly, a leader of about 2 metres is suggested. This rig is also suitable for shallow inshore reefs where the bottom is not too rough, otherwise try rig No. 4. All three rigs are fine from the beach or rocks, though when fishing off the rocks, the float rig No. 7C is best with the bait (dead or alive) suspended about 2 metres off the bottom.

How to hook

Impatience loses many mulloway. More often than not this fish will grab its food from the side and hold it first. Then the mulloway moves off slowly as it crushes and/or turns its prey so that it can swallow it, especially fish which it must swallow

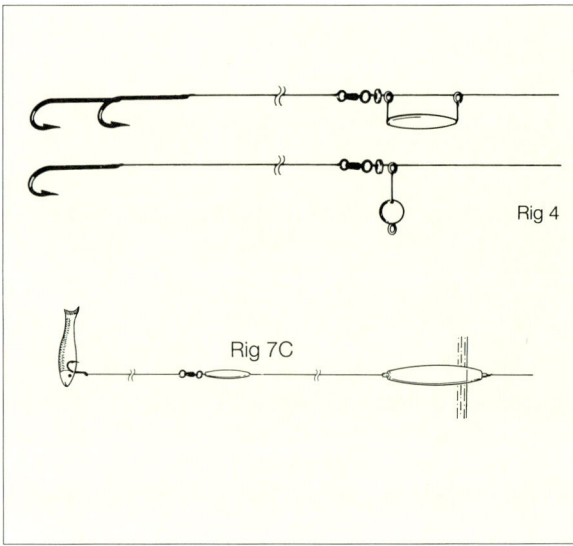

Perfect start to a perfect day: fine mulloway catch in W.A.

head first. (There are authenticated instances of large mulloway being captured by hand while floundering on the surface, choking because they had tried to swallow a fish tail first. The prey had raised its dorsal spines which were stuck in the mulloway's throat.) This slow swim is usually no more than 3 to 10 metres after which it moves off more rapidly. When this begins, that is the time to set the hook.

Hint

When fishing for mulloway with whole dead yellowtail, pilchards, mullet or garfish, bait your ganged hooks in the reverse manner — the *bottom* hook through the eye. This is particularly effective on school mulloway, which will often take the bait without the frustrating hesitation.

Another effective ploy is rather than ganging hooks in the normal eye-through-eye manner, tie or "snood" them separately on the line with 10 to 12 millimetres between them.

When using live fish pinned through the back, try a second hook swinging free on the side of the bait. This hook can be the hook tied to the end of the main eye, the hook holding the fish snooded above it; or it can be the bottom hook of a pair linked.

Edibility

The "soapie" mulloway is soft and lacks flavour. In fact any mulloway below 3 kilograms is not the best eating. Over the 3 kilogram mark the fish is excellent. It is probably better to fillet and skin the flesh, though cutlets from the larger fish are also popular. This is a fish which freezes well, provided that it is frozen while fresh. It can be cooked by most methods but mornay of mulloway is superb.

NANNYGAI

When is a nannygai a redfish, a bight redfish, a swallowtail, a
swallowtail nannygai, a red snapper or a yellow-eyed snapper? It
seems to largely depend on whether you accept the
recommended marketing name or the common
name used in various localities around Australia.
There is only one genus but five species, according to various
ichthyologists. Four are grouped here with the taxonomic
detail which separates them.
[**Note**: Some evidence exists that "nannygai" is the Aboriginal
word for juvenile snapper (red bream or cockney) but early
settlers confused the two fish — and perhaps researchers too.
One strong indication of this is that the fish now called
"nannygai" is fished in depths of water quite beyond the
resources of the Aboriginal people.]

NANNYGAI

Centroberyx affinis

OTHER NAME: **REDFISH**

Identification

This fish short-bodied fish has a deep oval shape. It
has a large head in comparison to the body, with
large eyes, the black pupil of which is circled in red.
There are several serrated ridges on the head and
the body has rough scales. All fins have sharp

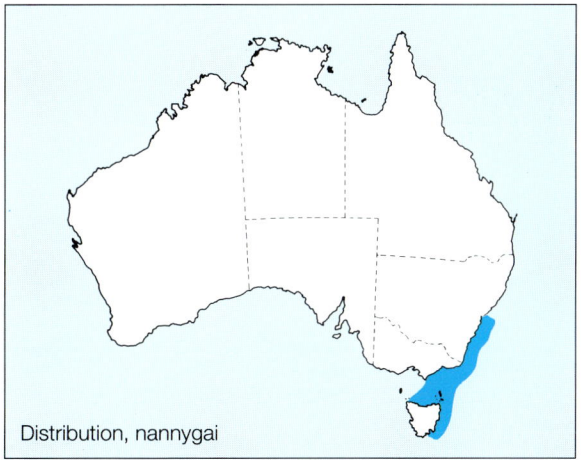

Distribution, nannygai

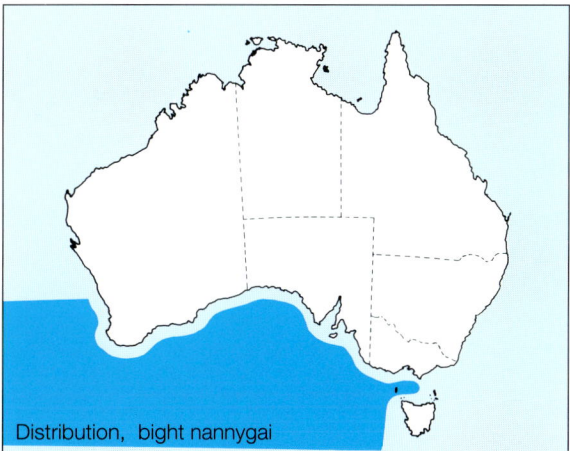

Distribution, bight nannygai

spines. The nannygai's colour is predominantly a silvery red on the head, body and tail, fading to a creamy orange towards the belly. There is a white edge on the fins.

Size
The nannygai grows to more than 50 centimetres in length.

Distribution
These fish are found in ocean waters (occasionally in deep harbours) south from central New South Wales, around eastern Victoria and on the north and east coasts of Tasmania.

NANNYGAI, BIGHT
Centroberyx gerrardi

OTHER NAMES: **RED SNAPPER, BIGHT REDFISH, BIGHT SNAPPER**

Identification
The largest of the nannygai, this fish is easily mistaken for *C.affinis*. To distinguish between them, this nannygai has only 6 spines in its dorsal fin compared to 7 in *C. affinis*. It also has a quite prominent white lateral line.

Size
This nannygai grows to at least 65 centimetres in length. The minimum length for a catch in Western Australia is 23 centimetres.

Distribution
The bight nannygai is found in small numbers as far east as Wilson's Promontory (Victoria) but becomes more abundant westward, through South Australia and in Western Australia as far north as Lancelin. It prefers reefs in deeper water.

NANNYGAI, SWALLOWTAIL
Centroberyx lineatus

OTHER NAMES: **REDFISH, SWALLOWTAIL**

Identification
This member of the family is more elongated than its relatives. It is also more red than orange on its back and tail with a much more silvery look to its body. It is easily identified by the long swallow-like tail.

Size
This fish grows to about 40 centimetres in length. The minimum legal length for this nannygai in Western Australia is 23 centimetres.

Distribution
The swallowtail nannygai inhabits deeper reef waters as well as shallow reefs close to deep water on the south coast of New South Wales and the Victorian, South Australian and Western Australian coasts.

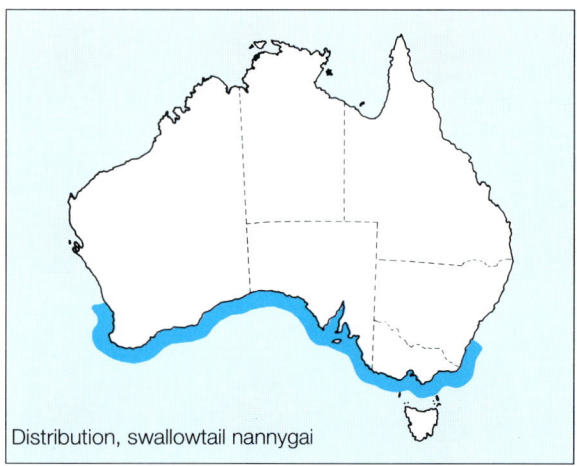

Distribution, swallowtail nannygai

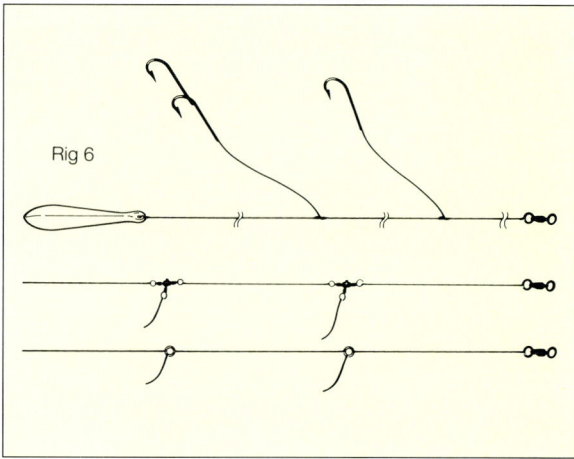

Rig 6

[**Note**: Two other smaller species of nannygai (genus *Centroberyx*) called "yellow-eyed" and "small-eyed" are found in the deep offshore waters of the Great Australian Bight andWestern Australia.
Two other similar fish that are related to the nannygai are the alphonsin *(Beryx splendens)* and the imperador *(Beryx decadactylus)*. Both these fish have only 4 spines in the dorsal fin. Anglers only rarely hook them from very deep waters.]

Breeding
Little is known.

Habits
Nannygai are invariably encountered in schools while fishing over or near reefs. They are carnivores, which eat fish, crabs, prawns, squid, etc.

When to fish
These fishes are usually taken during the daytime while fishing for other reef fish. They can be quite aggressive biters and respond well to bait on dark overcast days or at night.

Where to fish
Some of the species frequent shallower reefs from about 10 metres but are more likely to be found in deep water reefs of up to 200 metres. Drifting along the side of reefs is generally more productive than moving over a reef.

Tackle
On shallower reefs a handline, boat rod or medium-weight threadline or baitcasting rod and reels are all suitable. In the deeper water, handlines, boat rods or the gunwale-mounted winch type of reels are more commonly used. Because the more desirable species inhabit the same waters as nannygai, lines are in breaking strains to suit the wider range of fish, as are hook sizes.

Bait
The nannygai are ready feeders, taking any bait offered for snapper, morwong or other rock fish. If a school is encountered, a tough bait such as octopus tentacle stops them from stealing softer baits without reducing the likelihood of a strike.

Rigs
These fishes can be caught in multiples on a bottom rig such as No. 6, though other bottom rigs may be used.

How to hook
The nannygai, depending on their size, can steal soft baits from the large hooks that are usually used for snapper. But they do have a large mouth, so it is not worth changing to a smaller size. If the line is kept taut, a firm lift as a bite is felt usually hooks the nannygai. Once a school is discovered, anglers using multiple hook rigs occasionally wait until they feel that they have one or two fish before bringing them in.

Edibility
There is not a lot of flesh on small nannygai, but those at the top end of their size can yield a good fillet. The nannygai can be cooked by most methods and a whole fish stuffed and baked is very good eating.

PARROT-FISH
Scaridae

Most of the so-called parrot-fish caught by recreational anglers are nothing of the sort. They tend to be confused with tusk-fish and certain wrasses, which resemble parrot-fish and are similarly colourful. Moreover, all three fish occupy the same waters in varying populations, adding to the confusion. Parrot-fish, however, have a fundamental difference: a pair of fused heavy teeth in each jaw that give the impression of a parrot's beak. Hence the name. The teeth in their throat — called a pharyngeal mill — are even larger and stronger than those found in wrasses and some other fish.

 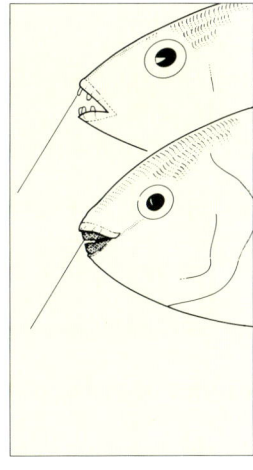

Tuskfish (top right) have peg-like teeth for crushing and tearing. Parrotfish (above & below right) have fused teeth for grazing on coral.

The parrot-fish's diet is also unusual. It exists on crushed coral, chewing off overgrowths which it pulps in those powerful throat teeth.

Some ichthyologists consider there may be fewer species of parrot-fish than is believed. It has been found that the fish are sexually dimorphic, resulting in a multiplicity of colours and even some differences in bone structure. They can also be differently coloured at various ages and it is possible that males and females are not the same colours. The most fascinating discovery about parrot-fish, however, is that they become disorientated and lost in the dark — or even if moved away from their usual location. They sleep on the bottom during the night, usually in a cave or under an overhang, and remain inactive on dark, clouded days.

The tusk-fish and wrasses (*see* entries) have peg-like teeth or canine-type teeth.

PERCH

Many saltwater perches are distinguished from the freshwater variety with the prefix "sea": the popular marine perches that are readily accessible to anglers may be found under the entry "sea-perches".

PERCH, ENGLISH
Perca fluviatilis

OTHER NAMES: **REDFIN, REDFIN PERCH, EUROPEAN PERCH**

This is an exotic perch that was introduced to Australia by early European settlers in Tasmania in 1861. Only ten fish survived the journey from England but another ten were imported, and this time released in a reservoir at Ballarat, seven of which were later transferred to a swamp which became Lake Windourie. Those seven fish produced all the English perch that are so widespread in Australia today.

Most biologists agree — with few reservations — that the English perch's predatory nature, combined with its prolific breeding, has had an adverse effect on native inland species. Though the prolific numbers of small perch or redfin are a food for Murray cod and to a lesser extent golden perch in some waterways, their competition for water space and a diet of such food as yabbies, shrimps and indigenous gudgeons and galaxiids, has had a net effect of reducing the numbers of cod and golden perch. English perch are also implicated in the decline of the trout cod in many areas and the Macquarie perch from some impoundments. And the careless introduction of these fish has replaced trout that were well established in some waters of Western Australia's south-west.

Identification

The English perch has an oval-elongate shape that is moderately deep in the body. There is a concavity above and behind the eye but from the back of the head it is markedly convex. Its spiny first dorsal fin is high from a long base, and separated narrowly from a high rear dorsal fin. The fish's colour is variable, the top of the body being a greenish-yellow to brownish, sometimes with a bluish tinge. The colour of its lower half fades to a greenish hue, with an off-white belly. There are six dark vertical bars or bands between the front of the first dorsal and the rear of the second dorsal fin, which become pointed at the belly region. The pelvic and anal fins are orange-red while the tail is grey with a red tinge. When frightened or captured, the body colour pales rapidly and the bands can disappear.

Size

English perch have been recorded at a weight of 10 kilograms. Even in Europe a larger fish has not been weighed. Depending on the populations in a waterway, English perch weighing from a few grams to about 2.5 kilograms may be caught by anglers.

Breeding

This fish is particularly fecund. Females disperse their eggs, after several males have selected the site, in late winter-early spring, when the water temperature reaches between 11°C to 12°C. Spawning takes place during the night, all the eggs being shed in a long ribbon over weeds or timber branches. In waters which the fish over-populate, males may mature when only 7 centimetres and females at 9 centimetres.

Habits

While small and juvenile (and in some overcrowded waters they can become stunted, so that mature fish resemble juveniles), these fish shoal in shallow waters near the banks. As they grow they disperse and the larger fish become solitary. English perches are basically bottom-dwellers of still waters, or at least very slow-running rivers. They spend much of the time adjacent to cover — rocks, timber, weed beds. In cold winters these fish retreat to deep holes. The only movement by the fish appears when they move to shallower depths in the spring-summer months. In floods they will swim against the current. In dams the fish are sometimes pelagic. The diet of redfin consists of other small fish (it is a cannibal) and shrimps, yabbies, crayfish, insects, insect larvae, worms, mussels, woodgrubs, etc. Although regarded as a cool to cold water species, not normally encountered in the cold fast-flowing Australian rivers, they are present in many such rivers to the upper lowland regions. On the other hand, English perch do not tolerate high

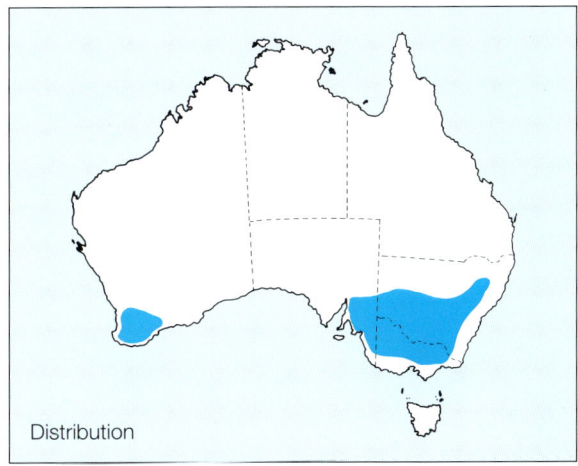

Distribution

temperatures of waters such as is found from time to time in the upper reaches of the Darling River. They require water with oxygen concentrations over 3 milligrams per litre. While these fish are found only in freshwater, they can withstand water with half the salinity of saltwater, which occurs in some inland lakes during droughts.

Distribution

Throughout many rivers, creeks and other waters, including irrigation channels, billabongs and swamps in southern, south-western, central and western New South Wales and parts to the north near the tablelands. Redfin are also widespread in Victoria, except the Gipsland area, in South Australia and south-west Western Australia, and in Tasmania.

When to fish

This fish is unlikely to be encountered in declared trout waters (as yet) so it may be fished for all year. It is less active, and reluctant to take baits or lures in extremely cold water when it retires to deep holes and becomes torpid. Otherwise the fish is available in the waters it inhabits and will bite at any time.

Where to fish

Try any current that is a backwater, or holes without noticeable flow, particularly if there are weeds or other underwater vegetation or obstructions such as rocks and timber. In lakes the fish will also be found with such shelters and usually close to the shore.

When a food source is discovered the English perch have an uncanny ability, especially in smaller sizes, to gather into large schools and totally clean out any food item available, then move to another

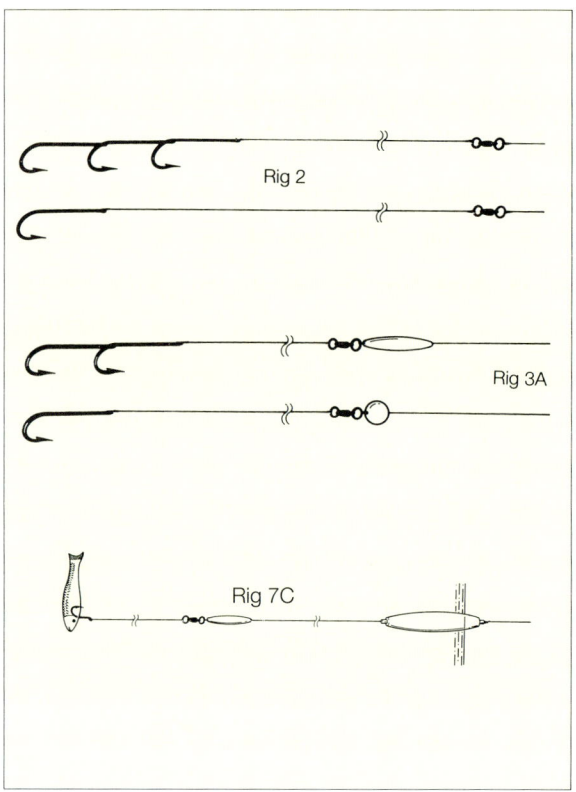

location. Even one fish finding a food supply attracts others.

Tackle

This can be worked by handline from the bank or from a small boat, though it need not exceed 5 kilograms breaking-strain. More convenient is a light threadline or baitcasting outfit, with a 3 to 5 kilogram line, which can be used for lure fishing, as well as with bait.

Bait

Small live redfin, yabbies, shrimps, worms, insects, grubs, etc. The fish will also respond to a wide range of lures, which are used for trout, such as spinners, spoons and small plugs and to jigging. They can be caught on weighted or wet flies.

Rigs

Depending on water depth and snags, try the unweighted rig No. 2 or lightly weighted No. 3 or 3A. The light quill float or bubble rig No. 7E, with the bait suspended close to the bottom, is excellent. Rig No. 2 is suitable for lures and for "yo-yoing" with lead-headed jigs.

How to hook

Being such a voracious and unfussy eater, the English perch really hooks itself. It is a strong fighter once hooked and good sport on light gear.

Edibility

The fish has a dry white flesh which is sweet to the taste. However, it is a real task to scale so is much better filleted and skinned. It is no more bony than a trout.

Other regulations

In Western Australia there is a closed season for redfin between June 1 and October 31 inclusive in waters of the Blackwood River upstream from Asplin, including all tributaries and the Arthur and Balgarap Rivers.

There is no size or quantity restriction on English perch in any State. There is a theory held by biologists that allowing unrestricted numbers to be taken by anglers reduces the population and allows fish to grow to a size at which they can really prey on native fish and trout. By restricting numbers caught from a waterway, the redfin could over-populate and become stunted, and be fodder fish for the Murray cod, golden perch and trout.

In either instance, these fish can reduce the numbers of native fish and trout. This is caused by the predation of the larval and juveniles or by competing for the organisms and other small items.

PERCH, ESTUARY
Macquaria colonorum

OTHER NAMES: **PERCH, GIPPSLAND PERCH, BASS (INCORRECTLY)**

Many anglers incorrectly call this fish a bass or just perch.
Some believe that there are not two perches, especially
old-timers on the north coast of New South Wales, which is
complicated by the fact that the two fish inhabit the same
stretches of coastal rivers at certain times of the year.

Identification
The estuary perch is an elongate-oval fish with a
slightly deeper, less cylindrical body than the
Australian bass. It has a sheen to its back that is also
apparent in the dark grey to dirty green colour of
its sides, which become a yellowish-white towards
the abdomen. Obvious features that separate it
from the bass are a dip above the eye and a deep
rise to the dorsal fin — the bass has a straight head
profile. Furthermore, unlike the bass, the estuary
perch does *not* have a white edge to the front of its
uniformly grey pelvic fin. The estuary perch can
also be identified by the number of gill rakers on
the first gill, having more than 16 , compared with
the 15 or less of the bass.

Size
Estuary perch reach 10 kilograms. They are
abundant in some Victorian waters, where they are
regularly caught measuring 54 centimetres long
and 4 kilograms in weight.
The minimum legal length for an estuary perch
catch in Victoria is 25 centimetres.

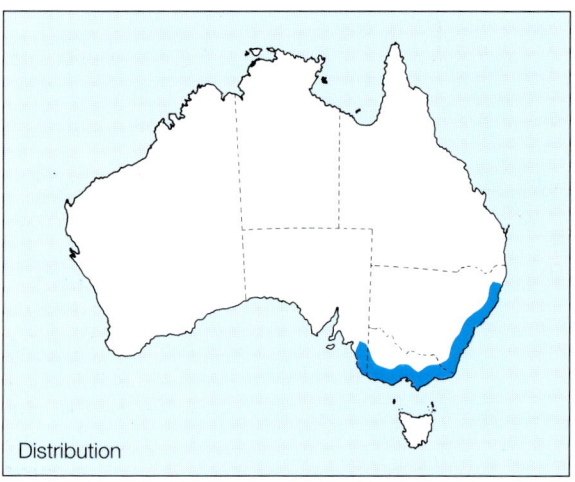

Distribution

Breeding

These fish breed in saltwater of a temperature of 14.5°C to 16°C in the lower waters of estuaries. This can be as early as July-August in New South Wales waters, but November-December in Victorian waters and the western end of its distribution. Estuary perch that have entered non-tidal freshwater will migrate downstream prior to spawning. Estuary perch are believed to mature earlier than bass.

Habits

The estuary perch live much more on the bottom than bass. They do not appear to "rise" for insects or food falling or struggling on the surface, consuming a less varied range of food items. Their diet consists of prawns, shrimps, worms, bivalves and small fish such as mullet, anchovy, sprats, smelts, gudgeons, etc.

While it is known to move beyond brackish water, the estuary perch are most likely to be encountered in the deeper and saltier water that bass will not enter.

Distribution

These perch are found in river estuaries south from about Richmond in New South Wales, along Victoria's coastline and on to the entrance of the Murray River in South Australia. They are particularly abundant in some coastal lakes in eastern Victoria, especially those not affected by closures due to weather or ocean conditions.

When to fish

These fish are present all year, though they are probably most abundant at the time of arrival in the lower reaches of the estuary before spawning. They take bait or lure — both day and night.

Where to fish

The best places to look for estuary perch are in deep holes, deep channels, along the edge of deep weed beds or banks, and in deep holes on the side of sand or mud banks over which the tide or current will carry food. They are often caught when fishing for bream or spinning for flathead.

Tackle

While a handline can be used, the ideal outfit for boat or bank is a light threadline or baitcasting rod of about 2 metres and reel. A line between 3 and 5 kilograms breaking-strain is sufficient. There is no need for a wire trace (although the nylon leader may be slightly heavier than the main line) and

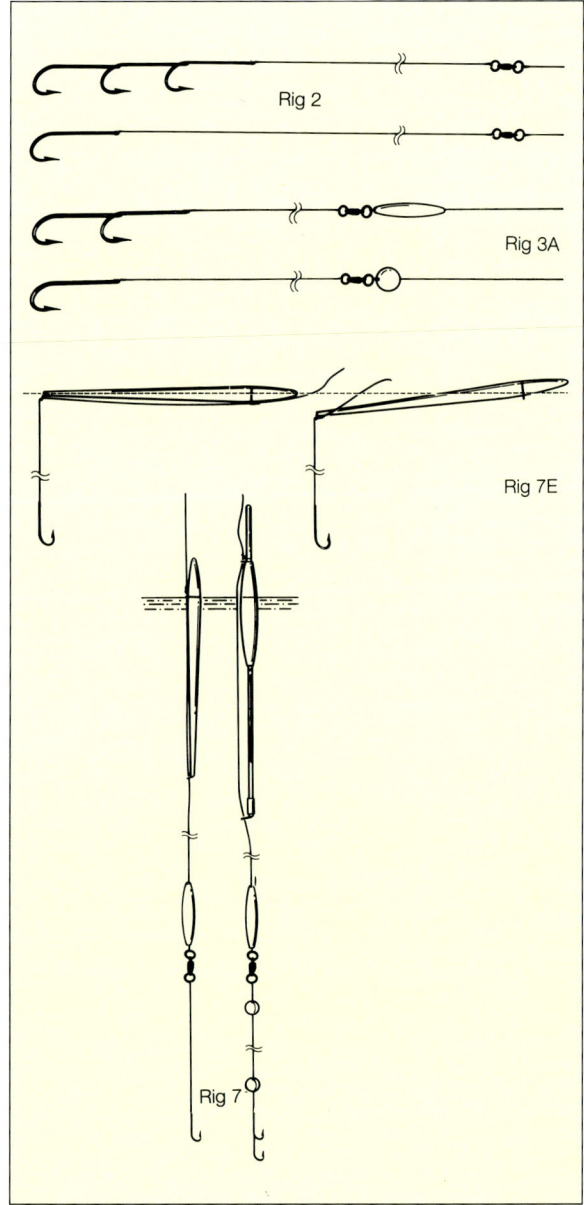

Rig 2

Rig 3A

Rig 7E

Rig 7

hooks of about 2 to 1/0 are large enough, depending on the bait.

Bait

Try live prawns, small fish, shrimps, mussels. Fillets of most fish are also effective, as long as they are fresh and light in colour.

Though the estuary perch is not as aggressive as its relative, the bass, it will nevertheless take deep-diving fish-like lures and some spoons.

Rigs

The unweighted or lightly weighted rigs No. 2 or 3A are suitable, so is a baited float rig No. 7 or 7E, depending on the water conditions.

How to hook

The estuary perch bite readily, showing some preference for a moving bait. Once the weight of the fish is felt it is only a matter of tightening the line to set the hook. They are a strong fish and fight well.

Edibility

The flesh is white, firm and tasty. It can be prepared by most methods for an enjoyable meal.

Other regulations

You may not fish for estuary perch — and bass for that matter — in Victoria from August 1 to November 30 inclusive.

Estuary perch are subject to heavy netting while pursuing mullet, bream, etc., in estuaries and ocean lakes. Some biologists believe that the construction of weirs and dams, which have been a cause of the decline of the bass (because of the resulting disruption to the bass's migration to freshwater where it grows and matures), has created some problems for the estuary perch by changing the flow into estuaries. However, pollution in many estuaries and the seasonal closure of some lakes, which prevents tidal flows freshening them, may be a more likely reason for the dwindling numbers of perch rather than netting by professionals.

PERCH, GOLDEN
Macquaria ambigua

OTHER NAMES: **YELLOWBELLY, CALLOP, MURRAY PERCH,
WHITE PERCH, MURRAY BREAM**

Biologists claim that European settlement has caused the decline of this fish's numbers and forced the constriction of its distribution in the Murray-Darling system. Without the successful hormone-induced breeding by State and private hatcheries, and the extensive stocking of public waters, it is doubtful that the golden perch would have remained the   mainstay of inland fishing. Over 3,000,000 have been released in dams or lakes in New South Wales since 1976 by the NSW State Fisheries, supplemented by the efforts of commercial hatcheries. Of all the Australian native fish, it is the golden perch that are the travellers. They undertake long-distance migration during floods or reasonable river rises in spring and summer. Tagged fish have been re-captured after movements exceeding 1,000 kilometres; one covered 2,300 kilometres from Berri in South Australia to Mungindi in Queensland. While the golden perch will use correctly designed fishways and can get over low weirs in floods, there are many dams and high-level weirs that prevent it reaching many of the areas it once inhabited in upper reaches of the rivers. Nor do golden perch tolerate the cool waters released from dams. Their battle for survival has also been influenced by siltation and pesticides where fertile river plains have been intensively farmed.

Identification

The golden perch can be either a fish of beauty or very ugly. From really turbid water they are likely to be a pale imitation of their normal colours, with a back of an anaemic whitish-yellow and a white belly. As the concentration of mud in the water is reduced, so the fish tend to be a light gold to bronze to olive-green. If taken from relatively clear water the fish appear a dark olive-green bronze to black, with a rich golden shade evident on their lower body and belly. The pectoral fins are usually a shade of yellow and the other fins tend to be dusky-coloured or cream, with a pink to red hue.

Golden perch are a deep-bodied fish, though the younger "yellowbellies" are well-proportioned before the exaggerated hump develops from the head to the body—a feature that is so pronounced in large specimens that it creates the impression that the head hasn't kept pace with the rest of the body. Having seen a 13 kilogram fish, the writer can only imagine the dwarfish head on the massive deep body of the largest recorded golden perch — 24.6 kilograms!

Size

The largest recorded golden perch, already mentioned, measured 76 centimetres in length. Fish above 5 kilograms, however, must be regarded as an excellent catch. Larger fish are more likely to be encountered in the warmwater dams where their growth rate is considerably faster than in rivers.

The minimum length for a legal catch of golden perch in South Australia is 33 centimetres; it is 30 centimetres in Queensland.

Breeding

Floods or even a rise in the level of the river,

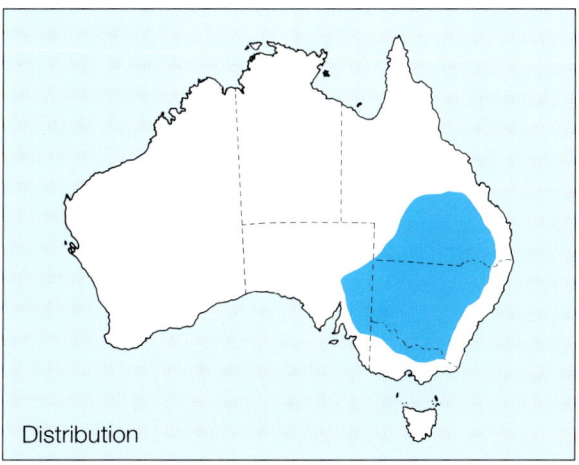
Distribution

provided the water temperature is over 20°C, can induce spawning, usually in the spring and summer. However, several separate spawning migrations can occur during good summers. Golden perch will congregate near river entrances to lakes before spawning. The eggs are semi-buoyant and must be kept suspended and floating by a current. A good survival rate of larvae depends on the abundance of plankton bloom. A mature female sheds over half a million eggs. This fecundity helps restore stocks in times when long droughts have effected populations. These fish rarely breed, if at all, in farm dams or impoundments without good river inflow and suitable water temperature during spring and summer.

Their extensive migration serves to concentrate breeding stocks and disperse young fish into new habitats. They distribute their floating ova downstream, ova that the females are able to hold to an advanced stage while waiting for suitable conditions. Coldwater releases from the dam barriers that restrict its movement have tended to push stocks out of the upper tributaries and down into the lower reaches of the Murray-Darling system.

Distribution

Once found throughout the Murray-Darling system, the golden perch have either disappeared completely or are at least very rare in many upper reaches of some tributaries. They adapt well to clear rocky waters, turbid slow-flowing waterways, creeks, billabongs and backwaters, and are remarkably common in many large shallow turbid lakes in New South Wales, particularly the dams along the south, central and northern tablelands, such as Burrinjuck, Wyangala, Copeton, Keepit and Burrendong. But such dams reduce the water temperatures downstream, which in turn drives the fish to lower reaches.

Golden perch are also found in some western Victorian lakes, the Lake Eyre and Bulloo drainage systems and the Dawson-Fitzroy river system in Queensland. They have also been introduced to new dams in Queensland. These fish can also be found in South Australian waterways. Efforts to translocate golden perch to Western Australia many years ago proved unsuccessful and the results of stocking in some Northern Territory coastal streams are still unknown.

Habits

Like the Murray cod, some golden perch station themselves in a productive food dispensary and seem to be territorial. Also like the cod, they are found around snags, fallen logs, submerged trees and rock drop-offs. They aggregate anywhere where there is an abundant supply of food, such as around flooded trees in dams. These opportunistic feeders eat shrimps, yabbies, small fish, worms. Research at Lake Keepit in New South Wales and in Queensland indicate that bony bream, in particular, and gudgeons, European carp and common carp, make up a major part of their winter diet while crustaceans are apparently more desirable in summer. Where land has been recently

inundated or when they reach freshly-filled billabongs or lagoons, adult fish will gorge themselves on terrestrial insects and crustaceans in summer.

When to fish

There are some man-made reasons which influence promising or hopeless fishing for golden perch, as with most inland natives. The river levels fluctuate when dams on tributaries make releases, when there are excessive demands for pumping or irrigation needs. This may hardly be noticeable in good seasons. Nature too can create floods in catchment areas from local downpours. There are periods when rivers are unfishable because of flooding, at others times they are so low that the fish are not interested in food.

Bearing this in mind, in rivers the golden perch will bite at any time, though afternoons and evenings are probably better, especially when there has been a slight rise in the water level or a slight fall, as when a river is returning to normal after a flood. The spring or autumn are usually better seasons than the middle of the summer.

Where to fish

This is easier: where food is plentiful, combined with good cover. Golden perch are found near deep rock faces; ridges which enter the river; rocky outcrops; against deep undercut banks; near submerged and fallen logs; among tree roots; and alongside weed beds. When a river is in a slow rise, especially where it meets another, the confluence is likely to hold golden perch, as is the bottom side of a weir on a river with fresh water flowing downstream.

Tackle

A handline is frequently used from banks and from boats when fishing for golden perch. These days, however, most anglers prefer a light or medium single-handed threadline or baitcasting rod, about 2 metres to 2.5 metres long, with a matching threadline or baitcasting reel that is spooled with about a 5 kilogram breaking-strain line. Such an outfit can be used for trolling, for bait-fishing, and for casting and retrieving lures. It will also handle a large Murray cod if you strike this bonus while fishing for golden perch. A good choice of hook is about a 1/0 in the Viking or French pattern.

Bait

Small bony bream, carp (*which an angler must not take from any waterway to another!*), and yabbies make

Rig 2

Rig 3A

Rig 1

Rig 9

Rig 10

Rig 11

excellent live bait. Golden perch will also readily take shrimps, large grasshoppers, mussels, etc. Many deep-diving active plugs and spoons will induce sudden strikes from golden perch when trolled or retrieved a t speeds fast enough to get the lure wobbling, darting or diving.

Rigs

Try the unweighted rig No. 2 or lightly-weighted rig No. 3A. Both are satisfactory. For casting and retrieving lures, depending on the maximum depth of the lure being tried, rig nos 9 or 10 will work. Trolling can be done with rig No. 11.

How to hook

The golden perch are not difficult to hook if in a feeding mood; however, they can be very difficult to entice in periods when the water is low, preferring to use up their body fat rather than expending energy on hunting food. When it does bite, the bite is definite, though it pays to give it a few seconds to get a live bait into its mouth before tightening to set the hook.

Hint

One of the most tempting baits for a golden perch is a small live fish or yabby fished under a float about a metre from the bottom. The signals transmitted by the vibration from these baits are likely to attract golden perch (and Murray cod) from their cover. Float or "bobber" rigs are usually much more effective than those which leave the bait sitting on the bottom.

Edibility

Golden perch have a firm white flesh and fish taken from clearer rivers are excellent, whatever the preparation. Larger fish from dams and muddy rivers are inclined to be fatty and the taste of their flesh gives an unpleasant hint of mud. However, if you skin, fillet and grill these fish, most of the fat is removed and the "muddy" taste disappears. A stuffed golden perch baked with some white wine added to the baking dish and garnished with browned onion rings in breadcrumbs is a delightful meal. These fish keep well, provided they are iced when caught.

PERCH, JUNGLE
Kuhlia rupestris

OTHER NAMES: **MOUNTAIN TROUT, BUFFALO BREAM**

The claims of some textbooks to the contrary, the jungle perch is a freshwater fish that is occasionally flushed from its normal habitat by floods: it is *not* an estuary dweller. The sad fact is that its numbers are now reduced in many streams and it has possibly disappeared from others.

Identification

Jungle perch have an elongate body. Their second dorsal fin is higher than the spines of the front dorsal to which it is joined. Colouring is variable but they are mainly a light tan to olive with a grey belly area. (It is speckled with brown-black spots.) These spots are joined in the young fish but separate as the size of their scales increase on bigger fish. It has a relatively large mouth and the bottom jaw extends beyond its snout. There is a blackish area, sometimes solid, in the tail.

Size

Jungle perch are reputed to grow to 3 kilograms but any fish caught today would be considered more than satisfactory at half this weight.

Breeding

Little has been authenticated regarding the spawning of jungle perch.

Habits

These fish prefer the fast-running well-oxygenated headwaters of streams, particularly waters with plenty of rocks. They are omnivorous, eating a wide range of aquatic inhabitants.

Distribution

Jungle perch are confined to an area along the coast of Queensland from about the Maroochy River to the Olive River on Cape York. They are not present on the western side of the Great Dividing Range. They can still be found in the headwaters of the rivers, but they have disappeared from many easily accessible waters.

When to fish

The best time to fish for jungle perch is during the day when lures or flies can be directed to likely fishing spots. Overfishing with bait is believed to be one reason for the diminished numbers of jungle perch.

Where to fish

One of the favoured spots for jungle perch is in bubbly or swift-flowing waters at the end of rocky sections, especially between rapids or stretches of quieter water.

Tackle

Use a light threadline or baitcasting outfit or light fly rod and reel. Line of about 3 kilogram breaking-strain is strong enough.

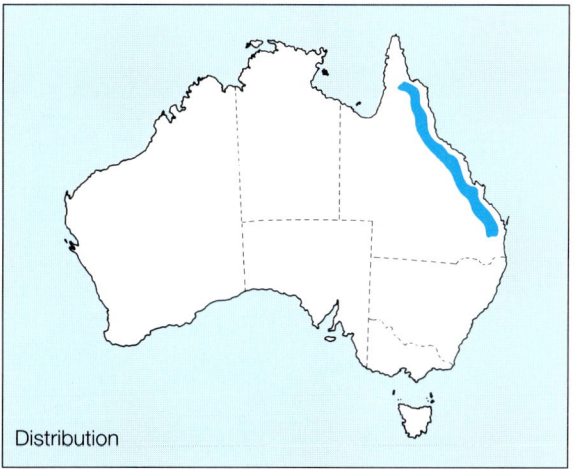
Distribution

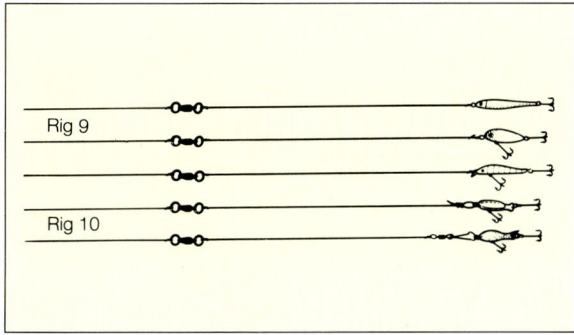

Bait

In the interests of preservation, anglers should confine their fishing for jungle perch to the lure or fly. Any small slow-working sub-surface lure will tempt the fish.

Rigs

On a fly rod, a sinking tip line and some of the larger wet flies are satisfactory. All you need is the lure rig No. 9 on a light threadline or baitcasting rod and reel.

How to hook

These fish are usually in clear waters and require the same cautious approach to the water as when fishing for trout. They are easily frightened, even a lure landing on the water will spook them. Jungle perch line up a lure and take it quite readily if the angler has cast properly and the lure is working well. These fish have surprising strength for their size.

Edibility

Unfortunately, the excellent eating qualities of the jungle perch, and their once prolific numbers in easily reached streams, led to greedy exploitation. Frankly, they are — or should be — a catch-and-release fish for today's thinking anglers.

PERCH, MACQUARIE
Macquaria australasica

OTHER NAMES: **BIG-EYE, SAD EYE, WHITE-EYE, SILVER-EYE, BREAM, BLACK BREAM, MURRAY BREAM, GOULBURN BREAM, MOUNTAIN PERCH, BLACK PERCH, MURRAY PERCH**

The once widespread distribution of the Macquarie perch can be judged from the many regional names of this fish. The decline of its populations in the past 50 years has been dramatic. Anglers fortunate enough to find them will have a rare opportunity to test their skill against this fine native game fish. A reverence for the Macquarie perch's fighting ability, combined with their scarcity, has led anglers to keep secret any locations where they can still be found in numbers — just to prevent further exploitation.
The Macquarie perch may not leap and dash like a trout, but they fight with a dour strength for long periods. On a weight for weight basis they must be valued as a challenging adversary. This noble native fish has suffered from the destruction of its habitat, predation by introduced species (research implicates both the redfin and trout), and over-fishing. The Macquarie perch should be recognised as a fish that deserves the protection of conservation, which Victorian Fisheries attempt to do with a closed season and a bag limit. An angler enjoying the great pleasure of catching one should be thankful — and refrain from taking even a legal number. There are some appalling records — and photographs — of up to 3 tonnes being taken from a single pool in the Goulburn River in Victoria!

The Macquarie perch was classified as "restricted" at the Conference on Australian Threatened Fish in 1985. This listing of a species means that it should be earmarked by Australian and State Fisheries authorities for suitable conservation measures to arrest any decline in distribution or abundance.

Both Victorian and New South Wales fisheries are presently cooperating to find the best technique to propagate Macquarie perch by hormone induced spawning. Some fish have been produced by stripping eggs from gravid (ripe) females and manually fertilising them with sperm from males.

Identification

Some of the names for this fish indicate a distinct feature which distinguishes it from other native fish, especially the silver perch. It possesses eyes with a large silver-white iris and a dark pupil. It has a relatively small head, small mouth and a rounded tail. There are deep conspicuous cavities high on the snout, around the eye, on the first bone of the gill cover. In larger specimens there is a pronounced slope from head to shoulder. Colours vary from almost black to a dark slate-grey with a hint of silver to bluish-grey, fading to off-white on the stomach with a bronze-yellowish tint. This fish changes to a darker colour when alarmed, if held in a keeper net, and at night. Its colour lightens during migration.

Size

Though there are records of Macquarie perch at 3.5 kilograms, any catch of 2 kilograms is an exceptional specimen today.

In Victoria, the minimum legal length for a catch is 25 centimetres. Care should be exercised when releasing undersized fish. They die when handled if water temperatures exceed 20°C.

Breeding

Macquarie perch require a water temperature about 16°C to spawn and will not migrate from deep water until the inflow from streams reaches 16.5°C, usually in mid-spring. The ova are slightly adhesive and stick to gravel or small boulders in water up to 60 centimetres deep. Spawning may occur over a period of two weeks. Macquarie perch will use the same rivers year after year.

Siltation has been an important contributor to the decline of this fish. Erosion from cleared lands and riverbanks fill deep holes and destroy a preferred habitat. Biologist Phil Cadwallader considers it significant that most river populations of Macquarie perch that are still in existence are in the upper reaches of catchments, where silt loads are not heavy and where there still are deep holes with shallow riffles. The fish's upstream spawning migration is prevented by dams — water releases from the bottom of dams are too cold for breeding by fish below them.

Habits

While a lone fish may be caught, it is more usual to find schools of varying size in the quieter currents of deep waterholes that have a sand or gravel bottom. In rivers, they are likely to aggregate in deep holes where the water enters across a sandbank or in disturbed water below rapids. Macquarie perch also seem to appreciate bankside growth over their waterhole, to provide shade and a source of food. In lakes they often dwell amongst submerged trees, moving closer to the shoreline in periods when the water is rising. The basic food of the Macquarie perch comprises insects and their larvae, earthworms, shrimps, frogs, tadpoles, small yabbies, wood grubs, crickets and the like.

Distribution

Once prolific in the cooler waters of the Murray-Darling system, right up to the source of many tributaries in mid and southern New South Wales and Victoria, populations are now confined to waters above a few impoundments. There are reasonable numbers in Lake Burrinjuck on the Murrumbidgee River and Lake Wyangala on the Lachlan River and some of the tributaries of these rivers in New South Wales. They have been reintroduced to the Queanbeyan River with a small stocking in Googong reservoir in recent years. In Victoria, Lake Dartmouth probably holds

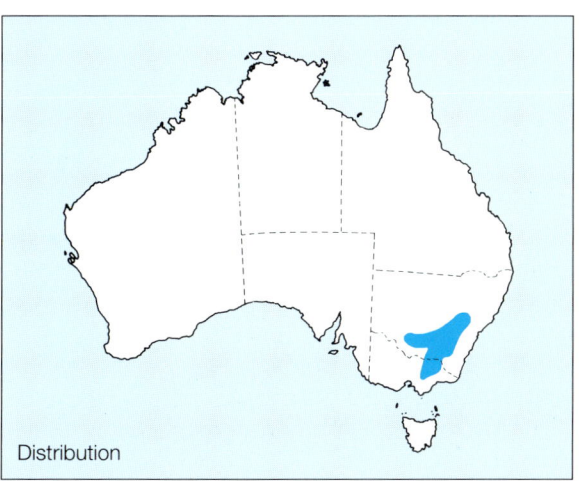

Distribution

the best stocks, with other populations in the Goulburn River catchment. Some Macquarie perch were introduced to the Yarra, Barwon and Wannon rivers in Victoria. These may be surviving.

There are populations in the upper reaches of the Shoalhaven and Nepean rivers in New South Wales, though it is yet to be positively established whether these fish are the same species.

When to fish
Macquarie perch are more likely to be caught from late spring through the summer months. Fish may be found schooling to make a spawning run, especially where there are rocky outcrops. In most lakes, Macquarie perch are likely to be caught by anglers fishing for trout or silver perch. This fish bites best early in the morning or in the late afternoon and will bite during the night.

[**Note:** Victoria has a closed season — usually from early November until late January — when fishing

Macquarie perch.

for Macquarie perch is not allowed. The dates can be changed because of water conditions and should be checked locally.

No closed season applies in New South Wales in the lakes where this fish is present, though in those streams that are closed for trout, Macquarie perch are afforded the same protection. But the trout season opens at the time the native fish begin their return from spawning and brood stock of Macquarie perch are extremely vulnerable to over-fishing by anglers at this time.]

Where to fish
The Macquarie perch is, in the main, a bottom-dweller where food is plentiful. This invariably means close to banks or weed-beds or amongst submerged trees, and along foreshores when impoundment water is rising. In rivers they like a deep hole on the downstream side of a sandbank and the disturbed water below rapids.

Tackle
The ideal tackle is a light single-handed, 2-metre long threadline or baitcasting rod and reel, with a line of 3 or 4 kilograms breaking-strain. This enables bait or lures (even weighted flies) to be used. Fly-fishing gear offers a challenging way to catch Macquarie perch.

Bait
Shrimps, small yabbies, woodgrubs, grasshoppers, crickets, earthworms and mudeyes are all taken.

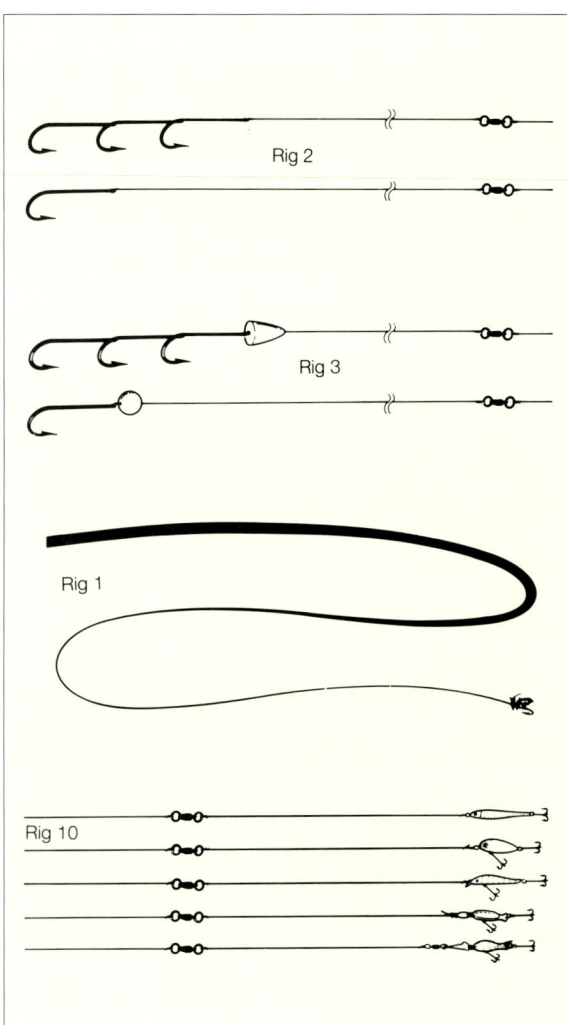

Rigs

Try to avoid weighting the bait rig No. 2. If the current or depth makes it necessary to use a sinker, use rig No. 3A with the minimum weight. Depending on the size of the bait, a hook between 1 and 4 completes the rig. Casting and retrieving lures (small deep-diving plugs and spinners and weighted flies) can be done with rig No. 9 or 10.

How to hook

The Macquarie perch is a firm biter. It rarely fiddles with its food. The hook is probably well into the mouth by the time the fish is felt, therefore tightening the line should result in a hook up.

Hint

Fish half a metre to a metre off the bottom with any of the recommended baits under a light pencil or quill float. With fly gear, fish a nymph-type fly close to the bottom. Late in the afternoon, when there are small rings similar to those created by sipping trout, use a tiny fly on a greased tippet. Macquarie perch sought on a fly are superb opponents for the most experienced trout fly fishers. They will find the same challenge and skill is needed to take them on wet teaser flies such as matukas.

Edibility

The Macquarie perch's white flesh has a firm texture and it is fine eating fish. But the experience of seeing a Macquarie perch and the sport of catching one *and then releasing it* can be much more memorable than trying to recall its marvellous taste.

Other regulations

Victoria places a legal limit of 10 Macquarie perch per angler per day.

PERCH, SILVER
Bidyanus bidyanus

OTHER NAMES: BIDYAN, BIDYAN GRUNTER, BLACK BREAM, SILVER BREAM, GRUNTER, BLACK GRUNTER

Silver perch have been condemned to shrinking numbers in many waters where they were once the most abundant fish. There is growing evidence that the silver perch is affected more than other native fish by water pollution, including chemicals used to control weeds and insects, urban run-off and sewerage inflow. The reaction of silver perch to pollution is actually considered by some water supply authorities to be a quicker and more efficient indicator of the presence of contaminants than sophisticated equipment.
Thankfully, its future — despite the fewer numbers — now seems assured because they have been successfully hormone-induced to breed by State operated hatcheries, with regular releases into impoundments and some rivers. They may never, however, return to such numbers that some inland anglers regarded them a nuisance that interfered with their pursuit of the more highly regarded Murray cod and golden perch.

Identification

An attractive, slim, elongate fish while young, the silver perch be,comes deeper bodied and compressed as it grows. The heads of large fish appear disproportionately small compared to the rest of their bodies. Their colour ranges from a light grey to almost black. The dorsal area and the belly is an off-white. This colour variation is the result of water turbidity. Young fish are mottled but this develops into a dark edge on the scales as the fish grows. The mouth is small and the tail slightly forked.

Size

This native fish grows to more than 60 centimetres in length and can exceed 8 kilograms but today such sizes are rare catches indeed.

The minimum legal length for a catch in South Australia is 33 centimetres.

Breeding

Silver perch require a rise in water level and the right temperature (about 23°C) to spawn. This occurs in the mid-spring to late summer, when the fish move upstream behind the peak of floods and spawn in shallow, warm waters. The fish have been seen to spawn in dams but the bottoms have to be clean for successful hatching and larval survival. Spawning is in schools with up to three males chasing a female to the water surface where the eggs and sperm are released. This occurs in the late afternoon and always before dark. They may move long distances upstream if the conditions of the water are suitable.

Habits

These fish can withstand temperatures of between 2°C and 37°C — the extremes for short periods only. Whether found in deep water in lakes or dams the fish are usually in schools, the numbers decreasing as the fish grow. They aggregate around submerged trees and rocky ridges which dip into water impoundments and in rivers they gather in agitated water below rapids, along sandbanks and against weir walls. The schools move about and these fish are opportunistic feeders. If you catch a single fish it is reasonable to suspect that others are nearby.

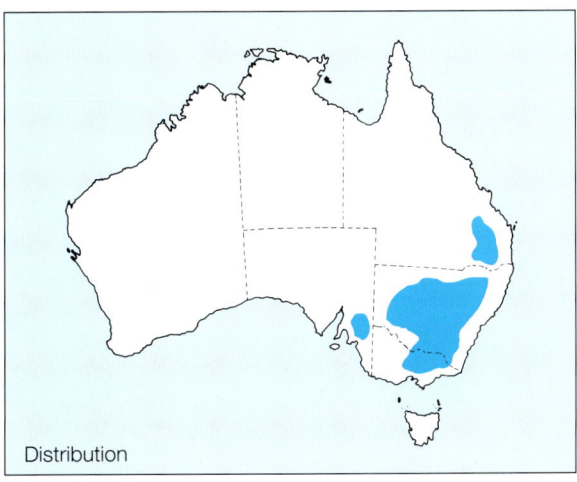
Distribution

These fish will bite at any time of the day. There are old-time anglers who contend that the larger-sized fish that are taken from a hole in the river are in fact residents. Adult silver perch are omnivorous, eating larger zooplankton, insects and their larvae, molluscs, worms, maggots and grubs. They are greedy feeders immediately after spawning.

The silver perch are flighty fish, easily scared. When these fish are sighted in clear water, take care not to frighten them.

Distribution

The distribution of silver perch has declined since European settlement. The construction of dams without suitable fish ladders has been one cause as well as predation from exotic fish and the deterioration of water quality. They can still be found over a wide area of the Murray-Darling drainage system but no longer progress as high as they once did. Silver perch are reasonably common in some rivers and impoundments in New South Wales, Victoria and South Australia. In recent years the newer dams in New South Wales and Queensland have been stocked with this fish.

When to fish

Though silver perch will sometimes feed at the surface, their favoured foods are found towards the bottom. They seem to eat at any time, but early to mid-morning can be a good time to catch them regularly.

Where to fish

A good place to look for silver perch in rivers is behind rocks below rapids or in the current as it slows down. The first place to try in dams is around submerged trees or over the edge of a sloping bank. The fish will be close to the bottom in these areas, but they will enter shallow areas to feed on insects such as grasshoppers or beetles landing on the water, and they can be taken on large flies and small spinners.

Tackle

In most waters, whether fishing from a boat or from the bank, a light or medium-weight single-handed threadline reel and rod is a good choice. It will help cast the light baits or lures and with a line of 3 to 5 kilograms breaking-strain it will also handle golden perch, Murray cod and trout which inhabit the same waters as silver perch. A light baitcasting outfit or even a handline can be used. Depending on the bait, hooks should be between sizes 4 and 1.

Rigs

Either the unweighted rig No. 2 or lightly-weighted rig No3 A are satisfactory. If you are using lures, try either rig No. 9 or 10.

Bait

Shrimps works extremely well with silver perch and worms are accepted readily. Other effective baits are grasshoppers, maggots, wood grubs, yabby tails and mussels. These fish take lures readily and any trout-sized spinners, wobblers, spoons and plugs are worth trying.

How to hook

Smaller silver perch can be a nuisance, picking a hook clean of the bait. A quick reaction to try to set the hook with a short lift is required when this happens. Larger fish, which swim higher from the bottom while seeking food, often grab the bait as it is sinking. A silver perch intent on a bait or lure doesn't miss too often.

Hint

A quill or bubble float (rig No. 7E), with a bait suspended above the bottom and allowed to move with the current or wind is always worth trying, in the shallow bays of lakes and dams particularly in the late afternoons and early evenings.

Edibility

The flesh of a silver perch is white, firm, dry but palatable. Some find the dryness requires a sauce to be added when the fish is served.

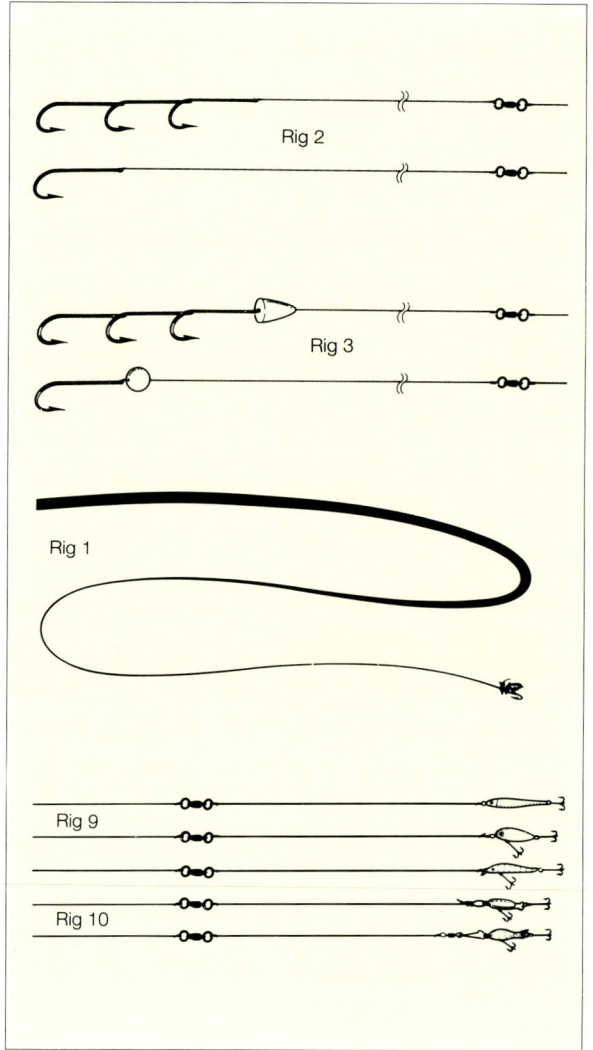

PIKE (SEA-PIKE)

The true pikes are large predatory freshwater fishes of the northern hemisphere and include the muskellunge of the USA. The seapikes of Australia are all marine fish. They too are predators, though not very large. Whether they are admired as a sport fish, or for food, seems to depend on the angler's perspective. In some areas they are well-regarded as both. There is some disagreement on the exact taxonomy of these fish, their distribution and their scientific names. And anglers don't help because they often apply the same names to the two or three species that are regularly caught in their region.

The marketing name recommended by the Australian Department of Primary Industries is striped seapike for one species, pike for the other: but several authorities even differ over whether the name should be hyphenated or two words— sea-pike or seapike. We settle for the former.

Striped seapike.

SEA-PIKE, STRIPED
Sphyraena obtusata

OTHER NAMES: **PIKE, LONG-FINNED SEA-PIKE, SNOOK, STRIPED PIKE, YELLOWTAIL SENNIT, BARRACUDA**

Identification

Striped sea-pike are elongated, rather streamlined fish. Their overall colour is a silvery white with a greenish to golden brown dorsal area. There is a distinct yellow-brown stripe from the snout to the base of the yellowish-coloured tail. The mouth is large and well-armed with sharp pointed teeth. The rear dorsal and anal fins are short based, almost identical and directly opposite each other. Its first dorsal fin begins level with the pectoral fin.

Size
These fish grow to around 50 to 60 centimetres long.

Breeding
Striped sea-pike are believed to spawn inshore near, or in, seagrass meadows.

Habits
These fish school in large numbers and swim swiftly, particularly around areas where there are large rocks or other underwater obstructions, such as wharves. They are ready to feed at most times of the day and will spend time during the afternoon hunting and eating over weed beds and seagrass meadows. Striped sea-pike are carnivorous, eating almost any small creature that moves.

Distribution
The striped sea-pike are found from Queensland, across the Northern Territory and down as far south in Western Australia as Albany. (Some sources suggest it only exists in southern Queensland waters, around the east and south coasts, including Tasmania, and then north to about Shark Bay in Western Australia.)

SEAPIKE, SHORT-FINNED

Sphyraena novahollandiae

(S. flavicauda is a short-finned seapike of tropical waters)

OTHER NAMES: **SNOOK, PIKE, SHORT- FIN PIKE, SHORTFIN SEAPIKE**

Identification
These short-finned seapikes are much longer and slimmer fish than the striped member of the family. They are usually silver with a greenish colour on the back and do not have the prominent stripes of their cousins. Their fins are a greenish-yellow. Some populations in the western area of their distribution are much darker, being quite brown with a blue-purple tinge. These fish can be

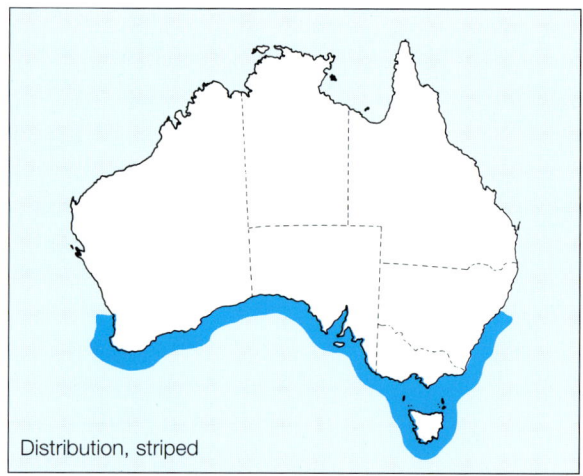

Distribution, striped

distinguished from other seapikes by the position of the first dorsal fin, which commences well to the rear of the pectoral fin.

Size
Short-finned seapike grow to more than a metre in length and up to 5 kilograms.
The minimum length for a legal catch in Western Australia is 28 centimetres; it is 36 centimetres in South Australia and Victoria.

Breeding
These pike are believed to spawn inshore.

Habits
Though these fish school, it is not unusual to see single fish or small numbers of fish, searching for food. Short-finned seapike are usually found around rocky areas, wharves and jetties and over weed beds and sand patches. These fast-swimming feeders are carnivores.

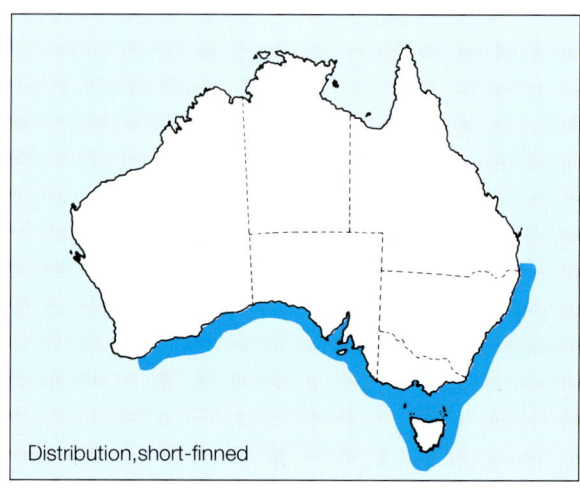

Distribution, short-finned

Short-finned seapike.

Distribution

The short-finned seapike is confined to the cooler southern areas of Australia, rarely extending past the lower northern coast of New South Wales or Jurien Bay in Western Australia. They are present all round Tasmania and are prolific in South Australia.

SEAPIKE, LONG-FINNED
Dinolestes lewini

OTHER NAMES: **PIKE, SNOOK**

[**Note:** This fish is not related to the striped or short-finned seapike. However, despite the fact that it belongs to a separate family, it is included here because the vast majority of anglers call it a pike.]

Identification

Long-finned seapike appear almost identical to the striped seapike, perhaps with a slightly deeper mid-section. They have a greenish to brown colouring over a silver body and a similar yellow-brown stripe along the side. These fish are easily distinguished from both the short-finned seapike and the striped seapike: they have a long-based anal fin, the leading edge of which is further forward on the body.

Size

These seapikes grow to about 90 centimetres in length.
The minimum legal size for a catch in Western Australia is a length of 33 centimetres.

Breeding

Little is known.

Habits

Often mistaken for the striped seapike, these fishes school over inshore coastal reefs and around rock headlands, wharves, etc. They are carnivores that feed on fish, crustaceans, and similar creatures.

Distribution

These fish prefer the cooler waters and are common in the waters of New South Wales from the central coast, south around Tasmania, west across Victoria, and north to the latitude of Rottnest Island in Western Australia.

The following information applies to all seapike.

When to fish

As a general rule the seapike gather in more numbers — or more accurately in a hungrier feeding mood — in the late afternoon and mornings. There are seasonal factors, which may be linked with food fish, and these seem to vary with the area. These fish tend to move on to shallow reefs, weed beds, seagrass meadows and sand areas at high tide.

Where to fish

Good locations are over weed beds, seagrass meadows and around rocks or over rocks and close to jetties and wharves. In fact, any place likely to attract small fish, crustaceans, and molluscs, is almost certain to attract seapike.

Tackle

Though good fighters that will sometimes leap out of the water— especially the short-finned species — the seapike are easily handled on a handline of 5 to 7 kilograms breaking-strain. However, a single-handed threadline or baitcasting rod and reel can be used for trolling, bait-fishing and casting lures in most areas — the exceptions being

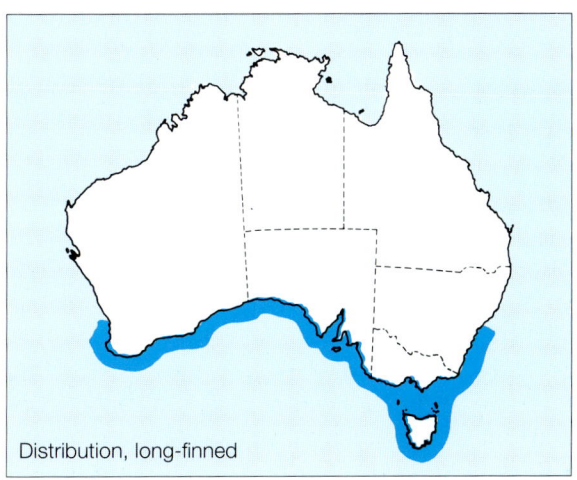

Distribution, long-finned

rocks and perhaps breakwaters or high wharves. For these locations, the more practical rods are about 3 to 3.5 metres long, of light-medium weight, to suit either threadline, overhead or sidecast reels. The lines for the rods need be no more than 5 kilograms breaking-strain. Single hooks, about size 1 or 2 with a long shank and a short, nylon-coated wire trace are suitable, but 2 or 3 ganged hooks (tarpon or viking-style) in the same sizes 2/0 to 4/0 with a heavy nylon leader prevent "bite-offs" from the pike's sharp teeth.

Bait

Small yellowtail, sprats, sardines, fillets of most fish, slivers of the pike's belly flesh, squid strips, etc. are all good baits.

The pike respond to many lures, particularly the metal spoon-types in the sizes of a small fish. (A short wire trace is a wise investment if using lures.)

Rigs

Depending on sea conditions, the unweighted or lightly-weighted rigs (No. 2, 3 or 3A) will suit the purpose. If using lures, the No. 9 rig with a short, light, wire trace is best. When trolling, especially for the short-finned seapike, you will find this rig adequate, as are rigs 1 or 11.

How to hook

If the bait is the right size, the seapike hook themselves as they hit a cast-and-retrieved or trolled bait or lure. If fish seem to miss, then the bait or lure may be too large; if you stop your retrieval, then the small seapikes will usually manage to swallow the bait.

Hint

Try three ganged hooks, baited with a triangular piece of the belly flap of a seapike. The pointed end of the bait should be long enough to extend 25 to 40 millimetres beyond the bend of the last hook — with enough left to wriggle as it is retrieved. The flap can be from any other white or silver-coloured fish or it may be strips of squid flesh.

Edibility

Seapikes are not a popular table fish in New South Wales and Queensland, where they are more often caught for live bait for mulloway, kingfish and as fillet bait for other fish. Nevertheless, all seapike are edible when cooked by most methods, though the short-finned seapike (or snook as it is more commonly called in South Australia), is probably the most popular and the tastiest.

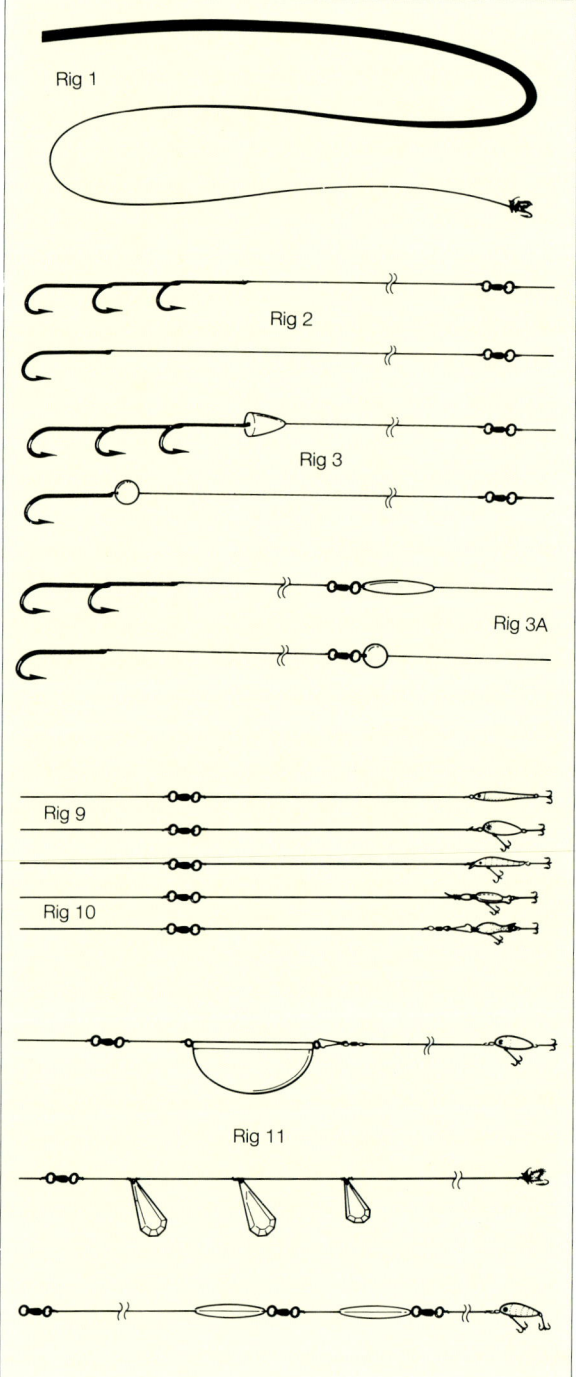

QUEENFISH

The four queenfish of Australian waters all occur in the tropical regions of the Indian Ocean and the western Pacific. Incorrect identification and the erroneous allocation of scientific names have pursued this species. So let the argument begin. The descriptions, distribution and other details of the four queenfish follow. Fishing methods that apply to all follow the individual descriptions.

The Talang queenfish.

QUEENFISH, BARRED
Scomberoides tala

OTHER NAME: **DEEP LEATHERSKIN**

Identification
This queenfish is a blue to bluish-green over a silvery white lower half. Between four and eight bar-like grey blotches are located above or across the lateral line. The fins of the fish are green with a dusky shade to them.

Size
The barred queenfish is the smallest of the four species, growing to about 45 centimetres in length.

QUEENFISH, DOUBLE-SPOTTED
Scomberoides lysan

OTHER NAMES: **LESSER QUEENFISH, ST. PETER'S LEATHERSKIN**

Identification
The upper body of the double-spotted queenfish is mainly a silvery blue to blue-green with a silver to white belly. Its identifying features are two rows of between six and eight grey circular blotches above and below the lateral line. These are never larger than the size of the eye. There is a black upper half to the front of the soft dorsal fin.

Size

The double-spotted queenfish grows to about a metre in length and 12 kilograms.

QUEENFISH, TALANG
Scomberoides commersonianus

(This fish is often referred to as *Scomberoides lysan.*)

OTHER NAMES : **LEATHERSKIN, WHITE-FISH, SKINNY FISH, GIANT DART**

Identification

The talang has a beautifully proportioned silvery white body that has a shiny light blue (or a faint green) dorsal area with just a tinge of gold below. All fins are usually a dusky yellow, though occasionally a brighter yellow. It may be positively identified by five to eight greyish oval blotches above or intersecting its lateral line. They are never smaller than the size of the eye.

Size

Talang queenfish grow to about a metre in length and about 15 kilograms.

QUEENFISH, NEEDLE-SCALED
Scomberoides tol

OTHER NAME: **SLENDER LEATHERSKIN**

Identification

This queenfish has the silver white colour on the lower part of its body. The dorsal area is blue. It has between five and eight small greyish-black oval marks above or through the lateral line. The front of the short, soft dorsal fin has a black tip.

Size

The needle-scaled grows to about half a metre.

Breeding

These fish are believed to spawn in summer, possibly in sheltered inshore waters or estuaries.

Habits

The pelagic queenfish swim swiftly, frequenting

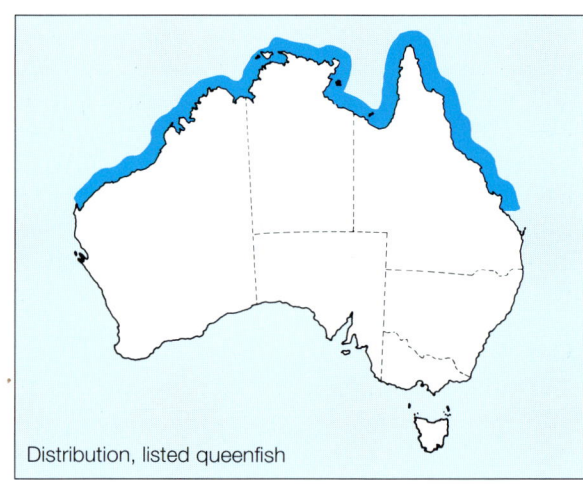

Distribution, listed queenfish

bomboras or rocky outcrops where there is a plentiful supply of small fish. They are an inshore species that are often found near headlands and in bays. They can also enter estuaries and can be found quite unexpectedly well up some creeks. They maraud when the tides push bait fish into a less turbulent corner of a bay. Their diet consists largely of small fish and crustaceans.

Distribution

All queenfish occur in the tropical inshore waters of the western Pacific and Indian Ocean, and those found in Australia are no exceptions. These fish are, however, most common north of about Rockhampton, around the northern coast, and as far south in Western Australia as Exmouth.

When to fish

Queenfish can be found all year round, but they are seen in the greatest numbers in bays and estuaries during the summer. They appear to be more active in the mornings, especially when the tide is flowing strongly — and particularly at the top of the tide near the entrance to a creek.

Where to fish

Though queenfish are caught around reefs in off-shore waters by bait-fishing or trolling, more are caught close in to rocky areas and in bays —and not infrequently in estuaries and creeks, especially in a deep hole that is out of the main body of water.

Tackle

The real sport fishing appeal of the queenfish can be experienced by using light tackle. However, because the angler will be fishing in waters which can produce barramundi, mangrove jack and some of the popular pelagic fish such as mackerel, a little prudence can save a lot of frustration. So, choose a medium weight threadline or baitcasting outfit with a 4 to 8 kilogram breaking-strain line. These can be used for trolling, lure tossing and fishing bait. A nylon-coated wire trace is usually a safeguard against toothier fish. Use strong hooks of about 4/0 to 8/0 for the larger fish, slightly smaller if the fish are not up to it.

Bait

Pilchards, garfish, etc. and fillets of almost any other fish are taken by queenfish. They like live bait; dead bait or fillets should be trolled or cast-and-retrieved.

Queenfish seem to find lures irresistible and this applies for any of the surface, sub-surface and popper models which are strong enough for tropical water fish. These fish can be moody and contrary sometimes, refusing one fast-worked lure for another which has a built-in action when retrieved or trolled at a slow speed. At other times quite the opposite occurs. When trolling a bait or casting-and-retrieving it, they may well refuse it at one speed, yet hit it at a higher speed.

Rigs

If the angler is willing to chance a "bite-off" from one of the toothier fish, a nylon-coated wire trace need not be used. Depending on the speed, rig No. 3 or 11 work for trolling. For casting and retrieving lures or bait, rig No. 2, 3 or 9 are suitable. Rig No. 3A will keep live bait swimming.

How to hook

The queenfish hooks itself. It can provide a thrilling aerial display or remain fighting powerfully underwater. Those which opt to stay down exhibit much more endurance than the acrobats. But a queenfish is never the angler's until it is exhausted and gaffed. They are clean fighters that rarely head for a reef refuge.

Hint

Most successful fishing for queenfish is done from small boats close in shore or in estuaries. The small boat angler can work around rocky outcrops, and troll or cast-and-retrieve to locations that large boats are unable to reach or to which shore-based anglers cannot cast. Nevertheless, shore-based anglers can find queenfish near any reef area, especially at the end of beaches and at the entrances to estuaries.

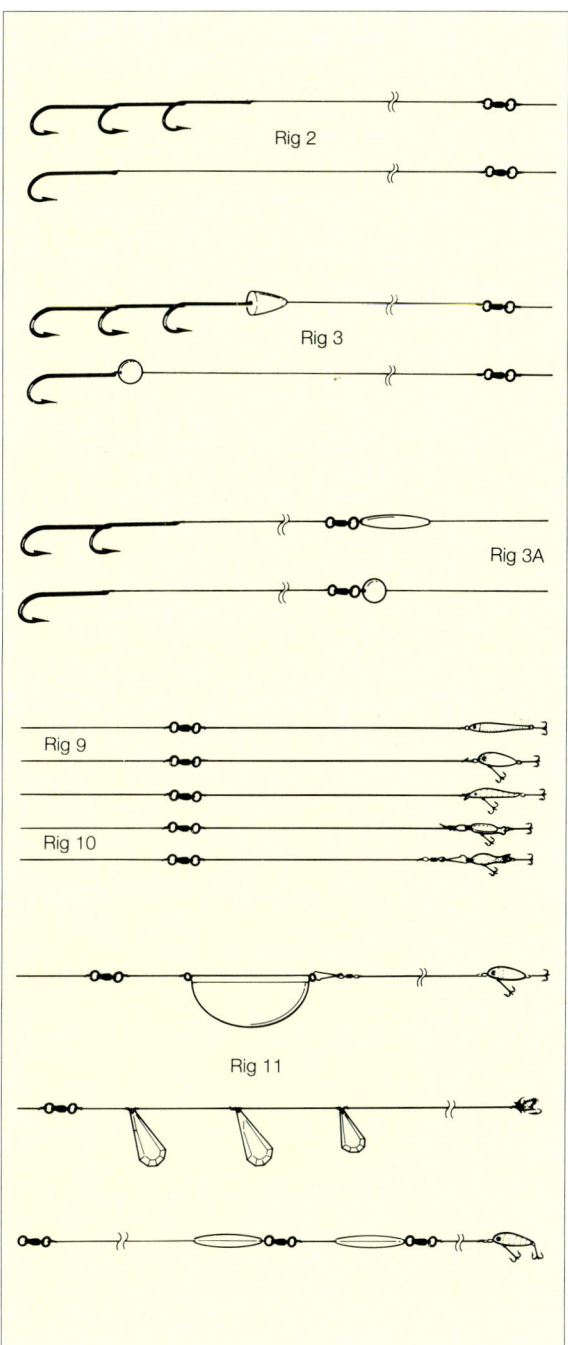

Edibility

The queenfish is more popular as a bait for big game fish or as fillets for reef fish than as a table fish. If the angler plans to eat it, then it must be killed, cleaned and kept on ice. It is a dry fish but skinned fillets are quite edible, though more palatable if prepared with a light spicy sauce.

The writer gratefully acknowledges the writings of John Gunn (CSIRO) for identification details of queenfish.

RAINBOW RUNNER
Elegatis bipinnulata

OTHER NAME: **RAINBOW KINGFISH**

This beautifully-coloured member of the Carangidae family and relative of the yellow-tail kingfish and trevallies is only within reach of anglers in the southern sections of Australia's east and west coast who fish well off shore — and they are not readily caught there! This situation changes, however, in the sub-tropical and tropical waters, where they are plentiful enough for boating anglers to enjoy a tussle with this fine fighting fish and excellent eating fish.

Identification

Rainbow runners resemble a slimmed-down version of a kingfish that is much more pointed from head to snout. Their dorsal area is a bright blue-green and their abdomen silvery white. A broad yellow band with two narrow blue margins extends from the eye to the caudal peduncle, though this tends to fade after death. The yellowish tail is large and deeply forked. Another distinguishing feature are two-rayed finlets between both the dorsal and anal fins and the tail. Very large specimens develop a deeper body.

Size

Rainbow runners are reputed to grow to 1.3 metres long and exceed 13 kilograms, but in Australian waters a fish weighing less than half this weight is more commonplace. (The largest rainbow runner on the records of the Australian National Sport Fishing Association, at December, 1987, weighed 3.4 kilograms.)

Breeding

Little is known.

Habits

These fish are pelagics, with schools of them roaming the blue water well off-shore. Only occasionally do they show themselves near the surface. Closer inshore they are found in areas of coral and rock reefs and it is not uncommon to encounter them among large predators such as sharks, barracuda and tanguigue. They move on and off reefs with the tides. As the fish grow, so the schools become smaller, with the large specimens often reduced to ones or twos. Rainbow runners are omnivorous, feeding on small fish, crustaceans, molluscs, etc. Their feeding habits are not unlike the tailor (*see* entry), often eating until food is literally filling their throats.

Distribution

Rainbow runners are common in the tropical regions of Australia, though they can be found in reasonable numbers as far south as the north coast of New South Wales and the Shark Bay area of Western Australia. In the summer months they can even stray to more southerly areas such as Bermgui (New South Wales) and Rottnest Island (Western Australia).

When to fish

In their main distribution zone, rainbow runners are about all year. The summer is the best time in the more southerly parts, when tongues of warm-water currents offer the best opportunity to find the fish. A depth sounder may also help by signalling their presence in the middle-lower depths of bluewater currents.

Where to fish

In the main, rainbow runners are taken by trolling other small fish, fish strips or lures along the edge of coral or rock reefs, islands and shoals. If a school

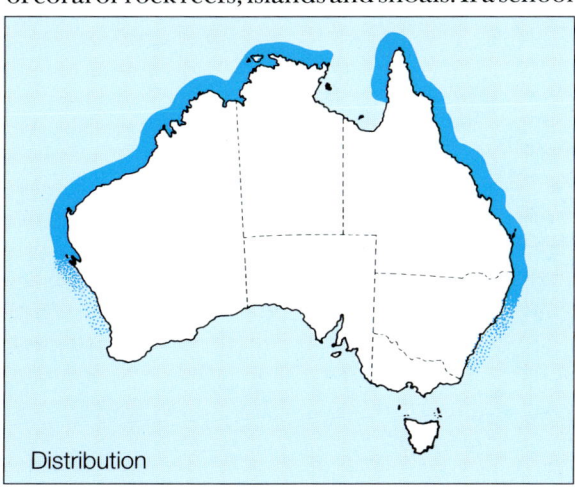

Distribution

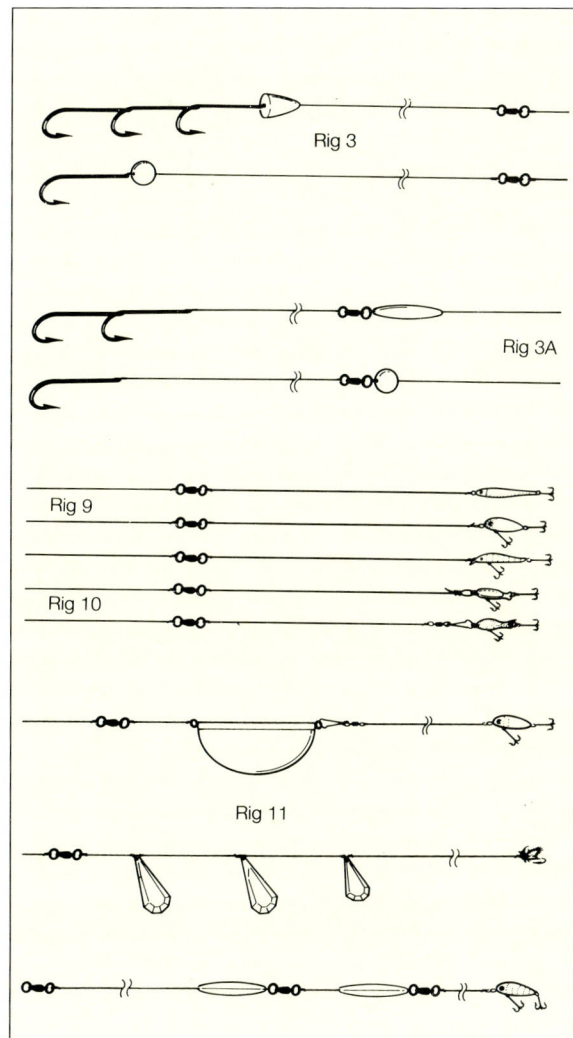

is discovered many anglers will change to casting and retrieving baits and lures as they drift within range.

Tackle

A frustrating element of fishing for rainbow runners is that they share their waters with larger species with teeth, because there is no doubt that they would otherwise offer excellent light-gear fishing. However, the likelihood of barracuda, tanguigue, wahoo, etc., taking bait or lure, makes lines between 5 and 10 kilograms breaking-strain, with a wire trace, a minimum requirement. Medium-size single-handed threadline or baitcasting outfits are adequate for trolling or casting and retrieving baits or lures.

Bait

Small fish such as garfish or pilchards, and fish-shaped fillets of these or such fish as mullet etc., make good baits. Rainbow runners respond to a wide range of lures, including small metal-headed and skirted styles, and plastic-bodied styles, as well as jigs. Baits may be on single or ganged hooks in a smaller size, say 3/0 maximum. Lures should also be limited to those of the smaller dimensions, because rainbow fish have small mouths.

Berley

Like their close relative, the yellowtail kingfish, rainbow runners can be attracted and held with a steady stream of fish pieces and scraps as berley. A problem, however, is that this berley is also likely to attract sharks.

Rigs

While an unweighted rig can be used, it may be necessary to weight the bait to get it down towards the fish, so rig Nos 3 or 3A are suggested with bait, and for lures rig Nos 9 and 11 (with the minimum of weight) are recommended for trolling.

How to hook

Being a pelagic, when a rainbow runner attacks a moving bait or lure you will invariably have a hook up. A hard-biting fish, they mostly rise towards the surface when hooked, rather than diving towards the bottom, and they make long runs. They have a soft mouth and the hooks can tear free if the angler attempts to *drag* in the fish.

Edibility

Game-fishing enthusiasts often use rainbow runners for skip-bait trolling for bigger game, but these fish are also very popular as a fine table fish in their own right.

As with all fish in the tropics, they should be killed, cleaned and placed on ice immediately they are caught. The white and moist flesh can be prepared in any manner.

ROCK-COD

The name rock-cod is given to a large group of fish that are members of the family Serranidae. Some of this family are called sea-perches, though they are *not* the same as the sea-perches listed under that entry in this book. A few are called sea bass. These fish inhabit rocky inshore waters and deepwater sea floors and reef areas around the Australian coastline. Exact numbers are largely a guestimate that is further confused by the variety of common or regional names they have been given over time. Moreover, even some of the scientific names remain a subject of debate — and their colour variations do not help. An arbitrary selection is given here, with a brief description highlighting any distinguishing features of a species. The rock cod's habits and recommended fishing methods follow the individual descriptions. [Scorpionfish, which are frequently called rock-cods, are described elsewhere in their correct entry.]

With two exceptions in this selection, all the rock-cods have a thick, oval-elongate body with a solid-spined first dorsal fin connected to a soft rear dorsal fin. The soft section of dorsal fin is often as high or higher than the spined section. The root of the anal fin is almost level with the soft dorsal. A rock-cod's pectoral fins are rounded, as is the tail. All rock-cods have large protruding eyes set close to both the forehead and the mouth.

Six-banded rock cod.

ROCK-COD, BLACK or SADDLED
Epinephelus damelii

Identification
This rock-cod can be easily mistaken for the estuary rock-cod. Its colour, however, is usually darker with more black and white blotches, tending to a ragged striping, that is generally apparent on the upper half of the body and head. There is an unmistakable black mark on the back between the dorsal fin and tail.

Size
This rock-cod is said to reach 1.5 metres in length.

Distribution
This fish may be found on coastal reefs from about Townsville in Queensland to Mallacoota in Victoria.

Special regulations
The saddled or black rock-cod (and the estuary rock-cod) are totally protected in New South Wales. Any caught must be returned to the water alive.

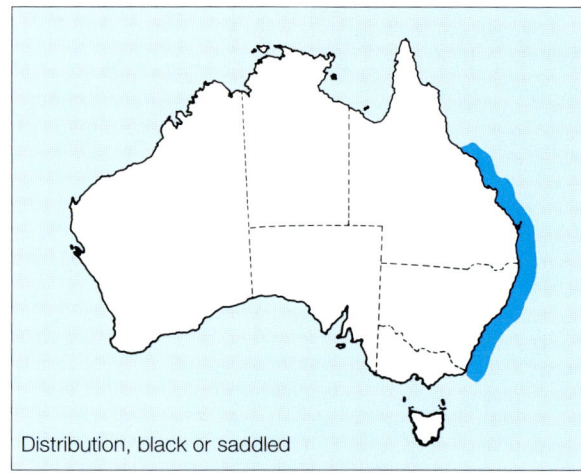
Distribution, black or saddled

ROCK-COD, CHINAMAN
Epinephelus rivulatis

Identification
The colour of this rock-cod is variable: from white through tan, pale brown, yellow-brown and deep reddish-brown. There can be 4 or 5 darker vertical bands on the body. The dorsal fin is yellow-tipped.

ROCK-COD, BREAKSEA
Epinephelides armatus

OTHER NAMES: **BLACKARSE COD, TIGER COD**

Identification
Like most cods, this species is variable in colour. Its colouring ranges from yellowish-orange with pink markings on the head (fish from deep water), to pale pink-brown, greenish-brown, grey-green and dark brown. A pale stripe is usually visible down the snout. It is distinguished by a black spot, which outlines the anus. This fish has a deeper body than other rock-cods of similar length.

Size
This rock-cod grows to 50 to 60 centimetres in length.

Distribution
This fish is only found in Western Australia, from the Recherche Archipelago to Shark Bay.

Breaksea rock-cod.

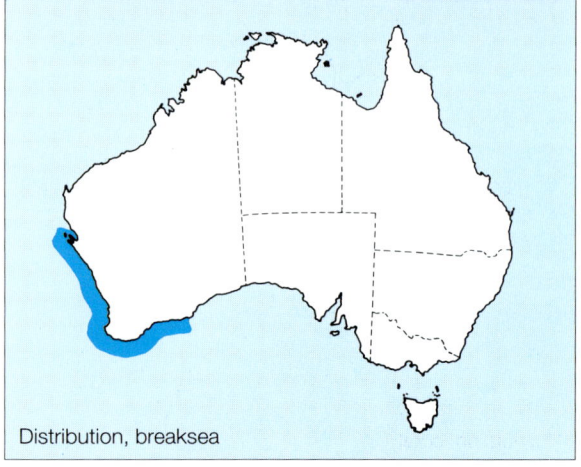
Distribution, breaksea

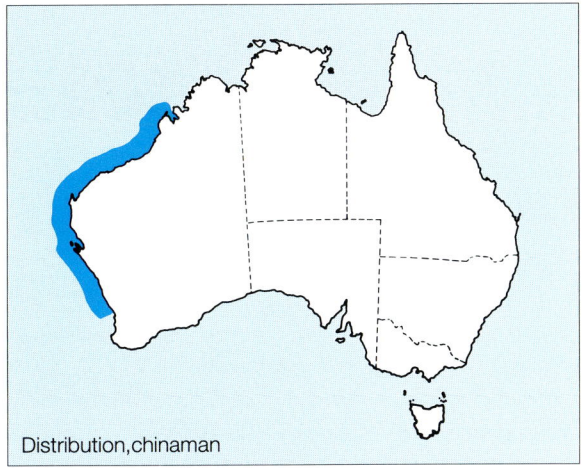

Distribution, chinaman

Size
This rock-cod grows to about 45 centimetres.

Distribution
This fish is found between Rottnest Island and the north-west of Western Australia and the Northern Territory.

ROCK-COD, CORAL
Cephalopolis miniatus

OTHER NAMES: **BLUE-SPOTTED ROCK-COD, CORAL TROUT (INCORRECTLY)**

Identification
The base colour of this rock-cod can be a brownish to bright red but it is covered with black-edged blue spots on the body and fins. (It is often mistaken for the coral trout but it has a deeper body and rounded tail.)

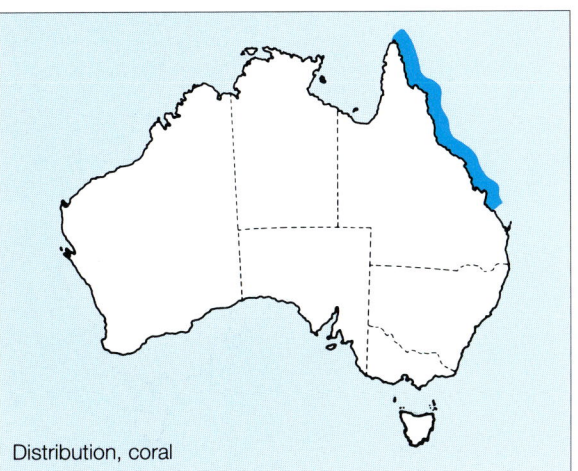

Distribution, coral

Size
Grows to about 50 centimetres.

Distribution
It is mainly found on the Barrier Reef from Gladstone northwards

ROCK-COD, ESTUARY
Epinephelus suillis
(Often described as *E. tauvina**)

OTHER NAMES: **GREASY COD, SPOTTED COD, GROPER, BROWN-SPOTTED COD**

Identification
This is a tropical species of rock-cod, though fair numbers are found in southern temperate waters. The predominant colour of the body is a fawn or mid-brown with yellowish tones. It has much darker cross-bands or bars on the body and head than other rock-cods, with numerous dark black-to-brown spots on the body. The older fish carry increased spotting.

Estuary rock-cod.

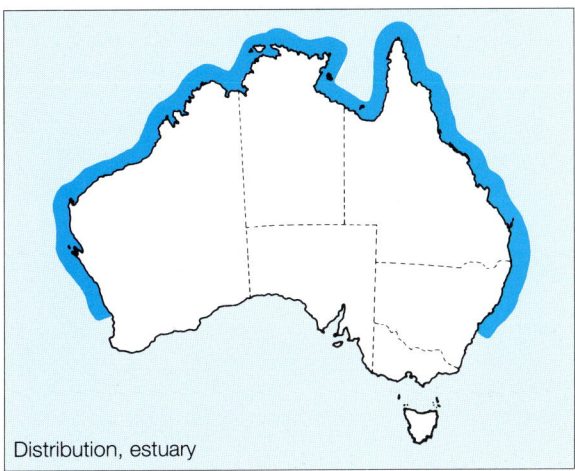

Distribution, estuary

Size

The estuary rock-cod reaches about 1.5 metres in length. The minimum legal length for a catch in Queenland is 35 centimetres.

Distribution

This rock cod exists throughout the tropical areas of Australia but it is also found as far south as the central coast of New South Wales and Rottnest Island in Western Australia. It inhabits inshore reefs and enters larger estuaries.

Special regulations

Both the estuary rock-cod (and the black or saddled rock-cod) are totally protected in New South Wales. Any caught must be returned to the water alive.

[*The estuary rock-cod is the same fish as the **malabar rock-cod** (previously *Epinephelus malabaricus*) of the Northern Territory and north-west area of Western Australia. *E. malabaricus* or maculatis is the brown-spotted rock cod of northern waters. *E. tauvina* is the greasy rock-cod of tropical waters. Neither of these fish is found in southern waters. Little wonder the angler is confused when there is such confusion among the experts.

Flowery rock-cod.

Identification

The body is a fawn colour, over which there are dense orange-brown spots, extending to the base of the fins. The spots are larger on the lower half and the belly. Large irregular black-brown blotches are scattered over the body. The top of the spined dorsal fin is dark at the edges and all other fins are a dark brown-to-black.

Size

This fish grows to about 40 centimetres.

Distribution

A tropical species, the flowery rock-cod is found from about Townsville around the tropical waters to about Broome. Though mainly a coastal reef-dweller, the flowery cod will sometimes be encountered in the deep water of mangrove estuaries and creeks.

ROCK-COD, FLOWERY
Epinephelus microdon

OTHER NAMES: **SMOOTH FLOWERY ROCK-COD, BLACK ROCK-COD, CARPET COD, FLOWER COD**

ROCK-COD, GREY-BANDED
Epinephelus septemfasciatus

Identification

The body of this cod is a variable grey colour, with brown to bronze tonings. There are six or seven

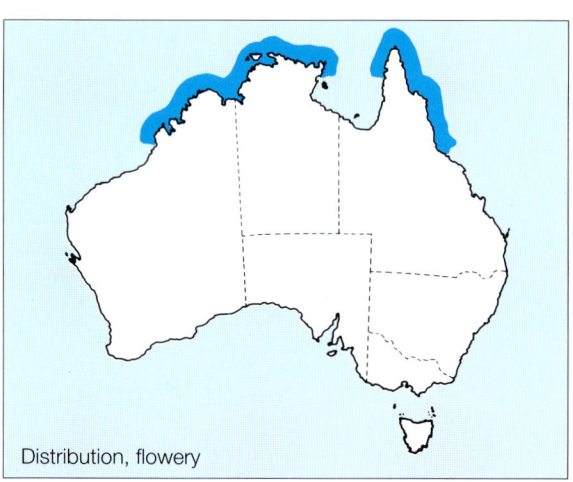

Distribution, flowery

Distribution, grey-banded

vertical bands on the body. The dark tail has a white edge.

Size
This rock-cod grows to about a metre in length.

Distribution
The grey-banded rock-cod is common on deep-water reefs, from about Evans Head to Mallacoota on the east coast, and from Albany to Jurien Bay on the west coast.

ROCK-COD, HUMPBACK
Cromileptes altivelis

OTHER NAMES: **HUMPBACK SEA-BASS, BARRAMUNDI COD**

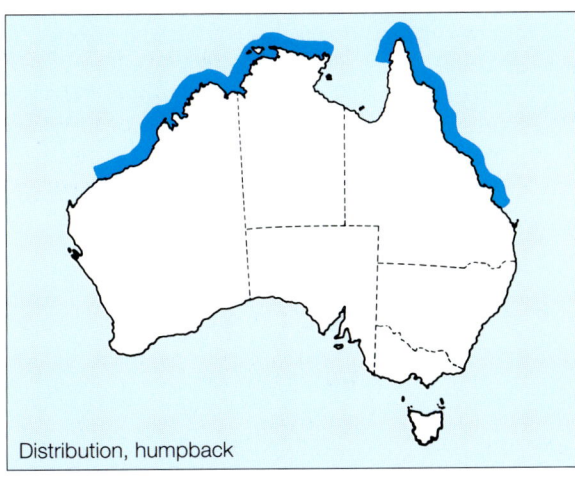

Distribution, humpback

Identification
This fish is easily identified. It has a remarkable small, flattened head, its eyes are very close to the mouth, and there is a steep rise to the dorsal area. The dorsal fins are long. The overall colour, including the fins, is a grey to purplish-brown and there are numerous, more or less evenly spaced, brown-black spots over the whole fish.

Size
The humpback rock-cod grows to about 50 centimetres in length.

Distribution
This fish is found in reef areas of varying depths from Gladstone in Queensland, across the top end, and south to about Dampier in Western Australia.

ROCK-COD, MAORI
Epinephelus undulatostriatus

OTHER NAMES: **MAORI, RED-SPECKLED ROCK-COD**

Maori rock-cod.

Identification
This fish is deeper-bodied than other rock-cods of a similar length. Body colouring is a yellowish-grey to a yellowish-brown. There are numerous golden tan to reddish-tan bands running obliquely across the body. There are golden edges to the rear dorsal fin, anal fin and tail.

Size
This fish reaches about 60 centimetres in length and can weigh from 4 to 5 kilograms.

Distribution
The Maori rock-cod is reasonably common in reefs off the south Queensland coast and extends south past Wollongong, but numbers decrease and catches at the southern end of the range are uncommon.

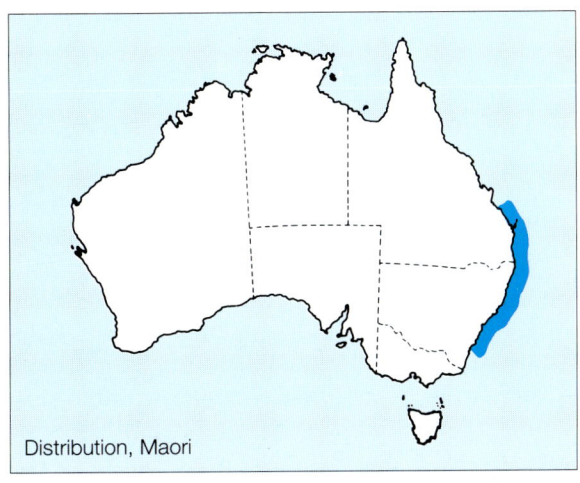

Distribution, Maori

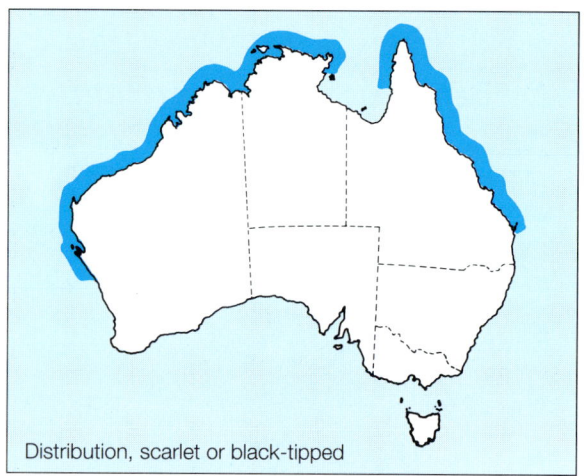

Distribution, scarlet or black-tipped

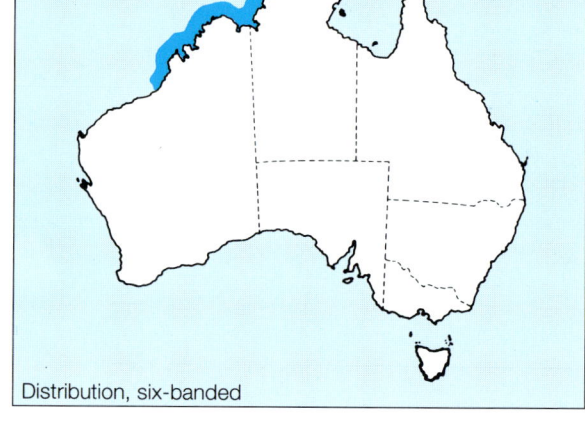

Distribution, six-banded

ROCK-COD, SCARLET or BLACK-TIPPED
Epinephelus fasciatus

OTHER NAMES:**BLACK-TIPPED GROPER, FOOTBALLER COD**

Identification
This cod is usually a pink-red to orange-red or scarlet. Six or seven vertical bands are sometimes apparent over the back, fading towards the belly. The edge of the spinous dorsal fin is dark to black-edged.

Size
This rock-cod grows to about 40 centimetres.

Distribution
These fish are found on reefs to about 60 metres in the tropical areas from south Queensland to the Abrolhos Islands (Western Australia.)

ROCK-COD, SIX-BANDED
Epinephelus sexfasciatus

Identification
This cod is fawn-coloured with a rosy shade to the lower head and abdominal area, with faint brown or lighter spots. Six brown bands (double this number in small fish: they merge as the fish grows) run from the dorsal fins to the belly. The pectoral fins are a reddish-yellow towards the edges and the rear dorsal fins are spotted in brown or black.

Size
The maximum length for this rock-cod is about 60 centimetres.

Distribution
The six-banded rock-cod is found in the north-west of Western Australia, the Northern Territory, and in tropical Queensland.

ROCK-COD, TIGER
Othos Dentex

OTHER NAMES: **HARLEQUIN FISH, CHINESE LANTERN FISH**

Identification
The tiger rock-cod is occasionally mistaken for a southern coral trout because (being more slender than other rock-cods) its body-shape and colouring is similar. The colour of the body can be red, orange-yellow, brownish-red, sometimes with dark patches in the head area. The upper half of the body is covered with blue spots of different sizes and there are large yellow spots or blotches below the lateral line.

Size
This fish grows to about 75 centimetres in length.

Distribution
The populations of this fish are depleted — mainly because of spearfishing — from the coastal reefs of Australian waters.

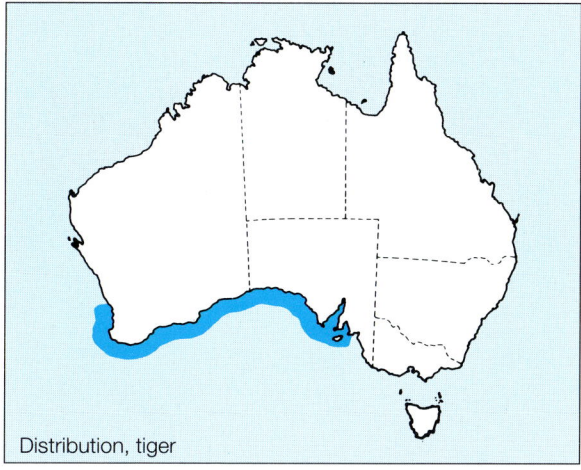

Distribution, tiger

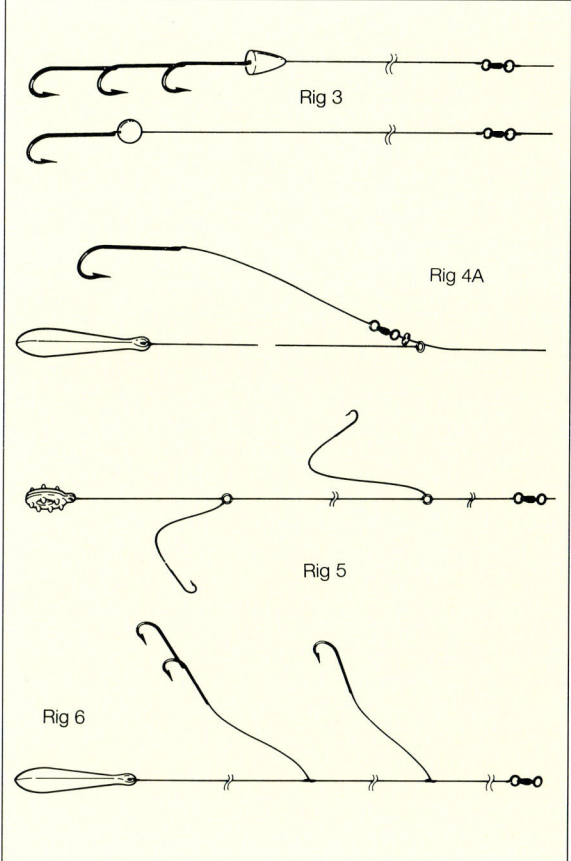

They can be found from about Victor Harbor in South Australia to north of Perth.
The following applies to all rock-cods.

Breeding

Only limited information is available. Many small or juvenile rock-cods of several species that are mostly located in deeper offshore reefs, can be found in shallow inshore waters (even rock pools) from time to time and also in tropical estuaries. Many members of the Serranidae family, to which rock-cod belong, are known to be hermaphrodites. They are usually female at maturity, though with a male organ, and are capable of laying eggs. At a later stage they turn into males. In the period between this change they are both — or neither — sex. The writer is unable to determine whether the rock-cods listed here experience this transformation.

Habits

Rock-cods do not pursue their prey. They are slow searchers for crabs, molluscs and shellfish, as well as the smaller fish of reef areas. Most rock-cods have a colouring that provides excellent camouflage and they can grab unsuspecting prey very smartly. All possess a capacious mouth.

When to fish

Anglers invariably hook a rock-cod during the daylight and at any time of the year.

Where to fish

Most rock-cod are caught while fishing for other reef species, such as snapper, morwong, coral trout, emperors etc. The rock fishers will occasionally hook a reasonably sized rock-cod while fishing on the bottom for reef species.

Tackle

Rock-cod are invariably hooked with outfits selected to catch other reef fish, especially the deck-mounted winch-type of reels, boat rods and handlines. Anglers fishing from the rocks will probably be using 3 to 4-metre rods with threadline, sidecast or overhead reels. The breaking-strain of the line is often much heavier than is necessary for rock-cod for the same reason.

Bait

All the rock-cods eat a wide variety of fish, fish fillets, crabs, octopus, squid, prawn, conjevoi, shellfish, etc.

Rigs

Those used for snapper, morwong, emperors etc., will catch rock-cods. Depending on the depth of the water and sea conditions, rig Nos 3, 4A, 5 and 6 are likely to find a rock-cod.

How to hook

The rock-cod does not pick. It gulps and usually hooks itself if the bait is moving, whether from a drifting boat or carried by the underwater currents.

Edibility

All the rock-cods have firm, moist, white flesh. Those caught in the tropics, particularly, should be cleaned and iced as soon as practicable. Most cod are a nice size to bake whole, but all yield solid fillets which can be prepared by most methods.

ROCK-COD, WIRRAH

Wirrah rock-cod.

The recreational angler is likely to hook several other rock-cods, the most common of which is the wirrah (several species of the genus Acanthistius) which inhabit inshore rocky and reef waters in the temperate waters around the Australian, from southern Queensland to Coral Bay in Western Australia and in waters of northern Tasmania.

The two most common are the **eastern wirrah** (*A. ocellatus*) and the **western wirrah** (*A. serratus*). These fish are deep-bodied, similar to the breaksea rock-cod or maori rock-cod, in shape. Both are good-looking fish. The eastern species is a greenish to darkish brown, spotted with dark-edged blue spots on both head and body. The western species can be a pale fawn to dark brown, with less non-blue spots on the head and dark stripes behind the eyes. Spots on the body are sometimes indistinct. Wirrahs can be separated from rock-cods in that they have 13 spines in their dorsal fins. Rock-cods never have more than between 9 and 11.

The wirrahs have firm, white flesh, but they are extremely tough and tasteless (another common name for them is "boot"!). While they can grow to 60 centimetres in length, it takes so long to prepare them — filleting and skinning are essential — that they hardly seem worth the effort. Steaming is probably the only suitable cooking method. But they are better released.

SAILFISH
Istuophorus platypterus

OTHER NAME: **BAYONET-FISH, PACIFIC SAILFISH**

This is often the first billfish tackled by small boat anglers,
simply because they can be encountered in waters where
such game fish as tanguige (narrow-barred spanish mackerel)
are sought — and reasonably close to the shore, especially
at certain times of the year in southern Queensland waters.
The angler who is ill-equipped has little chance of bringing a
sailfish alongside because of their often spectacularly airborne fighting ability.

Identification

The sailfish cannot be mistaken for a small marlin
because of its long sail-like dorsal fin, which is at
least twice the height of its body depth. The dorsal
area is a purplish-blue. This fades to a yellowish-
grey on the lower half of the body, the yellow
becoming brighter after death. The dull blue bars
on the body, that can light up when the fish is
hunting, tend to become blackish after death. The
rich blue dorsal fin often has dark or black blotches.
The ventral or pelvic fins are thin and extremely
long.

Size

The sailfish is known to grow to over 3.5 metres in
length and a weight of 100.24 kilograms — the
world all-tackle record. The Australian all-tackle
record as at December, 1988, was 88.75 kilograms,
caught at Lord Howe Island the previous year.

Breeding

It is generally agreed that the sailfish sheds floating
eggs in inshore waters. It is also widely accepted
that a female is accompanied by several males.
There is argument, however, about which time of
the year this occurs: some contending that breeding
takes place during the summer, others claiming
mid-winter. (Most of the obviously mature record-
setting fish have been caught between September
and February.) After a couple of weeks the fry of
sailfish are recognisable. They grow rapidly, a three-

year-old fish topping 40 kilograms. Small sailfish of around 3 to 7 kilograms are sometimes caught in Barrier Reef waters.

Habits

Sailfish prefer the warm waters of the tropics, between 22°C and 31°C but their movement is subject to sea conditions, food supply and currents. They can follow a current in 28°C to 29°C range, which often leads them further south in the summer.

These fish are known to feed from the bottom at depths of 200 metres, though they are usually found in the upper depths where they can find the schools of their favourite food items — garfish, pilchards, mackerel, mullet and many other fish, including tailor, yellowtail, flying fish, etc. Squid and octopus are also acceptable. Some sailfish, when opened, have revealed stomachs full of puffer or toadfish.

The sailfish appears to start feeding, according to some research, early in the day but they are usually much less fussy eaters in the late afternoon and evening. They will school in large numbers when feeding and often maraud bait fish and herd them into a ball. They are also likely to attack hard from below, their speed taking them above the surface. Much of their herding bait and feeding is done in choppy sea conditions. Their high dorsal sail is obvious as they cruise almost on the surface, while searching for food or "resting".

Distribution

Sailfish are found mainly in the sub-tropical and tropical off shore waters. They are found in New South Wales (about the central coast), throughout Queensland and as far south as Cape Leeuwin in Western Australia. Their appearance in southerly

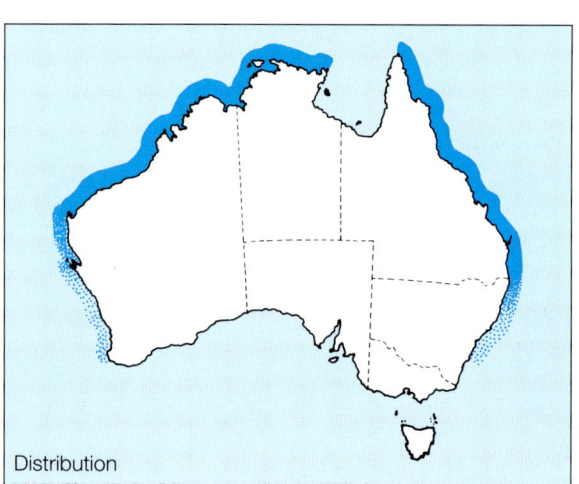

Distribution

temperate waters depends on warm-water currents, usually in mid-summer. They are often relatively common around Townsville on the east coast, and Exmouth Gulf on the west coast in the mid-winter period. Though there are more of them outside the Barrier Reef, they often enter the inside waters, around the Bribie Banks, and off the Gold Coast, when the water temperature rises above 21°C to 22°C. Migrating bait fish seem to influence these movements too.

When to fish

Indications are that warm water above 21°C is important to these fish and it may go as high as 30°C. They also seem to prefer the sea choppy or disturbed. The best times are from mid-morning until at least dark. Migrating bait fish are almost certain to attract sailfish.

Where to fish

The best waters are those which show the azure blue of a warm current or deeper waters along the edges of reefs.

Tackle

Anglers interested in records can fish with any line class, or bait or lure rigs that are approved by the Game Fishing Association of Australia — or rigs that comply with the rules of the Australian National Sport Fishing Association.

Obviously it depends on the size of the sailfish that are about, but lines of 6 to 10 kilograms breaking-strain are suitable as long as the reel (a heavy-duty threadline or at least a medium baitcaster) is powerfully geared and well maintained. From boats a single-handed or double-handed rod up to 3 metres is suitable, provided it has a fast-tip action and good power in the lower section.

Bait

Live or dead pilchards, garfish, mackerel, mullet and other small fish such as tailor, even trevally, are excellent bait. Fresh squid is also accepted and fish strips or fillets may be used.

Sailfish will also respond to a wide range of trolled or cast-and-retrieved lures; and taking a sailfish on a fly-fishing outfit with a saltwater fly is acknowledged as a fishing achievement.

Rigs

A live bait rig (often a lightly-weighted No. 3A) or lure rig No. 9 are popular with small boat anglers that have found a school of feeding sailfish. For trolling, use a single hook, two hooks ganged, or a

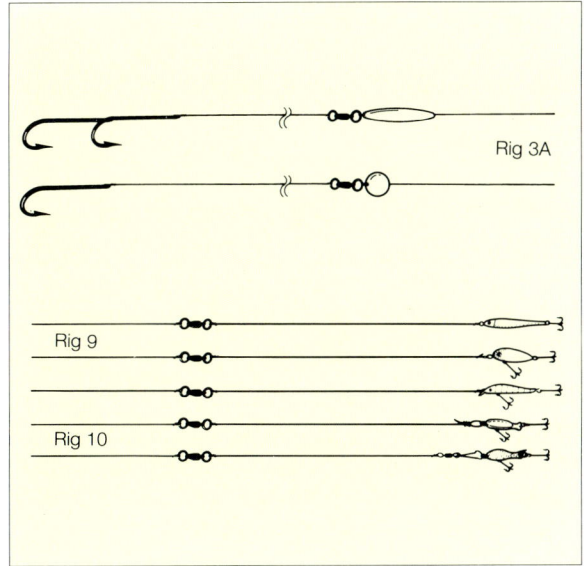

single hook with a sinker riding on the eye of the hook. Trolled baits are sometimes dressed with a plastic squid skirt. The bill of a sailfish is rough and can rasp through nylon leaders. If anglers are game enough to chance a lost fish, a nylon-coated wire trace doesn't have to be used.

How to hook
With trolled or cast-and-retrieved baits or lures, even flies, a sailfish can be very frustrating — following but not attacking. A change of speed or change to an erratic swimming action can often induce a bite. And when a sailfish bites it is generally hooked. With live bait or floated dead bait, it pays to wait until the fish is moving away freely before setting the hook.

The sailfish usually "rips and tears" and leaps. It is best to maintain a tension throughout the fight, not only to ensure that it doesn't throw a hook or lure but that it also tires the fish.

Edibility
Most anglers release sailfish unless intending to claim a record or being photographed with their first sailfish catch. Some retain a smaller specimen for mounting.

They are quite edible, especially when smoked, but there are many much more tasty fish that are much more easily caught.

SALMON, ATLANTIC
Salmo salar

This native of the northern hemisphere, from both sides of the ocean after which it is named, was one of the first fish to be successfully hatched from eggs transported to Australia. That was in Tasmania in 1864. Yet despite repeated attempts and considerable expense, the Atlantic salmon has not adjusted to this country and anglers lucky enough to hook one should release it. It is a splendid sport fish, probably one of the best, which makes spectacular leaps during its fight to break free. [**Note:** In recent years, this fish has been successfully farmed in Tasmania. This could stimulate research for an expanded release of the Atlantic salmon for recreational fishing.]

Identification

More slender than the brook, brown or rainbow trout, the Atlantic salmon, with a smaller head than the other three, is longer and narrower in the caudal peduncle. The tail is markedly forked in the young but it becomes much less pronounced as the fish mature. The Australian land-locked hatchery-bred species does not have the green-black and overall silvery sheen of sea-run fish: they are usually a dark shade of grey and dull silver. The dark spots on the back and sides have no halos or surrounds.

Size

Sea-run Atlantic salmon have been recorded weighing more than 43 kilograms. Though the largest one known in Australia has been less than

2 kilograms, two land-locked species in the United States and Canadian waters have been caught weighing 35 kilograms.

New South Wales regulations require that any catch of Atlantic salmon measuring less than 25 centimetres must be released.

Breeding

While it is successfully hatchery-bred in New South Wales, there is no record of it having bred in the wild where it has been released. (Non sea-run trout in the United States and Canada migrate to suitable cold streams in mid to late autumn to spawn.)

Habits

Australian-spawned Atlantic salmon probably behave much like the northern-hemisphere land-locked species, spending much of their life in the fast-flowing cool waters of rivers or creeks, or in the cooler depths of the lakes into which theese flow. These fish are known to follow the water temperature around a lake's shoreline, moving into deeper areas when the water warms. Unlike other northern salmon, the Atlantic salmon does not die when it spawns. It returns to the stream of its birth four or five times — provided it survives commercial and recreational anglers as well as its natural predators, especially during its period in the ocean.

Distribution

The fish is mainly confined to the Monaro, especially Lake Jindabyne and its tributary river, the Thredbo River. There may still be a few in Lake Burrinjuck or at least in a couple of the small rivers that flow into it. Lake Blowering has also been stocked.

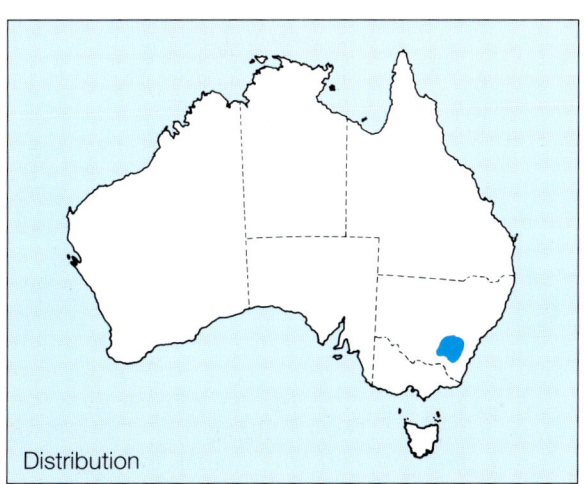

Distribution

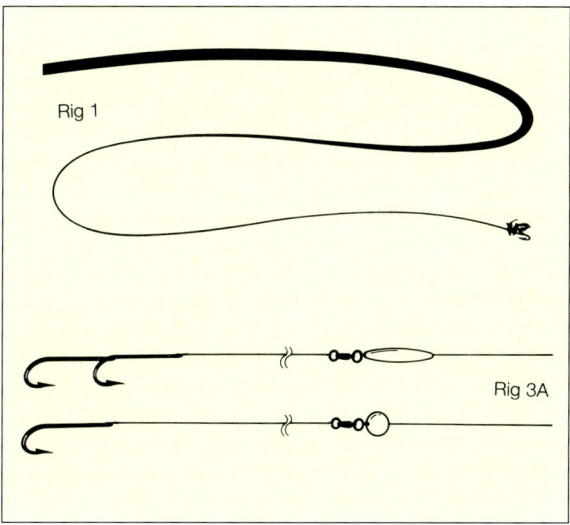

When to fish

Though Atlantic salmon may be fished in lakes all through the year and in those rivers declared trout waters when they are open to fishing, the best times are mid-spring through summer.

Where to fish

These fish may be found in the faster runs of the rivers or creeks. Other likely spots in lakes are where currents form from in-flowing water. It is also worth fishing from rocky ridges around lakes that descend into deep waters.

Tackle

Fly-fishing outfits with large wet flies, especially the matuka and streamer types, are eminently suitable. Single-handed threadline or baitcasting rods and reel may be used for bait-fishing or for trolling, with weighted flies or small but active — wobbling and darting — lures.

Bait

The carnivorous Atlantic salmon eats insects of all kinds, small fish, frogs, tadpoles, shrimp etc.

Rigs

Only a single rod and reel is permitted, and with no more than 2 hooks attached. Standard fly gear is successful, as are unweighted baits or lightly-weighted bait, and lures (Rigs 1 or 3A).

How to hook

If using fly gear, the timing for tightening the line to set the hook will really only come with experience. On the other hand, when using bait or lures, this fish tends to gulp them in and hooks itself.

Hint

Where permissible, try retrieving a small, light-coloured spoon downstream in rivers at a slightly faster rate than the current. This can often tempt an Atlantic salmon. If using a streamer or matuka fly, retrieving it very quickly can also attract a strike. If you tether the first Atlantic salmon caught, it often attracts others to the vicinity.

Edibility

The Atlantic salmon is one of the prized eating fish, whether fried, grilled, baked or broiled. Its flesh becomes a rich orange-red when cooked.

Other regulations

Apart from licence requirements, and the regulations governing size and the limitations on rods and lines, there are also closed seasons and waters that may only be fished by specific methods. Anglers fishing inland waters should obtain a copy of the current laws and regulations, which are available from better tackle shops, tourist centres and government fisheries departments.

The bag limit per angler per day in New South Wales is 10.

SALMON, AUSTRALIAN
Arripis trutta (Eastern)
Arripis truttaceus (Western)

OTHER NAMES: BLACK BACK, BUCK SALMON KAHAWAI (NZ); SMALLER SPECIMENS CALLED "NEWFISH", SALMON TROUT, BAY TROUT COLONIAL SALMON

Often described as the "poor man's marlin", these fine fish of
the sea-perch group were inappropriately named "salmon" by
Captain James Cook, when his crew caught them in New
Zealand waters — mainly because of their superficial
resemblance to the sea-run salmon that were so familiar to
the British sailors. There need be no such reservations,
however, regarding their quality as sporting fish. Australian
salmon provide exciting fishing with their leaping,
head-shaking and gill-flaring. Any angler who lands a
large specimen on light gear has had his skill tested
by a powerful opponent.

Identification

The Australian salmon's body is solid but streamlined, with a reasonably pointed head. It has a large mouth with rows of small sharp teeth in the jaws and mouth. A mature fish is silver, with a bluish or olive-green back that can be considerably darker in some specimens, hence "black-back". The colour of its sides fades to a silver or whitish belly, the faint but darker spots of the juvenile and immature disappearing as the fish ages. There is also a yellowish tinge on the side of some fish. The fins are a grey-green but the deep-forked tail is much darker.

The eastern and western sub-species appear to be identical and intermingle in some areas. The only difference between the two seems to be in the number of gill-rakers they have. Gill-rakers are used to sift plankton from the water.

Size

The eastern salmon is known to grow to about 5 kilograms but this weight could probably be doubled for the biggest of the western sub-species. A minimum legal size and/or a bag limit applies in some States. The minimum legal length for a catch

289

in South Australia is 23 centimetres; the minimum in Western Australia is 30 centimetres, coupled with a bag limit of 5 Australian salmon per angler per day; the minimum size in Victoria is 21 centimetres.

Breeding

The western salmon is believed to breed close the the West Australian coast off Busselton and the eastern salmon off Eden in New South Wales — both in autumn. The larval salmon from Western Australia move east to nursery areas along the western and southern coasts of Tasmania and the mainland coast between Lakes Entrance in Victoria and the mid-Bight coast of South Australia. They then return to Western Australia. The eastern larval salmon drift south to the eastern coast of Tasmania before moving north again. There is a possible overlap in the two populations around Tasmania and along the south-eastern parts of Victoria.

Habits

Australian salmon are pelagic fish that moves in schools. They start life as plankton-eaters but become carnivorous, eating krill, pilchards, sardines, whitebait, bluebait, garfish, mullet, squid, beach worms and the like. Sometimes a school can be seen feeding in a frenzy just beyond casting range from a beach or rock headland. They move about very quickly and can easily be scared, panic by a single fish spreading instantly through a large school. Australian salmon usually hug the coastline, rarely moving beyond the 40 metres depth.

Distribution

The main areas of adult populations range to just

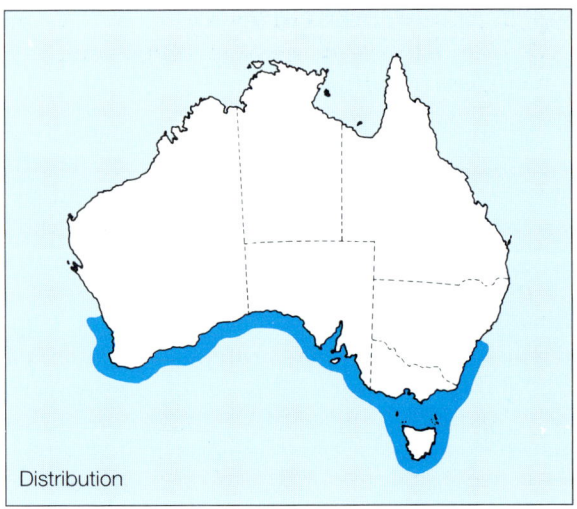

Distribution

north of Perth and east of Esperance in Western Australia, along the coasts of both South Australia and Victoria, in the Bass Strait and the northern half of Tasmania, and north along the coast of New South Wales to Newcastle — and even further north in some years. Migration begins in the south, moves north during summer, and returns to the south again in the autumn.

When to fish

This is governed to some degree by the seasonal migration, particularly on the western and eastern coasts. The fish is more likely to be encountered during the early morning before the waters brighten, in the late afternoon and into the evening.

Where to fish

Deep channels along beaches are popular hunting grounds for salmon, but they will move along rocky headlands and into inlets and bays as well as inside harbours and estuaries. When a school is found offshore, anglers in boats will do better trying to drift with the school while casting to the fish. Trolling can scatter the fish, causing the entire school to sound.

Tackle

Use good quality beach or rock-fishing rods, between 3.5 and 4 metres long, with matching threadline, overhead or side-cast reels. A 5 kilogram to 8 kilogram breaking-strain line is adequate. Smaller rods may be used around bays or harbours and when fishing from boats. Depending on the conditions, these outfits are all suitable for casting weighted or unweighted baits, and lures.

Australian salmon can be very exciting sport for those equipped with saltwater fly-fishing outfits and saltwater flies.

Bait

Australian salmon responds well to a variety of spoons and slicers. Even a little white or clear tubing, pushed on to a hook to give the impression of a small bait fish, can be effective. If using saltwater flies, try the blue/white or green shades.

These fish will take pilchards, sardines, whitebait, bluebait, garfish, mullet fillets, squid, beach worms, etc. but a small, live yellowtail or garfish is probably the best bait of all, particularly for larger fish.

Rigs

Unweighted baited hooks, rig No. 2, either single or ganged in two, three or four — depending on the size of the bait — seem to be the most successful.

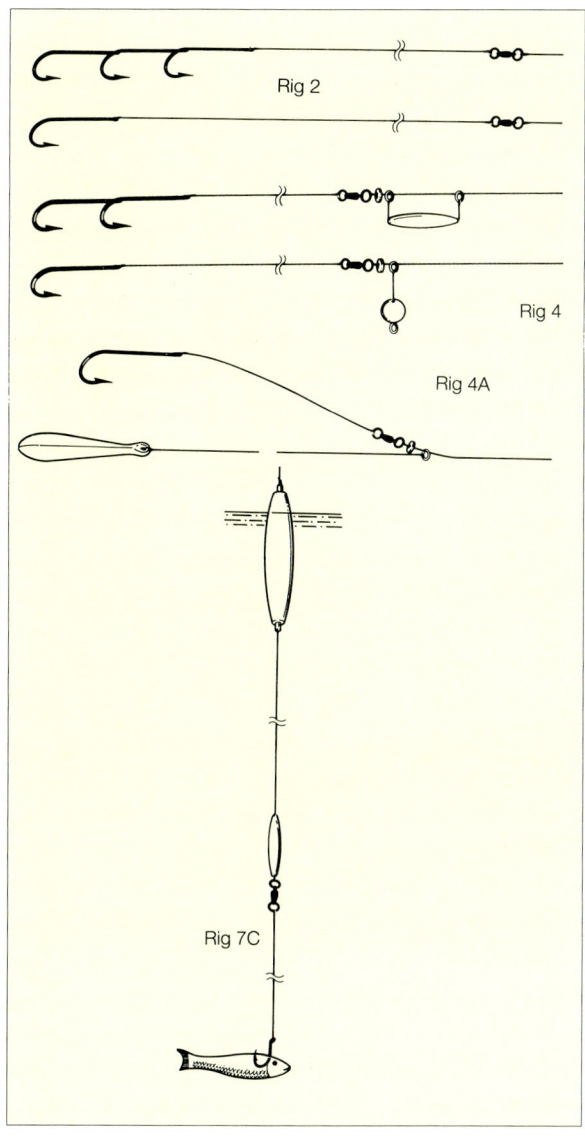

How to hook

Despite its robust display in a school of bait fish and its hectic acrobatics when hooked, the Australian salmon has a soft bite, often feeling more like a gentle pull. When this is felt, a firm lift of the rod will usually bury the hook in the fish's rather soft mouth. From that moment the angler will experience the power and energy of the salmon which can shake a hook free with its head-shaking "tail-walks". No Australian salmon is caught until it is beached or in the boat.

Hint

When a salmon school is biting freely, save bait by using only half pilchards or garfish on a single hook. Always put the hook through the stomach area of the head half and then through the eye. With the tail half, put the hook first through the butt of the tail and then through the stomach section of the cut fish.

Edibility

Australian salmon are generally regarded as poor eating, though there are recipes that improve the coarse dark flesh. Smoked fillets can be very good eating.

Other regulations

The maximum legal catch in Western Australia is 5 salmon per angler per day. Some beaches on the south coast and south-west coast of Western Australia are proclaimed fishing zones at certain times of the year. These dates are currently February 15 to May 31 for the south coast and March 1 to May 31 for the south-west. Professional salmon fishermen have priority on these beaches. Anglers may fish from the beaches or from a boat drifting or at anchor. However, trolling or simply moving about within 800 metres of the shoreline may scare salmon schools and interfere with commercial fishing operations.

If a sinker is necessary to increase casting distance or because of water conditions, it should be a running sinker (rig 4 or 4A). Any of the above baits suspended under a float are taken (rig No. 7C).

SAMSONFISH
Seriola hippos

OTHER NAME: **SEA KINGFISH**

Distinguishing this fish from the amberjack is fraught with
controversy and confusion — to the point where some anglers
grasp for the absurd "samberjack" when they cannot
tell the difference.

Identification

The body shape of this fish is less streamlined in
appearance than the amberjack, mainly because
the profile of the head is steeper from the mouth
to the beginning of the back. (It is even more
exaggerated in immature specimens.) The snout
is blunt. It is much more variable in colouring than
its relative, but alive it is usually more silver and the
back is a bluish-green with a bronze tone (compared
with the purplish-brown of the amberjack), which
fades to a yellowish-white below. After death, the
body may darken and the vertical bands, that are so
apparent in juveniles, tend to reappear. The
preoperculum or front gill cover does not go past
the middle of the eye. For positive identifications,
count the rays in its anal fin: they should number
no more than 17 (19 or more in the amberjack).

Size

The samsonfish reaches about 1.75 metres in
length. The Australian all-tackle record (as at
September, 1988) was 31.5 kilograms.
The minimum legal length for a catch in Western
Australia is 60 centimetres.

Breeding

The samsonfish occurs only in Australian waters
but very little is known of its spawning.

Habits

This fish inhabits coastal waters on the eastern and
western coasts of the continent. Schooling in small
numbers, then separating into pairs or even "loners"
as they grow, the samsonfish will mingle with
amberjacks and yellowtail kingfish. Preferring
reef areas, these fish eat many small bait fish such
as yellowtail, pilchards, sardines, etc., as well as
squid and octopus. They are less common in
shallower reefs than their cousins and usually
remain on the side of the reef where there is the
most current.

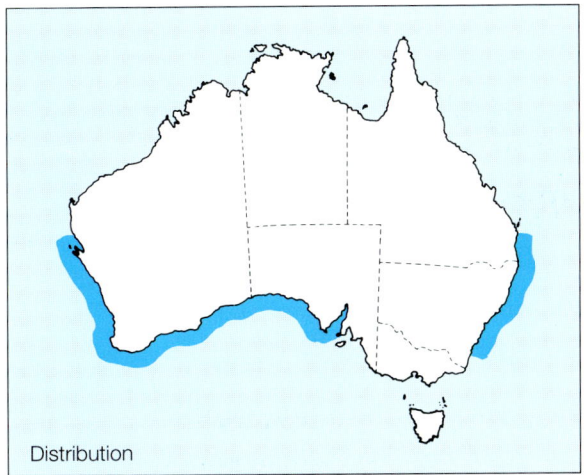
Distribution

Distribution

Reasonably common, particularly in Western Australian water, samsonfish can be found from about Shark Bay to the Yorke Peninsula in South Australia and on the eastern coast from southern Queensland waters to about Bermagui in southern New South Wales.

When to fish

Samsonfish are about most of the year but numbers vary, depending on the location, through the influence of the two currents on the coasts of Australia.

Where to fish

The best areas are beside off shore reefs, near the bottom. There are "hot-spots" around Jurien Bay and Rottnest Island in Western Australia and off the coast around Grafton on the north coast of New South Wales. Local knowledge is of great assistance.

Tackle

A handline can be used when fishing with bait, but by far the best tackle is a medium baitcasting or overhead rod and reel outfit, with about 10 to 15 kilograms breaking-strain line. There is no need to use a wire trace: a heavy nylon leader is sufficient.

Bait

Samsonfish seem to particularly enjoy yellowtail, small trevally and mullet. They will also take fresh dead fish and fillets of tuna, salmon, etc. Squid is also eaten.

The samsonfish will take lures, though they must be the deep-diving type, or jigs, especially when the fish are induced to rise from the bottom with berley.

Rigs

Sea conditions permitting, the lightest running rig No. 3A, 4 or 4A should be used. A hook size of about 6/0, with filleted fish bait or squid, or slightly smaller with live bait, will catch this fish.

How to hook

The samsonfish is a determined feeder, hitting lures hard and taking live or dead bait without hesitation. It derives its name from its strength and staying power, testing the angler's ability to use his gear at its optimum.

Berley

Fish pieces, cubes, etc. make excellent berley. It may be necessary to use some kind of weighted mesh bag to get it down to the bottom in deeper water. Around shallower reefs and in reasonably calm water conditions, the berley may simply be dropped over the side. As the fish follow the berley up, baits should be lifted as well. It is generally when the fish are induced higher that lures or jigging prove very effective.

Edibility

Up to about 10 kilograms, samsonfish are good eating but they must be cleaned and bled the moment they are caught. Skinned fillets, cooked in a light batter, are one easy way to prepare this tasty fish. Larger fish are coarse.

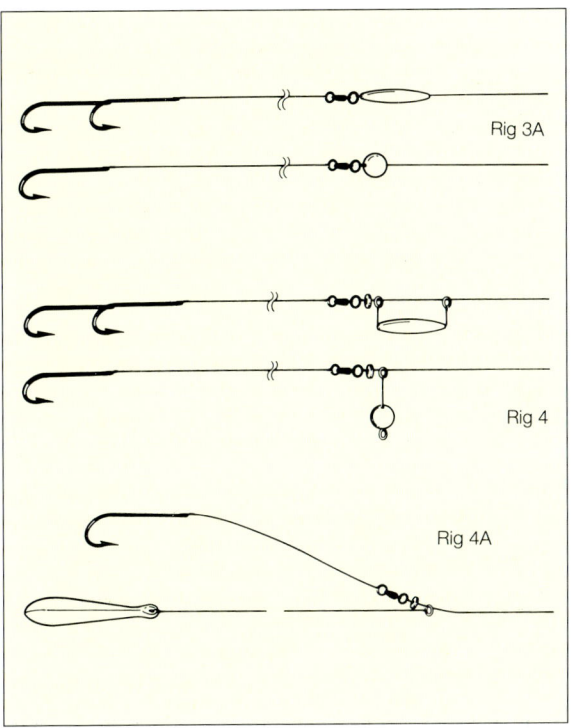

SARATOGA

Scleropages leichardti
Scleropages jardini

OTHER NAMES: **DAWSON RIVER BARRAMUNDI, DAWSON RIVER SALMON, NORTHERN SPOTTED BARRAMUNDI, GULF BARRAMUNDI**

The variety of other names for saratoga is being slowly whittled down and, though there are taxonomic differences, both are a challenge to the angler when sought with suitable equipment. Their rather solid cylindrical shape belies this fish's ability to hit a moving lure or bait with alacrity and leap furiously out of the water to fling lure or hook free.

Identification

The saratoga, whose lineage may well date back some 40 million years, is a herring-like fish with eyes placed for detecting food on the water surface or above. Its back is dark green, fading to a silver-grey around the belly. Its large scales, which are somewhat difficult to remove, especially if the fish is not cleaned quickly after killing, have single or several pink to red spots. This fish has a relatively large up-turned mouth and protruding lower jaw, with two short barbels. It has a small dorsal fin located close to its tail and a quite long anal fin.

Size

The *S. leichardti* is known to grow to almost a metre in length: the *S. jardini* reaches about half this size. The minimum legal length for either saratoga in Queensland is 35 centimetres.

Breeding

There may be some differences in the exact period of spawning by this fish, probably depending on water temperature — the different water temperature tolerance of each sub-species is one reason for the two classifications. We do know that spawning occurs between the end of September to the end of November. The female lays eggs in the low hundreds (compared with the millions deposited by the barramundi) and incubates the newly-hatched young in her mouth until the egg yolk disappears. It adapts to dams and will breed in them.

Habits

The saratoga is unlikely to be found in open running water, preferring still backwaters or billabongs with overhanging bankside vegetation and underwater root systems and weeds. It feeds on small fish, crayfish or yabbies, frogs, large terrestrial insects, etc. It often swims in small numbers in a type of feeding parade, just below the surface and a lure or bait cast near such a group usually results in one fish swooping on it. However, the way a saratoga hits a lure or bait dropped on to the water near the preferred shelter of lilies, tree limbs, etc., suggests that it is also territorial.

Distribution

The *S. leichardti* is in reasonable numbers in the waters of the Dawson River, from which it derives several of its other names, and its tributaries. It has been introduced to other coastal rivers south of this river and perhaps north to the Burdekin. *S. jardini* is the more northerly fish and is present in waters eastwards of the Adelaide River in the Northern Territory, rivers in the Gulf of Carpentaria, and Cape York, except the eastern side.

When to fish

Because of the wet season throughout the saratoga's distribution zone, during which rivers are frequently impossible to fish even when they are accessible, the best time is autumn to the end of winter, and early spring. Because the numbers of saratogas have declined in many of its former waters, anglers should avoid the spawning period (mid-spring onwards) to give this fish a chance to reproduce.

Where to fish

A saratoga is mainly found in sheltered waters, under lily pads, bank vegetation and tree overgrowth and alongside banks in still corners of

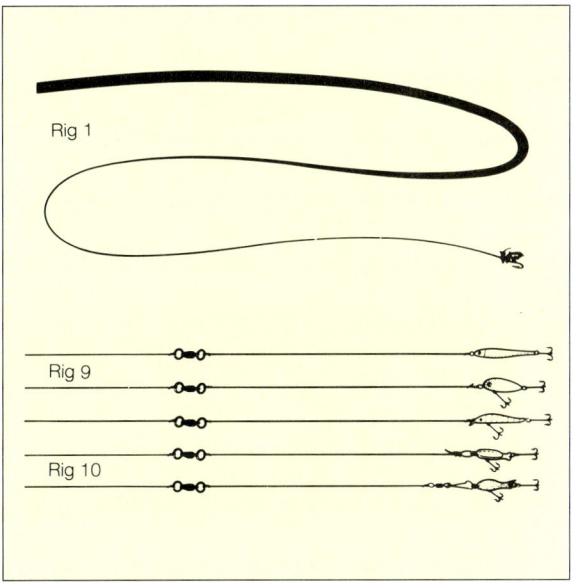

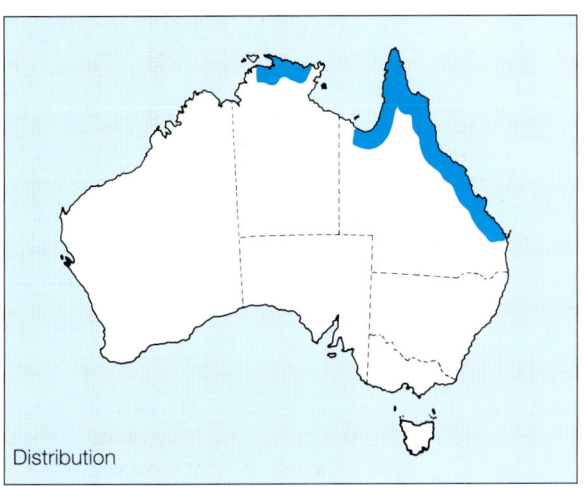
Distribution

rivers, backwaters, lagoons and billabongs.

Tackle

Light or medium threadline and baitcasting rod and reel outfits are adequate, but because the most desirable barramundi may occupy the same water, the medium-weight models may be more prudent. For the same reason, lines and leaders should be stronger and heavier than necessary to enjoy fishing for the saratoga.

Bait

While there is no legal requirement not to use a bait, the saratoga taken on one is likely to be hooked in the throat or deeper, making it extremely difficult to release it alive.

Rigs

The casting rig No. 9 or 10 and unweighted bait rig No. 1 is recommended. Hooks must be very sharp, because the mouth of the saratoga is hard and plate-like. Lures are more likely to hook in its lip area. Almost any surface or shallow-swimming lure or plug will tempt a saratoga. But a real triumph for the serious angler is to catch a saratoga on a fly-fishing outfit.

How to hook

Once a saratoga grabs a lure, firm pressure is required immediately if even the sharpest hook is to penetrate this fish's hard mouth, though if the reaction is quick enough it at least improves the chance of a lure's hook imbedding itself in the lip area.

Hint

Saratoga have a habit of following a lure. Stopping during retrieval may induce a quick grab.

Edibility

Only small saratogas have reasonable eating flesh. The flesh of larger fish is coarse and tasteless, requiring extra treatment and additives to improve it. Furthermore it is very bony.

There are fish with much more flavour than saratoga in many of the rivers it inhabits. For this reason — and because of its reduced numbers — it should be regarded as a catch-and-release fish.

[**Note**: The **lungfish,** *Neoeratodus forsteri,* which inhabits some Queensland freshwater rivers and has been introduced to others — between the Burnett River and the Coomera River south of Brisbane — bears some resemblance to the saratoga. Greenish-brown on top, with a yellow-to-orange abdomen, the lungfish (also called Burnett River Salmon) is of similar shape to the saratoga, though it can grow much larger, about two metres. It has large overlapping scales, limb-like fins and a pointed tail. Its head is small and pointed and it has very small eyes. The lungfish is totally protected by Queensland and Australian law.]

SCORPIONFISH

WIDELY KNOWN AS ROCK COD

Though conceding that the task is almost impossible, the author hopes that the use of their correct name here will encourage anglers to refer to scorpionfish as such instead of rock cods. It is a much more appropriate name. These members of the family *Scorpaenidae* are widespread in Australian waters and possess venomous dorsal spines that can cause painful wounds when they puncture the flesh. While unlikely to cause death, the severity of the poisoning depends on the size of the fish, the depth the spine or spines penetrate and the victim's sensitivity to the toxin. Nevertheless, all scorpionfish are edible, so much so that they are often referred to as "the poor man's lobster".
[**Note:** There are scorpionfish other than those listed which are quite common in tropical waters. They may be called scorpionfish or stingfish (*see* entry) or even gurnard perch. Some references claim that you can distinguish between scorpionfish and stingfish by counting the dorsal spines — 12 on scorpionfish and 13 on stingfish. Others disagree about this taxonomic detail.
The author suggests that anglers need trouble themselves less about counting dorsal spines than avoiding a sting!]

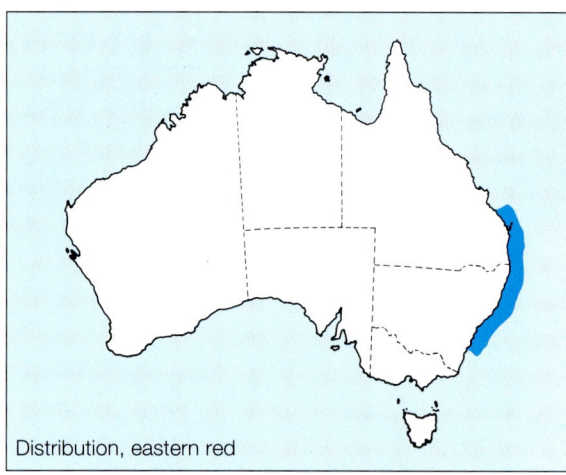

Distribution, eastern red

SCORPIONFISH, EASTERN RED
Scorpaena cardinalis

OTHER NAMES: **RED ROCK-COD, CARDINAL FISH, CORAL COD, PRICKLY HEAT, FIRECOD, BILLY BOUGAIN**

Identification

This fish's body is a solid, oval elongate. There are a few scales on the cheeks but none on the breast. Colours are variable, ranging from an overall bright crimson to a pale brown, with or without dark spots on lower half of body, or mottled blotches of red, white or brown. There is often a black blotch along top of first dorsal fin. Most have small but obvious tentacles on their body and small spines on the head. The red scorpion fish has 12 dorsal spines, all of which are venomous.

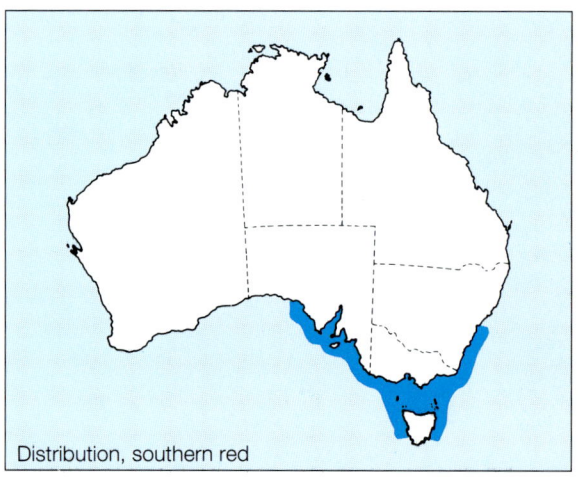

Distribution, southern red

Size

This scorpion-cod grows to 45 centimetres in length.

Distribution

The eastern red scorpion fish is found in coastal and inshore rocky areas from central Queensland to the Jervis Bay area of New South Wales.

SCORPIONFISH, SOUTHERN RED
Scorpaena papillosus

OTHER NAMES: **RED ROCK-COD, CHAINED SCORPIONFISH**

Identification

This fish is very similar to the eastern species, its colour varying from light pink through red to brown. Small specimens may have a purplish mark on back the of head. However, it has no spots on lower half of its body and the breast area is obviously scaled. Less obvious is the absence of body tentacles. The southern red scorpionfish has the same venomous 12 dorsal spines as its eastern counterpart.

Size

This scorpionfish grows to about 40 centimetres in length.

Distribution

The southern red scorpionfish inhabits coastal and estuarine reefs from the New South Wales central coast to Victoria, South Australian and Tasmanian waters. They are most common in Victoria and Tasmania.

SCORPIONFISH, WESTERN RED
Scorpaena sumptuosa

Identification

With a deeper and more hunched-back body, this scorpionfish can be bright red, red-brown or light brown with darker blotches or markings. The familiar 12 dorsal spines are similarly venomous.

Size

This scorpionfish grows to about 40 centimetres

Distribution

This fish is only found around the coastal reefs of south-western Western Australia.

Scorpionfish are usually caught while bait-fishing from the shoreline, or from boats in or near reefs. They neither bite nor fight with any vigour. They usually feel much like a clump of weed on the line when being reeled in.

Edibility

The larger specimens, handled carefully, are excelent eating, fried or grilled. However, when boiled, the superb white flesh may be eaten cold —

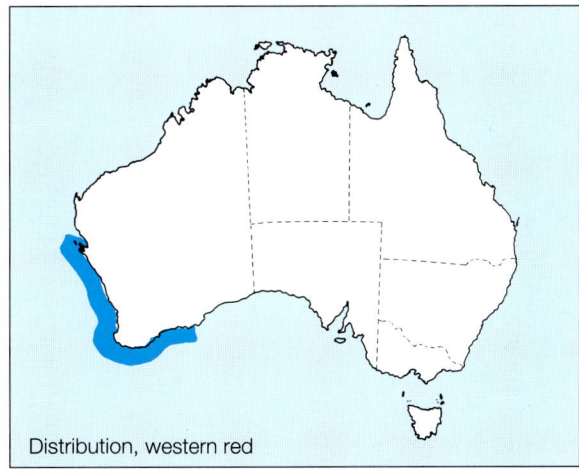

Distribution, western red

and many regard it the equal of crab or lobster.

SEA-PERCH

Sea-perches belong to the family Lutjanidae, which includes snapper, mangrove jack and the red emperor (*see* separate entries). An arbitrary selection is detailed here, based on this fish's wide distribution in Queensland, the Northern Territory and the north-west of Western Australia.

In several cases there are two common names, the use depending on the region. The confusion of other names clearly reflects the angler's experiences of trying to identify these fish. By whatever name, nevertheless, sea perch are generally excellent eating — the very serious exceptions being described in the three entries at the end of this section.

John's sea-perch.

SEA-PERCH, BLUE-SPOTTED OR MAORI
Lutjanus rivolatus

OTHER NAMES: **MAORI BREAM**

Identification

The deep oval-elongate body of the blue-spotted sea-perch varies from red right through the spectrum to olive on its top (some biologists claim such radical colour changes reflect the mood of the fish); a yellow hue can be identified in the vicinity of the lateral line; and the belly is an off-white. Each scale features a blue spot and thin wavy blue lines extend over the head.

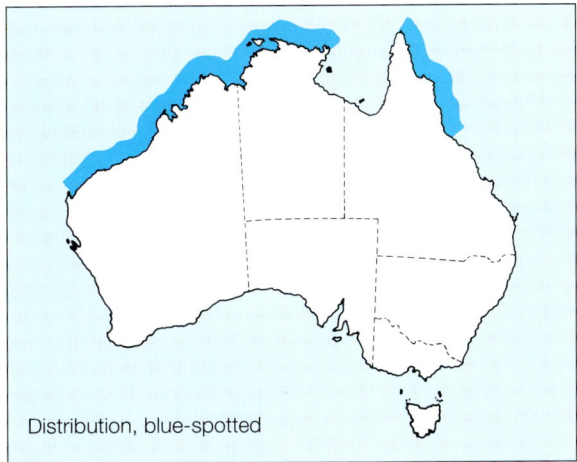

Distribution, blue-spotted

Size

This sea-perch grows to approximately 45 centimetres in length can weigh 10 kilograms.

Distribution

The blue-spotted or maori sea-perch can be encountered when fishing the deeper off-shore reefs, from about Townsville, in Queensland, across the top end, and down to the north-west of Western Australia.

SEA-PERCH, HIGH-BROW
Lutjanus erythropterus

OTHER NAMES: **RED BREAM, RED JEW, SMALL-MOUTHED NANNYGAI**

This fish (sometimes listed as *L. anguineus*) is confused with the scarlet or saddle-tailed sea-perch, especially in young or immature specimens, which bear the band through the eye, the prominent saddle on the back between the dorsal fin and tail, as well as narrow orange lines on the body. In these juveniles, the saddle has a faint silver edge. In more mature fish the silver is not apparent and the saddle rarely visible,

Identification

The body, which is crimson over the dorsal area, fades to a lighter shade towards the belly. There can be a deeper almost red colouring between the eyes and the red dorsal, pectoral, anal and caudal fins have a dark grey to black edge — a feature that is missing on their scarlet or saddle-tailed relatives.

The profile of the head of the high-brow is convex. The mouth of the saddle-tailed sea-perch is much smaller than the mouth of a scarlet sea-perch (hence one of its other names).

Breeding

Little is known.

Size

This fish is said to reach about 10 kilograms and 45 centimetres in length.

Distribution

A more northerly species, this fish prefers the more off-shore reefs in the waters from around Mackay, in Queensland, around the top end coastline and then down to the north-west area of Western Australia.

SEA-PERCH, MOSES OR RUSSELL'S
Lutjanus russelli

OTHER NAMES: **FINGERMARK BREAM, RED BREAM, RUSSELL'S SNAPPER**

Identification

The body is oval-elongate and its colours — in fish caught from off-shore waters — are variable, from violet-crimson to reddish-brown. Inshore species may be a lighter shade with a definite greenish tinge. The stomach area is silvery to off-white. Moses sea-perches are distinguished by the six to eight yellow-gold lines running longitudinally along

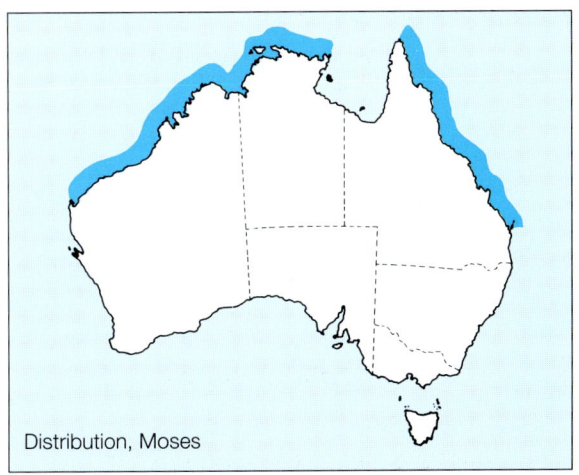

Distribution, Moses

the body, the dark oval spot below the middle of the dorsal fin, and the yellow to orange fins.

Size
This fish grows to about 22 centimetres in length.

Breeding
Little is known.

Distribution
This sea perch, which prefers inshore reefs and occasionally estuaries, can be found from the waters of southern Queensland, north and across the top end, and south to the North-West Cape in Western Australia.

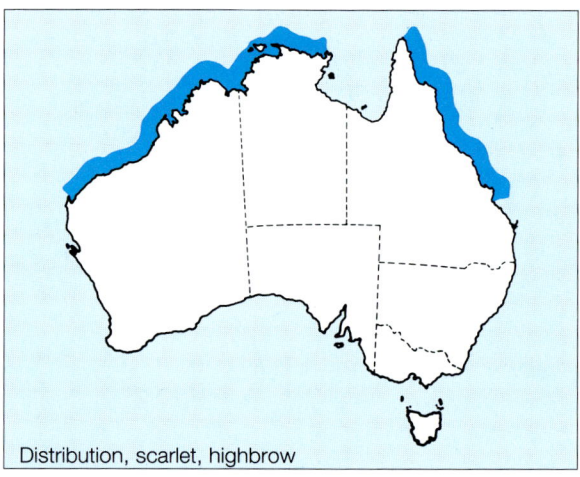
Distribution, scarlet, highbrow

SEA-PERCH, SCARLET or SADDLE-TAILED
Lutjanus malibaricus

OTHER NAMES: **RED BREAM, RED JEW, RED SNAPPER, NANNYGAI, LARGE-MOUTHED NANNYGAI, RED EMPEROR**

Scarlet sea-perch.

This fish is frequently mistaken for a red emperor. Moreover, its identification is not helped by it being marketed as a red emperor!

Identification
The scarlet sea perch, with its deep oval-elongate body, bears a remarkable resemblance to the red emperor. The body is also a uniform scarlet to crimson colour, compared with the salmon-pink to red colour of the emperor. In immature or juvenile specimens there is a broad dark-reddish band extending from the snout through the eye; a purplish-black saddle between the dorsal fin and the tail; and narrow orange lines on the body. In larger fish the saddle is faint. The profile of the head is straight or very slightly concave. All fins are about the same colour as the body (in red emperors

the top lobe of the tail usually has a red to black edge). A sure identification is the number of rays in the anal fin : the scarlet sea perch has a maximum of 9 compared with a minimum of 10 for the red emperor.

Size
Sea-perch grow to about 12 to 14 kilograms and 60 centimetres in length.

Breeding
Little is known.

Distribution
This is a tropical fish and though the occasional one is encountered in more southern waters, the scarlet or saddle-tailed sea-perches are more likely to be found north from Rockhampton in Queensland, around the northern coastline, and south to the North-West Cape in Western Australia.

SEA-PERCH, SPOTTED-SCALE or JOHN'S
Lutjanus johni

OTHER NAME: **RED BREAM**

Identification
With an elongate and smoothly oval body (a shallower shape than other sea-perches), the colouring of this fish is a silvery-green to olive-green, occasionally with a pinkish tinge. Dark lines run along the body above the lateral line, the result of a dark spot in the middle of these scales. In

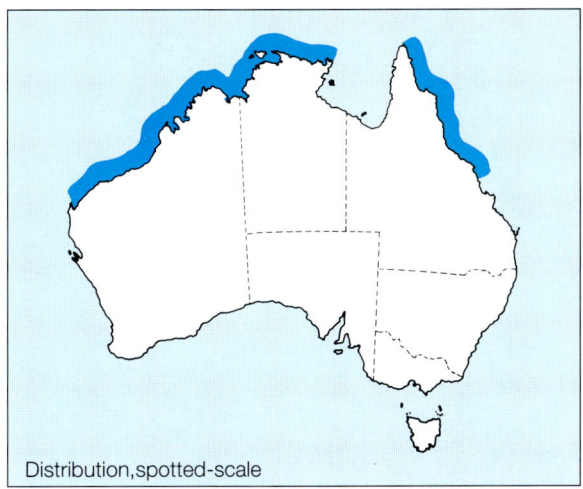

Distribution, spotted-scale

juveniles, a large black spot with a silver-white edge is clearly evident on the upper body, below the soft dorsal fin. This can be very faint on large fish.

Breeding
Little is known.

Size
The John's or spotted-scale sea-perch grows to about 40 centimetres in length.

Distribution
This is another sea-perch that is more common to the northern reef waters, from about Mackay in Queensland, around the coast of the top end, and down to the north-west of Western Australia.

Habits
The majority of sea-perches prefer the deeper off-shore reefs but some — the scarlet or saddle-tailed, Moses or Russell's and spotted scale or John's — are also caught around inshore reefs. The various species all school and some intermingle. All are carnivorous fish that feed on a variety of small fish, crustaceans and molluscs.

When to fish
Most sea-perches are present throughout the year. Sea and weather conditions, rather than the seasons, influence the prospects of a catch .

Where to fish
Sea-perches are more likely to be found along the edges of reefs and between openings in reefs, as well as near niggerheads scattered over a sand or rubble bottom.
The Moses or Russell's can be found hunting close

inshore and even in estuaries that have rock or reef formations.

Tackle
Most sea-perches are caught while fishing for other species, and a handline is quite practical, preferably with a breaking-strain of about 30 kilograms. A gunwale-mounted deck winch or reel, or a 2-metre boat rod with a winch type of reel, can also be used. So can medium to heavy single-handed threadline or baitcasting outfits with 12 to 15 kilogram breaking-strain lines. Lines of such strength are suggested because some of the other species that can be encountered may be very large. Strong hooks between 6/0 and 8/0 and a wire trace are also recommended. Medium-weight threadline or baitcasting outfits can be used.

Bait
Whole fish (if small) or halves of pilchards, garfish, mullet, etc. can be effective, as can be the fillets of almost any fish, squid and octopus.

Rigs
The bottom rig No. 6 with a sinker about half a metre below the bait can work well. One or two droppers may be used. The fish will take bait cast-and-retrieved or jigged. And they are not averse to snapping a variety of lures.

How to hook
The Lutjanus family are sometimes called snappers — and when they decide on a bait that is generally how they take it. When the hook is felt they soon demonstrate their strength and power and must be kept clear of rocky line-cutting habitats.

Edibility
Almost all sea-perches (see exceptions below) are esteemed table fish. Being a tropical fish, they should be cleaned and placed on ice as soon as they are caught. Small ones may be baked but the flesh is so firm and full of flavour that it can be prepared by most methods.

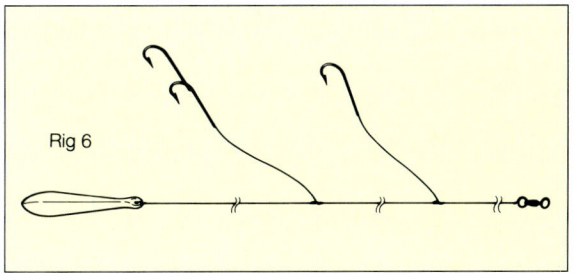

Rig 6

DANGEROUS SEA-PERCHES

(These fish must *not* be eaten — *see also* Ciguetara poisoning .)
The following sea-perches, if caught in Queensland waters,
should not be eaten. They have been implicated as the
cause of **Ciguetera poisoning**.

Sea-perch, chinaman-fish.

SEA-PERCH, CHINAMAN-FISH
Symphorus nematophorus

OTHER NAMES: **THREAD-FINNED SEA-PERCH, GALLOPER**

Identification
The profile of this fish is smoothly convex and
there is a deep groove or pit extending in front of
the eye. Its spined dorsal fin is lower than its soft
dorsal. Body-colour is a uniform red-orange with
dark, transverse patches. (Younger fish may be
brighter and have wavy blue lines along the body;
the fourth-to-seventh rays of the dorsal fin are long
and filament-like).
There is a low, scaly sheath on the dorsal and anal
fins. The tail is broad, almost straight, and it
displays blue spots.

Size
The chinaman-fish grows to about 60 centimetres
in length and can weigh about 15 kilograms.

Distribution
This fish is a common species in the reef waters of
North Queensland, from depths of about five to 50
metre. It is also found across the Northern Territory
and in the north-west region of Western Australia.
[**Note:** This fish is known as the **chinaman snapper**
in the Northern Territory and Western Australia.]

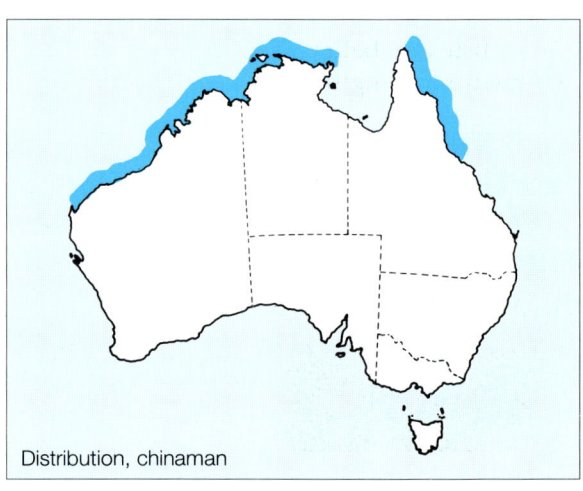

Distribution, chinaman

304

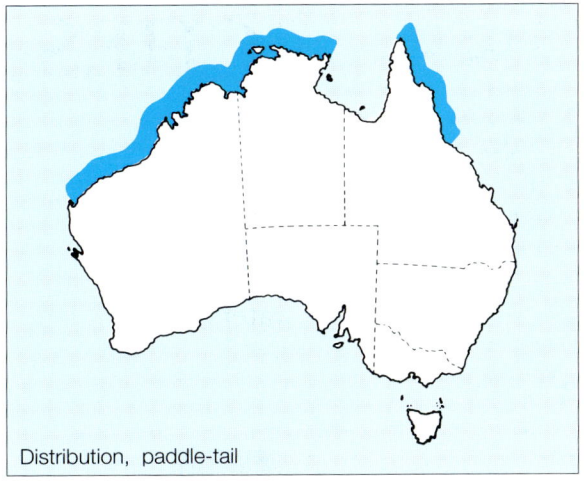

Distribution, paddle-tail

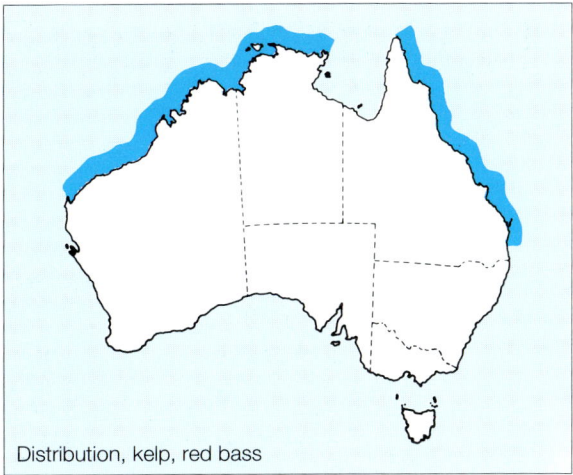

Distribution, kelp, red bass

SEA-PERCH, PADDLE-TAIL
Lutjanus gibbus

OTHER NAMES: **RED SNAPPER**

Identification

This fish is almost instantly recognised by the fairly obvious concave profile above the eye, creating a distinct hump-back appearance. The colour of the head and body is uniformly red to scarlet, slightly darker on some along the dorsal. The fins are dark red and the margins of the soft dorsal and anal fins are white. On some specimens, a yellowish patch has been noted on the top lip, over the eye and at the base of the pectoral fin.

The paddle-tail is, however, best identified by its broad tail, which is prominently forked but which has rounded lobes. The upper lobe is larger.

Size

These fish are believed to grow to about 60 centimetres in length.

Distribution

Paddle tail sea-perch may only occur in the most northern areas of the Queensland coast, but they inhabit waters along the Papua-New Guinea coastline, the Northern Territory and the north-west of Western Australia. It is a reef-dwelling species.

[**Note:** This fish is known as the **humpback snapper** in the Northern Territory and the north-west waters of Western Australia.

KELP SEA-PERCH or RED BASS
Lutjanus bohar

OTHER NAME: **KELP BREAM**

Identification

This fish has the typical sea-perch body, and its colour is a very dark red to red-brown along the dorsal area, from the tip of the snout to the tail. The sides are a lighter, rosy red. The belly is a silvery pink. Below the lateral line, and parallel to

Paddle-tail sea-perch.

Kelp sea-perch or red bass

it, there are some faint pink bands running back to the tail. There can also be a blush of yellow on the cheeks and throat. The spined dorsal fin is dark scarlet to black but always with a black base and edge; the pelvic fin, more than half of the anal fin, and the tail are a blackish red and the upper half of the pectoral fin is dark red.

This fish can be distinguished from a similar-looking relative — the mangrove jack — by the presence of the nostrils in a conspicuous groove or pit that extends forward from the eye.

Size

Kelp perch or red bass can be caught up to almost a metre in length and weighing about 12 kilograms.

Distribution

More common in the waters of the Great Barrier Reef, it can be found among the shoals and reefs of north Queensland. It is often caught on the outer reefs when trolling, employing a lure, or baitfishing for coral trout. Yet it has been caught as far south as Double Island Point and Cape Moreton.

[**Note:** This fish is called a **two-spot snapper** in the Northern Territory and north-west WA.]

SERGEANT BAKER
Aulopus purpurissatus

Though this fish is common enough for anglers to come across it sooner or later, the sergeant baker cannot be classified as either a sport fish or a desirable food fish.

Identification
These fish have an elongate shape with a well-developed dorsal fin, their colouring is mottled with blotches in pink, red and a purplish-blue. The dorsal fin and tail have oblique bands of crimson on a yellowish-pink background and the fins are mottled and spotted with an orange-red and yellow. The male has a long filament to the front of the first dorsal fin and the second dorsal fin is almost absent. Its mouth is capacious.

Size
The sergeant baker grows to about 74 centimetres.

Breeding
Little is known.

Habits
These fish inhabit rock and coral reefs and adjacent sand or rock rubble sea floors. During the day they appear to generally "rest" on a rock or rock shelf off the bottom, observing the surrounding area. They do not seem to move any distance. Any small fish or crustacean is acceptable food.

Distribution
The sergeant baker can be found in inshore waters as shallow as two metres and on reefs to more than 100 metres. Their range extends from southern Queensland, along the New South Wales coast to the eastern and northern coast of Tasmania, as well as across Victoria, South Australia and Western Australia, to about Coral Bay.

When to fish
Anglers are likely to catch one of these fish at any time of the year while rock fishing or fishing off shore reefs for other more desirable species.

Where to fish
Try fishing over or alongside reefs close to rubble floors or sandy areas.

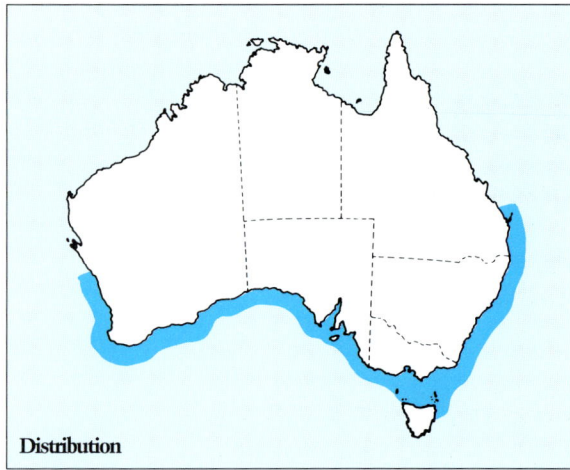

Distribution

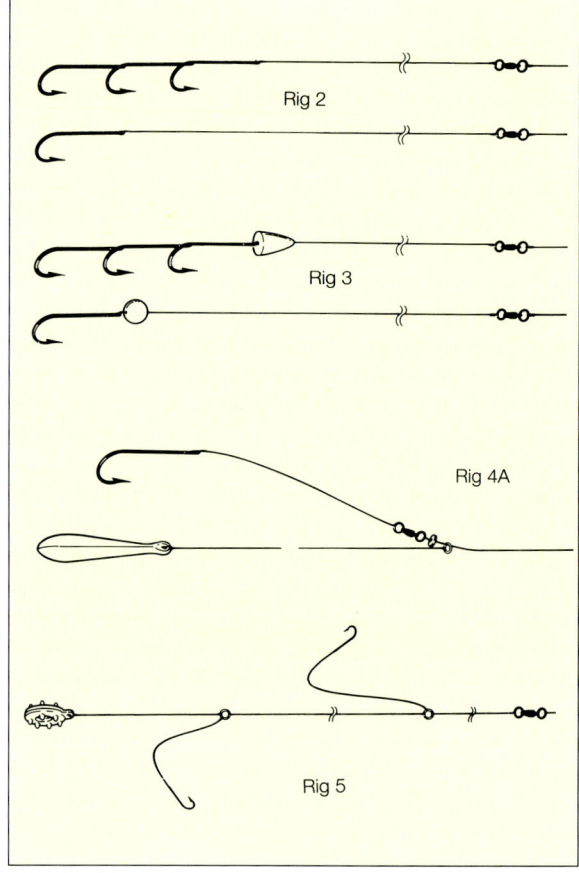

Tackle
These fish, which are invariably an unwelcome catch, are caught on handlines or rods.

Bait
Sergeant baker will take small fish such as yellowtail, pilchards, fillets of almost any fish, squid strips, prawns, etc.

Rigs
The rigs that are usually used for bottom fishing from boats or from the rocks, such as No. 4A and 5, will attract sergeant baker and, in shallow water, the unweighted or lightly weighted rigs No. 2, 3 or 4A will work. This fish is susceptible to a slowly-retrieved twister type of lure.

How to hook
Very often the first sign that a sergeant baker has taken the bait is a shaking or rattling feeling when it finds itself hooked. This fish is not a fighter.

Edibility
For a fish with firm white flesh (and a number of bones), it is remarkably tasteless, requiring sauce or dressing for those prepared to eat it.

SNAPPER
Chrysophrys auratus

OTHER NAME: COCKNEY, RED BREAM, SQUIRE, PINKIE, RUGGER, PINK SNAPPER, OLD MAN SNAPPER, REDDIE, OLD MAN RED

As a young "cockney" growing up in a harbour or bay, snapper are regarded as nuisance bait-stealers of the first order; as a "red bream" of legal size they make a good pan-fish; as a "squire" they should have been bigger; and finally, as a mature "snapper" they are a prized catch. They are all, of course, snapper, even though this fine fish has been given a name for its various stages of growth. What it is not, however, is a "schnapper", as so many restaurants (and others who cannot spell) would have us believe.

Identification

A snapper is unlikely to be mistaken for any other fish. When taken fresh from the water, the body is a glowing pink or deepish red with a scattering of blue spots that tend to be less distinct in older fish. The fins are pink, except for the pelvic and anal fins, which are a paler shade to creamy white. The well-known hump or bump of the forehead of older snapper may be a barely discernable rise or an exaggerated ugly protrusion — in some large fish it is hardly present at all. On older fish, the mouth is fleshy and pronounced, with four prominent strong canine teeth on the front of the upper jaw and six on the front of the lower jaw.

Size

Snapper can exceed 20 kilograms and 1.3 metres

in length in Australian waters, although this size is extremely rare (and probably only achieved by 50 years of age). Snapper are slow-growing fish. Research suggests that a South Australian snapper is probably 20 years old when it reaches 10 kilograms, growth rate being related to both the water temperature and the variety of food. Snapper from the north coast of New South Wales may well grow faster.

Despite views to the contrary, more large snapper are taken by recreational anglers from inshore waters than by professional fishermen working off-shore.

In Western Australia, the minimum legal length for a catch of snapper is 41 centimetres; the minimum size is 38 centimetres in South Australia; in Victoria it is 27 centimetres; in New South Wales the minimum size is 28 centimetres; and in Queensland the minimum size is 25 centimetres.

Breeding

Snapper reach sexual maturity when they are about 28 to 30 centimetres in length, or three to five years of age. Any angler who retains any below the legal sizes is reducing future stocks. These remarkable fish change sex during their lives! Biologists are aware that a small percentage are hermaphrodites, which change sex — males becoming females — at puberty, between three and four years.

The fish move inshore to spawn in about August/September — later along the southern coastline — which they complete by mid-summer, depending on the water temperature, about 18°C to 23°C being preferred.

Habits

The snapper inhabit inshore rocky areas and off

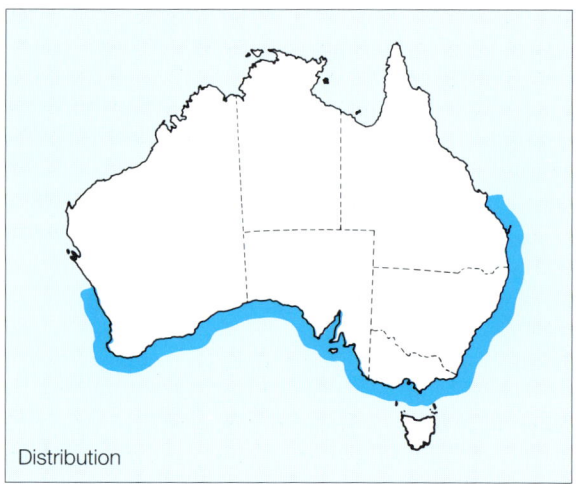

Distribution

Never too heavy to lift if you've caught it — one large snapper.

shore reefs to a depth of 200 metres, but large ones will occasionally enter estuaries and harbours. (The Gulf of South Australia and Port Phillip Bay are renowned for seasonal snapper runs). Their ideal habitat is a reef or broken reef area with a rubble bottom or other underwater obstruction such as a wreck or artificial reef. Such structures are particularly popular when they occur in relatively shallow waters.

The fish school and show considerable migration movements from one reef to another. South Australian research has shown that "middle-aged" snapper seem to stay away from the shallower gulf waters between the age of 5 and 12 years.

The same research suggests that snapper prefer prawns while young, but by the time they reach between 30 and 50 centimetres, they have developed more of an appetite for blue crabs. The older fish continue to eat blue crabs, sand crabs and molluscs, with a preference for mussels. Squid and small fish seem a minor part of this fish's diet. Its eating habits may be governed by availability, though research elsewhere indicates that crustaceans and molluscs are important foods, with small fish, squid, etc. a secondary part of their diet.

Distribution

Snapper range from about Cape Manifold in

Queensland south along the coast of New South Wales across Victoria, South Australia and north along the Western Australian coast north to about Coral Bay. Their numbers are fewer in Tasmanian waters.

When to fish

Snapper can be fished for throughout the year, sea conditions permitting. The shore-based anglers, or inshore boat anglers, will find them more readily from early spring through to autumn. It must be added, however, that while such timing is in general true, there are resident or visiting snapper in some areas throughout the year.

Heavy seas which pound the coastline and rip out conjevoi and drag out crabs from rocks, attract snapper inshore. Fishing from the rocks as the ocean is abating can produce large fish.

While acknowledging that there are exceptions, the accepted prime times for fishing inshore for snapper, at least close inshore or off the rocks, and in many bays, is the dawn — prior to sunrise and for about an hour after sun-up — and in the mid to late afternoon until after dark, and into the night. High tides that occur during these periods are also considered important because the fish will move in on a rising tide to feed. Snapper from deeper off-shore reefs are less conscious of time but usually bite better towards the top of the tide.

Where to fish

For small boat anglers the sides of reefs or around underwater structures with a sand or rubble area surrounding them are always worth trying. Modern electrical depth sounders, depending on their cost, will not only clearly delineate any underwater formations but they will also indicate fish by a series of dashes or other marks. This can save a great deal of time in locating the right areas. Inshore boat anglers can, depending on sea conditions, seek snapper close to the shoreline where there are deep, rocky bottoms and along the fringes of reefs jutting out from platforms or headlands.

Land-based anglers can find snapper off headlands or platforms where there are broken rocks over sand or rubble bottoms, and where there are holes within casting distance. Don't overlook those reefs or rock formations that can be found and fished at the ends of many beaches. In bays and gulfs, scallop and mussel beds are always likely to produce snapper.

Tackle

A handline on a caster or on a winch-type of reel fitted to the gunwale is practical, with the line being of from 15 to 20 kilograms breaking-strain. But much more convenient are rods about 1.8 to 2.5 metres, fitted with a threadline or baitcasting reel and spooled with line of 8 to 10 kilograms breaking-strain: they allow you to cast to the edges of white water and to fish with a minimum of weight.

If fishing from the shoreline, the rod should be between 3.5 and 4 metres long, of a style to correctly mount a sidecast, threadline or overhead reel with line of about 8 to 10 kilograms breaking-strain. All rods should have a medium-fast or multi-taper action, with some power towards the butt. A wire trace is unnecessary but a leader at least 50 per cent stronger than the main line is a necessary precaution.

Single, ganged or snooded pairs of extra strong hooks between 4/0 and 6/0 will handle most snapper, the size depending largely on the bait you wish to use.

Bait

If the scientists are right — and practical experience in this case seems to bear it out — crabs are the number one bait choice. However, the snapper also seem to enjoy small yellowtail, whole or half pilchards, mullet, tuna, mackerel and sweep fillets (which should be fresh). They like fresh bottle squid, whether live or dead, octopus tentacles, conjevoi, large beach worms, etc.

Snapper coaxed to the surface with berley will strike savagely at the soft plastic, wriggly twister-type of lure if it is cast and retrieved slowly or jigged near the bottom in deeper reefs.

Berley

Berley will improve the angler's chances of attracting snapper. Almost any mixture of prawns, fish pieces, crushed crabs and sea urchins work. Boiled rice with a can of fish-flavoured cat food stirred in is excellent. Commercially available "berley bombs" can be used on deepwater reefs, but the berley conconction can be dispensed with a weighted onion bag on shallower reefs.

For inshore waters, balls of the concoction — especially the soggy rice mixture — can be dropped in the water.

Rigs

The weight of a snapper rig is important. In deep water this means a sinker as light as possible to reach the bottom on the running rig No. 4A. This will also work in bays and gulf waters, although rig

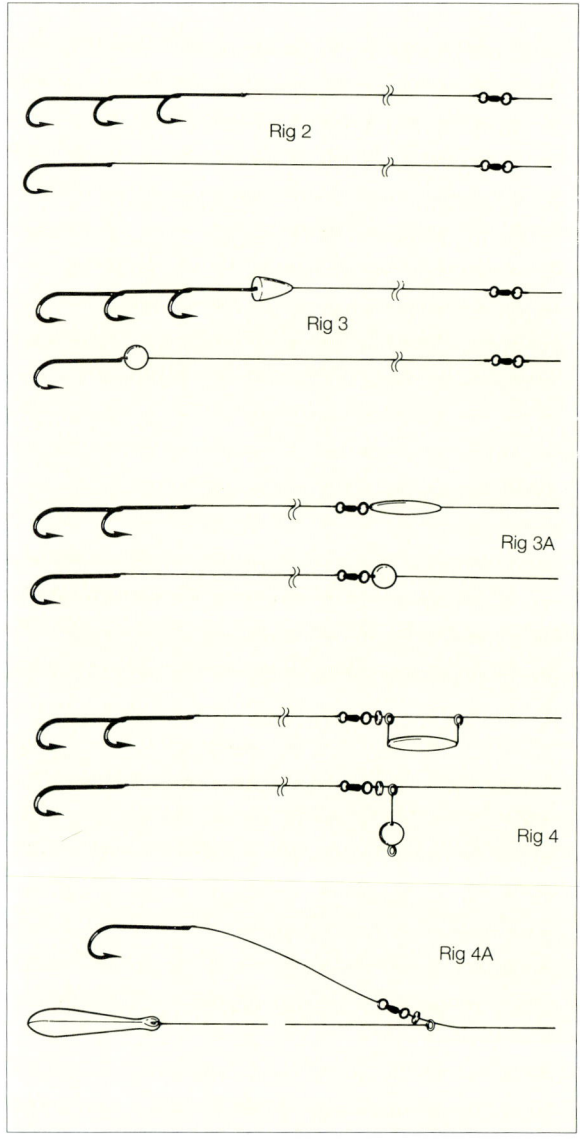

Rig 2

Rig 3

Rig 3A

Rig 4

Rig 4A

is another method of giving it some animation.

The snapper tends to mouth a bait so an over-anxious angler can easily pull it from the fish's mouth. If you suspect a snapper bite, then allow the fish to move off, perhaps for as much as 15 to 20 seconds, before firmly setting the hook. The fish caught on bait drifted in a berley trail show more alacrity in taking the bait.

The snapper will run hard and it will try to dive to deeper water, but rarely will it take refuge in rocks like some other reef fish. The angler who carelessly gives this fish too much loose line will often pay the price with the fish running around a snag. Snapper fight powerfully and they can invariably be identified by the series of bumps they transmit up the line. Provided tension is maintained, the snapper can be brought to the gaff or net or swum up on to the rocks.

Hint

Snapper eat fish head first. Small yellowtail, whole pilchards, etc. or half these and other fish (garfish for example, with the beak removed) can be fished most effectively if they are impaled on the hook so that the head is at the bend of the hook (the head is on the bottom hook on ganged or snooded hooks).

Sea urchins are extremely successful baits for snapper, especially during the inshore spawning migration. Fillets of European carp and eels from freshwater can also work.

When snapper are berleyed towards the surface from inshore reefs they will take lures and saltwater flies. Fitted with stronger hooks, the freshwater trout lures — Baltic minnow or Baltic flash — are effective jigs, as are many other minnow-style lures.

Edibility

The price that snapper bring at fish markets (or restaurants) reflects their value as table fare. They are excellent eating and will not disappoint, regardless of cooking method.

Other regulations

A mixed bag limit (10 fish per angler) applies to several fish, including snapper, in Western Australia. Check the regulations locally.

In South Australia 15 snapper per angler per day is the maximum catch permitted for fish measuring between 38 and 60 centimetres. If the fish exceed 60 centimetres then only 2 per angler are permitted. A bag limit for boats is also regulated, so check locally.

No. 4 (the type of sinker depending on the bottom) with a long trace can be very effective. If fishing from rocks, an unweighted or lightly weighted rig (No. 2, 3 or 3A) can be used. These rigs are also for inshore reefs and for fishing for snapper raised by berley.

How to hook

Snapper prefer a moving bait. So, success is more likely with a slow-moving bait while drifting in a boat or, if moored, a bait that is moving in the current.

If this is not possible, then try retrieving your bait with a slow, stop-start cranking action when fishing from the rocks or from a boat inshore. Suspending a bait beneath a float about a metre off the bottom

SNAPPER, LONG-SPINED
Argyrops spinifer

OTHER NAMES: **BOWEN SNAPPER,
FRYING-PAN SNAPPER**

Identification
This snapper has a deep pink colour with a silvery sheen that fades to a lighter shade on the lower sides and belly. The dorsal fin and tail are a pink to orange with red margins. The long dorsal spines are red and the pelvic and pectoral fins are pale pink to white. Each row of scales creates a broken, pinkish line. In profile it has a deep body and a steep head profile, fractionally convex near the eye. It is as beautiful as the better-known snapper, to which it is closely related.

Size
This snapper grows to about 50 centimetres.

Long-spined snapper.

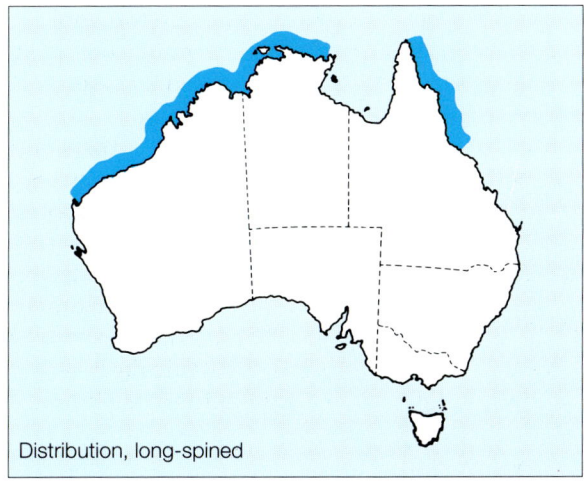
Distribution, long-spined

Breeding
Nothing definite is known.

Habits
Very similar to its relative, inhabiting reefs and rocky areas.

Distribution
This fish may be caught along the Queensland coastline and inhabits the waters of northern Australia and at least as far south down the West Australian coastas Exmouth.

The long-spined snapper is sometimes caught while fishing for other larger fish species on lines and hooks unsuited to its size.

Edibility
The flesh of the long-spined snapper is the equal of its relative and its size makes it a prized fish to serve whole.

[**Note:** Another snapper rarely caught, due mainly to its size, is the deep-sea snapper (*Dentex tumifrons*), also a shimmering pink fish, from the northern and north-western waters.]

313

SOLE

About 20 species of these flatfishes, similar to flounder, live in Australian waters. With the possible exception of two, soles can be distinguished from flounder by the absence of a separate tail; a sole's tail is part of its long dorsal and anal fins along the sides of its body which tapers to a terminal point. Members of the family *Soleidae* are usually more oval and are called, simply, soles. The slimmer members of the family *Cynoglossidae* are called tongue-soles. Soles can change their colour to suit the sand or silt bottom of the water. They can also camouflage themselves by displaying the patterns or colours of weeds or sea grasses in the area.

Many are less than 20 centimetres long, but anglers fishing for whiting may catch a worthwhile size on occasions. They can also be hooked when fishing for flounder because they inhabit the same waters. It can also happen when fishing for bait fish, particularly when the bait is rolled along the bottom. The largest soles are the **black**, **harrowed**, **peacock**, **narrow-barred** and **spotted** (all of which may be known by other names in some areas). They may reach a length of 27 to 35 centimetres. The **lemon**, **big-eye** and **patterned** tongue-soles grow to a size about 30 centimetres.

In Western Australia and Victoria, the minimum legal length for sole of any kind is 20 centimetres; in Tasmania the minimum is 23 centimetres.

All soles are excellent eating.

STINGFISH

WIDELY DESCRIBED AS GURNARD PERCH

The name stingfish is preferred rather than the often used gurnard perch. This is in line with a CSIRO reference. The name gurnard perch may have been derived from the wing-like pectoral fins, in some ways similar to those on members of the Triglidae family, the gurnards, and the perch-like shape of this fish.

Even an experienced angler is likely to call the stingfish a scorpionfish — if not a "rock-cod"! — and names considerably less scientific when pricked by one.

The fish looks much like a scorpionfish, although a side by side comparison shows that the stingfish has much larger eyes and much longer dorsal spines. The spines also protrude further beyond the rays of the dorsal than they do on the scorpionfish, where the spines hardly extend beyond the rays. Most stingfish have a very light pink, yellowish-to-light tan or mid-tan base colour with spotted or blotchy blackish brown bands across it.

STINGFISH
Neosebastus pandus

OTHER NAME: GURNARD PERCH

The fish is found in inshore reefs and weed areas of South Australia and Western Australia. It grows to 50 centimetres in length.

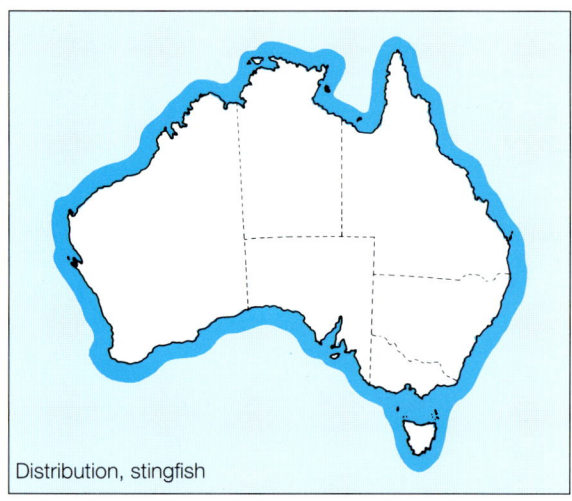

Distribution, stingfish

STINGFISH, BLACK-SPOTTED
Neosebastus nigropunctatus

OTHER NAME: BLACK-SPOTTED GURNARD PERCH

Inhabiting the deeper inshore reefs of South Australia and Western Australia, it grows to 40 centimetres in length.

STINGFISH, COMMON
Neosebastus scorpaenoides pereoides

OTHER NAME: COMMON GURNARD PERCH

This fish is common in Tasmanian waters but it is also found on coastal reefs off the central and southern coasts of New south Wales, Victoria and South Australia. Grows to about 50 centimetres.

STINGFISH, ORANGE-BANDED
Neosebastus entaxis

This is a common stingfish of the northern reefs of north-western Australia and tropical northern waters. It reaches about 40 centimetres in length.

STINGFISH, RED
Aholi colenus pereoides

OTHER NAME: RED GURNARD PERCH, OCEAN PERCH

This stingfish is found in the deeper off shore reefs of the central and southern coast of New South Wales, Victoria, Tasmania, South Australia and Western Australia. It grows to 50 centimetres in length.

Edibility
The stingfish have white firm flesh that is edible and similar in taste to scorpionfish.

Warning
Utmost care must be taken in killing and cleaning scorpionfish and stingfish. Even when the fish is dead, the spine an inflict a stab and release the venom. Prior to cleaning it is a good precaution to remove the dorsal and anal fins. Secateurs or side-cutters are excellent for this purpose.

SWEEP

There are three sweep along the southern coastline of Australia. Many do not realise that the juveniles that are sometimes encountered in numbers, when fishing for bait fish off the ocean rocks, can grow to a respectable size. The power of the sweep's fight can be judged by the surprising strength of the small ones when they are hooked.

SWEEP, BANDED
Scorpis georgianus

OTHER NAME: **TRUMPETER SWEEP**

Identification
Like all members of the sweep family, the body of this fish is deeply elliptical. As a rule, they are about twice as long as they are deep. They are a dark, greyish-brown, with a lighter-coloured belly. There are broad, darker, vertical bars on the head and body, extending into a prominent dorsal fin. The tail is dark and slightly forked. Juveniles are brownish-coloured, with orange bands, though this fades away to the adult colouring when they settle on a reef. There is a yellow tone to their lip and lower jaw. Scales are small and easily removed.

Size
The banded sweep grows to about 45 centimetres in length.

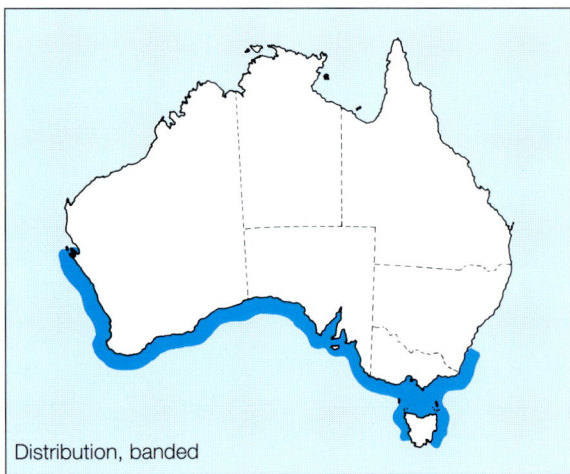

Distribution, banded

Breeding

Little is known, but sweep probably breed inshore or in estuaries.

Habits

A common inhabitant of the coastal reefs, this sweep can be found in large schools. They have a preference for stirred-up water and the turbulent underwater movement that can be found around rocks and reefs. These carnivorous fish eat prawns, shellfish, pipis, pieces of squid and fish, including pieces of their own kind. Often they will show a preference for pieces of dark-fleshed fish.

SWEEP, SEA
Scorpis aequipinnis

Distribution

They are fairly common south from about Coral Bay in Western Australia and across the Great Australian Bight as far as Kangaroo Island.

Identification

The sea-sweep is similar in shape to the banded sweep, but minus the latter's distinct bands. Its base colour ranges from a grey-black in western waters to a dark blue in the eastern range, both with a lighter grey shade over the belly. The lower lip and jaw have a yellow hue. The sea-sweep's tail is more forked than the banded sweep.

Size

This is the largest of the sweeps. It grows to a length of 60 centimetres.

Breeding

Little is known.

Habits

Sea-sweeps have a preference for deep off shore reefs, where schools of them may be encountered. They will be found in deep water with some turbulence close to rocks and offshore islands. Their food intake is similar to the banded sweep.

Distribution

This fish can be found from about Shark Bay in Western Australia across the southern coastline to about Kiama in southern New South Wales. It is also present in Tasmanian waters.
[**Note:** In Western Australia the minimum legal length for a catch of sweep is 23 centimetres — no differentiation is made between the species. All sweep caught in South Australia should be a minimum 21 centimetres long.
In Victoria, the sweep that is commonly referred to as a trumpeter sweep or banded sweep, must be a minimum of 23 centimetres long.]

SWEEP, SILVER
Scorpio lineolatus

Identification

The silver sweep is distinguished from the other two by the low lobe of the dorsal fin and a sharper vee to the forked tail. Its colour is a silver-blue grey to a dark grey. There is no yellow on the lower lip or jaw.

Size

The silver sweep grow to about 38 to 40 centimetres.

Distribution, silver

Habits

This sweep is extremely common on coastal and estuarine reefs, so much so that it can be a nuisance, the smaller fish being adept at stealing bait set for bigger game. It tends to move to offshore reefs as it grows, eating a similar range of food items as the banded sweep. It is certainly cannibalistic, often preferring pieces of its own kind to other bait. On occasions red-coloured flesh (and conjevoi) is taken more greedily than white flesh or light-coloured bait.

Distribution

The silver sweep is found on inshore and offshore reef areas from about Noosa Heads in Queensland to Tasmania. The populations thin out at both ends of its range, especially in eastern Victoria and Tasmania.

When to fish

Sweep are active all day and will feed whenever food is presented, although on some occasions they do show a preference for a particular type of food.

Where to fish

Sweep are a mid-water fish rather than a bottom-dweller. They can be present well above reefs and in mid-water levels around coastal rocks and rock faces. They seem to prefer areas that generate turbulent water. Look for them about inshore reefs and rocks where there are surface chop and white waters, and where there are upcurrents or tidal movement around reefs in deeper water.

Tackle

Many large sweep are hooked with outfits aimed at other fish species while fishing the rocks or off shore. To be successful with sweep, the lines should be lighter, the hooks smaller and the bait higher from the bottom than on rigs used for other reef fish, such as snapper.

Bait

Try small baits of prawn, conjevoi, pipi, mussel, etc., and pieces or small cubes of fish flesh, including sweep and skirt steak.

Berley

Any berley consisting of breadcrumbs, boiled rice, soaked laying pellets or dog biscuits, with some fish scraps or fish-flavoured cat food, will attract and hold sweep. Depending on the depth of water and turbulence, it can be thrown in by hand, used in a

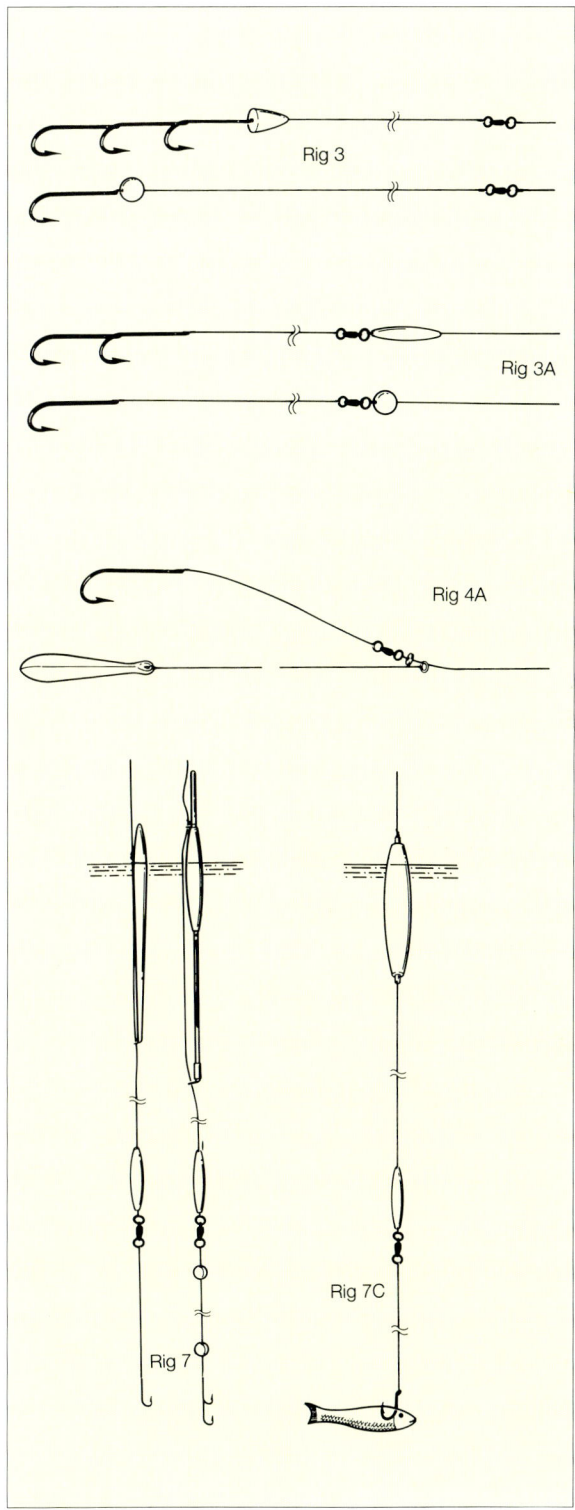

weighted porous onion bag, or in a perforated press-lid tin.

Rigs

If conditions are calm, use the unweighted rig No. 3, although such conditions are not the best for sweep. Lightly weighted rig No. 3A or a running rig No. 4A are better. A bait suspended under a float rig 7 or 7C, which can be adjusted for depth, is recommended where sea conditions permit, especially in inshore waters and off the rocks. For offshore deep water reefs, the bottom rig No. 6 with a smaller hook and bait on the upper dropper can be successful — leaving room for a larger hook on the lower dropper for other fish such as snapper.

How to hook

Sweep are fast biters and choosing the appropriate size hook for the size of the fish is crucial for good catches. A hook for even the largest sweep need be no bigger than about size 2.

It is important to maintain tension between the rod and bait so that any sharp response by the angler will be instantly effective at the working end of the line to set the hook. With a correctly weighted float rig, the pull of the float will often hook the fish before the angler tightens up.

Edibility

If cleaned and bled immediately they are caught — skinned if so desired — and filleted, the sweep's firm white flesh is excellent eating, particularly if cooked simply. The banded sweep is not as tasty but palatable nevertheless.

SWEETLIPS

The fish that is most popularly called "sweetlips" is found in the entry **Emperor, sweetlip,** where it properly belongs. The *real* sweetlips are quite unrelated to the emperors. Some of the larger ones have been selected in the following entry.

Painted sweetlips.

SWEETLIPS, BLACK
Plectorhinchus gibbosus

OTHER NAMES: **BLUBBER-LIP BREAM**

Identification

Its very fleshy thick lips are its most distinguishable feature, but its solid body of dark grey to dark brown, verging on black, separates it from other sweetlips. Another distinguishing feature is the obvious dip (hardly discernible on other members of the family) between the spinous and soft rays of the dorsal fin. Its mouth is also scarlet.

Size

This is probably the largest of the sweetlips, reaching a length of at least 60 centimetres and 5 kilograms.

Breeding

Little is known.

Habits

These fish prefer inshore waters, inhabiting rocky outcrops and reefs and headlands. It feeds on

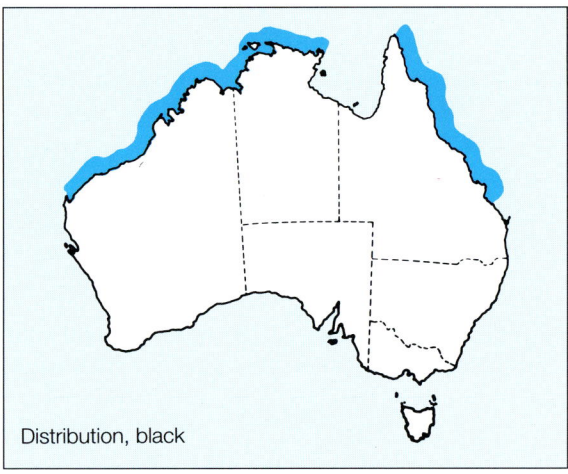

Distribution, black

prawns, crabs and other marine life including small fish.

Distribution

The black sweetlips is found in waters from central Queensland and across the north of the continent to about the north-west area of Western Australia.

SWEETLIPS, PAINTED
Diagramma pictum

OTHER NAMES: **BLACKALL, BLUEY, MORWONG, SLATE BREAM, THICKLIP, THICKLIP BREAM**

Identification

It is easy to see how some of its other names originated. The body shape is not unlike that of bream and the small mouth and thick lips are

similar to those of a morwong. The body colour of an adult painted sweetlips can be a brown to grey, and paler below. There is a profusion of brown to olive spots and sometimes yellow, on the upper sides and dorsal area. Occasional fish have faint yellow spots. There are olive-brown spots in the dorsal fin and tail. The other fins are mostly dark brown or black. There are scarlet patches inside the small mouth.

Size

The fish grows to about 40 centimetres in length.

Breeding

Little is known.

Habits

This fish, which inhabits reefs and other rocky areas, can also be found on sandy areas adjacent to reefs in inshore waters.

Distribution

The painted sweetlips is found in sub-tropical and tropical waters from northern New South Wales around the north of the continent and south to the North West Cape region of Western Australia.

SWEETLIPS, YELLOW-SPOTTED
Plectorhinchus flavomaculatus

OTHER NAMES: **GOLDEN-SPOTTED SWEETLIP, NETTED SWEETLIP, NETTED MORWONG (NO RELATION TO THE TRUE MORWONG), RUBBERLIPS**

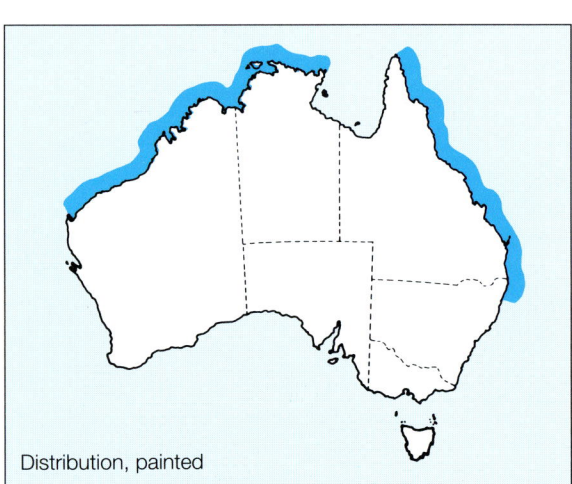

Distribution, painted

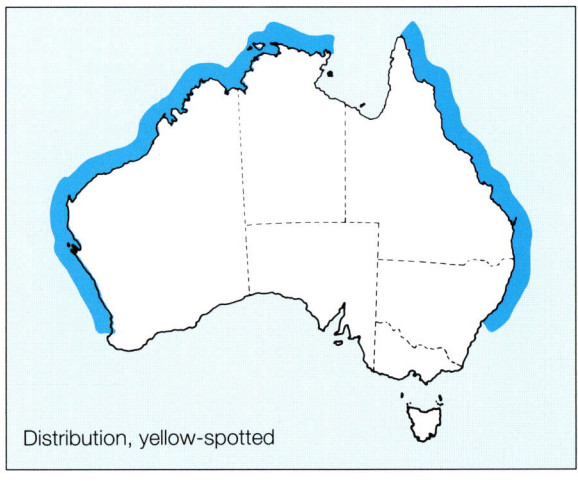

Distribution, yellow-spotted

Identification

The body of this fish is elongate and quite solid. Its base colour can be grey above a greenish-brown, with a mass of yellow or orange lines on the head and upper region of the body. The yellow lines on the head break into spots with age. The dorsal fin is a bluish-grey with wavy yellow lines and spots. The tail is black-spotted. The inside of the small mouth is bright orange.

Size

These fish grow to about 35 centimetres in length.

Breeding

Little is known.

Habits

This fish is a carnivorous reef-dweller that prefers sheltered coastal reefs. It is a retiring type of fish and an easy prey for spearfishers. Sweetlips eat prawns, crabs and some shellfish, as well as small fish.

Distribution

The yellow-spotted sweetlips can be found in reef areas from the middle of the New South Wales coast north through Queensland waters and across the top end of Australia and south to about Geographe Bay in the south-west of Western Australia. Its numbers are few in the southern parts, and even these are probably the result of fish wandering there in a warm current from the sub-tropical and tropical reef waters.

The following applies to all sweetlips.

When to fish

Sweetlips are present throughout the year.

Where to fish

The best spots to explore are amongst reefs, on the sand edges of reefs and in deeper water off headlands. The preferred habitat seems to be sheltered areas.

Tackle

Sweetlips can be handled easily on lines used for most reef species, but the fighting strength of this fish will not be appreciated. However, hooking sweetlips on the size of hooks generally used for reef fishing is fairly unusual, because their mouths are so much smaller — and these fish are reasonably quiet biters.

Bait

The best bait is undoubtedly prawns, with crab pieces as second choice, and some of the flesh of most shellfish. They are also caught with small fillets of fish.

Berley

Any mix of fish or crustacean pieces is likely to attract sweetlips.

Rigs

The chances of catching larger more welcome fish is greater than catching a sweetlips unless small hooks and soft baits are used, so those used for emperors, coral trout, etc., are suitable but the smaller hook poses a problem if a large fish takes the bait. Wire traces also inhibit sweetlips.

How to hook

It is usually an accident, but it can be likened to a hesitant bream bite.

Edibility

Sweetlips are not highly regarded as a food fish. If you wish to eat sweetlips, it is important they be killed, thoroughly bled and cleaned, skinned, filleted and kept cool. The flesh is somewhat coarse and is better if steamed or mornayed. Perhaps they are best allowed to swim free unless the angler is desperately hungry.

[**Note**: Many other sweetlips exist in the tropical waters of Australia. The three described here are representative of their habits. The methods of catching them apply to them all. They belong to the family Naemulidae, the same as the javelin-fish.

TAILOR
Pomatomus saltatrix

OTHER NAMES: **SKIPJACK, CHOPPERS, BLUEFISH**

There has been a marked decline in the number and size of tailor taken in the past decade from its strongholds on both sides of Australia. There are numerous theories why this excellent fish, which has thrilled more anglers than any other, should be on the decline in numbers and size. Some of the reasons are: the removal of a minimum size in New South Wales in the 1970s; over-exploitation by professional and amateur anglers in New South Wales, Queensland and Western Australia; the destruction of nursery habitats in estuaries; pollution, etc. As this entry is being prepared, co-operative research is being undertaken in all these States, which may produce some answers that can help build a more promising future for this very popular fish. All anglers will wish them speedy success.

Identification
Streamlined and powerful, the larger tailor grow, the more surly and pugnacious they look. Colouring is bluish-to-green on the back, fading to silver on the sides. The mouth is full of sharp shearing teeth. Anglers who carelessly unhook a tailor can have some nasty wounds inflicted on their hands.

Size
The tailor has been recorded at a length of 1.2 metres and 15 kilograms in weight in Australian waters. The largest tailor listed in the Australian National Sport Fishing Record Chart (as at December, 1988) is 12.10 kilograms caught, a fish caught at Shark Bay in Western Australia. In fact, almost all line-class records held by ANSA

members have been achieved in this area.

The minimum legal length for a catch in Western Australia is 25 centimetres; it is 23 centimetres in Victoria; and 30 centimetres in Queensland.

Breeding

No tailor larvae have been recorded in Australian waters, although very small juveniles have been taken from weed beds in Botany Bay. Tailor smaller than 10 centimetres are commonly found in most estuaries on the east coast and many on the west coast. Spawning occurs in waters offshore from Fraser Island, Queensland, in September. Tagging programmes indicate that these fish are from the northern area of New South Wales. A suggestion that breeding also occurs off the New South Wales coast may be fish from further south. New research being conducted may prove a theory long-held by many anglers that tailor from southern and northern regions have a circular migration rather than a south-north-south movement along the coast after spawning.

Habits

Tailor are pelagic fish that pursue and attack schools of baitfish. They are usually a surface to mid-water fish but sometimes "rest" in large schools on the bottom of a hole off a beach, particularly near an entrance to an estuary or near a broken reef off a beach.

Their migratory travel begins in mid-summer on the south coast of New South Wales around Gabo Island, though it is not clear if these fish are those which anglers flock to catch at Fraser Island about September. Tagging programmes are incomplete. There is an almost similar migration on the Western Australian coast. Really huge tailor are caught from mid-winter to spring, between Port Macquarie and Fraser Island in the east, and Dongara to Shark Bay on the western coast, the notable exception to this rule being the Shark Bay area, where there are always some big tailor present.

Tailor eat fish, squid and crabs but their favourites are pilchards, garfish, slimy mackerel, yellowtail, small mullet and sardines. Their ferocious attack on schools of the small fish attracts gulls and terns. Birds wheeling and diving around a particular spot at sea often announce the presence of a tailor school (diving sea birds are also a good sign that tuna, salmon and other pelagics are feeding).

Tailor seem almost to kill for the sake of it. It is not unusual, for instance, to catch a tailor that has attacked a lure despite its stomach and gullet being crammed full of food.

Tailor dislike bright sunlight and calm, clear water. They prefer some chop or white water but they will avoid areas of a beach where wave action clouds the water with sand.

Distribution

This pelagic can be found from Fraser Island in Queensland, south to Tasmania, across Victoria and South Australia, and along the West Australian coast as far north as Shark Bay. Populations are smaller in Tasmania and along the southern coastline.

When to fish

Tailor can be active throughout the day if it is overcast and dull, but the best periods are regarded as pre-sunrise dawn till the sun brightens the water, or the dusk into the evening. During the night tailor will make a number of fleeting visits to a beach, headland, or breakwater at different times, so the patient angler might enjoy several periods of exciting fishing.

The best times of the year to fish vary with the location.

Where to fish

The rock platforms or headlands on the extremities of beaches or estuaries are always worth trying for tailor, and so are breakwaters at river entrances. Tailor will also hunt along bays or inlets along rocky shores, often where migrating mullet and pilchards take shelter during the night. On beaches the foam-covered flats or deep channels are natural pathways for tailor searching for prey. In most cases, a rising to high tide, combined with choppy or disturbed water, produces the better fishing. Trolling near or over reefs and along the edges of white water near cliffs can also be rewarding —

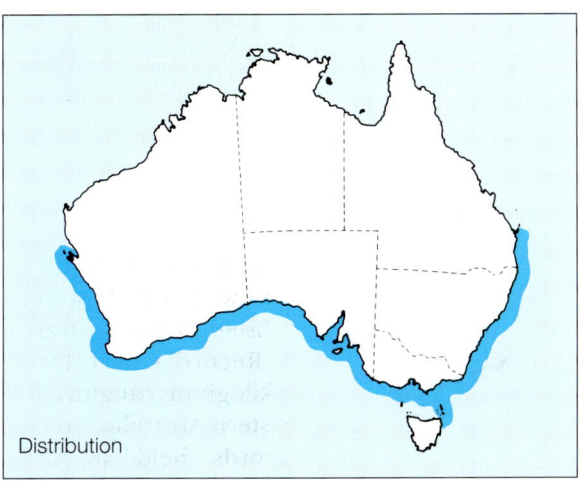

Distribution

A good sized tailor by anyone's standards.

provided the conditions allow such fishing to be conducted with safety.

Tackle

If fishing from a boat, a single-handed threadline or baitcasting outfit is suitable for trolling a bait or lure, as well as casting and retrieving the same. If, however, you are fishing from the beach or rocks, a good choice is a light to medium rod of about 3.5 metres to 4 metres long, with a fast or medium-fast tip. It is particularly convenient if the rod is balanced with either a sidecast, threadline or overhead reel. Lines can be between 5 and 8 kilograms breaking-strain (or lighter) with No. 4200 or 4202 Mustard or Tarpon hooks, "ganged" (linked eye-to-eye) in numbers to suit the size of the bait being used. The size of the hook also depends on the size of the bait. With ganged hooks, a wire trace is not usually required but some anglers use a short 20-centimetre length as a safeguard against the tailor's sharp teeth. A wire trace is essential with lures for large tailor.

Bait

The availability of blue pilchards make this bait a first choice, but sea garfish are also excellent. Nor will tailor reject yellowtail, small pike, mullet, slimy mackerel and squid. They will eat their own kind and fish-shaped slabs of almost any other fish can tempt them.

Most of the metal spoon-type lures and many minnow-type plugs, both sub-surface and surface swimming, will attract tailor. The soft plastic-bodied lures are excellent but vulnerable to the taylor's ripping teeth, which quickly tear them to pieces.

Berley

Laying or chicken pellets scattered on the surface near a school of tailor can hold them in an area, especially in quieter waters.

Rigs

When fishing from a boat, from the rocks or a breakwater, try the unweighted rig No.2 or, if the bait is required to be fished slightly deeper, rig No.3 with a small conical or barrel sinker. From the beach use either rig No. 4 or 4A. A satisfactory trolling rig is No. 11 with a barrel sinker on the swivel — or between a ring and a swivel, or two swivels.

How to hook

The tailor usually maims its prey in its first attack, nipping off the tail in a lot of cases. It is much better to resist setting the hook but continue to retrieve your line. The fish will strike again. If a steady pace is maintained the fish will usually be hooked. Sometimes a change of pace will induce or tease the fish when they are reluctant to bite. The same applies on a beach. When the bait has settled to the bottom (it should never be weighted so that it will not move with any current or sweep), it should be slowly retrieved towards the shoreline.

Hints

When pilchards or garfish, for example, are used on ganged hooks, the tail should be removed with the bottom hook, which should be impaled about 5 millimetres from the end of the fish. This aids casting, stops the fish revolving during retrieval and allows juices from the bait to ooze out, leaving a scent trail.

Tailor do not like revolving baits or lures. One that darts or dives or otherwise behaves like an injured fish is much more likely to be taken.

Some anglers, especially when fishing for "chopper" sized tailor, wire a treble hook to the bottom hook of a gang of hooks. Much more effective is a saltwater fly of a blue and white or green and white colour. If the bait is torn off without a hook-up, the tailor will very often hit the fly (this also works with salmon).

Edibility

Tailor are a soft fish. Allowing them to flop about on rocks or the bottom of boats, even the sand, bruises their flesh. They should be killed and bled immediately after they have been caught, and kept cool.

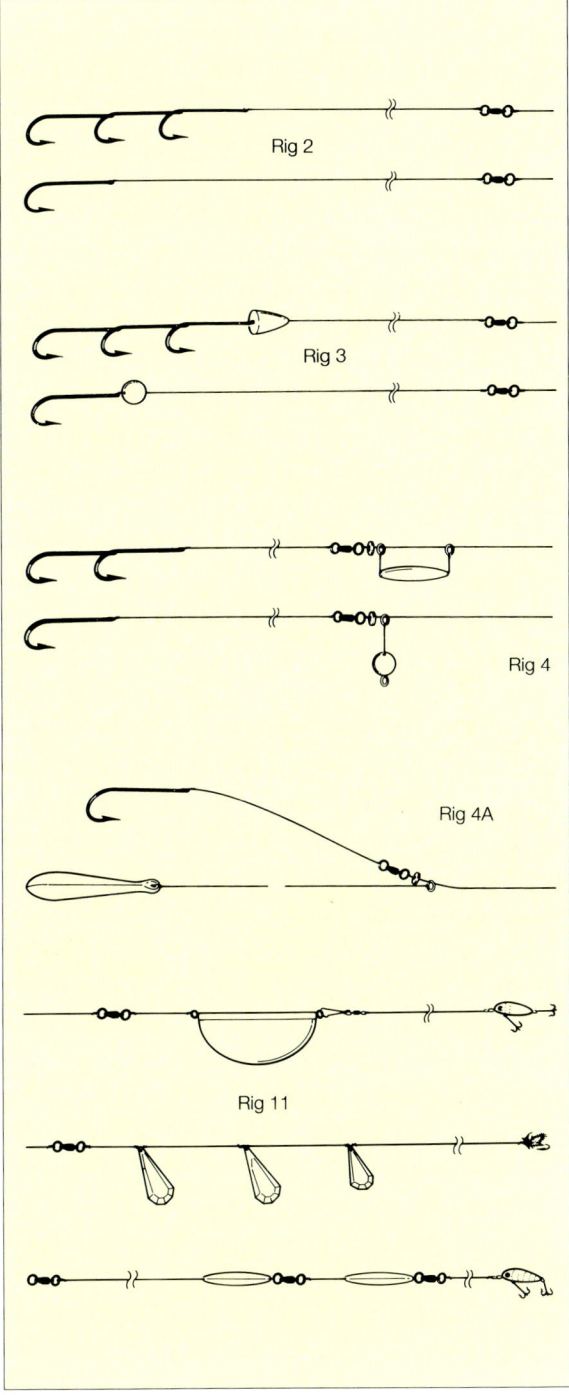

Tailor are one of the best and tastiest fish when simply cooked while fresh — such as a whole fish split open or fillets grilled with a little butter or margarine. They are also delicious smoked. Tailor are not a fish that freezes well.

TANGUIGUE
Scomberomorus commersoni

OTHER NAMES: **SPANIARD, NARROW-BARRED SPANISH MACKEREL, KINGFISH, SNOOK**

Though this fish has been traditionally known as the narrow-barred Spanish mackerel, the writer decided to accept the name under which this fish is listed by the International Game Fishing Association and the Game Fishing Association of Australia. This in no way implies that this prized fighting — and fine eating — speedster is the sole province of the expensively equipped game fishing fraternity. On the contrary, just ask any old salt who has caught this fish by floating a bait under a bobby-cork or balloon from a cliff or rock platform or from having cast-and-retrieved a lure!

Identification
This is by far the largest of the Scombridae or mackerel family. Though it resembles the wahoo (*see* entry), it can be distinguished by its more tapered first dorsal fin, the more central position of its second dorsal fin, and its deeply forked tail (the wahoo's second dorsal is much nearer the tail, which is almost straight rather than forked). The tanguigue's body is covered in up to 50 narrow vertical bluish-grey bars. It can also be distinguished by the very pronounced dip in its lateral line immediately below the second dorsal fin. It has a mouthful of sharp, finely serrated teeth.

Size
This fish can exceed two metres in length and more than 70 kilograms in weight. The Australian all-tackle record (as at September, 1988) was 38.75 kilograms for one caught at Rottnest Island off Western Australia. The world all-tackle record is 44.790 kilograms.

The minimum legal size for a tanguigue catch in Western Australia is 75 centimetres; in Queensland it is 45 centimetres.

Breeding
The eggs are semi-buoyant and float slowly to the

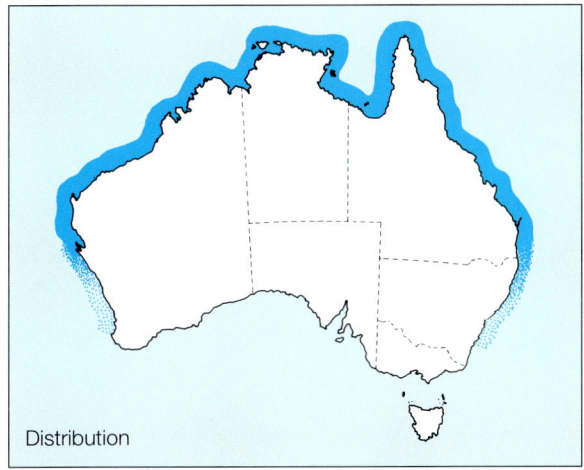

Distribution

Where to fish

Panic behaviour by small (and not so small) fish can indicate the savage attack of a tanguigue, though obviously they are not the only pelagic marauders in the ocean. If there are no visible signs of this fish, slow trolling with baits or lures along both the shallow and deeper edges of reefs, through openings in reefs and close to the tops of deeper reefs may find a lone large tanguigue. The fish generally prefer waters with a tidal rip or current, both inshore and near off shore islands. Live baits

bottom before hatching, in the summer period in the mid-tropical waters.

Distribution

A tropical fish, the tanguigue follows warm currents down the eastern and western coasts of Australia, where it is often caught in the April to May period as far as Montague Island, New South Wales and Geographe Bay, Western Australia. It is present in the tropical regions all year with increased numbers around between August and February.

Habits

The large tanguigue is not generally found in schools. As individuals, or in twos or threes, they tend to maintain a territory on a reef and will even hole up in deep water. When the smaller fish — up to 12 kilograms or so — are encountered in schools, they often feed frenziedly and will hit lures freely. The fish has a very catholic taste and eats many fish, from small snapper to wrasses and tuskfish and parrot-fish, from hardiheads to garfish and even its own relatives. It is also partial to squid.

When to fish

Though tanguigue are mainly tropical fish and may be found in varying numbers throughout the year, there are prime fishing times. Unseasonal occurrences are probably caused by favourable water currents and temperature. In the main, they are more likely encountered in the south of their range in late summer-autumn, but August through January are prime times in tropic and sub-tropic waters.

It is generally acknowledged that the time to expect tanguigue to bite is just after dawn and towards dusk. But deep-trolling or bait-fishing over the tops of reefs are worth the effort at other times of the day.

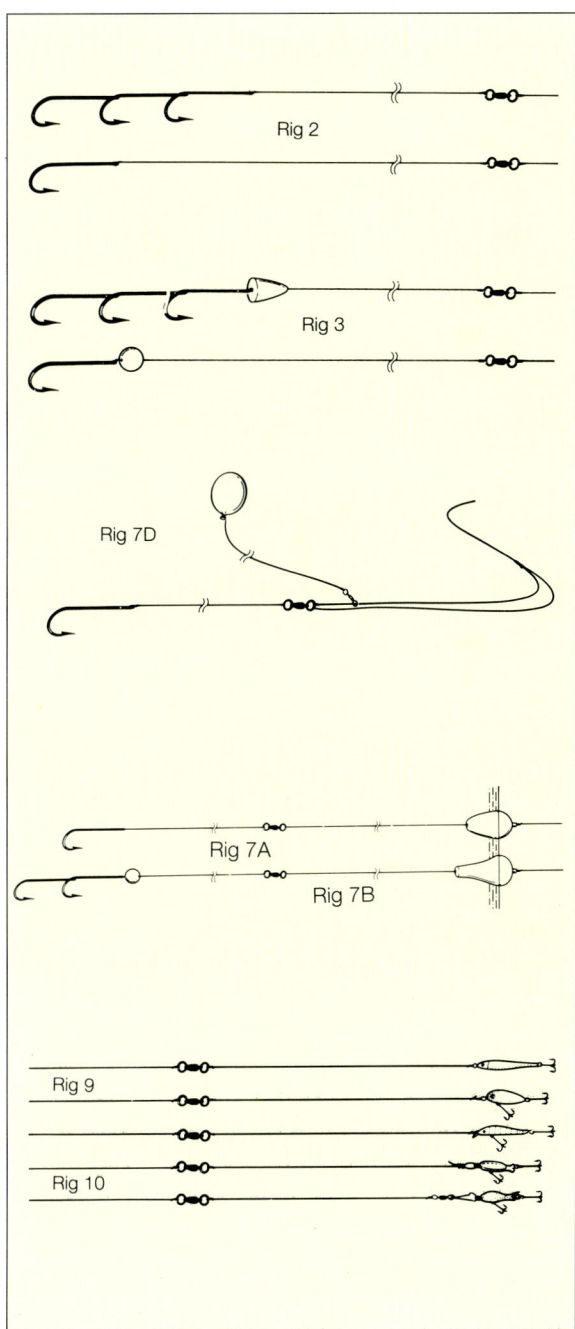

Rig 2

Rig 3

Rig 7D

Rig 7A

Rig 7B

Rig 9

Rig 10

near the bottom in deep water may also interest tanguigue.

Tackle

Handlines may be used for trolling and bait fishing, with a minimum breaking-strain of 30 kilograms. Rods should be medium or heavy, single or double-handed, threadline or baitcasting models, between 2 and 2.5 metres long. Use good quality reels, spooled with 6 to 10 kilograms breaking-strain line for the smaller tanguigue. It is probably wiser to fish with the top breaking-strain as large specimens or other favoured game fish can be encountered. Light game outfits and the powerful "stroker"-type rods are also sometimes used for this reason.

A wire trace may be unnecessary if using ganged hooks, but it is an insurance if using live bait or lures — and tanguigue have a broad taste in these.

Bait

The tanguigue is very catholic in its taste. Pilchards, garfish, hardiheads, mullet, herrings, striped sea-pike, yellowtail and similar fish are popular, whether trolled, used as floated baits or for casting and retrieving. Squid is sometimes used. The tanguigue, like its relatives, will take a wide range of lures — metal wobblers, spoons, minnows and the skirted types.

Berley

Fish scraps can be used to seek tanguigue in deeper water over reefs when bait-fishing. Success depends on getting it down towards the bottom.

Rigs

The unweighted bait rig No. 2 with heavy nylon leader or nylon-coated wire trace is satisfactory for fishing with baits. A light sinker rig No. 3A is suitable for reef areas with a reasonable bottom. For trolling, if records are to be considered, variations of the hook arrangement are required if they are to conform with Australian Game Fishing regulations, but rig No. 9 (or fished deeper via an outrigger) will be satisfactory. Rig No. 7D or 7E can be used with live baits where tide or wind can be used to take them out when fishing from land-based locations.

How to hook

Tanguigue are efficient predators. When they strike a moving bait or lure, they hit hard and fast, rarely missing.

If using a floating bait or live bait, it is best to give them a few seconds to swallow before setting the hook firmly. They should be allowed to run, but under pressure. These are not just surface fighters — they will dive deep too in their efforts to free themselves — and they can test the most experienced angler.

Hint

Despite their ability to swim and attack very fast indeed, the tanguigue will often prefer a slow-trolled bait or lure.

Edibility

The fish is highly regarded, cooked by any method, and is popular for sashimi. It should be bled and cleaned and placed on ice (or kept cool) as soon as it is caught. The body can be extremely slimy and this should be washed off. (Some references claim that this slime can cause infections or irritate some angler's skins so it is wise to wash the hands after handling the tanguigue.)

A word of caution

Infrequent cases of ciguetera poisoning (*see* entry) have been blamed on this fish. The writer can only repeat the tropical anglers' maxim: *eat only small portions of the larger carnivorous tropical species and less frequently.*

TARWHINE
Rhabdosargus sarba

OTHER NAME: **SILVER BREAM**

The tarwhine belongs to the same Sparidae family as the bream, and is superficially similar to them, particularly the yellowfin bream of ocean beach waters. In the main the tarwhine is a bonus catch for anglers seeking whiting or other surf and estuary fish.

Identification
The tarwhine has a deep body, with a smoother and more rounded contour than the bream from the snout to the front of the dorsal fin. The brilliant silvery colour of its body is streaked with golden bands from the gill covers to the tail. There is hardly any discernible change from the spines to the rays of its dorsal fin. Any doubts when trying to identify a tarwhine are certainly put to rest when you gut this fish: the black lining of its stomach cavity clearly distinguishes it from the bream.

Size
Tarwhine reach 70 centimetres in length and can weigh about 3 kilograms, although most catches are much smaller, usually less than 1.5 kilograms. The minimum legal length for tarwhine in Western Australia is 23 centimetres; the minimum in New South Wales is 20 centimetres.

Breeding
Little is known.

Habits
These fish school along surf beaches and also in estuaries, near the entrances. However, large tarwhine are often found in quieter backwaters of estuaries, though usually in only clean water conditions. The larger fish can also be found in

rocky areas at the ends of beaches and around ocean rocks adjacent to beaches. Turbulent water does not seem to disturb them. They are carnivorous fish, eating prawns, beach worms, shellfish, small fish such as whitebait, and sardines. They are more active during the day.

Distribution

Tarwhine can be found in sub-tropical and temperate waters on both the eastern and western coasts. On the eastern side they range from southern Queensland to the Gippsland Lakes in Victoria; in the west from Albany to Coral Bay.

When to fish

These fish seem to be present most of the year, though numbers vary. They are a daylight target; a particularly good time being the couple of hours before the top of the tide and an hour after it.

Where to fish

Tarwhine will follow tailor or salmon schools, perhaps feeding on the scraps left by these pelagics after they have attacked schools of bait fish. They are often found in the surf zone too, or close to it, where waves stir worms, crabs and shellfish from the sand. Gutters with rocks in them, or at least close to rocks, are also worth trying.

Tackle

Depending on the location and conditions, single-handed threadline or baitcasting rods and reels can be used, so can handlines. However, the most popular spots are usually from beaches or rocks: where a 3 metre to 4 metre light rod with a whippy tip, which can accommodate a sidecast or threadline reel, is probably the most practical outfit. Line need not exceed 3 to 5 kilograms

breaking-strain. Hooks between 2 and 1/0 size are suitable.

Bait

Tarwhine can be caught on prawns, yabbies, nippers, beachworms, small crabs, small fish and fillets.

Rigs

The weight should be just sufficient to hold the bait near the bottom. Running rigs No. 3, 3A and 4 will suit most surf conditions. If conditions permit, the unweighted rig No. 2 can be used.

How to hook

These fish bite voraciously, showing none of the wariness or finicky behaviour of bream. They usually hook themselves and fight so strongly that they can be a real problem to beach if a surf is running.

Edibility

Opinions vary about these fish. The soft white flesh deteriorates rapidly if not bled, cleaned — and remove the dark stomach lining! — filleted and cooled as soon as they are caught. They are quite tasty if eaten soon after having been caught but the flesh does not freeze well.

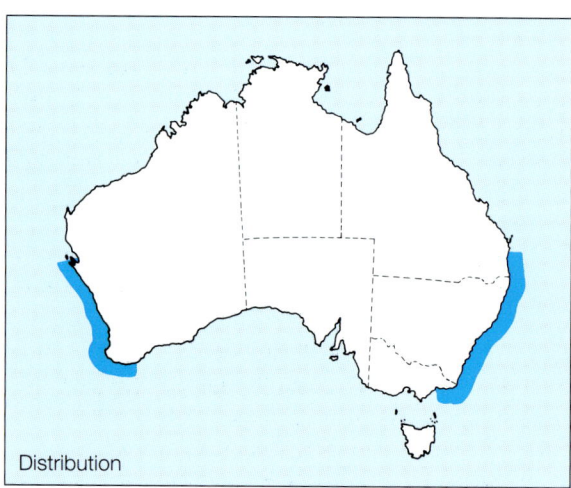

Distribution

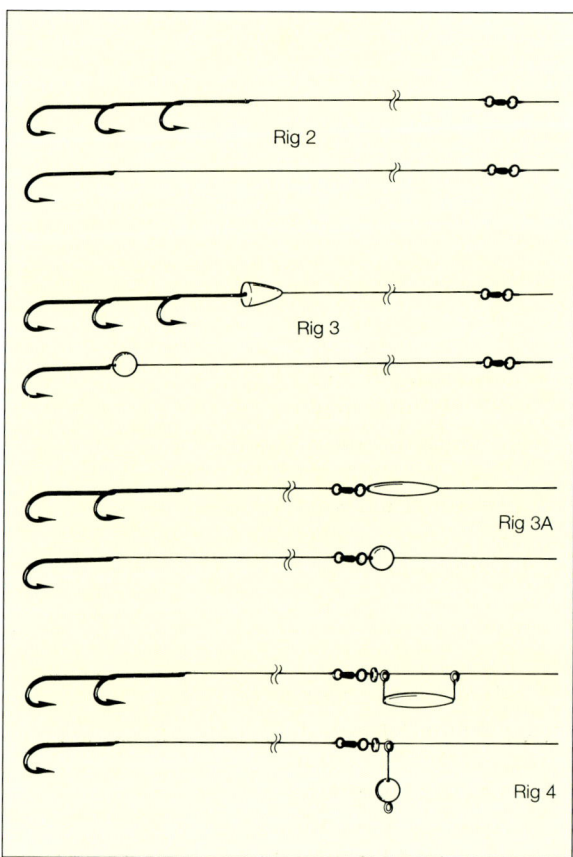

Rig 2

Rig 3

Rig 3A

Rig 4

TERAGLIN
Atractoscion aequidens

OTHER NAME: **TRAG, TERAGLIN-JEW**

This fish resembles a mulloway and is one that anglers may chance upon while fishing offshore reefs. But if they can pinpoint the locality with a depth sounder or other navigational aids, it is probably worth visiting again. Teraglin have a habit of lingering on or visiting a particular reef.

Identification

Though they resemble their close relatives, the mulloway, teraglin can be distinguished by the shape of their tail, being concave instead of convex. The rich yellow colour of the inside of the mouth and gill cover is another differentiating feature, as is the anal fin which is closer to the tail than on the mulloway. The overall colour is silver with bluish-black, sometimes brownish, tones. The dorsal fins have a yellowish colour.

Size

The fish grows to around a metre in length and about 12 kilograms, but the majority caught are between 3 and 5 kilograms.

Minimum legal length for a teraglin catch in New South Wales is 38 centimetres; the minimum in Queensland is 30 centimetres.

Breeding

Little is known.

Habits

The teraglin rarely ventures into the range of land-based anglers, although small fish have been found in some deepwater harbours or over rocky bottoms in estuaries. Lone fish are never encountered and they school in quite large numbers on some occasions.

During the day they appear to laze about the bottom, on or near reefs, but begin to eat, often voraciously, late in the afternoon and may eat throughout the night. They also eat well off the bottom and at night they will feed on the surface. Teraglin are carnivores: small fish, squid and octopus are the major items in their diet.

The teraglin is a warmwater fish.

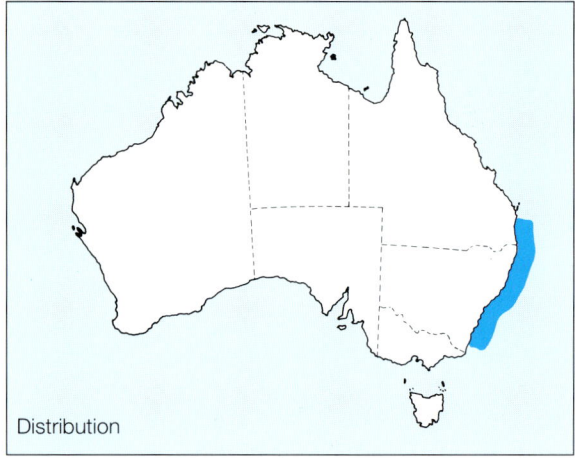

Distribution

Distribution

Confined to the east coast, from Double Island Point in Queensland to about Bermagui on the New South Wales south coast, teraglin are a summer fish in the south, moving north for the winter.

When to fish

It is unusual to catch a teraglin in the morning or middle of the day. Late afternoon and into the night — if anglers have a boat equipped to stay at sea — are the best times.

Where to fish

A depth sounder, particularly one of the new electronic models, is a real asset when trying to locate a school of teraglin, establishing what depth the fish are above a reef. Without a depth sounder, the angler should start fishing on the bottom and raise the bait a metre or so until the depth at which the teraglin are feeding is found. It can be a frustrating search. The fish can be found over reefs as shallow as 20 metres and up to about 50 metres. Anchoring the boat rather than drifting is the usual practice when schools of teraglin are located.

Tackle

A handline of about 15 kilograms breaking-strain can be used, so can a gunwale-mounted winch-type of reel with the same line. Short boat rods, threadline or baitcasting outfits, with line of about 8 or 10 kilograms breaking-strain are convenient. These should have a fast or medium-fast taper. A wire trace is unnecessary and hooks should be about 6/0 in size.

Bait

Use half-pilchards or garfish, fillets of mullet, slimy mackerel, yellowtail and tuna etc.

Berley

If conditions allow, berley can bring teraglin into a very concentrated area, often directly beneath the boat. It is better fed into the water rather than in a container on the bottom. It has to be used carefully because it can get caught in current and lead the fish away. Fish scraps and prawn heads make a suitable berley.

Rigs

Use a single hook rig, with a bean or barrel sinker of just sufficient weight to get the line towards the bottom (No. 3A) or a double hook rig such as rig No. 6.

How to hook

The fish is not a hard biter, tending to squash the bait before swallowing. A firm tightening of the line when a bite is felt usually hooks the fish. Despite their size and relationship to the mulloway, they do not fight hard and are easily brought to the boat.

Edibility

The flesh of a teraglin of any size has more flavour than a mulloway. It can be prepared by most methods.

[**Note:** Other fish related to the teraglin — and often referred to as "croakers" — exist in northern tropical waters and in the north-west waters of Western Australia. They are generally smaller and all mostly possess a wedge-shaped tail. *See a* Note in Mulloway entry.]

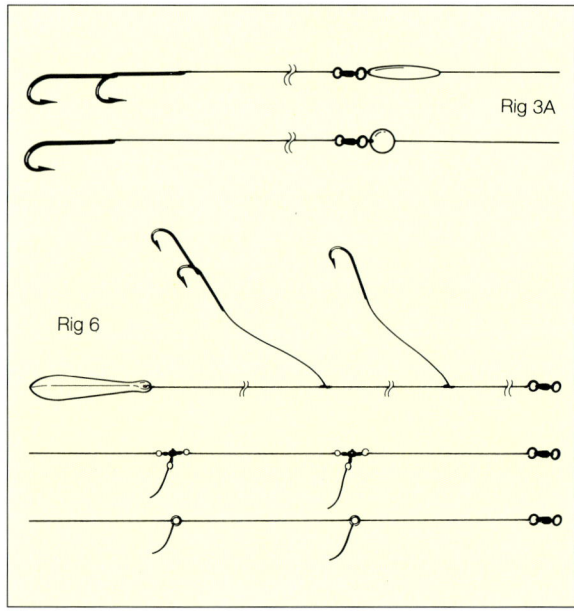

THREADFIN

Threadfin derive their name from the threads or filaments that stream from the base of their low pectoral fins. Of the several species that inhabit the same waters, the two larger species, which are generally more common, are dealt with in detail here. These fish offer excellent sport and make equally satisfying eating.

THREADFIN, GIANT
Eleumtheronema tetradactylum

OTHER NAMES: **TASSEL-FISH, BLIND TASSEL-FISH, BLUE SALMON, COOKTOWN SALMON, COLONIAL SALMON, KINGFISH, SALMON**

Identification
Identical in shape to the Sheridan threadfin, this fish is a dull blue-green on the dorsal area and white, with a yellowish tone, on the lower half. The fins are a generally a dull yellow, though the pectorals can be almost black. It can be distinguished from the Sheridan threadfin because it never has more than four filaments or "tassels" and it has broad rows of teeth that extend beyond the jaw. After death its eyelid becomes opaque.

Size
This fish is known to reach a length of 2 metres and a weight approaching 130 kilograms outside Australian waters. However, the largest taken under Australian National Sportfishing Association rules is 14.19 kilograms.

The minimum legal length for a catch of giant threadfin in Queensland is 40 centimetres.

THREADFIN, SHERIDAN
Polydactyl sheridani

OTHER NAMES: **BURNETT SALMON, KING SALMON, TASSEL-FISH, SALMON**

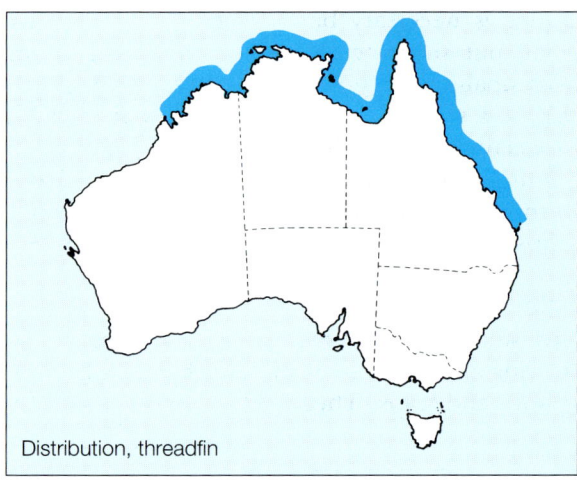

Distribution, threadfin

Identification

This species is an elongate fish, moderately compact, with a large forked tail. The upper half of its body is a greyish-blue and the abdomen silvery to off-white. The pectoral fins are a vivid yellow and the pelvic fin a lighter yellow. The other fins are dusky to grey. There is a high front dorsal fin well separated from the rear dorsal fin, which begins where the back dips towards the caudal peduncle.

The Sheridan threadfin can be distinguished from the giant threadfin by its five (rather than four) extremely long filaments, and the narrow bands of fine teeth along its jaw that do not extend past the jaws.

Size

This fish is said to grow to about 30 kilograms. The record in the Australian National Sportfishing Association record chart (at December, 1988) is 16.35 kilograms.

The minimum legal length for a catch of Sheridan threadfin in Queensland is 40 centimetres.

The following applies to both threadfin

Breeding

Little is known.

Distribution

Both species of threadfin are found in the rivers, creeks and sandflat areas of the tropics, from the Burnett River, in Queensland, in the Gulf of Carpentaria, extending across the Northern Territory, and south along the Western Australian coast. The giant threadfin is the species more likely to be encountered further south.

Habits

Threadfin are an inshore and estuary species, spending much of their time in turbid waters of muddy and sandy areas. They move with the rising tide, feeding on crabs, prawns and such small fish as mullet that forage in similar habitats. The threadfin will also ambush prey where a creek flows into more open water, sweeping food with it on a falling tide, or in a deep hole behind a sandbank. In clearer waters their tails and dorsal fins are often exposed as they chase food. They tend to be more abundant and more active prior to the start of the "wet" or monsoonal season.

When to fish

Many of the rivers and estuaries where threadfin are found are not only very difficult to get to, but they are often subject to flooding during the wet season. The period from about May through to October is much more pleasant and practical — and the threadfin can still be found. These fish bite day and night. Fishing with bait, whether live or not, often produces better-sized threadfins. Generally a rising tide over sand or mudflats is a favourable situation, as is the top of the tide or start of the ebb-tide at creek entrances.

Where to fish

The fish can often be seen feeding and may be approached in a canoe or drifting boat. They will enter quite shallow water over sand and mudflats. They are prepared to wait in a vicinity where food is brought towards them by an ebbing tide, such as a creek emptying into a larger waterway. The deep water behind sandbars is also worth a try.

Tackle

For bait-fishing, a handline of about 15 kilograms breaking-strain is a reasonable choice when fishing from the shoreline or a small boat. Medium-weight single-handed threadline or baitcasting outfits with a line of between 5 and 8 kilograms breaking-strain offers a broader choice — baits or lures can be cast and retrieved. A heavy nylon leader is necessary because the threadfin have small but sharp teeth. Threadfin can also be accompanied by unwelcome sharks and sword-fish, so a short length of wire trace is often used, especially when fishing with live bait. Hooks of about 4/0 to 6/0 size are safe sizes. If you link two or three together in these sizes for dead bait or fish strips, it overcomes any need for a wire trace.

Bait

Any small, live fish such as mullet, garfish and herring are almost irresistible to threadfin. So are prawns and crabs. These baits are also satisfactory when fished dead and fillets of other fish will usually be taken if threadfin are in a feeding mood. In clearer water during the day, threadfin will also take a variety of lures. These can be bibbed minnow-types, surface poppers and soft plastic styles as well as jigs (cast-and-retrieved). The writer has been unable to establish whether a threadfin has been caught on fly-fishing gear, but it would seem an excellent challenge for this style of fishing.

Rigs

If using dead bait, it should be weighted so that it can move slowly in the current. Running rigs No. 3A or 4 work well. These can be used with live bait, in which case rig No. 7A is extremely successful. Threadfin are often sought where tidal currents make it too difficult for a floating rig. For casting and retrieving, rigs No. 9 or 10 are satisfactory.

How to hook

The threadfins can behave in two distinct moods. On most occasions they will strike cast-and-retrieved lures, and even fish baits, with alacrity. On the other hand, they can be very divident takers of live bait or bait that is weighted to the bottom. If they are in the latter mood, then it is essential to allow them time to swallow and move off before setting the hook. As soon as the fish feels the hook, it explodes into action. They are clean fighters that leap and run with remarkable energy. The angler must tire this fish before attempting to net it or beach it.

Hint

The bait that is strangely overlooked, despite usually being plentiful where threadfin occur, is crab.

Edibility

Threadfin are a valuable commercial species with an excellent reputation as a fine food fish — every bit the equal of barramundi according to many northern anglers. As the fish grows larger, large bony nodules develop on the backbone, making filleting them in the normal manner difficult. They have firm white flesh of excellent flavour, which can be cooked by most methods.

[**Note**: Other threadfins likely to be encountered are the Grunther's or flat threadfin (*Polydactylus multiradiatus*) and the black-finned threadfin (*P. Nigripinnus*), which are occasionally found further south into sub-tropical waters.]

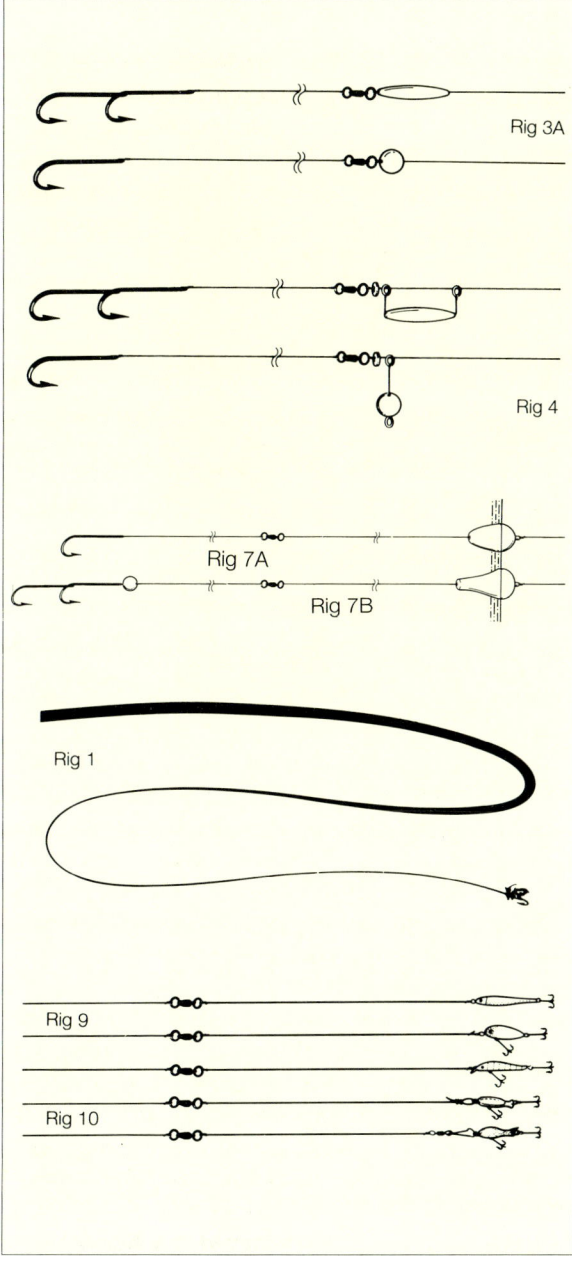

Rig 3A

Rig 4

Rig 7A

Rig 7B

Rig 1

Rig 9

Rig 10

TOMMY RUFF (ROUGH)
Arripis georgianus

OTHER NAMES: **ROUGHIE, RUFF, AUSTRALIAN HERRING**

It is about time biologists and fisheries publications settled on a spelling for this fish. The Macquarie Dictionary settles for "ruff" and perhaps that should be the standard. These fish are not herring, although widely called such, their only relative being the Australian salmon.

Identification

These tough little battlers can be mistaken for young or immature Australian salmon. Their distinguishing features, however, are much larger eyes, distinct black tips on the lobes of the tail, and the rough texture of their scales. Their colours are green over silver. Yellow-gold bars occur on the upper half of young fish, but these break zup into spots as the fish mature. The mouth is large.

Size

Tommy ruffs can grow to about 40 centimetres in length and they are said to weigh up to about half a kilogram, though such sizes are found only in the southern parts of their distribution.

The minimum legal length for a catch in Western Australia is 18 centimetres.

Breeding

These fish migrate westward and northward from the eastern end of their distribution on their spawning runs in late summer. They breed in the Geraldton area of Western Australia.

Habits

These fish school, travel and feed together. They hunt over shallow reefs, along beaches and in estuaries. They can be found along rocky shorelines. Being carnivorous fish, they will eat small whitebait, sardines, marine worms, etc., and they feed from the bottom to the surface.

Distribution

There is some doubt about tommy ruff extending east of Port Phillip Bay in Victoria, although reports

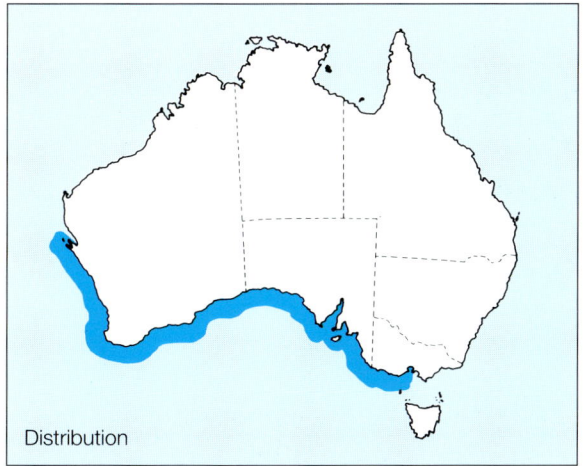

Distribution

of catches have come from southern New South Wales. The population of the fish increases towards the west and is abundant in the Southern Ocean, particularly off South Australia. While there are resident populations on the Western Australian coast, numbers there increase from late summer.

When to fish

The seasons dictate the presence of the greatest numbers of these fish: late spring to mid-summer is best in the east; autumn through winter applies in the west. Tommy ruff are usually fished for during the day.

Where to fish

Try the extremities of beaches and over reefs or from ocean rock-fronts first, though the tommy ruff does enter estuaries and bays. They can be caught from the shoreline or jetties and from boats.

Tackle

Handlines are adequate and efficient, provided the line never exceeds 8 kilograms breaking-strain. With light single-handed threadline or baitcasting outfits, however, you have a little more flexibility with locations. If you are fishing from a beach, along an open area of an estuary, or off the rocks, use a light rod of about 3 metres with a fast taper that is suited for either a threadline or sidecast reel. In this case, the line need only be about 5 kilograms breaking-strain. Hook style is probably unimportant but sizes of around 6 to 8 are satisfactory, and occasionally size 4. An indispensable item of tackle is a berley blob or a berley sinker.

Bait

Maggots (often called "gentles" in South Australia,

"wogs" in Western Australia) are considered the ideal bait. However, once biting, tommy ruff can be caught on pieces of almost any fish, as well as whole small whitebait, sardines and mullet strips fished on small, ganged hooks. Pieces or strips of squid and octopus are also taken, as is meat soaked overnight in pilchard or sardine oil.

Berley

There are almost as many "secret" concoctions used by anglers for tommy ruff as there are of "never-fail" berley recipes from the bream anglers! Boiled rice, breadcrumbs, bran and pollard, with minced old fish or mixed with cat food, will all work.

Rigs

Tommy ruff may be fished for with an unweighted rig No.2, but with a ring added, carrying two short leaders below the swivel. A variation of rig No. 4 substitutes a berley sinker or "bomb". (This is a wire cage that is filled with berley. In this case it is suspended on a longer dropper, sometimes with two hooks added on a ring below the swivel.) Another rig involves float fishing (No.7) with a

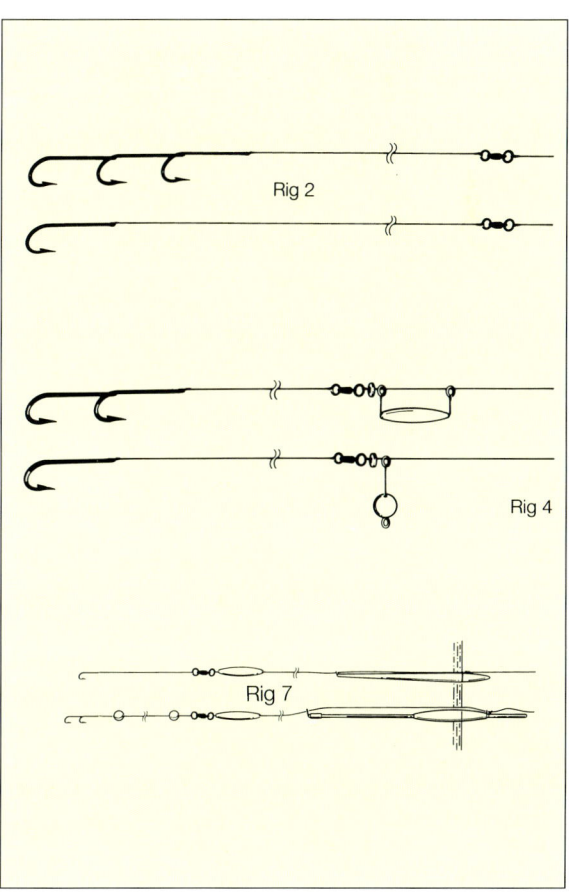

Rig 2

Rig 4

Rig 7

berley float or "blob" — a wooden or plastic bobby cork with a hole in it that is filled with berley — and again with one or two hooks on rings or swivels below the float.

In many cases lures of various kinds are substituted for baits on both the sinker or float rigs: multi-hooked bait-chasers that are commercially available can also be used.

The tommy ruff will take a wide range of lures — some as primitive as straws or plastic tubes fitted to the shank of a hook — especially the small sizes in spoons and slicers, provided they are bright and shiny.

How to hook

The secret of almost any rig used for tommy ruff is movement. Even with the berley sinkers the line should be retrieved slowly. A tommy ruff rarely misses. They fight aerobatically and tenaciously and they can throw or shake hooks free with vigorous leaping and twisting. A constant line tension between angler and fish is extremely important.

Hint

When fishing with standard lures, skittering them across the surface can often attract tommy ruff up from the bottom.

Edibility

These fish have a distinctive taste that is almost pungent. They are best grilled or fried whole after having been cleaned and scaled. They are excellent smoked.

TREVALLY

What trevally is that? Ask scientist, John Gunn, CSIRO Division of Fisheries Research, Hobart: "(Anglers) who have delved into the complex array of common or scientific names used for Australian carangids (trevallies) will have some idea of the state of confusion that surrounds the family's taxonomy. This confusion is primarily a consequence of inadequate and/or incorrect descriptions of species by many of the early workers.

"An important point towards reducing confusion has been the establishment of a world-wide list of standard common names and it is strongly recommended that these be adopted throughout Australia."

Such sound advice has been followed here with our selection of a representative number of trevallies. I acknowledge with thanks Mr Gunn's permission to use some of his work for the descriptions of the trevally that follow.

The giant trevally.

The big-eye trevally.

TREVALLY, BIG-EYE
Caranx sexfasciatus

OTHER NAMES: **GREAT TREVALLY, TURRUM**

Identification
The body of this trevally is relatively elongate, not deep, with a moderately steep but straight head profile and a slightly pointed snout. The eyes are large, the back third of them being covered by a clear adipose (fleshy) tissue. Adult big-eyes have a dusky to dark bluish-green upper body, with silver below. The second dorsal fin, anal fin and tail are all dark green to black, the last two fins having white tips, which becomes more obvious with age. The scutes — enlarged, sharply-pointed scales on this fish's lateral line — are mostly black. The curved half of the lateral line is moderately arched. Juveniles have a pale green to olive-green back, with silver below; the anal fin is yellow-green with a white tip. The tail is yellowish, apart from the black trailing edge and tip of upper lobe. It has similiar teeth to the giant trevally.

Size
The largest recorded length of a big-eye trevally is 75.7 centimetres.

Distribution
This trevally is most abundant in tropical waters. Its known southern limits are Sydney on the east coast and Kendren Island on the west coast.

TREVALLY, GIANT
Caranx ignobilis

OTHER NAME: **LOWLY TREVALLY**

Identification
The body of this fish is very deep, and deepest in large males. Its head profile is steep with a blunt mouth. Adult giant trevally vary in colour from silver-grey to black, being darkest on the upper body and head. Larger males exceeding 50 centimetres in length are often much darker than females of the same size. Small black spots or blotches are occasionally noticeable on the body and head.Juveniles are a silvery green above a silver-to-gold abdomen. Their soft dorsal, anal and caudal fins are pale green to yellow.
Giant trevally have an outer row of moderate to large conical teeth and an inner row of small, fine teeth in their upper jaw. There is a single row of smaller conical teeth in the bottom jaw.

Size
The largest recorded length of the giant trevally is 1.46 metres, though the Australian all-tackle record (at September, 1988) was only 37.6 kilograms. The world all-tackle record is 62.39 kilograms.

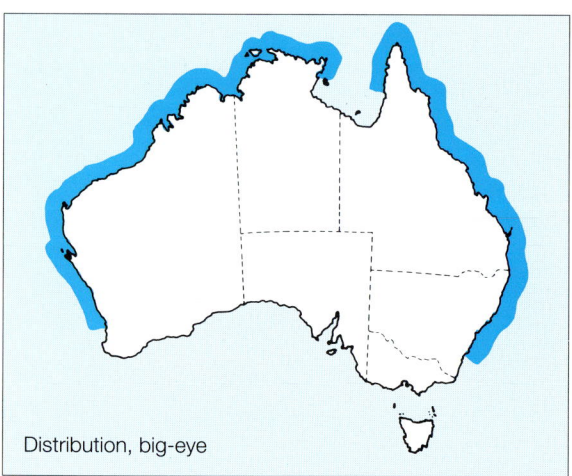

Distribution, big-eye

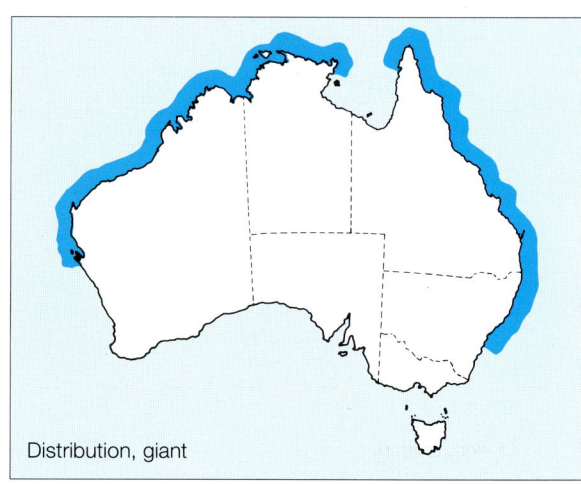

Distribution, giant

Distribution

These fish are normally abundant in Australia's tropical waters, though they are commonly encountered as far south as Sydney on the east coast and Coral Bay on the west coast.

TREVALLY, GOLDEN
Gnathanodon speciosus

Golden trevally.

Identification

The body of the golden trevally is elongate, though the dorsal profile is more convex than the stomach or ventral region. Juveniles of this trevally are a bright golden yellow with 7 to 11 vertical bars on the body, but this colour fades with age. The bars deteriorate into blotches in specimens over 50 centimetres, if they are apparent at all, and their positions are variable. The colour also varies after death, from silvery-white to a greenish-gold. The fins are pale or dusky grey, occasionally with a yellow tinge to them, and the tail has dark or dusky tips. Its schutes are few and small and weak. And it has no teeth on its jaws in specimens over 8 centimetres long. The tongue has fine, tooth-like projections.

Size

The largest known golden trevally was 1.1 metres long.

Distribution

These fish are common in the tropical regions of Australia, though the golden trevally has been recorded as far south as Sydney on the east coast and Denmark on the west coast.

TREVALLY, SKIPJACK
Pseudocaranx wrighti

OTHER NAMES: **SAND TREVALLY, SKIPPY**

[**Note**: This fish is often described in references as *Caranx georgianus*.]

Identification

Coupled with an identical profile, the colouring of this fish can lead to confusion with the white trevally. Both juveniles and adults have a body that varies from blue-green to a silvery green on the back, to a silvery white on the abdomen. The fins can be transparent to white, to yellow-green, to dusky green. There can be a yellow band along the mid-line of the body. There is a small but distinct black spot on the top of the gill cover. Another definite identifying feature is the gill raker count of 35 to 44, compared with the 29 to 34 of the white trevally. The shape of the hind or rear margin of the upper jaw is also different.

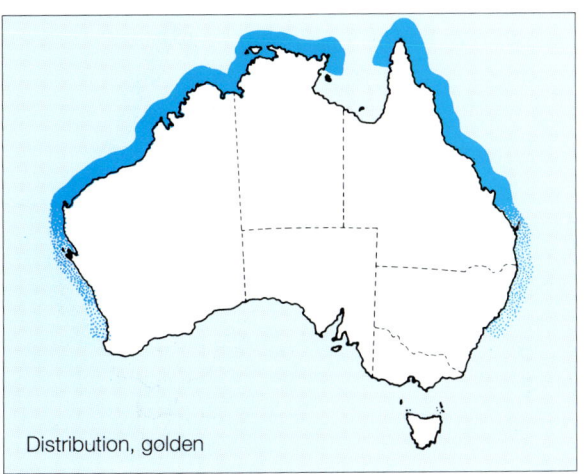

Distribution, golden

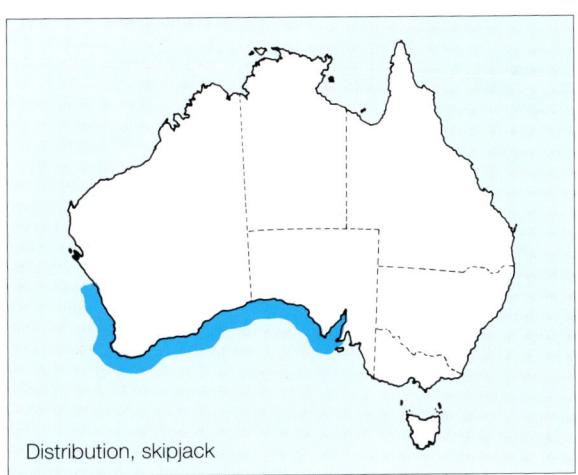

Distribution, skipjack

Skipjack trevally.

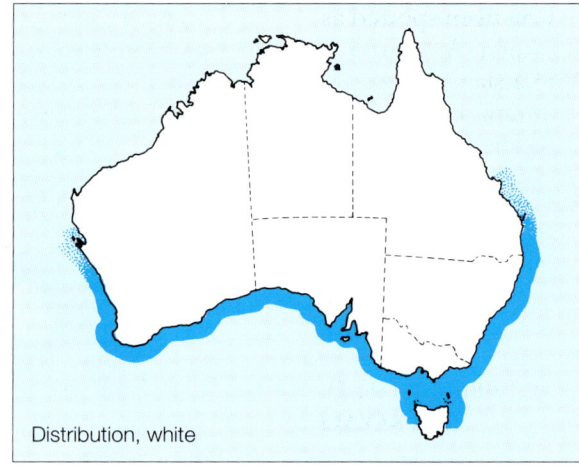

Distribution, white

Size

The skipjack trevally is smaller than the white trevally. Some references suggest 35 centimetres in length and a weight about 2 kilograms.

The minimum legal length for a catch in Western Australia is 20 centimetres.

Distribution

This trevally is endemic to Australian waters and it is distributed in temperate zones. It is most common in Western Australian waters, its most easterly distribution being recorded at Coffin Bay, in South Australia.

TREVALLY, WHITE
Pseudocaranx dentex

OTHER NAMES: **SILVER TREVALLY, BLUE TREVALLY (WA), SKIPPY, SILVER BREAM**

[**Note**: This fish is often referred to in references as *Caranx nobilis*]

Identification

The white trevally has a deep body similar to the skipjack trevally. Large males often develop a distinct hump above the eye. Juveniles and adults are the same colours, their bodies being blue-green to silvery-green above, and silvery below. A gold band is often present along the mid-line. Fins vary in colour from transparent white to a yellowish to dusky green. There is a large diffuse black spot on the upper gill cover compared to the distinct small spot on the skipjack. It has a gill raker count of 29 to 34.

Yellow-finned examples of this fish are more common on the central and northern coast of New South Wales.

Size

These trevally grow to about 90 centimetres and other records suggest a weight of about 8 to 12 kilograms around Lord Howe Island.

The minimum legal length for a catch in Western Australia, South Australia and Victoria is 20 centimetres

Distribution

There have been isolated reports of white trevally

White trevally.

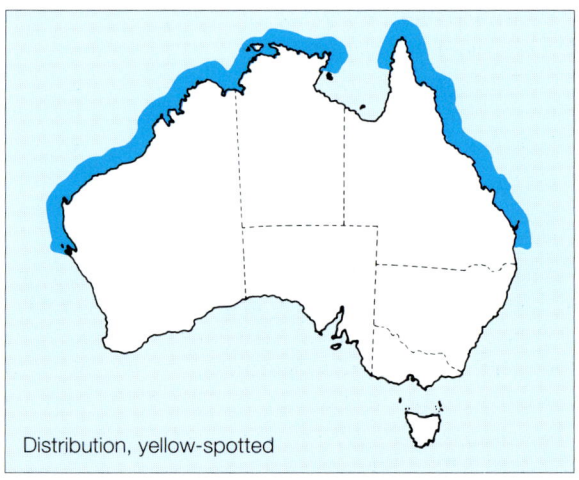

Distribution, yellow-spotted

having been spotted as far north as King Sound in Western Australia and One Tree Point in Queensland. Nevertheless, this species is most common in the temperate waters of southern Australia.

TREVALLY, YELLOW-SPOTTED
Carangoides fulvoguttatus

OTHER NAMES: **TURRUM, GOLD-SPOTTED TREVALLY, ALBACORE**

[**Note:** This fish has often been described in references as *Carangoides* or *Turrum emburyi*. However, *Carangoides fulvoguttatus* is the true **Turrum**, though other trevallies are, incorrectly, so described.)

Identification
The body of the yellow-spotted trevally, though quite deep in juveniles, becomes more elongate as the fish grows. Its head profile is straight and relatively steep. The colour at less than 15 centimetres is generally a uniform silver-grey with few, if any, small golden spots. Sometimes there is a hint of gold in the upper body and the fins are a dusky yellow.

By the time they are adult, the top of their bodies have become a blue-green to golden-green and silvery towards the abdomen. Numerous golden spots are visible over the upper two thirds of the body. There are also black spots on the gill cover, but these tend to be inconspicuous. The fins are a dusky yellow to green.

The yellow-spotted trevally can be distinguished from the big-eye and giant trevally by the rows of small sharp teeth in its jaws and the absence of the outer row of conical teeth.

Size
The maximum recorded length of a yellow-spotted trevally is 1.3 metres.

Distribution
These fish, which occur throughout the tropical waters of the Indian and western Pacific Oceans, are largely confined to the Australian tropics, though there have been isolated instances in which they have been recorded as far south as Maroochydore in Queensland and Coral Bay in Western Australia.

Yellow-spotted trevally.

The following applies to all trevally.

Breeding
All trevally are oceanic and group breeders, mainly throughout spring and summer periods.

Habits
Trevallies are schooling fish, especially during spawning migrations and as juveniles. The numbers in the schools of tropical trevally, however, are usually fewer. Large specimens are often found in a solitary state. These fish are never too far from a food source, being generally encountered along and over reefs, close in to rocky headlands, and it is not unusual to see them hunting on sand cays, beaches and in estuaries in the tropics. They are always active, always on the move, and almost always ready to accept a bait or lure. All are carnivores, eating fish, crustaceans, and molluscs. The golden trevally will take fish too, however, its protrusible mouth is much more specialised for extracting prawns, crabs, and other marine life from rocky and sandy areas, particularly around reefs.

When to fish
The mainly tropical species are present all year. Those caught in the south have usually been caught when they are following a warm current. Southern sea species bite best in the dusk to dark period of the day.

The temperate water species are more abundant in the most southern areas, from the middle to the end of summer. They can be prolific in autumn to early winter along the east coast of Victoria and southern New South Wales. The most promising months on the west coast are July and August.

Where to fish
Though trevallies are constantly moving, they are

likely to be found over or alongside reefs, near rocky shorelines and headlands, deep inlets and bays or harbours. In many of its tropical zones, trevally can be seen feeding in the clear waters, a rare luxury indeed in more southern waters.

The common temperate water species — skipjack trevally and white trevally — are usually encountered in schools over reefs, and around ocean rocks and headlands. They will, however, invade harbours, bays and estuaries and they are often caught from wharves and jetties, even from some sandy beaches. These fish are determined fighters for their size.

Tackle

Many of the tropical trevally are hooked while fishing the bottom for other species. Despite the fact that lines so used are invariably more than adequate in breaking-strain, the trevally will usually fight so long and hard that they may well snap a line on sharp rocks. Such breaks tend to be accidents, however, because trevally fight cleanly in open water and they can usually be boated if the gear and the angler are up to the task. Many anglers in tropical waters prefer to look for the larger fish in clear areas near headlands or reefs and then cast-and-retrieve lures. These outfits are usually medium to heavy single-handed or double-handed threadline or baitcasting rods and reels. It depends both on the sporting instincts and the experiences of the angler, but the line can be from 6 to 10 kilograms breaking-strain. Single or twin ganged hooks (three or four ganged hooks if it a better arrangement for the bait), up to a size of about 6/0 are satisfactory.

None of the trevallies, it should be noted, are surface fighters. They stay down deep in their efforts to free themselves. Most can be handled on a handline of 8 to 12 kilograms breaking-strain. If fishing from boat or wharf, you may prefer a boat rod, or a single-handed, medium-weight threadline or baitcasting outfit, including a 4 to 6 kilogram breaking-strain line. When fishing from the rocks, try a medium-weight rod for either sidecast, threadline or overhead reel, spooled with about 8 to 10 kilogram breaking-strain line for the trevally of southern waters. Hooks can be smaller, used singly or ganged — from 2 to 2/0 depending on the bait or the size of fish encountered.

Bait

Try whole fish (for the temperate water species, these should be small such as whitebait), fish fillets, slivers of squid, prawns, and limpets and mussels.

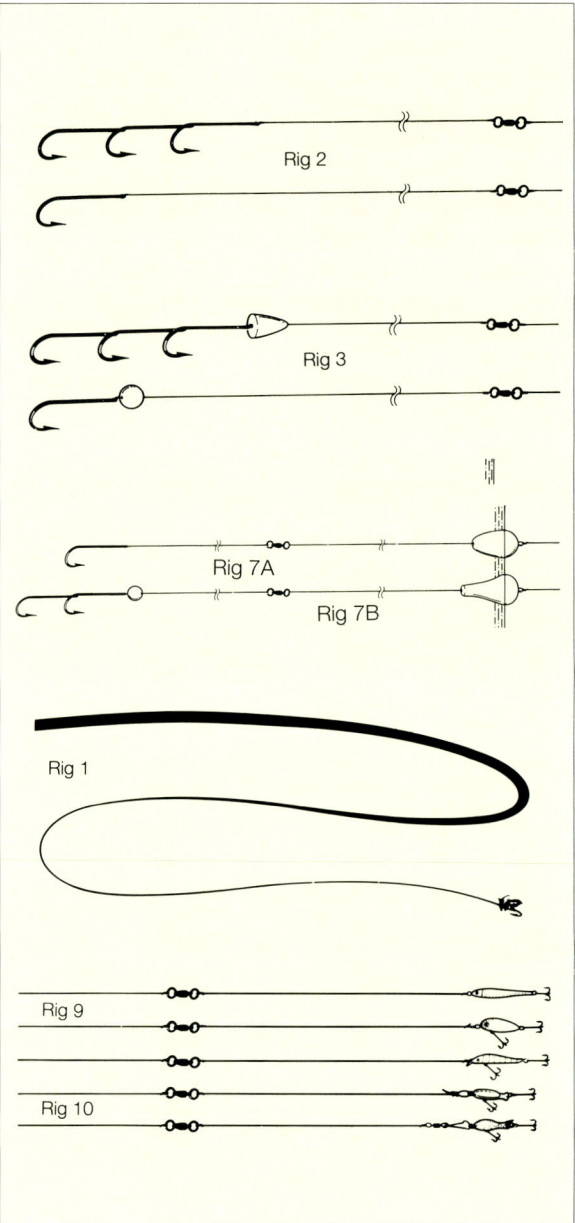

All trevallies will respond to lures, the larger members of the tropics often rising to take shallow-running or popper styles. For the southern trevally, small metal spoons, plastic-bodied lures, or the twister type of lures, all work well — especially when a school can be held with berley.

Rigs

The standard lure-casting rig No. 9 or 10 is suitable for trevally. But when fishing in the north, add a long, heavy leader, because the large tail of these fish is capable of badly chafing the line in a lengthy fight. The leader need only be about 50 per cent stronger than the main line for temperate species.

If fishing from a boat the unweighted rig No.2 or lightly weighted rig No.3 is recommended. If conditions allow, a bait suspended about mid-water beneath a float (rig No. 7A, for example) can be very effective.

How to hook

The larger trevally very seldom miss a lure or a bait (especially of live). The southern species, on the other hand, can be missed, even though they slurp the bait. The most likely cause of such a miss is a hook that is too large or too small for that particular school of fish. Trevally have tough mouths, so hooks should be sharp, thopugh even then their powerful efforts can tear them free.Whatever the size of a trevally, it will not surrender until it is tired.

Berley

A berley of boiled rice or breadcrumbs and bran, mixed with fish-flavoured cat food, will attract and hold trevally. Fishing an unweighted bait, or slowly retrieving a small lure through a good berley trail, is an excellent method for catching them.

Edibility

If the tropical species are retained for eating, they are usually juveniles of up to about 50 centimetres. All trevally should be killed, bled, gutted and filleted as soon as caught, and then iced, or at the very least kept cool.

They are very suitable for smoking and if some regard their flavour as too strong, they are palatable, especially if dressed with a robust sauce.

TROUT, BROOK
Salvelinus fontinalis

OTHER NAMES: **BROOKIE, RED SPOTTED BROOK TROUT**

Though this fish is a char rather than a trout, it is arguably the best-looking of the introduced freshwater species in Australia. It is one of numerous varieties of chars that exist in the coldwater lakes of Europe and possibly Siberia. The brook is native to the north-eastern region of the United States of America and some Canadian waters.

It is less wily than the brown trout and responds well to fly, lure and bait-fishing, offering excellent sport in its natural habitats. In many US States, it is a catch-and-release fish. A great deal of time and money has been spent breeding brook trout, especially in New South Wales, with minimal results for anglers. The reason may be unsuitable waters or the withering competition for food from brown trout and rainbow trout. Any angler landing a "brookie" should regard it as a bonus.

Identification

There is a distinct hump near the dorsal fin of mature male brook trout, which contrasts sharply with the streamlined shape of true trout and salmon. This hump does not occur on the female.

Their backs are usually a dull olive-green, with pale green wiggly patterns that form into creamy spots on the sides. They also have red spots surrounded by bluish circles on their sides. The dorsal and

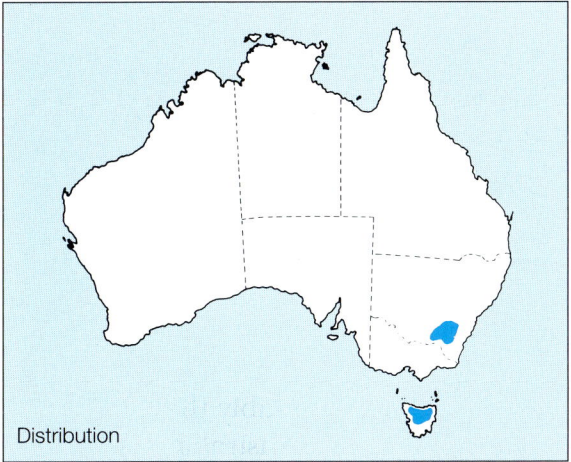

Distribution

taking surface food, they frequently linger on or near the surface, apparently filling their mouth before sinking again.

Distribution
Apart from the population in Clarence Lagoon, in Tasmania, these fish have been introduced elsewhere. In New South Wales some streams, and Lake Jindabyne, on the Monaro, have been stocked with hatchery-bred brook trout. Catches by anglers are not common.

When to fish
The brook trout's preference for colder waters means it is more active in early spring and autumn, prior to the spawning migration. In summer it

caudal fins have dark, wavy patterns. The abdomen is a cream to silver colouring, the males showing an orange tint. Pelvic fins, anal fins and caudal fins have white leading edges. The brook trout's scales are smaller than those of the true trout.

Size
Chars grow to 50 kilograms elsewhere in the world, but any brook trout of more than 6 kilograms is considered large. A brook trout reaching 2 kilograms in Australian waters would be exceptional.
In Tasmania, the minimum legal length for a catch is 22 centimetres; the minimum in New South Wales is 25 centimetres.

Breeding
Brook trout spawn and migrate to the gravel sections of running streams in autumn through to early winter. With the exception of a small self-sustaining population in Tasmania's Clarence Lagoon, brook trout in other waters in Tasmania and in the Monaro lakes and rivers in New South Wales, are released from hatcheries. There is no evidence of spawning in the wild in New South Wales.

Habits
Studies in the United States have shown that these fish do much better in waters where other fish — especially trout — do not compete for the same food. This may also be the reason that brook trout are invariably scattered in such waters, aggregating only when there is an increase in food, such as an abundance of stoneflies or mayflies occurring. The carnivorous brook trout have an appetite for almost any aquatic or terrestrial insect or animal — and other fish, including their own kind. When

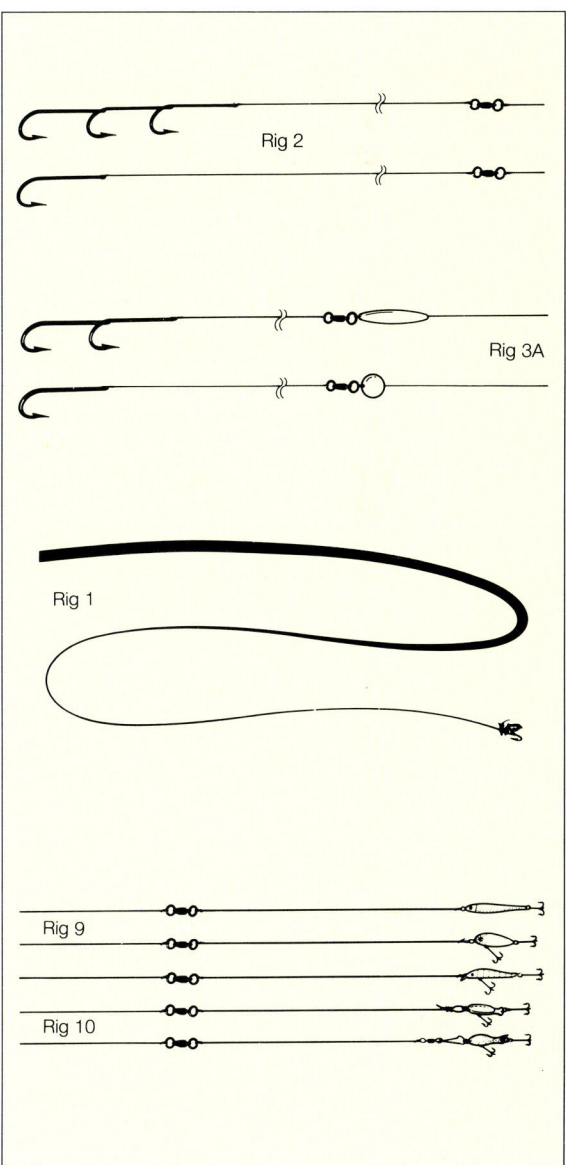

seeks the cooler depth of lakes during the hot weather, but will rise to terrestrial insects blown on the water, especially in early morning and late afternoon.

Fishing times are controlled in some States. All inland waters are closed in Tasmania during June and July. New South Wales streams are generally closed between midnight on the Queen's Birthday weekend in June until midnight of the Friday before Labor Day in October. Check with your local fisheries department or angling clubs.

Where to fish

Try fishing the faster running water, or in holes at the bottom of rapids, where the water is well-oxygenated; or in deep waters close to lake shores, especially where a creek or spring flow enters.

Tackle

Fly rod and reel are appropriate tackle, using either floating or sinking lines, and any of the popular patterns in dry and wet flies. Alternatively, a light single-handed threadline or baitcasting outfit, with a 2 to 4 kilograms breaking-strain line, will offer the flexibility of casting and retrieving lures *or* using bait.

Bait

Brook trout will respond to large insects, mudeyes, grasshoppers, yabbies, shrimps, earthworms and grubs, amongst other baits.

Rigs

Depending on water current and depth, use either an unweighted bait or a light running sinker, fished to move with the current (rig No.2 or 3A). Spinners, wobbling-type lures, deep-diving plugs and floating-diving plugs can be cast-and-retrieved. Many of these can be trolled with keels or attractors to fish deep water in lakes (rig No. 11). A collection of teaser-type flies, nymph patterns, and grasshoppers and beetle patterns, both wet and dry, should be in the fly fisherman's fly box.

Trolling does not appear to be as successful as fly-fishing or cast-and-retrieve methods with lures and bait (rigs No. 2 or 9).

It is a good idea to check with local fishing equipment suppliers for the most popular lures and flies.

How to hook

The brook trout, which is much less wary than brown trout, takes wet or dry flies readily. It usually hooks itself when it strikes a spinner or lure, or when it takes a moving, floating bait. Brook trout are also less diffident than the browns when mouthing or swallowing a still bait: stopping the line as it moves away and lifting the rod will set the hook.

Hint

Fishing an unweighted bait in deep water, close to an in-flowing creek or spring, can catch a brook trout in the restricted waters they inhabit. When a fish can be observed taking several surface insects in succession — and disappearing briefly in between — a larger dry fly should be floated past to tempt it.

Edibility

Many regard the brook trout as better eating than either the brown trout or rainbow trout.

Other regulations

The bag limit in New South Wales is 10 brook trout per angler per day; in Tasmania the bag limit is 12, although this number is proportionately reduced if blackfish, freshwater crayfish, and other trout are caught. The grand total cannot exceed 12 fish, whatever the mix.

TROUT, BROWN
Salmo trutta

This native of Europe and western Asia was introduced to Australia in 1864, first in Tasmania and later in Victoria. Tributaries of the Murrumbidgee were stocked in 1888. A year later a few coastal rivers and some western and New England streams were stocked. Brown trout are now widespread in the streams and lakes of Victoria, southern New South Wales, and along the central and northern tableland waters. They are prolific in Tasmania and limited populations exist in some small waterways in South Australia and the south-west of Western Australia.

Brown trout have an adverse affect on some native species, especially some of the galaxiids. Biologists believe that this imported fish — as a result of competition for food and by predation — may be responsible for the decline and disappearance of the indigenous trout cod and the markedly reduced numbers of the Macquarie perch and river blackfish. Where brown trout and rainbow trout inhabit the same waters, the brown appears to dominate. In many waters, especially in deep impoundments where cold water releases are made, the brown trout thrives. Though many stocks are maintained or supplemented by hatcheries, this trout is self-propagating in streams that have suitable spawning areas. Its growth is often limited only by over population creating a shortage of food.

Brown trout will enter salt water from coastal streams but return for spawning. Probably the wiliest of the trouts, the brown is an excellent angling species.

Identification

This elongated streamlined fish has a long head and a large mouth. Its colours are extremely varied. In rivers and streams it is predominantly a light brown or tawny brown on the back, slightly silvery on the sides, and displays black spots on the dorsal area, its sides and its head. Many anglers contend that a brown trout spawned in the wild has a tawny or golden hue rather than a silvery colour over the the lower part of its body. The spots spread below the lateral line, particularly towards the head, and they are often surrounded by a halo. There are also irregular reddish spots on the sides. The tail is square, or truncate, with a shallow fork.

Size

The size of brown trout depends on the level of the local population and the consequential availability of food. It has been recorded up to 14 kilograms in Australia. Young fish can be distinguished by between nine and 14 narrow, bluish parr marks (dark vertical marks like thumb prints) along the lateral line.

The minimum legal size for a catch — below which brown trout must be released — is 22 centimetres in Tasmania; 28 centimetres in South Australia; 30 centimetres in Western Australia; 25 centimetres in New South Wales; and 25 centimetres in Victoria.

Breeding

Spawning occurs from April to July, but it can vary, probably because of water temperatures or conditions. Spawning areas are almost always the

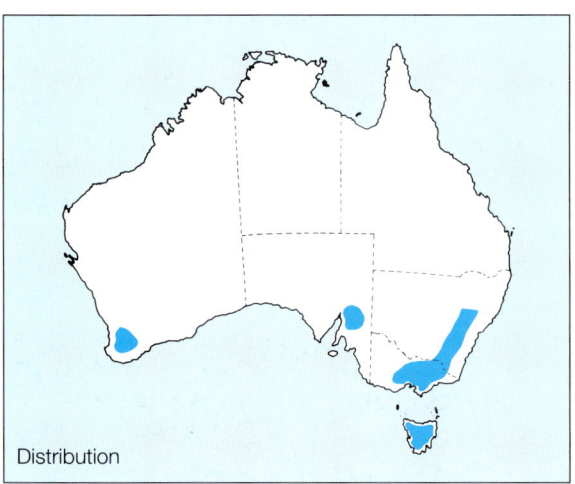

Distribution

small tributaries of rivers with gravel beds and a suitable water velocity. The ova is deposited in excavations made by the female, over which a male releases milt. This is then covered by the female.

Habits

The smaller browns tend to form shoals in favourable locations but they become solitary and territorial when they grow. Research in Victoria has shown that one-year-old brown trout will range over almost 400 metres of a stream but by two years they restrict their movement to 60 metres. Tasmanian angling research indicates that more browns are caught in or close to weed beds and near the shoreline of lakes; and that night fishing is probably twice as successful as day fishing in both zones. Far fewer browns are caught in open waters or near the surface. This same research showed the brown ate more crustaceans and caddies than other trout.

Brown trout feed on a wide range of crustaceans, such as yabbies and shrimps, aquatic insects, molluscs and small fish, worms and grubs, crickets, and insects which fall on the water, especially grasshoppers and Christmas beetles.

Distribution

Probably the most abundant trout in Australia, the brown is not only widespread, but reproducing in many waters, including lakes and impoundments in Tasmania and Victoria, and in the cooler mountain streams of the Great Dividing Range in New South Wales. There are some populations in the headwaters of a number of eastern-flowing streams in New South Wales. The fish exists in streams in the hills near Adelaide and in rivers and impoundments in Western Australia's south-west, between Perth and Albany.

When to fish

Regulations govern the periods when fishing is permitted in some waters in some States. All inland waters are closed in Tasmania during June and July. New South Wales generally closes its streams between midnight of the Queen's Birthday weekend in June until midnight of the Friday before Labor Day holiday in October. In Western Australia, some waters are closed between May 1 and August 1, others between May 1 and November 30 inclusive. In Victoria, it can be May 1 to the day before the second Saturday in December, both days being inclusive. Obviously it is best to check with your local fisheries department or angling club.

Bait-fishing, spinning and wet-fly fishing are usually

most productive in the spring. Where browns make a run for the sea in Tasmania and the coastal streams in Victoria, spinning the estuaries can be rewarding in this period. During summer, bait-fishing with grasshoppers is often successful and dry-fly fishing tends to come into its own. Prior to spawning in autumn, brown trout often become so hungry that they can be taken by bait, lures and flies.

Where to fish

Whether fishing with bait or using lures, more successful results with brown trout come from fishing along the edge or on top of weed beds, alongside undercut banks and below bank overgrowth —and in the deep corners of holes in streams, where a large specimen may have taken up residence.

With flies, wet teaser types such as streamers or matukas are very effective. So are nymph patterns. A heavy hatching of terrestrial insects, or perhaps grasshoppers blown on to the water, can induce browns to the surface to feed, especially in the late afternoon.

Tackle

For bait fishing, lure fishing and trolling — from bank or boat — a light to medium threadline or baitcasting rod and reel is adequate. Monofilament line of between 3 and 5 kilograms breaking-strain (slightly heavier if deep trolling with larger lures) is all that is needed. Large weighted matuka or streamer flies (where permitted) can also be used on this gear.

Small streams or larger waterways will determine the choice of fly rod, and the type and weight of line, but a floating line with a sinking tip should be your first choice if you are after brown trout in particular.

Bait

Try scrub worms or earthworms (rather than tiger worms), grasshoppers, shrimps, yabbies, mussels, crickets, Christmas beetles, wood or wattle grubs, mudeyes etc.

Rigs

Depending on water current and depth, use either an unweighted bait or a light running sinker, fished to move in the current (rig No.2 or 3A). Spinners, wobbling lures, deep-diving plugs, and floating-diving plugs, can all be cast and retrieved. Many of these can be trolled with keels or attractors when fishing deep lake waters (rig No. 11). An

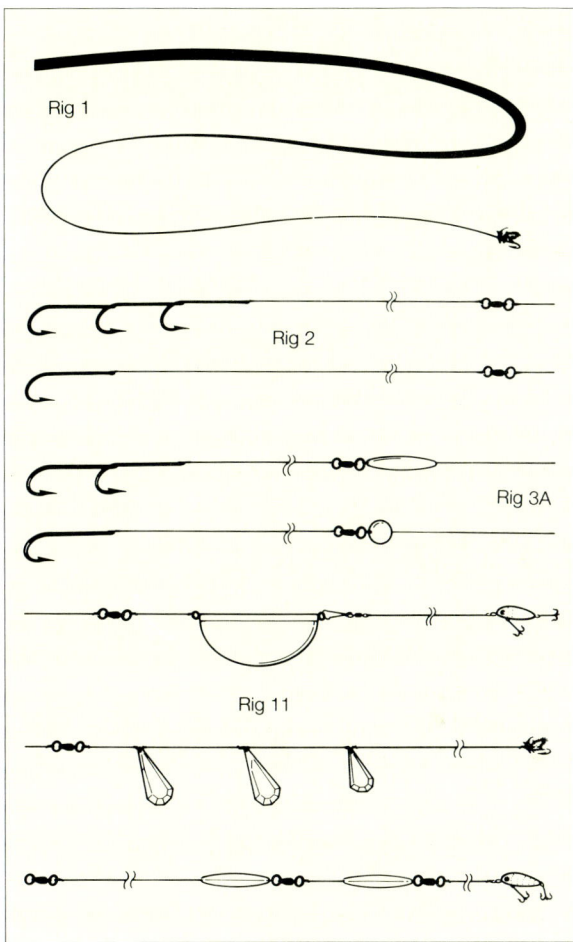

adequate selection of the teaser type of flies, nymph patterns, grasshoppers and beetle patterns, both wet and dry, should be in the angler's fly box. Check with local fishing equipment suppliers for the most effective lures and flies.

How to hook

Brown trout can be unpredictable. At times they hit a bait or lure hard and hook themselves; at others they tend to pick at a bait and often a slight lift-and-sink or stop-start retrieve will induce them to take the offering.

It is a good idea to allow the trout to move away for one or two metres with a bait before lifting the rod to set the hook. A fish seen to follow a lure or fly (or inspect it) can often be tempted with a change to a smaller size.

Hint

When using bait in streams, cast so that it is carried past likely trout holding locations on the current. At night, especially in lakes, fish bait under a "flip" float rig 7E, allowing the wind to move it about close to the shore .

Edibility

The brown trout is good eating, either fried or grilled, but many believe it is overrated. It is best when eaten very soon after having been caught. The flesh of a brown may be white or pink, almost red, the latter indicating it has been feeding mostly on water-fleas and crustaceans.

Other regulations

Apart from minimum sizes and closed seasons, there are regulations governing the number of fish an angler may keep. Moreover some waters are declared fly only, lure only etc., and even the number of rods an angler is permitted. These vary from State to State, but any angler contemplating fishing for freshwater fish should obtain a current guide for the relevant State from the better fishing tackle suppliers, tourist centres or fisheries departments.

In New South Wales the daily bag limit is 10 per person; in Victoria it is 5 per person in certain waterways; in Western Australia it is 10 per person; and in Tasmania it is 12 per person. (This number is reduced if blackfish or freshwater crayfish or other trout are caught.

The grand total of such a mixed bag may not exceed 12 fish.)

No bag limit applies in South Australia.

TROUT, CORAL
Plectropoma maculatum

OTHER NAME: **LEOPARD COD**

The coral trout has an aura of glamour about it. Anglers visiting the north for the first time tend to put this fish high on their wanted list — along with the barramundi — and it is well worth the effort. This fish of considerable beauty is, however, rarely cooperative. The coral trout can be difficult to find and a hard-fighting sporting fish if hooked. It is also a premium food fish.

Identification

It is important to realise that the coral trout is not always the bright red colour that identification photographs tend to show. Fish of such rich colour are usually taken from the deeper waters of its habitat. Those from the shallow areas tend to be a dull pink to brown. (After death, even the most vivid specimens become much duller.) Whatever the shade of red, the coral trout's body is covered with bright blue spots that are slightly paler on all fins and the tail. Its large eyes are red, with a blue to purple outline, and black pupils.

The coral trout is a somewhat compressed elongate fish, with a pronounced curve to its back. The front spined dorsal fin is lower than the back dorsal fin. The caudal peduncle is thick and the tail broad, almost straight. Coral trout have large mouths with small teeth, though some of their outer teeth are much larger and quite sharp.

Size

Though the coral trout has been recorded at more than 23 kilograms, a fish of more than 8 kilograms is not common. The larger sizes are more common along the north-west coast of the continent.

The minimum legal length for a coral trout in Queensland is 35 centimetres.

Breeding

Little is known, but this is one of the many hermaphroditic fish, which change sex during their life. In heavily fished areas, taking too many large fish may upset the balance of males and females.

Habits

This fish is a coral dweller. While it has been caught in much deeper waters, the coral trout seems to be more at home in waters up to 30 metres. It holes-up in caves and crevices in coral outcrops, from which it emerges to prey on small fish, crustaceans and molluscs. It is a fish that is caught in the day and at night — and a very fast swimmer when chasing a lure.

Distribution

Coral trout can be found from the southernmost end of the coral reef outcrops on the Queensland coast, around the north of Australia, and down to about the Abrolhos Islands near Geraldton, in Western Australia. It has been caught in some tropical areas by land-based anglers, where the water is clear and the coral occurs within casting range.

When to fish

Because reef fishing has its navigational and weather hazards, the most popular time is during the day in the dry season. However, the coral trout will certainly take baits at night, as boating anglers equipped with advanced navigational aids and depth sounders have found.

Where to fish

A coral trout is always a pleasant possibility while fishing for other reef fish, usually on the drift past the edge of coral cays and outcrops, in water to 25 metres. It is also found in much shallower water, as shallow as 3 metres at the rim.

Tackle

Heavy handlines are needed, probably no less than 30 kilograms breaking-strain, because there are many other large fish that inhabit the same territory as the coral trout. The same applies when trolling. Recently, the most popular outfit has been a short rod of about 2.5 metres, with a fast-medium taper and a powerful mid to butt section, which allows anglers to apply plenty of pressure to the fish. The reel is usually a heavy baitcasting type, spooled with line of about 12 kilograms breaking-strain. The same rod built to accommodate a heavy duty threadline reel will do the job. These outfits allow trolling, bottom-fishing and floating bait methods, as well as casting and retrieving baits and lures.

Bait

The coral cod is caught on fillets or cubes of almost any fish, small whole fish such as hardiheads, pilchards, garfish, mullet, etc. and octopus tentacles.

Rigs

The unweighted bait rig No. 2 is suitable for the shallower waters, but as the depths increase, the lightly-weighted bait rig No. 3 may be needed. Depending on the bottom, which invariably has snags, the bottom rig No. 6 with the sinker attached by a lighter line may save some hooks. The casting and retrieving of bait or lures can be done with rig No. 9. The use of ganged hooks can replace a wire trace but the leader must be heavy.

How to hook

The coral trout is less of a gulp-and-swallow feeder than many other fish caught in its territory. It grabs hard and is usually hooked in the mouth. It has to be stopped by the maximum pressure the angler's handline or rod and reel outfit can apply, or the fish will reach the sanctuary of reef caves or dash around coral niggerheads, either of which usually means a lost fish.

Hint

When trolling or casting lures, the lead-headed jigs with the upturned hook will reduce the odds of hooking coral instead of the fish. Those with replaceable plastic tails (have a good supply of these) seem to work on most fish in the vicinity of coral reefs.

Edibility

Coral trout, as with any fish caught in the tropics, is

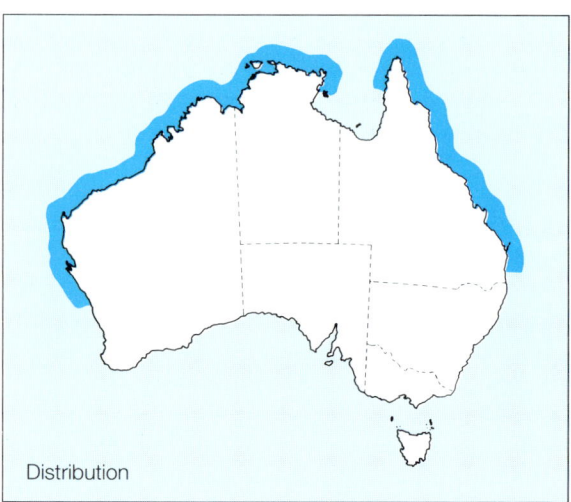

Distribution

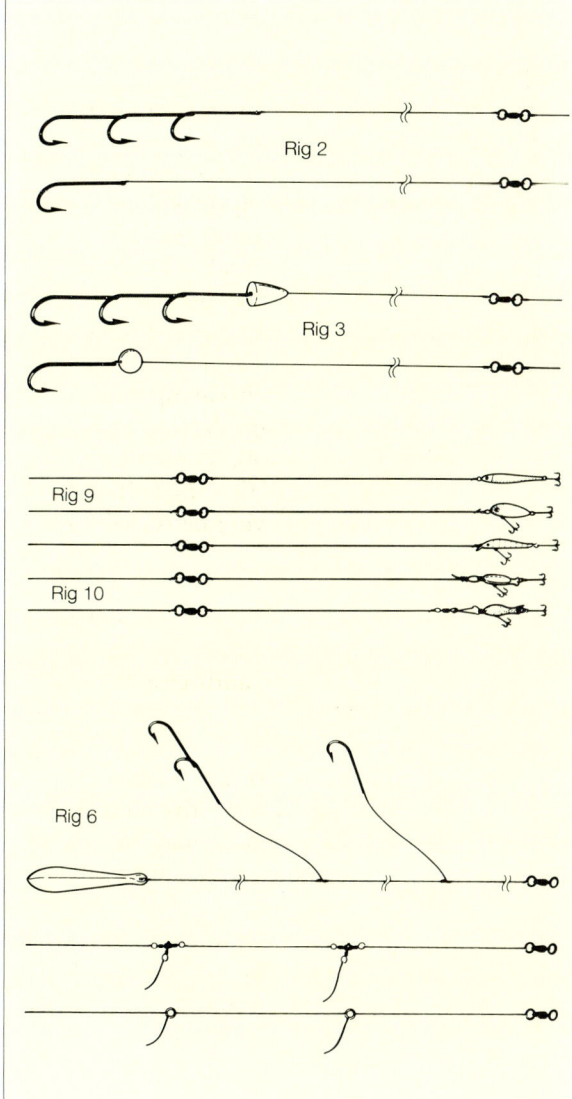

Rig 2

Rig 3

Rig 9

Rig 10

Rig 6

best cleaned immediately and kept on ice, whether filleted or whole. The flesh is firm, tender and white, with excellent flavour. A whole fish, stuffed with ingredients that will not overpower the fish's flavour, is a delightful meal.

[**Note**: Another fish, whose precise taxonomic status exacts considerable argument, is also called a coral trout. Known locally as the Chinese footballer, footballer-trout or tiger-trout, it is caught in the same locations as the true coral trout. It is mainly a yellowish-green to olive-brown, and dark on the back and head. It has four or five bands of irregular shape, from the dorsal area to the stomach. It has blue spots, which are particularly vivid on the yellow to orange coloured fins. It is not known how big this fish grows, but it has been caught at around the 60 to 80-centimetre length. The real bonus is that it is every bit as edible as the real thing.]

TROUT, CORONATION

Variola louti

OTHER NAMES; **FAIRY COD, LUNAR-TAILED ROCK COD**

This fish, which is fairly widespread in tropical regions, is known as far south as Noosa. It is one of the most beautiful of reef fish. Its overall colour is a brilliant orange-red, with small, purplish splashes or spots all over its body. The dorsal and anal fins have a swept-back style and the tail is a deep, sickle shape. These fins are edged in yellow at the trailing end, as are the pelvic fins and pectoral fins. The coronation trout has a straighter mouth and larger lower jaw than the coral trout. It occupies the same habitats, grows only to about 80 centimetres, and can be caught by the same methods. It is also excellent eating.

An almost identical fish, called the **white-finned moontail bass** (*Varicola albimarginata*), inhabits the waters of the Northern Territory and the north-west of Western Australia. Its head and body are deep red, which becomes more orange on the abdomen. It has a network of small crimson or purplish spots and yellow lines over the head and body. The outer half of its pectoral fins are yellow, but the edge of the caudal fin is white.

TROUT, RAINBOW
Salmo gairdneri

[**Note**: Recent research in the US suggests that this fish may be a char rather than a trout. These biologists recommend that the scientific name should be *Oncrhynchus mykiss*.]

The rainbow trout, which is a native of the west coast of the United States, Canada and Alaska, was introduced to Australia in 1894. It requires constant re-stocking, however, once the more aggressive brown trout is introduced to compete with it. The rainbow will run to sea from rivers with easy access to the ocean and seem to disappear — unlike brown trout which returns to the river it leaves.

For the first-time trout angler, the rainbow offers the best opportunity to catch a trout. Smaller ones often display a singularly suicidal tendency to take a spinner or retrieved bait.

Identification

Though very similar in shape and features to the brown trout, a mature rainbow — while varying considerably in colour as a result of its habitat, size, and sexual condition — has a pinkish blush or red band along the sides of the body. Most rainbow trout that live and spawn in streams display a more intense colour than lake residents, the latter being lighter, brighter and more silvery. The stream-dweller also has large numbers of small black spots scattered above its lateral line and over most of its sides, but very few — if any — are evident on fish from lakes. These fish can be a bluish-green on the back with quite silvery sides. The tail is moderately forked, though it does tend to be square in large specimens.

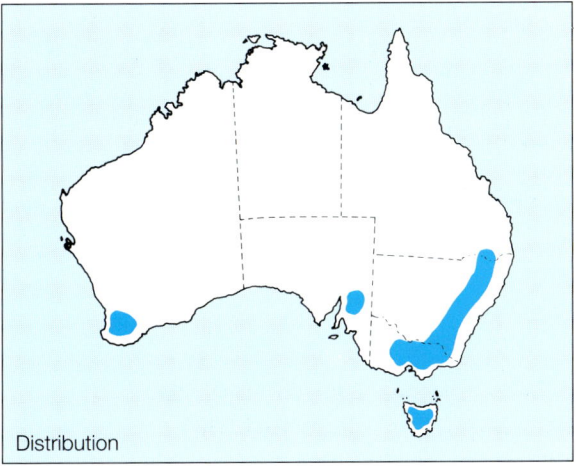
Distribution

Size

You are unlikely to catch a rainbow trout in Australia over 5 kilograms, though the largest recorded was 9.3 kilograms. Most taken by anglers are between 0.5 kilograms and 1.5 kilograms, depending on waters.

The minimum legal length for rainbow trout is the same as for other trout in all States: 22 centimetres in Tasmania; 25 centimetres in New South Wales; 28 centimetres in South Australia; 30 centimetres in Western Australia; and 25 centimetres in Victoria.

Breeding

Spawning occurs from August to September in most areas of Australia. The trout move into the small tributaries of rivers or lakes, where there is a gravel bed beneath a current, often above a deep pool. During the period when the female prepares an excavation for the eggs, the males chase each other in a hectic mood. Breeding of the rainbow trout, as with brown trout, is well established in hatcheries in Australia.

Habits

Rainbow trout prefer cool, aerated water, particularly swift-flowing rivers and creeks. In Australia, however, the rainbow are often more numerous in lakes than in running water, possibly because of better food resources. Generally much more active than browns, rainbow trout also grow faster. Their diet is extensive, including aquatic and terrestrial insects, crustaceans, worms, grubs etc., and other small fish. Local research seems to be gathering the conviction that the rainbow trout is largely responsible for the disappearance or dramatic decrease of many of Australia's native galaxiids.

Distribution

These trout are widespread in both streams and lakes of Tasmania and Victoria, and in the waters and impoundments of the southern, central, and northern regions of the Great Dividing Range in New South Wales. There is a small population near Warwick in Queensland, in the hills behind Adelaide in South Australia, and in some streams in the south-west of Western Australia.

When to fish

The ideal time to fish is from spring, throughout the summer, and into autumn. Better catches are made when the water temperature has not affected the metabolism of the fish — and during seasonal hatches of midges and insects.

The period for fishing some waters in some States is controlled by regulations. All inland waters are closed in Tasmania during June and July. New South Wales generally closes its streams between midnight on the Queen's Birthday weekend in June until midnight on the Friday before Labor Day in October. In Western Australia some waters are closed between May 1 and August 31, others between May 1 and November inclusive. In Victoria it can be from May 1 to the day before the second Saturday in December, inclusive of both days. Check with local fisheries departments or angling clubs.

Where to fish

Seek out well-oxygenated waters in rivers, or pools below rapids. Also, try the shaded areas of lakes, especially those close to weed beds, amongst trees, and where a river current is still visible.

Tackle

Use a fly rod and reel with either floating or sinking lines and the most popular patterns in dry and wet flies. A light single-handed threadline or baitcasting outfit, with a 3 to 4 kilograms breaking-strain line, will provide the flexibility to cast-and-retrieve lures or bait. A slightly stronger line is suggested for trolling.

Bait

The rainbow trout will take worms, beetles, tadpoles, frogs, grasshoppers and wood grubs etc.

Rigs

As with brown trout, the rig depends on water current and depth. Use either an unweighted bait or a light running sinker, so it can move in the current (rig No.2 or 3A). Spinners, the wobbling type of lures, deep-diving plugs and floating-diving

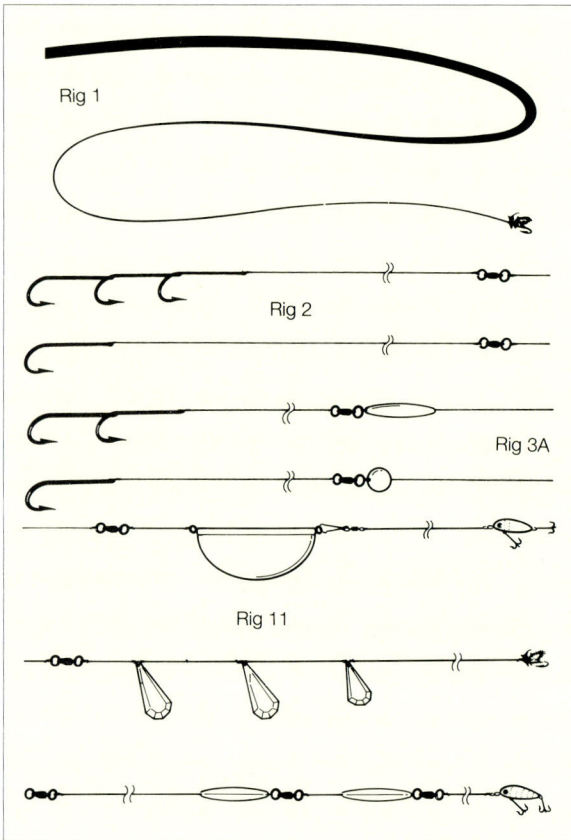

Rig 1

Rig 2

Rig 3A

Rig 11

plugs can all be cast and retrieved. Many of these can be trolled with keels or attractors when fishing deep lake waters (rig No. 11). An adequate selection of the teaser type of flies, nymph patterns, grasshoppers and beetle patterns, both wet and dry, should be in the angler's fly box.

It is a good idea to check with local fishing equipment suppliers for the most popular lures and flies.

How to hook

If fishing with a dry or wet fly, the critical timing for setting the hook comes only with experience, because the line must be tightened without a jerk. Matuka, or the streamer type of fly, worked erratically, often results in a rainbow hooking itself

— as they do when lures, especially bright spinners, are cast-and-retrieved or trolled. After what appears to be a nibble, allow a bait to be taken a metre or so before stopping the line and lifting the rod.

Hint

A relatively new technique involves casting a tiny lead-headed jig upstream in rocky rapids, and allowing it to tumble down in the current. It is proving very successful and it is often worth lifting the rod as soon as the jig stops. Sometimes its movement is caused by a rock, but it is often the grab of a rainbow trout!

Rainbow trout can prove to be very tough adversaries when caught on suitably light gear. Their fight is usually remarkably spectacular, with plenty of airborne gymnastics.

Edibility

The flesh of the rainbow trout is white or pink, depending on the diet of the fish. Many regard the pink flesh to have a richer flavour than the white. It is good eating whether lightly fried, grilled or baked.

Other regulations

Apart from minimum sizes and closed seasons, there are regulations limiting the number of trout an angler may keep as well as waters declared fly-only, lure-only etc., and even the number of rods permitted. These vary considerably, so anglers contemplating fishing for freshwater fish should obtain a current guide for the relevant State from better fishing tackle suppliers, tourist centres or fisheries departments.

In New South Wales the bag limit is 10 per angler per day; in Victoria it is 5 per angler per day in certain waterways; in Western Australia it is 10 per angler per day; and in Tasmania 12 per angler per day. This number is reduced if blackfish or freshwater crayfish and other trout are caught: the grand total may not exceed 12 fish, whatever the mix. There is no bag limit in South Australia.

TRUMPETER

There are several sea-perch in Australian waters (family Teraponidae) that are commonly referred to as trumpeters. And even the little mado — an innocuous bait-stealing fish of estuaries and inshore waters — are often called trumpeters. Here, however, "trumpeter" is properly confined to fish belonging to the family Labrididae of the south and south-eastern waters of the continent, though they are mostly associated with Tasmania.

TRUMPETER, TASMANIAN or "REAL"
Latris lineata

OTHER NAMES: **STRIPED TRUMPETER, STRIPEY**

Identification

This trumpeter has an elongate, oval body, which is identically curved on the dorsal area above the gill cover, and on the belly — from the base of the pectoral fin to the end of the dorsal fin and the anal fin, which ends very close to the tail. The head is long and pointed. The base colour of the body is a yellow-green, but lighter in the belly area. The head is an olive-brown and three dark brown to blackish stripes run the length of the body. The upper stripe starts at the snout and passes through the eye, the middle stripe starts at the end of the mouth and the bottom one at the top of the gill cover. The dorsal fins are a fawn to light brown. The tail is dark brown and the other fins are dusky to fawn.

Juveniles are lighter in colour than adults, with a fourth, shorter yellowish stripe on the fins.

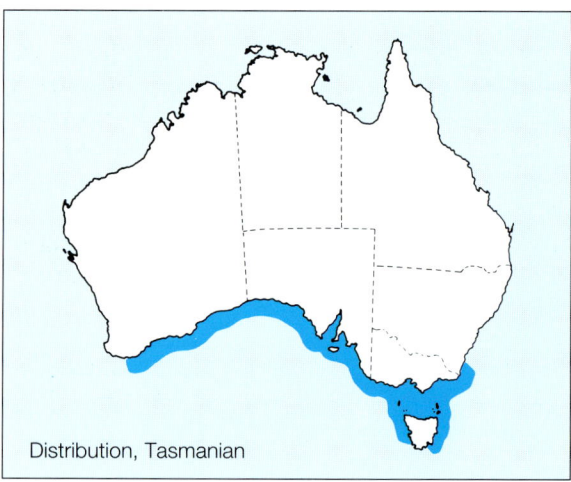

Distribution, Tasmanian

Size

The Tasmanian or "real" trumpeter grows to about 1.2 metres and exceeds 25 kilograms. A specimen over 10 kilograms is regarded as exceptional. The minimum legal length for a catch in Tasmania is 33 centimetres.

Breeding

The fish move from deep offshore reefs to coastal reefs to spawn in the summer.

Habits

Trumpeters inhabit the deeper offshore reefs, rarely being caught in less than 40 metres of water. They dislike dirty water and are more common in cooler waters. Their food consists of crustaceans and any small fish that moves, though they mix freely with other reef fish.

Distribution

The Tasmanian trumpeter is most prolific in Tasmanian waters, though it can be found in southern coastal waters of New South Wales (to Montague Island), Victoria, and the south of Western Australia, to around Albany.

When to fish

The trumpeter is around all year, but it only seems to visit the shallower inshore reefs during the summer months. The best fishing time is usually in the morning period. Sea conditions often prevent small boats reaching the trumpeter's preferred habitat.

Where to fish

The ideal place to fish is over or alongside deep, offshore reefs. A boat equipped with a good depth sounder is almost a necessity. Very heavy commercial and recreational fishing in past years has reduced inshore numbers.

Tackle

Handlines, or short boat rods with the winch type of reels, are probably the best choice. The line's breaking-strain should be a minimum of 20 kilograms and hooks should be about 4/0 to 6/0 in size.

Bait

Trumpeter will take any fresh fish fillets or cubes, and octopus. However, a very popular bait is fillets of fresh barracouta.

Rigs

In most cases, rigs will need a heavy sinker to reach the Tasmanian trumpeter. Depending on depth, the bottom rigs — running No. 4A or deep-sea rig No. 6 — are suitable.

How to hook

It helps if the bait is drifting or being moved by the current. Tasmanian trumpeters are not hesitant biters in most instances. Their grab for the bait, combined with the movement of the bait, usually results in a hook-up. Unfortunately, the depths at which they are caught and brought to the surface reduce their fighting ability.

Edibility

The trumpeter's flesh is tasty, whether baked,

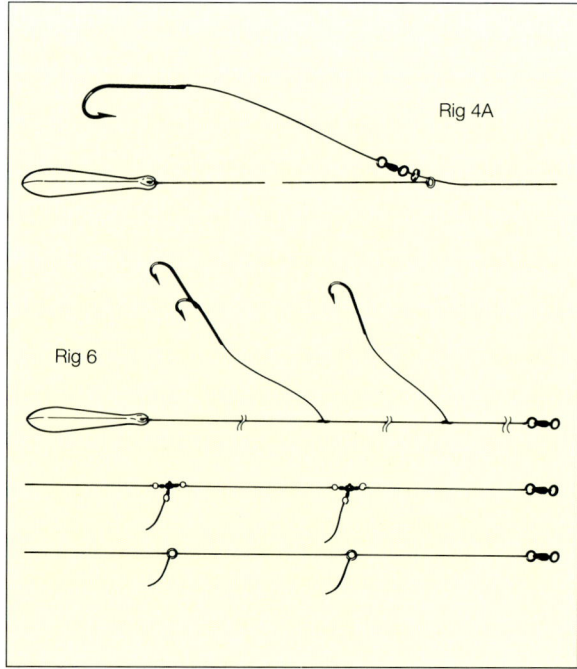

Rig 4A

Rig 6

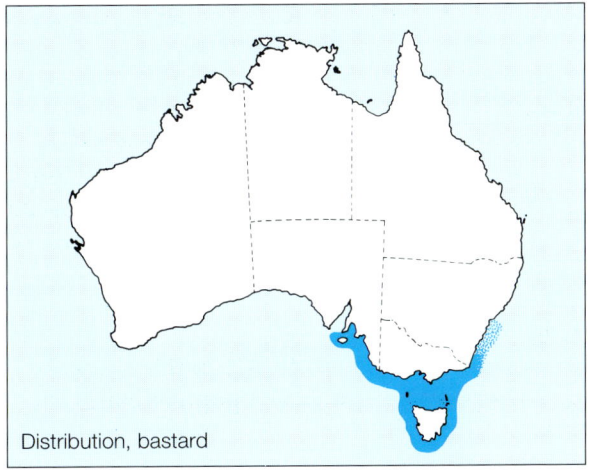

Distribution, bastard

fried, grilled or boiled. It is a very good fish for smoking.

TRUMPETER, BASTARD
Latridopsis forsteri

OTHER NAME: **SILVER TRUMPETER**

Identification
This fish could be mistaken for a morwong with its deep oval elongate shape. However, the pectoral fins lack the long filaments that characterise the morwong. The snout is also less rounded. The body colour is a silver-grey with the upper half a brownish-orange. There are darker shades near the dorsal fin. Juveniles may be predominantly a shade of red.

Size
This fish grows to about 65 centimetres in length and may weigh as much as 3 kilograms.

Breeding
Little is known.

Habits
These fish are omnivores. They eat a wide range of small fish, crustaceans, shellfish, etc. The juveniles often school in vast numbers but adults are more likely to be encountered singly or in ones and twos. They prefer reefs and rock areas.

Distribution
Bastard trumpeters are reasonably common in the deeper inshore and offshore reefs of Tasmania, and are occasionally found in waters from Sydney south, around Victoria and on to South Australia.

When to fish
These fish are around all year, but morning or evening appear to be the better fishing times.

Where to fish
The bastard trumpeter can be found on or near reefs in deeper inshore and offshore waters.

Tackle
Handlines are quite suitable, as are boat rods with the winch type of reels, spooled with line of about 10 kilograms or more breaking-strain. Hooks should be about 1/0.

Bait
Try prawns, shellfish flesh, particularly mussels, and marine worms.

Rigs
Depending on the depth of water, bottom rigs No. 4A, 5, or 6 can be effective (*see* previous entry for rigs 4A and 6).

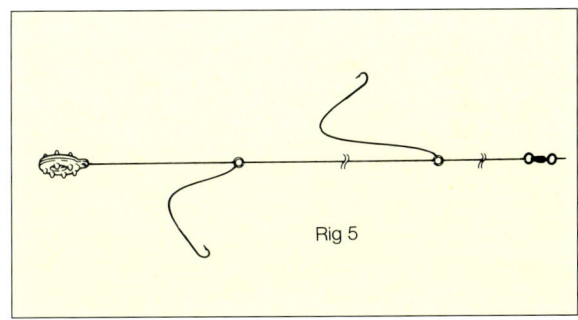

Rig 5

How to hook
This fish is usually a soft biter but it takes the bait quickly. As soon as the weight of the fish is felt, a quick tightening of the line is generally enough to hook it.

Edibility
The flesh is quite white and tasty. It can be prepared for the table by most methods.

TUNA

The three species of tuna dealt with first are those reasonably accessible to anglers fishing from the shore or a boat. Small tunas can generate the same excitement and rewards as the really mighty tunas — it is a matter of degree. Even relatively novice anglers, with quite basic outfits, have a chance of experiencing the speed and power of these fish — not just the very serious game fishers, with their splendid pursuit boats and lavishly expensive game gear (though it undoubtedly helps). All tunas are torpedo-shaped with one common characteristic. While they vary in size — and only some visit inshore waters — they are all very swift predators, forever on the move in search of prey, especially schooling fishes and squid. The feeding tuna are generally of a similar size , with the larger fish aggregating in the smallest numbers.

All tunas — and their relatives the mackerels — swim with their mouths slightly open to ensure more water is forced across their gills. They require a high oxygen intake because of their extreme muscular activity, which depends on a more abundant supply of blood than is found in other fish. Because of this, they swim and feed almost continuously, especially the long-tail tuna, which has no swim bladder.

Tunas will be about only where and when the water is clean, free of sand, algae, weeds or pollutants, which may clog their gills and inhibit their intake of oxygen.

Two members of the family appear elsewhere under other names. Fishing tackle and methods are combined for some.

Striped tuna or skipjack.

BONITO

(*see* entry BONITO)

TUNA, ALBACORE

(*see* entry ALBACORE)

TUNA, LARGE-SCALE

(*see* entry MACKEREL, SHARK)

TUNA, FRIGATE
Auxis thazard

OTHER NAMES: **FRIGATE MACKEREL,
LEADENALL**

Identification

When alive, the frigate tuna (which is thicker through the body than the mackerel with which it is so frequently listed) has a deep blue back. This colour fades into a silvery, faintly-blue white on the belly. There are worm-like stripes on the back, less distinct than on the kawa kawa tuna. It is easily distinguished from the kawa kawa by the wide space between its two dorsal fins.

Size

The frigate tuna grows to about 55 centimetres in length and 2 kilograms, though the majority taken are usually half this size.

Habits

This fish is basically a surface feeder, which eats

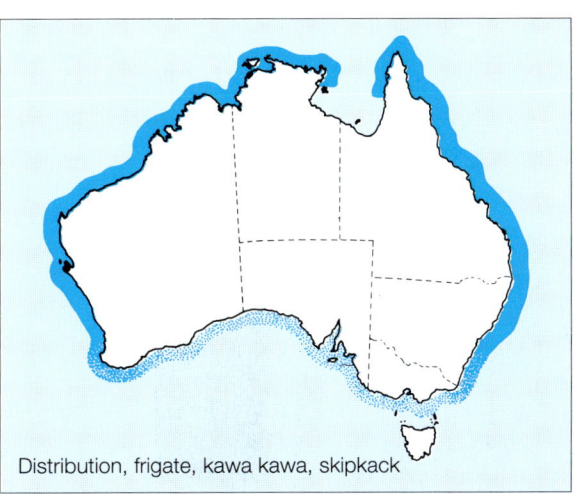

Distribution, frigate, kawa kawa, skipkack

small fish such as whitebait and squid. They prefer a water temperature of 14°C to 24°C. In the southern part of their range, their presence often also indicates that yellowfin and marlin are around.

TUNA, KAWA KAWA
Euthynnus affinis

OTHER NAMES: **MACKEREL TUNA, LITTLE
TUNA**

Kawa kawa tuna.

Distribution

While it appears sporadically or seasonally in some waters, it is more common from the mid-coast of New South Wales up through the tropical waters of the north, and down to the north-west coast of Western Australia.

Identification

Having a colouring and stripe pattern on its back very similar to the frigate mackerel, this fish is identified by its long-based front dorsal fin being only marginally separated from its second dorsal fin. The back is a somewhat lighter and greener blue and the wavy greenish stripes are more pronounced. There are from two to five dark spots above the ventral fin.

Size

The kawa kawa tuna may reach about a metre in length and about 10 kilograms in weight. Six people (at September, 1988) share the all-tackle record with a fish at 9.07 kilograms, all having been caught in the central coast of New South Wales.

Habits

These fish school and feed on small fish, whitebait, pilchards, sardines, yellowtail, etc., and squid. They are mainly surface feeders that, when hunting, will follow their prey close into rock-fronts and behind the breaker-line along beaches.

Distribution

Regarded as a tropical species, they are nevertheless fairly common in the southern temperate waters of the east and west coasts, ranging as far south as Cape Leeuwin in Western Australia and Eden on the New South Wales south coast.

TUNA, SKIPJACK
Katsuwonis pelamis

OTHER NAME: **STRIPED TUNA**

Identification

The dorsal area of the body is a dark blue, sometimes lighter near the tail, that darkens after death. The skipjack is distinguished by the dark stripes on its sides and abdomen, which occasionally appear as broken patches.

Size

The skipjack tuna reaches a length of about 1.1 metres and a weight of 20 kilograms. The Australian all-tackle record (at September, 1988) is 11.50 kilograms. The world all-tackle record is 19 kilograms.

Habits

This schooling fish is a surface feeder that follows migrating small fish. It also eats squid. As with most tunas, the fish tend to school with fish of a similar size. Their preferred water temperature is 15°C to 27°C. Their presence may indicate that yellowfin tuna, kingfish or marlin are in the vicinity.

Distribution

Though it is a tropical species, it can frequently be encountered in schools in the more southern waters of the east and west coast. Interestingly, the Australian Game Fishing Association records indicate that small fish are caught in the tropics in the winter period; larger fish are taken from spring and through the summer in southern Queensland; further south, including Tasmania, the better catches are in late autumn.

The following applies to frigate, kawa kawa and skipjack tuna.

When to fish

There are always the odd lost members of these tuna that may be encountered in most of their distribution range. As a general guide, winter is the time for them in the tropics, spring to mid-summer in the sub-tropical and northern temperate waters, and late summer to autumn is better in the south. Water temperatures and currents are another factor that can influence this generalisation.

The duller light of early morning or late afternoon can be more productive, as can overcast days. And a smooth flat sea is never as rewarding with these tuna as a sea with some chop or waves.

Where to fish

Gulls, terns and other sea birds will gather when any tunas are feeding offshore, diving for scraps, pieces of fish or maimed prey. Tunas will often give themselves away when they break the surface in their attacks. Without such signs, trolling may intercept their path, the lure or bait diverting them from their cruising pattern, for they never stop hunting.

Tackle

When fishing from boats, the fish may be trolled with handlines or boat rods fitted with the winch type of reels. The most effective tackle, however, is a light to medium single-handed threadline rod and reel, or a baitcasting rod and reel, spooled with 4 to 6 kilograms breaking-strain line. These outfits provide for trolling with lures or bait, casting-and-retrieving to a school, or drifting with unweighted bait. If fishing with live bait, or casting-and-retrieving lures from rocks, use a 3-metre to 4-metre medium rod, with a fast to fast-medium taper. Rods can be overhead, threadline or side-cast. The line needs to be about 8 to 10 kilograms breaking-strain. Wire traces are unnecessary and hooks and lures should not be too large — up to 3/0, depending on the tuna and its size.

Bait

These three tunas will often attempt to swallow the trolled baits and lures that were meant for larger fish; at other times they can contrarily refuse fish that are not exactly the size of their normal prey. In general, the best baits are the smaller sizes of fish such as yellowtail, garfish, mullet, pilchards, sardines, whitebait or fish-shaped fillets, and squid. If in doubt, fish with smaller baits or lures.

All three tuna will respond to the above fish, fished live under a float, with the mackerel tuna (and bonito) often being caught close in to the rocks. These three tuna are also excellent game fish on saltwater flies and some of the small plastic-bodied fish-shaped lures. It is difficult to choose the right size but "smaller" is invariably the best way to go. White-painted barrel sinkers, cast-and-retrieved at high speed, can be remarkably successful.

Rigs

Try the unweighted rig No. 2. A lightly-weighted rig No. 3A can be used for casting-and-retrieving bait and lure. The barrel sinker weighted or keel type of rig (No. 11) are suitable for trolling with small baits or lures.

How to hook

In most instances, the fast strike of a tuna results in a hook-up. With floated bait it is often wise to allow the fish to run until they have turned the bait to a swallowing position, which is often indicated by the fish slowing or stopping. These tuna won't break the surface in their attempts to escape but they will fight hard. The mackerel tuna makes the longest and hardest runs and it will seek rock obstructions when hooked from an ocean front.

Edibility

The frigate, in particular, and small kawa kawa and skipjack tuna, are popular trolling baits for larger game fish and for sharks. And their flesh is a good bait for many other fish, especially reef species. If

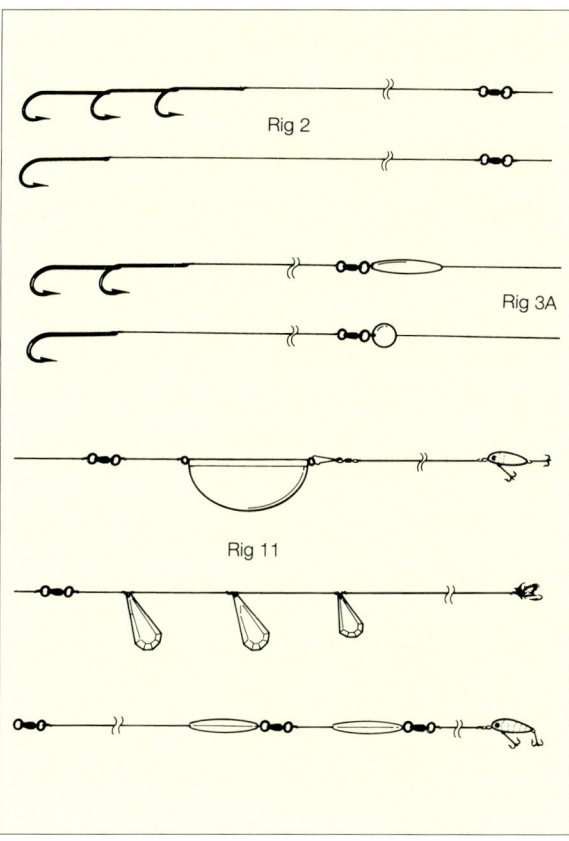

required for eating, the fish should be killed, bled, cleaned and filleted, and then placed on ice as soon as it is caught. The flesh is red, but it can be made a more acceptable white colour by dipping it in boiling water. It can be palatable when crumbed and fried.

TUNA, BIG-EYE
Thunnus obesus

Identification

Small specimens of this fish are sometimes confused with similarly-sized yellowfin. The pectoral fins of the big-eye are of moderate size and they end directly below the beginning of the second dorsal fin (yellowfin's pectoral fins always end *past* the beginning of its more elongated second dorsal). This tuna's eye is also larger than the yellowfin's. If still in doubt, examine the liver: there are no dark streaks in the big-eye's liver, unlike the yellowfin's. The big-eye's colour is a blue-black on the upper part, fading to a silver-grey below. Its finlets are yellow with a broad, but blotchy, black edge.

Size

The big-eye tuna is believed to reach about 2.4 metres in length. The Australian all-tackle record caught under the rules of the Australian Game Fishing Association is 120 kilograms (at September, 1988). The world record is 197.31 kilograms.

Habits

This is an off shore member of the tuna family, living and hunting out beyond the continental shelf. Reports of juveniles having been sighted in estuary waters and inshore areas of tropical waters may be the result of confusion with other species.

Distribution

There are very few line-class records of this fish taken in Australian waters. The record all-tackle fish was taken off Bermagui in April. One other big-eye tuna weighing 56.24 kilograms was caught off Port Lincoln in May. Some immature fish have been taken in Queensland waters. The fish is regarded as widespread in waters of the right temperature, from the Great Australian Bight north around Australia and south to Eden on the south coast of New South Wales.

This tuna is a prime target for commercial long-line fishers.

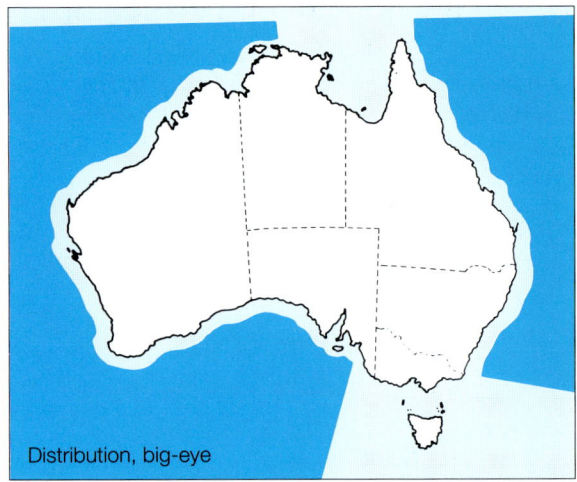

Distribution, big-eye

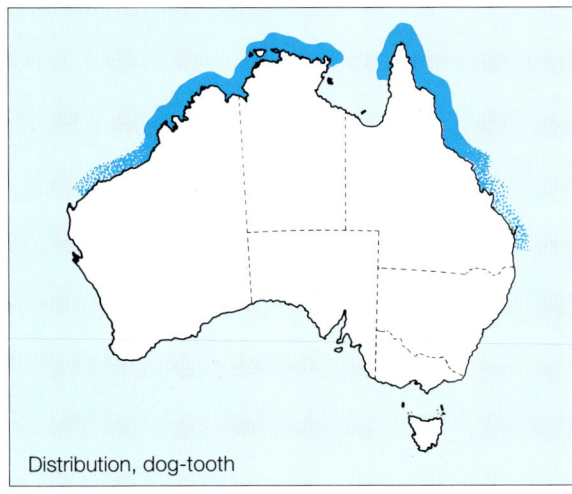

Distribution, dog-tooth

Dog-tooth tuna.

TUNA, DOG-TOOTH
Gymnosarda unicolor

OTHER NAMES: **SCALELESS TUNA, WHITE TUNA, PEG-TOOTH TUNA**

Identification

Though more properly a bonito, this tuna is identified by its lack of scales and obvious canine teeth — of which anyone unhooking this fish should be cautious. The body is generally more elongate than other large tuna, and it is a dark blue fading to a greyish-white belly. Its lateral line is undulating. Its long-based front dorsal is not as high as those of other tuna, nor does it taper as steeply towards the second dorsal. The pectoral fins are very short, only about half the height of the front dorsal. The fins and tail are a dullish grey with yellowish undertones.

Size

This tuna has been caught in Australian waters at almost 90 kilograms, although the Australian all-tackle record (at September, 1988) was only 69.62. Well-known game-fishing authority, Peter Goadby, believes the dog-tooth tuna is potentially the largest and longest in the Australian tropical waters, despite yellowfins and big-eyes having been recorded at more than 100 kilograms.

Habits

These fish are usually encountered in August and through the summer months, beyond the openings between reefs. There appears to be fewer of them than other tuna and their large eyes suggest that they are probably a deeper-swimming fish. If this is the case, it is possible that the dog-tooth is in fact a bottom-feeding fish that rarely surfaces.

Distribution

Distribution is confined to the more northern tropical waters of Australia, from Cairns on the east coast, across the top end, to about the Rowley Shoals on the west coast.

TUNA, LONG-TAIL
Thunnus tonggol

OTHER NAMES: **NORTHERN BLUEFIN TUNA, ORIENTAL BONITO**

Identification

This fish gets its name from its slender body, which is very noticeable between the rear dorsal and anal fins, giving the impression of a long tail. The body is dark blue with a grey tone on the dorsal area and a silvery white belly. The finlets have yellow blotches on them and the fins are a mid-grey to dark-grey. This fish has no swim bladder.

Size

Long-tail tuna grow to about 1.5 metres. The Australian and world all-tackle record (at September, 1988) was 35.9 kilograms. In fact, most of the world records for this fish have been set by anglers in Australian waters.

Habits

This tuna is mainly coastal, eating a broad range of fish as well as squid and cuttlefish, all of which they attack with astonishing ferocity. Probably the most fearless of the tuna, they come almost up to the

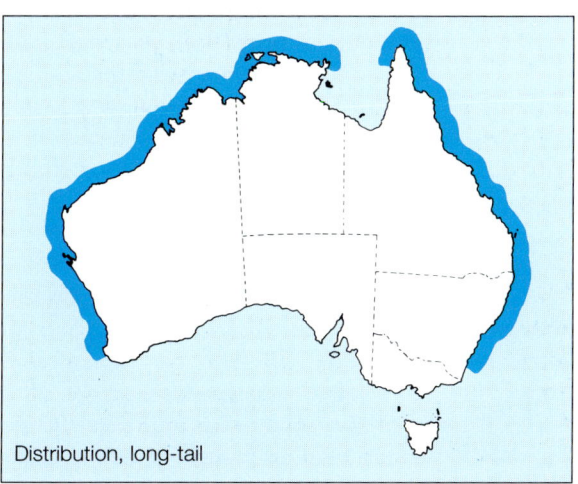
Distribution, long-tail

boat when attracted by berley. This fish is regarded as one of the strongest on a power-to-weight ratio and it probably produces the longest runs of any tuna. They prefer a water temperature from 19°C to 23°C, though they have been caught in waters approaching 30°C.

Distribution

Long-tail tuna are basically a tropical species, though they are found in waters north from Cape Leeuwin in Western Australia, across the top end, and south to Eden on the New South Wales far-south coast. The Australian Game Fishing records show that small fish, under 10 kilograms, are caught in the winter period in the northern waters of the continent. The size of the catches generally increases during spring and summer, with the large specimens being caught from the central New South Wales coast to Bermagui in late summer to early autumn. The occasional larger specimen is caught in Moreton Bay in the July to August period.

TUNA, SOUTHERN BLUEFIN
Thunnus maccoyii

Identification

The southern bluefin tuna has a robust body and relatively short pectoral fin. Its colour is dark blue on the dorsal area and silvery white below. The finlets are yellow with a black edge, compared with the blotched yellow of the long-tail tuna. This fish does have a swim bladder.

Size

The southern bluefin grows to about 2.4 metres in length. The Australian all-tackle record (at September, 1988) is 125.75 kilograms, caught off the Tasmanian coast. The world record is 158 kilograms.

The minimum legal length for a catch in Victoria is 70 centimetres.

Habits

This tuna breeds in the waters towards Indonesia and migrates to the south-east to start its Australian coastline migration at about Exmouth in Western Australia. It moves across the Great Australian Bight and part of the population passes around

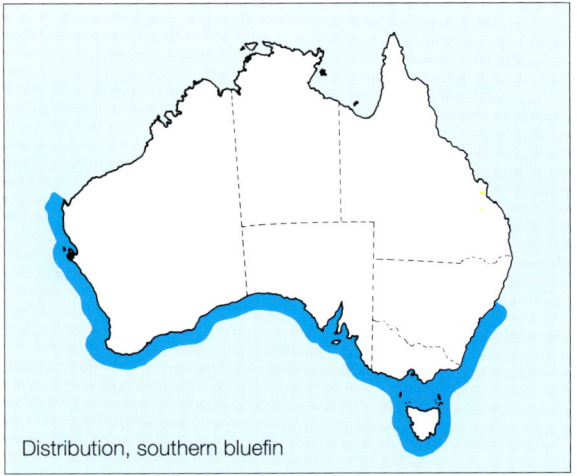
Distribution, southern bluefin

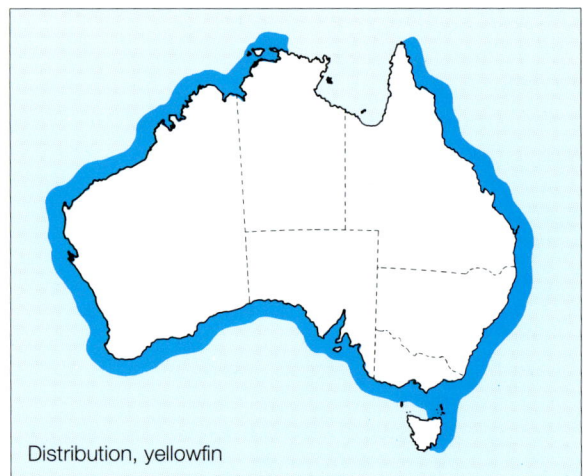
Distribution, yellowfin

Tasmania. Some move north off Tasmania's east coast; others continue to New Zealand. These fish travel extensively, one tagged as a yearling was recaptured in the Atlantic more than three years later. They prefer cooler water in the range of 10°C to 21°C. The younger fish, weighing about 10 to 15 kilograms, are those likely to be encountered by land-based anglers. They eat only small fish; they have a real fondness for squid; and make incredible line-stripping and gear-busting runs.

Distribution

These tuna are found from Exmouth south, across the southern coastline, around Tasmania, and north to about Port Macquarie, New South Wales.

The southern bluefins have become very rare on the southern and eastern coasts of Australia, due to uncontrolled exploitation in past years. One can only hope that the management policies and catch quotas imposed by the Australian Government on commercial fishing fleets sees them become as common to recreational anglers as they once were.

Special Regulations

A legal bag limit of 5 southern bluefins per day applies in Western Australia.

Yellowfin tuna.

TUNA, YELLOWFIN
Thunnus albacares

OTHER NAME: **ALLISON TUNA**

Identification

Apart from some similarities with the big-eye, a yellowfin is hard to confuse. The first dorsal and long scythe-shaped second dorsal and anal fins are a bright yellow, as are the pectoral fins and margins of the tail. The pectoral fins reach back past the beginning of the second dorsal fin. The finlets are yellow with a well-defined black edge.

Size

Yellowfin tuna are reputed to grow to 2.1 metres. The all-tackle record for a fish in Australian waters is 102 kilograms (at September, 1988). The world all-tackle record is 176.35 kilograms.

Habits

This fish is usually found in waters between 16° C and 27° C, where it feeds on such fish as yellowtail, pilchards, slimy mackerel, other small tuna, etc., and squid. The schools of yellowfin invariably contain a number of larger-sized members. This fish will visit deep open water locations along ocean fronts.

Distribution

The yellowfin tuna is wide-ranging and reasonably abundant along the Australian east coast, where it is a viable land-based game fish. It is found in all States. Recent results of tagging along the New South Wales coast by recreational anglers seems to suggest that the inshore population has a circular migration. They spend the winter in northern New South Wales waters and move south with warm currents until about May, when they return to the north in late autumn. These tuna do not appear to extend far offshore.

The following applies to big-eye, dog-tooth, long-tail, southern bluefin and yellowfin tunas.

Tackle

These tuna are usually fished for with gamefishing outfits, the line class depending on the skill of the angler, particularly those who are seeking a record. For the non-record seekers, however, heavy duty baitcasting or overhead reels, on short rods with powerful butt sections, are recommended. A roller-tip at least is suggested. Line should be a minimum of 10 kilograms breaking-strain, usually with a double-line and leader (a wire trace is unnecessary). Special-designed hooks are used — termed "tuna" and "special tuna" — but other strong-forged patterns may be used.

An essential item in the tackle box is a thermometer to gauge the water temperature.

Bait

These tuna will take live yellowtail, slimy mackerel, and almost any small fish. Dead bait and fillets, or cubes of pilchards can also work.

All the larger members of the tuna family will respond to trolled lures, especially the skirted and squid types. And the trolling speed is usually fairly high. Occasionally, long-tail, yellowfin and southern bluefin tuna will be caught by the high-speed retrieval of lures by land-based fishers.

Rigs

The double-line and leader rig, or a long leader with a swivel some distance back from the hook, is used to drift live bait and cubed bait. It may be lightly-weighted to get the bait closer to the depth required. Floats (or balloons) are used when fishing from the rocks.

Weighted trolling rigs are sometimes used with dead bait or fish fillets.

How to hook

Yellowfin is the larger member of the tuna family that the recreational anglers are most likely to come across. This tuna can be caught with live bait floated from a rock platform that juts out into deep clear water. It can also be caught by trolling or fishing live bait in a berley trail. The angler should give the fish time to swallow the bait — allowing the fish to run for 30 to 60 seconds — before setting the hook.

However, for those recreational anglers with a boat sufficiently seaworthy to venture well offshore, the method in simple terms is to berley with cubes of fish to attract the yellowfin to the boat. Then drift a hook with a similar sized bait in the berley. After its first sizzling run, the yellowfin may fight deep or just beneath the surface. It is usually a long circular swim as the angler tires the fish and works it boatside. This method also works for the northern bluefin.

Edibility

Any of the larger tuna that are to be eaten need to be bled and gutted when caught, and kept cool or iced. The white-fleshed tunas are considered better eating but the yellowfin flesh can be bleached by dipping it in hot water.

They are excellent for sashime and may be fried, grilled or prepared by other methods, especially steamed and served with a sauce.

TUSKFISH

These colourful fish are often confused with parrot-fish, or even wrasses. They tend to be on the small side; however, a good tuskfish is not only a testing challenge for the sporting angler but a satisfying meal for the most fastidious fish-eater. Colours and patterns vary in all tuskfish, depending on age, sexual maturity and habitat. Those listed here are representative of the many in the sub tropical and tropical reef areas of Australia.

TUSKFISH, BLUE or BLACK-SPOT
Choerodon schoenleinii

OTHER NAMES: **PARROT-FISH, BLUE GROPER, BLUE-BONE**

Identification
This fish has an olive-green body, with a blue cast on the top and more yellow on its abdominal area.

There are bright blue stripes on each side, forming lines on the body near the tail. These fish can have yellow "cheeks" and red flashes in their blue dorsal fins. The throat is yellow to orange and there is usually a dark spot on their body, near the end of the soft rays of the dorsal fin. Tuskfish have a blunt head, a solid body, a powerful tail, and four prominent curved canine teeth at the front of their mouths.

Size
This fish may reach about 1 metre and exceed 15 kilograms, though they are rarely caught at anywhere near this size.

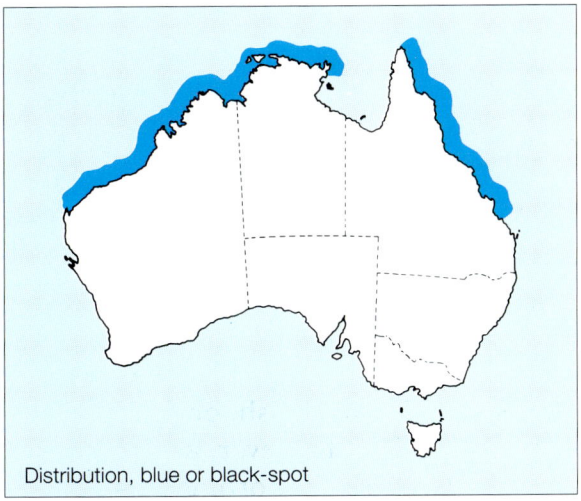

Distribution, blue or black-spot

Distribution

These fish are present on the Great Barrier Reef, north of Rockhampton, and from around the tropical areas of Western Australia, down to the south-west.

TUSKFISH, BLUE-BONE

Choerodon albigena

OTHER NAMES: **BLUE TUSKFISH, BLUE-FISH, BLUE GROPER, GREY TUSKFISH, PARROT-FISH**

Identification

The dominant colour of this tuskfish is blue-green, with lighter cheeks. There is usually a pale blotch apparent below the soft dorsal fin. Both the dorsal and anal fins have blue edges and the anal fin additional bright blue and yellow stripes. The tail is a dark blue-purple. The teeth are bluish and, when filleted, this same colour can be seen in the bones.

Size

The blue bone tuskfish has been recorded at 70 centimetres in length and over 8 kilograms but it is usually taken at 1 to 3 kilograms.

Distribution

This is one of the most common tuskfishes, which is found on coral reefs north from Rockhampton. It is only occasionally seen in more southerly waters.

TUSKFISH, PURPLE
Choerodon cephalotes

OTHER NAMES: **PURPLE PARROT, GREEN PARROT**

Identification

The body shape is typical of the species, being blunt and solid with strong fins — that is, more truncate than slightly rounded, as in many tuskfish — and a tail. Its colour is olive to a purple-blue (rosy in juveniles) and pale blue, with alternating blue and yellow vertical lines in the front part of the body: these break-up into yellow-edged blue spots towards the tail. The purple tuskfish has blue lines around the eyes, and yellow or orange spots on the cheeks. There are blue and yellow markings in the dorsal fins, giving a varigated appearance.

Size

This tuskfish grows to about 37 centimetres.

Distribution

The purple tuskfish is found in more northern areas of the Great Barrier Reef, and in tropical waters across the top end and down to the north-west of Western Australia.

The purple tuskfish.

TUSKFISH, VENUS
Choerodon venustus

OTHER NAMES: **BLUE PARROT, BLUE-SPOTTED GROPER, PINK-SIDED TUSKFISH, PARROT-FISH**

Identification

The venus tuskfish varies in colour, from green to bright red and darker along the dorsal area. Both head and body are covered in numerous bright blue spots. The obvious canine or peg teeth are strong, especially the front pair. The tail is dark with bluish parallel bars and it is straighter than other tuskfish.

Size
The venus tuskfish grows to 55 centimetres long and a weight of about 4 kilograms.

Distribution
A most abundant fish in reef waters the length of Queensland and into northern New South Wales waters.

The following applies to all tuskfish.

Breeding
Little is known.

Habits
The tuskfish seems to live a life of leisure, browsing around coral reefs, or lazily swimming over reef flats or the sandy areas between reefs…and eating. They can often be seen "resting" in caverns and under rock ledges. Theirs is a mainly carnivorous diet, including crustaceans, shellfish and marine worms — with small crabs being a particular favourite. They are inactive at night, sometimes seen lying on their sides — probably asleep — by divers.

When to fish
Tuskfish are day feeders.

Where to fish
Sometimes they can be spotted browsing in the clear northern reef waters and a bait can be dropped towards them. In reality, however, they are more often caught when fishing for other species alongside overhanging reef ledges or near caverns.

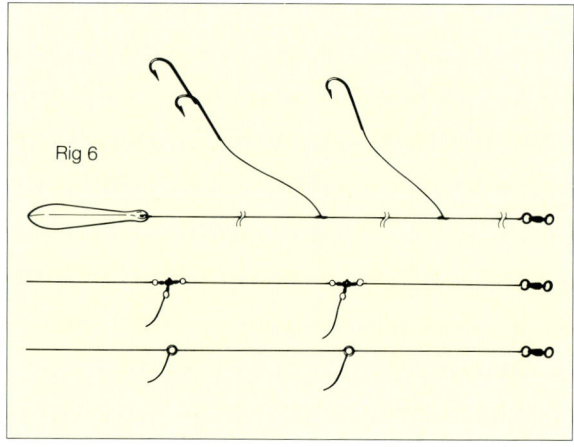
Rig 6

Venus tuskfish.

Tackle
Tuskfish are usually caught on tackle being used for bottom fish for other species such as emperors. Handlines, deck-mounted winch-type of reels, boat rods and medium to heavy threadline or bait-casting outfits can be used. Because most anglers are seeking other fish, lines are usually heavier and the hooks larger than are necessary to catch this fish.

Bait
These fish are less interested in fish bait than they are in shellfish, prawns, marine worms and small crabs or crab pieces, which are much better bait, provided other small reef fish don't pick them clean before a tuskfish can get to them.

Rigs
Try any of the bottom rigs (No. 6) used for other reef species such as snapper, morwong, emperors, etc. An extra strong hook of about size 1/0 to 2/0 is a realistic size for tuskfish, which have a relatively small mouth.

How to hook
The tuskfish's teeth equip it to grab and tear its preferred food free. It accepts a loose bait to its liking quite quickly. When hooked, it displays remarkable power and can reach line-cutting shelter if the angler allows it any leeway during the initial stage of tiring it.

Edibility
The flesh of tuskfish is white, firm and flaky, not like the mushy softness of its relatives, the wrasses. It is excellent eating, however prepared.

[**Note**: Some find the greenish-blue bones of the tuskfish off-putting, though the colour does not indicate anything is wrong with the fish. Such sensitivity, however understandable, can lead to the waste of a fine food fish.]

WAHOO
Acanthocybium solandri

OTHER NAME: **JACK MACKEREL**

This near perfect example of a streamlined predator can be very unpopular with game fishers trolling baits for marlin. On the other hand, it is a welcome catch for anglers fishing in some competitions because it scores well.

Identification

At first glance the wahoo resembles a tanguige (narrow-barred spanish mackerel) with its vivid vertical blue stripes. The body is a bright blue on top and silvery blue below and some of the two dozen or so bars are doubled or V-shaped. The bars are most pronounced ("lit up") when the fish is first caugh: They fade after death. Its longer, higher and spinous dorsal fin distinguishes it from the tanguige, as does its longer head and more pointed snout. The lower jaw protruding beyond the movable upper jaw is another difference.

Size

Wahoo grow to 2.1 metres in length and may weigh as much as 70 kilograms. The Australian all-tackle record (at September, 1988) was 47 kilograms. The world all-tackle record was 67.58 kilograms.

Breeding

Little is known.

Habits

While small juvenile wahoo sometimes school, adults appear to be lone hunting-machines, forever marauding other fish, slashing their prey in attacks of devastating speed. Wahoo have an uncanny knack of stripping the bait from hooks and they will often shadow or trail a lure of bait for some time before they close in.

These fish have a preference for waters where the temperature ranges from 21°C to 30°C. The charts of recorded fish indicate they make a southern migration down the east coast with the warm currents of late summer. This may indicate a spawning run as well.

Distribution

The wahoo is a tropical species that is nevertheless found in numbers on the southern coast of New South Wales. Its range is regarded as north from Exmouth Gulf in Western Australia, around the tropical coastline, and south down the east coast as far as Bermagui in New South Wales.

When to fish

Water temperature is important and, provided it is right, the wahoo can appear at any time. However, general opinion has it that wahoo are more likely

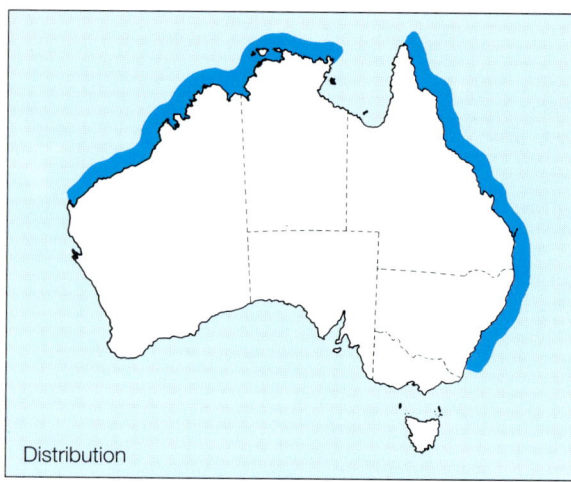

Distribution

hook the fish, though it has a reputation for ripping trolled fish clean off the hooks without being impaled. The fight is furious but brief: wahoo lose stamina more rapidly than such fish, as tanguigue.

Edibility

The wahoo are excellent table fish, provided that they are bled and cleaned and treated carefully. They are suitable for most methods of cooking.

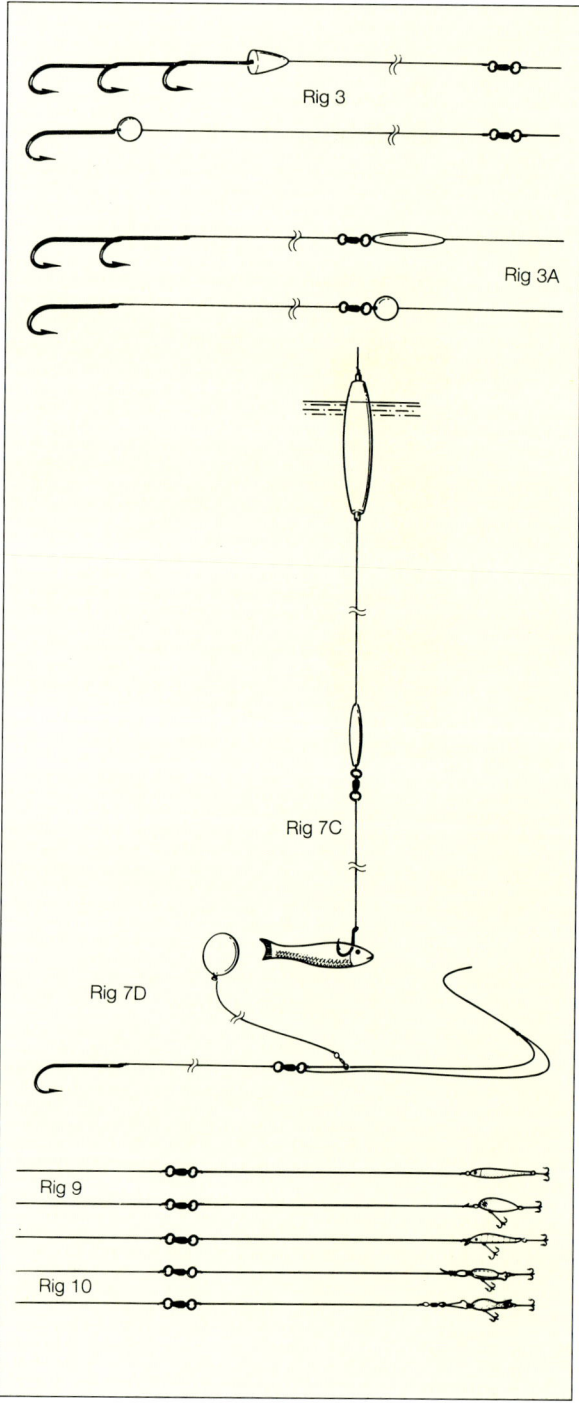

to be caught in the morning and the late afternoon. [The writer recalls a late afternoon attack from below by a wahoo, when fishing for kingfish (with a yellowtail some 3 metres below a float). The wahoo took the yellowtail *and* float, and cleared the water by 2 metres. The gear was inadequate and the wahoo was free within 20 seconds.]

Where to fish

Try wherever there is a suitable current of the right temperature, usually offshore or along the edges of deep-water rocks.

Tackle

The minimum reel required is a quality medium-to-heavy baitcasting or overhead model, or perhaps a light game reel. A line of about 10 kilograms is the lightest breaking-strain that can seriously be considered, unless fishing for juveniles.
Rollered game rods or the short "stroker" type of rods, with plenty of power, are suitable for trolling bait or lures, and even drift fishing with dead bait.

Bait

The wahoo is not fussy: it will take almost any fish, whole or in large fillets. It will relish all knuckle-head style, feathered and skirted lures, as well as active metal lures.

Rigs

Any approved game fishing record or trolling rigs are suitable. However, rigs such as No. 3, 3A or 9 may be used for casting baits or lures. Rig Nos. 7C or 7D are suitable for live bait and rig No. 11 for trolling. Use a nylon-coated or plain wire trace.

How to hook

The ferocity of a wahoo attack is almost certain to

WAREHOU
Seriolella brama

OTHER NAMES: SNOTTY, SNOTTY OR SNOTGALL TREVALLY, HADDOCK, SEA-BREAM

The warehou is one of the mainstays of rock anglers and inshore small-boat anglers in Tasmania. Some anglers mistakenly believe that this fish cannot be taken with rod and line.

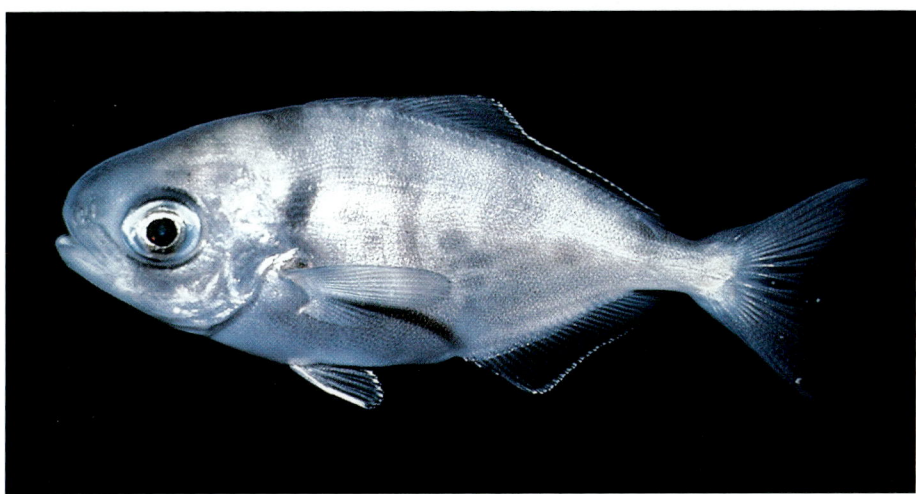

Identification
With a shape much like a trevally, the colouring of this fish is greyish-green on smaller specimens taken from shallow inshore waters. Those caught in deep waters are more of a steel blue. A dark blotch is evident at the top of the gill cover and fainter blotches on the sides. It has a low, short-based and spinous dorsal fin, and its pectoral fins are long and pointed.

Size
These fish are reputed to grow to 70 centimetres in length. The Australian record is about 3.7 kilograms.

Breeding
Little is known.

Habits
The larger more mature warehou prefer rocky bottoms in deep off shore waters, but schools of smaller fish enter the shallow coastal waters of Tasmania from the late summer to early autumn. Juveniles can occasionally be seen among the tentacles of jellyfish, according to some reports. These fish are carnivorous, with a distinct preference for shellfish, but they also eat bluebait and whitebait.

Distribution
Warehou are found in waters off the southern coast of New South Wales, across Victoria and on to South Australian waters. It is most common, however, in Tasmanian waters.

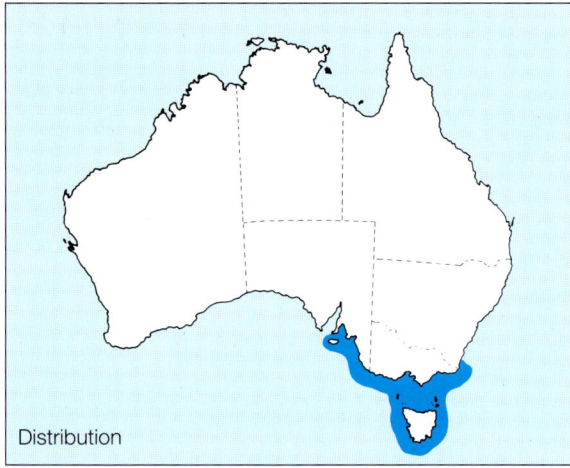

Distribution

When to fish

The warehou is around all the year on deep-water reefs but rock-based anglers and small-boat anglers have the best chance to catch them during the late summer and early autumn.

Where to fish

This fish inhabits rocky bottoms in both deep-water and rock bottoms inshore, especially where they can expect a good yield of shellfish and mussels.

Tackle

Handlines on casters, gunwale-mounted deck winches, or short boat-rods with a winch type of reel, are suitable for deep-water fishing. Lines need to be about 10 kilograms breaking-strain upwards for the heavy sinkers that are needed to reach the bottom offshore. In shallow water, single-handed threadline or baitcasting outfits, with 5 to 8 kilograms breaking-strain line can be used. The same line on a 3-metre to 4-metre light or medium rod, with either sidecast, threadline or overhead reel, should be adequate for fishing from the rocks. Hooks of about 1/0 will suit the baits used for warehou. If using whitebait or bluebait, gang two or three hooks together.

Bait

The warehou has a liking for mussels or similar shellfish but they will take prawns, bluebait, whitebait and other fish bait.

Berley

Use crushed mussels and other shellfish, with some boiled rice or breadcrumbs, if you want to improve your catch when fishing from the rocks.

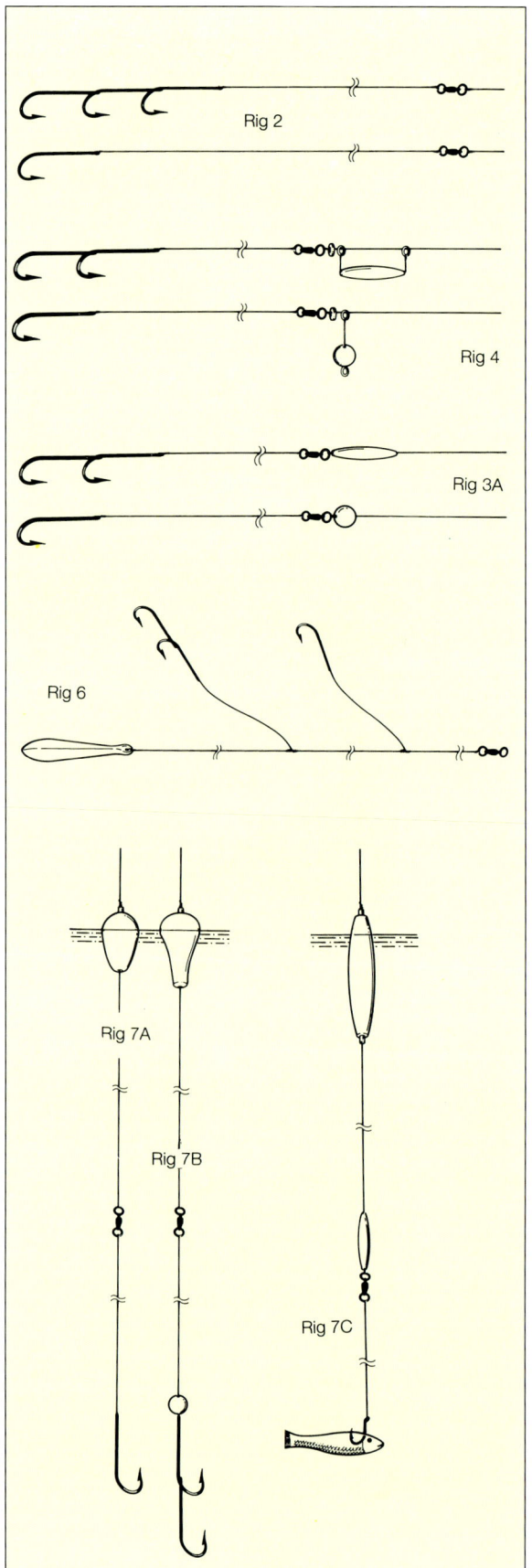

Rigs

Depending on water depth and conditions, bottom rigs Nos 4 or 6 are satisfactory. From the rocks, an unweighted or lightly-weighted rig No. 2 or 3A make a good choice. You may also enjoy a measure of success with one of the float rigs Nos 7B or 7C.

How to hook

Warehous are mid-water feeders, so inshore anglers will do much better if their bait sinks slowly or floats in a berley stream. They can be finicky, soft biters. They require a sharp response when the bite is felt. The warehou's oval body generates plenty of pull when hooked.

Hint

The floated bait method keeps the bait moving about off the bottom where warehou seem to swim.

Edibility

The flesh is tasty eating prepared by any method.

TREVALLA, SPOTTED
Scriobella punctata

OTHER NAME: **MACKEREL TREVALLA**

This fish can be encountered while fishing for warehou, although schools are unlikely to be found in shallow water. Slightly more elongated than the warehou, it is a deeper blue in the upper body with a profusion of small dark spots along the sides.
Only those anglers fishing the deepest off shore waters might catch another member of the family, the **deep-sea trevalla** (*Hyperoglyphe antarctica*) also called blue-eye or blue nose, or big-eye. This is the fish now marketed as blue-eye.
Both fish are top class table fish.

WHITING

These fish offer pleasant angling with basic equipment, and
they inhabit waters that are easily and safely fished from the
shoreline or small boats. Usually plentiful, whiting bite freely
and — on the right light gear — put up a good fight. And
if all this was not enough, whiting are also one
of the best eating fish.
All whiting are slim, rounded fish, most with a silver stripe
along the body and a pouting mouth designed for grubbing
for shellfish, worms and crabs on the bottom. All have much
the same habits.

King George whiting.

WHITING, EASTERN SCHOOL
Sillago flindersi

OTHER NAME: **SCHOOL WHITING,
BASS STRAIT WHITING**

Identification
The light sandy-coloured dorsal area on the whiting
has red-rusty spots which form wide oblique bands,
much more distinct than those of the closely-
related southern school whiting.

Size
This whiting reaches a maximum of 32 centimetres
in length.

Distribution
Eastern school whiting is the one least caught by
the angler. It is found in the deeper coastal waters
from Moreton Bay in Queensland, south along
New South Wales to Westernport in Victoria, and
off Tasmania.

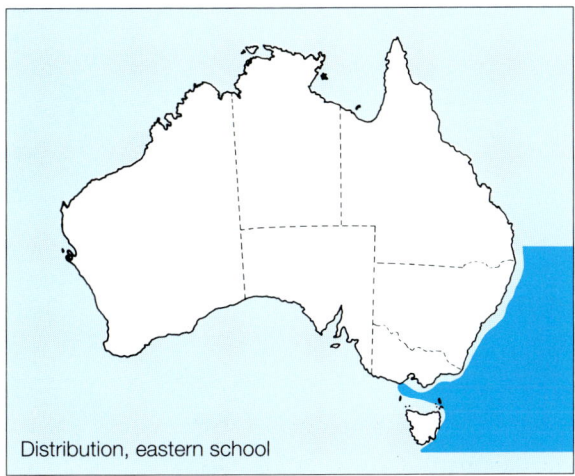
Distribution, eastern school

WHITING, KING GEORGE
Sillaginodes punctata

OTHER NAMES: **KG (KAYGEE), SPOTTED WHITING**

Identification

This is the largest and most distinguishable whiting. Its base colour is variable, from light brown to blackish-brown above with silver y fawn to gold hues below. The body is covered in dark brown spots, some forming worm-shape patterns.

Size

This whiting is known to reach 70 centimetres in length and more than 4 kilograms in weight.
The minimum legal length for a catch in Western Australia is 25 centimetres; 23 centimetres plus a bag limit of 30 per angler per day in South Australia; in Victoria the minimum is 27 centimetres.

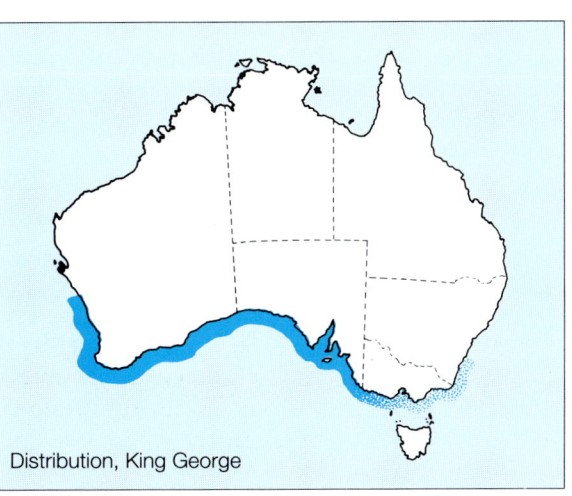
Distribution, King George

Distribution

This prized whiting is found in patchy numbers in the southern waters of Australia, particularly on the south coast of New South Wales, as far north as Lake Illawarra. The King George whiting is also found in Victoria but it increases in numbers the further west you go. They are reasonably common in Western Australia, extending beyond Lancelin. They can be found occasionally in the north-eastern waters of Tasmania.

WHITING, SAND
Sillago ciliata

OTHER NAMES: **SUMMER WHITING, BLUE-NOSED WHITING**

WHITING, YELLOW-FINNED
Sillago schombergkii

Identification

These two relatives are distinguished from other whiting by an absence of the usual silvery stripe along the body. They also have a more uniform silver-light yellow colouring, but without spots or bands. Both fish have yellow ventral fins and anal fins, but there is a distinct dusky blotch on the base of the sand whiting, an eastern species.

Size

The minimum legal limit for a catch is 22 centimetres in Western Australia; 24 centimetres in South Australia; and 27 centimetres in New South Wales.

Distribution

Large schools are found over the sandy bottoms of coastal beaches, bays, estuaries and coastal lakes. The eastern sand whiting is found from central

Sand whiting.

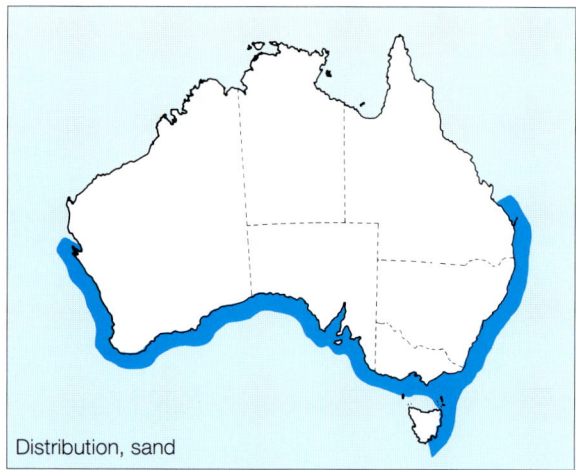

Distribution, sand

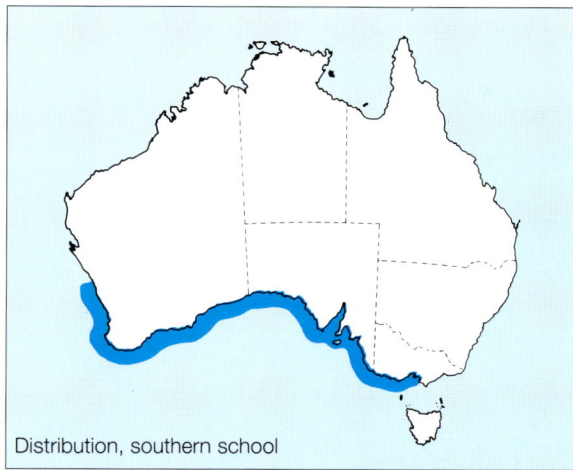

Distribution, southern school

Queensland, south along New South Wales, off Victoria and along the east coast of Tasmania. The yellow-finned whiting becomes increasingly abundant from St Vincent Gulf in South Australia and westwards along the coast, and along the coast of Western Australia to about Shark Bay. It obtains its other common name because of its presence in prolific numbers in most areas during the summer. Other whiting confined to more northern areas are the **northern sand** *Sillago schana* and the **golden lined** *Silago analis*, which do intermix with the sand whiting in the northern parts of the latter's distribution range.

WHITING, SOUTHERN SCHOOL
Sillago bassensis

OTHER NAMES: **SCHOOL WHITING, SILVER WHITING, SAND WHITING**

Identification
This close relative of the eastern school whiting has fine brownish spots — so faint as to be almost indistinct — that form thin streaky lines on the back.

Size
The maximum size of this whiting is about 36 centimetres in length. The minimum legal size for a catch in Western Australia is 22 centimetres.

Distribution
An abundant species in sandy areas of the shallow coastal waters of South Australia and Western

Australia as far north as Geraldton. They are also found in Westernport Bay in Victoria.

WHITING, TRUMPETER
Sillago maculata

OTHER NAMES: **WINTER WHITING, SAND WHITING, DIVER WHITING**

Identification
Trumpeter whiting have a slightly different colouring on the east and west coasts. The eastern member has elongated brown blotches on the back reaching to the lateral line; the western member's blotches are rounded.

Size
These whiting reach about 30 centimetres in length.

Distribution
Trumpeter whiting are usually found in large schools over the sand or silt bottoms of coastal bays, lakes and estuaries, and earned one of their popular common names with their presence in the cooler parts of of the year.

Trumpeter whiting.

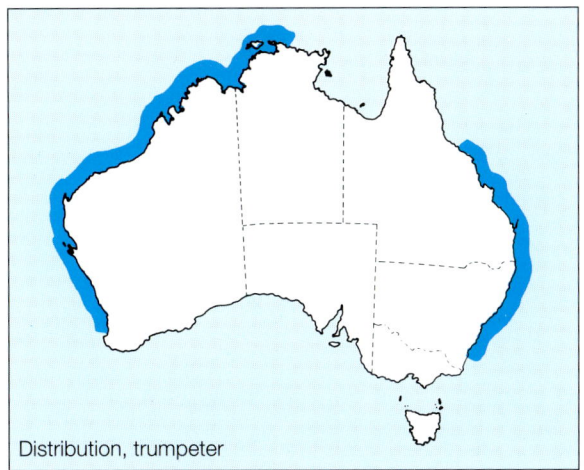

Distribution, trumpeter

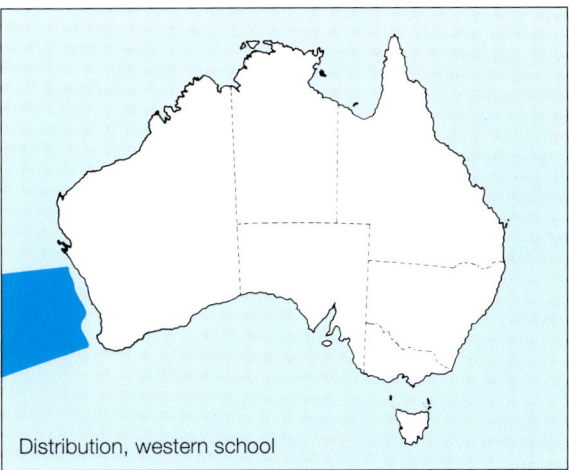

Distribution, western school

WHITING, WESTERN SCHOOL

Sillago vittata

OTHER NAME: **BANDED WHITING**

Identification

This is the western relative of the eastern school whiting. It is distinguished by its slightly wider stripes and a very dark blotch on the base of the pectoral fins.

Size

Western school whiting grows to only about 30 centimetres in length.
A minimum legal limit of 22 centimetres applies to any catch in Western Australia.

Distribution

This whiting is limited to a stretch of the Western Australian coast, from about Geraldton to Coral Bay. It favours deeper off-shore sandy bottoms.

The following applies to all whiting.

Breeding

The King George whiting seems to be the best researched in this regard. They spawn offshore in late winter and the hatchings are only a few weeks old when they aggregate inshore to protected waters, where they remain until they reach about 3 years of age, or about 40 centimetres long. Research indicates that a fully mature KG has never been caught inside West Australian estuaries or bays.

The visits of the other whiting suggest they are late winter-and-summer spawners and sand whiting in New South Wales are believed to have spawning periods from November to March, at the mouths of estuaries or in the open sea.

Habits

Whiting, with the exception of the King George, are usually found in schools with sandy or fine gravel and shell bottoms. These may be off surf beaches, bay beaches or inside estuaries or coastal lakes. Though they will feed in very shallow water, the eastern school whiting and western school whiting will not venture inside the surf areas along beaches. By contrast, immature and undersized school whiting, especially the western species, can be prolific around estuary mouths. These species (of legal size!) are in deeper, sandy, offshore waters. Trumpeter whiting can be found in numbers on lightly-silted bottoms with weed beds. They nose along the bottom, seeking marine worms, crustaceans, molluscs, etc.

King George whiting like broken rocky bottoms with sand, weed or seagrass beds. Only those KGs that have not reached breeding age are caught in estuaries or bays.

Whiting are wary fish, alert to the danger of predators above them. Shadows from boats, anglers or even rods can scare them. They like the cover of foamy water on beaches and are less likely to feed in shallow areas in bright sunshine. Overcast and rainy days seem to give them a false sense of security, as does twilight.

When to fish

Whiting can be around most of the year but from spring through the summer period is when numbers are more prolific. The trumpeter, however, offers good fishing during the winter in eastern estuaries and lakes. The best times are undoubtedly in the morning, and late afternoon into the evening, when better catches are usually made.

Where to fish

Clear, sandy shallow and lightly-silted bottoms are the favourite feeding grounds for trumpeter. Sandy bottoms with rocks and weeds seem to be the best for KG whiting. Tidal runs or surf rips do not seem to worry whiting, the water movement helping to uncover much of their favourite food items. These fish are unlikely to be found in still backwaters. The high tide usually fishes best.

Tackle

If fishing from shore locations or in a small boat, try a light handline with a 5 kilograms breaking-strain line. Light or medium threadline rods, even baitcasting rods, coupled with reels spooled with 3 to 5 kilograms breaking-strain line are also very convenient when fishing from boats and some estuary locations, as well as jetties. A light flexibly-tipped rod of about 3.5 metres, with either a threadline or sidecast reel spooled with similar weight line, is ideal for broad exposed bays and beaches. Hook sizes about size 4 or 8, standard or long-shanked, are adequate for most whiting — the smaller size for smaller fish (remember that the higher the number in hooks, the smaller they are). After size 1, larger hooks are the opposite, number 1/0, 2/0, 3/0, etc. increasing in size.

Bait

The number one bait for whiting is probably worms, whether fishing estuaries or beaches, even off-shore. The worms may be bloodworms, squirt worms, wrigglers, sand or beach worms. They also will eat pink yabbies and nippers, pieces of pipi and prawns. The trumpeter whiting will also bite if offered slivers of squid. Small bluebait or whitebait are used on small, ganged hooks offshore when pursuing the very large King George whiting.

Rigs

The most widely used rig is the lightly-weighted No. 3A with a sinker just heavy enough to hold the bottom. You can use a ball, bean, barrel or channel sinker with a trace of between 30 and 40 centimetres. In some estuaries, a second dropper is often used from another swivel further along the main line,

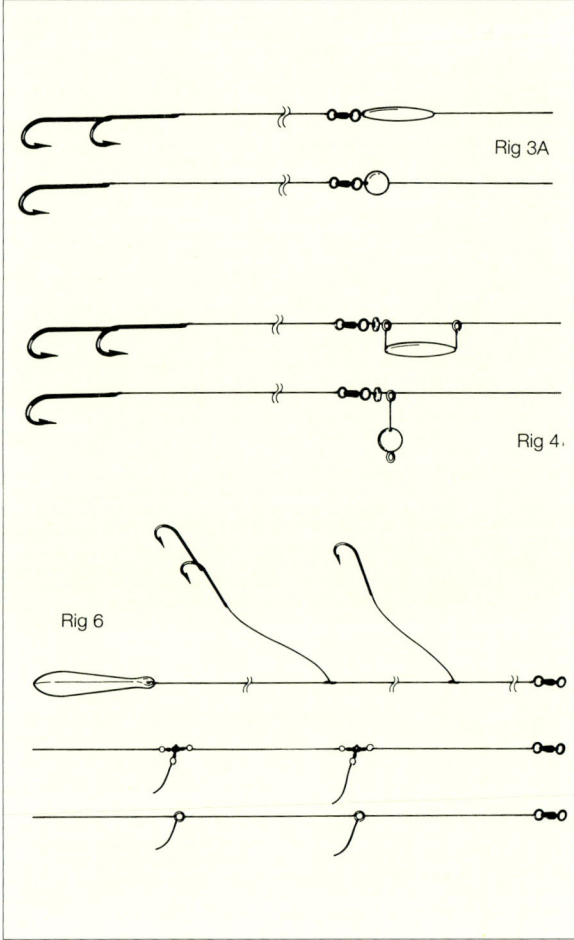

but is more likely to catch bream than whiting off the bottom. On beaches with some side sweep, the alternative rig No. 4 can be substituted. From boats offshore in rocky areas where King George whiting may be encountered, a bottom rig No. 6 with droppers from two three-way swivels may also be used.

The addition of a short length of red plastic or rubber tubing to the working end of the line at the eye of the hook helps attract whiting to the bait.

How to hook

Whiting may be fished from a moored or drifting boat as well as from the shoreline. A moving bait is the more successful. This can be achieved, if not drifting, by slowly retrieving the bait across the sand. The angler should be able to feel the weight of the sinker at all times. Small whiting are quick and bite with a series of taps, often so fast it is impossible to react. By keeping the bait on the move, you will enhance your prospects of hooking a whiting. Whiting fight vigorously, and they are often only hooked through the lip. So,if given any slack line, they can tear themselves free, particularly with their body-twisting.

Hint

Two or three small crabs, such as soldier crabs (though any will do) on a long-shanked hook is irresistible to most whiting. Such bait may be picked off by small whiting but large whiting, such as King George, do not hesitate to take them straight into their mouths.

Whiting will also take the tiny lead-headed jigs, with red plastic, worm-like bodies, if retrieved slowly along sandy bottoms.

Edibility

Only the exceptional King George may need filleting. Whiting are generally better cleaned, gutted and lightly fried whole. Fillets of large specimens are best pan-fried or lightly grilled with a sprinkling of lemon juice. They are one of the best of the marine fishes for texture and taste.

WRASSE

Most of the numerous wrasses caught by anglers are small and strikingly colourful. They can be a nuisance, taking baits being used to tempt the popular rock and reef fishes. Wrasses also are referred to incorrectly as parrot-fish (their obvious teeth separate wrasses from this fish) and groper, but a few are worthwhile angling fish — and better to eat than some other fish popular fishes. An arbitrary selection of wrasses follow:

WRASSE, BLUE-THROATED
Pseudolabrus tetrieus

OTHER NAMES: **BLUE-HEAD, KELPIE**

Identification
Males are usually a brown to bluish-grey, with whitish cross bands. The latter are often less evident on females, which can be coloured from a green to an ochre. The male's gill region is a bluish-grey.

Size
The blue-throated wrasse grows to about 50 centimetres in length.

Habits
These fish live on inshore and estuarine reefs, where they feed on a variety of shellfish, crustaceans and worms.

Distribution
The blue-throated wrasse can be found from the Illawarra area of southern New South Wales, south to Victoria, Tasmania, and along the South Australian waters to near the West Australian border.

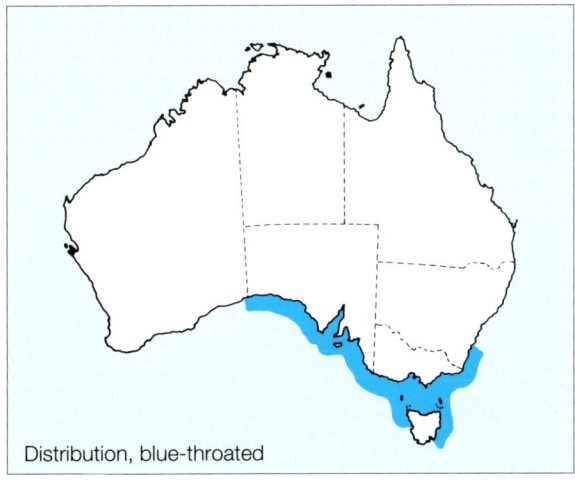

Distribution, blue-throated

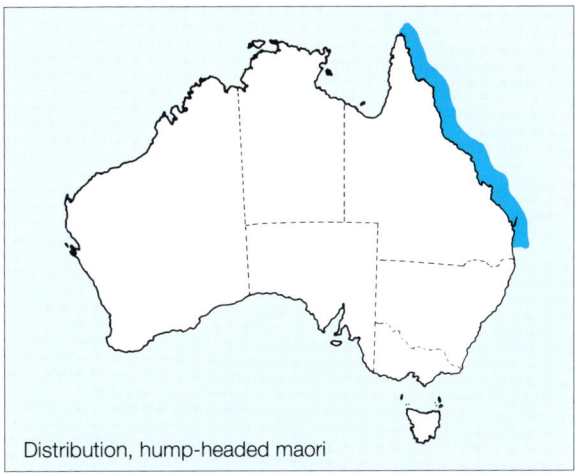

Distribution, hump-headed maori

WRASSE, HUMP-HEADED MAORI

Cheilinus undulatus
Coris undulatus

OTHER NAME: **BLUE-TOOTH GROPER, DOUBLE-HEADED PARROT-FISH, GIANT WRASSE, MAORI WRASSE**

This is the giant of the wrasses, a fish exceeding 50 kilograms being seen if not caught in tropical waters. (Some reports claim that a "blue-tooth groper" caught at Hayman Island was well over 2 metres and weighed almost 200 kilograms.)

Hump-headed maori wrasse.

Identification

The younger fish do not have the fleshy hump on the forehead which gives the fish its name. They are solid, oval-elongate fish, with long soft dorsal fins and anal fins, and a big rounded tail. The body colour is usually a blackish-purple-green, fading to a lighter, sometimes rosy, shade towards the stomach. Each scale has a wide vertical violet bar edged with orange. There are dense scribblings of yellow, blue, orange and red on its head, cheeks and throat. The colours fade rapidly on death. The scales are large and become an angling trophy, often being about 8 centimetres across on medium sized fish.

Size

These wrasses are believed to grow to about 1.5 metres in length 25 to 60 kilogram specimens are not uncommon.

Habits

The hump-headed maori wrasse is a reef-dweller that eats crustaceans and shellfish — nor is it averse to a piece of fresh fish. Their strong jaws and large conical teeth can crush large shellfish.

Distribution

They mainly inhabit the deeper reefs north of Mackay.

WRASSE, MAORI

Ophthalmolepis lineolatus

Identification

This fish is easy to identify. It has distinctive bright

blue lines on the head, snout and cheeks, together with the red-brown to orange-brown band along the dorsal area, above a white band on the side. Males have a charcoal grey stripe along their side under the white band; females do not.

Size

The maximum length of the fish is about 40 centimetres.

Habits

The maori wrasse is found on rocky reefs from 2 to 40 metres, where it feeds on shellfish, crustaceans, worms, etc. It is believed to be particularly territorial.

Distribution

It is a common inhabitant of deeper offshore reefs, along the eastern, south-eastern and south-western coasts. Its range extends from the north coast of New South Wales to Wilson's Promontory in Victoria, and from Kangaroo Island off South Australia to the Houtman Abrolhos islands in Western Australia.

WRASSE, PURPLE
Pseudolabrus fucicola

OTHER NAME: **SADDLED WRASSE,
YELLOW-SADDLED WRASSE, KELPIE,
SOUTHERN WRASSE**

Identification

Despite the wide base colour variations – dark green, purplish-brown, tannish-green and brown — there are always five creamy blotches along the base of the dorsal fin, which can often form faint vertical bars over the dorsal fins and body into the female. The face often has pale yellow marks in the region of the eye and nose.

Size

This fish grows to about 50 centimetres.

Habits

The purple wrasse is a shallow inshore and estuarine dweller.

Distribution

This fish is mainly caught from the south coast of New South Wales around the coast to about Cape Jaffe in South Australia. It is more common in Victorian and Tasmanian waters.

WRASSE, SENATOR
Pictilabrus laticlavius

Identification

The body colour can be brownish, reddish-brown, greenish or a yellow-brown. The male has brown-to-red stripes along the body and a dark blotch above the leading edge of the anal fin.

Size

This wrasse grows to about 35 centimetres in length.

Habits

The senator wrasse is fairly common in rocky parts and the weedy rock areas of shallow coastal waters, where it feeds on shellfish, crustaceans and worms.

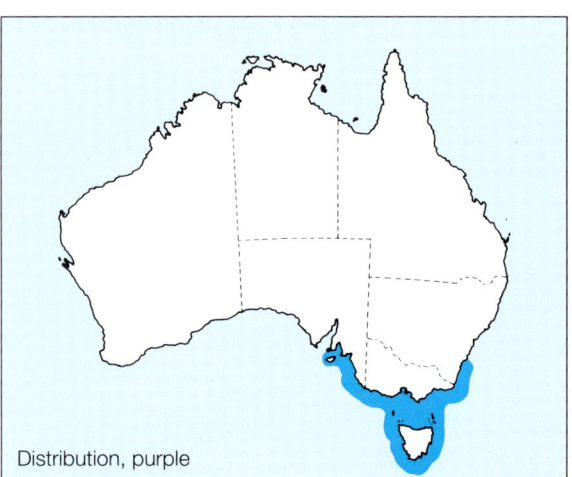

Distribution, purple

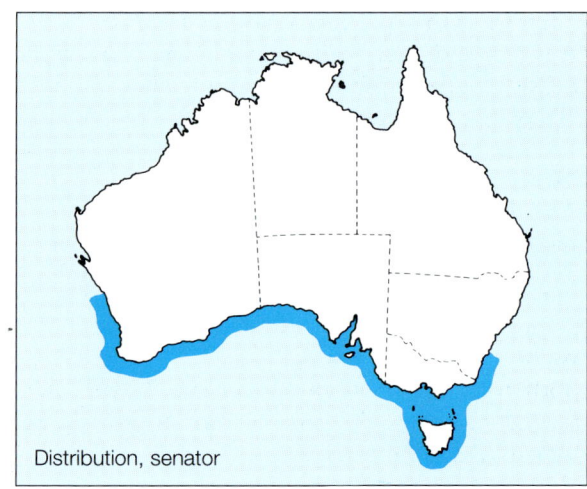

Distribution, senator

Senator wrasse.

Triple-tail wrasse.

Distribution

It is found south from the far north coast of New South Wales, around the southern coast of the continent, including Tasmania, and north to Abrolhos islands in Western Australia.

WRASSE, SCARLET-BREASTED MAORI
Cheilinus fasciatus

WRASSE, TRIPLE-TAIL MAORI
Cheilinus trilobatus

Identification

The soft rays of the dorsal fins and anal fin, that sweep back towards the tail, give the triple-tail maori wrasse its name. Mostly green in colour, this fish has scarlet lines and spots on its head and throat, and scarlet stripes on the scales.

The scarlet-breasted maori is distinguished by a tan body with 6 or 7 dark vertical bars, and an olive-brown head that features red lines around the eyes. The front of the belly and back of the head are bright scarlet.

Size

The triple-tail maori wrasse grows to about 70 centimetres and the scarlet-breasted maori wrasse about half that size.

Habits

Both wrasses dwell on the Great Barrier Reef, feeding largely on shellfish and crustaceans, though they may graze on coral.

Distribution

The triple-tail are more common in the northern area of the tropics; the scarlet-breasted are found the whole length of the Great Barrier Reef.

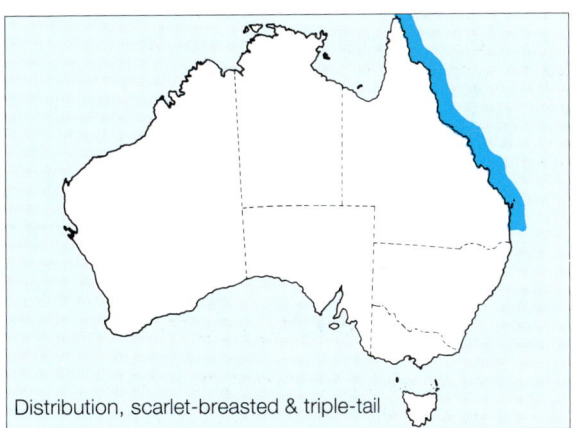

Distribution, scarlet-breasted & triple-tail

WRASSE, THICK-LIPPED
Hemigymnus melapterus

OTHER NAMES: **BLACK-EYED, THICK-LIP**

Identification

It is almost impossible to mistake this fish because of its extremely thick, fleshy, green protruding lips. Colour varies with size and age, but they are mainly a bluish-green. The head area is a much paler olive-green to green, with discernible wiggly green lines on the reddish area of the forehead. This red becomes black on death.

Size

The thick-lipped wrasse grows to about 60 centimetres in length.

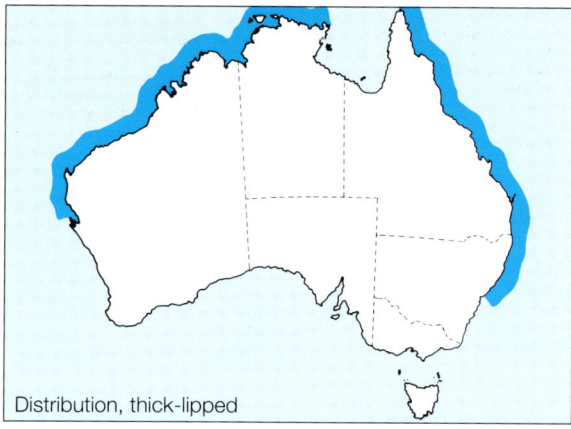
Distribution, thick-lipped

Habits
These fish eat shellfish and crustaceans, and they may also browse on coral. They are often more common among the spearfishers' catches because they live in reef caverns and under ledges much of their lives.

Distribution
The thick-lipped wrasses inhabit the full length of the Great Barrier Reef and as far south as the central coast of New South Wales. They are also found in the waters across the top end of Australia and south to about Shark Bay in Western Australia.

The following applies to all wrasses.

Breeding
It is known that many members of the wrasse family change sex — when needed! A male may maintain a harem of females but if anything happens to him, the largest female changes sex and then accommodates the remaining females.

When to fish
Wrasses may be caught at any time of the year. The southern species seem to become more active in the duller light of the late afternoon, but they are unlikely to be caught after dark, when they tend to hole-up for the night.

Where to fish
Depending on the species, these fish are caught near or on estuarine inshore and offshore reefs — invariably while bottom fishing for more welcome species.

Tackle
The wrasses are caught on any of the gear used for bottom fishing. Handlines, the winch-type of reels, or boat rods are all suitable when fishing from a boat. So are short single or double-handed threadline or baitcasting outfits. A 3 to 4 metre long rod with a sidecast, threadline or overhead reef is best when fishing from the rocks. Line breaking-strains are invariably heavier than is necessary because anglers are usually after other larger fish (excepting, of course, the hump-headed maori wrasse!). Around 15 kilograms breaking-strain is suggested as a minimum, and stronger in northern waters.

Bait
Try mussels and other shellfish, prawns, conjevoi and even fish flesh.

Rigs
The wrasses are caught on the various rigs used for bottom species. For inshore waters rigs No. 3 or 4A are suitable. For deeper fishing, rigs 4A or 5 may be used. The style and weight of the sinker depends on the depth of water, currents and bottom terrain.

How to hook
The wrasse's bite is much like many others: sometimes it will nibble the bait softly; at other times it will grab the offering with forthright purpose.

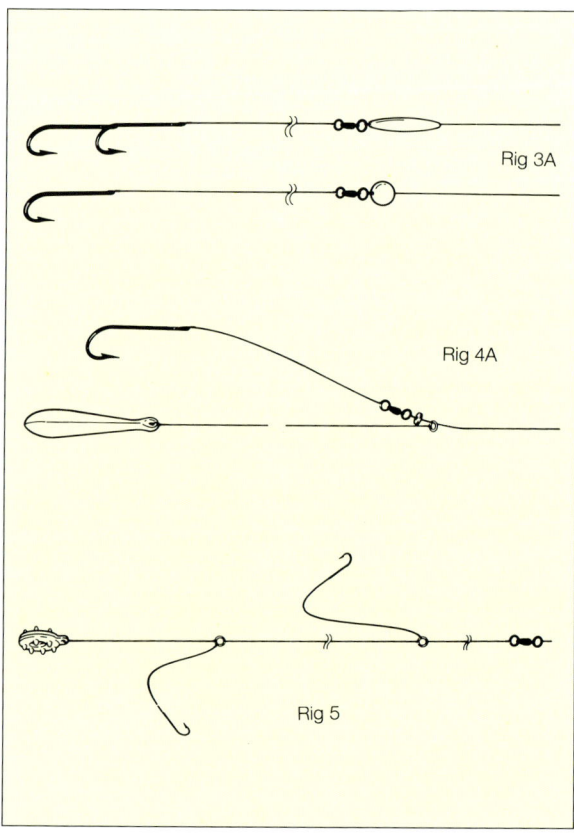
Rig 3A

Rig 4A

Rig 5

When hooked, the larger fish tend to dive for the shelter of line-snagging territory, but this is not really an issue when using heavy gear.

Though one of the smaller wrasses, the maori wrasse of southern waters has surprising power and it will give an angler a hard fight on light line. The hump-headed maori wrasse of the tropics is all brute strength and it has beaten the best of anglers with the finest gear.

Edibility

The tropical wrasses are regarded as excellent table fish, the flesh being white, flaky and tasty, however prepared. The southern species, even in the smaller sizes, have soft flesh, which is palatable. But they are only acceptable if no other fish are biting. Wrasses are best pan-fried in a light batter or grilled with a sprinkling of lemon juice — and never over-cooked.

YELLOWTAIL

Trachurus novaezelandiae

OTHER NAMES: **YAKKA, SCAD, YELLOWTAIL SCAD**

How many anglers were introduced to this fish as a child?
Fishing with their first equipment, be it a discarded handline, a
"handed-down" rod and reel, or a sparkling new outfit, kids are
still catching them today. So are thousands of adults, who seek
this fish as bait. After all, it is one of the best for an amazing
array of marine species, from flathead to marlin, john dory
to wahoo, tailor to tuna.

Identification

This fish is *not* a juvenile yellowtail kingfish. It is a
slim and streamlined fish that is very strong for its
size. Those yellowtails that have spent time in
estuaries or bays are often a brownish colour on
the dorsal area, while those taken from coastal
waters are more bluish-green. There is a hint of
yellow along the lateral line and the tail, of course,
is yellow. The line of scutes (raised scales) from the
head to the tail, separate them from the two other
fish — scads and cowonyoung — that are so often
caught in the same places as the yellowtail.

Size

Yellowtail grow to about 25 centimetres in length.

Breeding

Little is known.

Habits

Schools of yellowtail are commonly found in bays,
harbours, estuaries and along coastal rocks. They
are carnivorous, eating shellfish flesh, prawns, crabs,
the flesh of most other fish, and red meat, etc.

Distribution

These fish are found in the waters of Queensland,
New South Wales, Victoria, Tasmania, South
Australia and Western Australia.

When to fish

Yellowtail are around in varying numbers
throughout the year.

Where to fish

They can be found around wharves, jetties,
breakwaters, and deep water in rocky bays, especially

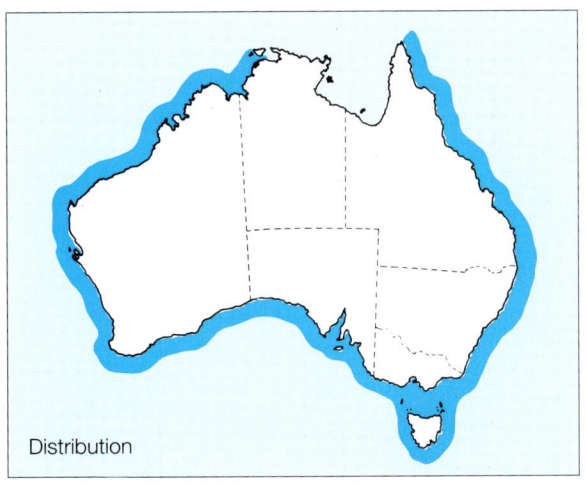

Distribution

with a habitat offering refuge from predators.

Tackle

A light handline of 2 to 4 kilograms breaking-strain, or a single-handed light threadline rod and reel with about the same weight of line, is ideal. Hooks should be sizes 6 to 10, depending on the size of the fish in the school. Long-shanked hooks make it quicker and easier to unhook, especially if the fish are to be retained as live bait.

Bait

Yellowtail will eat anything, but they will nevertheless display a frustrating preference for a particular bait from time to time. Pieces of prawn are rarely refused, nor are pieces of garfish. Fresh mado flesh can also be effective. Sometimes yellowtail prefer a red meat or a piece of pilchard. It's better to have a couple of choices to offer them.

Rigs

The most used rig is a hook on a leader, with a small split-shot sinker squeezed on to the line about 15 to 25 centimetres above the hook. If using a rod, a tiny swivel with the smallest (00) ball sinker above the swivel is suitable. In calm waters and windless conditions, a weight may be unnecessary. Commercially available multi-hook bait chasers dropped to the bottom — and slowly jigged to the surface — can also work. A tiny bit of bait added to the hooks is sometimes more productive on these.

How to hook

In sheltered waters, yellowtail can be finicky biters: a very slow retrieval of the bait will often hook them, but the reaction of the angler should be fast in setting the hook. In coastal waters, once they "come on the bite" they tend to be more voracious and hook themselves. They fight hard — that's why the use of a handline is suggested, particularly for kids. The direct hand-over-hand contest is an educational experience.

Berley

A berley can attract and hold these fish. Popular ingredients are dehydrated potato, minced potatoes, minced fish scraps, breadcrumbs, pollard, bran, etc. Sometimes the lot is mixed in with fish oil or canned cat food, crumbled dog biscuits, etc.

Hint

The yellowtail is very sensitive to the presence of predators, which it probably detects by smell. Avoid using the flesh or oil of predators in the berley you plan to use, such as salmon, tailor, tuna, etc. One of the most successful berlies is boiled rice mixed with canned pilchard cat food, or minced old yellowtail, mado and sweep.

Edibility

There is nothing wrong with a large yellowtail, split open and fried or grilled. They smoke very well.

[**Note:** Often mistaken for the yellowtail are the **southern mackerel scad** (*Decapterus muroadsi*), which are generally larger and slimmer, with a dorsal area varying from bluish-green to greyish-green, and a more prominent yellow stripe. Only the top lobe of the tail is yellow. They lack the large scutes on the curved front portion of the lateral line. Though a tropical species, schools of these fish can be found

A boy in pursuit of yellowtail — and anything that moves.

as far south as Sydney on the east coast and Fremantle on the west coast during the summer. While they may be a different species, their value as a bait fish does not change, nor does the closely related **Russell's mackerel-scad** *(Decapterus russelli)*, which can be identified by its very slim body and lack of any scuta on the front part of its body and any yellow in the tail. This fish has a similar distribution to the southern mackerel-scad. These fish grow to 30 and 40 centimetres respectively.

Every so often, the ocean schooling or roaming **cowanyoung** *(Trachurus declivis)* **or jack mackerel**, invade harbours or maraud along ocean rock formations. They are frequently mistaken for large yellowtail. Usually the hooks being used for yellowtail are too small for the fish. The strength they exhibit when hooked can snap the lighter lines. They have a secondary lateral line of scutes, which extend forward past the middle of the body. They display no yellow in their body or fins. Jack mackerel grow to about 60 centimetres. They like a moving bait and are rarely missed with a larger hook, size 4 to 1/0, depending on the fish in the school.

These fish are not as popular for bait, other than with game fishers for trolling, and they can be eaten. The flesh, however, tends to be dry.

INDEX

INDEX

INDEX

INDEX

INDEX

PHOTOGRAPHIC CREDITS

BOOTH, G. (Bonito, Kingfish, Marlin, black, Wahoo) CLAYTON (Bream, yellowfin, Dart x 2, Whiting, Sand) CSIRO (Emperor, Flathead, Flathead, halibut, Goatfish, Jobfish, green, Leatherjacket, Mahi-Mahi, Queenfish, Rainbow Runner, Rock-cod, flowery, Rock-cod, six banded, Seaperch, John's, Seaperch, kelp bohar, Seaperch, paddletail, Seaperch, scarlet, Trevally, big eye, Trevally, giant, Trevally, golden, Trevally, skipjack, Tuskfish, blue, Tuskfish, purple, Wrasse, tripletail) CUSACK, R. (Groper, baldchin, Jewfish, Mulloway, Whiting, king george) FEDERAL PUBLISHING (Hairtail, Marlin, striped) HARRISON, R. (Saltwater, Albacore, Barramundi, Bonefish, Catfish, Cod, Murray, Emperor, long nosed, Milkfish, Perch, estuary, Perch, golden, Perch, jungle, Salmon, aust, Samsonfish, Saratoga, Tuna,

dog tooth, Herring, ox-eye, Threadfin) INGRAM, B. (Cod, murray) IJOBSON, F. (Freshwater, Perch, macquarie, Perch, silver) JULIUS, A. (Grunter, sooty) JOYCE, R. (TRANNIES) (Amberjack, Carp, european, Dory, john, Goatfish, Herring, giant, Javelinfish, yellow, Jewfish, Leatherjacket, Mangrove Jack, Rock-cod, maori, Rock-cod, wirrah, Seapike, striped, Seapike, short finned, Snapper, Stingfish, Trumpeter, tasman, Tuskfish, venus, Tuna, mackerel, Tuna, yellowfin) KUITER, R. (Barracouta, Cobia, Cod, beardie, Flathead, Flounder, Groper, eastern blue, Groper, queensland, Groper, western blue, Mackerel, shark, Morwong, sth blue, Morwong, jackass, Milkfish, Mullet, diamond, Nannygai, Rock-cod, breaksea, Trout, rainbow, Tuna, frigate, Warehou, Wrasse, blue throat, Wrasse, senator) LOCKWOOD, (FEDERAL PUBLISHING). (Hairtail) MENSFORD, S. (Mulloway, Snapper) MORRISON, R. (Saltwater) SCOTLAND, M. (Blackfish, rock Bbarfish, Boarfish,

Flathead, Kingfish, yellowtail, Leatherjacket, Morwong, red, Scorpionfish, Sweetlips, painted, Trevally, yellow spot, Wrasse, hump-head) SIMPSON, T. (Sailfish) SQUIRES, I. (Birds Nest, Saltwater, Bream, pikey, Flounder, long tooth, Goatfish, Luderick, Rock-cod, estuary, Sergeant Baker, Sweep, silver, Tanguigue, Trevally, white, Yellowtail) STANLEY, P. (Rock-cod, chinaman) STEPTOE, W. C. (Bass x 2, Perch, Pearl, Tailor) STRICKFUSS, B. (Cobia) THURBAN, A. (preparation) TRANNIES (Cod, murray, Gurnard, Mackerel, qld school, Morwong, blue, Mullet, sea, Mullet, yellow-eye, Perch, redfin, Salmon, atlantic, Scorpionfish, Snapper, long spined, Sole, Stonefish, Teraglin, Tommy Ruff, Tarwhine, Whiting, trumpeter, Yellowtail) TURNBULL, J. (Freshwater, Trout, brook, Trout, brown) WILSON, B. (Drummer) ZAVODNY, A. (Trout, coral)